T0202539

# Lecture Notes in Artificial Intelligence 11374

Subseries of Lecture Notes in Computer Science

More information about this series at http://www.springer.com/series/1244

Dirk Holz · Katie Genter ·
Maarouf Saad · Oskar von Stryk (Eds.)

# RoboCup 2018:
# Robot World Cup XXII

*Editors*
Dirk Holz
X: The Moonshot Factory
formerly Google [x]
Mountain View, CA, USA

Maarouf Saad
Ecole de Technologie Supérieure
Montreal, QC, Canada

Katie Genter
The University of Texas at Austin
Austin, TX, USA

Oskar von Stryk
Technical University of Darmstadt
Darmstadt, Germany

ISSN 0302-9743         ISSN 1611-3349   (electronic)
Lecture Notes in Artificial Intelligence
ISBN 978-3-030-27543-3       ISBN 978-3-030-27544-0   (eBook)
https://doi.org/10.1007/978-3-030-27544-0

LNCS Sublibrary: SL7 – Artificial Intelligence

This Springer imprint is published by the registered company Springer Nature Switzerland AG
The registered company address is: Gewerbestrasse 11, 6330 Cham, Switzerland

# Preface

RoboCup fosters robotics and AI research by setting formidable challenges, which bring researchers from around the world together through publicly appealing competitions and organized scientific meetings. RoboCup 2018 was held in the Palais des congrès de Montréal, Montréal, Québec, Canada, during June 18–22, 2018. The competition had 2,350 participants from 39 countries with over 1,000 robots competing in various disciplines. In the RoboCupJunior leagues the focus is on the technical education and development of middle and high school students through project-oriented robotic challenges. The research-oriented major leagues were held in the areas of: RoboCup Soccer, with five leagues spanning simulated robots to full-size humanoid robots competing in soccer; RoboCup Rescue, with three leagues investigating how robots can support first-responders in emergency situations; RoboCup@Home, with three leagues where the development of service robots in everyday environments is promoted; and RoboCup Industrial, with two leagues exploring future uses of robots in industrial applications.

This book highlights the approaches of champion teams from the competitions and documents the proceedings of the 22nd annual RoboCup International Symposium that was held at the Palais des Congrès on June 22, 2018. Due to the complex research challenges set by the RoboCup initiative, the RoboCup International Symposium offers a unique perspective for exploring scientific and engineering principles underlying advanced robotic and AI systems. The highly experimental and interactive character of RoboCup, along with its unique opportunities to benchmark and validate research progress, provides a natural forum where novel ideas and promising technologies can be disseminated across a large and growing community.

For the RoboCup 2018 Symposium, a total of 53 submissions were received. The submissions were carefully reviewed by the 69 members of the international Program Committee who generously helped to read and evaluate each of the submissions. Each paper was scored and discussed by three reviewers. The committee ultimately decided to accept 32 regular papers and one paper for a special track on open source hard- and software for an overall acceptance rate of 60%. Among the accepted papers, 10 were selected for oral presentations and the remainder were presented as posters. In addition, the poster session featured 18 projects that RoboCup funded for the promotion and development of RoboCup Leagues.

The RoboCup 2018 Symposium was fortunate to have three invited keynote speakers:

- Yoshua Bengio (Université de Montréal): "Deep Learning for AI"
- Jeannette Bohg (Stanford): "On the Role of Structure in Learning for Robot Manipulation"
- Torsten Kroeger (Karlsruhe Institute of Technology): "Robot Manipulation: Real-time Motion Planning, Hybrid Control, and Reinforcement Learning"

Yoshua Bengio, who recently received the Turing Award, discussed deep learning as a highly capable machine learning approach inspired by brains, learning multiple levels of representation and different levels of abstraction. Jeannette Bohg focused on motion-based segmentation of an unknown number of simultaneously moving objects and a method for predicting the effect of physical interaction with objects in the environment. Torsten Kroeger presented a talk on robot manipulation. His focus was on embedding multiple sensors - force/torque, vision, and distance - in the feedback loops of motion controllers and the new robot applications involved.

Their three exciting presentations helped to attract over 500 participants to the symposium.

The Award Committee selected one best paper, printed first in the book: Best Paper Award for Scientific Contribution: Thomas Gabel, Philipp Klöppner, Eicke Godehardt, and Alaa Tharwat: "Communication in Soccer Simulation: On the Use of Wiretapping Opponent Teams."

We want to thank the members of the Program Committee and our additional reviewers for their time and expertise to ensure the quality of the technical program, as well as the members of the Award Committee for their work during the symposium. Our thanks go to the local Organizing Committee, who supported us in the preparation and running of the symposium. The support and efforts of our local co-chair, Maarouf Saad, are especially acknowledged by all other symposium co-chairs. We also thank all the authors and participants for their contributions and enthusiasm. Finally, we are grateful to the General Chair of RoboCup 2018, Sara Iatauro, who dedicated her complete time and energy, as well as the members of the Organizing Committee and all team members who helped to make RoboCup 2018 a very special cooperative event. As symposium co-chairs, we had the great pleasure of working together and seeing each other in Montreal. We sincerely thank the entire RoboCup community for their support and friendship!

December 2018

Dirk Holz  
Katie Genter  
Maarouf Saad  
Oskar von Stryk

# Organization

## Symposium Co-chairs

Dirk Holz                 X: The Moonshot Factory - formerly Google [x], USA
Katie Genter              The University of Texas at Austin, USA
Maarouf Saad              Ecole de Technologie Superieure, Canada
Oskar von Stryk           TU Darmstadt, Germany

## Program Committee

H. Levent Akin            Bogazici University, Turkey
Hidehisa Akiyama          Fukuoka University, Japan
Minoru Asada              Osaka University, Japan
Jacky Baltes              National Taiwan Normal University, Taiwan
Sven Behnke               University of Bonn, Germany
Joydeep Biswas            University of Massachusetts Amherst, USA
Joschka Boedecker         University of Freiburg, Germany
Ansgar Bredenfeld         Dr. Bredenfeld UG, Germany
Stephan Chalup            The University of Newcastle, Australia
Kai Chen                  University of Science and Technology of China, China
Xiaoping Chen             University of Science and Technology of China, China
Esther Colombini          Unicamp, Brazil
Anna Helena Reali Costa   University of São Paulo, Brazil
Bernardo Cunha            University of Aveiro, Portugal
Klaus Dorer               Hochschule Offenburg, Germany
Farshid Faraji            Bonab Azad University, Iran
Thomas Gabel              Frankfurt University of Applied Sciences, Germany
Reinhard Gerndt           Ostfalia University of Applied Sciences, Germany
Justin Hart               The University of Texas at Austin, USA
Masahide Ito              Aichi Prefectural University, Japan
Ulrich Karras             RoboCup Germany Regional Committee, Germany
Thierry Karsenti          University of Montreal, Canada
Piyush Khandelwal         The University of Texas at Austin, USA
Gerhard Kraetzschmar      Bonn-Rhein-Sieg University, Germany
Gerhard Lakemeyer         RWTH Aachen University, Germany
Nuno Lau                  University of Aveiro, Portugal
Olivier Ly                LaBRI - Bordeaux 1 University, France
Patrick MacAlpine         The University of Texas at Austin, USA
Sebastian Marian          Elrond Network, Romania
Ehsan Marjani             Islamic Azad University, Iran
Mauricio Matamoros        Universität Koblenz-Landau, Germany
Eric Matson               Purdue University, USA

| | |
|---|---|
| Tekin Meriçli | Carnegie Mellon University, USA |
| Çetin Meriçli | Carnegie Mellon University, USA |
| Francois Michaud | Université de Sherbrooke, Canada |
| Kazuhito Murakami | Aichi Prefectural University, Japan |
| Tomoharu Nakashima | Osaka Prefecture University, Japan |
| Daniele Nardi | Sapienza University of Rome, Italy |
| Tim Niemüller | RWTH Aachen University, Germany |
| Asadollah Norouzi | Singapore Polytechnic, Singapore |
| Oliver Obst | Western Sydney University, Australia |
| Maike Paetzel | Uppsala University, Sweden |
| Paul G. Plöger | Bonn-Rhein-Sieg University of Applied Science, Germany |
| Mikhail Prokopenko | The University of Sydney, Australia |
| Caleb Rascon | Universidad Nacional Autónoma de México, Mexico |
| Luis Paulo Reis | University of Porto - FEUP/LIACC, Portugal |
| Javier Ruiz-Del-Solar | Universidad de Chile, Chile |
| Thomas Röfer | Deutsches Forschungszentrum für Künstliche, Intelligenz GmbH, Germany |
| Soroush Sadeghnejad | Amirkabir University of Technology, Iran |
| Benjamin Schnieders | University of Liverpool, UK |
| Raymond Sheh | Curtin University, Australia |
| Masaru Shimizu | Chukyo University, Japan |
| Saeed Shiry | Amirkabir University of Technology, Iran |
| Marco Simoes | Universidade do Estado da Bahia (UNEB), Brazil |
| Jivko Sinapov | The University of Texas at Austin, USA |
| Frieder Stolzenburg | Harz University of Applied Sciences, Germany |
| Komei Sugiura | NICT, Japan |
| Yasutake Takahashi | University of Fukui, Japan |
| Federico Tombari | Technical University of Munich, Germany |
| Flavio Tonidandel | Centro Universitario da FEI, Brazil |
| Arnoud Visser | University of Amsterdam, The Netherlands |
| Ubbo Visser | University of Miami, USA |
| Sven Wachsmuth | Bielefeld University, Germany |
| Alfredo Weitzenfeld | University of South Florida, USA |
| Timothy Wiley | The University of New South Wales, Australia |
| Aaron Wong | The University of Newcastle, Australia |
| Junhao Xiao | National University of Defense Technology, China |
| Sebastian Zug | Universität Magdeburg, Germany |

## Additional Reviewers

| | |
|---|---|
| Philipp Allgeuer | University of Bonn, Germany |
| Alexander Biddulph | The University of Newcastle, Australia |
| Domenico Bloisi | University of Verona, Italy |
| Huseyin Coskun | Technical University of Munich, Germany |
| Hafez Farazi | University of Bonn, Germany |

| | |
|---|---|
| Josiah Hanna | The University of Texas at Austin, USA |
| Amirhossein Hosseinmemar | University of Manitoba, Canada |
| Trent Houliston | The University of Newcastle, Australia |
| Meng Cheng Lau | University of Manitoba, Canada |
| Maria Teresa Lazaro | Sapienza University of Rome, Italy |
| Jakob Mayr | Technical University of Munich, Germany |
| Arul Selvam Periyasamy | University of Bonn, Germany |
| Pedro Peña | University of Miami, USA |
| Stefan Schiffer | RWTH Aachen University, Germany |
| Vida Shams | Amirkabir University of Technology, Iran |
| Akira Taniguchi | Ritsumeikan University, Japan |
| Alaa Tharwat | Frankfurt University of Applied Sciences, Germany |
| Ruben van Heusden | University of Amsterdam, The Netherlands |
| Jonathan Vincent | Université de Sherbrooke, Canada |
| Shun-Cheng Wu | Technical University of Munich, Germany |
| Behnam Yazdankhoo | University of Tehran, Iran |

# Contents

## Poster Presentations

# Best Paper Award

# Communication in Soccer Simulation: On the Use of Wiretapping Opponent Teams

Thomas Gabel[(✉)], Philipp Klöppner, Eicke Godehardt, and Alaa Tharwat

Faculty of Computer Science and Engineering,
Frankfurt University of Applied Sciences,
60318 Frankfurt am Main, Germany
{tgabel,godehardt,aothman}@fb2.fra-uas.de,kloeppne@stud.fra-uas.de

**Abstract.** Inter-agent communication has been playing an important role in soccer simulation 2D since its introduction. Its primary usage has been to communicate with teammates in order to share state observations to fill gaps in the players' world models, to announce near future actions like passes or requesting passes, as well as for sharing and synchronizing on locker room agreements. In this paper, by contrast, our focus is on the communication of the opponent team. We present an approach for wiretapping and decoding opponent communication and systematically evaluate its impact. Our main finding is that a team that wiretaps its opponent and exploits intercepted information appropriately, can boost its own playing performance significantly.

## 1 Introduction

When multiple agents need to act independently of one another, under real-time constraints, and under a partial view of the world, inter-agent communication is one mean to mitigate the challenges of distributed decision-making and of coordinating agent behaviors. In robotic soccer, we face all of these challenges, with different nuances across leagues. Given that robotic soccer represents also a highly competitive domain, it is standing to reason that nearly any team exploits the granted possibilities of communication to the extent the rules of the respective RoboCup league permit. As a consequence, the question arises whether some team might gain an advantage, if it decides to wiretap its opponent and if it – assuming that it somehow understands the contents of foreign communication – exploits such eavesdropped information during its own decision-making process. This is the research question that we are going to explore for the 2D simulation league, subsequently.

We start off by providing relevant background information on the mechanics and the general role of communication in soccer simulation (Sect. 2), before we present the core ideas of an approach to learn the meaning of opponent communication in Sect. 3 [4]. The task will be cast as a supervised learning problem where deep convolutional neural networks will do the actual work of decoding some foreign language message to readable data. Since the belonging implementation has

D. Holz et al. (Eds.): RoboCup 2018, LNAI 11374, pp. 3–15, 2019.
https://doi.org/10.1007/978-3-030-27544-0_1

been realized using the TensorFlow (TF) framework [1], we advocate Sect. 4 to a brief review of software engineering challenges encountered when incorporating the TF-based implementation into an existing RoboCup team. In Sect. 5, we return to our research question and empirically evaluate the quantitative impact of our approach. In so doing, we introduce various communication-related modifications to our team FRA-UNIted, including the aforementioned wiretapping ideas, and assess its performance against the current world champion (Helios [2]). Besides reporting and visualizing the remarkable impact, we critically discuss the approach before we conclude (Sect. 6).

## 2   Background

In what follows, we outline the general mechanics of communication in the 2D simulation league and discuss relevant related work.

### 2.1   Communication in RoboCup's Soccer Simulation 2D League

While direct communication among agents is prohibited, each agent is allowed to broadcast a string of up to 10 characters in each of the 6000 time steps that a regular game is made of. Such say messages are received by the Soccer Server [9] and are handed on to those players in the subsequent simulation cycle which had put their listening attention to the sender. Each agent can maximally hear one message from a teammate plus one message from an opponent at a time.

```
9,0  Recv HELIOS2017_10: (kick 86.8 63.1)(turn_neck -73)(attentionto our 11)(say "BybzQQ(u9U")
9,0  Recv FRA-UNIted_5: (dash 100 -0)(turn_neck 7.65998)(say "72gtaUuDWT")(attentionto our 4)
9,0  Recv HELIOS2017_2: (turn -53.967)(turn_neck -31)
9,0  Recv HELIOS2017_4: (dash 60)(turn_neck -1)
9,0  Recv FRA-UNIted_4: (dash 100 -0)(turn_neck -89.2104)(say "6zfuDWN9VT")(attentionto our 6)
9,0  Recv HELIOS2017_11: (dash 100)(turn_neck 0)(say "PzdAc_")
```

**Fig. 1.** Excerpt of the text log file of RoboCup 2017's final match (shortened).

Figure 1 shows an excerpt of the text log file of the 2017 final match, which among other things reveals which actions were taken by some of the players during time step 9. Most interestingly, some of the players made use of communication by issuing say messages of up to 10 chars length, though, from a human perspective, it seems nearly impossible to understand the contents of these strings. In this regard, we refer to Sect. 5.2, where we exemplarily and empirically reason on the actual contents of such say messages.

### 2.2   Related Work

Communication is an active field of research in the multi-agent systems community and, specifically, in robotic soccer. There has been a lot of work on communication across leagues (e.g. in the MidSize league [8] or in the 3D simulation league [7]). For the 2D league, communication has been an important building block ever since, though the rules on how to communicate, as enforced by the Soccer Server [9], have changed over the years. In early work, Stone and Veloso [12] focused on developing techniques for inter-agent communication in unreliable, low-bandwidth environments, assuming that agents can communicate 256 bytes every two time steps. Starting with the change from Soccer Server version 7 to 8 in 2002, the maximum length of players' say messages has, however, been limited severely (to the 10 chars mentioned), rendering "plain text" communication nearly useless. The general potential for communication to improve distributed decision-making in multi-agent systems is also considered in [13]. Our experimental methodology is, to some extent, in line with [10], who theoretically and empirically evaluated the utility of varying communication protocols in soccer simulation, and with [15] to which we relate our work more thoroughly in Sect. 5. Finally, we point the reader to the related work section in [15] for an excellent overview on multi-agent communication and coordination.

## 3   Eavesdropping Opponent Agent Communication

In this section, we aim at providing a concise overview of the approach to eavesdrop and decode intercepted messages sent by an opponent soccer simulation team, which has first been presented in [4]. The basic idea of this approach is to pose the problem as a supervised learning task and to leverage state-of-the-art deep learning techniques for recognizing the meaning of messages heard. The authors make the obvious assumption that the contents of an intercepted message bears information whose transmission is beneficial to the opponent team, containing match-related data such as (1) ball-related, (2) player-related, (3) pass-related, or (4) team strategy-related junks of information. While the authors of [4] have primarily concentrated on (1) and (3), the focus of the paper at hand is on pass-related information, more specifically on the recognition of adversarial pass announcements, as well as on the quantitative impact that wiretapping the opponent agents can have on our own team's playing performance.

### 3.1   Learning Problem Formalization

Defining the problem as a supervised learning task, a set of training patterns $\mathbb{P} = \{(x^p, t^p)|p = 1, \ldots, |\mathbb{P}|\}$ is required. An input vector $x^p$ corresponds to a say message $\mathcal{C} = (c_s, \ldots, c_0)$ with $s < 10$ and literals $c_i$ from the alphabet $A$ of 94 printable ASCII-128 characters. So, the discrete set of transmittable messages is $\mathcal{A} = \cup_{i=0}^{9} A^i$ which in our setting boils down to $|\mathcal{A}| \approx 5.1 \cdot 10^{19}$.

In regard to the target values $t^p$, however, we arrive at two sub-tasks relevant to the specific task of opponent pass announcement recognition:

(a) The problem of classifying whether an intercepted say message $\mathcal{C}$ contains a pass announcement or not. Accordingly, it holds $t^p \in \{true, false\}$.

(b) Given that the classifier from (a) states that $C$ contains a pass announcement, the next logical challenge is to extract details of the pass announcement from $C$, such as its starting point or velocity. Thus, we obtain a classical regression problem with $t^p \in \mathbb{R}^l$ ($l = 4$ in case of pass announcements, as $x$ and $y$ components of the start position and velocity characterize the pass).

If we proceed on the assumption that the opponent team under consideration does announce its pass (this is a valid assumption for the 2D league), the training data set can be compiled easily by running a large batch of matches against the considered opponent team, recording its communication as well as observing its actual passes played. If, in so doing, a pass is accompanied by a say message $C$ sent simultaneously to or shortly before the pass is played, then it is likely that $C$ contains a pass announcement plus details of the intended pass.

## 3.2   Bit-Level Representation of Communicated Messages

As pointed out, the goal is to build and train a deep neural network into which some representation of the say message $C$ is fed and whose output neuron(s) provide(s) decoded pass-related information. Intuitively, it seems tempting to feed a numeric representation of each letter $c_i$ (e.g. its ASCII code) into the first layer of the network. Such an approach might indeed be expected to yield good results, if the payload to be transmitted is generally not distributed across multiple chars and if certain pieces of information were known to be located at a fixed position within $C$. Given the limited communication bandwidth, however, these assumptions are unrealistic to be made. Accordingly, in [4] it has been suggested to employ a bit level representation of $C$. Among other merits, such a representation will contain bit patterns that hint to the type of data encoded in the message as well as patterns that can be decoded to pass parameters[1].

Most importantly, a bit representation allows for the utilization of convolutional neural networks [5,6] that perform one-dimensional convolution on the bit sequence in order to detect features that allow for classifying a message as containing a pass announcement or for extracting pass parameters. Therefore, any say message $C \in \mathcal{A}$ is mapped to a bit sequence $b(C)$ using a function $b : \mathcal{A} \rightarrow \{0,1\}^B$ where $B$ is determined by the length of the message and the size of the underlying alphabet (in our case $B = 10\lceil \log_2 94 \rceil = 70$).

The authors of [4] suggest different ways of defining that function $b$, discussing in detail the motivation, advantages and limits of each suggested bit level encoding. In the rest of this paper, we stick to the "Base-$|\mathcal{A}|$ Bit Level Representation" ($b_{|\mathcal{A}|}$) which, according to [4], makes some assumptions on how opponent teams might have encoded their say messages, and which has brought about superior empirical results when using it as the basis of the decoding approach.

---

[1] Under the assumption, that the opponent team does not employ some form of sophisticated data encryption or compression techniques before broadcasting messages. Hence, we proceed on the assumption that communicated data is not encrypted.

### 3.3   Model Architecture and Performance

We utilize the same deep convolutional neural network architecture as the one described in [4] (two convolutional layers, ReLu activations, max pooling, fully connected final layers, dropout, Adam optimizer) with one minor exception: For the task of extracting the numeric pass details ($x/y$ of pass start position and velocity) we do not employ a single trained model with an output vector of length four, but four separately trained models with the same base architecture, but a single output neuron each (one of these for each of the four pass announcing variables, $p_x$, $p_y$, $v_x$, $v_y$). With four models using a single output neuron each and trained separately, we were able to achieve better generalization capabilities, i.e. the average test errors of the to-be-predicted four numeric pass details were significantly smaller compared to the monolithic model with a four-dimensional output (even when the latter was allowed to be trained for a much longer time).

For the general empirical performance of the approach, we again refer to [4]. Most notably, it is possible to train a reliable pass announcement classifier with as little as 50 sample passes observed (accuracy of 98.6%). For 20k training examples, the accuracy increases to 99.2%. Inferring pass announcement details reliably requires substantially more training samples. However, with 20k passes in the training data set, the average error of the pass start position is less than one meter (on the 2D playing field with 105 m length and 68 m width), and the average pass velocity error is generally less than $0.1\frac{m}{step}$ (where $v_{x/y} \in [-3\frac{m}{step}, 3\frac{m}{step}]$).

Based on these definitions, implementations and the reported decoding accuracies, our idea was to incorporate this approach to eavesdrop and understand opponent team communication into our competition team. This raised two questions. First, what engineering effort is required to make such an approach practically usable in an existing soccer simulation team. And second, what are the benefits in terms of possibly increased playing performance, if we succeed in enabling our team to reliably decode and exploit opponent team communication.

## 4   Implementation Within the FRA-UNIted Framework

The learning approach outlined above had first been implemented in a prototypical manner utilizing TensorFlow's well-documented Python API. However, deploying this approach within the FRA-UNIted competition team, which is implemented in C++ entirely, issued quite an engineering challenge.

- Doing classification/regression with the trained networks utilized via Python scripts and using inter-process communication with our C++-based agent binary would have been a first option. But the resulting IPC overhead in conjunction with the need to possibly set up TF on competition machines render this approach impractical from our point of view.
- Porting the entire approach to C++ did not represent a valid option, too, since TF's C++ API does not enable access to optimizer classes such as the Adam optimizer for training the decoding models.

– We thus had to opt for a hybrid approach where the network topology definition and the training process of the deep networks takes place in the Python world. During matches, stored networks (TF checkpoints) are loaded via TF's C++ API and are utilized by our agent via a shared TF library that we built and that is dynamically loaded by the FRA-UNIted agent.

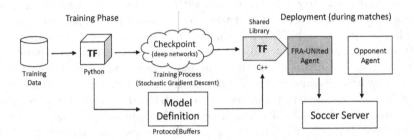

**Fig. 2.** Python scripts define the topology of the deep networks and use previously gathered data for training. Training results and model definitions are stored in separate files. The latter are generic for all teams, while the former are different for each opponent team we face. Via TF's C++ API, both files are then utilized by our agent.

The specific challenges and hurdles of creating and utilizing a shared C++ library that contains vast parts of TensorFlow as well as the technical and engineering details of our corresponding implementation can be found in our current team description paper [3].

## 5 Empirical Evaluation

In [15], the authors have presented the results of a study to measure the efficiency of inter-agent communication and its influence on the general playing performance of robotic soccer simulation teams. While in that paper the focus has been on the analysis of the structural and functional connectivity of the graph of communicating players, our main interest is on quantifying the differences in playing strength of a team that applies varying communication behaviors which is related to the notion of design points used by the authors of [15].

### 5.1 Communication Behavior Variants (CBV)

In all our experiments, we abbreviate our team FRA-UNIted as *Team A*. The version with which *Team A* participated in last year's world championships (RoboCup 2017) represents our baseline, labeled *A_Baseline17*. We selected the current world champion (Helios [2]) as the opponent (calling it *Team B*) against which to compare. More specifically, we selected both, its 2017 champion binary as well as its predecessor from RoboCup 2016 (labeled *B_Baseline17* and *B_Predecessor16*, respectively). In order to reliably quantify the contribution of communication to the overall performance of *Team A*, we adapted its baseline version, thus yielding the four communication behavior variants (CBVs) considered subsequently.

(a) *A_Baseline17*: Version of *Team A* used at the RoboCup 2017 tournament.
(b) *A_NoComm*: While no change to the agents' playing behavior has been made, the agents of *Team A* no longer use *any* form of inter-agent communication. So, this CBV should perform worse than the baseline.
(c) *A_NoOwnPasses*: Again, there is no change in the agents' playing behavior, but passes that are intended and/or are being played will no longer be communicated among the players of *Team A*. All other aspects of team-internal communication (like communicated player information or ball data) remain untouched.
(d) *A_OppPassExploit*: This communication behavior variant is in the center of our interest since it represents the baseline version enhanced by the implementation of the approach to eavesdrop and understand opponent pass announcements, whose basic ideas are described in Sect. 3.

It is important to stress that the actual *exploitation* of an intercepted opponent pass announcement in (d) has intentionally been implemented in a straight-forward manner in order to facilitate an utmost fair assessment of the impact of the approach. Each decoded opponent pass announcement is treated in exactly the same manner as a pass announcement received from a teammate (like in (a) or (b)). Accordingly, no additional logic or special cases for opponent passes were programmed, which allows us to assess the benefits of having wiretapped the opponent team as accurately as possible. Hence, from the point of view of an *A_OppPassExploit* agent, there are just "a few more" pass announcements compared to the baseline version of the agents. As a consequence, the advantage of (d) over (a) is, essentially, time: An *A_OppPassExploit* agent will, in general, know earlier about an opponent pass than a baseline agent and, thus, will be able to react on this faster. Besides the changes mentioned, the only necessary modification of *A_OppPassExploit* agents compared to their baseline counterparts concerned their listening attention-to behavior: In order to be able to reliably receive say messages from the opponent ball holder $h$, the listening attention had to be put to $h$ instead of putting it to some teammate (as a baseline agent would do, by contrast), if $h$ controls the ball.

## 5.2 Distribution of Communication Data

In order to assess the communication restrictions imposed on the *A_NoComm* and *A_NoOwnPasses* CBVs, it is advisable to quantify the amount of communication data that is on average received by a *A_Baseline17* agent. We refer to the publicly available source code release of *Team A* which reveals the inner workings of its communication policy [11]. Table 1 shows that 70% of all communicated pieces of information are player-related, i.e. positions of teammates or opponents recently seen. By contrast, pass-related information make up for only 0.8% of all communicated data chunks, corresponding to 96.3 pass announcements and 2.6 pass requests per player per game on average. Moreover, that table summarizes the average distribution of the total amount of data sent among the five considered types of soccer-related information (in total number of bits received and the corresponding share of communication channel usage per type). Essentially, only 1.7% of the overall communication bandwidth is used for announcing passes to teammates.

**Table 1.** Utilization of the communication channel by *A_Baseline17*: besides overhead (headers etc.), 4 soccer-related categories of information are shared across agents.

|  | Overhead | Ball-Rel | Pass-Rel | Player-Rel | Strategy-Rel |
|---|---|---|---|---|---|
| Avg. number of payload units | 714.4 | 615.5 | 98.9 | 8535.8 | 3030.4 |
| Sent per match (total and share) |  | 5.0% | 0.8% | 69.5% | 24.7% |
| Avg. amount of bits sent per match | 3571.9 | 104.4k | 3102.8 | 153.6k | 15151.9 |
| Share of comm. channel usage | 1.9% | 5.6% | 1.7% | 82.6% | 8.2% |

As a consequence, *A_NoOwnPasses* agents (which do not receive pass announcements from teammates) disregard circa 0.8% of all data chunks that are communicated in our team, which makes up for 1.7% of the overall data payload. By contrast, *A_Baseline17* disregards nothing, and *A_NoComm* disregards the entire communication.

### 5.3  Empirical Methodology

All four communication behavior variants of *Team A* were matched against both versions of *Team B*. For each combination, 5000 matches were played in order to form score averages and, hence, to account for the stochastic nature of the Soccer Server. To assess the overall team playing strength and to analyze the impact of altered communication schemes, we adopt the perspective of *Team A* and, for the rest of this paper, focus on the following performance measures.

- $\mu_a$: average number of goals scored during a single match by *Team A* with belonging standard deviation $\sigma_a$, calculated over the set of matches played.
- $\mu_b$: average number of goals scored by *Team B*, i.e. the average number of goals conceded by *Team A* with belonging standard deviation $\sigma_b$.
- $\mu_p$: expected number of points *Team A* gains from a match against *Team B* on average, when a victory is rewarded with three points, a draw with one, and a defeat with none.

Given that the modifications to the communication behavior of the CBVs will most likely have affected the standard deviations of the performance measures considered, we applied an unequal variance t-test (also known as Welch test [14]) in order to determine whether any empirically observable change of $\mu_a$ or $\mu_b$ is statistically significant (and if so, at which confidence level).

## 5.4    Results

Figure 3 shows the variability in playing strength of the four *Team A* CBVs considered. Here, *A_Baseline17* is considered as the baseline (100%) against which the three other variants are compared with respect to the relative amount of goals scored and conceded against both versions of *Team B*. Consistently, an increased utilization and exploitation of communicated information brings about an increased overall performance. Interestingly, when playing against *B_Baseline17*, the activation of our wiretapping and opponent pass announcement decoding approach yields an increase in the number of goals shot by 8.8% and a simultaneous decline in the number of goals conceded by 4.4%.

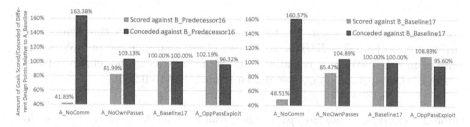

**Fig. 3.** Taking CBV *A_Baseline17* as the ground truth, these charts visualize the relative changes in $\mu_a$ and $\mu_b$ when the other three considered CBVs are matched against *Team B* (left: against *B_Predecessor16*, right: against *B_Baseline17*).

While Fig. 3 shows performance measures relative to *Team A*'s baseline, the left chart in Fig. 4 highlights absolute values of $\mu_a$ and $\mu_b$ for all combinations of CBVs of *Team A* having played against both *Team B* versions. The lengths of the line segments in both data series convey a good impression of how the overall playing capabilities of *Team A* are impacted by switching off/on the entire team-internal communication, just team-internal pass announcements, and eavesdropping and exploiting opponent pass-related communication. Apparently, the impact and usefulness of the opponent pass decoding, is more distinct when playing against *Team B*'s 2017 champion version than when playing against its 2016 predecessor, though the former has, of course, a generally higher playing strength than the latter. It is also worth noting that, when testing against *B_Baseline17*, the gain/loss of switching on/off the exploitation of *Team B*'s decoded pass announcements is almost as pronounced as the one resulting from switching on/off our team-internal pass announcements.

The right part of Fig. 4 concentrates on the expected points $\mu_p$ to be obtained when playing against the two versions of *Team B*, but just focuses on a comparison of the two CBVs *A_Baseline17* and *A_OppPassExploit*. To do so, it visualizes the share of matches won/drawn/lost by *Team A* as well as the exact value of $\mu_p$ (secondary axis). With respect to opponent *B_Predecessor16*, the exploitation of heard opponent pass announcements reduces the percentage of games lost by roughly 1%, increasing the share of draws accordingly, thus resulting in an

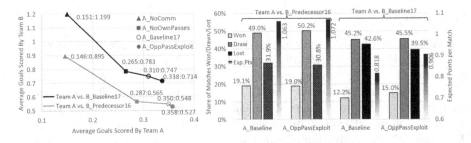

**Fig. 4.** Left: Average scores of the four *Team A* CBVs when facing both *Team B* versions considered. Right: Share of matches won/drawn/lost as well as expected points $\mu_p$ when *A_Baseline17* and *A_OppPassExploit* face both *Team B* versions.

improvement of $\mu_p$ by about 1%, too. By contrast, when evaluating against the current world champion *B_Baseline17*, we observe an increase of $\approx$3% in the share of matches won at a constant level of draws, which amounts to a 10.8% growth of the expected points per match (from 0.818 to 0.906).

**Table 2.** Performance measures $\mu_a$ and $\mu_b$ for all CBV pairings. $p_a$ and $p_b$ stand for the error levels at which a change in $\mu_a$ and $\mu_b$ (i.e. a change from $\mu_{a/b}^{A\_Baseline17}$ to any other $\mu_{a/b}$ value) is statistically significant.

| Opponent | Measure | CBV with conf. level of a significant change vs. *A_Baseline17* | | | | | |
|---|---|---|---|---|---|---|---|
| | | *A_NoComm* | $p_{a/b}$ | *A_NoOwnPass* | $p_{a/b}$ | *A_Baseline17* | *A_OppPassExp* | $p_{a/b}$ |
| B_Prede- | $\mu_a \pm \sigma_a$ | $0.146 \pm .490$ | .001 | $0.287 \pm .536$ | .001 | $0.350 \pm .578$ | $0.358 \pm .575$ | .25 |
| cessor16 | $\mu_b \pm \sigma_b$ | $0.895 \pm .966$ | .001 | $0.565 \pm .730$ | .1 | $0.548 \pm .746$ | $0.527 \pm .739$ | .1 |
| B_Base- | $\mu_a \pm \sigma_a$ | $0.151 \pm .380$ | .001 | $0.265 \pm .506$ | .001 | $0.310 \pm .553$ | $0.338 \pm .555$ | .01 |
| line17 | $\mu_B \pm \sigma_b$ | $1.199 \pm 1.135$ | .001 | $0.783 \pm .895$ | .01 | $0.747 \pm .878$ | $0.714 \pm .842$ | .025 |

Table 2 summarizes the values of performance measures $\mu_a$ and $\mu_b$ for $n = 5000$ game repetitions for each CBV playing against both *Team B* versions. Also, we report the significance levels at which the null hypothesis for the Welch test has to be rejected (null hypothesis: performance measure did not improve/worsen (compared to *A_Baseline17*) due to switching on/off the communication feature of the respective CBV). While the test statistic allows us to confirm the expected changes at very low error rates in most cases, for the evaluation of *A_OppPassExploit* versus the older 2016 version of *Team B* we can attest the expected improvements in $\mu_a$ and $\mu_b$ at an error level of 0.1 and 0.25, only.

## 5.5 Discussion

In the experimental evaluation at hand, our selected opponent (*Team B*) was the current world champion. Thus, all conclusions refer to this opponent in the first place. However, as pointed out by [4], similar or even better communication learning performance can be expected, when playing against other 2D top teams. Besides, by having selected the currently best team in the world, we have set a high standard and it is standing to reason that our findings can be generalized to (at least several) weaker teams. Clearly, when switching to another opponent a separate decoding model in the form of a deep convolutional neural network would have to be trained beforehand. Also, we should emphasize the fact that the advantages reported can only be exploited in real tournament games under the assumption that the opponent does not change or encrypt its communication.

The disk space requirements of *Team A* increase substantially, when incorporating the presented approach into our team. Having consumed 6.9 MB in total in its RoboCup 2017 version (*A_Baseline17*), the new working binary (*A_OppPassExploit*) now requires 110 MB where 96 MB are consumed by the created TensorFlow shared library and 7.3 MB are due to newly trained neural networks for communication decoding.

The computational burden caused by the TensorFlow-based opponent communication decoding is acceptable. On a 4-core i7 with 3 GHz (with all 22 players plus 2 coaches plus the Soccer Server running in parallel on this single machine) *without* GPU support a say message classification requires between 3 and 4 ms. The subsequent determination of pass start and velocity vectors costs between 9 and 10 ms on average. Given that during competitions teams are allowed to employ several machines (typically only 3–4 agents play on a multi-core machine, i.e. a separate CPU core is available for each agent), the mentioned calculation times are likely to be around or even below 1.5 ms. With respect to the required training times of the deep neural networks, which of course strongly depend on the hardware used and on the availability of powerful GPUs, we refer to the numbers we reported in [4].

It is worth noting that an agent of CBV *A_OppPassExploit* does receive, decode, and exploit 66.2 passes from *Team B* during one full match on average, and that this is almost 70% of the number of pass announcements they receive from their own teammates (96.3 on average per game). However, a substantial amount of these opponent pass announcements are "safe passes" which, despite the fact that we hear and understand them, by no means, allow for tackling the pass receiver or in conquering the ball, immediately. We found that an *A_OppPassExploit* agent gets to know that an opponent pass is being played on average 2.2 time steps earlier than an *A_Baseline17* agent which has to rely on its (restricted, noisy, and non-omnidirectional) vision system to see the pass. Given the comparatively small number of exploitable opponent passes and, hence, intuitively small qualitative influence on the overall course of the game, the reported quantitative impact on the general playing strength of *Team A* is remarkable.

# 6   Conclusion

It has been argued by numerous authors that the utilization of team-internal communication is highly beneficial in soccer simulation 2D. In this paper, we

have substantiated that claim by two means. On the one hand, we have compared the empirical playing strength of our team (FRA-UNIted) when disabling
certain paths of communication across teammates. On the other hand, we have
utilized a deep learning-based approach for decoding the contents of say messages
broadcast by the opponent team. In so doing, we could show that the playing
performance of a team that wiretaps an opponent and exploits intercepted information (in our case pass announcements) can be boosted significantly.

Since the mentioned deep learning-related part of the approach relies on a
TensorFlow-based implementation, a critical question concerns the practicability
of our approach. Powerful machine learning libraries and their APIs evolve fast.
In regard to the fact that our team binary should retain easily deployable on
any machine (e.g. during competitions or for reproducibility) it was our goal
to utilize the required TensorFlow functionality into our team with as little
installation or maintenance effort as possible. Hence, our delineations in Sect. 4
(and, in addition, in our current team description paper [3]) are meant as an aid
for teams in the simulation league and beyond which intend to merge their team
sources with TensorFlow utilizing its C++ API.

# References

1. Abadi, M., et al.: TensorFlow: large-scale machine learning on heterogeneous systems (2015). http://tensorflow.org/. Software available from tensorflow.org
2. Akiyama, H., Nakashima, T., Fukushima, T.: HELIOS2017: Team Description (2017). www.robocup2017.org/file/symposium/soccer_sim_2D/TDP_HEL
   IOS2017.pdf. Supplementary to RoboCup 2017: Robot Soccer World Cup XXI
3. Gabel, T., Klöppner, P., Godehardt, E.: FRA-UNIted - Team Description 2018
   (2018). http://tgabel.de/cms/fileadmin/user_upload/documents/Gabel_EtAl_FU-
   18.pdf. Supplementary material to RoboCup 2018: Robot Soccer World Cup XXII
4. Gabel, T., Tharwat, A., Godehardt, E.: Eavesdropping opponent agent communication using deep learning. In: Berndt, J.O., Petta, P., Unland, R. (eds.) MATES
   2017. LNCS (LNAI), vol. 10413, pp. 205–222. Springer, Cham (2017). https://doi.
   org/10.1007/978-3-319-64798-2_13
5. Goodfellow, I., Bengio, Y., Courville, A.: Deep Learning. MIT Press, Cambridge
   (2017)
6. LeCun, Y.: Generalization and network. Design strategies. Technical Report CRG-
   TR-89-4, University of Toronto (1989)
7. MacAlpine, P.: Multilayered skill learning and movement coordination for
   autonomous robotic agents. Ph.D. thesis, University of Texas at Austin, USA
   (2017)
8. Mota, L., Reis, L.: An elementary communication framework for open co-operative
   RoboCup soccer teams. In: Proceedings of the 3rd International Workshop on
   Multi-Agent Robotic Systems, pp. 97–101. SciTePress, France (2007)
9. Noda, I.: Soccer server: a simulator of RoboCup. In: Proceedings of the AI Symposium 1995, pp. 29–34. Japanese Society for Artificial Intelligence (1995)
10. Prokopenko, M., Wang, P.: Evaluating team performance at the edge of chaos. In:
    Polani, D., Browning, B., Bonarini, A., Yoshida, K. (eds.) RoboCup 2003. LNCS
    (LNAI), vol. 3020, pp. 89–101. Springer, Heidelberg (2004). https://doi.org/10.
    1007/978-3-540-25940-4_8

11. Riedmiller, M., Gabel, T., Schulz, H.: Brainstormers 2D: public source code release 2005. Technical Report, University of Osnabrück (2005). http://sourceforge.net/projects/bsrelease/files/bs05publicrelease.documentation.pdf
12. Stone, P., Veloso, M.: Communication in domains with unreliable, single-channel, low-bandwidth communication. In: Drogoul, A., Tambe, M., Fukuda, T. (eds.) CRW 1998. LNCS, vol. 1456, pp. 85–97. Springer, Heidelberg (1998). https://doi.org/10.1007/BFb0033376
13. Stone, P., Veloso, M.: Multiagent systems: a survey from a machine learning perspective. Auton. Robots **8**(3), 345–383 (2000)
14. Welch, B.: The significance of the difference between two means when the population variances are unequal. Biometrika **29**, 350–362 (1938)
15. Zuparic, M., Jauregui, V., Prokopenko, M., Yue, Y.: Quantifying the impact of communication on performance in multi-agent teams. Artif. Life Robot. **22**(3), 357–373 (2017)

# Oral Presentations

# Multi-Robot Fast-Paced Coordination with Leader Election

Ricardo Dias[(✉)], Bernardo Cunha, José Luis Azevedo, Artur Pereira,
and Nuno Lau

DETI/IEETA, University of Aveiro, Aveiro, Portugal
ricardodias@ua.pt, mbc@det.ua.pt, {jla,artur,nunolau}@ua.pt

**Abstract.** Coordination in Multi-Robot Systems is an active research
line in Artificial Intelligence applied to Robotics. Through coordination,
a team of robots can efficiently achieve their pre-defined global objective. From a wide range of multi-agent coordination sub-topics, one of
the current open issues is task assignment and role selection in fast-
paced environments. In homogeneous teams, where robots have the ability to dynamically change roles, working in highly dynamic and stochastic environments, it is important that any solution is able to perform and
achieve results while complying with realtime constraints. In this paper,
we balance the advantages and disadvantages of completely decentralised
solutions and centralised ones, and then present our solution for leader
election among a team, which is based on the Raft algorithm and tack-
les two of its limitations. The proposed solution was implemented in a
real team of soccer-playing robots and the experimental results are thoroughly presented and discussed.

## 1 Introduction

In Multi-Agent Systems, several interacting intelligent agents pursue a goal by
performing a set of tasks. To do so, they need to share information and coordinate to maximize the group gain. Among different topics that orbit around
multi-agent coordination [13], one of the most common is task assignment. In
particular, when dealing with homogeneous teams, where any agent can assume
any available role, fixing the role per agent would not be the wisest decision, since
it would restrict the ability to dynamically change roles between team members,
therefore decreasing the overall performance. On the other hand, dynamically
assigning roles in a team can have some associated costs, namely processing time
and computing power.

One environment that has been empowering research in multi-agent coordination on autonomous and mobile robots is the RoboCup [7] - an event that occurs
annually since 1997 and gathers together researchers and robotics enthusiasts
from all around the world in a series of competitions around *R-Sports* (Robotic-
Sports) and a symposium. Among the different leagues present in RoboCup,
one of the strongest theme is robotic soccer, for which the Federation defined a
bold objective: *"By the middle of the 21st century, a team of fully autonomous*

© Springer Nature Switzerland AG 2019
D. Holz et al. (Eds.): RoboCup 2018, LNAI 11374, pp. 19–31, 2019.
https://doi.org/10.1007/978-3-030-27544-0_2

*humanoid robot soccer players shall win a soccer game, complying with the offi-
cial rules of FIFA, against the winner of the most recent World Cup".*

One of the RoboCup soccer leagues is the MSL (Middle-Size League) [14], a
league that is very challenging, not only in terms of regulations, but also due to
its rich environment (Fig. 1) - complex and semi-structured - that provides an
excellent testbed for autonomous robotic teams in stochastic and highly dynamic
environments.

**Fig. 1.** Middle-Size League finals in RoboCup 2013 at Eindhoven, Netherlands

The reason why a robotic soccer match has proved over the years to be
an excellent testbed is because it resembles more the real world than typical
pre-conceived research lab setups, especially due to its natural characteristics:
agents must be resilient both to unexpected situations (because the opponent
team actions can only be predicted up to a certain point) and to expeditious
changes of the world state at any time.

In this league, teams play with 5 field robots (including the goalkeeper)
and an auxiliary computer that usually acts as the coach, providing the user
interface for visualisation and establishes the link between the referee signals
and the playing robots. Humans are not allowed to interact with any system
that is taking part in the match. Additionally, since the coach computer is not
allowed to have sensors and there are no extra sensors installed around the field,
the playing robots must act as a sensor network for the coach, providing it with
the necessary information to base its decisions on.

The work described in this paper was accomplished within the MSL context,
more specifically in the CAMBADA (Cooperative Autonomous Mobile roBots
with Advanced Distributed Architecture) team [10], the MSL Robotic Soccer
team from the University of Aveiro. The project was founded in 2003 and is currently hosted by the IEETA IRIS (Intelligent Robotics and Intelligent Systems)
group.

For inter-robot communications, this team uses the Realtime Data Base
(RtDB) middleware [1], that provides seamless access to the complete state of

the team using a distributed database, partially replicated to all team members. Robots push information such as perceived ball position, self pose belief, coordination signals provided to achieve team-work tasks and other state variables. A portion of the information present locally on an agent is periodically and asynchronously broadcasted to all team members by a running process ('comm') that runs on each robot processing unit.

In a fast-paced and highly dynamic environment such as the RoboCup MSL, if task assignment constantly relied on negotiation techniques, they could easily become timely ineffective, due to the strict timing restrictions of the application and the delays caused by the negotiation itself. This is why fully-distributed techniques have generally been avoided for applications with realtime constraints. However, roles switch occurs with a low frequency, thus promoting the use of the coach computer to perform role selection among the team. However, as it will be discussed later, this constitutes a major single point of failure that, in the case of an actual collapse, may compromise the performance of the team.

In this paper, a thorough description of the leader election mechanism implemented in the CAMBADA team is described. We will start by discussing the coordination techniques widely used and described in the literature in Sect. 2. In Sect. 3, we formally describe the consensus problem and present two of the most reputable solutions to solve it, as well as their limitations. Sections 4 and 5 describe the proposed solution and its results, respectively. We finally conclude the paper with some final considerations on Sect. 6.

## 2   State of the Art

### 2.1   Distributed Assignment

In multi-agent systems, a common distributed approach is to dynamically assign roles locally (on each agent) based on a set of pre-defined policies that depend on their world-state *belief*. These policies must be defined in a way that guarantees convergence and avoid conflicts between intentions and/or actions [4]. This is often achieved using policy reconstruction methods, which make explicit predictions about an agent action, by explicitly running the decision-making algorithm of that agent, using shared plans [5] or by using a learned model of the other agent behaviour [3,6]. Some related work can achieve coordination when in low-communication and time-critical environments, provided that agents can periodically have full connectivity [15].

However, each agent has a slightly different world-state *belief* at a given time. Assuming that it would be possible to, in a real application, take an instant snapshot of the *beliefs* of all agents at the same time and, by looking into them, we would find (slight) differences between them. This is due to the fact that the information residing on the agent world state is affected by many disturbances (starting on the measurement itself, partial observance, unideal modelling, noise, integration errors and even network delays). Therefore, the obvious drawback of the distributed approach is that agents are basing their decisions upon different *beliefs*, which can easily lead to lack of consensus and conflicting decisions. Most distributed policies designed to reach a consensus on task assignment are based on the fact that there is a common world state *belief* for all agents, which in real realtime highly dynamic applications is rare.

To overcome this problem the agents can, instead of deciding locally and instantly committing to that decision, broadcast the intention and then use distributed negotiation algorithms to deal with any conflicts [17]. However, this approach is dependent on the network conditions and negotiation is not practical when the application demands a high level of reactivity.

## 2.2  Centralised Assignment

As opposed to fully distributed approaches, centralised architectures rely on a single agent to control and monitor the action plans of all other agents. Since this coordinator agent gets to decide on the final plan (which includes all agents partial plans), any conflicts between agents' plans can be taken into account during the planning process.

Centralising the decision to achieve consensus has some advantages over a distributed approach:

- Centrally solves the problem of *tightly-coupled coordination* that arises whenever there are one or more actions of one agent that affect the optimal action choice of another team member, since the decisions are based on a single belief of the world state.
- From a software architecture point of view, it is simpler to implement and maintain.

Albeit these positive aspects, a completely centralised approach has three main drawbacks with respect to decentralised solutions:

- **No redundancy.** The coordinator agent constitutes a single point of failure - if it fails, the whole team may fail due to lack of coordination.
- **Network delays can propagate to actions.** Decisions need to be communicated to the agents, which takes time that, in some applications, depending on the authority level of the coordinator agent, may be critical.
- **Limited scalability.** A higher number of agents will require higher computational power on the coordinator agent to process and to devise a plan for the complete team of agents.

## 2.3  Centralised Assignment with Leader Election

When scalability is not a priority, some systems rely on centralised decision taken by one of the participating agents. However, network delays make it unfeasible for the leader to make realtime decisions when the environment requires a high level of reactivity. Therefore, the leader has to provide the team high-level coaching hints that will work towards a group consensus, while leaving low-level decisions (the fast-paced action that needs to be taken locally) to the other team-members.

The election of the coordinator agent is a fundamental part of this type of architecture to overcome a possible faulty coordinator. In case the coordinator fails, the agents need to recognise a coordinator failure and then coordinate to find the next leader - the agent that will replace the previous one.

# 3   The Consensus Problem

The consensus algorithms described below were designed to achieve consensus between processes or between server clusters, but in this section, we will refrain from using the term *agent* or *server* and will use the more inclusive term *node*. Consensus is a general term used to describe a state where participating nodes on a system agree on something, bound under certain conditions.

When applied to Multi-Agent Systems, consensus algorithms allow a group of agents to work coherently, enabling the system as a whole to survive in the event of sporadic failures of one or more of its members. For example, consensus algorithms have been successfully implemented for distributed storage on server clusters using log replication [11], as well as in robotic networks [9].

## 3.1   Paxos

Over the last decade, Paxos [8] has dominated the subject of consensus algorithms for software systems. Paxos has either been applied to or influenced many systems to solve a consensus problem. Multi-Paxos [16] is also referred in the literature - it was proposed as an optimisation to Paxos, since it essentially skips one step, which has no impact on coherence, provided that the leader remains the same and online for a long period of time.

However, the (Multi-)Paxos algorithm, which was conceived upon a complex theoretical model makes it less convenient to implement in real-world systems: in order to properly run it on practical systems, significant changes to its architecture are required [2].

## 3.2   Raft

As a response to the concerns mentioned above, Diego Ongaro and John Ousterhout have developed the Raft [12] protocol, with understandability and implementability as a primary goal, but without compromising the correctness or efficiency of the (Multi-)Paxos. Using techniques such as decomposition and state space reduction, the authors have not only been able to separate leader election, log replication and safety, but also reduce the possible states of the protocol to a minimal functional subset.

**Assumptions.** The following three assumptions are made by Raft:

- **Machines run asynchronously:** there is no clock synchronisation between different systems and there are no upper bounds on message delays or computation times.

- **Unreliable links:** possibility of indefinite networks delays, packet loss, partitions, reordering, or duplication of messages.
- **Unreliable nodes:** processes may crash, may eventually recover, and in that case rejoin the protocol. Byzantine failures are assumed not to occur (Fig. 2).

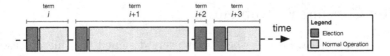

**Fig. 2.** Timeline of example execution of Raft, adapted from [12]. In three of the presented *terms*, a leader was elected after an election period. Only in *term i + 2*, consensus was not reached during the election process, so a new election stars.

**Consensus by Strong Leadership.** Raft achieves the consensus by a strong leadership approach. In steady-state, a node in a Raft cluster is either a *LEADER* or a *FOLLOWER*. There can only be one leader in the cluster and when the leader becomes unavailable, an election occurs, and nodes can become *CANDIDATE*s.

In the original Raft system applied to log replication, the *LEADER* is fully responsible for managing log replication to the followers (the remaining nodes) and regularly informs the followers of its existence by sending heartbeat messages. Upon receiving this heartbeat, a *FOLLOWER* node resets a timer and whenever it reaches a timeout value the node can become a *CANDIDATE* to initiate a new election.

Each leader is elected for a *term* - a discrete temporal identifier (counter). At most, one leader can be elected in a given *term* and the event of a new election marks the start of a new *term*.

During an election, three situations can occur:

1. The majority of the nodes vote for the *CANDIDATE*, meaning this node can switch to the *LEADER* state and start sending heartbeat messages to others in the cluster to establish authority.
2. If other *CANDIDATE*s receive a packet, they check for the *term* number. If the *term* number is greater than their own, they accept the node as the leader and return to *FOLLOWER* state. If the *term* number is smaller, they reject the packet and still remain a *CANDIDATE*.
3. The *CANDIDATE* neither loses nor wins. If more than one node becomes a *CANDIDATE* at the same time, the vote can be split with no clear majority. In this case, a new election begins after one of the *CANDIDATE*s times out.

**Limitations.** Two main limitations have been identified in the Raft protocol:

- **1 and 2 active nodes corner-cases:** when there are less than 3 nodes available, Raft will fail to elect a leader, because it is impossible to achieve the majority of votes in either of the cases.

– **No prioritisation:** nodes are equally probable of becoming the leader. In some heterogeneous clusters, the user might want to defer the leadership to a node that has more computing power available.

## 4 Proposed Solution

Our leader election solution is based on the Raft algorithm for that purpose, with some adaptations to overcome the aforementioned limitations. Furthermore, we have integrated it in the RtDB middleware as an asynchronous service. By doing so, the information from the current leader is available for all agents at any time without re-configuration.

### 4.1 Timing Parameters

Three crucial aspects to consider when implementing this solution are the parameterisation of the sending frequency of heartbeat packets ($f_{HB} = 1/\Delta T_{HB}$), the heartbeat timeout ($T_{max,HB}$) and the election timeout ($T_{max,E}$). Despite Raft originally suggesting times in the order of tens or hundreds of milliseconds, the selection of these times depend a lot on the application, fail-frequency and the communication medium between nodes.

In most mobile robotic teams, the robots communicate with each other in one or more of the many different available forms of radio communication. In this particular application, robots are using the Wi-Fi (IEEE 802.11a standard) in a spectrally dense environment, with strict bandwidth limitations (currently 2.2 Mbit/s).

To select the heartbeat frequency $f_{HB}$, a trade-off between delay in the start of a new election and bandwidth expense has to be considered, while accounting for the actual role of the leader and the frequency that its orders change. This is important because the robots will follow the latest available order while a new leader is being elected.

The heartbeat timeout $T_{max,HB}$ should be selected in line with the packet loss experienced in the testbed environment. For example, when selecting an heartbeat timeout that is more than twice the maximum heartbeat packet period, then a new election will occur when two consecutive heartbeats are not received from the leader.

The election timeout $T_{max,E}$ accounts for the time we allow the exchange of vote packets and is important whenever no majority of votes is achieved by any of the candidates.

Based on these assumptions, the values were selected as follows, with the ranges defining the limits of random uniform distributions.

$$40\,\text{ms} \leq \Delta T_{HB} \leq 60\,\text{ms} \tag{1}$$

$$250\,\text{ms} \leq T_{max,HB} \leq 400\,\text{ms} \tag{2}$$

$$T_{max,E} = 100\,\text{ms} \tag{3}$$

## 4.2  The Backup State

To tackle the first limitation (failure to achieve majority in an election with less than 3 active nodes), apart from *LEADER, FOLLOWER* and *CANDIDATE* states in the original Raft algorithm, we have introduced the *BACKUP* state, which is triggered whenever there is only 1 or 2 active nodes in the system. The complete state machine is present in Fig. 3.

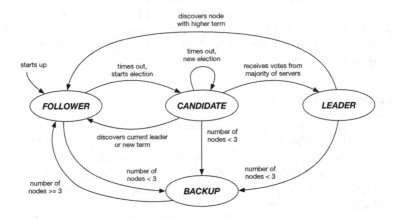

**Fig. 3.** State machine of the proposed solution

A node maintains a dynamic dictionary of timers, indexed by the peer ID. The timer belonging to a peer node is reset whenever a heartbeat or acknowledge packet is received. The active nodes list is determined by the peer IDs in the dictionary that have an elapsed timer lower than the heartbeat timeout. When in a *BACKUP* state, the leader is determined by the lowest ID among the active nodes.

## 4.3  Preferred Leader Agent

In our particular application, in order to free computational resources from the robots, it is wise to give preference to a coach computer to be the leader, whenever it is available, while keeping the leader election functionality active as a redundancy mechanism for when it fails.

In order to achieve this priority for the coach agent, while keeping harmony and consistency among the voting agents and the voting process, we skip the heartbeat timer reset on the coach agent. When joining the network, the coach agent will start as a follower and will start receiving the heartbeat packets from the current leader, updating its *term* accordingly, but ignoring the heartbeat timer reset step. When reaching the heartbeat timeout, the coach agent will start a new election in a higher *term* and the previous leader will retreat. This constitutes the only situation when an agent intentionally takes over the team leadership.

## 5   Experimental Setup and Results

To test this solution, an experimental setup has been devised with 5 computers running the communication process with the leader election algorithm described in the previous section and an experiment coordinator. The coach agent was disconnected. The coordinator was impaired from becoming the leader, but participates in the voting phase and is responsible for monitoring the leader selection evolution, measuring times and forcing periodic communication failures (each 5 s, approximately) on the elected leader, hence triggering a new election, and logging data for offline analysis. The setup is depicted in Fig. 4.

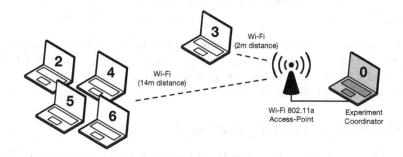

**Fig. 4.** Experimental setup

The system has been setup and worked for 16 h and 37 min, producing a total number of 11970 *terms*. From this dataset it is possible to statistically analyse the performance of the proposed solution with respect to *term* period, election time, occurrence of simultaneous multiple candidates in an election, leader attribution distribution and also the number of failed elections due to lack of majority in the voting process. Among all samples, the measured *term* time was $5000.15 \pm 92.73$ ms (mean and standard deviation), which is consistent with our experimental setup described above.

### 5.1   Failed Elections

Having the coordinator participating in the voting rounds, makes it possible to tie a voting, because the total population consists of 6 agents. A failed election occurs whenever none of the candidates receives the majority of votes. From the total number of 11970 *terms*, there were 2 registered failed elections.

### 5.2   Election Time

Election times were inspected (Fig. 5) and it was verified that they follow a distribution that is consistent with the selected heartbeat timeout time $T_{max,HB} \in$ [250 –400] ms, picked by a random uniform distribution on that range.

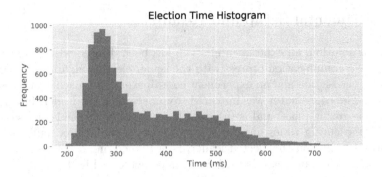

**Fig. 5.** Election time histogram

It is also important to mention that apart from the results presented on Fig. 5, there were 5 other samples with higher election times, namely: 1.1, 2.2, 2.6, 2.7 and 2.8 s. These 5 samples were not included in the Figure to improve visibility of most samples in the plot.

### 5.3 Simultaneous Multiple Candidates

The occurrence of multiple candidates for election was also analysed. These results are shown in Fig. 6 (with the y axis in a logarithmic scale), were we can see that in 97.4% of the samples there is only one candidate, 2.5% two candidates and 0.03% (only 3 times in the whole run) three candidates, which was the maximum count for multiple candidates in a single round.

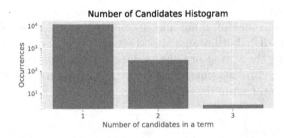

**Fig. 6.** Number of candidates histogram - y axis in logarithmic scale

### 5.4 Leadership Attribution

A uniform distribution of leaders among the eligible agents was expected, however there are small differences between the agents, as shown in Fig. 7a Since agent 3 (the laptop closer to the access-point) showed the maximum number of wins in elections, we wanted to investigate further if this was merely a coincidence or if the relative position to the access-point would affect the priority of being selected as a leader when there are multiple candidates.

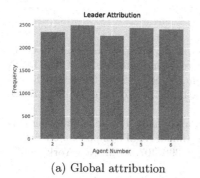

(a) Global attribution

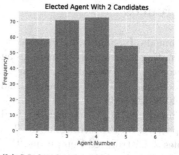

(b) Multiple candidates attribution

**Fig. 7.** Leadership attribution analysis

To test that hypothesis, we analysed the leader attribution in the *terms* for which there were more than one candidate (Fig. 7b). These results do not show a clear higher chance of agent 3 to become a leader in conflict situations. Because in this setup many external factors can influence the communication medium, further tests must be performed with laptops' positions shuffled between runs.

## 6   Conclusion

After discussing the original Raft approach to achieve consensus on machine clusters, two main limitations have been identified - a corner-case when there are only 1 or 2 active nodes and the lack of prioritisation among agents to become a leader. A solution that is based on the Raft leader election protocol has been described and successfully implemented to overcome the aforementioned limitations.

An experimental setup has been created to test our leader election solution, by continuously forcing a new election. The obtained results are in line with the timings set for the asynchronous activity of this mechanism, set accordingly to the requirements of the application - in this case, a robotic soccer team.

In a nutshell, the proposed solution is suitable to select a leader among the team agents. It accounts for the possibility of having a preferred leader agent, providing a fault-tolerant and reliable redundancy mechanism whenever the leader becomes inactive.

**Acknowledgement.** This research is supported by Portuguese National Funds through Foundation for Science and Technology (FCT), in the context of the project UID/CEC/00127/2013 and by European Union's FP7 under EuRoC grant agreement CP-IP 608849.

# References

1. Almeida, L., Santos, F., Facchinetti, T., Pedreiras, P., Silva, V., Lopes, L.S.: Coordinating distributed autonomous agents with a real-time database: the CAMBADA project. In: Aykanat, C., Dayar, T., Körpeoğlu, İ. (eds.) ISCIS 2004. LNCS, vol. 3280, pp. 876–886. Springer, Heidelberg (2004). https://doi.org/10.1007/978-3-540-30182-0_88

2. Chandra, T.D., Griesemer, R., Redstone, J.: Paxos made live: an engineering perspective. In: Proceedings of the Twenty-Sixth Annual ACM Symposium on Principles of Distributed Computing, PODC 2007, pp. 398–407. ACM, New York (2007). https://doi.org/10.1145/1281100.1281103

3. Farouk, G.M., Moawad, I.F., Aref, M.M.: A machine learning based system for mostly automating opponent modeling in real-time strategy games. In: 12th International Conference on Computer Engineering and Systems (ICCES), pp. 337–346, December 2017. https://doi.org/10.1109/ICCES.2017.8275329

4. Groen, F.C.A., Spaan, M.T.J., Kok, J.R., Pavlin, G.: Real world multi-agent systems: information sharing, coordination and planning. In: ten Cate, B.D., Zeevat, H.W. (eds.) TbiLLC 2005. LNCS (LNAI), vol. 4363, pp. 154–165. Springer, Heidelberg (2007). https://doi.org/10.1007/978-3-540-75144-1_12

5. Grosz, B.J., Hunsberger, L., Kraus, S.: Planning and acting together. AI Mag. **20**(4), 23 (1999). https://doi.org/10.1609/aimag.v20i4.1476

6. Hsieh, J.L., Sun, C.T.: Building a player strategy model by analyzing replays of real-time strategy games. In: 2008 IEEE International Joint Conference on Neural Networks (IEEE World Congress on Computational Intelligence), pp. 3106–3111, June 2008. https://doi.org/10.1109/IJCNN.2008.4634237

7. Kitano, H., Asada, M., Kuniyoshi, Y., Noda, I., Osawa, E.: RoboCup: the robot world cup initiative. In: The First International Conference on Autonomous Agent, Agents 1997, pp. 340–347 (1997). 10.1.1.50.5425

8. Lamport, L.: The part-time parliament. ACM Trans. Comput. Syst. **16**(2), 133–169 (1998). https://doi.org/10.1145/279227.279229

9. Montijano, E., Sagüés, C.: Robotic Networks and the Consensus Problem, pp. 9–19. Springer, Cham (2015). https://doi.org/10.1007/978-3-319-15699-6_2

10. Neves, A., et al.: CAMBADA soccer team: from robot architecture to multiagent coordination (chap. 2), pp. 19–45. I-Tech Education and Publishing, Vienna (2010)

11. Oki, B.M., Liskov, B.H.: Viewstamped replication: a new primary copy method to support highly-available distributed systems. In: Proceedings of the Seventh Annual ACM Symposium on Principles of Distributed Computing, PODC 1988, pp. 8–17. ACM, New York (1988). https://doi.org/10.1145/62546.62549

12. Ongaro, D., Ousterhout, J.: In search of an understandable consensus algorithm. In: Proceedings of the 2014 USENIX Conference on USENIX Annual Technical Conference, USENIX ATC 2014, pp. 305–320. USENIX Association, Berkeley (2014)

13. Reis, L.: Coordination in multi-agent systems: applications in university management and robotic soccer. Ph.D. thesis, FEUP, July 2003

14. Soetens, R., van de Molengraft, R., Cunha, B.: RoboCup MSL - history, accomplishments, current status and challenges ahead. In: Bianchi, R.A.C., Akin, H.L., Ramamoorthy, S., Sugiura, K. (eds.) RoboCup 2014. LNCS (LNAI), vol. 8992, pp. 624–635. Springer, Cham (2015). https://doi.org/10.1007/978-3-319-18615-3_51

15. Stone, P., Veloso, M.: Task decomposition, dynamic role assignment, and low-bandwidth communication for real-time strategic teamwork. Artif. Intell. **110**(2), 241–273 (1999). https://doi.org/10.1016/S0004-3702(99)00025-9

16. Van Renesse, R., Altinbuken, D.: Paxos made moderately complex. ACM Comput. Surv. **47**(3), 42:1–42:36 (2015). https://doi.org/10.1145/2673577
17. de Weerd, H., Verbrugge, R., Verheij, B.: Negotiating with other minds: the role of recursive theory of mind in negotiation with incomplete information. Auton. Agent Multi-Agent Syst. **31**(2), 250–287 (2017). https://doi.org/10.1007/s10458-015-9317-1

# Visual SLAM-Based Localization and Navigation for Service Robots: The Pepper Case

Cristopher Gómez[1], Matías Mattamala[1(✉)], Tim Resink[3],
and Javier Ruiz-del-Solar[1,2]

[1] Department of Electrical Engineering, Universidad de Chile, Santiago, Chile
{cristopher.gomez,mmattamala,jruizd}@ing.uchile.cl
[2] Advanced Mining Technology Center, Universidad de Chile, Santiago, Chile
[3] Delft University of Technology, Delft, The Netherlands
p.w.resink@student.tudelft.nl

**Abstract.** We propose a Visual-SLAM based localization and navigation system for service robots. Our system is built on top of the ORB-
SLAM monocular system but extended by the inclusion of wheel odometry in the estimation procedures. As a case study, the proposed system is
validated using the Pepper robot, whose short-range LIDARs and RGB-
D camera do not allow the robot to self-localize in large environments.
The localization system is tested in navigation tasks using Pepper in two
different environments: a medium-size laboratory, and a large-size hall.

## 1 Introduction

Pepper is the official robot used in the RoboCup@Home Standard Platform
League. It presents several advantages for human-robot interaction such as its
friendly appearance but has important limitations such as its reduced sensing
and computing capabilities. In contrast to custom robots which generally rely
on expensive LIDARs for metric localization and navigation, which work in both
indoor and outdoor environments, Pepper has short-range LIDARs and an RGB-
D camera that provide reliable localization only in small indoor rooms, being
unable to provide useful information to localize the robot in large environments.
This is a big deal for Pepper, which is expected to be used not only in homes,
but also in public places like hospitals, shopping malls, and schools.

To address this issue, we built upon the recent advances of visual SLAM systems to develop a visual-SLAM based self-localization solution aided by wheel
odometry, which allows Pepper to self-localize and navigate in large environments. The reason to include odometry in the visual estimation procedures is
to recover the metric scale (unknown in typical pure-visual schemes) and to

---

C. Gómez, M. Mattamala, T. Resink—Equal contribution.

D. Holz et al. (Eds.): RoboCup 2018, LNAI 11374, pp. 32–44, 2019.
https://doi.org/10.1007/978-3-030-27544-0_3

make the visual system more robust to tracking failures. This is vital for navigation tasks that require a "continuous" localization hypothesis to work. The proposed solution is based on an open-source visual SLAM system, ORB-SLAM [10], which is extended by the inclusion of the wheel's odometry in the estimation procedures.

In Sect. 2 we present a brief overview of modern SLAM systems. Then, in Sect. 3 we describe some basic notation as well as relevant characteristics of the Pepper robot. Afterwards, we present our localization and navigation approach in Sect. 4. In Sect. 5 we present two experiments of localization and navigation with the Pepper robot in different environments. Finally, Sect. 6 concludes the work with discussion and recommendations for future developments along this line.

## 2   Visual SLAM

Visual SLAM has been a hot topic during the last years since it presents a low-cost solution for applications that require localization and mapping features such as augmented reality, virtual reality, and autonomous systems (e.g. autonomous cars, inspection drones). Being originally formulated as a filtering problem, nowadays optimization-based approaches are preferable by its superior accuracy at similar computational cost [13]. Optimization-based approaches model the problem as a *factor graph* which probabilistically relates several variables -such as poses and landmarks-, by the so-called *factors*, that correspond to sensor measurements or physical constraints between the variables [1]. An example of a visual SLAM system is shown in Fig. 1.

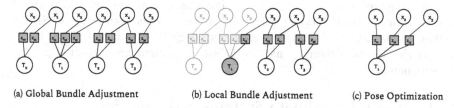

(a) Global Bundle Adjustment          (b) Local Bundle Adjustment          (c) Pose Optimization

**Fig. 1.** Different factor graphs related to optimization approaches in ORB-SLAM. Circles denotes variables such as map points and keyframes within a visual SLAM scheme; white are active, gray fixed. Squares denote factors or measurements.

The factor graph can be formulated as a non-linear least squares problem [1] that aims to find the states $\mathcal{X}^* = \mathcal{X}_1, ..., \mathcal{X}m$ that minimize the error between the measurements $\mathcal{Z}_i$, and an *observational model* $h_i(\mathcal{X}_i)$ that "predicts" the expected measurement given the state $\mathcal{X}_i$[1]:

---

[1] The operator $\boxminus$ generalizes the concept of subtraction for non-Euclidean spaces. Please refer to Hertzberg *et al.* [5] for a complete treatment.

$$\mathcal{X}^* = \arg\min_{\mathcal{X}} = \sum_{i=1}^{m} \|h_i(\mathcal{X}_i) \boxminus \mathcal{Z}_i\|_{\boldsymbol{\Omega}_i}^2 \tag{1}$$

The same formulation holds for the visual case, where the states correspond to selected camera poses of the trajectory -keyframes- and also the map representation -3D points, surfels, voxels, etc.-, and the measurements are reprojections of the map into the image plane.

Regarding some actual systems, different solutions have been developed for monocular and stereo/depth sensors. We are concerned about monocular solutions since cameras are ubiquitous in current robots while being "cheap" sensors in comparison to the other two; they also can work in both indoor and outdoor environments. Monocular visual SLAM systems are either *feature-based* that utilize just some features in the image, such as ORB-SLAM [10], or direct methods that exploit the complete information from every image as in LSD-SLAM [3].

The main issue with monocular systems is that they require a moving camera in order to estimate the depth of the scene, as well as depending on an unknown scale factor that maps the estimated states to physically consistent dimensions. The typical approach to solve the problem relies on the usage of different sources of information that provides the scale, such as inertial measurements units (IMU); however, this increases the computational requirements of the estimation problem, since the number of states increases [12].

The utilization of visual localization systems in the RoboCup@Home has been disregarded since most of the custom robots could afford accurate but expensive LIDAR systems [2,7], which provide a simpler solution. Nevertheless, since the range of Pepper's LIDARs and depth camera are defined by the manufacturer, and the RoboCup@Home SSPL (Social Standard Platform League) forbids the use of additional sensors, it is unfeasible for the robot neither localize nor navigate in large environments. For this reason, we propose a visual approach for the localization problem based on an open-source visual SLAM system, ORB-SLAM [10], and we present a strategy to solve visual SLAM issues (mainly the lack of a metric scale) by aiding the system with wheel odometry measurements.

## 3     Platform, Coordinate Systems and Notation

### 3.1     Notation

To prevent confusion in notation, we follow the conventions of Paul Furgale[2]:

- Coordinate frame A is notated as $\underrightarrow{\mathcal{F}}_A$.
- Homogeneous transformation matrix $_o\mathbf{T}_{WC} \in SE(3)$ represents the pose of the camera frame $\underrightarrow{\mathcal{F}}_C$ with respect to the world frame, $\underrightarrow{\mathcal{F}}_W$, seen from frame $\underrightarrow{\mathcal{F}}_O$. A vector expressed in world frame W, $_W\mathbf{v}$ can be hereby transformed to the camera frame C by the rotation matrix $\mathbf{R}_{WC} \in SO(3)$, as $_C\mathbf{v} = \mathbf{R}_{WC}\,_W\mathbf{v}$

---

[2] http://paulfurgale.info/news/2014/6/9/representing-robot-pose-the-good-the-bad-and-the-ugly.

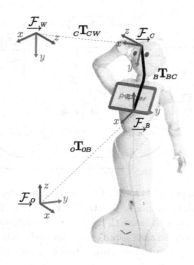

**Fig. 2.** Coordinate frames used in this work, we follow the classic conventions with X red, Y green and Z blue. $\mathcal{F}_C$ denotes the camera frame, $\mathcal{F}_O$ the odometry frame and $\mathcal{F}_B$ the body's. Pepper picture is based on Philippe Dureuil's. (Color figure online)

– The homogeneous transformation matrix $_C\mathbf{T}_{WC}$ will be abbreviated to $\mathbf{T}_{WC}$ for reader convenience unless otherwise indicated.

## 3.2   Pepper Robot

Pepper is a wheeled humanoid platform. It has a mobile omnidirectional base and 20 degrees of freedom, including an actuated pelvis and neck. It has two Omnivision OV5640 cameras, located in the forehead and the mouth, in addition to an RGB-D sensor in the eyes. Additionally, the base has three LIDARs and an IMU. In order to access the sensors and control the robot, Softbank provides an API to its middleware, NAOQi.

Since we base our system in the ROS framework, we access sensing and perform control through the `naoqi_driver` ROS package. We principally use the images from the forehead camera at a 640 × 480 pixels resolution, as well as the internally computed odometry measurements; the algorithmic details about the latter are unknown to the user.

We considered two main reference frames for this work (Fig. 2): On the one hand, the odometry frame denoted by $\mathcal{F}_O$ describes the pose of the robot relative to the initial pose, as defined in ROS REP 105[3]. We use this frame to describe the pose of the robot's torso (body) computed by the internal wheel odometry, denoted by $_O\mathbf{T}_{OB}$. On the other, ORB-SLAM has its own reference frame (world) $\mathcal{F}_W$ that depends on the initialization of the system, hence it may change every

---

[3] http://www.ros.org/reps/rep-0105.html.

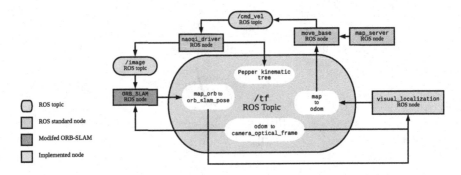

**Fig. 3.** Overview of our proposed system. The camera images are feed to the ORB-SLAM system together with the camera position with respect to the odometry frame (*odom*). An estimated camera position with respect to an arbitrary fixed frame is given as output by ORB-SLAM. The `visual_localization` node takes this information and the Pepper kinematic information to compute a transformation between the standard fixed frame *map* and the *odom* frame.

time the system is reset. The estimate provided by ORB-SLAM corresponds to the world position with respect to the camera pose, $_c\mathbf{T}_{cw}$.

# 4 Localization and Navigation System

Our visual SLAM-based localization and navigation system for Pepper consist of three main components, which are shown in Fig. 3. Firstly, an ORB-SLAM-based localization and mapping system, which uses a single RGB camera located in Pepper's forehead, and odometry measurements computed by the proprietary Pepper's software. The second component correspond to the `visual_localization`[4] ROS node that transforms ORB-SLAM's camera pose estimate to a transformation between the standard *map* frame and the *odom* frame. Finally, the node `move_base`[5] executes the navigation process.

## 4.1 ORB-SLAM-based Localization

Our localization system maintains the same software architecture with 3 parallel threads, original from ORB-SLAM2 [11]: incoming images are processed in the *Tracking* thread, creating new map points and estimating the current camera pose $\mathbf{T}_{cw}$ in world frame $\mathcal{F}_w$; a *Local Mapping* thread which builds on the map and the keyframes and frequently performs local bundle adjustments to update the positions of map points and camera poses at the keyframes; a *Loop Closing* thread which detects loops in the trajectory and propagates a correction through the trajectory poses and the map. In addition, we implemented the following improvements:

---

[4] https://github.com/ristofer/visual_localization/.
[5] http://wiki.ros.org/move_base.

**Tracking Modifications.** We changed the Tracking thread to process not only images but also odometry measurements, obtained directly from ROS. Odometry measurements are computed within the Pepper's internal software and published in ROS through NAOqi wrappers with respect to the *odom* frame, shown as $\mathcal{F}_o$ in Fig. 2. Our ROS-compatible wrapper for ORB-SLAM subscribes the tf topic and images, and requests an odometry measurement every time a new image is received, obtaining a synchronized pair image-odometry. Later, every time a new keyframe is created after a successful camera tracking, the odometry information is also included in the keyframe.

In addition, since the original behavior of ORB-SLAM is to stop providing camera poses when camera tracking fails, and wait until a relocalization, which is not a desirable strategy while navigating[6], we set the camera estimation equal to the odometry prediction. This ensures a continuous camera pose hypothesis for planning tasks but requires that the metric scale is initialized.

**Metric Scale Initialization.** We did not utilize any general system initialization solution as in [9] but preferred a multi-step approach as in [12]. We first wait until the pure visual SLAM system is initialized and the unscaled map built, to then compute the scale from the odometry information between keyframes.

By comparing the relative translations between keyframes as predicted by ORB-SLAM $\Delta\mathbf{p}_o(i-1,i)$ and the odometry $\Delta\mathbf{p}_w(i-1,i)$, the scale can be retrieved and the map and keyframe poses can be updated by the method of Horn [6] (Eq. (2)). However, the initial map is subject to major change in the early stages of the mapping. Therefor the scale correction is done after a fixed number of $N$ keyframes have been created, ensuring a satisfactory converged map and thus a reasonably reliable scale correction. The success of this strategy only depends on the environment's size and the motion performed by the robot; an additional discussion is given in Sect. 5.

$$s = \frac{\sqrt{\sum_i^N \|\Delta\mathbf{p}_o(i-1,i)\|^2}}{\sqrt{\sum_i^N \|\Delta\mathbf{p}_w(i-1,i)\|^2}} \tag{2}$$

After the scale update, a Global Bundle Adjustment (Global BA) is performed to guarantee an optimal map reconstruction.

**Local Mapping.** Every time a new keyframe is created, *Local Mapping* performs an optimization in a subset of the complete trajectory updating both the poses and the map -the so-called *local window*. The parts of the trajectory to be optimized are keyframes in the neighborhood of the last added keyframe, and also map points being observed by those; the neighbors are selected by the so-called *covisibility graph* [10]. This operation on the local window ensures an efficient optimization process even in large maps.

---

[6] Unless high-level behaviors to detect failures are considered.

Since the initialization procedure makes the current trajectory and map *metrically consistent*, it is possible to fuse the visual information with wheel odometry information to avoid drift. This is done by adding odometry factors or *constraints* between keyframes. In order to do so, the odometry measurement is mapped from the odometry frame $\mathcal{F}_o$ to the camera frame $\mathcal{F}_c$ by using Pepper's forward kinematics. Hence, we compute the difference between the odometry measurements $i-1$ and $i$, $_c\mathbf{T}_{C_{i-1},C_i}$, between all the keyframes in the local window, which hopefully match the difference between the keyframes' pose, $(\mathbf{T}_{C_{i-1}W}\mathbf{T}_{C_iW})$. The error between the odometry's and ORB-SLAM's differences are defined in the minimal representation of the pose, i.e. 6-dimensional, which is achieved by using the *logarithm map* of SE(3):

$$\varepsilon_{odo} = \mathrm{Log}_{\mathrm{SE}(3)}\left(_c\mathbf{T}_{C_{i-1},C_i}^{-1}\mathbf{T}_{C_{i-1}W}\mathbf{T}_{C_iW}^{-1}\right). \tag{3}$$

This residual is defined for every pair of keyframes within the local window; additionally, keyframes with neighbors which are not in the local window, are also added as fixed nodes in the optimization. The corresponding optimization problem that minimizes visual error terms $\varepsilon_{vis}$ (as defined in [10]) and odometry terms $\varepsilon_{odo}$ (Eq. (3)), is:

$$\mathcal{X}^* = \arg\min_{\mathcal{X}} = \sum_{(i,k)}\|\varepsilon_{vis}\|_{\mathbf{\Omega}_{vis}}^2 + \sum_{(i-1,i)}\|\varepsilon_{odo}\|_{\mathbf{\Omega}_{odo}}^2 \tag{4}$$

The optimization problem in Eq. 4 is solved with the graph optimization framework *g2o*[8] using fixed information matrices $\mathbf{\Omega}_{odo}, \mathbf{\Omega}_{vis}$. The resulting keyframe poses and map points are then updated, and the *Local Mapping* thread awaits until a new keyframe is added from *Tracking*.

**Localization Mode and Map Reuse.** ORB-SLAM provides the option to localize in a previously built map, disabling the SLAM capabilities. This localization can run in a single thread, hence requiring a fraction of the computational requirements compared to the full ORB-SLAM system. Nevertheless, in order to perform localization-only, it is required a map that was built in the same session.

Since this is not generally the case, we use map saving capabilities (taken from a fork of ORB-SLAM[7]) and implemented a different behavior for the system when it is launch with a pre-built map, that first tries to relocalize and then continue mapping incrementally. These minor changes allowed us to build maps even during different sessions once the relocalization is successful.

### 4.2    Navigation

For the navigation part, we assume the ORB-SLAM's map was already built, so we can rely on the localization mode.

---

[7] https://github.com/Alkaid-Benetnash/ORB_SLAM2.

The pose estimation performed by ORB-SLAM is 6-dimensional since it considers a camera freely moving in the space, which would be an overkill to perform planning with Pepper. In order to use ORB-SLAM's estimates within a planar navigation framework, we developed the `visual_localization` node, which takes the estimated position of the camera with respect to the ORB-SLAM world frame and computes a transformation between the ROS standard *map* and *odom* frames. This transformation represents the Pepper position in the ORB-SLAM map based on the estimated pose of the Pepper's camera and its kinematic information.

The `move_base` package is used to navigate. Our localization system basically replaces the `amcl`[8] package in the ROS Navigation Stack. The `move_base` package uses the pose estimate provided by the localization system and Pepper's laser readings to compute the cost map necessary for planning. Thus, lasers are not used for localization, but for obstacle detection and path planning.

## 5   Experiments and Results

### 5.1   Experimental Setup

We considered two real environments of the Faculty of Physical and Mathematical Sciences of Universidad de Chile to test our system: *Mechatronics Laboratory* and *School Building South Hall*. The chosen places were different in size, furniture, and visual features complexity, being the latter of paramount importance for the visual SLAM system.

- The Mechatronics Laboratory (Fig. 4a) is a $10 \times 9\,m^2$ space. The main furniture are rolling chairs and work tables. It is a feature-rich space comparable to the RoboCup Arena; however, it has various windows that enable the pass of natural light.
- The School Building South Hall (Fig. 4b) has an area of $16 \times 27.5\,m^2$. It is an open space with pillars and doors, but generally feature-less, making it the most challenging environment for our system.

To have a ground truth reference, a Google Tango Tablet is used (Fig. 4c).

### 5.2   Experiments

**Mapping.** The first experiment considered a localization and mapping task; this was performed in both the Mechatronics Lab (Fig. 4a) and South Hall (Fig. 4b). We remote controlled the robot to build a three dimensional map to be later used for localization. Table 1 compare different mapping results through the *Absolute Trajectory Error* [14], a metric that calculates the root mean square error $RMSE$ defined as $\left(\frac{1}{N}\sum_i^N \|p_{e_i} - p_{gt_i}\|^2\right)^{1/2}$ between the localization estimate $p_{e_i}$ and the ground truth $p_{gt_i}$ through all the time indices.

---

[8] http://wiki.ros.org/amcl.

**Fig. 4.** *Left:* Mechatronics Lab. *Center:* South Hall. *Right:* Pepper with Google Tango Tablet attached for ground truth measurements.

**Table 1.** Absolute Trajectory Error (ATE) in meters, for each place and axis. A mapping experiment was performed in the Mechatronics Laboratory and in the South Hall. The estimated trajectory and the ground truth was used to calculate the ATE.

| Place | ATE X [m] | ATE Y [m] | ATE Z [m] |
|---|---|---|---|
| Mechatronics Laboratory | 0.270 | 0.249 | 0.080 |
| South Hall | 0.619 | 0.849 | 0.390 |

During all the experiments we noticed that the robot must move smoothly and preferably sideways in order to triangulate the initial map; pure rotational factors must be avoided despite the offset between the head camera and the base's axis of rotation. The initial displacement is primordial to recover a reliable scale factor as well. However, this also depends on a parameter that sets the number of keyframes to wait until the scale is recovered with Eq. 2, which is set empirically.

Regarding mapping, as is expected from a feature-based visual SLAM system, the number of points and quality of the map increases in feature-rich environments. In addition, compared to LIDAR mapping, visual mapping requires significantly more time. This because map creation depends on the field-of-view (FOV) of the camera, which is very narrow in Pepper, requiring to map the same place from multiple views in order make it useful for robust localization. LIDAR does not suffer from this issue since localization is performed by point cloud alignment rather than feature matching. However, feature matching has the advantage of providing instantaneous relocalization when the robot is lost since places are uniquely defined by a bag-of-words representation [10].

**Localization and Navigation.** We performed a second experiment to test the localization and navigation in a known place, i.e., with a pre-built map. This was also executed in the Mechatronics Laboratory and South Hall.

We commanded the robot to navigate without operator help to a relative point with respect to its initial pose, which exploited the localization capabilities of our system in a known environment. Localization results are shown in Figs. 5 and 6.

Our experiments show the performance of the system, which uses both visual localization and odometry fusion (highlighted in gray) and odometry-only local-

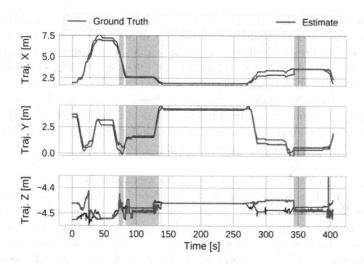

**Fig. 5.** Navigation test on the Mechatronics Laboratory. The estimate of the localization system is compared to ground truth. Grey areas in the graph indicated when the robot is correctly localized with ORB-SLAM. When the robot is not localized, an odometry estimate is used

ization when the robot is lost (in white). In the navigation experiment in the Mechatronics Lab, showed in Fig. 5, Pepper correctly navigated through the test. However, between seconds 275 and 350 there exists a considerable drift between the ground truth and the localization estimate. These problems can result in reaching an erroneous navigation goal or even collide if no safety procedures are considered. We believe that a cause of this issue was the lack of viewpoints during the mapping step, as mentioned in the previous experiment.

Regarding South Hall experiments, the multiple discontinuities in the localization estimate (Fig. 6, Z axis) made navigation unfeasible. This was caused by the large distance between the robot and the landmarks in this environment, which was not the case of the Mechatronics Lab. Since visual SLAM systems are based on optimization and Pepper's FOV is narrow, it is more difficult to correctly estimate the pose because the triangulation uncertainty is higher; this is a known problem in visual systems [4].

However, in both experiments we noticed that localization is robust to changes in the environment, like a change in furniture position and, if the map is correctly built, there is minimal (if not zero) accumulation of drift error.

## 5.3   Discussion

The previous experiments evidence several advantages but also challenges of our proposed system. We summarizes them as follows:

*Advantages.* Our localization system is not affected by Peppers' LIDARs short range, which is one of the main limitations of it in RoboCup environments. Since we used the map created visually, the robot is able to localize with a single look by exploiting the relocalization capabilities of ORB-SLAM. Our scale recovery solution also allowed us to perform metric mapping despite using a single camera. In addition, since the motion estimation is based on features, it is robust to partial occlusions, and odometry is used when no visual features are tracked. All these advantages demonstrate that it is possible for our system to localize the robot in RoboCup@Home arenas successfully.

*Challenges.* Despite the previous advantages, we cannot avoid to mention some challenges and difficulties we noticed during our experiments. The first one relates to illumination changes, which can deteriorate hugely visual tracking. If we set the camera exposure to automatic we can deal with dynamic lighting, but the system is more susceptible to motion blur, which is still an issue despite the robot performs planar motion; the main cause of this is joint backslash. If the environment has non-variable illumination, we recommend to fix the camera exposure to diminish those problems. The second challenge regards glossy surfaces, which produce fake landmarks because of reflections. Despite ORB-SLAM is able to deal with outliers that do not match the predicted motion, it is still an open challenge in our opinion. Finally, localization turns noisier when the landmarks are far away, which is caused by the optimization procedures and the point's triangulation uncertainty.

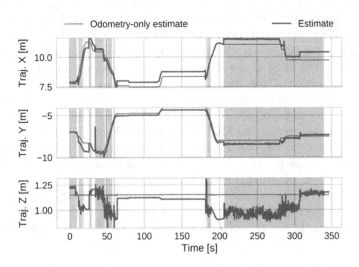

**Fig. 6.** Navigation test on the South Hall. The robot tries to navigate but the localization system does not work correctly.

# 6 Conclusions

In this work, we presented a localization system for a Pepper robot based on a visual SLAM system. Our solution, built upon ORB-SLAM, was focused on developing a self-localization system able to deal with large environments despite the LIDARs' short range. In order to do so, we presented an approach that fused visual and wheel odometry information. We tested the system in two real environments, showing the feasibility performing SLAM and navigation with our system with the current Pepper sensors, despite displaying some issues such as weakness to illumination changes, ambiguities to glassy surfaces and far landmarks.

Nowadays we are working towards an on-board implementation of the self-localization system on Pepper, which will allow us to perform a more exhaustive evaluation and comparison with other sensors such as lasers. In the future, we would like to improve robustness to illumination changes and reducing the noisy behavior in large environments.

**Acknowledgments.** This work was partially funded by the FONDECYT 1161500 project.

# References

1. Cadena, C., et al.: Past, present, and future of simultaneous localization and mapping: toward the robust-perception age. IEEE Trans. Robot. **32**(6), 1309–1332 (2016)
2. Cheng, M., et al.: Synthetical benchmarking of service robots: a first effort on domestic mobile platforms. In: Almeida, L., Ji, J., Steinbauer, G., Luke, S. (eds.) RoboCup 2015. LNCS (LNAI), vol. 9513, pp. 377–388. Springer, Cham (2015). https://doi.org/10.1007/978-3-319-29339-4_32
3. Engel, J., Schöps, T., Cremers, D.: LSD-SLAM: large-scale direct monocular SLAM. In: Fleet, D., Pajdla, T., Schiele, B., Tuytelaars, T. (eds.) ECCV 2014. LNCS, vol. 8690, pp. 834–849. Springer, Cham (2014). https://doi.org/10.1007/978-3-319-10605-2_54
4. Hartley, R., Zisserman, A.: Multiple View Geometry in Computer Vision. Cambridge University Press, Cambridge (2004)
5. Hertzberg, C., Wagner, R., Frese, U., Schröder, L.: Integrating generic sensor fusion algorithms with sound state representations through encapsulation of manifolds. Inf. Fusion **14**(1), 57–77 (2013)
6. Horn, B.K.P.: Closed-form solution of absolute orientation using unit quaternions. J. Opt. Soc. Am. A **4**(4), 629 (1987)
7. Iocchi, L., Holz, D., Ruiz-Del-Solar, J., Sugiura, K., Van Der Zant, T.: RoboCup@Home: analysis and results of evolving competitions for domestic and service robots. Artif. Intell. **229**, 258–281 (2015)
8. Kümmerle, R., Grisetti, G., Strasdat, H., Konolige, K., Burgard, W.: G$^2$o: a general framework for graph optimization. In: IEEE ICRA, pp. 3607–3613 (2011)
9. Martinelli, A.: Closed-form solution of visual-inertial structure from motion. Int. J. Comput. Vis. **106**(2), 138–152 (2014)

10. Mur-Artal, R., Montiel, J.M., Tardos, J.D.: ORB-SLAM: a versatile and accurate monocular SLAM system. IEEE Trans. Robot. **31**(5), 1147–1163 (2015)
11. Mur-Artal, R., Tardos, J.D.: ORB-SLAM2: an open-source SLAM system for monocular, stereo, and RGB-D cameras. IEEE Trans. Robot. **33**(5), 1255–1262 (2017)
12. Mur-Artal, R., Tardos, J.D.: Visual-inertial monocular SLAM with map reuse. IEEE Robot. Autom. Lett. **2**(2), 796–803 (2017)
13. Strasdat, H., Montiel, J.M.M., Davison, A.J.: Visual SLAM: why filter? (2012)
14. Sturm, J., Engelhard, N., Endres, F., Burgard, W., Cremers, D.: A benchmark for the evaluation of RGB-D SLAM systems. In: IEEE ICRA, pp. 573–580 (2012)

# Visual Mesh: Real-Time Object Detection Using Constant Sample Density

Trent Houliston$^{(\boxtimes)}$ and Stephan K. Chalup

School of Electrical Engineering and Computing, The University of Newcastle,
Callaghan, NSW 2308, Australia
trent@houliston.me, stephan.chalup@newcastle.edu.au

**Abstract.** This paper proposes an enhancement of convolutional neural networks for object detection in resource-constrained robotics through a geometric input transformation called Visual Mesh. It uses object geometry to create a graph in vision space, reducing computational complexity by normalizing the pixel and feature density of objects. The experiments compare the Visual Mesh with several other fast convolutional neural networks. The results demonstrate execution times sixteen times quicker than the fastest competitor tested, while achieving outstanding accuracy.

**Keywords:** Convolutional neural network · Deep learning ·
Ball detection · Graph transformation · TensorFlow · Machine vision

## 1 Introduction

This paper introduces a Visual Mesh that defines an input transformation for convolutional neural networks (CNN). By normalizing object size, the Visual Mesh accounts for differences in an object's appearance when detecting and localizing it. This allows simpler network architectures to be used and reduces oversampling, improving the computational performance substantially.

CNNs require powerful hardware to perform in real-time. Despite this, some networks have been developed to run on constrained hardware with limited success. Speck et al. [13] built a CNN for detecting the coordinates of a soccer ball on an image. When implemented on their target platform it ran in 26 ms and had an accuracy of 58% in $x$ and 52% in $y$. The accuracy dropped to less than 30% in distances over two meters. Therefore, this approach had limited success in object localization.

Faster and more accurate systems have been developed that only perform object classification. These systems utilize color segmentation to provide proposals for a CNN to classify. As a result they were much faster than systems that localize objects, however, color segmentation is sensitive to changes in lighting conditions and must be manually calibrated. Javadi et al. [7] utilized such a system for detecting humanoid robots. The best performing network ran in 2.36 ms with 97.56% accuracy per proposal on an Intel Core i5 2.5 GHz. Cruz et al. [5]

© Springer Nature Switzerland AG 2019
D. Holz et al. (Eds.): RoboCup 2018, LNAI 11374, pp. 45–56, 2019.
https://doi.org/10.1007/978-3-030-27544-0_4

developed a system to classify Aldebaran NAO robots. This network executed in
$\approx 1\,\text{ms}$ per proposal. Albani et al. [2] and Bloisi et al. [3] utilized a similar technique for ball detection. This system was implemented on an Aldebaran NAO
robot and processed 14–22 frames per second as the only process running. The
reliance on color segmentation for proposals limits these networks to color coded
environments.

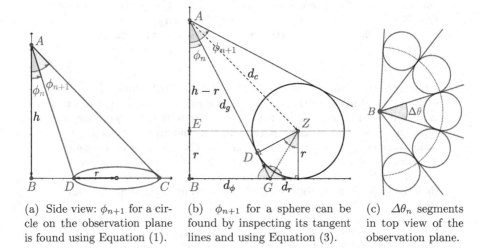

(a) Side view: $\phi_{n+1}$ for a circle on the observation plane
is found using Equation (1).

(b) $\phi_{n+1}$ for a sphere can be
found by inspecting its tangent
lines and using Equation (3).

(c) $\Delta\theta_n$ segments
in top view of the
observation plane.

**Fig. 1.** Geometry for calculating $\phi_{n+1}$ and $\Delta\theta_n$.

## 2   Visual Mesh Geometry

The Visual Mesh detects objects that lie on a plane at a known distance and
orientation from the camera. This plane is referred to as the observation plane.
The geometry of the Visual Mesh can be described using Fig. 1 where the camera
is assumed to be at point $A$. The target object's geometry determines the pixel
resolution, i.e., the placement of points in the Visual Mesh. The geometry for
two target object shapes are analyzed in this paper: Circles are appropriate for
detecting two-dimensional objects on the observation plane (Fig. 1a). Spheres
are appropriate for three-dimensional objects that have an approximately equal
extension in all dimensions (Fig. 1b). More complex objects such as cylinders
could also be modeled.

For establishing the Visual Mesh two orthogonal angular components have to
be determined. These are $\Delta\phi_n$ and $\Delta\theta_n$ and are given by the angular diameters
of the target object with respect to points $A$ and $B$. The height $h$ of the camera
above the observation plane and the radius $r$ are required to calculate the mesh.

The first component is $\Delta\phi_n := \phi_{n+1} - \phi_n$ and is determined by the inclinations $\phi_n$ from directly below the camera. A series $\phi_n$, $n = 0,..,N$ is given
recursively by function $f : \mathbb{R} \to \mathbb{R}$, $\phi_{n+1} = f(\phi_n) = \phi_n + \Delta\phi_n$ where $\phi_0 = 0$.

The second component, $\Delta\theta_n$, is measured around point $B$ in the observation plane and depends on $\phi_n$ for both, circle and sphere objects (Fig. 1c).

The inclinations $(\phi_n)_{n=0,...N}$ induce a series of nested concentric cones with vertex at $A$ and center axis orthogonal to the observation plane. Each of these cones is radially segmented at its basis by $\Delta\theta_n$ and the tangent rays from $B$.

## 2.1   Circle

The geometry for circles is shown in Fig. 1a. $\phi_{n+1}$ for a circle is calculated by adding the diameter $2r$ of the circle to its distance $\overline{BD}$ to obtain

$$\phi_{n+1} = \tan^{-1}\left(\tan(\phi_n) + \frac{2r}{h}\right) \tag{1}$$

Figure 1c shows the geometry for $\Delta\theta_n$ within the 2D observation plane where

$$\Delta\theta_n = 2\sin^{-1}\left(\frac{r}{h\tan(\phi_n)}\right) \tag{2}$$

This formulation of $\Delta\theta_n$ has a singularity when the center of the object is closer than its radius making it more difficult for the mesh to detect objects directly below the camera.

## 2.2   Sphere

For spheres $\Delta\phi_n$ is determined by the sphere's shadow from a virtual light at $A$ and it decreases more slowly with $n$ than for circles. Figure 1b shows how $\phi_{n+1}$ is calculated. Using the triangle $\triangle AEZ$ and edges $\overline{AE}$ and $\overline{EZ}$ gives

$$\begin{aligned}
\phi_{n+1} &= 2\tan^{-1}\left(\frac{d_\phi + d_r}{h - r}\right) - \phi_n \\
&= 2\tan^{-1}\left(\frac{r\sec(\phi_n)}{h - r} + \tan(\phi_n)\right) - \phi_n
\end{aligned} \tag{3}$$

The calculation of $\Delta\theta_n$ is the same as for circles and uses Eq. (2).

## 2.3   Object Dependent Sample Density

The current description guarantees one point in the mesh for the target object. For use in computer vision, multiple sample points per object are required. Let's assume our object requires $k$ pixels to be recognizable. In the Visual Mesh this $k$ corresponds to the number of intersections of the $\phi_n$ rings with the object. A $\phi_n$ ring is obtained by rotating vector $\overrightarrow{AD}$ about the axis $\overrightarrow{AB}$. If $\Delta\phi_n$ and $\Delta\theta_n$ are reduced, the spacing between the $\phi_n$ rings will be decreased which leads to more intersections with the target object.

An increase in the number of sample points for the circle model can be achieved by dividing $\Delta\theta_n$ in (2) by $k$ and also the diameter of the circle by $k$, i.e., replacing $2r$ in (1) by $2r/k$.

In the sphere model $k$ sample points can be achieved by creating a version of the mesh where the original sphere is replaced by smaller spheres so that the original sphere intersects with $k$ $\phi_n$ rings associated with the smaller spheres (Fig. 2). If $k$ is expressed as fraction $k = \frac{p}{q}$, $p, q \in \mathbb{N} - \{0\}$, the equation relating the radii of the spheres is given by $f^q(\phi_0, r_0) = f^{pq}(\phi_0, r_1)$ where $r_0$ is the radius of the target and $r_1$ is the radius of the small spheres in the mesh. A solution for $r_1$ can be obtained numerically.

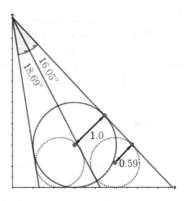

**Fig. 2.** Multiple sample points on a sphere can be calculated by finding the smaller sphere's radius.

### 2.4 Graph Structure of the Mesh

**Fig. 3.** The Visual Mesh projected onto an image. Note that four $\phi_n$ rings pass through the ball regardless of its location.

A mesh can be generated using the points around $\phi_n$ rings (see arcs in Fig. 3). In each $\phi_n$ ring, points are separated by $\Delta\theta_n$. This ensures that the number of points within an object falls within a small range ($\pm 1$ in $\phi$ and $\theta$). Each point is connected with edges to the two adjacent points on the same $\phi_n$ ring as well as to the two nearest points on the $\phi_{n\pm 1}$ rings. The single point below the camera is connected by six equally spaced points. Projecting these points onto an image creates a mesh structure as shown in Fig. 3.

Another method to view the mesh is to project the $\phi_n$ rings onto concentric circles as in Fig. 4. Due to perspective, the size of objects decreases in distance within the original image, while the Visual Mesh ensures objects are always the same size.

### 2.5 Network

Once the image data has been transformed by the Visual Mesh, it exists as a graph, rather than a grid of pixels. The pixels no longer have nine neighbors, but six. This changes how convolutions occur when executed on the graph.

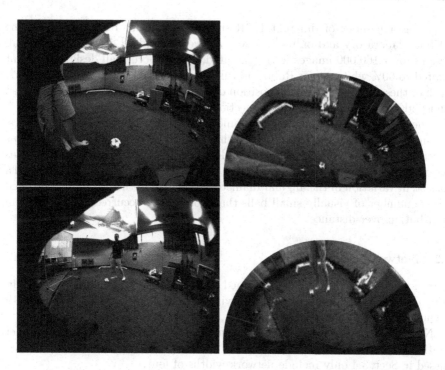

**Fig. 4.** The Visual Mesh projected in concentric rings. Due to perspective, the size of the ball decreases with distance in the original (left). In the Visual Mesh, the ball has always a similar size (right).

For example, a 3 × 3 convolution in a typical CNN accesses eight pixels around a central pixel. The equivalent operation in the graph accesses points with a graph distance of one, its six neighbors. This has a positive impact on performance, as two fewer values need to be considered. Larger convolutions would be equivalent to operating on points at a larger maximum graph distance. For example, a 5 × 5 convolution would operate on all points that have a maximum graph distance of two to the central point.

## 3    Evaluation of the Visual Mesh

### 3.1    Dataset

A semi-synthetic dataset with masks that segment out the ball was created for training. By using 360° high dynamic range (HDR) images to provide image-based lighting, along with physics-based rendering, realistic semi-synthetic scenes were generated. From this, the mask images, as well as the camera orientation and position can be obtained.

Using a number of different HDR scenes taken from RoboCup 2017, the NUbots' laboratory and online[1], as well as over a hundred different soccer ball designs, over 160,000 images were generated. These soccer ball designs were not limited to 50% white as per RoboCup rules and included balls of various colors. Each of these images varied the position of the soccer ball and switched between equisolid and rectilinear camera projections.

The distance of the balls from the camera varied between zero and ten meters. The intensity of the lighting varied in the scene. The rendered soccer ball was selected from a set of 140 different models. The distribution of distances was designed to provide a uniform variation in the pixel size of the ball. This allowed a consistent variation in the angular diameter of the ball in the image. It prevented a large number of visually small balls that would have occurred with a uniform distribution over distance.

## 3.2   Network Architecture

Each node in the Visual Mesh performed a $3 \times 3$ convolution using its six neighbors. These layers were stacked to varying depths from two to nine and with output widths varying from two to eight, resulting in a fully convolutional net.

Networks of width four performed significantly better than networks of other widths as the hardware utilized can vectorize on four elements. The results discussed in Sect. 3.4 only include network widths of four.

Networks were also tested with ReLU [9], ELU [4] and SELU [8]. SELU consistently outperformed ELU and ReLU in terms of training time and network accuracy. SELU is computationally more expensive than ReLU but is similar to that of ELU. Results in Sect. 3.4 only include those tested with SELU.

The network depths used for evaluation were three, five, and nine layers. These were chosen as their receptive fields were half, one and two ball radii, respectively. This ensured the networks had sufficient contextual information to correctly classify the ball.

In addition to these Visual Mesh networks, similar CNNs using a regular hexagonal grid were trained. These networks allowed a comparison between the Visual Mesh and a network that has equal computational cost due to selecting the same number of pixels. This network provides a comparison to an equivalent network without the constant sample density of the Visual Mesh.

## 3.3   Training

The training of these networks was undertaken using the TensorFlow library [1]. The pixel coordinates from the Visual Mesh and the indices of each pixel's six neighbors were used to apply the Visual Mesh at each layer. Once this gather step was performed, the neural network steps were undertaken as normal.

When training these neural networks, the number of ball points and non-ball points were balanced. This was achieved by selecting an equal number of points

---

[1] HDRI Haven https://hdrihaven.com/.

from each class. The backpropagation gradients were only calculated from the selected points.

This method was chosen instead of the traditional method of weighting the gradients intentionally. The majority of non-ball points in training images are grass. As a result, the initial networks experienced over-fitting on the field.

Once the initial network was trained, the error in its classification of each point in the image was used as a probability to select that point. This resulted in fewer grass points selected in future training. This resampling was run twice, with the probabilities added together with a 5% baseline probability. This greatly improved the accuracy in subsequent training.

In addition to these networks, five convolutional network architectures were fine-tuned on this dataset. These networks were SSD MobileNet and RCNN Inception V2 trained using TensorFlow [1,6] and YOLOv1 [10], YOLOv2 [11] and YOLOv3 [12] trained using Darknet[2]. These networks were chosen as they were regarded as some of the fastest real-time networks.

## 3.4    Results

**Precision.** In addition to the Visual and hexagonal meshes, five typical CNNs were also evaluated. Their results were measured using a 75% IoU. 75% was chosen as 50% was considered a poor match. With 50% IoU, the center of the detection can be at the edge of the object.

As shown in Fig. 5a, the accuracy of the Visual Mesh consistently outperforms the hexagonal mesh of an equivalent size. Increasing the depth of the network increases its performance.

The performance of the Visual Mesh remains approximately constant as distance increases. However, as shown in Fig. 5c the performance of the hexagonal mesh, as well as the other CNNs degrades with increased distance. Note that as the generated data was made uniform over pixel size rather than distance, the number of sample images falls off as distance increases. The fewer samples increase noise in the plot.

The performance of the Visual Mesh exceeds the performance of the hexagonal mesh even when the number of points in the object is the same. The number of points in both tested networks are equal at 2.5 m. Figure 5b shows the number of points in the Visual Mesh stays constant over distance, except for a peak at 0 m. This peak is when points are directly below the camera. This is a singularity point for the Visual Mesh as it is currently implemented. The hexagonal mesh has a decreasing number of points as distance increases.

**Detections.** Figure 6a shows a typical set of detections from each of the trained networks. YOLOv1 is omitted as it performs strictly worse than YOLOv2. The Visual Mesh has a good detection while the hexagonal mesh has several false

---

[2] Darknet http://pjreddie.com/darknet/.

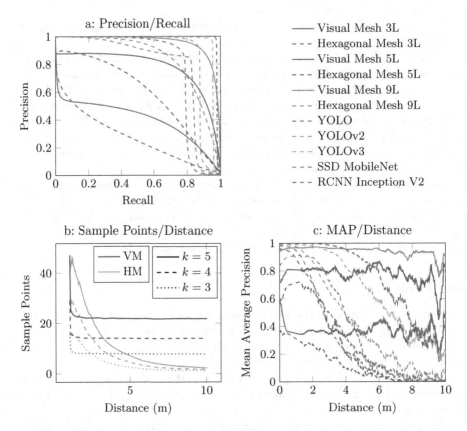

**Fig. 5.** (a) The Precision/Recall curve over all data. (b) The number of sampled points in an object over distance (VM is Visual Mesh HM is Hexagonal Mesh). (c) The Average Precision of the detectors over distance.

positives. The five other networks all detect the ball. YOLOv2 has a lower confidence than the other networks on the dataset. SSD MobileNet, YOLOv2 and YOLOv3's bounding boxes are less accurate across the dataset.

The Visual Mesh excels at distant detections as shown in Fig. 6b. Except for the Visual Mesh and RCNN Inception V2, none of the other networks detect the ball. RCNN Inception V2 has a poorly fitted bounding box. This is typical of distant balls in the dataset.

Figure 6c shows how the Visual Mesh is able to use scale to identify target objects. The hexagonal mesh found many false positives on objects that had a different size than expected, but similar appearance as the target.

**Execution Performance.** Each network was tested on the CPU and GPU from the Intel NUC7i7BNH as well as on an NVIDIA 1080Ti. The input images were $1280 \times 1024$ for all networks. SSD MobileNet and RCNN Inception V2 were not executed on the Intel GPU as TensorFlow does not support OpenCL at this

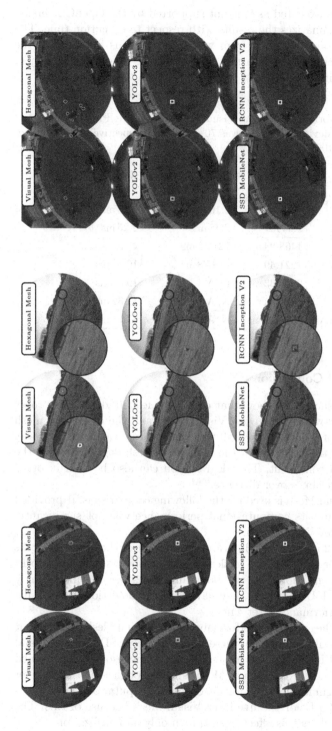

(a) Detection on an empty field. All networks achieve acceptable performance. However, the hexagonal mesh has some false positives.

(b) Detections at extreme distance. Only the Visual Mesh achieves a good detection. RCNN Inception V2 detects but IoU of the bounding box is < 50%.

(c) Detection on a field with a robot. The mesh has many false positives on the robot, while the other detectors perform well.

**Fig. 6.** Example detections where confidence intervals are represented by colors: Red >50%, Yellow >75% and White >90% (Color figure online)

time. YOLOv3 was not executed as it is not supported by the OpenCL version of Darknet. Table 1 summarizes the results with respect to execution time. The times for all networks are measured from when the image is first sent to the algorithm until the inferences are returned. Therefore, the time taken to project Visual Mesh points is included.

**Table 1.** Execution performance: For the Visual Mesh on the Iris Plus Graphics and the NVIDIA 1080Ti the device utilization was 70% and 35% respectively. For all other cases utilization was at 100%.

|                     | Intel Core i7 7567U | Intel Iris Plus Graphics 650 | NVIDIA 1080Ti |
|---------------------|---------------------|------------------------------|---------------|
| Visual Mesh 5       | 1.64 ms             | 2.10 ms                      | 2.18 ms       |
| Visual Mesh 9       | 2.44 ms             | 2.48 ms                      | 2.25 ms       |
| YOLOv1              | 1468.24 ms          | 721.13 ms                    | 17.55 ms      |
| YOLOv2              | 1221.49 ms          | 613.73 ms                    | 16.13 ms      |
| YOLOv3              | 2651.33 ms          | N/A                          | 19.00 ms      |
| SSD MobileNet       | 37.76 ms            | N/A                          | 11.32 ms      |
| RCNN Inception V2   | 1521.32 ms          | N/A                          | 47.75 ms      |

### 3.5  Discussion and Conclusion

The results for the Visual Mesh show that consistent feature density improves the accuracy of the network. When the Visual Mesh and the hexagonal mesh had an equal number of points on the ball the Visual Mesh was more accurate. As distance increased, the accuracy of the hexagonal mesh degraded while the Visual Mesh remained consistent. This degradation can also be seen in other networks as accuracy declines over distance.

The nine-layer Visual Mesh is used for the following comparisons. It provided the highest accuracy and its computational performance was not significantly worse than the five-layer Visual Mesh.

RCNN Inception V2 and YOLOv3 performed the best of the other networks tested. While the other CNNs failed to detect distant objects, these networks continued to detect them. However, the bounding boxes became increasingly inaccurate. At a lower IoU threshold they have a higher detection rate. Visual Mesh exceeds their performance after 4 m.

As seen in Table 1, the execution performance of the Visual Mesh exceeds that of the other convolutional networks. Of these networks, only SSD MobileNet and the Visual Mesh could be considered for real-time use on resource-constrained systems. The performance of the Visual Mesh is fast enough that the transfer times of images is a significant factor for GPU based computation. The NUC's CPU outperforms its GPU for the five-layer Visual Mesh because of this. The NVIDIA 1080Ti also suffers this effect, resulting in only 35% utilization.

The Visual Mesh has a number of advantages beyond its accuracy and speed. As objects always have a similar number of points additional post-processing options are available to improve accuracy. Within detected areas, metrics such as graph diameter can be used to filter out irrelevant areas. Additionally the best fitting subgraph can be used to remove invalid points in a detection.

Higher resolution does not increase the computational cost of the Visual Mesh. The number of points that are projected onto the image does not change for the same camera lens and orientation. However, increased resolution will allow the Visual Mesh to project points that are a greater distance from the camera. If the resolution of the camera is insufficient for the level of detail requested, the Visual Mesh will begin sampling the same pixel multiple times. The Visual Mesh is still accurate with limited amounts of this duplicated data. However, as the amount of information decreases, the accuracy of the network will decline.

As the distance to objects increases, typical networks must learn to account for the differences in scale that occur. Often these differences are not well represented in the training data or, can be biased in the training data. This can require additional training data to be generated by scaling. For the Visual Mesh, this is not necessary as the object will always appear the same size. This reduces the complexity of training as well as the complexity of the required network.

As the Visual Mesh is always oriented relative to the observation plane, the resulting network is better able to handle changes in the orientation of the camera. This form of transformational invariance only applies to rotations in the camera, not rotations on the object. This can reduce the amount of training required if the object can be assumed in a particular rotation. For example, if extended to detect the goal posts the training data would not need to be modified for different orientations of the camera as they would always be normal to the observation plane. Without this invariance, training for goal posts would have to include multiple orientations.

Networks based on the Visual Mesh also have an independence to the lens used. As the sample points are always in the same place in the world, changing to a different lens geometry does not change the points. This makes it easier to train using data from different lenses and apply trained networks to new lenses.

The presented formulation of the Visual Mesh has two primary limitations. One concern is that it cannot function when the height of objects are greater than or equal to the height of the camera. In these cases, the Visual Mesh correctly predicts that all objects are visible on the horizon. This results in a single line of points. In practice, this does not afford good detection performance. The second limitation is that objects that are directly below the camera fall into a singularity. When in this singularity, twice as many points intersect with the objects until they move beyond this position. This increases the complexity that the Visual Mesh must learn.

The training and execution code for the Visual Mesh is available at https://github.com/Fastcode/VisualMesh.

**Acknowledgments.** TH was supported by a Australian Government Research Training Program scholarship and a completion scholarship from 4Tel Pty. Ltd.

# References

1. Abadi, M., et al.: Tensorflow: a system for large-scale machine learning. In: Proceedings of the 12th USENIX Conference on Operating Systems Design and Implementation, OSDI 2016, pp. 265–283. USENIX Association, Berkeley (2016)
2. Albani, D., Youssef, A., Suriani, V., Nardi, D., Bloisi, D.D.: A deep learning approach for object recognition with NAO soccer robots. In: Behnke, S., Sheh, R., Sariel, S., Lee, D.D. (eds.) RoboCup 2016. LNCS (LNAI), vol. 9776, pp. 392–403. Springer, Cham (2017). https://doi.org/10.1007/978-3-319-68792-6_33
3. Bloisi, D., Duchetto, F.D., Manoni, T., Suriani, V.: Machine learning for realistic ball detection in robocup SPL. CoRR abs/1707.03628 (2017)
4. Clevert, D.A., Unterthiner, T., Hochreiter, S.: Fast and accurate deep network learning by exponential linear units (ELUs). CoRR abs/1511.07289 (2015)
5. Cruz, N., Lobos-Tsunekawa, K., Ruiz-del Solar, J.: Using convolutional neural networks in robots with limited computational resources: detecting NAO robots while playing soccer. CoRR abs/1706.06702 (2017)
6. Huang, J., et al.: Speed/accuracy trade-offs for modern convolutional object detectors. CoRR abs/1611.10012 (2016)
7. Javadi, M., Azar, S.M., Azami, S., Ghidary, S.S., Sadeghnejad, S., Baltes, J.: Humanoid robot detection using deep learning: a speed-accuracy tradeoff. In: Akiyama, H., Obst, O., Sammut, C., Tonidandel, F. (eds.) RoboCup 2017. LNCS (LNAI), vol. 11175, pp. 338–349. Springer, Cham (2018). https://doi.org/10.1007/978-3-030-00308-1_28
8. Klambauer, G., Unterthiner, T., Mayr, A., Hochreiter, S.: Self-normalizing neural networks. In: Guyon, I., et al. (eds.) Advances in Neural Information Processing Systems 30, pp. 971–980. Curran Associates, Inc. (2017)
9. Nair, V., Hinton, G.E.: Rectified linear units improve restricted Boltzmann machines. In: Proceedings of the 27th International Conference on International Conference on Machine Learning, ICML 2010, pp. 807–814. Omnipress, USA (2010)
10. Redmon, J., Divvala, S.K., Girshick, R.B., Farhadi, A.: You only look once: unified, real-time object detection. CoRR abs/1506.02640 (2015)
11. Redmon, J., Farhadi, A.: YOLO9000: better, faster, stronger. In: 2017 IEEE Conference on Computer Vision and Pattern Recognition (CVPR), pp. 6517–6525 (2017)
12. Redmon, J., Farhadi, A.: YOLOv3: an incremental improvement. CoRR abs/1804.02767 (2018)
13. Speck, D., Barros, P., Weber, C., Wermter, S.: Ball localization for robocup soccer using convolutional neural networks. In: Behnke, S., Sheh, R., Sariel, S., Lee, D.D. (eds.) RoboCup 2016. LNCS (LNAI), vol. 9776, pp. 19–30. Springer, Cham (2017). https://doi.org/10.1007/978-3-319-68792-6_2

# Fast Multi-scale fHOG Feature Extraction Using Histogram Downsampling

Mihai Polceanu[✉], Fabrice Harrouet, and Cédric Buche

LAB-STICC, ENIB, Brest, France
{polceanu,harrouet,buche}@enib.fr

**Abstract.** Object detection is crucial for autonomous robotic systems to interact with the world around them but, in robots with low computational resources, deep learning is difficult to take advantage of. We develop incremental improvements to related work on feature approximation and describe an adaptive fHOG feature pyramid construction scheme based on histogram downsampling, together with a SVM classifier. Varying the pyramid level to which the scheme is applied gives control over the trade-off between precision or speed. We evaluate the proposed scheme on a modern computer and on a NAO humanoid robot in the context of the RoboCup competition, *i.e.*, robot and soccer ball detection, in which we obtain significant increase (1.57x and 1.68x on PC and robot respectively) in pyramid construction speed relative to our baseline (the dlib library) without any loss in detection performance. The scheme can be adapted to increase speed while trading off precision until it reaches the conditions of a state-of-the-art power law feature scaling method.

**Keywords:** Vision for robotics · Object detection ·
Feature approximation · Histogram of Oriented Gradients

## 1 Introduction

Object detection has seen tremendous progress in the past years, which stemmed both from hand-crafted features and the relatively recent convolutional neural networks (CNN). As CPUs improved and with the advent of cheaper GPU processing, some subfields witnessed super-human image recognition accuracy.

Our focus is however on conditions where the system is required to function with low computational resources. Such conditions can be found in the Standard Platform League (SPL) of the RoboCup soccer competition. Here, teams must use the commercially available SoftBank NAO humanoid robot without hardware modifications. The resources available in this setup are an Intel Atom 1.6 GHz processor with one thread and 1GB of RAM. Although sufficient for vision, these resources must be shared by several processes to perform locomotion, localization and strategic behavior necessary for the soccer match, hence in reality, object

D. Holz et al. (Eds.): RoboCup 2018, LNAI 11374, pp. 57–69, 2019.
https://doi.org/10.1007/978-3-030-27544-0_5

detection can only account for a small amount of resources (roughly 5% CPU in the implementation we used for this work) when the robot is in motion.

The main tasks for computer vision in this competition are the detection of lines, goal posts, the ball and other robots (teammates and opponents). For humanoid detection we turn to the subfield of pedestrian detection, where Histograms of Oriented Gradients (HOG) continue to play an important role since their invention in 2005 [5]. HOG consists in dividing an image into cells, computing the gradient of each cell, binning gradients into a histogram of main orientations and finally normalizing over blocks of cells to produce features (originally 36-dimensional) that are used for training a Support Vector Machine (SVM) classifier over a sliding window. Later, [8] introduced a refined version of HOG features (commonly referred to as Felzenszwalb HOG or fHOG) which proved more robust for pedestrian but also generic object detection. Despite its high popularity, HOG-like (HOG, fHOG, or other variants) feature extraction is known to be slow, although more energy efficient than more accurate CNNs [19].

While many other flavors of object detectors have been proposed, most combine HOG-like features with other types to obtain better results under different conditions. Our main focus is to accelerate fHOG feature extraction in order for it to run on a robotic platform with low computational resources, while maximizing detection precision.

We first discuss existing work on feature approximation and how our work differs from the state-of-the-art method [6]. We then present a series of evaluations on a modern computer (Intel Core i7, 2.60 GHz) to observe how our choices have an impact on detection quality and execution speed. All results are obtained using a single execution thread and averaged over multiple runs to ensure validity. From these evaluations we make several observations that lead to an adaptive scheme that gives control over the trade-off between average precision and execution speed. Finally we validate the results on the chosen robotic platform, where we obtain higher execution time compared with the modern computer as expected, due to the lower quality processor, but still observe significant improvement relative to the baseline.

## 2   Related Work

The Histogram of Oriented Gradients is a widely used feature descriptor, first proposed for human detection by [5]. The intuition behind this approach is that the shape and appearance can be characterized by the distribution of local edge directions (intensity gradients). The main steps in obtaining a HOG-based detector, as originally described by [5], are to compute gradients that are binned in histogram of 9 dominant directions (bins), which are then normalized over blocks of 4 cells and finally concatenated to obtain the HOG features ($9 \times 4 = 36$ dimensional). These features are then fed as input to a SVM classifier that is trained with the corresponding labels such as pedestrians. Afterwards, [8] improved upon the result with insights gained from applying Principal Component Analysis

(PCA) to reduce the dimension of the initial features while retaining the same performance and used additional contrast sensitive components to improve overall performance.

Our work falls in the concept of feature approximation, notably used by [7] to significantly increase the speed of the feature pyramid construction for non scale invariant features like HOG. The feature pyramid is constructed by downsampling the image by a factor, *i.e.*, a smaller image is obtained by downscaling the original by a chosen fraction. For example, downsampling a $640 \times 480$ image by a $4/5$ factor means that the obtained image is $640 * 4/5 = 512$ pixels wide and $480 * 4/5 = 384$ pixels high. The main intuition is that instead of downscaling the image and extracting features at each level of the pyramid, intermediary levels could be *approximated* using nearby feature maps. Approximating intermediary pyramid levels is complementary to other works focusing on optimized variants of HOG, such as faster cell-based scanning [18], heavy use of parallelism [12] and different approaches to computing gradients [4].

Successive image down-sampling and calculating features at each pyramid level are computationally expensive. Taking advantage of the generally fractal structure of natural images, it is possible to obtain similar performance by only downsampling and computing the features for each halved image; *i.e.*, at each octave [6]. In-between, the features are approximated (upsampled and downsampled) from the ones directly calculated at each octave, which directly leads to higher execution speed that is crucial for embedded systems [11].

Regarding the context of application, object detection in the RoboCup Soccer competition (standard platform league) has been achieved with (generally manually tuned) detectors based on color segmentation [13, 16] or color histograms [17], statistical modeling [2], line detection, rough shapes [3], or simply as non-green patches which differentiate themselves from the green football field [10]. We note that some approaches [16] make use of smaller image sizes and regions of interest (instead of sliding windows) to limit the search space in the image to improve performance; this technique is complementary to our work on analyzing the effects of feature approximation on performance.

In our experiments, we use the object detector provided by Dlib [14] which uses the well known 31-dimensional feature extraction method described by [8] (fHOG) together with Max-Margin Object Detection (MMOD) [15] which improves training efficiency. While other implementations exist (such as OpenCV and others), our focus is on studying the impact of feature approximation, regardless of particular implementation. Final detections are obtained by applying non-maximum suppression on the ensemble of overlapping detection boxes. Dlib represents one of the most efficient implementations of state-of-the-art classical object detection and is used by both academia and industry. Throughout this work, our contribution is compared to the current implementation of fHOG-based SVM classifier in Dlib as primary baseline.

# 3    Image and Histogram Downsampling

The first important observation is that the main bottleneck in computing fHOG features resides in calculating the gradient histogram which happens before computing the final feature map. Most modern processors provide Single Instruction, Multiple Data (SIMD) instructions, which have the same execution time and electricity consumption as their scalar counterparts, but handle 16 bytes of data simultaneously which, for our purposes, enables 4 floating point operations instead of one. This is also the case for the Intel Atom 1.6 GHz processor of the NAO robot used in our research. However, computing histograms involves the decision of which bin is associated with each data point, and therefore cannot be fully vectorized. This observation led us to consider avoiding successive histogram computations, similar to how other authors avoid direct feature extraction.

Another important aspect to consider is that the bulk of computational expense rests in the first few levels of the pyramid that use large scale images. For example, for a 10-level pyramid that uses 4/5 downscaling factor on a 640 × 480 image, computing features for each level costs 36.70%, 23.23%, 14.81%, 9.54%, 6.02%, 3.91%, 2.53%, 1.52%, 1.07% and 0.67% of the total time, respectively.

We can identify three aspects of the fHOG feature extraction algorithm that can be accelerated: (a) The level to which the scheme is applied, (b) Image downsampling strategy and (c) Histogram downsampling strategy. Here we describe each of these aspects, and then put them to the test in the following section, in comparison with related state-of-the-art schemes.

All tests are performed on a dataset that contains images from the publicly available SPQR dataset [1] and also includes new frames coming from robots during test matches in different lighting conditions and of lower resolution. Lower resolution images were upscaled to 640 × 480 which is the chosen resolution of our evaluation, as this is the real image size that is usable from the NAO robot camera; in fact, the output of the camera is 960p/30fps (1280 × 960) and is provided in YUYV format (also known as Y'UV422), but processing the full sized image exhausts much of the resources available on the robot [9]. For training and testing, we only consider the Y value which can very efficiently be read directly from the raw camera output. The images in the enhanced dataset have been randomized and divided into 100 training images (50 with horizontal flip added) and 98 test images, amounting to 190 and 185 positive examples respectively. The training set was kept small to avoid excess robot pose variation which makes training a HOG detector inefficient (*i.e.* the resulting vignette becomes blurred); this proves to obtain acceptable accuracy without the need to train multiple detectors for several poses which drastically increase the amount of resources required, while in practice it also allows training for a different object with few on-site images.

## 3.1 Approximating Levels

As seen previously, it is most important to approximate lower levels of the pyramid (*i.e.* larger image sizes), as they have the highest cost in terms of computation time. Throughout this work, we evaluate different downsampling strategies by applying them up to a certain level of the pyramid. Applying each scheme up to a level means that some or all intermediary levels are approximated from histograms from a lower level (source level depends on each scheme). After doing a hyperparameter (pyramid downscaling factor; C and risk gap of SVM; and box matching threshold) search (grid followed by random search) on the Dlib fHOG object detector [14] which we use as a baseline, we chose to use a 4/5 downscale factor which in our implementation leads to a pyramid with 10 levels (0–9). In the following, we report the precision and execution time of each approach by applying the scheme (approximating histograms) up to a given level exclusively, while higher levels are computed in the same way as the baseline; this way, results at level 1 are equivalent for all schemes and baseline since the scheme is not applied to any level. Starting from level 2 and up to 9, the charts illustrate the effect of the chosen scheme on performance and speed. We also include level 10, which means that the entire pyramid (levels 0–9) is approximated, using the chosen scheme.

## 3.2 Image Downsampling

Constructing smaller scale images is originally performed in the Dlib baseline at each pyramid level using bilinear interpolation, while histograms and features are also extracted at each level. The power law based feature approximation approach [6] proposes to only subsample images at each octave (ratio of 1/2) while approximating the intermediary final features (as opposed to histograms in our work). To test how approximation influences performance, regardless of octaves, we approximate histograms up to a given level while downsampling images for the higher levels in two ways: in the first scheme (dubbed *slow* method in the following) we continue to downsample images from each previous level, even if these intermediary images are not used for feature extraction, and in the second scheme (dubbed *fast* method) we do not keep intermediary images, but downsample from the original image directly to the level up to which the scheme is applied (see Fig. 1 for clarification). While significantly faster, one may argue that this method can lead to important information loss for higher levels (smaller image scales), due to the fact that entire pixels are ignored in the downsampled image.

We put this intuition to the test, and evaluate quality when skipping several levels when downsampling image. We note that using the *fast* approach, we obtain "pixelated" parts of the image, where gradient information is lost, but this only becomes clear when the gap between downsampled images increases, in our case, further than 4 or 5 levels. We therefore expect that having at least some intermediary images, such as in the case of the power law approach [6] which subsamples images at each octave, should improve results.

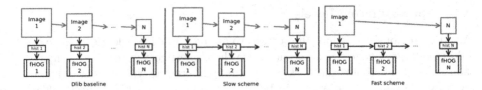

**Fig. 1.** Image downsampling approaches of Dlib baseline (left), *slow* (center) and *fast* (right) schemes applied up to level $N$.

To study the impact of the two image downsampling strategies, we measure speed and performance at each level in the pyramid. To visualize the progression in function of level, we plot the average execution time (Fig. 2 left) obtained by a single image pyramid, measured for 10 configurations. Each configuration $i$ consists in an fHOG detector that performs feature downscaling using the respective image downsampling strategy (*slow/fast*) until level $i-1$ and then, from level $i$ onwards it performs the default feature extraction (which corresponds to downsampling the image and extracting features at each step).

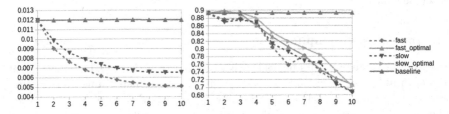

**Fig. 2.** Average execution time (in seconds) on modern computer (left) and average precision (right) of *slow* vs. *fast* image downsampling when applying each scheme up to each level of the pyramid (yielding multiple configurations of each scheme). Dotted lines show the performance of the detector in each case using the same hyperparameters initially found for the baseline. Because features differ when approximation is used, we retrained each configuration on the same dataset to obtain the true average precision for each level (indicated as "optimal" in figure), being equivalent to having a different model per configuration.

As expected, the *fast* approach is more desirable in terms of execution time. However, we find that the performance of extracted fHOG features depends on the quality of the image at higher levels, but remain robust to drastic downsampling at lower levels. Figure 2 (right) shows that, with hyperparameter tuning for each configuration, *slow* downsampling outperforms the *fast* method overall. However, this also implies a significant loss in execution speed. Nevertheless, we note that for the first few levels, the performance difference is not as pronounced.

Therefore, if the approximated gap between downsampled images is small enough, the *fast* downsampling strategy should retain enough information to minimize performance loss while offering good execution speed gains.

## 3.3  Histogram Downsampling

In this work, we refer to "histogram" as the frequency of gradients binned into each of the 18 orientations described by [8] that is computed *before* calculating the final 31-dimensional fHOG features, while [6] describe feature downsampling on *final* features. Downsampling final features would seem much faster, because recomputing and normalizing them is directly avoided, however it turns out that the time lost on this process is regained in our approach because the downsampling is done on 18 dimensions instead of 31. This leads to very similar runtime for both approaches, but we observe higher performance loss in scaling final features. This loss could be alleviated by smoothing the feature maps as [6] propose, but this would inevitably lead to slower runtime only to reach detection performance similar to our approach. In all experiments we use downsampling on 18-dimensional histograms and then compute and normalize the 31-dimensional fHOG features.

As with images, histograms can be downscaled using bilinear interpolation of bins between adjacent cells, either by always starting from the first level and obtaining the rest (which we dub *direct* method), or by successively obtaining level $i+1$ from level $i$ (*progressive* method), see Fig. 3 for clarification. Because the algorithm requires histograms for all levels, the *progressive* method yields faster overall computation time as the source histogram is smaller, but leads to additional blur that, contrary to the case of images, decreases detection accuracy.

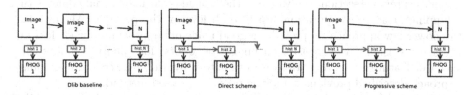

**Fig. 3.** Dlib baseline (left) and histogram downsampling schemes – *slow* (center) and *fast* (right) – applied up to level $N$.

In the following we evaluate execution speed and performance of each method, by successively applying it up to a given level ranging from 2 to 10, where 10 is actually a completely approximated pyramid, the entire pyramid has 10 levels (0–9) as in the previous results. From Fig. 4 we observe that the speed of both *progressive* and *direct* schemes are very similar, with little loss at higher levels for the *direct* histogram downsampling.

As for the *slow* and *fast* schemes, we compute the average precision of the detector using *progressive* and *direct* histogram downsampling with hyperparameters of the baseline and with best scores after a parameter search for each level. Results in Fig. 4 show that *direct* downsampling outperforms *progressive* by a small but real margin. We must note however that this advantage only appears after a few levels, where the blur introduced by the *progressive* method accumulates.

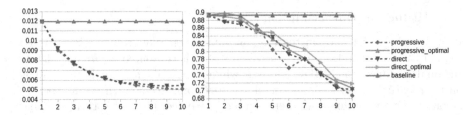

**Fig. 4.** Average execution time (in seconds) on modern computer (left) and average precision (right) of *progressive* vs. *direct* histogram downsampling. Dotted lines show the performance of the detector in each case using the same hyperparameters initially found for the baseline.

## 4   Adaptive Feature Pyramid Construction

It is clear that a trade-off exists between detection performance and the frame-rate at which the algorithm can run. While it is ideal to obtain accurate detections, in real setups such as the RoboCup competition the robot must also spend computational resources on other tasks, such as maintaining balance while walking. In fact, resource consumption varies throughout the game, depending on the situation. Therefore, it is desirable to have an adaptive control of the trade-off between accuracy and speed, while maximizing detection precision (*i.e.*, minimizing false positives).

In the previous section, we evaluated the drop in performance that comes with "skipping" feature computations up to each level of the pyramid. Meanwhile, the power law approach [6] provides a good trade-off: approximately 4% loss in average precision (in our setup, on images of robots) for almost doubling the speed of feature extraction. Here we evaluate a hybrid[1] between the skipping approach described previously and the power law based method.

We begin by skipping feature extraction up to level $N$ exclusively, while retaining it at levels that coincide with a 1/2 downscale of the image (octave). This way, we obtain a method that is bounded in speed and average precision by the original baseline (upper bound) and the power law based results (lower bound). The setup presented herein uses 4/5 downscale from one level to the next, therefore octaves correspond roughly to levels 3, 6 and 9. The proposed scheme skips levels excepting those corresponding to octaves and applying the scheme up to (but excluding) level $N$, thus we have equivalence between levels 3–4, 6–7 and 9–10 as the same conditions are met.

We note that the approximation of levels following an octave is done using the result that was obtained from a downsampled image, therefore the quality of the histogram is superior to the case where the approximation had continued from the first level, as is the case in the previously described results.

In Fig. 5 we compare our approach with the original algorithm, power law method and the previously described level skipping strategies. As with the optimal versions of previous strategies, we performed a hyperparameter search and

---

[1] Full code and dataset available at: https://github.com/polceanum/fast.fhog.

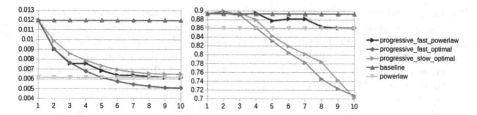

**Fig. 5.** Average execution time in seconds (left) and average precision (right) of studied feature approximation methods. Baseline and power law based approaches [6] shown as a straight lines, due to no level parameter.

retrained each configuration on the same dataset (equivalent to having a different model for each level to which the scheme is applied).

We observe the importance of retaining image downsampling at octave intervals as described by [6]. Applying our scheme up to level 4 does not sacrifice average precision, even though the most computationally expensive levels are approximated. At higher levels, average precision gradually decreases until it matches its lower bound, the power law baseline.

As the previous experiments have shown, gains in execution speed are significant especially for the first few levels of the pyramid. Figure 5 illustrates how execution time drops with each level, on the modern computer. At level 4, which had no average precision loss, the scheme offers 1.57x speed increase relative to the original algorithm. Increasing the level up to which the scheme is applied to 7 gives a 1.87x speed increase with only ~1% decrease in average precision.

We note that the *slow* image downsampling strategy could give slightly higher average precision results, but the loss in execution speed would be much higher.

## 5   Results

The processor equipped on the NAO v4 robot platform is, according to our estimates, approximately 25 times slower than the modern CPU on which we ran the evaluation. This is due to several factors such as lower frequency, less processor cache and other aspects which are outside the scope of this paper. These differences impose a hard standard on what algorithms can be run on this model of robots.

We evaluated the scheme on the NAO robot, obtaining gains in execution speed similar to the PC version (see Table 1). In fact, the speed increase is 1.68x without average precision loss relative to the dlib baseline, which is higher than the PC version, due to optimizations that are not available on the robot. At level 7, we obtain 1.95x speed increase with only 1.14% loss in average precision, while at level 10 (which is equivalent to the power law approach) the speed increase is 2.05x but the loss rises to 3.21%.

**Table 1.** Summary of proposed scheme performance. Average precision (AP), feature extraction execution time in milliseconds on modern computer (TMC) and on robot (TR), false positives per image (FPPI) and miss rate (MR) are shown for each level up to which the scheme is applied. For total detection time that includes SVM classification, add ~7 ms to TMC and ~117 ms to TR. Small FPPI variations most probably due to different SVM hyperparameter C values for each level.

| Level | 1 | 2 | 3–4 | 5 | 6–7 | 8 | 9–10 |
|---|---|---|---|---|---|---|---|
| AP | 89.3% | 89.4% | 89.4% | 87.7% | 88.2% | 87.0% | 86.1% |
| TMC | 11.9 | 9.0 | 7.5 | 6.8 | 6.3 | 6.2 | 6.1 |
| TR | 298.2 | 227.1 | 177.0 | 162.3 | 152.4 | 148.9 | 145.3 |
| FPPI | $5.4 \times 10^{-2}$ | $8.6 \times 10^{-2}$ | $3.7 \times 10^{-2}$ | $2.1 \times 10^{-2}$ | $3.2 \times 10^{-2}$ | $4.3 \times 10^{-2}$ | $3.7 \times 10^{-2}$ |
| MR | 11.3% | 8.6% | 10.2% | 11.8% | 11.3% | 12.9% | 13.5% |

We note that the time needed to compute the feature pyramid on the robot is still elevated, and thus more optimizations will be required. However, the ~150 ms drop with minimal loss in average precision is an important improvement in this case. To retain smooth motion and cognition, the algorithm can be broken down into multiple steps, and tracking can be performed in between. The important aspect is that the number of false positives per image is low, while some such cases are actually correct hits which were not annotated in the dataset (see Fig. 6).

**Fig. 6.** Robot (a–d) and ball (e–h) detection examples and extreme lighting conditions (i). Note: true positives in (a, b); false negative in (c) (fallen robot was not annotated in the dataset; false negatives in (d, h) due to excessive blur and similar background; detection in cluttered image (e); near (f) and far (g) detections. Slight box mismatches due to sliding window size; over time, detected bounding boxes vary slightly, especially visible in the extreme lighting scenario.

Results on ball detection are also satisfactory with the ability to detect soccer balls that are close and far away. We do note however that when the background has very similar color and texture, detection does not perform well. The algorithm is relatively robust to lighting conditions, as well as to a reasonable amount of motion blur. We notice that a limitation is represented by situations in which the objects "blend in" with the background. Outside the scope of the RoboCup competition, we expect that our approach will offer a better, adjustable trade-off between average precision and execution speed. For more difficult object detection problems, if hardware resources are more readily available, finer sampled image pyramids may improve results, and the gain from approximating intermediate levels becomes much more pronounced.

# 6 Conclusions and Future Work

In this work we provided a detailed evaluation of the trade-off between feature extraction speed and detector average precision, at each level of the feature pyramid. In our experiments, we used histogram downsampling instead of final feature downsampling used in related work. Results showed that this trade-off is not linear and that average precision is not lost by skipping the first few levels of the pyramid, which in fact account for a major part of the total computation time. We compared these results with the dlib library and with a state-of-the-art method based on image downsampling power law as baselines. Based on this analysis, we developed a hybrid method which is upper bounded by dlib and lower bounded by the power law approach in both execution time and average precision. We significantly improved the execution time compared to the dlib library and obtained a better trade-off than proposed by [6]. In practice, the proposed method can be adapted, by changing the level up to which it is applied, to favor average precision or execution speed. This way, on a modern computer, we obtain 1.57x increase in pyramid construction speed without any loss in average precision, ~1% average precision loss with 1.87x speed increase, and finally the same results as power-law approach when reaching the lower bound.

Execution speed gains are retained on the robot implementation, where we obtain 1.68x speed increase compared to the baseline with no loss and 1.95x increase with ~1% average precision loss, compared with 2.05x obtained with the power law baseline that presents ~3% average precision loss.

Following from the observation that the first few levels of the pyramid account for the majority of execution time, and that in our approach we compute the first level (level 0), extra time should be saved by upscaling level 0 from higher levels. Future work will include performance evaluation of this idea, as well as vectorizing histogram downsampling to the extent possible, including adopting complementary optimization techniques from related work. While this work improved the execution speed of the algorithm, the resulting framerate is still low on the NAO robot and requires further optimization (including vectorization which is not fully taken advantage of in this work), however it is possible to divide the feature pyramid extraction and object detection algorithm into steps that can be executed over multiple cognition cycles and couple the detection process with computationally cheaper tracking.

**Acknowledgements.** We thank the RoboCanes team of the University of Miami for providing their RoboCup software platform for our research. We also thank François

Lasson for help with hyperparameter search, and anonymous reviewers for their valuable feedback. The work in this paper was partially funded by the ANR project SOMBRERO (ANR-14-CE27-0014).

# References

1. Albani, D., Youssef, A., Suriani, V., Nardi, D., Bloisi, D.D.: A deep learning approach for object recognition with NAO soccer robots. In: Behnke, S., Sheh, R., Sarıel, S., Lee, D.D. (eds.) RoboCup 2016. LNCS (LNAI), vol. 9776, pp. 392–403. Springer, Cham (2017). https://doi.org/10.1007/978-3-319-68792-6_33

2. Brandão, S., Veloso, M., Costeira, J.P.: Fast object detection by regression in robot soccer. In: Röfer, T., Mayer, N.M., Savage, J., Saranlı, U. (eds.) RoboCup 2011. LNCS (LNAI), vol. 7416, pp. 550–561. Springer, Heidelberg (2012). https://doi.org/10.1007/978-3-642-32060-6_47

3. Budden, D., Fenn, S., Walker, J., Mendes, A.: A novel approach to ball detection for humanoid robot soccer. In: Thielscher, M., Zhang, D. (eds.) AI 2012. LNCS (LNAI), vol. 7691, pp. 827–838. Springer, Heidelberg (2012). https://doi.org/10.1007/978-3-642-35101-3_70

4. Cao, T.P., Deng, G.: Real-time vision-based stop sign detection system on FPGA. In: 2008 Digital Image Computing: Techniques and Applications, DICTA 2008, pp. 465–471. IEEE (2008)

5. Dalal, N., Triggs, B.: Histograms of oriented gradients for human detection. In: IEEE Computer Society Conference on Computer Vision and Pattern Recognition, vol. 1, pp. 886–893. IEEE (2005)

6. Dollár, P., Appel, R., Belongie, S., Perona, P.: Fast feature pyramids for object detection. IEEE Trans. Pattern Anal. Mach. Intell. 36(8), 1532–1545 (2014)

7. Dollár, P., Belongie, S.J., Perona, P.: The fastest pedestrian detector in the west. In: British Machine Vision Conference, vol. 2, p. 7 (2010)

8. Felzenszwalb, P.F., Girshick, R.B., McAllester, D., Ramanan, D.: Object detection with discriminatively trained part-based models. IEEE Trans. Pattern Anal. Mach. Intell. 32(9), 1627–1645 (2010)

9. Genter, K., et al.: UT Austin Villa: project-driven research in AI and robotics. IEEE Intell. Syst. 31(2), 94–101 (2016)

10. Gudi, A., de Kok, P., Methenitis, G.K., Steenbergen, N.: Feature detection and localization for the RoboCup Soccer SPL. Project report, Universiteit van Amsterdam, February 2013

11. Hemmati, M., Niar, S., Biglari-Abhari, M., Berber, S.: Real-time multi-scale pedestrian detection for driver assistance systems. In: 2017 54th ACM/EDAC/IEEE Design Automation Conference (DAC), pp. 1–6. IEEE (2017)

12. Iandola, F.N., Moskewicz, M.W., Keutzer, K.: libHOG: energy-efficient histogram of oriented gradient computation. In: International Conference on Intelligent Transportation Systems (ITSC), pp. 1248–1254. IEEE (2015)

13. Khandelwal, P., Hausknecht, M., Lee, J., Tian, A., Stone, P.: Vision calibration and processing on a humanoid soccer robot. In: 2010 The Fifth Workshop on Humanoid Soccer Robots at Humanoids (2010)

14. King, D.E.: Dlib-ml: a machine learning toolkit. J. Mach. Learn. Res. 10(Jul), 1755–1758 (2009)

15. King, D.E.: Max-margin object detection. arXiv preprint arXiv:1502.00046 (2015)

16. Menashe, J., et al.: Fast and precise black and white ball detection for robocup soccer. In: Akiyama, H., Obst, O., Sammut, C., Tonidandel, F. (eds.) RoboCup 2017. LNCS (LNAI), vol. 11175, pp. 45–58. Springer, Cham (2018). https://doi. org/10.1007/978-3-030-00308-1_4
17. Metzler, S., Nieuwenhuisen, M., Behnke, S.: Learning visual obstacle detection using color histogram features. In: Röfer, T., Mayer, N.M., Savage, J., Saranlı, U. (eds.) RoboCup 2011. LNCS (LNAI), vol. 7416, pp. 149–161. Springer, Heidelberg (2012). https://doi.org/10.1007/978-3-642-32060-6_13
18. Mizuno, K., Terachi, Y., Takagi, K., Izumi, S., Kawaguchi, H., Yoshimoto, M.: Architectural study of HOG feature extraction processor for real-time object detection. In: 2012 IEEE Workshop on Signal Processing Systems (SiPS), pp. 197–202. IEEE (2012)
19. Sze, V., Chen, Y.H., Einer, J., Suleiman, A., Zhang, Z.: Hardware for machine learning: challenges and opportunities. In: 2017 IEEE Custom Integrated Circuits Conference (CICC), pp. 1–8. IEEE (2017)

# Combining Simulations and Real-Robot Experiments for Bayesian Optimization of Bipedal Gait Stabilization

Diego Rodriguez[✉], André Brandenburger, and Sven Behnke

Autonomous Intelligent Systems, Computer Science, University of Bonn,
Bonn, Germany
{rodriguez,behnke}@ais.uni-bonn.de, andre.brandenburger@uni-bonn.de
http://ais.uni-bonn.de

**Abstract.** Walking controllers often require parametrization which must be tuned according to some cost function. To estimate these parameters, simulations can be performed which are cheap but do not fully represent reality. Real-robot experiments, on the other hand, are more expensive and lead to hardware wear-off. In this paper, we propose an approach for combining simulations and real experiments to learn gait stabilization parameters. We use a Bayesian optimization method which selects the most informative points in parameter space to evaluate based on the entropy of the cost function to optimize. Experiments with the igus® Humanoid Open Platform demonstrate the effectiveness of our approach.

## 1 Introduction

Walking is a crucial task for legged robots. The state-of-the-art walking controllers and generators typically require a fine-tuned parametrization that due to its complexity is determined by experts. This puts a constraint on the applicability of these methods. They can be used mainly by the people who designed them. In recent years, learning approaches have been proposed in order to reduce the amount of work and expert knowledge required to tune these methods [7,18]. This implies thus to perform experiments to estimate parameters. Consequently, sample-efficient learning approaches are required in order to reduce the hardware wear-off induced by the experiments. One way to reduce the need for real-robot experiments is to use simulations, which are cheaper to perform but do not fully represent reality. This point is particularly relevant for low-cost robots whose hardware is not as precise as expected. In this paper, we propose a method to combine simulations and real-robot experiments to optimize gait parameters, specifically to learn activation values of corrective actions that act on top of an open-loop bipedal gait generator. The optimization uses a state-of-the-art sample-efficient Bayesian method which selects the most informative points in parameter space to evaluate based on the entropy of a cost function (Fig. 1).

---

D. Rodriguez and A. Brandenburger—Both authors contributed equally.

© Springer Nature Switzerland AG 2019
D. Holz et al. (Eds.): RoboCup 2018, LNAI 11374, pp. 70–82, 2019.
https://doi.org/10.1007/978-3-030-27544-0_6

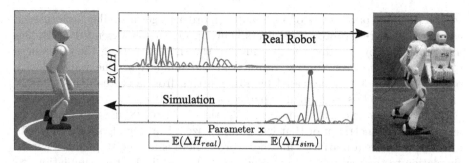

**Fig. 1.** Combining multiple sources of information for learning gait parameters **x**. Based on the largest relative entropy $\mathbb{E}(\Delta H)$ of a cost function $J$, a walking sequence is performed in simulation or with the real robot. The number of walking sequences performed with the real robot is reduced by using simulations.

## 2    Related Work

Several learning methods have been used to optimize manipulation or locomotion parameters [1,7,9,12,18,20]. Most of the methods are based on Bayesian optimization—due to its high sample efficiency. Deisenroth et al. [9], for example, developed a Bayesian approach to tune a cart-pole system, whereas Berkenkamp et al. [6] proposed to use Bayesian optimization to safely tune robotic controllers for quadrotors. Moreover, Marco et al. [16] combined Bayesian optimization with optimal control to tune LQR regulators. In contrast to these approaches, Akrour et al. [1] suggested to direct the optimization process by using a search distribution, however, the optimization loses expressibility on a global scope since it only optimizes locally. Even though these methods take advantage of the sample efficiency of the Bayesian optimization, the robotic hardware is worn off unnecessarily in the learning process, especially in the initial stages where the controllers do not possess any prior knowledge.

Specifically for the problem of gait parameter optimization, Calandra et al. [7] suggested a Bayesian optimization in order to replicate a given target trajectory for a bipedal robot. Based on only real experiments, the algorithm was able to find a stable gait. Because only the real hardware was used for all experiments, we expect a considerable wear-off of the robot. On the other hand, Heijmink et al. [12] proposed a method to learn gait parameters and impedance profiles in simulation for a quadruped robot. This was accomplished by using the PI$^2$ algorithm with a cost function consisting of speed tracking, energy consumption, joint limits, and torques. Although the results were validated in the real hardware, no transfer between simulation and the real hardware was addressed. Similarly, Hengst et al. [13], use a simulator to learn gait parameters that will be tested in the real robot. This is a reinforcement learning approach that learns the ankle joint position of the stance leg and the placement of the swing foot.

There exist several approaches that have transferred knowledge gathered in simulation to real robotic platforms. Farchy et al. [10], for example, learn several dynamic parameters of a simulator in order to get a similar performance compared with real-robot experiments. This approach was extended by Hanna and Stone [11] by learning the dynamics of the simulator using the differences of the actions between the real world and the simulation. The walk velocity of the NAO robot was increased by 43% starting from a state-of-the-art walk engine. Nevertheless, a human expert was required to select the appropriate parameters to be learned. Additionally, Cutler and How [8] uses a simulator to learn a nonparametric prior that will parametrize a learning algorithm that acts directly on the real platform, in other words, there is an one-step transfer from simulation to the real robot. In a recent work, Rai et al. [18] uses simulations to build a lower-dimensional space which is later used to learn gait parameters on the real hardware. Although this approach was able to achieve good results for a 9-dimensional controller with only 20 iterations, it requires—due to its informed kernel structure—a large amount of precomputed simulator data.

## 3   Preliminaries

### 3.1   Gaussian Process Regression

Given a training set $\mathcal{D} = \{(\mathbf{x}_i, y_i) | i = 1, \ldots, n)\}$ of $n$ observations, a Gaussian Process attempts to infer the relationship between the inputs and the targets given some *prior* knowledge. The observations are assumed to be corrupted by normally distributed noise $\epsilon \sim \mathcal{N}(0, \sigma^2)$, such that

$$y = f(\mathbf{x}) + \epsilon \tag{1}$$

$$f(\mathbf{x}) \sim \mathcal{GP}(\mu(\mathbf{x}), k(\mathbf{x}_i, \mathbf{x}_j)), \tag{2}$$

where $\mu(\mathbf{x})$ is the prior mean, which can be uniform, and $k(\mathbf{x}_i, \mathbf{x}_j)$ is the kernel also called the covariance function. Using a kernel allows us to transform the input space into a higher-dimensional feature space such that a non-linear map from the input vector $\mathbf{x}$ to the function value $f(\mathbf{x})$ can be inferred. The kernel models the uncertainty of the mean estimate and encodes how similar $f(\mathbf{x})$ is expected to be for two vectors $\mathbf{x}_i$ and $\mathbf{x}_j$. A high value of $k(\mathbf{x}_i, \mathbf{x}_j)$ would mean that the posterior value of $f(\mathbf{x}_j)$ is significantly influenced by the value of $f(\mathbf{x}_i)$. Note that using kernels we do not need to know the shape of the corresponding feature space, because only the inner products in the input space are required.

### 3.2   Bayesian Optimization

Bayesian optimization is a gradient-free sample-efficient framework that optimizes a cost function $f(\mathbf{x})$ using statistical models. Its goal is to find a global optimum of a cost function which is typically expensive to evaluate. In our case, it would imply to wear-off the hardware of the robot by performing walking experiments. This optimum is found by minimizing a posterior mean function. Often, the mean and covariance of $f(\mathbf{x})$ are described by a Gaussian Process.

The points to evaluate $f(\mathbf{x})$ are selected through an *acquisition function*, which also trades off exploration and exploitation, i.e., to select promising points were the optimum might be and to reduce the uncertainty about $f(\mathbf{x})$.

A prominent example of those acquisition functions is *Entropy Search* (ES) [14]. ES is based on the expected change of entropy $\mathbb{E}[\Delta H(\mathbf{x})]$, such that the point to evaluate in the next iteration is the one that offers most information (highest entropy change). The location of the minimum is approximated by a non-uniform grid, which, upon convergence, will be peaked around the actual minimum. The acquisition function for ES is defined as:

$$\mathbf{x}_{t+1} = \arg\max_{\mathbf{x}\in X}(\mathbb{E}[\Delta H(\mathbf{x})]). \tag{3}$$

The approximations to make ES computationally tractable can be found in [14].

## 3.3  Multi-Fidelity Entropy Search

Marco et al. [15] extends the ES algorithm to integrate multiple sources of information (Fig. 2). The resulting method is called *Multi-Fidelity Entropy Search* (MF-ES) and typically trades off real experiments with simulations. MF-ES optimizes the cost function

$$J_{real}(\mathbf{x}) = J_{sim}(\mathbf{x}) + \epsilon_{sim}(\mathbf{x}) \tag{4}$$

over a parameter set $\mathbf{x} \in X$. The key idea is to model the cost on the physical system $J_{real}$ as the cost in simulation $J_{sim}(\mathbf{x})$ plus a systematic error $\epsilon_{sim}(\mathbf{x})$. This error $\epsilon_{sim}$ can be a complex transformation, which is learned by the Bayesian optimization. MF-ES defines two kernel functions $k_{sim}$ and $k_\epsilon$, which model the cost on simulation and the difference to the real experiments, respectively. In this manner, the kernel is expressed as:

$$k(\mathbf{a}_i, \mathbf{a}_j) = k_{sim}(\mathbf{x}_i, \mathbf{x}_j) + k_\delta(\delta_i, \delta_j)k_\epsilon(\mathbf{x}_i, \mathbf{x}_j), \tag{5}$$

where $\mathbf{a} = (\delta, \mathbf{x})$ is an augmented vector in which $\delta$ indicates if a real experiment was performed and $k_\delta(\delta_i, \delta_j) = \delta_i\delta_j$ is a kernel indicator that equals one if both evaluations were performed with the real robot. Accordingly, two real experiments are expected to covary stronger than evaluations containing simulations.

Since $k_\epsilon$ is modeled inside the GP, we do not need to address explicitly the mapping between $J_{sim}$ and $J_{real}$; we only require assumptions about the difference between simulation versus real experiments in form of a mean and a covariance function. Additionally, $\delta$ has to be explicitly incorporated into the acquisition function of the optimization—otherwise only real experiments would be selected, because they deliver more information about the target function. This is done by introducing weight parameters $w_i$ for both information sources. Thus, the acquisition function is expressed as

$$\mathbf{x}_{t+1} = \arg\max_{\mathbf{x}\in\mathbb{R}^d, i\in\{\text{sim},\text{real}\}} \left(\frac{\Delta H_t(\mathbf{x})}{w_i}\right). \tag{6}$$

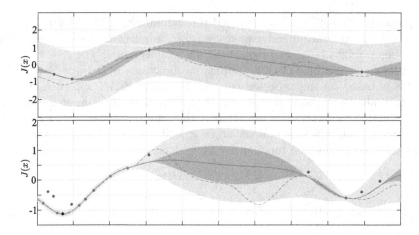

**Fig. 2.** Combination of simulation (blue dots) and real-robot (red dots) experiments in a synthetic example. The dashed red line represents the true cost function. Top: simulation experiments condition the mean posterior (red line) of the cost function of the physical system $J_{real}$ and influence considerably the simulation uncertainty (blue shaded), but the uncertainty of the real system (red shaded) is only slightly affected. Bottom: this uncertainty is significantly reduced by real-robot experiments. Note that the difference of the simulation data points and $J_{real}$ is captured by $\epsilon_{sim}$ (Eq. 4) The influence of simulation costs to the real system uncertainty is encoded in Eq. (5). (Color figure online)

### 3.4  Bipedal Walking with Feedback Mechanisms

In this section, we briefly describe the gait we want optimize [3]. The gait is based on an open-loop gait pattern generator as presented in [5]. It essentially produces high-dimensional trajectories for omnidirectional walking given a desired target velocity vector. The open-loop gait makes use of: the joint space, the inverse, and the abstract leg representations [17]. The abstract leg space is a representation of the leg pose, consisting of the leg extension, leg and foot angles, and is, in contrast to representations in Cartesian or joint space, designed for easy use for walking. The gait starts from a halt pose in the abstract space and incorporates several motion primitives such as leg lifting and leg swinging, also defined in the abstract space. The resulting pose is converted into the inverse space where more motion primitives are incorporated. Finally, the open-loop gait outputs a joint trajectory by converting the resulting inverse pose into the joint space.

In order to improve the stability and robustness of the robot, feedback mechanisms were added to the open-loop gait [3]. The orientation of the robot is represented by fused angles [2]. Using the deviations $d_\alpha$ and $d_\beta$ of the fused roll $\alpha_B$ and fused pitch $\beta_B$ from a desired orientation, e.g., from an upright torso pose, the activation value **u** of different corrective actions is calculated.

The elements of $\mathbf{u}$ can be considered as the strength of corresponding corrective actions (feedback mechanisms) which are then applied to the open-loop gait in the abstract or inverse space. The corrective actions include: *arm swinging, hip movement, COM shifting, ankle tilting, and support foot tilting.* In order to obtain the activation values $\mathbf{u}$, the deviations $d_\alpha$ and $d_\beta$ are passed through a feedback pipeline composed of integrators, derivatives, mean filters and smooth deadband filters to produce a PID vector $\mathbf{e} \in \mathbb{R}^6$. This vector is then multiplied by a gain matrix $\mathbf{K_a} \in \mathbb{R}^{m \times 6}$ to generate the activation values of the corresponding $m$ corrective actions.

# 4   Gait Parameter Learning

As explained in Sect. 3.4, the gait is composed of two main components: an open-loop central pattern generator and feedback mechanisms. In this paper, we address the problem of optimizing of the feedback mechanisms. Specifically, the activation gains $\mathbf{K}_a$ of the corrective actions will be optimized.

## 4.1   Cost Function

The fused angle deviations $d_\alpha = \alpha_{des} - \alpha$ (pitch) and $d_\beta = \beta_{des} - \beta$ (roll) give us an estimate about the unintended tilt of the robot induced by walking. These measurements are, however, very noisy. We apply thus a mean filter and a smooth deadband to $d_\alpha$ and $d_\beta$ as proposed in [3]. In other words, we end up with the proportional part $e_{P\alpha}$ and $e_{P\beta}$ of the fused feedback vector $\mathbf{e}$. So, we define the stability criterion of the entire gait as the integral of $e_{P\alpha}$ and $e_{P\alpha}$ along the gait duration $T$

$$\int_0^T \|e_{P\alpha}(\mathbf{x})\|_1 + \|e_{P\beta}(\mathbf{x})\|_1 dt \,. \tag{7}$$

This stability criterion will be part of our cost function. Additionally, we introduce a penalty term that smoothly regularizes the parameter $\mathbf{x}$. The penalty term is a logistic function of the form:

$$\nu(\mathbf{x}) = \frac{s}{1 + \exp\left(-\gamma(\|\mathbf{x}\|_2 - \lambda\|\mathbf{x}_{max}\|_2)\right)} \,, \tag{8}$$

where $\mathbf{x}_{max}$ is the upper bound of $\mathbf{x}$, $\lambda$ is a factor that affects the position of the transition, $s$ represents the magnitude of the penalization and $\gamma \in \mathbb{R}$ controls the smoothness of the phase transition.

Since corrective actions in the sagittal plane are only activated by the fused angle pitch $\alpha$ and in the lateral plane by the fused angle roll $\beta$, we propose a cost function for the parameters $\mathbf{x}_l$ that have an effect on the lateral plane and another cost function for the parameters $\mathbf{x}_s$ that affect the sagittal plane:

$$J_\alpha(\mathbf{x}_l) = \int_0^T \|e_{P\alpha}(\mathbf{x}_l)\|_1 dt + \nu(\mathbf{x}_l) \tag{9}$$

$$J_\beta(\mathbf{x}_s) = \int_0^T \|e_{P\beta}(\mathbf{x}_s)\|_1 dt + \nu(\mathbf{x}_s). \tag{10}$$

In order to overcome the intrinsic error of the simulator, i.e., same parameters yield different results, we perform $N$ evaluations in simulation with the same parameters and incorporate their mean into the cost function for the simulation:

$$\bar{J}_{sim,i}(\mathbf{x}) = \frac{1}{N}\left(\sum_{i=1}^N \int_0^T \|e_{Pi}(\mathbf{x})\|_1 dt\right) + \nu(\mathbf{x}), i \in \{\alpha, \beta\}. \tag{11}$$

For real-robot experiments, we set $J_{real}$ as given by Eqs. (9) and (10). In both (simulations and real-robot experiments), if the robot falls, a large cost is assigned to $\mathbf{x}$.

To define the kernel function of the optimization (Eq. (5)), we used the Rational Quadratic (RQ) kernel for $k_{sim}$ and $k_\epsilon$. The RQ kernel introduces three parameters ($\sigma_k^2$, $\alpha$ and $l$) to be tuned, also called hyperparameters. The $l$ parameter roughly determines the distance of two points to significantly influence each other, the scale factor $\sigma_k^2$ determines the problem-specific signal variance, and $\alpha$ is a relative weight of large-scale and small-scale variations.

## 4.2   Termination Criteria

The most simple and frequently used criterion to stop global optimization algorithms is based on the number of iterations. Whereas this condition works fine for problems that are fast to compute, it looses applicability when iterations become more expensive. We propose a termination criterion which is based on entropy. We formulate a criterion that stops the algorithm as soon as the relative entropy $\mathbb{E}[\Delta H(\mathbf{x}_t)]$ reaches a defined value. Moreover, to ensure that outliers do not lead to a premature stop, we apply a saturated filter to the relative entropy (Fig. 3) defined for each iteration $t$ with a velocity factor $0 < v < 1$ as:

$$(1 - v)\mathbb{E}[\Delta H(\mathbf{x}_{t-1})] + v\mathbb{E}[\Delta H(\mathbf{x}_t)]. \tag{12}$$

This criterion is applied after a minimum number of iterations since a bad prior mean can lead to a low relative entropy right after the first iteration. The entropy termination criterion is also combined with a maximum number of iterations criterion in case the relative entropy threshold is not reached mainly because the prior assumptions might not represent reality well enough.

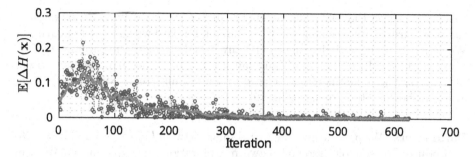

**Fig. 3.** Unfiltered (blue) and filtered with $v = 0.9$ (orange) relative entropy. The latter is used to terminate the optimization. Iterations after the magenta line can be skipped because of their very low information gain. (Color figure online)

## 5   Evaluation

### 5.1   Experiment Setup

**Robot Platform.** We test our approach on the igus® Humanoid Open Platform [4]. The robot has in total 20° of freedom: 6 for each leg, 3 for each arm and 2 for the neck. The links of this platform are fully 3D printed. The robot is 92 cm tall and weights 6.6 kg. The platform incorporates an Intel Core i7-5500U CPU running a 64-bit Ubuntu OS and a Robotis CM730 microcontroller board, which electrically interfaces with its Robotis Dynamixel MX actuators. A 3-axis accelerometer and gyroscope sensors are also contained in the CM730, for a total of 6 axes of inertial measurement.

**Software Architecture.** Due to the limited computational power of the robot, the optimization and simulations are performed on a desktop PC with a Core i7-4890K CPU and 8 GB of RAM. The simulations are carried out in Gazebo 2.2 with a real-time factor of 1.5. We use ODE as the dynamics engine without constraint force mixing and an error reduction parameter of 0.2. The geometries of the joint links are approximated using convex hulls. The joints are controlled using the *ros_control* package. To avoid induced noise in the simulation, the simulator is reset after each performed trial. The Bayesian optimization run in Matlab 2017b. All the components required for the gait are implemented in C++ and executed on the robot's computer. The interprocess communication is implemented using the ROS middleware.

**Scenarios.** We propose two scenarios to evaluate our approach. We initially perform a 2D optimization to learn the P- and D-gain of the *Ankle Tilt* corrective action. In the second scenario, a 4D optimization to learn the P- and D-gains of the *Swing Arm* and *Ankle Tilt* actions is performed. In both scenarios, there are no other feedback mechanisms active. To avoid artifacts coming from the transient of a robot in a static configuration, all experiments start with the robot walking on the spot. The walking sequence is then defined as walking on the spot during three seconds and then walking forward with a speed of 0.3 m/s. We do not bias the optimizer specifying any initial values of the parameters. We compare the results of our algorithm against manually tuned parameters devised by experts. These parameters were used by the winning team NimbRo TeenSize at the RoboCup 2017 competition [19].

**Parameters.** We parametrize the kernel function with $l = \left(\frac{\mathbf{x}_{max}}{8}\right)$ and $\alpha = 0.25$ to produce a reasonable trade-off between exploration and exploitation. We use the same values of $l$ and $\alpha$ for $k_{sim}$ and $k_\epsilon$. The standard deviation of $k_{sim}$ is set to $\sigma_{sim} = 2.48$ and the standard deviation of $k_\epsilon$ is set to $\sigma_\epsilon = 2.07$ for the 2D optimization, whereas $\sigma_{sim} = 2.07$ and $\sigma_\epsilon = 1.79$ are set for the 4D optimization. The prior means are set to $\mu_{sim} = 53.3502$ and $\mu_\epsilon = -37.1385$. These values are chosen from initial experiments. Additionally, the penalty function $\nu(\mathbf{x})$ is parametrized with $\lambda = 0.75$ and $s = 7.5$ to punish parameters larger than $\lambda\mathbf{x}_{max}$. The smoothness of the phase transition is set to $\gamma = 6$. The effort of the simulation and real-robot experiments are set to $w_{sim} = 10$ and $w_{sim} = 50$, respectively, i.e., a real-robot walking sequence is five times as expensive as a simulated one.

### 5.2   Experimental Results

**2D Optimization.** The algorithm performed in total 126 iterations, from which 20 walking trials were carried out with the real robot. This implies that approximately one real robot walking trial was required for every five simulations, which shows the applicability of the integration of simulation and real robot experiments for learning the activation value of the *Ankle Tilt* corrective action. The optimized values yielded a cost of 9.3, while the manually tuned ones resulted in a cost of 13.77. Thus, the optimization process found parameters that are approximately 32% better than the manually by-expert-tuned parameters. The resulting posterior is depicted in Fig. 4. The difference in the cost of the simulation compared to the cost with the real robot is mainly caused by the noise of the simulator, e.g., by modeling errors of the floor impacts.

Our approach was compared with a Random Search algorithm that greedily searches for the optimal value by corrupting the current best guess with uniform noise at each iteration. We applied this algorithm on the same experimental setup and a maximum of 25 real-robot experiments. With a cost of 11.04, the parameters of the random search outperformed the manually tuned ones. However, our method performed 20 real experiments and yielded 15% better results than random search. Additionally, the evaluations of the random search caused one fall of the robot which never occurred with our approach.

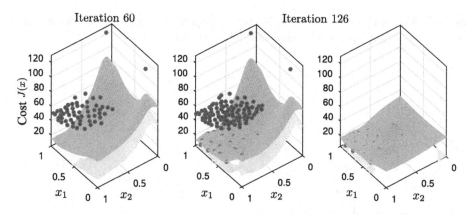

**Fig. 4.** Optimization of the parameters for the *Ankle Tilt* corrective action. The purple mesh resembles the posterior mean while the gray mesh shows the covariance. At the first iterations, the algorithm decided to perform only simulations (blue). Once enough information has been gathered in the simulation, real experiments (red) are carried out. To stress the contribution of the simulation, the rightmost plot shows the posterior considering only real-robot experiments. (Color figure online)

**4D Optimization.** For the 4D optimization, 301 iterations were carried out: 271 in simulation and 30 with the real robot, i.e., in average one real-robot experiment is required for every nine simulations. The resulting parameters were evaluated against manually tuned parameters, performing with the real robot 15 walking sequences for each set of parameters. The optimized parameters yielded an average cost of 10.38 and resulted, in comparison to the manually tuned gait with a mean cost of 16.28, in an improvement of 35%. In order to evaluate only the contribution of the stability in the cost, we subtract the penalty term of the cost; the resulting performance of the optimized parameters is 53% better than the manually tuned parameters.

Moreover, we compared the measured fused angle deviation (not fused angle feedback) and its integral during five trials. As expected, during the first three seconds (walking on spot) there are no significant differences. However, as soon as the robot starts walking forward, the deviations start to diverge and the difference between the set of parameters becomes apparent. In general, the optimized parameters reproducibly generate deviations of lower amplitude. The difference becomes more apparent observing the integral of the mean absolute deviation $\bar{D}_\alpha = \int_0^T \mathbb{E}\left[\|d_\alpha\|\right] dt$ depicted in Fig. 5.

A remarkable property of our approach is the fact that the real robot did not fall a single time during the optimization process, because parameters that resulted in a fall in simulation were ruled out without the need for real-robot experiments. Furthermore, the optimized gait looks qualitatively more stable and generally walks with a more upright torso compared to the manually tuned parametrization. A video of the gait with the optimized parameters is available online[1]. The optimized gait was also tested in a very rough terrain, where the robot successfully traversed a series of debris (Fig. 6).

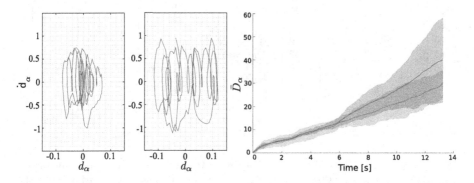

**Fig. 5.** Phase plots of the optimized (left) and manually (middle) tuned parameters for our gait. For clarity, only one walking sequence is displayed but all the evaluated sequences show a similar behavior. Right: integral of the mean absolute fused angle deviation $\bar{D}_\alpha$ of the optimized (red) and the manually tuned (blue) parameters. The shaded regions cover the values within two standard deviations ($\pm 2\sigma$). (Color figure online)

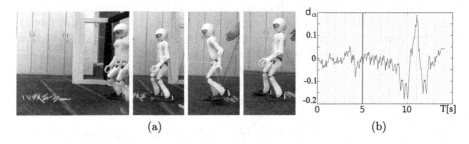

**Fig. 6.** Evaluation of the optimized gait parameters on very rough surfaces (artificial grass with small debris). (a) Evaluation setup (leftmost) and pictures of the robot traversing the debris. (b) The corresponding fused angle deviation over time. The magenta line indicates the moment of contact with the debris.

## 6   Conclusions

We presented an approach to trade off simulations and real-robot experiments for learning gait parameters based on a state-of-the-art Bayesian optimizer. We showed how the gait stability was improved with the parameters found by our approach. During the optimization process, the real robot did not fall a single

---

[1] http://www.ais.uni-bonn.de/videos/RoboCup_Symposium_2018.

time, which shows that the algorithm was successfully generalizing the information gathered from the simulation. This generalization also leads to a lower number of required physical experiments, which enables the applicability of our approach.

We observed a limitation of our method to be applied in higher dimensions. We hypothesize to solve this issue by using dimensionality reduction methods and by performing the optimization in a lower-dimensional space. Additionally, in the future, we also want to learn the hyperparameters of the kernel during optimization.

**Acknowledgements.** The authors would like to thank Alonso Marco from the the Max Planck Institute for Intelligent Systems for providing the MF-ES implementation. This work was partially funded by grant BE 2556/13 of German Research Foundation.

# References

1. Akrour, R., Sorokin, D., Peters, J., Neumann, G.: Local Bayesian optimization of motor skills. In: Proceedings of the 34th International Conference on Machine Learning (PMLR) (2017)
2. Allgeuer, P., Behnke, S.: Fused angles: a representation of body orientation for balance. In: International Conference on Intelligent Robots and Systems (IROS) (2015)
3. Allgeuer, P., Behnke, S.: Omnidirectional bipedal walking with direct fused angle feedback mechanisms. In: International Conference on Humanoid Robots (Humanoids) (2016)
4. Allgeuer, P., Farazi, H., Schreiber, M., Behnke, S.: Child-sized 3D printed igus humanoid open platform. In: International Conference on Humanoid Robots (2015)
5. Behnke, S.: Online trajectory generation for omnidirectional biped walking. In: Proceedings of IEEE International Conference on Robotics and Automation (ICRA) (2006)
6. Berkenkamp, F., Schoellig, A.P., Krause, A.: Safe controller optimization for quadrotors with Gaussian processes. In: IEEE International Conference on Robotics and Automation (ICRA) (2016)
7. Calandra, R., Gopalan, N., Seyfarth, A., Peters, J., Deisenroth, M.P.: Bayesian gait optimization for bipedal locomotion. In: Pardalos, P.M., Resende, M.G.C., Vogiatzis, C., Walteros, J.L. (eds.) LION 2014. LNCS, vol. 8426, pp. 274–290. Springer, Cham (2014). https://doi.org/10.1007/978-3-319-09584-4_25
8. Cutler, M., How, J.P.: Efficient reinforcement learning for robots using informative simulated priors. In: IEEE International Conference on Robotics and Automation (ICRA) (2015)
9. Deisenroth, M.P., Fox, D., Rasmussen, C.E.: Gaussian processes for data-efficient learning in robotics and control. IEEE Trans. Pattern Anal. Mach. Intell. **37**(2), 408–423 (2015)
10. Farchy, A., Barrett, S., MacAlpine, P., Stone, P.: Humanoid robots learning to walk faster: from the real world to simulation and back. In: Proceedings of the International Conference on Autonomous Agents and Multi-Agent Systems (AAMAS) (2013)

11. Hanna, J.P., Stone, P.: Grounded action transformation for robot learning in simulation. In: Association for the Advancement of Artificial Intelligence Conference (AAAI) (2017)
12. Heijmink, E., Radulescu, A., Ponton, B., Barasuol, V., Caldwell, D.G., Semini, C.: Learning optimal gait parameters and impedance profiles for legged locomotion. In: IEEE-RAS 17th International Conference on Humanoid Robots (Humanoids) (2017)
13. Hengst, B., Lange, M., White, B.: Learning ankle-tilt and foot-placement control for flat-footed bipedal balancing and walking. In: 11th IEEE-RAS International Conference on Humanoid Robots (Humanoids) (2011)
14. Hennig, P., Schuler, C.: Entropy search for information-efficient global optimization. J. Mach. Learn. Res. **13**(Jun), 1809–1837 (2012)
15. Marco, A., et al.: Virtual vs. real: trading off simulations and physical experiments in reinforcement learning with Bayesian optimization. In: Proceedings of the IEEE International Conference on Robotics and Automation (ICRA) (2017)
16. Marco, A., Hennig, P., Bohg, J., Schaal, S., Trimpe, S.: Automatic LQR tuning based on Gaussian process global optimization. In: IEEE International Conference on Robotics and Automation (ICRA) (2016)
17. Missura, M., Behnke, S.: Self-stable omnidirectional walking with compliant joints. In: 8th Workshop on Humanoid Soccer Robots, International Conference on Humanoid Robots (2013)
18. Rai, A., Antonova, R., Song, S., Martin, W.C., Geyer, H., Atkeson, C.G.: Bayesian optimization using domain knowledge on the ATRIAS biped. In: IEEE International Conference on Robotics and Automation (ICRA) (2018)
19. Rodriguez, D., et al.: Advanced soccer skills and team play of RoboCup 2017 teensize winner nimbro. In: Akiyama, H., Obst, O., Sammut, C., Tonidandel, F. (eds.) RoboCup 2017. LNCS (LNAI), vol. 11175, pp. 435–447. Springer, Cham (2018). https://doi.org/10.1007/978-3-030-00308-1_36
20. Röfer, T.: Evolutionary gait-optimization using a fitness function based on proprioception. In: Nardi, D., Riedmiller, M., Sammut, C., Santos-Victor, J. (eds.) RoboCup 2004. LNCS (LNAI), vol. 3276, pp. 310–322. Springer, Heidelberg (2005). https://doi.org/10.1007/978-3-540-32256-6_25

# Learning Skills for Small Size League RoboCup

Devin Schwab[✉], Yifeng Zhu, and Manuela Veloso

Carnegie Mellon University, Pittsburgh, PA 15217, USA
digidevin@gmail.com

**Abstract.** In this work, we show how modern deep reinforcement learning (RL) techniques can be incorporated into an existing Skills, Tactics, and Plays (STP) architecture. STP divides the robot behavior into a hand-coded hierarchy of plays, which coordinate multiple robots, tactics, which encode high level behavior of individual robots, and skills, which encode low-level control of pieces of a tactic. The CMDragons successfully used an STP architecture to win the 2015 RoboCup competition. The skills in their code were a combination of classical robotics algorithms and human designed policies. In this work, we use modern deep RL, specifically the Deep Deterministic Policy Gradient (DDPG) algorithm, to learn skills. We compare learned skills to existing skills in the CMDragons' architecture using a physically realistic simulator. We then show how RL can be leveraged to learn simple skills that can be combined by humans into high level tactics that allow an agent to navigate to a ball, aim and shoot on a goal.

**Keywords:** Reinforcement learning · Robot software architecture · Autonomous robots

## 1 Introduction

RoboCup soccer is an international competition where teams of researchers compete to create the best team of autonomous soccer playing robots [22]. Multiple leagues from simulation, to full humanoid leagues compete each year. In this work we focus on the Small Size League (SSL) RoboCup, which is a challenging, fast paced, multi-agent league.

The Skills, Tactics, and Plays (STP) [3] software architecture has been used by the 2015 winning champions, CMDragons. STP is a hierarchical architecture consisting of three levels. Skills are coded policies that represent low-level tasks, used repeatedly in a game of soccer. These are tasks such as: dribbling the ball, navigating to a point, etc. Tactics combine skills into behaviors for a single

This research is partially sponsored by DARPA under agreements FA87501620042 and FA87501720152 and NSF grant number IIS1637927. The views and conclusions contained in this document are those of the authors only.

D. Holz et al. (Eds.): RoboCup 2018, LNAI 11374, pp. 83–95, 2019.
https://doi.org/10.1007/978-3-030-27544-0_7

robot. Typical tactics are roles such as: attacker, goalie, defender, etc. They are typically coded as state machines, where specific skills are called in each state. Plays are how multiple tactics are coordinated. Each robot is assigned a tactic based on cost functions, and then the robots execute these tactics independently.

In prior years, all levels of the STP architecture have been written by hand using classical robotics algorithms. Low-level policies such as navigation can use algorithms such as an RRT [9], while the tactic state machines have been written by intuition and improvement through extensive testing. Writing new skills is a large investment of human time and coding. Ideally, these low-level skills could be learned automatically, and then reused by the human-coded tactics in order to save time and man-power.

Recently, deep reinforcement learning (Deep RL) techniques have made major breakthroughs in performance. Deep Q-Networks (DQN) [13,14] have been used to learn policies from pixels in Atari that exceed human performance. More recently, Deep RL has been used to beat human performance in the game of Go [17,18]. Outside of games, Deep RL has been used to learn complex continuous control tasks such as locomotion [7]. It is therefore an attractive idea to use Deep RL for SSL RoboCup. However, it is unclear how best to learn policies in such a complex, multi-agent, adversarial game.

In the rest of this paper, we explore how Deep RL can be used to automatically learn skills in an STP architecture. While it would also be useful to learn tactics and plays, skills are small enough problems to be effectively learned using Deep RL in a short amount of time. Tactics are much more complicated, and plays would require multi-agent RL algorithms, therefore, in this work we focus on learning skills. A learning algorithm can be implemented once and then applied to learn many different skills. Whereas, each hand-coded skill will require it's own implementation, testing and tweaking. By learning skills, human coders can spend time working on the more complicated tactics and plays. We show that after skills are learned using Deep RL they can be effectively combined by humans into useful tactics.

## 2    Small Size League (SSL) RoboCup

Figure 1 shows an example of the CMDragons SSL robot. The robots are approximately 18 cm in diameter and move omni-directionally. The robots can kick at various speeds both flat along the ground and through the air. The robots also have spinning dribbler bars, which apply backspin to the ball.

Figure 1 shows an overview of the field setup. Overhead cameras send images to a central vision server. The vision server uses colored patterns to determine ball position and robot field positions, orientations, ID and team. This information is sent to each team at 60 Hz. Teams typically use a single computer that sends radio commands to all robots on the field. Therefore, centralized planning and coordination can be used.

The full game of SSL has many different parts: kickoff, free kicks, penalty kicks, main game play, etc. In this work we focus on skills that can be useful

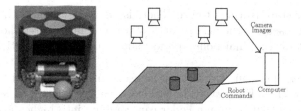

**Fig. 1.** (Left) A typical Small Size League (SSL) robot and ball. (Right) SSL field setup. Overhead cameras capture dot patterns on the tops of robots to determine positions, orientations, team and robot ID. Ball position is also determined from color. A central computer publishes this position information to each team. Teams then send radio commands to their robots on the field. (Color figure online)

in many different parts of the game: namely capturing the ball on the dribbler, and aiming and shooting at the goal.

## 3   Related Work

Deep RL algorithms, such as Deep Q-Networks (DQN), Asynchronous Advantage Actor (A3C) and others, have been shown to work in complex Markov Decision Processes (MDPs) such as Atari games and the game of Go [12–14,17]. There have also been some initial successes in applying Deep RL to continuous control tasks using policy gradient methods such as Deep Deterministic Policy Gradients (DDPG), Trust Region Policy Optimization (TRPO) and Proximal Policy Optimization (PPO) [10,15,16]. Unlike traditional RL, Deep RL algorithms can often work from low-level features such as joint angles or even pixels. This can alleviate the need for domain specific feature engineering.

Our work is not the first attempt to apply learning to RoboCup domains. Many techniques have been developed and applied for the game of Keep-away [20]. In Keep-away, teams or robots must learn to coordinate by moving and passing the ball so that an opponent team cannot steal the ball. Many techniques have been applied including genetic algorithms [1,8,11] and reinforcement learning [21,23].

Multiple groups have applied genetic programming techniques to learn team robot soccer policies [1,8,11]. Genetic programming uses genetic algorithm optimization techniques with a set of composable functions in order to "evolve" a program capable of completing some objective. Prior attempts have had limited success, either relying heavily on carefully hand-coded sub-policies or failing to learn cooperative team behaviors.

Reinforcement learning (RL) based approaches have also been popular in this domain [4,21,23]. Stone et al. [21], utilized an options [19] like framework. The low-level controls were hand-coded. The agent learned to call these sub-policies at the appropriate times. They were able to successfully train in up to a 4 teammates vs 3 opponents scenario. While their approach was successful, a significant amount of effort went into determining the proper low level actions and the proper state-features to use. There is also no guarantee that the higher level features chosen are the best possible features. The features chosen can have a large impact on the final policy performance, and are in practice difficult to choose.

Most of these previous works have focused on learning multi-agent policies in sub-games, such as Keep-away. In this work, we are focused on learning small single agent skills that a human coder can combine into higher level behaviors in the STP architecture.

There has been more recent work on applying Deep RL to single agent skills with parameterized action spaces [5,6]. In Hausknecht, Chen and Stone [5], existing Deep RL techniques were extended to work in an action space that combines discrete and continuous components. They then learned a policy from demonstrations, that allowed the agent to navigate to the ball and score on an empty goal. Hausknecht and Stone [6] later extended this work to learn ball manipulation in this setting completely from scratch. Both of these approaches demonstrated the applicability of Deep RL based algorithms to robot soccer, however, they learned an end-to-end policy to go to the ball and score on the goal. It would be difficult to divide up this policy after training and use the different parts in other contexts. In this work, we aim to learn small reusable skills that can be combined by human written tactics.

## 4    Approach

### 4.1    Algorithm

In this work we use the Deep Deterministic Policy Gradient (DDPG) algorithm to train our skills [10]. DDPG is an actor critic, policy gradient algorithm that has been shown to work for continuous action spaces in complex control tasks. Like DQN, DDPG uses a target network for the actor-critic along with a replay memory. Samples are collected and stored in a replay memory. Batches of the samples are used to optimize a critic network which estimates the Q-value of a state-action input. Then the actor network, which takes in a state and returns a continuous action, is optimized to maximize the critic's estimate. We use DDPG in this work, because it is well studied and has been shown to work on a variety of interesting continuous control tasks [10].

### 4.2    Simulation

We train our skills in the CMDragons simulator. This simulator is physically realistic including configurable amounts of radio latency, observation noise and different robot dynamics models. This simulator has been used to develop the existing STP. The API of the simulator is similar to the real robots, so that a network trained on the simulator can then be run directly on a real robot.

To train the skills we setup different initial conditions in the simulator and applied the DDPG algorithm. When training the simulation is set in "step mode", meaning that the simulation will only advance when a new command is sent. This guarantees that when training, the extra computation time for updating the network does not cause the agent to miss observation steps. However, when we evaluate the skills we set the simulator to real-time mode. In this mode, the physics runs in real time, and if the agent takes more than 16ms to send a command, then it will miss control time steps.

## 4.3    Skills

All of the skills use a vector of relevant state features as the input. While Deep RL algorithms such as DDPG can work with pixel based inputs, the state vector allows us to directly include information about velocities. The state-vector representation also requires less computation than an image based representation.

**Go to Ball Skill.** go-to-ball is a skill where the robot learns to navigate to the ball and get the ball on it's dribbler. The go-to-ball environment uses positions and velocities in the robot's own frame. By making the coordinates relative to the robot, the learned policy should generalize to different positions on the field better.

The state input for go-to-ball skill is as follows:

$$s = (P_x^B, P_y^B, V_x^R, V_y^R, \omega^R,$$

$$d_{r-b}, x_{top}, y_{top}, x_{bottom}, y_{bottom}, x_{left}, y_{left}, x_{right}, y_{right})$$

where $P_x^B$ and $P_y^B$ are the ball position, $V_x^R$ and $V_y^R$ are the robot's translational velocity, $\omega^R$ is the robot's angular velocity, $d_{r-b}$ is the distance from robot to ball, $x_{top}$ and $y_{top}$ are the closest point on the top edge of the field to the robot, $x_{bottom}$ and $y_{bottom}$ are the closest point on the bottom edge of the field to the robot, $x_{right}$ and $y_{right}$ are the closest point on the right edge of the field to the robot, and $x_{left}$ and $y_{left}$ are the closest point on the left edge of the field to the robot.

The action space of this skill is robot's linear velocity, and angular velocity, which are: $(v_x^R, v_y^R, \omega^R)$.

The terminal condition for training go-to-ball skill is that if the robot has the ball on its dribbler, the episode ends and is marked as a success. If the robot fails to get the ball on its dribbler in 10 s, the episode ends and is considered a failure.

**Aim and Shoot Skill.** aim-to-shoot is a skill where the robot learns to aim towards goal and take a shot. In this skill, we assume that the robot already has a ball on its dribbler.

The state input is as follow:

$$s = (P_x^B, P_y^B, V_x^B, V_y^B, \omega^R, d_{r-g}, \sin(\theta_l), \cos(\theta_l), \sin(\theta_r), \cos(\theta_r))$$

where $V_x^B$ and $V_y^B$ are the x and y translational velocity of the ball, $d_{r-g}$ is the distance from the robot to the goal, $\sin(\theta_l)$ and $\cos(\theta_l)$ are the sine and cosine of the angle of the left goal post with respect to the robot's orientation, $\sin(\theta_r)$ and $\cos(\theta_r)$ are the sine and cosine of the angle of the left goal post with respect to the robot's orientation, and the remaining state components match the go-to-ball skill. We use the sine and cosine of the angle, so that there is not a discontinuity in the input state when the angle wraps around from $-\pi$ to $\pi$.

The action space of aim-to-shoot skill contains robot's angular velocity, dribbling strength and kick strength: $(\omega^R, dribble, kick)$.

The terminal condition for training aim-to-shoot skill is that if the robot has kicked and scored, the episode ends and is considered as a success. Otherwise, the episode ends with the following failure conditions: the ball is kicked but does not go into the goal, ball is not kicked yet but the ball has rolled away from the dribbler, or the episode reaches the maximum episode length of 1.6 s.

**Reward Functions.** We use reward shaping to help speed up the learning. In the go-to-ball , our reward function is:

$$r_{total} = r_{contact} + r_{distance} + r_{orientation}$$

where,

$$r_{contact} = \begin{cases} 100 & \text{ball on the dribbler} \\ 0 & \text{ball not on the dribbler} \end{cases}$$

$$r_{distance} = \frac{5}{\sqrt{2\pi}} \exp(\frac{-d_{r-b}^2}{2}) - 2$$

$$r_{orientation} = \frac{1}{\sqrt{2\pi}} \exp\left(-2\frac{\theta_{r-b}}{\pi^2}\right)$$

where $\theta_{r-b}$ is minimum angle between the robot's dribbler and the ball.

For the aim-to-shoot skill, the agent gets positive reward when it kicks towards the goal and negative when it kicks away from the goal. We also want the robot to shoot as fast as possible on the goal, so we scale the reward by the ball velocity. Kicking fast towards the goal gives higher reward. The reward function for aim-to-shoot skill is as follows:

$$r = \begin{cases} 0.05(\alpha - \beta)|V^B| & \alpha > \beta \\ (\alpha - \beta)|V^B| & \alpha < \beta \end{cases}$$

where, $\alpha$ is the angle between left goal post and right goal post, $\beta$ is the larger angle of one of the goal posts relative to robot's orientation.

## 4.4    Go to Ball and Shoot Tactic

We combined the `go-to-ball` skill and the `aim-to-shoot` skill into a tactic that can go to the ball, get the ball on the dribbler, turn towards the goal and shoot. Figure 2 shows a flow-chart for the tactic state machine. The robot starts out using the trained `go-to-ball` skill. Once the ball is near the dribbler (defined by $d_{d-b} \leq 35$ mm, where $d_{d-b}$ is the distance from the dribbler to the ball), the robot transitions to a fixed "drive forward" skill. The drive forward skill just turns on the dribbler and moves the robot forward for 1 s. After the skill completes, if the ball is no longer near the dribbler (i.e. $d_{d-b} > 35$ mm), then the robot starts the `go-to-ball` skill again. Otherwise, the robot starts the learned `aim-to-shoot` skill. If the ball is lost during the `aim-to-shoot` , then the robot transitions back to go to ball and tries again.

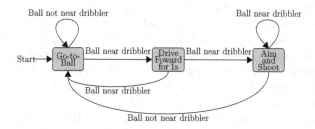

**Fig. 2.** Flowchart of Go to ball and shoot tactic.

# 5    Empirical Results

In this section we evaluate the learning performance and the final policy performance of our skills. We also evaluate the performance of our tactic composed of the two learned skills and one hard-coded skill.

## 5.1    Skill Learning

Tables 1 and 2 shows the hyperparameters used while training both skills. We used an Ornstein-Uhlenbeck noise process [10]. The table also shows the layer sizes for the actor and critic networks. Each layer is a fully connected layer. The hidden layers use ReLU activations, the final layer of the actor uses a tanh activation. The final layer of the critic uses a linear activation. Layer-norm layers were inserted after each hidden layer [2]. When training each skill we initialize the replay memory with examples of successful trajectories. This has been shown in the past to improve the convergence speed of DDPG [24].

During the training of `go-to-ball` skill, we start by collecting 50,000 steps of demonstrations of a good policy as part of the replay memory "burn-in". These samples initialize the replay memory before collecting samples according to the current actor and noise policy. To get these good demonstrations, we spawn the robot at an arbitrary position on the field so that is facing the ball. We then drive the robot forward until it touches the ball. During the actual training, the robot must learn to reach the ball from arbitrary positions and orientations.

For the training of `aim-to-shoot` skill, we initialize the replay memory with 10,000 samples from a good policy. To get these initial samples we spawn the robot near the goal, facing the goal, and then kick the ball at full strength. During the actual training, the robot must learn to orient itself and the ball towards the goal and then kick.

Figure 3a shows the learning curve from training the go-to-ball skill. The initial part of the curve shows the initial policy demonstrations used to seed the replay. While there is variance in the final policy performance, we see that the agent takes about 500,000 training samples before it has converged to an acceptable policy. Figure 3b shows the average episode length while training. There is a large difference in the maximum number of steps taken to successfully complete an episode between the initial policy and the final policy.

We tested the learned go-to-ball skill against the existing go-to-ball skill. The existing skill moves the robot in a straight line while turning to face the ball. We spawn the ball in a random location of the field. Then the robot is also spawned at a random position and orientation. We then run the skill until either 10 s has elapsed or the ball has been touched on the dribbler.

Figure 4 shows a histogram of the times taken for the go-to-ball skill to get to the ball from 1000 different runs. We can see that while the learned skill has more variance in the times, the max time is still within approximately 2 s of the max time taken by the baseline skill. While the learned skill may take slightly longer, it does reach the ball as intended. The discrepancy in time is likely due to an inability of the DDPG algorithm to perfectly optimize the policy given the training samples. Table 3 shows the success rate of both policies. We see that the baseline is always successful, and the trained policy only failed to get the ball in a single run.

Qualitatively, the path the learned skill takes is very different from the baseline. The baseline is very consistent, moving in a straight line and slowly turning to face the ball. The learned policy's path curves slightly as it adjusts it's orientation to face the ball. Sometimes there are also overshoots in the learned policy. Figure 7 shows an example of a sequence of frames which includes part of the learned `go-to-ball` skill.

Figure 6 shows the training curve for the `aim-to-shoot` skill. This skill's learning curve is more unstable than the `go-to-ball` skill. However, we were still able to utilize the learned policy to aim and score on the goal.

Figure 5a shows the time taken to shoot by the baseline and Fig. 5b shows the time taken to score by the learned policy. Both the baseline and the learned policy were tested on 1000 different runs with different initial conditions. Each run, the robot is spawned at some position, with some orientation, with the ball on the dribbler. We then run the policy and measure the time taken to score. From the figures, we see that again, learned policy takes about 2 s longer to

**Table 1.** Hyperparameters used for `go-to-ball` skill

| Name | Value |
|------|-------|
| Critic learning rate | $1 \times 10^{-3}$ |
| Actor learning rate | $1 \times 10^{-4}$ |
| Critic size | $300, 400$ |
| Actor sizes | $300, 400$ |
| Replay mem size | $1,000,000$ |
| Noise parameters | $\theta = 0.15, \mu = 0,$ $\sigma = 0.3$ |

**Table 2.** Hyperparameters used for `aim-to-shoot` skill

| Name | Value |
|------|-------|
| Critic learning rate | $1 \times 10^{-4}$ |
| Actor learning rate | $1 \times 10^{-4}$ |
| Critic size | $200, 300, 300, 300$ |
| Actor sizes | $200—300, 300, 300$ |
| Replay mem size | $600,000$ |
| Noise parameters | $\theta = 0.15, \mu = 0,$ $\sigma = 0.3$ |

**Table 3.** Success rate for `go-to-ball` skill

| Name | Value |
|------|-------|
| Baseline | 1.0 |
| Trained policy | 0.999 |

**Table 4.** Success rate for `aim-to-shoot` skill

| Name | Value |
|------|-------|
| Baseline | 0.71 |
| Trained policy | 0.772 |

score the goal on average. We believe the learned policy takes longer because the reward function prioritizes accuracy over time, whereas the hand-coded policy was designed to shoot at the first available opportunity.

Table 4 shows the success rate of the baseline `aim-to-shoot` skill vs the success rate of the learned `aim-to-shoot` skill. While the baseline takes shots on goal faster, we see that the learned policy is actually more accurate by approximately 6%. This makes sense, as our reward function gives negative rewards for failures, so the agent will be incentivized to prioritize good aim over time taken to score.

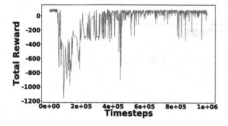

(a) Total reward vs Number of Samples while training `go-to-ball` skill. Higher is better. Initial part of the curve shows replay memory burn-in.

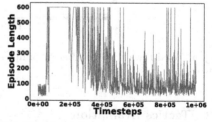

(b) Number of time-steps vs Number of samples while training `go-to-ball` skill. Each time-step is equal to 0.16ms. Lower is better. Initial part of the curve shows replay memory burn-in.

**Fig. 3.** Training curves for `go-to-ball` skill.

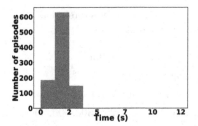

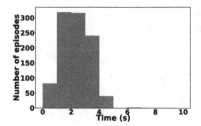

(a) Time taken by existing `go-to-ball` skill.

(b) Time taken by neural network `go-to-ball` skill.

**Fig. 4.** Comparison of existing `go-to-ball` skill vs learned `go-to-ball` skill.

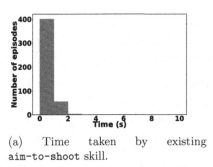

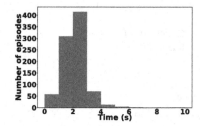

(a) Time taken by existing `aim-to-shoot` skill.

(b) Time taken by neural network `aim-to-shoot` skill.

**Fig. 5.** Comparison of existing `aim-to-shoot` skill vs learned aim-to-shoot skill.

**Fig. 6.** Total reward vs number of samples while training `aim-to-shoot` skill. Higher is better.

## 5.2 Tactics Evaluation

In order to be useful in an STP hierarchy, the learned skills must be easily composable by human coders. The tactic state machine from Fig. 2 was implemented using the learned `go-to-ball` and `aim-to-shoot` skills. To evaluate the performance, we executed the state machine across 500 different runs. Each run, the robot was spawned at a random location on the field with a random orientation.

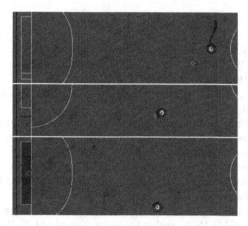

**Fig. 7.** Sequence of key-frames from execution of go to ball and shoot tactic using learned skills. The blue circle shows the robot. The blue line shows the history of the robot's trajectory. The orange circle is the ball and the orange line shows the trajectory of the ball. The following link contains videos of the simulated policy: https://goo.gl/xB7VAE (Color figure online)

The ball was also spawned at a random location on the field. We then run the tactic until either (1) a goal is scored or (2) the maximum time of 15 s elapses. The tactic was able to succeed 75.5% of the time. On average the tactic took 7.49 s with a standard deviation of 3.87 s.

## 6   Conclusion

In this work we have shown that Deep RL can be used to learn skills that plug into an existing STP architecture using a physically realistic simulator. We have demonstrated learning on two different skills: navigating to a ball and aiming and shooting. We showed that these learned skills, while not perfect, are close in performance to the hand-coded baseline skills. These skills can be used by humans to create new tactics, much like how hand-coded skills are used. We show that using a simple state machine, the two skills can be combined to create a tactic that navigates to the ball, aims, and shoots on a goal. Given these results, we believe that reinforcement learning will become an important part in future competitions. Future work will address how well the learned policies transfer from the simulation to the real robots.

# References

1. Andre, D., Teller, A.: Evolving team Darwin united. In: Asada, M., Kitano, H. (eds.) RoboCup 1998. LNCS, vol. 1604, pp. 346–351. Springer, Heidelberg (1999). https://doi.org/10.1007/3-540-48422-1_28
2. Ba, J.L., Kiros, J.R., Hinton, G.E.: Layer normalization. arXiv preprint arXiv:1607.06450 (2016)
3. Browning, B., Bruce, J., Bowling, M., Veloso, M.: STP: skills, tactics and plays for multi-robot control in adversarial environments. J. Syst. Control Eng. **219**, 33–52 (2005). The 2005 Professional Engineering Publishing Award
4. Fernandez, F., Garcia, J., Veloso, M.: Probabilistic policy reuse for inter-task transfer learning. Robot. Auton. Syst. **58**, 866–871 (2009). Special Issue on Advances in Autonomous Robots for Service and Entertainment
5. Hausknecht, M., Chen, Y., Stone, P.: Deep imitation learning for parameterized action spaces. In: AAMAS Adaptive Learning Agents (ALA) Workshop, May 2016
6. Hausknecht, M., Stone, P.: Deep reinforcement learning in parameterized action space. In: Proceedings of the International Conference on Learning Representations (ICLR), May 2016
7. Heess, N., et al.: Emergence of locomotion behaviours in rich environments. CoRR (2017). http://arxiv.org/abs/1707.02286v2
8. Hsu, W.H., Gustafson, S.M.: Genetic programming and multi-agent layered learning by reinforcements. In: GECCO, pp. 764–771 (2002)
9. LaValle, S.M., Kuffner Jr., J.J.: Randomized kinodynamic planning. Int. J. Robot. Res. **20**(5), 378–400 (2001)
10. Lillicrap, T.P., et al.: Continuous control with deep reinforcement learning. In: Internal Conference on Learning Representations (2016). http://arxiv.org/abs/1509.02971v5
11. Luke, S., Hohn, C., Farris, J., Jackson, G., Hendler, J.: Co-evolving soccer softbot team coordination with genetic programming. In: Kitano, H. (ed.) RoboCup 1997. LNCS, vol. 1395, pp. 398–411. Springer, Heidelberg (1998). https://doi.org/10.1007/3-540-64473-3_76
12. Mnih, V., et al.: Asynchronous methods for deep reinforcement learning (2016). http://arxiv.org/abs/1602.01783v2
13. Mnih, V., et al.: Playing atari with deep reinforcement learning (2013). http://arxiv.org/abs/1312.5602v1
14. Mnih, V., et al.: Human-level control through deep reinforcement learning. Nature **518**(7540), 529–533 (2015)
15. Schulman, J., Levine, S., Moritz, P., Jordan, M.I., Abbeel, P.: Trust region policy optimization. CoRR, abs/1502.05477 (2015)
16. Schulman, J., Wolski, F., Dhariwal, P., Radford, A., Klimov, O.: Proximal policy optimization algorithms. arXiv preprint arXiv:1707.06347 (2017)
17. Silver, D., et al.: Mastering the game of go with deep neural networks and tree search. Nature **529**(7587), 484–489 (2016). https://doi.org/10.1038/nature16961
18. Silver, D., et al.: Mastering the game of go without human knowledge. Nature **550**(7676), 354 (2017)
19. Stolle, M., Precup, D.: Learning options in reinforcement learning. In: Koenig, S., Holte, R.C. (eds.) SARA 2002. LNCS, vol. 2371, pp. 212–223. Springer, Heidelberg (2002). https://doi.org/10.1007/3-540-45622-8_16

20. Stone, P., Kuhlmann, G., Taylor, M.E., Liu, Y.: Keepaway soccer: from machine learning testbed to benchmark. In: Bredenfeld, A., Jacoff, A., Noda, I., Takahashi, Y. (eds.) RoboCup 2005. LNCS, vol. 4020, pp. 93–105. Springer, Heidelberg (2006). https://doi.org/10.1007/11780519_9

21. Stone, P., Sutton, R.S., Kuhlmann, G.: Reinforcement learning for RoboCup soccer keepaway. Adapt. Behav. **13**(3), 165–188 (2005). https://doi.org/10.1177/105971230501300301

22. The RoboCup Federation: RoboCup (2017). http://www.robocup.org/

23. Uchibe, E.: Cooperative behavior acquisition by learning and evolution in a multi-agent environment for mobile robots. Ph.D. thesis. Osaka University (1999)

24. Vecerik, M., et al.: Leveraging demonstrations for deep reinforcement learning on robotics problems with sparse rewards. CoRR (2017). http://arxiv.org/abs/1707.08817

# Real-Time Scene Understanding Using Deep Neural Networks for RoboCup SPL

Marton Szemenyei[1]([✉])(iD) and Vladimir Estivill-Castro[2](iD)

[1] Budapest University of Technology and Economics, Budapest, Hungary
szemenyei@iit.bme.hu
[2] Griffith University, Brisbane, QLD, Australia

**Abstract.** Convolutional neural networks (CNNs) are the state-of-the-art method for most computer vision tasks. But, the deployment of CNNs on mobile or embedded platforms is challenging because of CNNs' excessive computational requirements. We present an end-to-end neural network solution to scene understanding for robot soccer. We compose two key neural networks: one to perform semantic segmentation on an image, and another to propagate class labels between consecutive frames. We trained our networks on synthetic datasets and fine-tuned them on a set consisting of real images from a Nao robot. Furthermore, we investigate and evaluate several practical methods for increasing the efficiency and performance of our networks. Finally, we present RoboDNN, a C++ neural network library designed for fast inference on the Nao robots.

**Keywords:** Computer vision · Deep learning ·
Semantic segmentation · Neural networks

## 1 Introduction

Deep learning [10] is rapidly revolutionising the field of computer science. While deep neural networks (DNNs) have many usages, they are now undoubtedly the most popular technique in the field of intelligent perception, especially computer vision. In RoboCup, especially in the SPL league, several teams [7,12,15,17, 19] have used CNNs to classify relevant objects on the soccer field. However, due to the limitations of the robot's hardware, these networks were relatively shallow and were designed to classify fixed-resolution image patches only. This straightforward design meant that the teams had to use separate object-proposal methods to feed their network with candidate image regions.

We propose an end-to-end real-time object detection method for the Nao robots using deep neural networks. Our method combines two separate networks to achieve high accuracy at reasonable speed. The first network is a deep neural network trained to perform semantic segmentation (pixel-wise classification) on the image from the robot's camera. The second is a smaller network, trained to propagate the class labels from the previous image onto the next. Our system

© Springer Nature Switzerland AG 2019
D. Holz et al. (Eds.): RoboCup 2018, LNAI 11374, pp. 96–108, 2019.
https://doi.org/10.1007/978-3-030-27544-0_8

is capable of localizing four foreground classes (ball, robot, goalpost, and field line), without the use of a separate object proposal system.

Furthermore, we also report on the comparison of methods to accelerate deep neural networks. These techniques include using field edge detection to reduce the image size without decreasing the resolution of the relevant image parts, and pruning the weights of the neural network. We also compare with different network structures and show how to find the optimal accuracy/runtime trade-off.

Finally, we present RoboDNN, a lightweight C++ deep neural network library. RoboDNN is a forward-only library, designed for maximum performance on the Nao robot. The library has no dependencies, and does not use new constructs of the C++11 standard, facilitating compilation for the Nao. Moreover, we designed RoboDNN using the strictest compiler settings. Our implementation also offers compatibility with the popular Pytorch [1] DNN framework, with the ability to import neural nets trained using Pytorch. The RoboDNN library, the code and datasets are all available on our website [2].

## 2 Related Work

The availability of high-quality datasets and computational resources has enabled the training DNNs, once some numerical problems were surpassed [9]. The use of deep learning is perhaps most prominent in the field of computer vision, where DNNs are used for standard classification [13] and (semantic or instance) segmentation tasks [21,23]. Fast architectures, such as YOLO [20] exist for object detection, however, segmentation provides a more complete understanding of the scene. Also YOLO struggles with cluttered objects, which is frequent in robot soccer scenes.

Semantic segmentation aims to achieve visual scene understanding. The objective is to segment the image by classifying each pixel individually. The simplest way to achieve this with neural networks is to use a classification network, and replace the final fully connected layers by (usually $1 \times 1$) convolutional layers. This network can output a segmented image at a lower resolution, which can be upsampled using techniques, such as bilinear upsampling [5]. Other works [25] employ a superpixel segmentation method, and classify these superpixels individually in order to approximate object boundaries with higher accuracy.

The SegNet architecture [5] uses so-called unpooling layers to upsample the feature maps. In SegNet the max pooling layers in the first half of the network store the index of the maximum value and share this information with the corresponding unpooling layer. This extra piece of information allows the unpooling layer to recover the spatial information lost during downscaling. Nonetheless, the full feature map is not recovered, since the non-maximum values are permanently lost. Several important advances have improved the accuracy of SegNet-based segmentation, especially when it comes to capturing the fine details of objects. The first of these improvements is the Fully Convolutional Network (FCN) architecture [23], which introduced shortcuts (skip connections) from the front layers of the network. By adding shortcuts from early layers, the final layer has more information on the fine-resolution details of the image, resulting in better approximation of object boundaries. Shortcuts also improve the convergence properties of deep neural networks considerably [11].

Choosing the upscaling and downscaling methods in the network can also affect the performance significantly. The FCN network uses strided convolutions instead of pooling. It introduces costly transposed convolutional layers instead of unpooling to implement learnable downsampling and upsampling operations [23]. Wang et al. [24] introduced the dense upsampling convolution operation (DUC), which was shown to increase the accuracy further, but again, at a considerable increase of computational cost.

The field of view of the final classification neuron also influences the accuracy of the segmentation network, since it determines the amount of contextual information the final neuron can use to determine the class of each pixel. Chen et al. [6] showed that using dilated/atrous convolutional filters increases the performance without increasing the computational cost. Pooling operations may also be atrous [6], resulting in a similar improvement.

While convolutional neural networks have achieved staggering accuracy in numerous applications, their power comes with a high computational cost. Such high computational cost seems to prohibit the use of CNNs on board of mobile and embedded platforms. While several methods have been proposed for reducing the size and computation required for neural networks, the most relevant to our application is pruning [4]. During the pruning process, a ranking method is used to order the weights or neurons of a layer by importance, then a fixed percentage of the least important neurons/connections are deleted/set to zero. Next, the network is fine-tuned while keeping the pruned elements at zero value. Several ranking methods exist ranging from brute-force methods, that only use the magnitude of the weights to more complex ones, such as pruning weights so that the change in the network's loss function would be minimal [18].

**Computer Vision in RoboCup.** Achieving human-level vision and scene understanding is an essential component of achieving RoboCup's goals and the RoboCup environment has steadily changed from featuring objects that are easy to recognize using low-level features, such as colour, to ones that greatly resemble objects used in human soccer. The vision pipelines used by the competing teams have changed in tandem, going from human-engineered vision methods [16,22] to pipelines relying increasingly on machine learning. Several teams have used convolutional neural networks either for binary classification tasks [7,17] or to detect several relevant object categories [15,19]. These methods, however, use CNNs for classification only, therefore they still require a separate object proposal method, and the quality of the system may largely depend on the efficiency of the algorithm used to generate candidates for classification. A further disadvantage is that running the same neural network on potentially overlapping image regions is wasteful, since the same features are computed twice.

Hess et al. [12] present a high-quality virtual RoboCup environment created in Unreal Engine. Their work allows to easily create large datasets of realistic images of a soccer field along with pixel-level semantic labelling. Since the performance of a trained neural network is highly dependent on the quality and quantity of the training data, and creating a large hand-labelled database is highly time-consuming, their work was profoundly valuable for our research.

## 3   Preparation of the Training Data

To ensure the quality and amount of the training data for training the semantic segmentation network, we created a synthetic image set of 5000 images [12]. We used 100 different random sets of environmental variables, and generated 50 images with each setting. The images were separated into train and test sets randomly, using an 80–20 division. The automatically generated labels are available as PNG images, and contain labels for all five relevant categories (background, ball, robot, goal and line).

In addition, we extended the challenge to allow for the creation of image sequences instead of independent scenes. We used this mode to create a dataset of 800 images to train the label propagation network. This database also features 100 individual image sequences with different random scene parameters. In each sequence, however, the position and orientation of the camera and field objects only changes marginally between consecutive frames.

Synthetic images are an excellent way of pre-training a network on a large dataset, yet due to the differences between a synthetic and a real environment we require a database of real images to fine-tune the network. But the pre-training allows a much smaller dataset for fine tuning than would be otherwise required. For these reasons, we created a real semantic segmentation database consisting of 570 images taken at 3 separate locations: at the venue of RoboCup17, at the venue of IJCAI17 and in our lab at Griffith University. The images are from the top camera, since these usually contain more complex scenes, justifying the use of neural networks. A portion of this database consists of image sequences, which are used as a dataset for label propagation.

We manually annotated the images using a tool of our own creation. Our tool provides several ways to aid the annotation process, such as tools for drawing polygons and lines, as well as square and circular brush tools. The program also uses the superpixel segmentation method proposed by Li and Chen [14] to speed up the labelling process. In the case of successive images, the tool is able to use dense optical flow to approximate the labels of the next image. Using the tool, it is also possible to mark the edges of the field, setting pixels and labels outside the field to black and background respectively. This dataset can be used for detection easily by computing bounding boxes for the connected label components.

Despite having a fair number of real images, they were considerably less varied than the synthetic images, since they included only three locations with their unique environmental settings (such as lighting and carpet colour). To compensate for this disadvantage, we used aggressive, unique data augmentation in addition to standard techniques, such as flipping images horizontally. To emulate changes in lightning conditions, we applied random changes in the

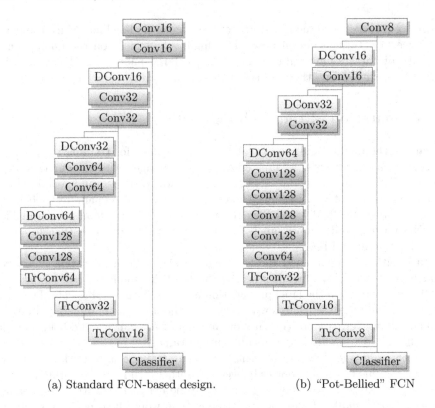

(a) Standard FCN-based design.          (b) "Pot-Bellied" FCN

**Fig. 1.** Our architectures: green nodes are strided convolution, while red nodes are transposed convolution. We have batch normalization in every node. (Color figure online)

brightness and contrast of the images. To introduce further variation into the dataset, we also applied random shifts to the hue and saturation of our pictures, which may help the robots with unique carpet colours. In Sect. 6 we show that our data augmentation techniques improve the accuracy of the trained models greatly.

## 4   Model Selection and Training

We used the Pytorch framework [1] for training the network. We applied stochastic gradient descent (SGD) optimisation with momentum and weight decay regularisation. During training, we used an adaptive learning rate schedule, which reduced the learning rate of the network after $N$ consecutive epochs in which the validation loss could not fall below the current lowest value. We made a slight modification to Pytorch's learning rate scheduler, to allow us to reload the current best model in every learning-rate reduction event. We remark that this variation results in the optimiser finding a new optimum more often after reducing the learning rate. Table 1 displays the hyperparameters used for pre-training and fine-tuning the semantic segmentation and label propagation networks.

The nature of the scenes specific to robot soccer fields offers a major challenge. Typical soccer images offer few pixels belonging to objects of interest. In our datasets, the ratio of background pixels is around 93–94%. Moreover, the rest distribute somewhat unevenly amongst the relevant classes. This uneven dataset usually complicates convergence and may result in a final network that is heavily biased towards making false negative-type errors. We stress that this imbalance stems from the distribution of classes *in the individual images themselves*. Therefore it is not possible to re-sample the training set.

We propose two solutions to overcome this difficulty. First, we selected the images for the training set so that they would contain a relatively high percentage of pixels from objects of interest (so called foreground). Second, we used a weighted version of the 2-dimensional negative log-likelihood (NLL) loss function, which is implemented in Pytorch, encouraging the network to emphasize more the relevant object categories.

The next challenge is to define an efficient and powerful network structure. Our review of the literature suggests an architecture based on FCN [23], using strided convolution for downsampling and transposed convolution for upsampling, as well as employing dilated convolutions to increase the field of view of the final classification layer. But, we avoided using DUC for upsampling, due its higher computational requirements. This first design (refer to Fig. 1a) had three modules consisting of convolutional and downsampling layers, combined with three upsampling layers.

Most CNNs used for semantic segmentation are relatively waist-heavy, meaning that the middle section of network, where the feature map has the smallest spatial dimensions has the largest number of filters. This has obvious advantages when it comes to memory consumption and computational efficiency. In our experiments, we decided to push this feature even further, using few and shallow layers to downsample the feature map quickly, then using a larger number of deep convolutional layers at the lowest level, followed by a similarly shallow and quick upsampling. In Sect. 6 we demonstrate that this network structure is much more efficient, providing better accuracy for lower computational cost. Figure 1b illustrates our new alternative, the "Pot-Bellied" (PB-FCN) architecture.

Our training procedure consists of three steps. First, the first half of the segmentation network is trained on the dataset provided using Hess et. al [12] generation for classification. We modified the dataset by separating the background and field line classes. Next, the full segmentation network is trained on the synthetic database. Finally, the full segmentation network is fine-tuned on the real database. The training procedure for the label propagation network is similar, except the first step is omitted.

**Table 1.** Hyperparameters used for the training procedures.

| Parameter | LR | Momentum | Decay | Reduction | Patience | Batch | Epochs |
|---|---|---|---|---|---|---|---|
| Segmentation | 0.1 | 0.5 | 1e−3 | 0.5 | 20 | 32 | 200 |
| Fine-tune | 0.01 | 0.1 | 1e−3 | 0.5 | 50 | 8 | 500 |
| Label prop | 0.2 | 0.5 | 1e−5 | 0.5 | 10 | 16 | 100 |
| LP fine-tune | 0.05 | 0.1 | 1e−5 | 0.5 | 25 | 8 | 250 |

## 5    Real-Time Implementation

To ensure real-time performance of our object detection pipeline, we must employ several techniques to improve the speed of the trained neural network. For the Nao hardware, these improvements are critical, since the networks resulting from training as in the previous section require approximately 1 s to run on a Nao V5 robots using the Darknet library [20]. For all our experiments, we used $160 \times 120$ images in YUV colour space.

The first technique we employ is weight pruning: since convolution is implemented as a matrix multiplication, setting weights to zero increases the efficiency significantly, even when an extra operation (checking if the weights are zero) is introduced. We used a brute-force pruning technique, simply setting 75% of the smallest weights in every layer to zero, and then fine-tuning the network, while forcing the pruned weights to remain zero. We found, that this technique reduced the runtime of the network by approximately 70%.

Moreover, our vision pipeline includes a hand-crafted field detection system, which is used by our network to crop part of the image (the outside the field is usually the top part of the image). This approach comes with two advantages. First, it reduces the number of pixels to be processed without reducing the level of detail. Second, if the network is trained on images where the parts outside the field are omitted, it avoids learning complex backgrounds outside the field (which are easily confused with field objects). While this technique provides considerable improvement in the networks speed, this improvement is highly dependent on the robot's position in the field. For this reason, we used uncropped images when comparing the execution times of different models and methods.

Our second technique for increasing the speed of our pipeline is label propagation. Here, we estimate the labels of the next image by using the labels of the previous one. We can achieve a considerable increase in speed, by only running the main neural network every 10 or 20 frames, and provided that accurate label propagation can be implemented using a significantly faster algorithm.

We first employed Gunnar Farneback's dense optical flow (OptFlow method) algorithm [8] to move the labels to their new location. While the algorithm's speed was satisfactory, the accuracy suffered. Namely, small, single-pixel errors would accumulate over time, constantly eroding small objects. Also, the optical flow-based method is completely unable to handle faster movements or new objects appearing in the image (or partially seen objects sliding in).

**Table 2.** Accuracy variations from the *baseline* by the training techniques.

| Technique | Baseline | Augment. | Field | Reload | Prune |
|-----------|----------|----------|-------|--------|-------|
| TPA | 97.72 | 0.61 | 0.31 | 0.09 | −0.18 |
| MCA | 92.19 | 2.55 | 0.82 | 1.08 | −0.8 |
| MIoU | 75.57 | 6.66 | 2.36 | 0.19 | −0.4 |

This problem can be remedied by training a neural network to predict the labels of the next image from the labels of the previous one. Since this is much easier, than predicting the labels from the raw image, we used considerably smaller version of PB-FCN (Fig. 1), which would run at approximately twice the speed of the segmentation network (PB-FCN-LP method). The network takes an 8-channel input, consisting of the Y channels of the two images, their difference and the 5-channel label image. For numerical reasons, the binary labels were scaled between −1 and 1. The label propagation network was trained using sequential the synthetic and real datasets mentioned in Sect. 3. We used the same data augmentation techniques, and trained the network to be able to predict the new labels in both ways (previous-to-next and vice versa), since the vast majority of movements might occur in both directions.

Since this method combines knowledge about the visual appearance of the classes and the movement between the images it is arguably able to account for the appearance of new objects and handle larger movements. Moreover, for the same reason, the label propagation network has some form of self-correcting ability, thus misclassifying a pixel in one frame does not mean that the error will be carried on until the next run of the segmentation network. We observed during our experiments that the label propagation network seemed to be able to incrementally correct the mistakes made by the segmentation network, especially when the robot was not moving (Fig. 2).

While implementation could use an existing library, the target platform (Nao robot) is a challenge. For example, Caffe [3] is a relatively old library with numerous dependencies, making it difficult to compile for the Nao robot. While the newer Darknet [20] has no dependencies, it lacks support for several important features we used in our design, such as dilated convolutions and affine batch normalization. Thus, we created our own C++ library called RoboDNN, based on Darknet, implementing the most common neural network layers. Our library is designed for inference only, therefore all code for training the networks was stripped. Our library has no external dependencies, does not require C++11, and - like all of MiPal's code - compiles using the strictest compiler settings.

The current version of RoboDNN is compatible with Pytorch. Our code includes support for dilated convolutions, output padding for transposed convolutions, and layers for affine batch normalization. Thus, RoboDNN is fully compatible with neural networks trained in Pytorch, and we provide code to export the weights Pytorch models along with the library. Our library is also

**Table 3.** Comparison of the different neural network architectures.

| Model | FCN | PB-FCN | PB-FCN-VGA | ResNet-DUC | OptFlow | PB-FCN-LP |
|-------|------|--------|------------|------------|---------|-----------|
| TPA | 98.42 | 98.50 | **98.87** | 98.71 | 95.82 | 96.52 |
| MCA | 94.95 | 94.40 | **96.50** | 94.88 | 86.15 | 90.7 |
| MIoU | 80.31 | 81.30 | **84.00** | 83.98 | 82.70 | 79.15 |

optimized for maximum efficiency, including support for accelerating pruned networks, running on cropped images and several in-place operations for memory efficiency.

# 6   Results

We now demonstrate experimentally the virtues of our design and training method. First we evaluate the accuracy across model design and learning techniques. Second, we asses the speed of our pipeline on the Nao V5 robots. Figure 3 shows some of the best and worst results of the segmentation.

**Tests on Accuracy.** We use three measures to evaluate accuracy. The first is the percentage of pixels classified correctly, called Total Pixel Accuracy (TPA). Taking the average of TPA per class is what we call Mean Class Accuracy (MCA). These two measures are relevant because our class imbalance. Note that TPA will favour models that are more likely to err on the side of background, but MCA will be higher for models that are more likely to make false positive predictions. The third measure is Mean Intersection over Union (MIoU), which (on our dataset) prefers models with minimal confusion between foreground classes.

We now demonstrate the change in accuracy provided by our data augmentation operations, field extraction, reloading learning rate scheduler, and pruning. We measured the improvements of these techniques separately on a fine-tuned PB-FCN network. Table 2 presents variations in accuracy from the baseline. The results indicate that our techniques increase the accuracy considerably, while our brute-force pruning retains most of the predictive power.

Table 3 compares four different models: The standard FCN-based model, our PB-FCN used on both $160 \times 120$ and $640 \times 480$ (PB-FCN-VGA) resolution images, and a fourth model using ResNet152 [11] and deep DUC upsampling. From these results, we can draw several conclusions. First, PB-FCN is slightly more powerful compared to the standard FCN structure. Second, a comparatively shallow PB-FCN loses surprisingly little accuracy compared to the ResNet152 model, and even outperforms it considerably when used at VGA resolution.

Lastly, we compare our pruned, fine-tuned PB-FCN-based label propagation network with the optical-flow based method (see Table 3). Note that neural label propagation clearly outperforms the optical-flow method. Moreover, optical flow

**Table 4.** Detection results on our validation set.

| Model | PB-FCN | PB-FCN-VGA | ResNet-DUC | BBN-L | BBN-MC | BBN-L | BBN-MC |
|-------|--------|------------|------------|-------|--------|-------|--------|
| Accuracy | 95.53 | **98.86** | 95.36 | 83.36 | 81.39 | 95.39 | 94.89 |
| False pos. | 2.69 | **1.00** | 2.32 | 26.19 | 21.58 | 5.27 | 4.45 |
| False neg. | 4.47 | **1.14** | 4.64 | 16.64 | 18.61 | 4.61 | 5.11 |

**Table 5.** Comparison of the execution times of different models.

| Model | PB-FCN | Pruned | VGA | FCN | ResNet | Opt-flow | Neural LP | BBN-L | BBN-MC |
|-------|--------|--------|-----|-----|--------|----------|-----------|-------|--------|
| Time (ms) | 1480 | 380 | 2850 | 640 | 8000 | 80 | 170 | 70 | 22 |
| FpS | 0.7 | 2.6 | 0.35 | 1.56 | 0.125 | 12.5 | 5.9 | 14 | 46 |

produces slightly better MIoU results due to the heavily unbalanced dataset (optical flow introduces minimal confusion between foreground classes). We used the real-image dataset for all the results in this section.

**Comparison Against Other Solutions.** We also compare our results against the networks used by other teams. First, we evaluate the first half of our PB-FCN network against the classification results reported by Hess et al. [12] using the same test dataset. Our algorithm clearly outperforms theirs, producing 96.66% accuracy compared to 94.4% and 93.52% with their BBN-L and BBN-M-C models respectively. Moreover, we managed to achieve this result on a significantly smaller dataset, consisting of 9,000 images per class only (compared to 25,000 per class). This improvement is largely due to our data augmentation methods.

Since to our knowledge this is the first work to publish semantic segmentation results in the context of robot soccer, there is no established baseline to compare our method against. We are also aware that other teams may use an object detection method instead of a pixel-wise classification algorithm. For this reason, Table 4 presents the performance of our networks in a detection task by simply counting the percentage of relevant objects that were correctly detected. Note, that a portion of false negatives and false positives may be objects that were incorrectly merged or separated by our network.

We also evaluated BBN-L and BBN-M-C on this dataset by providing it with all the relevant image patches, as well as three background patches per image to measure the false positive rate. This setting is equivalent to an object candidate generation method with zero false negative rate and here our PB-FCN clearly outperforms the two other networks. The comparison is fair since we test all classification networks on patches extracted form our training database.

**Evaluating Execution Time.** We tested the execution time of our entire vision pipeline on a Nao V5 robot, using the top camera image. We used a single core to run the neural network, and we ran the pipeline with other soccer subsystems active. Table 5 shows the execution time of the pruned versions of

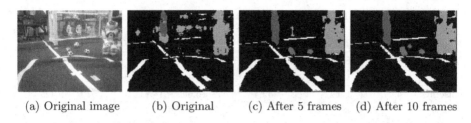

(a) Original image　　(b) Original　　(c) After 5 frames　(d) After 10 frames

**Fig. 2.** The self-correcting ability of the label propagation network.

**Fig. 3.** A few examples of good (top) and bad (bottom) results.

the models compared in the previous subsection. For reference, we also included the non-pruned version of PB-FCN. The results show a clear improvement as a result of pruning, and that PB-FCN outperforms the vanilla FCN in speed as well. We remark that the data shows that running a relatively shallow network on a higher resolution image seems to be much faster than running ResNet on a downscaled version, while providing superior accuracy.

In Table 5 we also present the comparison of label propagation using optical flow and CNNs. The results show that the extra accuracy coming with the neural network comes at lower speeds. Still, the fully neural vision pipeline runs at 6 frames per second, which is sufficient to enable real-time reactions at robot soccer speeds. For reference, we include our measurements of the speed of the neural network used by Hess et al. [12]. The comparison shows, that although we could achieve significant improvements in accuracy and the neural network's efficiency, it is still several times slower than other methods.

## 7　Conclusion

In this paper, we presented a deep neural network-based method for scene understanding in the context of robot soccer. Our method uses a semantic segmentation network and a separate label propagation net to increase the frame rate of the vision system. With our experiments, we demonstrated the efficiency of our method, including the improvements we achieved using our data augmentation techniques, pruning and field-edge cropping. Our method has superb accuracy at satisfactory speed.

We also presented large semantic segmentation and label propagation datasets consisting of synthetic images, as well as small real datasets for the same tasks, including a tool for manual pixel-wise labelling of images. Finally, we presented a Pytorch-compatible C++ deep neural network library designed for fast inference on the Nao robots supporting the acceleration techniques discussed in this paper. Our library has been designed to compile for the Nao robots using the strictest compiler settings.

**Acknowledgments.** Our research was supported by NVIDIA and Erasmus Mundus PANTHER.

# References

1. http://www.pytorch.org
2. http://3dmr.iit.bme.hu/research/robocup/index.html
3. http://caffe.berkeleyvision.org
4. Anwar, S., Hwang, K., Sung, W.: Structured pruning of deep convolutional neural networks. ACM J. Emerg. Technol. Comput. Syst. **13**(3), 1–11 (2017)
5. Badrinarayanan, V., Kendall, A., Cipolla, R.: SegNet: a deep convolutional encoder-decoder architecture for image segmentation. IEEE Trans. Pattern Anal. Mach. Intell. **39**(12), 2481–2495 (2017)
6. Chen, L., Papandreou, G., Kokkinos, I., Murphy, K., Yuille, A.L.: DeepLab: semantic image segmentation with deep convolutional nets, atrous convolution, and fully connected CRFs. IEEE Trans. Pattern Anal. Mach. Intell. **PP**(99), 1 (2017)
7. Cruz, N., Lobos-Tsunekawa, K., Ruiz-del-Solar, J.: Using convolutional neural networks in robots with limited computational resources: detecting NAO robots while playing soccer. In: Akiyama, H., Obst, O., Sammut, C., Tonidandel, F. (eds.) RoboCup 2017. LNCS, vol. 11175, pp. 19–30. Springer, Cham (2018). https://doi.org/10.1007/978-3-030-00308-1_2
8. Farnebäck, G.: Two-frame motion estimation based on polynomial expansion. In: Bigun, J., Gustavsson, T. (eds.) SCIA 2003. LNCS, vol. 2749, pp. 363–370. Springer, Heidelberg (2003). https://doi.org/10.1007/3-540-45103-X_50
9. Glorot, X., Bengio, Y.: Understanding the difficulty of training deep feedforward neural networks. In: Proceedings of the Thirteenth International Conference on Artificial Intelligence and Statistics, pp. 249–256 (2010)
10. Goodfellow, I., Bengio, Y., Courville, A.: Deep Learning. MIT Press, Cambridge (2016)
11. He, K., Zhang, X., Ren, S., Sun, J.: Deep residual learning for image recognition. In: IEEE Conference on Computer Vision and Pattern Recognition (CVPR), pp. 770–778 (2016)
12. Hess, T., Mundt, M., Weis, T., Ramesh, V.: Large-scale stochastic scene generation and semantic annotation for deep convolutional neural network training in the RoboCup SPL. In: Akiyama, H., Obst, O., Sammut, C., Tonidandel, F. (eds.) RoboCup 2017. LNCS, vol. 11175, pp. 33–44. Springer, Cham (2018). https://doi.org/10.1007/978-3-030-00308-1_3
13. LeCun, Y., Bottou, L., Bengio, Y., Haffner, P.: Gradient-based learning applied to document recognition. Proc. IEEE **86**, 2278–2324 (1998)

14. Li, Z., Chen, J.: Superpixel segmentation using linear spectral clustering. In: IEEE Conference on Computer Vision and Pattern Recognition (CVPR), pp. 1356–1363 (2015)

15. Menashe, J., et al.: Fast and precise black and white ball detection for RoboCup soccer. In: Akiyama, H., Obst, O., Sammut, C., Tonidandel, F. (eds.) RoboCup 2017. LNCS, vol. 11175, pp. 45–58. Springer, Cham (2018). https://doi.org/10.1007/978-3-030-00308-1_4

16. Metzler, S., Nieuwenhuisen, M., Behnke, S.: Learning visual obstacle detection using color histogram features. In: Röfer, T., Mayer, N.M., Savage, J., Saranlı, U. (eds.) RoboCup 2011. LNCS, vol. 7416, pp. 149–161. Springer, Heidelberg (2012). https://doi.org/10.1007/978-3-642-32060-6_13

17. Javadi, M., Azar, S.M., Azami, S., Ghidary, S.S., Sadeghnejad, S., Baltes, J.: Humanoid robot detection using deep learning: a speed-accuracy tradeoff. In: Akiyama, H., Obst, O., Sammut, C., Tonidandel, F. (eds.) RoboCup 2017. LNCS, vol. 11175, pp. 338–349. Springer, Cham (2018). https://doi.org/10.1007/978-3-030-00308-1_28

18. Molchanov, P., Tyree, S., Karras, T., Aila, T., Kautz, J.: Pruning convolutional neural networks for resource efficient inference. arXiv:1611.06440 (2016)

19. O'Keeffe, S., Villing, R.: A benchmark data set and evaluation of deep learning architectures for ball detection in the RoboCup SPL. In: Akiyama, H., Obst, O., Sammut, C., Tonidandel, F. (eds.) RoboCup 2017. LNCS, vol. 11175, pp. 398–409. Springer, Cham (2018). https://doi.org/10.1007/978-3-030-00308-1_33

20. Redmon, J.: Darknet: open source neural networks in C (2013–2016). http://pjreddie.com/darknet/

21. Ronneberger, O., Fischer, P., Brox, T.: U-Net: convolutional networks for biomedical image segmentation. In: Navab, N., Hornegger, J., Wells, W.M., Frangi, A.F. (eds.) MICCAI 2015. LNCS, vol. 9351, pp. 234–241. Springer, Cham (2015). https://doi.org/10.1007/978-3-319-24574-4_28

22. Schwarz, I., Hofmann, M., Urbann, O., Tasse, S.: A robust and calibration-free vision system for humanoid soccer robots. In: Almeida, L., Ji, J., Steinbauer, G., Luke, S. (eds.) RoboCup 2015. LNCS, vol. 9513, pp. 239–250. Springer, Cham (2015). https://doi.org/10.1007/978-3-319-29339-4_20

23. Shelhamer, E., Long, J., Darrell, T.: Fully convolutional networks for semantic segmentation. IEEE Trans. Pattern Anal. Mach. Intell. **39**(4), 640–651 (2017)

24. Wang, P., et al.: Understanding convolution for semantic segmentation. arXiv:1702.08502 (2017)

25. Xing, F.Z., Cambria, E., Huang, W.B., Xu, Y.: Weakly supervised semantic segmentation with superpixel embedding. In: IEEE International Conference on Image Processing (ICIP), pp. 269–1273 (2016)

# Training a RoboCup Striker Agent via Transferred Reinforcement Learning

Warren Blair Watkinson II$^{(\boxtimes)}$ ⓘ and Tracy Camp ⓘ

Department of Computer Science, Colorado School of Mines, Golden, CO 80401, USA
{wwatkinson,tcamp}@mines.edu

**Abstract.** Recent developments in reinforcement learning algorithms have made it possible to train agents in highly complex state and action spaces, including action spaces with continuous parameters. Advancements such as the Deep-Q Network and the Deep Deterministic Policy Gradient were a critical step in making reinforcement learning a feasible option for training agents in real world scenarios. The viability of these technologies has previously been demonstrated in training a RoboCup Soccer agent with no prior domain knowledge to successfully score goals; however, this work required an engineered intermediate reward system to direct the agent in its exploration of the environment. We introduce the use of transfer learning rather than engineered rewards. Our results are positive, showing that it is possible to train an agent through a series of increasingly difficult tasks with fewer training iterations than with an engineered reward. However, when the agent's likelihood of success in a task is low, it may be necessary to reintroduce an engineered reward or to provide extended training and exploration using simpler tasks.

**Keywords:** Reinforcement learning · Transfer learning ·
Multiagent systems

## 1 Introduction

An elusive goal in artificial intelligence is the training of a robotic agent to solve problems or to act within a domain without being specifically programmed, modeled, or provided with heuristics to direct its behavior. Reinforcement learning techniques, in which an agent can explore and develop an understanding of its environment on its own, have the potential to realize that goal. The most interesting applications of reinforcement learning are in domains having extremely large or continuous state or action spaces. Despite several recent advances that have yielded excellent results in these types of domains, reinforcement learning continues to have challenges in domains where an agent must follow a long sequence of actions before it achieves a goal. These challenges are especially pronounced when the actions available to an agent have continuous parameters. The compounding effect of the long action sequence along with the infinite number of actions available to the agent at each step in the sequence may make it impossible for the agent to successfully explore the environment to reach a goal state.

© Springer Nature Switzerland AG 2019
D. Holz et al. (Eds.): RoboCup 2018, LNAI 11374, pp. 109–121, 2019.
https://doi.org/10.1007/978-3-030-27544-0_9

The most common way to deal with the divide between an agent's initial state and a goal state is with intermediate rewards. Some domains have naturally occurring intermediate rewards, such as video games, where points might be earned for destroying enemies. Using reinforcement learning, an agent will explore its options within the game and quickly learn the value of actions that destroy enemies. If destroying enemies eventually leads to winning the game, the intermediate rewards will help direct the agent toward a winning goal state. Where the domain does not have naturally occurring intermediate rewards, the reinforcement learning scenario designer might engineer intermediate rewards that he or she believes will lead an agent toward an ultimate goal state. For example, in a video game where an agent starts on the extreme "left side" of a world with the goal of reaching the extreme "right side," such as in Super Mario Brothers on the 8-bit Nintendo Entertainment System (NES), an intermediate reward might be given every time the agent successfully advances toward the right. While these intermediate rewards address the lack of feedback between an agent's initial state and goal state, this approach will be suboptimal since the agent would likely not take shortcuts or other optimizations along the way. As an alternative to this intermediate reward approach, we explore a method of *transfer learning* in the RoboCup Soccer domain.

Transfer learning is the idea that the experience an agent gains while learning one task can help it successfully learn a different task. In this paper, we explore the viability of using transfer learning to train a robotic soccer striker agent to successfully score a goal. A striker agent has the problem we described previously. Specifically, from a random start state, the number of actions the agent must correctly select in order to score a goal, including moving to the ball, dribbling the ball toward the goal, and eventually scoring, is extremely large, and at each new state, the agent has nearly an infinite number of actions from which to choose. In order to overcome this challenge of exploration, we first train an agent on a simple goal scoring task followed by a series of increasingly difficult tasks.

In the sections that follow, we summarize background on reinforcement learning using Markov Decision Processes (MDPs) and recent advances that have seen success in the application of reinforcement learning approaches in large and continuous domain and action spaces, such as in RoboCup Soccer. We also provide an overview of the approach we took to train a RoboCup Soccer striker agent in 2d simulation and the results of our simulations. Lastly, we discuss our conclusions and future research opportunities.

## 2 Background

### 2.1 Reinforcement Learning and Markov Decision Processes

The most common approach in reinforcement learning problems is to model the domain as an MDP [14]. In an MDP, an agent perceives that it is in some state $s \in S$ within the environment where $s$ is a feature vector: $s = \langle x_1, x_2, \ldots, x_n \rangle$. The agent chooses an action $a \in A$, which causes the agent to enter a new state according to a transition function $T: S \times A \rightarrow S$, a probability distribution mapping each state and action pair to the resulting state of the environment after the action is executed. The agent receives a numerical reward according to a reward function $R: S \rightarrow \mathbb{R}$ which is a mapping of each state to the instantaneous numerical award for arriving in that state. Usually, the

MDP is designed such that most states yield a reward of 0 and the goal state yields a positive reward. An agent's policy $\pi: S \rightarrow A$ is a probability distribution that governs which action the agent will choose from a particular state.

In a typical reinforcement learning problem, the agent can observe (or partially observe) its state $s$ and is aware of the set of actions $A$ available, but it does not know $R$ or $T$. Some reinforcement learning approaches attempt to directly learn the model $R$ and $T$. Other approaches seek to estimate the action-value or the state-value, which is the discounted value of a present action or state in earning a future reward according to a discount factor $\gamma$. The effectiveness of an agent is determined by how well its policy obtains rewards over the long run. The goal of reinforcement learning is to find an optimal policy $\pi^*$ that maximizes future rewards. When the state or action space is relatively small, developing such a policy is trivial (as the entire environment could be explored by the agent). On the other hand, many domains,

**Table 1.** Approximate state and action space for various games

| Game | State space | Action space |
|---|---|---|
| Tic-tac-toe | $10^3$ | 4.5 |
| Checkers [2] | $10^{18}$ | 2.8 |
| Backgammon [16] | $10^{20}$ | 20 |
| Chess [4] | $10^{46}$ | 35 |
| Go [18] | $10^{127}$ | 181 |
| RoboCup Soccer[a] | $10^{408}$ | $10^{320}$ |
| Starcraft 2 [10] | $10^{1685}$ | $[10^{50}, 10^{200}]$ |

[a]The RoboCup Soccer state space is a lower-bound estimate using 22 players, their positions and velocities, and individual stamina. To calculate the RoboCup state space, we assume the ball and each of the 22 players can be in one of 680 × 1050 positions on the field with a velocity in one of 360° and a magnitude as one of 10 values. Furthermore, each player has a stamina [0, 8000]. When we consider that these features are actually continuous and that each player may have many different player characteristics, the state space is far greater than this estimate. The actions used to calculate the action space is the subset of RoboCup actions available to the agents in our simulations.

such as RoboCup Soccer, have such vast state and action spaces that it would be impossible to directly explore every possible state and action sequence. For example, see Table 1 for the state and action space complexity of various domains. In such domains, it is helpful to use reinforcement learning techniques that approximate an action-value or state-value by inferring similarities between various states. These action-value or state-value functions can then be used to discover an optimal policy.

## 2.2  Large and Continuous State and Action Spaces

Some of the earliest reinforcement learning work in 2D RoboCup Soccer [11] developed aggressive defensive behaviors in RoboCup defenders. Using a neural network to optimize the action-value function, Riedmiller et al. saw a significant increase in the success of an agent using learned behavior over hand-coded behavior. This success relied on significant reductions in the state and action space. For example, the learning agents used only the dash and turn commands and the parameters were discretized such that only 76 actions were available to each agent. The state space was also significantly reduced, as the set of starting states was limited to 5,000, and an episode would proceed for 35 time steps. While this seminal work was significant, to fully realize reinforcement learning in the large state and action space of RoboCup soccer, algorithmic advances were necessary.

In 2015, Mnih et al. developed the Deep-Q Network (DQN), an Artificial Neural Network (ANN) to estimate the action-value function [9], and demonstrated that an agent could learn to play Atari games, which involve highly complex state spaces. The DQN developed by Mnih et al. received game state information in the form of screen pixels. The DQN would output one of 18 discrete joystick commands that directed the agent's behavior, and the agent received the change in game score as reward. The DQN uses an *experience replay*, a stored vector of experiences $e_t = \langle s_t, a_t, r_t, s_{t+1} \rangle$, at each time step $t$. All previous experiences are pooled together and sampled randomly during the gradient-descent update of the ANN. This experience replay has several advantages when approximating the action-value function. First, each sample can be reused many times to update the ANN, increasing the efficiency of data collected as the agent explores the environment. Second, because sequential states tend to be very similar, sampling from the experience replay avoids using highly correlated experiences to update the network. Finally, the experience replay approach provides an off-policy mechanism for developing an action policy. This is advantageous because samples in an on-policy mechanism can become saturated with states dictated by the current action policy. This saturation could lead to limited exploration of the state space and a policy that stagnates at a local optimum. The DQN also utilized a target network that would follow the actual ANN at a rate of *tau* ≪ 1. The target network generated the target action-values used to update the network, thereby stabilizing learning. These benefits combine to make DQNs effective in high-dimensional state spaces. Mnih et al. demonstrated the success of the DQN in reinforcement learning on 49 Atari games; their trained agent learned to play Atari games at a human-expert level of performance with only the raw frames from the Atari game as input.

Another significant advancement in reinforcement learning [12] concerns the Deep Deterministic Policy Gradient (DDPG). In DQN, the policy gradient is estimated stochastically over an integration of both the action and state spaces, and it was believed that a deterministic policy gradient could not be found without a model-based learning approach. Silver et al. proved that a deterministic descent policy gradient can be integrated over state spaces alone in model-free learning. Lillicrap et al. incorporated the deterministic descent policy gradient into DQN in 2016 [8] creating the DDPG. This key advancement extended DQNs to allow agents to select actions with continuous parameters.

The DDPG is an actor-critic network where both the actor and critic is an ANN. The input to the actor network is the state feature vector. The actor network has two linear output layers. The first output layer selects discrete actions, and the second output layer provides continuous parameter values that correspond with the actions. The actor's outputs are then provided as inputs to the critic network with the state feature vector. The critic network generates an estimate of the action-value. Back-propagation of the critic network calculates the gradients of the action-value function with respect to the action. These gradients are provided as input to the actor for back-propagation, and the actor updates the agent's policy.

Hausknecht and Stone extended the DDPG actor-critic network by implementing an *inverting gradients* technique that reduces the magnitude of the gradient as it approaches its bounds and then inverts the gradient when the parameter exceeds its bounds. The inverting gradients method reduces the tendency of the critic to demand that the actor push the continuous parameters outside the parameter bounds [5]. They also introduced other enhancements to the DDPG algorithm including a hyperparameter $\beta$ as a ratio of on-policy and off-policy learning updates. These enhancements stabilized the learning of the agent and yielded more consistent results from the DDPG algorithm.

Their results are impressive; after approximately 3 million iterations, they trained a RoboCup Soccer striker agent to score a goal against an expert goalie. As it would be impossible for an agent to discover the correct sequence of actions leading to a goal state in such a large and continuous state and action space, Hausknecht and Stone used an engineered intermediate reward. To direct the exploration of the agent within the soccer domain, the intermediate rewards provided up to one point for approaching the ball, up to three points for moving the ball toward the goal, and finally, five points for scoring a goal.

### 2.3 Transfer Learning

Despite extensive use of transfer learning techniques in reinforcement learning [15], we are aware of only one instance where transfer learning has been used in RoboCup Soccer. Torrey et al. [17] trained agents in RoboCup Keepaway [13] and transferred the knowledge gained to agents in Half-Field Offense [6]. Keepaway is a RoboCup part-task simulator in which *M keepers* keep the ball away from *N takers*. Half-Field Offense is a game in which *M* attackers attempt to score against *N* defenders. In their experiments, the authors of [17] initialized the reinforcement learning keepers with *advice* such as "when a taker is close, pass the ball to a teammate." Over a series of Keepaway games, the learning keeper agents refined the advice. A human user then mapped the refined advice learned in the Keepaway task to appropriate scenarios in the Half-Field Offense task. Thus, the learning attacker agents in Half-Field Offense benefited from the refined advice learned in Keepaway. Torrey et al. discovered that, initially, Half-Field Offense attackers without advice outperformed attackers receiving advice; however as learners continued learning and refining the advice over many games, the attackers which received advice outperformed attackers with no advice.

In [17], agents started with domain awareness. In particular, agents understood the meaning of state features, such as the distance to the ball, and they had the ability to perform fairly high level tasks, such as kick the ball to a distant teammate. We are not aware of any other use of transfer learning to support reinforcement learning in RoboCup Soccer, and certainly none where the agents are starting *tabula rasa*. In the following section, we describe an approach using transfer learning to train a RoboCup Soccer striker agent to score on a goal with no prior domain knowledge.

## 3    Methodology

### 3.1    Overview

Our experiments leveraged the idea of *learning from easy missions* [3,15]. To train a striker agent, we used a DDPG actor-critic network similar to the one used in [5]. Previous work used *reward shaping*, or an engineered intermediate reward, which is an artificial reward signal rather than a reward based directly on the actual goal. In our work, we trained an agent over a series of successively difficult learning phases. The action-value function approximation learned in previous phases, along with the replay memory, was preserved in the transfer, and allowed the agent to "jump start" its learning

**Table 2.** Agent learning phases

| | Ball$_x$ | Ball$_y$ | Dist | | Ball$_x$ | Ball$_y$ | Dist |
|---|---|---|---|---|---|---|---|
| Phase1 | 1.6 | [-13.6,13.6] | 0.0 | Phase1 | 1.6 | [-13.6,13.6] | 0.0 |
| Phase2 | [10.5,26.3] | [-20.4,20.4] | 0.0 | Phase2 | [10.5,26.3] | [-20.4,20.4] | 0.0 |
| Phase3 | [10.5,26.3] | [-20.4,20.4] | 0.1 | Phase3 | [10.5,26.3] | [-20.4,20.4] | 0.1 |
| Phase4 | [10.5,26.3] | [-20.4,20.4] | 5.0 | Phase4 | [10.5,26.3] | [-20.4,20.4] | 5.0 |
| Phase5 | [42,52.5] | [-27.2,27.2] | ~ | Phase5 | [42,52.5] | [-27.2,27.2] | ~ |
| Phase6 | [42,52.5] | [-27.2,27.2] | ~ | Phase[6-10] | [42,52.5] | [-27.2,27.2] | ~ |

(a) Experiment 1: Empty Goal Task          (b) Experiment 2: Defended Goal Task

Starting ball positions represent the location of the ball relative to the center of the goal opening and to the goalie in meters. Ball$_x$ and Ball$_y$ define the ball's position relative to the goal where Ball$_x$ is the ball's distance away from the goal line, and Ball$_y$ is the ball's distance away from a line bisecting the goal opening. Where scalar values are depicted, such as 1.6, every trial started with the ball in the same position. Range values, such as [10.5,26.3], depict trials where the ball was placed stochastically between those values. Dist is the distance the agent is placed away from the ball beyond the agent's kickable range. A dist of ~ is designated for where the agent was placed stochastically on the field without regard to where the ball was placed. The first five learning phases between the two experiments were identical, with the exception that the defended goal task had a stationary goalie in the center of the goal opening.

in the new phase. Through reinforcement and transfer learning, we trained agents to perform in two different experiments in Half-Field Offense: an empty goal experiment (*Experiment 1*) and a defended goal experiment (*Experiment 2*).

In the empty goal experiment, we trained an agent to start from somewhere on the right half of the soccer field, run to the ball positioned randomly on the same side of the field, and then kick the ball into an undefended goal. In the defended goal experiment, we also trained an agent to run to the ball and kick it into a goal, but this time the goal was defended by an Agent2d [1] hand-coded expert goalie. Agents in *Experiment 1* used 59 egocentric features such as distance and angle to the goal, ball, and other landmarks on the field. Each feature was a scalar value ranging from [−1, 1]. The game state was fully observable to the agent. As a low-level feature set, these features represented a fundamentally basic viewpoint in the agent's frame of reference and did not include synthesized features, such as the direction of the largest angle between the goalie and a goal post, which a programmer might synthesize for the agent based on an understanding of how to successfully score. Agents in *Experiment 2* had an additional nine features representing information about the goalie. The agents had four discrete actions and a total of six continuous parameters: dash, with continuous parameters of power and degrees; turn, with a continuous parameter of degrees; tackle, with a continuous parameter of degrees; and kick, with continuous parameters of power and degrees.

We trained the agents using a simple reward, i.e., five points for a goal. Since the agent received no other feedback for positive behavior, such as advancing the ball to the goal or attempting a shot on the goal, we used a series of increasingly difficult learning phases, transferring the agent's learning from one phase to the next.

### 3.2 Training Experiences

The series of learning phases listed in Table 2 represent our attempt to train the agent to understand how its behavior affects the environment and how it can score goals. *Experiment 1, Phase1* is a simple task in which the agent and ball are placed at a random

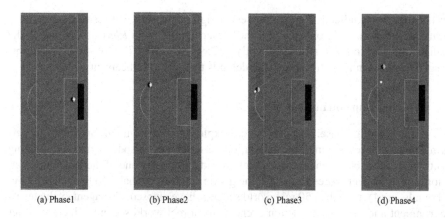

(a) Phase1          (b) Phase2          (c) Phase3          (d) Phase4

**Fig. 1.** Sample starting positions of *Learning Phases 1* through *4*

position directly in front of the goal. To be successful, the agent simply needs to kick the ball with any amount of power in the direction of the goal. By the end of this task, the agent should understand the effect of kicking the ball, with a marginal understanding of kick direction and power. Building on its former experience, *Phase2* places the agent with the ball at a random position near the penalty line in order to have the agent develop a greater understanding of kick direction and power. In *Phase3*, the ball is placed at a random position near the penalty line, but the agent is placed just outside its kickable range from the ball. In this phase, the agent learns to move toward the ball in order to kick it, thus it learns about movement and direction of movement. *Phase4* keeps the ball at a random position near the penalty line, but the agent is moved further away from the ball. This phase requires the agent to sustain a movement direction over time to approach and kick the ball. *Phase5* places both the ball and the agent at a random position on the field. This phase brings all of the previous learning of the agent together as the agent is expected to run across the field and, through a series of kicks, score on an empty goal. In *Phases 1* through *5* the agent is able to fully observe its state without noise (full-state information is used), regardless of what its sensors actually perceive. *Phase6* has the agent observe its environment through noisy and limited sensors (standard view used in RoboCup competitions). This phase demonstrates how effectively an agent, having learned in a fully observable simulation, can transfer its knowledge to a partially observable and noisy version of the same task. To assist with limited and noisy sensors, the agent has an underlying layer which updates an approximate world model by integrating information over multiple observations. This layer also governs the focus and direction of the visual sensor so that the agent can update and maintain its world model. This layer was not controlled by our DDPG (Fig. 1).

The first five phases are common to both experiments, with the exception of the addition of a goalie in the defended goal experiment. In *Phases 1* through *5* of the defended goal experiment, the goalie is stationary in the center of the goal. In these phases, the goalie makes no attempt to intercept the ball, but if the ball hits the goalie, the ball is "captured" and no goal is scored. In *Phase6*, the goalie is permitted to move, but because the hand-coded goalie possesses significant skill, we restrict the goalie's ability so it can move in only 10% of the server iterations. In *Phases 7, 8,* and *9,* the goalie is allowed to move more frequently in 25%, 50%, and 75% of server iterations, respectively, and in *Phase 10,* the goalie defends the goal at full capacity.

### 3.3  Training Implementation

In a given learning phase, an agent would explore its environment and learn to perform a task by executing multiple simulation episodes. An episode begins with starting positions as described in the previous section and ends under one of the following conditions: (1) the agent scores a goal, (2) the goalie captures the ball, (3) the ball goes out of bounds, or (4) more than 50 real world seconds have elapsed. The agent evaluates its environment and executes an action every $1/10$ of a real world second, which we refer to as an iteration. Thus, a single episode can have up to 500 iterations, though many episodes are much shorter.

We trained four agents in each of our two experiments, for a total of eight agents. In *Experiment 1, Agent$_1$* and *Agent$_2$* progressed from one learning phase to the next immediately after demonstrating a 96% success rate against the goal. *Agent$_3$* and *Agent$_4$* progressed to the next learning phase after completing 500,000 iterations of the current learning phase. Similarly, in *Experiment 2, Agent$_5$* and *Agent$_6$* progressed to the next learning phase after demonstrating a 96% success rate, and *Agent$_7$* and *Agent$_8$* progressed after completing 500,000 iterations.

### 3.4  DDPG Architecture Details

We employed a similar actor-critic network as in [5]. Both the actor and critic had the same network architecture consisting of four fully connected layers with 1024, 512, 256, and 128 units. Inputs to the actor network were the 59 or 68 (if a goalie is present) state features. Inputs to each neuron in the hidden layers were first processed through a leaky rectified linear unit (ReLU) with a negative slope of 0.01. The actor network had two linear output layers. The first was for the four discrete actions, and the second was for the six continuous parameters. These outputs were provided as inputs to the critic network, in addition to the 59 or 68 state features. The critic had the same hidden layer architecture as the actor network, and provided a scalar representing the approximated action-value. The actor used the feedback from the critic to update the agent's policy. The critic's update to the actor regarding the parameter gradient was bound according to the inverting gradients algorithm.

We used the Caffe Deep Learning Framework by Berkeley Artificial Intelligence Research with the Adam [7] solver using the hyperparameters identified in [5] that yielded the best results through experimentation: a $10^{-5}$ learning rate for the actor and $10^{-3}$ for the critic; 20% on-policy updates, and 80% off-policy updates; and $\tau$ of 0.001 to temper the rate of change in learning. At initialization, the agent selected all actions at random, and over the first 10,000 actions we anneal this stochastic selection linearly to 10%, favoring the best action according to our trained policy 90% of the time. We use a reward discount rate $\gamma$ of 0.99.

**Table 3.** Performance of each agent in the empty goal experiment

|  | Full observability | | Partial observability | |
|---|---|---|---|---|
|  | Iter ($10^3$) | Goal rate | Iter ($10^3$) | Goal rate |
| [5] | ~1500 | 1.00 | N/A | N/A |
| $Agent_1$ | 710 | 1.00 | 980 | 1.00 |
| $Agent_2$ | 820 | 1.00 | 890 | 1.00 |
| $Agent_3$ | 2290 | 1.00 | 2620 | 1.00 |
| $Agent_4$ | 2300 | 1.00 | 2580 | 1.00 |

We estimate that it was approximately 1,500,000 iterations to train the agent in [5] after which it was able to consistently score against an empty goal. We note the authors of [5] did not present results for a scenario with partial observability.

## 4   Results

Overall, the agents trained in the empty goal experiment performed exceedingly well. Alas, those trained against the defended goal ultimately stopped learning and failed when the goalie was allowed to move more quickly (i.e., in *Phases 6–10*). We found it necessary to reintroduce a shaped reward to assist the agent's learning. Figure 2 shows the change in the agents' performance (with respect to goal percentage) as the agents experienced additional iterations. For the sake of space, the figures depict only the odd-numbered agents; the even-numbered agents had a similar performance compared to their odd-numbered counterpart. The following sections discuss our results in more depth.

### 4.1   Empty Goal Experiment

In the empty goal experiment, we found that our transfer learning phases provided a responsive learning opportunity from one phase to the next. In general, $Agent_1$ and $Agent_2$, which transferred to the next phase immediately after demonstrating success in the current phase, had an initial significant drop in performance when assigned to the new phase. These agents, however, returned to an acceptable degree of performance in the course of training (see Fig. 2a, transitions from *Phase1* to *Phase2* and from *Phase2* to *Phase3*). In *Phase5* and *Phase6*, we continued training the agents until they reached flawless performance. The iterations required to reach this level of performance are reported in Table 3. Despite the early struggles with a new phase, $Agent_1$ and $Agent_2$ learned the empty goal task more quickly than any previous benchmark. Moreover, all four agents learned the empty goal task in the fully observable scenario (*Phase5*) and were able to transfer that learning successfully to the partially observable scenario (*Phase6*).

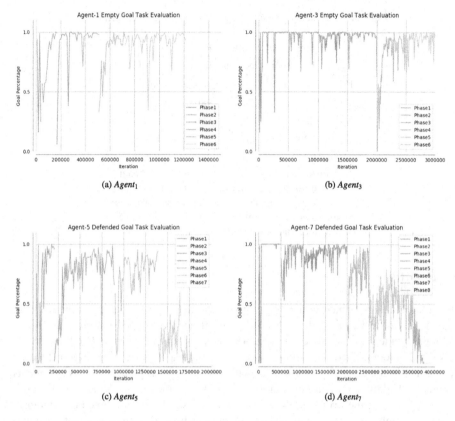

**Fig. 2.** Performance of agents in empty and defended goal experiments

## 4.2 Defended Goal Experiment

In contrast, the agents learning in the defended goal experiment had a much more difficult time. $Agent_5$ and $Agent_6$, which transitioned immediately to the next phase after becoming an expert in the current phase, initially struggled with the new phase (similar to $Agent_1$ and $Agent_2$) but were able to eventually learn the skills necessary to advance in the first five phases (see Fig. 2c). $Agent_7$ and $Agent_8$, which continued to practice the phase for a full 500,000 iterations before advancing, adapted more quickly to the new phase. After completing the first five phases in which the goalie was immobile, all four agents had significant difficulties as the goalie's capabilities increased. $Agent_5$ and $Agent_6$ struggled with the goalie at 25% capacity and were not able to continue to the next phase. $Agent_7$ and $Agent_8$ performed slightly better, but stopped learning with a goalie at 50% capacity. All four agents, when faced with a goalie that would block their goal attempts, would eventually stop attempting to score and simply run off the field. We suspect this result occurred because the agents prefer exploration behaviors when prior experience indicates the likelihood of success using previous strategies is marginal.

In summary, as the goalie's ability increased, the agents stopped attempting a shot in favor of exploring other avenues for earning a reward. We, therefore, experimented with reward shaping [15]. After training agents in *Phase5*, we provided agents with a proportional reward for moving the ball toward the goal, up to a max of three points. This artificial reward encouraged the agents to move the ball toward the goal. With this modification, all agents eventually learned to score against a skilled goalie at full ability.

**Table 4.** Performance of each agent with shaped reward

|            | Iter ($10^3$) | Goal rate |
|------------|---------------|-----------|
| $Agent_5$  | 2950          | 0.97      |
| $Agent_6$  | 2730          | 1.00      |
| $Agent_7$  | 5210          | 0.96      |
| $Agent_8$  | 4370          | 0.92      |
| $Agent2D$  | N/A           | 0.96      |
| *HELIOS*   | N/A           | 0.98      |

Table 4 summarizes the number of iterations required for each of these modified agents to reach a performance threshold, using transfer learning for *Phases 5–10* and shaped rewards for *Phases 6–10*. Remarkably, the agents quickly learned how to defeat the hand-coded goalie. The performance of most of the agents equaled or exceeded that of both the Agent2D base and the 2016 championship team *HELIOS* attacker (Table 4). With this alternative, we duplicated some of the efforts of [5], but demonstrate that shaped rewards can work alongside transfer learning.

### 4.3 Other Observations

Early performance in a learning experiment was not a consistent indicator for how well the agents would ultimately succeed in that learning phase. For instance, the initial performance of $Agent_7$ and $Agent_8$ in *Phase5* was around 1% in terms of successful goals (Fig. 2d), but over time, their performance improved such that they were eventually scoring in over 90% of the scenarios. On the other hand, when $Agent_7$ and $Agent_8$ started *Phase8*, they were scoring 30% and 40% of the time; within 500,000 iterations, however, the performance dropped to zero, and the agents stopped attempting shots on the goal.

We also observed that more practice with a phase did not create a disadvantage when transitioning to the next phase. Indeed, those agents having more experience adapted to the new task more quickly.

We now consider our ad-hoc experiment using the shaped reward signal. After the agents learned how to successfully score consistently against the goalie, we removed the reward for advancing the ball towards the goal. Our preliminary results indicate that the agents continued to attempt goals against the goalie, and, despite no incentive for unsuccessful shots on the goal, they maintained a high level of performance.

Overall, there appears to be promise in utilizing the transferred learning approach in complex domains with large and continuous action and state spaces. Our approach, however, does introduce additional variables. For example, we believe the success and rate of learning is dependent upon the specific learning phase tasks chosen. If the gap between phases is too great, or if the learning phase tasks were performed in a different order, we expect the results would be different, e.g., agents either failing to learn the task or learning the task more quickly. With respect to the defended goal task, we suspect one issue is the learning phases have too large a gap between them. That is, in our experiment the goalie develops skill more quickly than the striker can learn. If we could improve the skill of the goalie more gradually, perhaps the striker would learn to score through successive learning phases.

## 5    Conclusions and Future Work

We have applied a novel approach of transfer learning in the RoboCup Soccer domain by training agents via a series of learning phases of increasing difficulty. Using a DDPG with replay memory, we are able to select optimal actions in continuous action parameter space to meet a simple, single objective: score on a goal.

We found the agents exhibit no negative transfer in the range of iterations we're using for training. In fact, agents with more experience in the environment adapted more quickly to novel tasks than agents with less experience. On the empty goal task, our agents exceeded previous benchmarks in reinforcement learning, suggesting that transfer learning of increasingly complex tasks can reduce learning time when compared to all other known techniques. In addition, skills learned in a fully observable state are transferable to a partially observable state when the agent maintains an approximate world model integrated over several observations.

Our results with the defended goal task are less positive. Specifically, when the rewards received were too scarce, the agents stopped attempting to earn the reward and instead turned to exploring the model. We found that in those situations, it may be necessary to introduce reward shaping to help direct the agent's behavior toward successful strategies. After the agent has learned a policy which yields a higher probability of success, it appears as though we can remove the "training wheels" without ill-effect. That is, after the agent develops a policy yielding a higher probability of success, the agent continues to learn, successfully scoring while it improves its performance, even without the shaped reward.

As for future research, we would like to explore whether longer training times beyond 500,000 iterations would prove effective in the defended goal task. We would also like to adapt our transfer and reinforcement learning approach to train a striker agent and a goalie in tandem. After some initial orientation to the state and action space, we would like to see if it is possible to bring both a novice attacker and a novice goalie online together to learn as they compete against one another.

Further development toward principled methods for determining whether an agent can successfully learn via learning phases would be valuable to the reinforcement learning community. As it is, early performance in a target learning task provides little to no indication as to whether or not the agent will demonstrate continued learning over the long term. Finally, we'd like to explore other domains for reinforcement learning in continuous parameter action space. Pushing the DDPG model into more complex domains will help to further our understanding of the opportunities and limitations of the DDPG reinforcement learning model.

# References

1. Akiyama, H.: Agent 2D Base Code 3.1.1 (2012). https://osdn.net/projects/rctools/releases/ p4887
2. Allis, L.V.: Searching for Solutions in Games and Artificial Intelligence. Ponsen and Looijen, Wageningen (1994)
3. Asada, M., Noda, S., Tawaratsumida, S., Hosoda, K.: Vision-based behavior acquisition for a shooting robot by using a reinforcement learning. In: IAPR/IEEE Workshop on Visual Behaviors, Seattle, Washington, June 1994
4. Chinchalkar, S.: An upper bound for the number of reachable positions. Int. Comput. Chess Assoc. J. **19**, 181–183 (1996)
5. Hausknecht, M., Stone, P.: Deep reinforcement learning in parameterized action space, pp. 1–12. arXiv preprint arXiv:1312.5602, February 2016. arXiV:1511.04143v4
6. Kalyanakrishnan, S., Liu, Y., Stone, P.: Half field offense in RoboCup soccer: a multiagent reinforcement learning case study. In: Lakemeyer, G., Sklar, E., Sorrenti, D.G., Takahashi, T. (eds.) RoboCup 2006. LNCS, vol. 4434, pp. 72–85. Springer, Heidelberg (2007). https:// doi.org/10.1007/978-3-540-74024-7_7
7. Kingma, D.P., Ba, J.: Adam: a method for stochastic optimization. arXiv preprint arXiv:1412:6908, December 2014
8. Lillicrap, T., et al.: Continuous control with deep reinforcement learning. In: Proceedings of the International Conference on Learning Representations, San Juan, Puerto Rico, May 2016
9. Mnih, V., et al.: Human-level control through deep reinforcement learning. Nature **518**(7540), 529–533 (2015)
10. Ontañón, S., Synnaeve, G., Uriarte, A., Richoux, F., Churchill, D., Preuss, M.: A survey of real-time strategy game AI research and competition in StarCraft. IEEE Trans. Comput. Intell. AI Games **5**(4), 293–311 (2013)
11. Riedmiller, M., Gabel, T., Hafner, R., Lange, S.: Reinforcement learning for robot soccer. Auton. Robots **27**(1), 55–73 (2009)
12. Silver, D., Lever, G., Heess, N., Degris, T., Wierstra, D., Riedmiller, M.: Deterministic policy gradient algorithms. In: International Conference on Machine Learning, June 2014
13. Stone, P., Sutton, R.S., Kuhlmann, G.: Reinforcement learning for RoboCup soccer keepaway. Adapt. Behav. **13**(3), 165–188 (2005). 0301
14. Sutton, R., Barto, A.: Reinforcement Learning: An Introduction. MIT Press, Cambridge (1998)
15. Taylor, M.E., Stone, P.: Transfer learning for reinforcement learning domains: a survey. J. Mach. Learn. Res. **10**, 1633–1685 (2009)
16. Tesauro, G.: Temporal difference learning and TD-Gammon. Commun. ACM **38**(3), 58–68 (1995)
17. Torrey, L., Walker, T., Shavlik, J., Maclin, R.: Using advice to transfer knowledge acquired in one reinforcement learning task to another. In: Gama, J., Camacho, R., Brazdil, P.B., Jorge, A.M., Torgo, L. (eds.) ECML 2005. LNCS, vol. 3720, pp. 412–424. Springer, Heidelberg (2005). https://doi.org/10.1007/11564096_40
18. Tromp, J., Farnebäck, G.: Combinatorics of go. In: van den Herik, H.J., Ciancarini, P., Donkers, H.H.L.M.J. (eds.) CG 2006. LNCS, vol. 4630, pp. 84–99. Springer, Heidelberg (2007). https://doi.org/10.1007/978-3-540-75538-8_8

# Playing Soccer Without Colors in the SPL: A Convolutional Neural Network Approach

Francisco Leiva[✉], Nicolás Cruz, Ignacio Bugueño, and Javier Ruiz-del-Solar

Advanced Mining Technology Center and Department of Electrical Engineering,
Universidad de Chile, Santiago, Chile
{francisco.leiva,nicolas.cruz,ignacio.bugueno,jruizd}@ing.uchile.cl

**Abstract.** The goal of this paper is to propose a vision system for humanoid robotic soccer that does not use any color information. The main features of this system are: (i) real-time operation in the NAO robot, and (ii) the ability to detect the ball, the robots, their orientations, the lines and key field features robustly. Our ball detector, robot detector, and robot's orientation detector obtain the highest reported detection rates. The proposed vision system is tested in a SPL field with several NAO robots under realistic and highly demanding conditions. The obtained results are: robot detection rate of 94.90%, ball detection rate of 97.10%, and a completely perceived orientation rate of 99.88% when the observed robot is static, and 95.52% when the observed robot is moving.

**Keywords:** Deep learning · Convolutional Neural Network ·
Robot detection · Ball detection · Orientation detection ·
Proposals generation

## 1 Introduction

The perception of the environment is one of the key abilities for playing soccer; without an adequate vision system it is not possible to determine the position of field's features or to self-localize. It is also impossible to determine the position of the ball and the other players, which is necessary in order to play properly. Given that the soccer environment is highly dynamic and has a predefined physical setup, most of the current vision systems use color information.

In the case of the SPL and the former Four-Legged League, the first generation of vision systems analyzed colored objects which were then segmented [1,2]. Year by year, the restriction of having colored objects in the field was relaxed: (i) the number of colored beacons was first reduced and then beacons were not used anymore, (ii) the goals were first colored and solid, then non-solid, and finally white, (iii) the ball used to be orange, and since 2016, black and white.

---

F. Leiva and N. Cruz—These authors contributed equally to this work.

D. Holz et al. (Eds.): RoboCup 2018, LNAI 11374, pp. 122–134, 2019.
https://doi.org/10.1007/978-3-030-27544-0_10

However, still most of the teams use color information to detect field features (e.g., lines and their intersections), other players and the ball. Very recently, Convolutional Neural Networks (CNNs) have been used for detecting the robots and/or the ball (e.g., [3–6]), but even in these cases, the CNN-based detectors require object proposals which are usually obtained using color information. Therefore, to the best of our knowledge, color-free vision systems have not been used in robotic soccer, at least not in the SPL. Some of the main reasons are: (i) the challenge of achieving real-time operation when using limited computational resources, (ii) the problem of training deep detectors without having very large databases, and (iii) the challenge of having fast and color-free object proposals.

The goal of this paper is to propose a color-free vision system for the SPL. The main features of this system are: (i) real-time operation in the NAO robot, and (ii) the ability to detect the ball, the robots, their orientations, the lines and key field features very robustly. In fact, our ball, robots and robots' orientation detectors are highly performant; they obtain the highest reported detection rates.

## 2    Playing Soccer Without Color Information

In this section we present the proposed vision system. Section 2.1 broadly explains the general characteristics and functioning of the vision framework, while Sects. 2.2, 2.3, 2.4, 2.5 and 2.6 detail the operation of each of its main modules.

### 2.1    The General Framework

The main feature of our framework is that it manages to detect the ball, other players, their orientations, and key features of the field without using any color information: all the processing is performed on grayscale images. This is done by following a cascade methodology (inspired in [16]) that combines classical approaches widely used in pattern recognition and modern CNN-based classifiers.

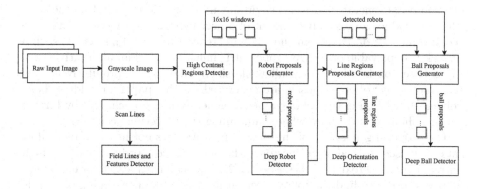

**Fig. 1.** Block diagram of the proposed vision system.

The proposed vision framework is illustrated in Fig. 1. While the detection of lines and field features is done by using a set of rules and heuristics, both the detection of the ball and the other robots is done by means of object proposals and their subsequent classification using CNNs. This cascade approach takes advantage of the information previously extracted from the image to use it in benefit of following processing modules.

## 2.2   High Contrast Regions Detection

Since the robots and the ball used in the SPL possess high contrast, an effective approach to know where to search for them is to find high contrast regions in the images. To do this, the grayscale input images are scanned using windows of 16 × 16 pixels. Regions outside the field boundaries and within the body of the observer robot are discarded. The remaining windows are used to construct histograms of pixels, which are used to estimate thresholds for image binarization using Otsu's method [7]. Windows with thresholds over a predefined value are considered as important, since they may be close or within another robot or the ball. Since the chosen threshold for the selection of windows could be restrictive and leave out image regions belonging to objects of interest, a morphological dilation operation is applied on the previously selected windows, which means that all the 16 × 16 pixels blocks adjacent to selected windows are also considered as high contrast regions.

## 2.3   Robot Detection

In [3] we presented a robot detector based on CNNs, capable of operating in real time. The system was based on the classification of color-based robot proposals (generated by B-Human's robot perceptor [8]). This was modeled as a binary classification problem where proposals could be labeled as robots or nonrobots. The system processed hypotheses in ∼1 ms with an average accuracy of ∼97%. Although this system achieved a very high performance, it possessed some major drawbacks. First, while the CNN classifier was very robust to noise and variations of the illumination, the same did not apply to the color-based robot proposal generator. Adverse environmental conditions could lead the algorithm to produce an excessive amount of object hypotheses, or none at all. The second drawback derived from the CNN inference time of ∼1 ms. While such a network is deployable on a NAO robot, it is much slower than alternative algorithms based on heuristics or shallow classifiers, and can be prohibitively slow when too many robot proposals are generated. In this paper we address both problems by changing the robot proposals generation approach, and by further reducing the inference times while maintaining the detection accuracy.

The proposal generation of this new framework does not use any color information: it uses vertical scan lines over all the image $x$-coordinates where high contrast regions were detected (see Sect. 2.2). The scan lines search for luminance changes in order to find the robots' feet positions, and by performing geometric sanity checks, the proposal generator provides a set of bounding boxes which may contain the robots' body. Most checks are similar to the rules used in the B-Human player detector [8], but applied to a grayscale image. This approach is more robust to changes in lighting since it relies on contrast information rather than heuristic color segmentation.

The obtained grayscale image regions are then fed to a CNN, which we call *RobotNet*, that classifies the proposals as robots or non-robots. This CNN is based on the architecture described in Sect. 3.1. Using grayscale image regions allows the system to perform in real time for a large number of robot proposals, since the reduction of input channels greatly reduces the CNN's inference time.

## 2.4   Robot Orientation Determination

Inspired on [10], we propose an improved Vision-Based Orientation Detection for the SPL League, which makes use of CNNs in order to achieve much better prediction accuracy than the original system. The general architecture of the module is presented in Fig. 2.

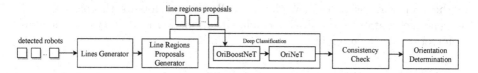

**Fig. 2.** Robot orientation module pipeline.

This system uses the bounding boxes of the *Detected Robots* as inputs. Over these regions, the set of points that compose the robots' lower silhouette [10] is calculated by the *Lines Generator* module, which extracts a region corresponding to the robot's feet and analyses its Contrast-Normalized Sobel (CNS) image [11] by using vertical scan lines. Over each scan line pixel an horizontal median filter is applied and its response is compared to a threshold. Pixels with a filter response below the threshold are considered as part of the lower silhouette. Then, by iterating for each scan line, the subset of points that make up a closed convex region can be obtained by using Andrew's convex hulls algorithm [12]. For each consecutive pair of points of the convex set we calculate a line model in field coordinates. Each line model is then validated with the set of points of the lower silhouette, by using a voting methodology akin to the RANSAC algorithm [17]. The line with the higher number of votes is selected as the *first line*. Once the linear model has been chosen, a *second line* may be generated by iterating over the remaining pairs of convex points. This line must comply with a series of conditions such as a minimum and maximum length and approximate orthogonality to the first line in order to be accepted as valid.

To estimate the orientation of the observed robot, the lines are classified to determine the robot's direction. To do this, a region that includes the robot's feet and legs is constructed around each line by the *Line Regions Proposals Generator* module. The regions are then classified by the *Deep Classification* module which is based on CNNs, whose structure is shown in Fig. 4. For each of the line's regions a CNN that measures its quality, *OriBoostNet*, is first applied. Regions with too much motion blur or that were incorrectly estimated are discarded to decrease the number of wrong orientation estimations. If a region is accepted, it is then fed to a second CNN, *OriNet*, that in turns classifies it as a side, front or back region. Afterwards, we perform a *Consistency Check* by imposing that no more than one region of each class must exist. This further reduces the number of incorrect orientation estimations. Finally, the *Orientation Determination* is performed by combining the rotation given by the inverse tangent from two points belonging to the analyzed line, with the direction of the line determined by its class. The resulting orientation is added to a buffer that stores the last 11 measurements and a circular median filter is applied over it. In order to avoid invalid results, we consider the direction as valid only for a small period of time if no new samples are added to the buffer.

## 2.5 Ball Detection

In the proposed vision framework, the ball detector follows the paradigm of proposal generation and subsequent classification. Figure 3 shows the general architecture of this module.

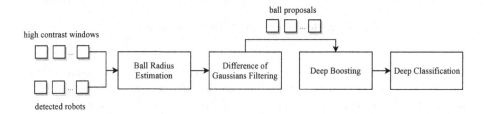

**Fig. 3.** Ball detection module pipeline.

Our ball proposal generator is inspired on the hypothesis provider developed by the HTWK team [13]. The main differences between both approaches are: (i) we only use grayscale images, (ii) we use a different method to estimate high contrast regions (see Sect. 2.2), and (iii) we use the robots' detections in order to improve the generation of proposals.

The proposal generator uses the high contrast regions and the robots' detections to provide the ball hypotheses. To accomplish this task, the generator performs a pixel-wise scan over all image windows that were detected by the high contrast detector and over image regions corresponding to the detected robots' feet. During this stage, a *Ball Radius Estimation* is calculated for every analyzed position in image coordinates.

The next stage consists in a *Difference of Gaussians* (DoG) *Filtering*. During this process, DoG filters' local responses are calculated for each scan coordinate.

The support regions of the filters are dependent on the estimated ball radii, so we are actually searching for blobs by means of the same approach used by the SIFT algorithm [15]. Additional DoG responses are calculated in front of the other robots' feet given that the ball may be in these regions. Finally, only the highest responses are used to construct a set of proposals, whose size depends on the estimation of the radius of the ball.

To perform the ball detection, the proposals are fed to a cascade of two CNNs which classifies them as ball or non-ball. The first CNN, *BoostBallNet*, performs *Deep Boosting* to both limit the proposals' number to a maximum of five, and sort them based on their confidence. The second CNN, *BallNet*, performs *Deep Classification*, meaning that it processes the filtered hypotheses to detect the ball. Both networks are extremely fast and accurate, having execution times of 0.043 ms and 0.343 ms, and accuracy rates of 0.965 and 0.984, respectively.

### 2.6  Field Lines and Special Features Detection

The field lines and features detection follow the same algorithm released by B-Human [8]. The main difference with respect to the original approach, is that in the proposed framework no color information is used. To do this, a set of vertical and horizontal scan lines are used, which save transitions from high-to-low and low-to-high luminance. This allows the detection of a set of points which are then fed to the B-Human's algorithm in order to associate them with lines and other features such as the middle circle, corners and intersections.

## 3  Design and Training of the CNN-Based Detectors

In this section we focus on the design and training methodologies used to obtain highly performant CNN based classifiers for our vision framework. Section 3.1 presents the network architectures of our classifiers and Sect. 3.2 describes the active learning-based algorithm that was developed to train them.

### 3.1  Base CNN

The proposed vision system makes use of several classifiers based on CNNs. While these CNNs are used for different purposes, their architectures remain similar across all the developed modules and are based on the work presented in [3], with slight variations to achieve higher speeds while maintaining accuracy. The main component of these architectures is the extended Fire module, which was developed in [3] inspired on the original Fire module proposed in [9]. This module concatenates the outputs produced by filters of different sizes in order to achieve increased accuracy while being computationally inexpensive. Small filters are used to extract local information across channels, while bigger filters obtain global information which is more spatially spread out. The information obtained at different scales is then combined into a single tensor and fed to the next layer. This allows the network to extract and work with both local and detailed features as well as broad, global features. Following this approach allows the training of performant models, but concatenating the information of several filters could be prohibitively expensive in terms of computational cost. To account for this, a $1\times1$ filter is placed at the beginning of each Fire module to compress the size of the representation that correspond to the input of the subsequent larger and more expensive filters. In contrast with the previous miniSqueezeNet version, all newly developed CNNs have grayscale image inputs. Since most of the computational cost of the network correspond to the first convolutional layers, this translates in sharply reduced inference times, and an accuracy loss of about 0.01. Another change is the use of leaky ReLU [18] instead of ReLU as activation functions. Previously, we used ReLU in most layers, however, this sometimes resulted in the "dying ReLU" problem while training (no gradients flow backward through the neurons). The use of leaky ReLU solves this, while incurring in no accuracy loss. All CNNs were developed using the Darknet library [14]. A diagram of the new CNN structure is presented in Fig. 4.

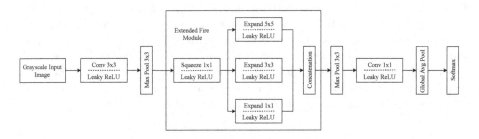

**Fig. 4.** Modified MiniSqueezeNet network structure.

## 3.2   Active Learning Training Methodology

In order to train the classifiers, we implemented an active learning-based algorithm that automatically selects and pseudo-annotates unlabeled data.

We start by initializing the parameters of the CNNs by training them using publicly available datasets (e.g., SPQR datasets [4]). However, if we directly use the obtained CNN weights in our vision framework, the classifiers behave poorly because there is a distribution mismatch between the samples present in the public datasets, and the ones that our proposal generators output.

To address this problem, the classifiers must be trained using the same kind of samples that would actually reach the networks during games. To accomplish this, the vision system is deployed on the NAO robot and data is collected using the proposal generators. Each proposal is then stored in the robot's memory with a label annotated by the CNN. To get uncorrelated data, we set a constraint for the object hypotheses to be saved: for the robot proposals, data is acquired periodically in accordance to a predefined time step; for the ball proposals, samples can only be saved if no other proposals with the same position and estimated radius were previously collected. The next stage consists in actively checking the data saved by the observer robot, and manually annotate the samples that were incorrectly labeled. We then aggregate this data to the original dataset and re-train the models.

The above process is repeated until the CNNs reach a high performance. By doing this, we are progressively aggregating correctly labeled samples to provide enough training data for robust feature learning, but also aggregating hard examples which the models fail to correctly infer, to actively shape the decision boundary of the classifiers.

After we obtain proficient models by following the described methodology, we further enhance them by switching to a bootstrap procedure. To do this, we add confidence-based constrains to collect new training data in environments where the object we want to detect is absent. For instance, if we are getting false positives from the ball detector, we would set the NAO robot to collect data from proposals with high confidence in environments were no balls are present. The samples collected would then be used to re-train the ball classifiers.

This active learning-bootstrap procedure results in a dramatical improvement in the performance of the classifiers after only a few iterations, and also allows the fine tuning of the CNN parameters by means of using data aggregation when an abrupt domain change occurs. Since the inputs to our models have relatively low dimensionality, the space used in the NAO memory during the data collection process is very small, for instance, 1,000 robot proposal samples weight about 3 MB. This procedure, combined with the automatic selection and labeling of the new samples, make the training process extremely time-wise efficient.

## 4   Results

### 4.1   CNN Classification

Table 1 shows the model complexity (number of CNN parameters), average inference time (on the NAO robot), and accuracy for each developed CNN.

**Table 1.** Performance of the developed CNNs.

| Model | RobotNet | BoostBallNet | BallNet | OriBoostNet | OriNet |
|---|---|---|---|---|---|
| Input size | $24 \times 24 \times 1$ | $12 \times 12 \times 1$ | $26 \times 26 \times 1$ | $12 \times 12 \times 1$ | $24 \times 24 \times 1$ |
| No. of parameters | 884 | 125 | 444 | 246 | 657 |
| Inference time (ms) | 0.382 | 0.043 | 0.343 | 0.059 | 0.329 |
| Accuracy | 0.969 | 0.965 | 0.984 | 0.962 | 0.984 |

Results show that the classifiers achieve very high performance while maintaining low inference times, which proves that their use is suitable for real time applications such as playing soccer. This also validates the effectiveness of the proposed methodology for the design and training of the classifiers. Finally, this also proves that the use of color information is not necessary to detect robots or balls when using expressive classifiers such as CNNs. In fact, the CNN used in the robot detector achieves a similar accuracy rate that the model proposed in [3], while being approximately 2.75 times faster.

## 4.2 Robots, Ball and Field Features Detection Systems

For the robots and ball detectors, results are divided on proposal generation and module performance. We replicated typical and challenging game conditions in order to acquire about 600 processed frames by an observer robot. Several lighting conditions were imposed while collecting these frames in order to test the robustness and reliability of our modules. The analysis of these frames allowed the extraction of empirical results in relation to the performance of the proposals generators and each detector, which are shown in Table 2.

Results show that the robots and ball proposals generators achieve high recall rates, while producing an average number of hypotheses per frame that can be processed in real time by the subsequent classifiers. Given the recall rate of the ball proposals module and the percentage of true positives of the boosting stage, the overall detection module has a very high detection rate. In fact, our ball detector outperforms B-Human's implementation, which achieves an overall accuracy rate of 0.697 when testing it under the same conditions.

Finally, the field lines and features detector was tested by comparing the difference between the real and the estimated robot pose. The estimation was obtained by using the field lines and features detected by our module. By using this approach we calculated a mean squared error of 40.07 mm, which indicates that our detector is very accurate and reliable.

**Table 2.** Performance of the robots and ball detection systems.

| Module | Robot detector | Ball detector |
|---|---|---|
| Avg. proposals per frame | 3.05 | 10.3 |
| Proposals recall | 0.972 | 0.993 |
| Overall accuracy | 0.949 | 0.971 |

## 4.3 Robot Orientation Determination

In Fig. 5 we present a comparison between the B-Human algorithm proposed in [10], our base orientation determination system, and its output after applying a circular median filtering. For this experiment, the observer and the observed robot are static and placed at a distance of 120 cm from each other. For each measurement the observed robot was rotated 22.5° around its axis. As in [10], we

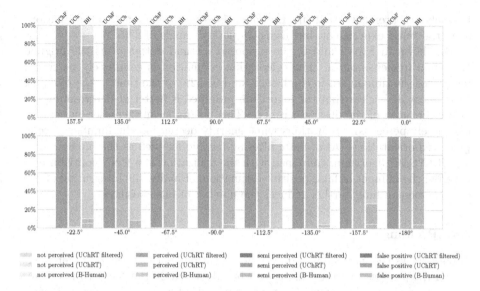

**Fig. 5.** Results obtained for the first experiment. Graph shows a performance comparison between raw (UCh) and filtered (UChF) estimations for our orientation detector and a B-Human system replication (BH).

define a *false positive* as any estimation that deviates more than a tolerance angle of 11.25° from the ground-truth. The orientation is classified as *semi perceived* when the rotation can be determined but the facing direction is unknown. The class *not perceived* corresponds to any frame where the orientation could not be calculated, while an orientation estimation is *perceived* if it does not deviate more than a tolerance angle of 11.25° from the ground-truth orientation.

In Fig. 6 we show the results obtained when testing our system in a dynamic environment, where the observed robot is moving at a speed of 12.0 cm/s, while the observer remains static. The observed robot is rotated in 45° around its axis

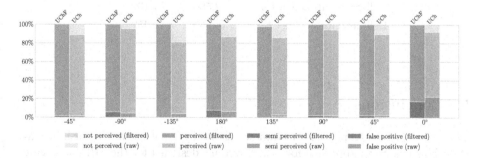

**Fig. 6.** Dynamic experiment results. Graph shows a performance comparison between raw (UCh) and filtered (UChF) estimations for our orientation detector.

for each measurement. We define the same classes for the orientation estimations as in the static experiment, but using a tolerance angle of 22.5°.

As shown in Figs. 5 and 6, the proposed method outperforms the original B-Human implementation. The orientation estimation is completely perceived 99.88% of the time in static conditions, and 95.52% of the time in the dynamic experiment. It is clear that the algorithm proposed is better at determining the facing direction of the observed robots. This results in an increased number of completely perceived orientations while sharply decreasing the number of semi perceived orientations. Also, noise filtering techniques such as the median filter and RANSAC algorithm, combined with the utilization of a CNN contribute to lowering the number of false positive estimations. Finally, the integration of the circular median filter further reduces the number of false positives.

### 4.4 Profiling

Table 3 shows the maximum and average execution times for the different modules of the proposed vision framework when deployed on the NAO v5 platform. The results obtained show that the proposed color-free vision system is deployable on platforms with limited processing capacity (such as the NAO robot). In addition, they prove the importance of the dimensionality reduction of CNN-based classifier inputs, and how this design decision impacts the performance of the system from a time-efficiency point of view.

**Table 3.** Vision framework profiling.

| Module | Max. (ms) | Avg. (ms) |
|---|---|---|
| High contrast regions detector | 2.755 | 1.478 |
| Field lines & features detector | 2.909 | 1.300 |
| Robot proposals generator | 2.692 | 1.083 |
| Robot detector | 2.417 | 0.939 |
| Robot orientation detector | 4.537 | 1.366 |
| Ball proposals generator | 2.506 | 1.132 |
| Ball detector | 6.959 | 2.452 |

## 5    Conclusions

This paper presents a new vision framework that does not use any color information. This is a novel approach for vision systems designed for the SPL, achieving very high performance while being computationally inexpensive.

The proposed vision system we present introduces four new modules: a redesigned robot detector, a visual robot orientation estimator, a brand new ball detector, and finally, a color-free field lines and features detector. All modules developed for this paper are able to run simultaneously in real-time when deployed on the NAO robot, and greatly outperform our previous perception system.

Furthermore, we demonstrate that CNN-based classifiers are a useful tool to solve most of the perception requirements of the SPL, and generally translate in an overall better performance of the corresponding module when coupled with good region proposal algorithms, and proper design and training techniques.

**Acknowledgements.** This work was partially funded by FONDECYT Project 1161500 and CONICYT-PFCHA/Magíster Nacional/2018-22182130.

# References

1. Veloso, M., Lenser, S., Vail, D., Roth, M., Stroupe, A., Chernova, S.: CMPack-02: CMU's Legged Robot Soccer Team. Carnegie Mellon University Report (2002)
2. Zagal, J.C., Ruiz-del-Solar, J., Guerrero, P., Palma, R.: Evolving visual object recognition for legged robots. In: Polani, D., Browning, B., Bonarini, A., Yoshida, K. (eds.) RoboCup 2003. LNCS (LNAI), vol. 3020, pp. 181–191. Springer, Heidelberg (2004). https://doi.org/10.1007/978-3-540-25940-4_16
3. Cruz, N., Lobos-Tsunekawa, K., Ruiz-del-Solar, J.: Using convolutional neural networks in robots with limited computational resources: detecting nao robots while playing soccer. In: Akiyama, H., Obst, O., Sammut, C., Tonidandel, F. (eds.) RoboCup 2017. LNCS (LNAI), vol. 11175, pp. 19–30. Springer, Cham (2018). https://doi.org/10.1007/978-3-030-00308-1_2
4. Albani, D., Youssef, A., Suriani, V., Nardi, D., Bloisi, D.D.: A deep learning approach for object recognition with NAO soccer robots. In: Behnke, S., Sheh, R., Sariel, S., Lee, D.D. (eds.) RoboCup 2016. LNCS (LNAI), vol. 9776, pp. 392–403. Springer, Cham (2017). https://doi.org/10.1007/978-3-319-68792-6_33
5. Speck, D., Barros, P., Weber, C., Wermter, S.: Ball localization for robocup soccer using convolutional neural networks. In: Behnke, S., Sheh, R., Sariel, S., Lee, D.D. (eds.) RoboCup 2016. LNCS (LNAI), vol. 9776, pp. 19–30. Springer, Cham (2017). https://doi.org/10.1007/978-3-319-68792-6_2
6. Menashe, J., et al.: Fast and precise black and white ball detection for RoboCup soccer. In: Akiyama, H., Obst, O., Sammut, C., Tonidandel, F. (eds.) RoboCup 2017. LNCS (LNAI), vol. 11175, pp. 45–58. Springer, Cham (2018). https://doi.org/10.1007/978-3-030-00308-1_4
7. Otsu, N.: A threshold selection method from gray-level histograms. IEEE Trans. Syst. Man Cybern. **9**(1), 62–66 (1979)
8. Röfer, T., et al.: B-Human Team Report and Code Release 2017 (2017). http://www.b-human.de/downloads/publications/2017/coderelease2017.pdf
9. Iandola, F.N., Moskewicz, M.W., Ashraf, K., Han, S., Dally, W.J., Keutzer, K.: SqueezeNet: AlexNet-level accuracy with 50x fewer parameters and <1 MB model size. CoRR (2016). http://arxiv.org/abs/1602.07360
10. Mühlenbrock, A., Laue, T.: Vision-based orientation detection of humanoid soccer robots. In: Akiyama, H., Obst, O., Sammut, C., Tonidandel, F. (eds.) RoboCup 2017. LNCS (LNAI), vol. 11175, pp. 204–215. Springer, Cham (2018). https://doi.org/10.1007/978-3-030-00308-1_17

11. Röfer, T., Müller, J., Frese, U.: Grab a mug - object detection and grasp motion planning with the Nao robot. In: IEEE-RAS International Conference on Humanoid Robots (HUMANOIDS 2012), Osaka, Japan (2012)
12. Andrew, A.M.: Another efficient algorithm for convex hulls in two dimensions. Inf. Process. Lett. **9**(5), 216–219 (1979)
13. Nao-Team HTWK: Team Research Report (2018). http://www.htwk-robots.de/ documents/TRR_2017.pdf?lang=en
14. Redmon, J.: Darknet: open source neural networks in C (2013–2016). http:// pjreddie.com/darknet/
15. Lowe, D.G.: Int. J. Comput. Vis. **60**, 91 (2004). https://doi.org/10.1023/B:VISI. 0000029664.99615.94
16. Viola, P., Jones, M.: Rapid object detection using a boosted cascade of simple features. In: Proceedings of the 2001 IEEE Computer Society Conference on Computer Vision and Pattern Recognition, CVPR 2001, vol. 1. IEEE (2001)
17. Fischler, M.A., Bolles, R.C.: Random sample consensus: a paradigm for model fitting with applications to image analysis and automated cartography. Commun. ACM **24**(6), 381–395 (1981)
18. Maas, A.L., Hannun, A.Y., Ng, A.Y.: Rectifier nonlinearities improve neural network acoustic models. In: Proceeding of the ICML, vol. 30. no. 1 (2013)

# Poster Presentations

# End-to-End Deep Imitation Learning: Robot Soccer Case Study

Okan Aşık[✉], Binnur Görer, and H. Levent Akın

Department of Computer Engineering, Boğaziçi University, 34342 Istanbul, Turkey
{okan.asik,binnur.gorer,akin}@boun.edu.tr

**Abstract.** In imitation learning, behavior learning is generally done using the features extracted from the demonstration data. Recent deep learning algorithms enable the development of machine learning methods that can get high dimensional data as an input. In this work, we use imitation learning to teach the robot to dribble the ball to the goal. We use B-Human robot software to collect demonstration data and a deep convolutional network to represent the policies. We use top and bottom camera images of the robot as input and speed commands as outputs. The CNN policy learns the mapping between the series of images and speed commands. In 3D realistic robotics simulator experiments, we show that the robot is able to learn to search the ball and dribble the ball, but it struggles to align to the goal. The best-proposed policy model learns to score 4 goals out of 20 test episodes.

## 1 Introduction

In robot learning, it is a challenging problem to collect training data set in real-world environment. One possible solution is to isolate the problem from the entire robotic system. For example, object detection, which is a highly important problem in robotics vision, can be addressed separately in development of a home service robot. Image data can be captured from the robot camera without requiring fully functional robotic system and can be used with supervised or unsupervised learning methods. In contrast to supervised and unsupervised learning, reinforcement learning is inherently hard for real-world robotics as it requires direct interaction with the environment. Let's consider the problem of high-level behavior (task) learning such as learning to play soccer. Reinforcement learning is based on the exploration of the state-action space and the iterative improvement of the values of experienced state-action pairs. That exploration takes many time steps and may harm the robot during the interaction with the environment. Therefore, it is not feasible to use direct reinforcement learning for behavior learning in robotics.

One of the most common approaches to solve behavior learning is the imitation learning. The imitation learning can be classified as one of the supervised learning approaches since the learning model imitates data provided by demonstration. A demonstrator controls the robot to complete a specific behavior (task)

© Springer Nature Switzerland AG 2019
D. Holz et al. (Eds.): RoboCup 2018, LNAI 11374, pp. 137–149, 2019.
https://doi.org/10.1007/978-3-030-27544-0_11

using the robot. During the demonstration, data is collected from the sensors and actuators of the robot. By using many demonstration sessions, a data set is created that can be used to learn sensor-actuator tuples. In this study, we use imitation learning to dribble the ball to score a goal using a humanoid robot.

These behavior learning approaches require a symbolic representation of the behavior. This representation determines the abstraction of the problem. For example, in the case of the ball dribbling behavior, we can represent the world of the robot as the pose of the robot and the position of the ball on the field. To be able to construct a learning problem and apply it in real-world, we need to have robot perception algorithm that is able to calculate the pose of the robot and the position of the ball. Most of the behavior learning approaches in the literature uses this level of abstraction in learning [3,10,11,13]. However, this level of abstraction requires solving complex perception problems such as determining its own pose using the features extracted from the camera image. In this study, we learn the behavior using the camera image as an input to our machine learning model. Therefore, the basic robotics problems such as perception, localization, and planning would be inherently learned by our model.

We create a training data set that is collected while a teacher realizes the behavior on the robot. The dataset consists of images taken from the robot camera and movement commands. Instead of recruiting a human teacher to make the task to the robot a number of times, we use a robotics software developed for the robot soccer as a teacher. The simulation environment makes it easy to code the behavior since we have the pose of the robot and the ball without running any perception or localization algorithm. We train a deep learning model using the training data set. The model that can replicate the same speed commands given the images achieves the imitation learning without requiring any complex solutions to subproblems in the task.

The robot soccer problem is a partially observable problem because the robot cannot sense the current state of the environment using its own onboard sensors. Therefore, a policy that maps the current perception to an action command may have suboptimal behavior. Therefore, we propose to use recurrent convolutional neural network since it has the capability of estimating the current state from a series of perceptions. In addition to the recurrent convolutional neural network, we also propose to use a hierarchical model to divide the ball dribbling behavior into sub-skills such as searching for the ball and aligning to the goal and a more basic convolutional neural network approach to compare the performances.

We measure the learning performance of our models on the test demonstration data set. On the test data set, we achieved an average error of 0.16, 0.17, and 0.14 with the convolutional neural network, hierarchical convolutional neural network, and recurrent convolutional neural network policies, respectively. The error is calculated as the average Euclidean distance between two action vectors. Also, we count the number of goals scored in 20 test episodes; CNN scores 3 goals, H-CNN scores 3 goals, and R-CNN scores 4 goals. In this study, we show that we can teach a humanoid robot to carry out a complex task that requires perception and planning using deep imitation learning. We test our method on a realistic robotics simulator, but our future aim is to evaluate the approach using real robots.

# 2    Related Work

Imitation learning is a promising research area since it has the potential of enabling non-technical domain experts to teach their expertise to a computational machine. There are many ways of demonstrating a behavior to a robot such as teleoperation and exoskeleton suit. In this study, a high-level behavior control software controls the robot in simulation, and raw sensor readings and mid-level actions are collected as demonstration data set. Our mid-level actions are 2D speed commands. We use teleoperation based data demonstration and direct state-action policy representation according to the categorization of Husseion *et al.*, and Argall *et al.* since we learn state-action mapping [2,7].

This study is based on end to end deep learning. The first study shows that an agent can learn to play Atari using the screen inputs as the state of the game [14]. Although end to end learning is a reinforcement learning method, its key feature is that the policy representation is powerful enough to learn without abstracting the state or action of the problem. For example, in Atari learning, state is the screen of the game and action is joystick command so that no feature engineering is involved. Our study also uses sensor inputs (camera images) without any feature engineering, but the actions have an abstraction since humanoid walking problem is still quite complex to be used in such end to end learning. Also, most of the end to end learning approaches use deep convolutional neural network to represent the expected reward of state-action pairs. However, we represent our policy as a simple mapping function that maps states to actions. We could also use reinforcement learning, but it would take quite long time to learn to score a goal. We know that if the reward is deep in reinforcement learning problems, it gets harder to learn (consider the Atari game *Montezuma's Revenge* [14]).

We structure our related work in two subsections; end to end deep learning and ball dribbling behavior. In the first section, we overview the methods using end to end deep learning. In the second section, we overview the methods that directly issue the ball dribbling behavior.

## 2.1    End to End Learning

The first study that combines deep learning and reinforcement learning is done by Mnih *et al.* [14]. They achieved human-level atari game playing by using a deep convolutional neural network to represent the policy that evaluates the expected reward of state-action pairs. Their most important contribution is using the state representation as the actual screen of the game as if a human player perceives the game. This approach is also the most important part of our work where relevant features are automatically discovered by the convolutional neural network instead of human-engineered features.

Guo *et al.* use Monte Carlo Planning algorithm to collect data that will be used to train the convolutional neural network [4]. Although Monte Carlo Planning has better performance than reinforcement learning algorithms, it is quite slow compared to neural networks. They show that reinforcement learning that uses the data generated by Monte Carlo Planning improves the performance. This is also one of the inspiration for this study where an expert software is used to teach an end-to-end neural network policy. However, we do not represent policy as a Q-function [18], but as a state-action mapping function. Another work that combines the Monte Carlo planning and deep learning is the amazing Alpha Go that beats the Go champion [16].

One of the most important robotics application of the end-to-end deep learning method is the study that learns to manipulate objects using the raw camera images [12]. The robot learns to send joint commands to motors using a convolutional neural network. In contrast to them, we generate high-level motion commands to control the 2D motion of the robot using 2D speed commands. They improve the performance of their method by using many different pre-processing and pre-learning methods. In contrast to them, we train the whole network at once using the data generated by the demonstrator.

Husseion et al. combine the deep imitation learning with active learning to learn to navigate in the 3D maze [6]. The use of imitation learning in 3D simulation environment to solve such complex tasks are also our aim. In contrast to their work, we use realistic 3D robotics simulator.

## 2.2  Ball Dribbling Task

One of the early studies that aim to learn to dribble the ball in robot soccer is done by Latzke et al. [10]. They use imitation learning to improve the performance of reinforcement learning algorithm. The data generated by the teacher is used to initialize the reinforcement learning policy. They train a humanoid robot to dribble the ball to the empty goal. They report a reduction in training time and increase in the learning performance when imitation data and function approximation is used. Leottau et al. propose two layer approach for humanoid robot ball dribbling [11]. They use a fuzzy logic controller for alignment to the ball and reinforcement learning to push the ball towards the goal. Although pushing the ball towards the goal after the alignment seems a simple task, in addition to the dribbling the ball as fast as possible, they try to keep the ball possession, i.e. keep the ball as close as possible. Therefore, they use reinforcement learning to optimize for two conflicting goals; being as fast as possible, but also keeping the ball as close as possible. Mericli et al. propose to use a corrective human feedback system to teach the robot to dribble the ball through stationary defender robots [13]. The main contribution of the work is the combination of hand-coded behavior with the active demonstration of the human. The performance of the ball dribbling, that is the time to scoring a goal, is improved by the integration of the demonstrations. All these ball dribbling tasks have lower ambitions compared to our work. They use the model of the problem, robot perception, and localization and solve one of the subtasks of the behavior, that is ball dribbling.

## 3 Methods

This study consists of two parts; dataset creation and the training of deep neural networks. In imitation learning, the dataset is created by an expert who knows how to control the robot to carry out a task. In this study, we use a hand-coded behavior on B-Human simulation environment instead of a human expert. We define a behavior that searches the ball, goes towards the ball, aligns to the goal, and dribbles the ball to the goal. The collected data set, a set of image-speed tuples, is used to train the convolutional neural networks with three different architectures. These neural networks learn to predict robot speed commands based on the images taken from the cameras.

### 3.1 Dataset Creation

RoboCup Standard Platform League (SPL) is a competition where robot soccer teams compete using 5 Nao robots. B-Human is one of the successful teams in SPL and they make their robot software publicly available[1]. They provide all their software with a 3D robotics simulation software called SimRobot with the modules that can both run on the robot and in the simulator. A screenshot of the simulator can be seen in Fig. 1a. In this study, we use the SimRobot simulation environment and robot software [15].

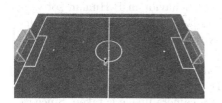

(a) A screenshot of SimRobot simulator.

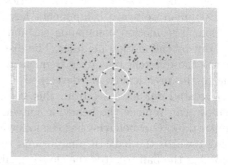

(b) The position of robots (red points) and balls (blue points) of the dataset

**Fig. 1.** (**left**) SimRobot environment and (**right**) robot and ball positions (Color figure online)

The Nao robot that is used in SPL has two cameras, one views the forward (top camera) and another one (bottom camera) is aligned to view the feet of the robot. These cameras do not (almost) overlap. Although we can get the images from those cameras at different resolutions, most of the teams use 640 × 480 for

---

[1] https://github.com/bhuman/BHumanCodeRelease.

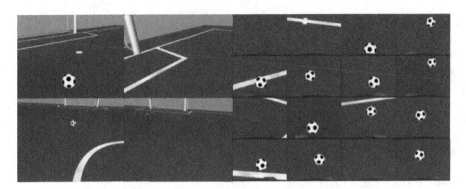

Fig. 2. A series of sample pre-processed images. The **bigger** images on the left are top camera images, the **smaller** images on the right are bottom camera images.

the top camera and 320 × 240 for the bottom camera. Those cameras provide images at 33 Hz.

We use the images of these two cameras as input our learning approach. We pre-process images to lower the dimensionality of images to able to use as input. We scale and convert images to gray-scale. Scaling is done by averaging the pixel values corresponding to a particular region by Thumbnail provider of B-Human software module [15]. We scale top camera images to 160 × 120 resolution and bottom camera images to 80 × 60. A series of sample images can be seen in Fig. 2.

B-Human software components have two main categories; cognition and motion. The motion commands calculated by the cognition modules are carried out by the motion modules. The distinction between these two processes is due to the different operating frequencies of motors and sensors. In this study, due to the practicality, we developed a simple behavior in B-Human software and created our data set from this behavior. However, we can safely assume that we can replace the behavior software with a human operator and collect similar data. Our behavior has the following components; searching for the ball, going towards the ball, turning around the ball to align to the closest goal and dribbling the ball towards the closest goal. By default, the software calculates a speed command at every time step when a new camera image is taken. Since we aim to learn a policy that maps image to speed commands, we create a motion command when images from both top and bottom cameras are taken. Therefore, at the current time step, if we have not received images from both cameras, we repeat the last command. Otherwise, if the images captured from two cameras processed separately, the predicted actions for each of them may conflict.

We create our dataset by selecting random robot position in 4 m by 4 m area on the center of the field, and random ball position in 4 m by 2 m area on either side of the field. We choose the position of the ball such that the ball is at least one meters away from the center line of the field. In this way, we aim to choose a side for the ball where the robot will score a goal. The random positions of the robots and balls can be seen in Fig. 1b. Data collection starts when the robot starts to move and ends when the robot scores a goal. We created our dataset using 100 episodes with the random ball and robot positions. Our dataset has $160 \times 120$ and $80 \times 60$ grayscale images with speed commands (speed commands consist of forward, left and turn speeds).

## 3.2   Deep Imitation Learning

There are two important research questions of the imitation learning; handling the states that are not part of the learning and the generalizing capability of the model and representation. A teacher demonstrates the expected behavior by controlling the robot at every time step. That way, we construct state-action tuples. By using this demonstration data, we learn the policy of the task. If the teacher's demonstrations cover very limited part of the state space or the learning model is not able to generalize well, the performance of the imitation learning decreases.

In this study, we use convolutional neural networks as our learning models. In this way, we are able to directly use camera images as input to our learning model. This is called end-to-end learning since we do not use intermediate feature extraction approach. In other words, the model itself learns to extract useful features based on the task. This approach is closer to the human's cognition where real neural network processes the image and produces an action.

When the state is fully observable by the robot, the direct state-action mapping has the capability of representing the optimal policy taught by the teacher assuming that the dataset encompasses every state. However, when the problem is partially observable, where a single observation is not enough to infer the world state, our learning model needs to learn to infer action from a series observations. For example, in the robot soccer problem, the robot perceives the world from its cameras. Therefore, the robot can perceive only a small part of the field. If there is a ball in the camera, the robot knows the position of the ball, but if the ball is not in the field of view of the camera, the robot does not know the current state of the world about the ball. A convolutional neural network (CNN) can only map the current image to an action so that previous actions or images does not affect the choice of the action. However, the robot soccer behavior needs the information of previous camera images to act properly. Therefore, we extend basic CNN with a hierarhical neural network (H-CNN) and recurrent convolutional neural network (Recurrent-CNN).

**Convolutional Neural Network (CNN).** This is the straightforward neural network to learn state-action mapping. We assume that the images taken from two cameras of the robot are powerful enough to learn the behavior operated by the teacher. To be able to process the two images having different resolutions, we have two different channels of input layers. The first hidden layer consists of 16 units for top camera image and 8 for bottom camera image 5 by 5 convolutional filters that convolve the images with stride 2. After the convolution, a 2 by 2 maximum pooling filter is used. The second hidden layer consists of 32 for top

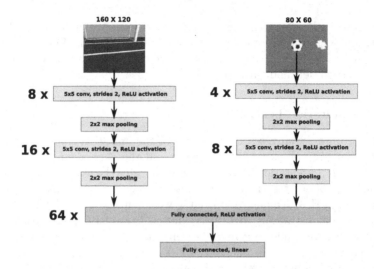

**Fig. 3.** The architecture of deep convolutional neural network

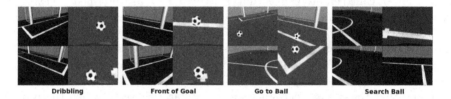

**Fig. 4.** Sample representative images from different clusters.

camera image and 16 for bottom camera image 5 by 5 convolutional filters that convolves the images with stride 2. After the convolution, a 2 by 2 maximum pooling filter is used. We also used ReLU [9] activation function after every convolutional layer. After this four layers, we have a fully connected layer with 128 units and ReLU activation. The last layer is a fully connected linear output layer with three units. The layers of the neural network model can be seen in Fig. 3.

**Hierarchical Convolutional Neural Network (H-CNN).** We propose a hierarchical approach to learn a behavior that consists of sub-behaviors or skills. For example, our robot soccer behavior consists of four sub-behaviors such as searching the ball, going to the ball, aligning to the goal and dribbling the ball. Our assumption is that our demonstration data including the actions can be clustered into four classes where each may correspond to a sub-behavior. A set of example images from different clusters can be seen in Fig. 4. Therefore, we first cluster the whole data into a predetermined number of classes. Then, we learn a separate convolutional neural network with the same architecture as Fig. 3

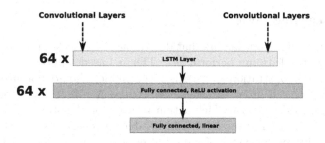

**Fig. 5.** The Recurrent-CNN with LSTM layer

for each cluster. During the test phase, we find the closest cluster to the given images and use the learned CNN of that cluster.

For the clustering, we first create histograms of images with 5 bins. We concatenate the top and bottom histogram features. Then, we use the K-Means clustering algorithm [1] to cluster the whole dataset. After the clustering, we obtain a different demonstration dataset for each cluster. Finally, we train a CNN for each of these datasets.

**Recurrent Convolutional Neural Network (Recurrent-CNN).** We also propose a recurrent convolutional neural network model (Recurrent-CNN) to learn the mapping between a series of states and a series of actions. We augment the CNN model proposed in Sect. 3.2 by adding a Long-Short Term Memory (LSTM) layer after the convolutional layers as seen in Fig. 5. LSTM cells have the capability to learn to keep which part of the data in its memory and which part to forget [5]. It is shown that LSTM is the state of the art method on sequence learning [17].

The LSTM layer of Recurrent-CNN has 64 units. It is trained using a 100 time step window of data that corresponds to approximately three seconds of the data sequence. We empirically determine the window size in order to balance the training time and the performance. We test and evaluate the model by sliding a 100 time step window over the data sequence.

## 4   Experiments and Results

Our training data set consists of 100 episodes where every episode includes a complete robot soccer behavior as explained in Sect. 3.1. We train all of our three models using ADAM neural network optimization algorithm [8]. We used different maximum iterations for different models since we used fixed processing time. Finally, we measure the overall training error as the root mean square of the Euclidean distance between the true action vector and predicted vector. We also measure the performance of the models on 20 test episodes that is not used in training.

## 4.1  The Learning Performance

One of the most important factors that determine the success of imitation learning methods is the learning performance. This is based on how well the model can learn the demonstration data. Also, the model should not memorize all the demonstrations in order to avoid over-fitting. A robust imitation learning method is supposed to learn which action to take for the states which are not in the demonstration. The model should be able to generalize for new states as well. The learning performance of an imitation learning model can be measured by the average error on the demonstration data. The generalization performance can be measured by the average error on the test demonstration data.

**Table 1.** The performance of CNN models

| Models | # of Training iterations | Training error | Test error | Goals scored |
|---|---|---|---|---|
| CNN | $10^6$ | 0.12 | 0.16 | 3 |
| H-CNN | $15 \times 10^4$ | 0.15 | 0.17 | 3 |
| Recurrent-CNN | $3 \times 10^3$ | **0.036** | **0.14** | **4** |

The overall performance of different models can be seen in Table 1. The R-CNN has the best performance by having the least training error and least test error. Test and training errors are reported as the average distance of the calculated speed vector and the demonstration speed vector. The training results are provided over all training data and the test results are provided on the data from 20 new episodes. When we observe the overall learned behavior, we see that robot struggles to find the direction of the goal and turns around while dribbling the ball. However, the robot robustly performs searching for the ball, moving towards the ball and dribbling the ball actions. When we measure the number of goals scored in test scenarios, the robot scores 4 goals using R-CNN, 3 goals using CNN and 3 goals using H-CNN models over 20 test episodes. The trajectories of the robot with R-CNN model and demonstration trajectories are seen in Fig. 6. The left trajectories present the goal scored ones, the right trajectories present some of the failed ones.

## 4.2  Discussion

There are two important research questions about imitation learning; how to represent and collect demonstration data, and how to represent and optimize the policy. Our approach generates demonstrations from an expert software such that the behavior of the robot is consistent. By using a software for the collection of the demonstration data, we minimize the possibility of demonstrator errors and instability.

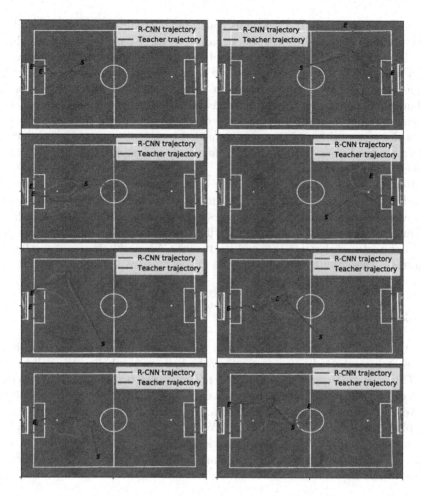

**Fig. 6.** The comparison of robot trajectories while running test episodes. The **left** figures show goal scored episodes. The **right** figures show some of the failed test episodes.

Since demonstrator errors are minimized, the success of our approach basically depends on the data representation and model selection for the policy. We use deep convolutional neural networks (CNN) to represent our policies because they enable us to represent the demonstration data as camera images. It is known that CNNs perform well on visual classification and detection tasks [9]. The dataset we generated can be viewed as a machine learning dataset for visual regression task. However, basic use of CNN comes with the assumption that we can infer the expected action using camera images of the current time step. Although the problem is not fully observable, we see that the performance of different policy representations (CNN, H-CNN, Recurrent-CNN) are close. This might be due to the possible overlap between training data set and test data set. We argue that learned models are able to memorize some of the training cases to reduce the error, but not able to generalize or memorize the whole task.

When we investigate the behaviors generated with different learning models, we see that all of the models are able to carry out three basic subtasks; searching the ball, going towards the ball, and dribbling the ball. However, they generally fail to align with the goal. This is due to the demonstration behavior. The demonstration behavior decides to align to the goal when the ball is close to dribbling and orientation of the robot is not towards the goal. However, the behavior does not use the robot images to carry out aligning to the goal behavior. It uses the true position of the robot provided by the simulator. Hence, how to align to the goal using only the camera images is not explicitly exhibited in the demonstration data.

Although the real world application of this method is limited, the policy learned in the simulation can be further improved with less amount of real-world data. Also, we keep the CNN architectures as small as possible to be able to have real-time performance. On a laptop having 2.8 GHz cpu[2], the forward pass of CNN architecture takes 0.0018 s, and Recurrent-CNN architecture takes 0.0021 s on average. Based on these statistics, we expect near-real-time performance on Nao robot.

## 5    Conclusion

Using the deep imitation learning method, we learned a basic robot soccer behavior of searching the ball, moving towards the ball, and dribbling the ball to the goal. Our proposed convolutional neural network uses two images from two different cameras of the robot as input. We created our dataset using RoboCup SPL team B-Human software modules and carried out our experiments using SimRobot 3D realistic robot simulator. We show that using quite a few samples, we can learn simple robot soccer behaviors using end-to-end training. In the future, we aim to scale our method to more complex behaviors on real robots in real environments.

**Acknowledgments.** This project is supported by Turkey Technology Team Foundation (T3).

## References

1. Alpaydin, E.: Introduction to Machine Learning. MIT Press, Cambridge (2014)
2. Argall, B.D., Chernova, S., Veloso, M., Browning, B.: A survey of robot learning from demonstration. Robot. Auton. Syst. **57**(5), 469–483 (2009)
3. Aşık, O., Akın, H.L.: Solving multi-agent decision problems modeled as Dec-POMDP: a robot soccer case study. In: Chen, X., Stone, P., Sucar, L.E., van der Zant, T. (eds.) RoboCup 2012. LNCS (LNAI), vol. 7500, pp. 130–140. Springer, Heidelberg (2013). https://doi.org/10.1007/978-3-642-39250-4_13
4. Guo, X., Singh, S., Lee, H., Lewis, R.L., Wang, X.: Deep learning for real-time Atari game play using offline Monte-Carlo tree search planning. In: Advances in Neural Information Processing Systems, pp. 3338–3346 (2014)

---

[2] Intel 7700HQ 4 cores 2.8 GHz, 32 GB 2400 MHz RAM.

5. Hochreiter, S., Schmidhuber, J.: Long short-term memory. Neural Comput. **9**(8), 1735–1780 (1997)
6. Hussein, A., Elyan, E., Gaber, M.M., Jayne, C.: Deep imitation learning for 3D navigation tasks. Neural Comput. Appl. **29**, 1–16 (2017)
7. Hussein, A., Gaber, M.M., Elyan, E., Jayne, C.: Imitation learning: a survey of learning methods. ACM Comput. Surv. (CSUR) **50**(2), 21 (2017)
8. Kingma, D.P., Ba, J.: Adam: a method for stochastic optimization. arXiv preprint arXiv:1412.6980 (2014)
9. Krizhevsky, A., Sutskever, I., Hinton, G.E.: ImageNet classification with deep convolutional neural networks. In: Advances in Neural Information Processing Systems, pp. 1097–1105 (2012)
10. Latzke, T., Behnke, S., Bennewitz, M.: Imitative reinforcement learning for soccer playing robots. In: Lakemeyer, G., Sklar, E., Sorrenti, D.G., Takahashi, T. (eds.) RoboCup 2006. LNCS (LNAI), vol. 4434, pp. 47–58. Springer, Heidelberg (2007). https://doi.org/10.1007/978-3-540-74024-7_5
11. Leottau, L., Celemin, C., Ruiz-del-Solar, J.: Ball dribbling for humanoid biped robots: a reinforcement learning and fuzzy control approach. In: Bianchi, R.A.C., Akin, H.L., Ramamoorthy, S., Sugiura, K. (eds.) RoboCup 2014. LNCS (LNAI), vol. 8992, pp. 549–561. Springer, Cham (2015). https://doi.org/10.1007/978-3-319-18615-3_45
12. Levine, S., Finn, C., Darrell, T., Abbeel, P.: End-to-end training of deep visuomotor policies. J. Mach. Learn. Res. **17**(1), 1334–1373 (2016)
13. Meriçli, Ç., Veloso, M., Akın, H.L.: Task refinement for autonomous robots using complementary corrective human feedback. Int. J. Adv. Robot. Syst. **8**(2), 16 (2011)
14. Mnih, V., et al.: Human-level control through deep reinforcement learning. Nature **518**(7540), 529 (2015)
15. Röfer, T., et al.: B-Human team report and code release 2017 (2017). http://www.b-human.de/downloads/publications/2017/coderelease2017.pdf
16. Silver, D., et al.: Mastering the game of go with deep neural networks and tree search. Nature **529**(7587), 484–489 (2016)
17. Sutskever, I., Vinyals, O., Le, Q.V.: Sequence to sequence learning with neural networks. In: Ghahramani, Z., Welling, M., Cortes, C., Lawrence, N.D., Weinberger, K.Q. (eds.) Advances in Neural Information Processing Systems 27, pp. 3104–3112. Curran Associates, Inc. (2014). http://papers.nips.cc/paper/5346-sequence-to-sequence-learning-with-neural-networks.pdf
18. Sutton, R.S., Barto, A.G.: Introduction to Reinforcement Learning, vol. 135. MIT Press, Cambridge (1998)

# Designing Convolutional Neural Networks Using a Genetic Approach for Ball Detection

Georg Christian Felbinger(✉), Patrick Göttsch, Pascal Loth, Lasse Peters, and Felix Wege

RobotING@TUHH e.V., Hamburg University of Technology, Hamburg, Germany
hulks@tuhh.de, https://hulks.de

**Abstract.** At RoboCup 2017, the HULKs reached the Standard Platform League's quarter finals and won the mixed team competition together with our fellow team B-Human. This paper describes the design of a convolutional neural network used for the detection of the black and white ball - one of the key contributions that led to the team's success. We present a genetic design approach that optimizes network hyperparameters for a cost effective inference on the NAO, with limited amount of training data. Experimental results demonstrate that the genetic algorithm is able to optimize the hyperparameters of convolutional neural networks. We show that the resulting network is able to run in real-time on the robot with a very precise classification in generalization test.

## 1 Introduction

In 2016, a black and white patched ball was introduced into the Standard Platform League (SPL). While in previous years color based approaches [2,5] were sufficient to achieve a acceptable detection and classification performance, the new ball requires more sophisticated techniques. Requirements for a detection algorithm comprise a robust detection and classification in dynamically changing environments, as well as a cost-effective real-time computation on the NAO.

Approaches based on convolutional neural networks (CNN) for object detection led to promising results in RoboCup SPL [7,8]. However, hyperparameters for the structural setup of such networks need to be chosen carefully. Genetic approaches as described in [4] and [9] can be used to determine an optimized network topology. Stanley and Miikkulainen described the evolution of fully connected network topologies [10]. The idea can easily be applied to other model components, e.g. convolutional layers. A similar genetic approach was used by Sun, Xue, and Zhang to automatically discover good architectures of CNNs [11].

This paper presents a genetic framework to design CNNs for real-time applications on computationally weak hardware by simultaneously optimizing the classification performance and inference complexity. Our approach considers a bounded capability to collect large amounts of training data and allows the user to prioritize true negative rate and true positive rate suitable for a specific task.

© Springer Nature Switzerland AG 2019
D. Holz et al. (Eds.): RoboCup 2018, LNAI 11374, pp. 150–161, 2019.
https://doi.org/10.1007/978-3-030-27544-0_12

The detection of a black and white ball on the NAO robot is used to demonstrate the performance of the framework.

Section 2 outlines the general idea of a genetic algorithm as well as the components used to assemble a CNN. Section 3 describes the resulting search space and the fitness function used for the genetic optimization. Section 4 presents the process of data acquisition. Herein the techniques used to generate and setup training data are described. Finally, in Sect. 5 the conducted experiments are presented and the evaluation results are discussed.

## 2   Prerequisites

### 2.1   Genetic Algorithm

The method used in this work follows a genetic algorithm pattern [4]. The basic elements are chromosomes or individuals $c \in S$, a possible solution in given k-dimensional search space $S$. The algorithm works in an iterative manner with a fixed number of generations $N$. A set of $n$ chromosomes used during iteration $j$ is called population $P_j = \{c_1, ..., c_n\} \subset S$. The initial population $P_0$ is generated randomly. In each generation $j \in [1, N]$ the population of the previous iteration is evaluated using a fitness function $f(c) : \mathbb{C}^k \mapsto \mathbb{R}$. Given the individuals fitnesses of the previous population a set $S_j$ is selected from $P_{j-1}$ as parents. In the next step a mutation function will be applied to every element in $S_j$. Finally, mutated parent elements are recombined yielding the next generation $P_j$.

#### 2.1.1   Selection
The selection is done using the following steps. According to a given clipping parameter $c \in [0, 1]$ individuals in the lower $c$th percentile is dropped. The minimal fitness within the population is given by $\min_{k \in [1,n]}(f(c_k))$. Given the other $m$ individuals the probability of survival is calculated by Eq. (1).

$$p(c_i) = \frac{f(c_i) - \text{minscore}}{\sum_{j=1}^{m} (f(c_j) - \text{minscore})} \tag{1}$$

Hence, the individual with the lowest fitness value is assigned to the survival probability zero. According to this distribution, $n$ elements are sampled for mutation and reproduction.

#### 2.1.2   Mutation
For every value within chromosome $c$ a new value will be sampled based on a given mutation probability $p_m$. If a gene is to be replaced a new random value is chosen.

#### 2.1.3   Reproduction
In the reproduction phase the selected and mutated chromosomes are pairwise randomly sampled. Each pair yields two new children. For every value within the chromosome of a child, the corresponding parent value is chosen randomly.

## 2.2  Convolutional Neural Networks

In our recent work [7] convolutional neural networks showed promising results in the field of object detection. The following briefly describes the basic components used for our CNN structure.

### 2.2.1  Convolutional Layer

In this work multiple two-dimensional convolutions are used, i.e. an input image with $q$ channels is mapped to an output image with $k$ channels. Equation (2) shows the computation of a convolutional layer.

$$y_{i,j,k} = \sum_{di,dj,q} x_{i+di,j+dj,q} \cdot m_{di,dj,q,k}$$

$$x \in \mathbb{R}^{i \times j \times q}, m \in \mathbb{R}^{di \times dj \times q \times k} \tag{2}$$

### 2.2.2  Pooling Layer

Pooling layers reduce every dimension of each image channel by applying a function to neighboring pixels using a $2 \times 2$ mask. In this paper $\max(a,b,c,d)$ (maximum value of arguments) and $\text{avg}(a,b,c,d)$ (arithmetic mean of arguments) are used.

### 2.2.3  Normalization Layer

Batch normalization layers are used to increase the learning rates and to reduce the sensitivity to the initialization of the weights [6]. During training normalization is calculated batch-wise. For input vectors $[1,m] \in \mathbb{N}$ it is calculated by Eq. (3).

$$\text{BN}_{\gamma,\beta}(x_i) = \gamma \cdot \frac{x_i - \mu_B}{\sqrt{\sigma_B + \epsilon}} + \beta \tag{3}$$

The scale $\gamma$ and offset $\beta$ are trainable parameters which get optimized due to the training problem. The batch mean is element-wise computed by $\mu_B = \frac{1}{m} \sum_{j=1}^{m} x_j$. The batch variance is also element-wise computed by $\sigma_B = \frac{1}{m} \sum_{j=1}^{m} (x_j - \mu_B)$.

For the inference mean and variance are approximated by a moving average approach during training [6, pp. 4]. Mean $\mu_n$ and variance $\sigma_n$ after $n$th batch can be computed recursively using a moving average.

## 3  Genetic Design of Convolutional Neural Networks

To find an optimal topology of the CNN the genetic algorithm mentioned in Sect. 2.1 is used. Each topology set corresponds to a single individual within the search space. CNN structure and search space are specified in this chapter.

## 3.1  Network Structure

The uniform structure used for all evaluated individuals is given in Fig. 1. The input is a YCbCr candidate image of arbitrary quadratic size. It is resized to a fixed quadratic size using nearest neighbor interpolation. Then, multiple convolutional layers are applied. The next step is a batch normalization layer. Finally, multiple fully connected layers are applied. The output is a vector representing the class scores.

Each individual specifies the remaining hyperparameters within this structure. These are the input size, number of convolutional and fully connected layers as well as their internal configuration. Each convolutional layer is parameterized with a mask size, pooling type and activation function. Likewise, the parameters of a fully connected layer consists of the size and activation function.

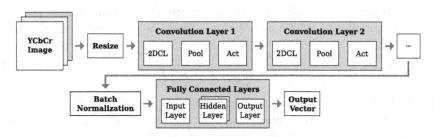

**Fig. 1.** General structure of a CNN. Each convolutional layer consists of a two dimensional convolution mask (2DCL) followed by a pooling layer (Pool) and an activation function (Act). The convolved and normalized image is fed into multiple fully connected layers yielding the final output vector.

## 3.2  Search Space

The search space for the genetic algorithm consists of parameters described in Sect. 3.1 with the value ranges described in the following. The size of the quadratic input image is sampled within the range $[8, 16] \in \mathbb{N}$. The amount of convolutional layers is limited to two. For each convolutional layer the number of kernels is chosen from $[1, 5] \in \mathbb{N}$. The kernel size is equal within each convolutional layer and is either two or three in both dimensions. Either no pooling, max-pooling or avg-pooling is used in the pooling layer. The activation function for the CNN and the fully connected layer is either tanh or rectified linear unit (ReLU). There are four fully connected layers at maximum each with a number of neurons within $[2, 20] \in \mathbb{N}$.

## 3.3  Fitness Function

We optimize classification performance and inference complexity at the same time. In the fitness function classification performance is represented by the true negative and true positive rate. Inference complexity is approximated asymptotically.

### 3.3.1 Classification Performance

For each network a $k$-fold cross validation was performed which yielded $k$ values for true negative rate $TNR_{nk}$ and true positive rate $TPR_{nk}$. In order to approximate a lower bound of these performance metrics the difference of mean and variance were used in the fitness function. The $TPR_n$ and $TNR_n$ for a network $n$ was computed by:

$$TPR_n = \text{Avg}(TPR_{n1}, ..., TPR_{nk}) - \text{Var}(TPR_{n1}, ..., TPR_{nk}) \tag{4}$$

$$TNR_n = \text{Avg}(TNR_{n1}, ..., TNR_{nk}) - \text{Var}(TNR_{n1}, ..., TNR_{nk}) \tag{5}$$

where Avg is the arithmetic mean and Var is the variance.

### 3.3.2 Inference Complexity

The complexity of a network was asymptotically approximated and linearly scaled. The complexity $cc$ of a convolutional layer $i$ is approximated by Eq. (6).

$$cc_i = \frac{I_x \cdot I_y \cdot I_c \cdot m_x \cdot m_y \cdot m_c}{\hat{I}_x \cdot \hat{I}_y \cdot I_c \cdot \hat{m}_x \cdot \hat{m}_y \cdot \hat{m}_c} = \frac{I_x \cdot I_y \cdot m_x \cdot m_y \cdot m_c}{\hat{I}_x \cdot \hat{I}_y \cdot \hat{m}_x \cdot \hat{m}_y \cdot \hat{m}_c} \tag{6}$$

Symbols $I_x, I_y, I_c$ correspond to layer input size and depth, $m_x, m_y, m_c$ to amount and size of the convolution masks in this layer. While $\hat{I}_x, \hat{I}_y, \hat{m}_x, \hat{m}_y, \hat{m}_c$ represent maximum values as defined by the Sect. 3.2.

The complexity $cf$ of the fully connected part is approximated by Eq. (7).

$$cf = \frac{\sum_{i=1}^{k} s_i \cdot s_{i-1}}{\sum_{i=1}^{k} \hat{s}_i \cdot \hat{s}_{i-1}} \tag{7}$$

The number of hidden layers is denoted by $k$ and the size of layer $i$ by $s_i$. The input vector size is $s_0$.

Hence, the final complexity of a network topology with $j$ convolutional layers is

$$c_n = 1 - \frac{\sum_{i=1}^{j} cc_i + cf}{j + 1}. \tag{8}$$

### 3.3.3 Resulting Fitness Function

Given the approximation of classification performance and inference complexity the resulting fitness function is chosen as follows:

$$f_n = 0.7 \cdot TNR_n^2 + 0.25 \cdot TPR_n^2 + 0.05 \cdot c_n. \tag{9}$$

In our case for the desired behavior of the ball detection, the $TNR$ is much more important than the $TPR$. Hence, this component is assigned the largest weight. The search space is already limited to topologies which are feasible for inference on the target system. Therefore, the inference complexity is weighted with a very low weight in the fitness function. If networks have similar classification performance the smaller network is preferred. These weights were chosen based on empirical considerations.

For networks with a good classification performance it is disproportionally difficult to further increase the *TNR* and *TPR*. Thus, the *TNR* and *TPR* are squared in the fitness function.

# 4   Data Acquisition

## 4.1   Data Setup

The data used for training and evaluation of the classifier were collected during various events (RoboCup 2017, Iran Open 2017, German Open 2017, weekly test games). It consists of 16880 positive examples (candidate images containing a ball) and 23876 negative examples (candidate images not containing a ball). During training negative examples are subsampled randomly to ensure that in every cross-validation set the same amount of positive and negative examples are present.

## 4.2   Candidate Generation

The training data is collected directly on the robot to ensure equally sampled data during training and inference. This allows an iterative process consisting of the following steps.

1. Training a network with the collected data.
2. Running the newly trained model in a test environment while collecting data not yet seen by the network.
3. Labeling newly collected data and evaluating classification performance based on the test set.

### 4.2.1   Generating Seeds
In the first step of the candidate generation the algorithm determines seeds for possible candidates. The image is segmented using vertical scan lines on every second column of the image. The two dimensional gradient is computed along the scan lines. Whenever this gradient exceeds a preconfigured threshold a new segment along this scan line is created. The median of five pixels equally distributed over the segment determines the color of the segment. A seed is the central pixel of a segment which passes a series of checks.

1. The luminance of the corresponding region must be lower than 100 which naturally corresponds to the black patches of the ball.
2. The corresponding ball radius in pixels $r_p$ at the seed's position is determined by projecting the assumed ball onto the image. If the ratio $r_s = \frac{l_s}{r_p}$ of the segment's length $l_s$ to the pixel radius is not within the range $[0.1, 0.7]$ the seed is dropped.

3. Neighboring areas of the black patch are checked. Therefore the luminance in eight directions around the seed with a distance of $\frac{r_p}{2.5}$ are sampled. All of those sampled values must be slightly higher than the luminance of the seed. Also, five of those values must have a significant difference in luminance.

If all conditions match, the seed is used for the candidate generation.

### 4.2.2   Merging Seeds To Candidates

Seeds are merged into a single candidate if they are close to each other. First, an empty set of candidates is initialized. For every seed in the image it is checked if there is a nearby candidate with a maximum distance of a ball diameter in pixels. If a candidate is found the current seed will be merged into that candidate by taking the mean of the position and radius. Otherwise a new one with position and radius of the current seed is added. Afterwards candidates are filtered such that only candidates based on at least two seeds remain.

### 4.2.3   Reprojection of Found Balls

Our existing software framework features a filter to estimate the ball state. The physical model of the ball is used to predict the ball position in the current image which yields another candidate.

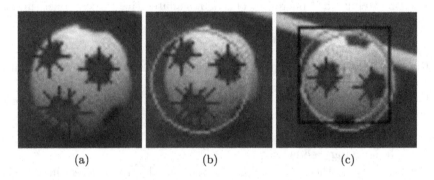

(a)                    (b)                    (c)

**Fig. 2.** Visualization of ball candidates [3, pp. 17–18]. (a) Seed is corresponding to the center of the black patches on the ball. (b) Merged seeds and projection of the corresponding ball radius. (c) Reprojected ball from result of the ball filter (green circle bounded black rectangle). (Color figure online)

## 5   Experiments and Evaluation

The computational power of the NAO is severely limited. Therefore, designing the CNN using the genetic algorithm is done offline on a more powerful machine. The resulting network is transferred to the robot and is evaluated in a final generalization test. The classification performance is measured based on labeled data collected by the candidate generation.

## 5.1 Setup

In every experiment 15 generations with 50 networks in each generation were evaluated. The worst 10% in each generation were excluded from reproduction. The mutation probability was set to $\frac{1}{16}$ according to the maximum number of degrees of freedom of the given search space.

The algorithm should be able to design a CNN as a solution to the ball detection problem considering a limited amount of training data. To show that this can be achieved three experiments were conducted, sampling 25%, 50% and 100% of the available training data.

## 5.2 Results

For the experiment with 25% of the data the best networks in the last generation reached a TNR of 0.91 to 0.95 with a TPR of about 50% to 75%. The resulting network has a very small sample size of $8 \times 8$, one convolutional layer of four masks and only three hidden layers in the fully connected part.

With 50% of data the best networks in the last generation reached a TNR of about 0.93 with a TPR above 0.85. Networks with one large convolutional layer and mainly three hidden layers in the fully connected part dominated this experiment.

With the full amount of data the best networks in the last generation reached a TNR of about 0.95 with a TPR above 0.90. While the sample size and convolutional layers remained similar to those in the second experiment, the fully connected part converged to four hidden layers instead of three.

## 5.3 Evaluation

In early generations of the first experiment networks with a very high TNR also had a very low TPR as Fig. 3a illustrates. These individuals were eliminated due to the weights of the fitness function. Networks of the last generation were highly biased to reject input which yields a high TNR while having a poor TPR. Classification performance in the second experiment was significantly higher. Therefore, not only individuals with a bad TNR were eliminated but also the TPR converged over time. Figure 3b shows that there were no outliers with a TPR below 0.70 in later generations. Figure 3c shows that later generations of the final experiment also formed a very dense cluster. Hence, the algorithm could not really find a much better solution throughout generations but was able to select better networks and remove outliers.

The network having the highest score in the last generation is considered to be the resulting network. Table 1 shows a summary of those networks in each experiment. Networks became more complex while increasing the amount of data resulting in better classification performance.

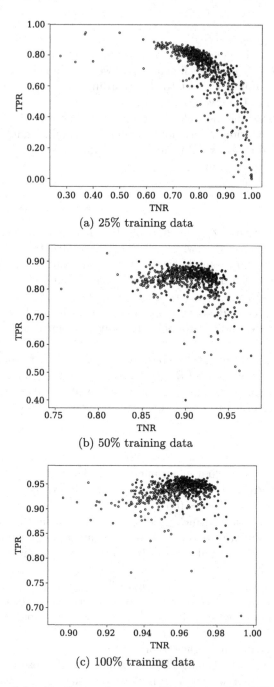

(a) 25% training data

(b) 50% training data

(c) 100% training data

**Fig. 3.** Evolution of classification performance. Note that scaling differs between experiments as the overall results got better. Results of the first generation are plotted with white filled circles. Results of the following generations are plotted in increasingly darker shades of gray.

**Table 1.** Overview of the resulting networks of experiments. Column *Exp* lists the number of the experiment. The second column *Data* corresponds to the amount of data used. Columns *TNR*, *TPR* and *Comp* show the components of the fitness function. Note that the *TNR* and *TPR* parts are the lower bound approximations described in Eqs. (4) and (5). Column *Score* corresponds to the resulting score.

| Exp | Data | TNR | TPR | Comp | Score |
|---|---|---|---|---|---|
| 1 | 25% | 0.921 | 0.700 | 0.732 | 0.856 |
| 2 | 50% | 0.932 | 0.853 | 0.663 | 0.899 |
| 3 | 100% | 0.972 | 0.958 | 0.638 | 0.922 |

## 5.4   Generalization Test

The best network of the last generation that was trained with all of the training data is subjected to a final generalization test. This final network is evaluated with data collected in another environment which can be considered to be a proper generalization test because no data from these testing conditions was used during training. The classifier predicted 4989 of 5687 positives and 12680 of 12730 negatives correctly resulting in a $TNR = 0.99$ and a $TPR = 0.87$.

## 5.5   Runtime Analysis on the NAO Robot

The whole ball detection including the resulting network running on the NAO was evaluated. For this test we fixed the number of generated candidates per image to the average amount five to get stable measurement results. Figure 4 shows the result of those measurements. With an average runtime of about 8 ms on the top and 4 ms on the bottom camera we reached our real-time criteria which is 30 ms for a vision cycle.

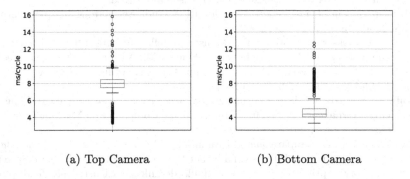

(a) Top Camera              (b) Bottom Camera

**Fig. 4.** Runtime of the ball detection including the resulting network on the NAO. The green line indicates the mean of the runtime. The interquartile range is shown by the blue box. The upper black bar illustrates the 0.75-quantile, respectively the lower black bar the 0.25-quantile. The circles correspond to outliers. (Color figure online)

## 6   Conclusion

The goal of this paper was to optimize the topology of neural networks with respect to classification performance and inference complexity simultaneously. We presented a genetic framework that was successfully applied to the problem of black and white ball detection using little computational power. Our experiments showed that a genetic approach is able to identify a small yet efficient network suitable for a specific classification task. The presented optimization strategy obtains suitable hyperparameters even with limited amount of training data. However, the optimization of the architecture needs a lot of computation time as the algorithm has to train and evaluate plenty of CNNs, in our case 2250 networks. Thus, applying the presented optimization strategy to classification problems that require significantly more complex networks may be infeasible.

In order to enhance convergence speed future work should focus on evaluating different variants of genetic algorithms such as elitism [1]. Additionally, we would like to apply the approach to multiclass problems using a modified fitness function.

## References

1. Baluja, S., Caruana, R.: Removing the genetics from the standard genetic algorithm. Technical report CMU-CS-95-141. Pittsburgh, PA: Carnegie Mellon University, May 1995
2. Budden, D., Fenn, S., Walker, J., Mendes, A.: A novel approach to ball detection for humanoid robot soccer. In: Thielscher, M., Zhang, D. (eds.) AI 2012. LNCS (LNAI), vol. 7691, pp. 827–838. Springer, Heidelberg (2012). https://doi.org/10.1007/978-3-642-35101-3_70
3. Felbinger, G.C.: A genetic approach to design convolutional neural networks for the purpose of a ball detection on the NAO robotic system. Project Work, October 2017. https://www.hulks.de/_files/PA_Georg-Felbinger.pdf
4. Harbich, S.: Einführung genetischer Algorithmen mit Anwendungsbeispiel. Universität Magdeburg, December 2007
5. Härtl, A., Visser, U., Röfer, T.: Robust and efficient object recognition for a humanoid soccer robot. In: Behnke, S., Veloso, M., Visser, A., Xiong, R. (eds.) RoboCup 2013. LNCS (LNAI), vol. 8371, pp. 396–407. Springer, Heidelberg (2014). https://doi.org/10.1007/978-3-662-44468-9_35
6. Ioffe, S., Szegedy, C.: Batch normalization: accelerating deep network training by reducing internal covariate shift. In: International Conference on Machine Learning, pp. 448–456, March 2015
7. Kahlefendt, C.: A Comparison and Evaluation of Neural Network-based Classification Approaches for the Purpose of a Robot Detection on the Nao Robotic System. Project Work. April 2017. http://www.hulks.de/_files/PA_Chris-Kahlefendt.pdf
8. Menashe, J., et al.: Fast and precise black and white ball detection for RoboCup soccer. In: Akiyama, H., Obst, O., Sammut, C., Tonidandel, F. (eds.) RoboCup 2017. LNCS (LNAI), vol. 11175, pp. 45–58. Springer, Cham (2018). https://doi.org/10.1007/978-3-030-00308-1_4
9. Mitchel, M.: An Introduction to Genetic Algorithms A Bradford Book. The MIT Press, Cambridge (1999). ISBN 0-262-63185-7

10. Stanley, K.O., Miikkulainen, R.: Evolving neural networks through augmenting topologies. Evol. Comput. **10**(2), 99–127 (2002). http://nn.cs.utexas.edu/?stanley:ec02
11. Sun, Y., Xue, B., Zhang, M.: Evolving deep convolutional neural networks for image classification. In: CoRR abs/1710.10741 (2017). arXiv: 1710.10741. url: http://arxiv.org/abs/1710.10741

# ImageTagger: An Open Source Online Platform for Collaborative Image Labeling

Niklas Fiedler[1,2]($\boxtimes$), Marc Bestmann[1,2], and Norman Hendrich[2]

[1] Hamburg Bit-Bots, Department of Informatics, University of Hamburg,
Vogt-Kölln-Straße 30, 22527 Hamburg, Germany
{5fiedler,bestmann}@informatik.uni-hamburg.de
[2] TAMS, Department of Informatics, University of Hamburg,
Vogt-Kölln-Straße 30, 22527 Hamburg, Germany
hendrich@informatik.uni-hamburg.de
http://robocup.informatik.uni-hamburg.de

**Abstract.** The need for labeled training data for object recognition in RoboCup increased due to the spread of deep learning approaches. Creating large sets of training images from different environments and annotating the recorded objects is difficult for a single RoboCup team.

This paper presents our tool *ImageTagger* which facilitates creating and sharing such data sets. The tool is already being successfully used in RoboCup Soccer, and a large amount of labeled data is publicly available. Other leagues are invited to use this tool to create data for their contexts.

**Keywords:** RoboCup · Open source · Image labeling · Deep learning

## 1 Introduction

The approaches for object recognition in RoboCup Soccer evolved significantly during the last few years. This was triggered by rule changes in multiple leagues, replacing the simple color-coded environment with a realistic one. Combined with the increase of the field size and the change to artificial grass ball and goal recognition got more difficult, and previously popular algorithms, e. g. [5] were not able to reliably detect objects over large distances anymore. Therefore, many teams started to use different kinds of machine learning techniques [4,11,12]. A huge amount of labeled images is needed for training deep neural networks, which requires a lot of image recording and labeling. Furthermore, in order to achieve good training sets, multiple recording locations, e. g. different RoboCup competitions and various objects have to be used.

This makes it very difficult for a single team, especially for a new one, to achieve large, high-quality training sets. This problem also exists in other leagues, e. g. RoboCup@Home, where objects and environment change from year to year.

The workload can be lowered by either providing a tool which enables faster labeling or by sharing training data with other teams. We tried to achieve both

© Springer Nature Switzerland AG 2019
D. Holz et al. (Eds.): RoboCup 2018, LNAI 11374, pp. 162–169, 2019.
https://doi.org/10.1007/978-3-030-27544-0_13

by implementing an online tool called *ImageTagger*. It provides intuitive user interfaces for labeling images, for verifying annotations and for managing image sets. The labels are saved internally in a common format to ensure compatibility but can be exported in user-defined formats, so that no changes in the existing training processes of the teams are needed. The integrated user and permission management system allows the team admins to decide which of their image sets are be public or private. While these features allow collaboration in any RoboCup league, this paper will focus on our results in the soccer context.

The remainder of the paper is structured as follows: first, already existing tools are compared to ImageTagger in Sect. 2. The core features of our tool are explained in Sect. 3 and an evaluation of the tool is provided in Sect. 4. The paper concludes with a summary and an outlook to future work in Sect. 5.

## 2 Related Work

Manual labeling of images for object recognition is a common task since it is needed for many supervised learning approaches. Therefore, many different tools

**Table 1.** List of commonly used image labeling tools compared by compliance to requirements for collaboration of RoboCup teams.

| | Online | Open Source | Label Types (shapes) | Label Categories | Export Format | User/Permission Management | Verification | Label Import | Image Preloading | Image Upload | Image Management |
|---|---|---|---|---|---|---|---|---|---|---|---|
| sloth [6] | | ✓ | user definable | user definable | self impl. | 0 | | 0 | 0 | 0 | 0 |
| Ratsnake [8] | | (free) | polygon, grid | user definable | multiple | 0 | | 0 | 0 | 0 | 0 |
| LabelImg [9] | | ✓ | polygon | user definable | PASCAL VOC | 0 | | 0 | 0 | 0 | 0 |
| via [7] | ✓ | ✓ | multiple | free text | JSON, CSV | | | | 2 | ✓ | |
| Rhoban Tagger [3] | ✓ | ✓ | binary | admin defined | JSON | 1 | ✓ | | | | |
| LabelMe [10] | ✓ | ✓ | polygon | free text | XML | | | | | ✓ | ✓ |
| Labelbox [2] | ✓ | | admin defined | admin defined | JSON, CSV | ✓ | | | ✓ | ✓ | ✓ |
| **ImageTagger** | ✓ | ✓ | multiple | admin defined | user definable | ✓ | ✓ | ✓ | ✓ | ✓ | ✓ |

[0] Not applicable in an offline tool    [1] Users start in training mode
[2] Images are stored in the browser cache

already exist. Though, none of the programs presented in Table 1 offers the combination of labeling with other features (e. g. online image access, user, and annotation management) needed to allow collaboration between teams.

Proprietary products are difficult to use in a community like RoboCup because they are not customizable enough to fit the specific requirements of the environment. Furthermore, teams cannot contribute to the development and implement desired features for the whole community.

Offline tools are afflicted by multiple problems such as the installation process and compatibility issues. The main reason to exclude them from our options is the image and label management. Multiple team members need to coordinate their work and progress, and the files they are working with.

Most of the competing online tools require a lot of server-side management of images and annotations, which makes it difficult for multiple teams and users to work together efficiently. While a cloud could handle the image exchange between multiple users, it lacks useful metadata about these image collections (e. g. location or description of the situation) and most notably the labels in a universal format. For online tools, the image preloading feature is essential to overcome the latency to the server which gets significantly high for large images and high distances between the users and the server. The ability to export the labels in a format defined by the teams themselves is required for sharing the image and label data. In this domain, the ImageTagger offers customizability comparable to self-implementation of the export for every user. In the RoboCup environment, the amount of label categories is rather limited. It proved to be a faster way to label only one category at a time, which is easily applicable in the RoboCup environment.

## 3    ImageTagger Overview and Features

ImageTagger provides an efficient browser-based user interface for all required tasks: image labeling, verifying annotations, up- and downloading images/labels, managing users and teams, and the definition of image and label categories. The

**Fig. 1.** Exemplary labels from categories common in RoboCup soccer. Precise labels are created to allow learning of exact object localization.

software is written in Python, using the web framework Django. Its key features are explained in the following subsections.

## 3.1   Manual Labeling

The *annotation view* allows the user to create labels (Fig. 1) on images. The ImageTagger offers tools to create bounding box, polygon, line and point annotations (Fig. 2). Since this is a highly repetitive task, it has to be done as fast as possible. Therefore, the images are sorted in a list which can be filtered by existing label types (e. g. ball). The user then iterates through the images using shortcuts, leaving the mouse free for creating annotations. Successive images get preloaded while the user creates an annotation for the current image, allowing a fast transition to the following image. An option to keep the last annotation enables faster labeling since the image sets are often created sequentially and require only a small adaption in the position of the label between two images. Labels can be marked as "blurred" and "concealed". Existing annotations are listed below the image and can be drawn into the image if needed. The option to label a category as "not in the image" allows users to create negative data.

**Fig. 2.** The *annotation view* while creating a ball annotation. On the **left** is a list of images which can be filtered for missing annotations. In the **center**, the image is displayed and an annotation can be created. On the **right**, controls are provided, most of which can also be accessed via keyboard shortcuts for speed.

## 3.2   Automated and Offline Labeling

ImageTagger enables users to upload existing labels to its database. This upload feature allows users to share labels between multiple instances of ImageTagger, to restore local backups of labels and to migrate existing training data which was created with other tools.

Some deep learning methods, e. g. deep FCNNs, are not applicable during RoboCup games due to their runtime, but they can be used to create labels automatically. The results do not need to be optimal since users can verify the labels after uploading them (cf. Sect. 3.3).

### 3.3   Label Verification

To ensure sufficient accuracy and quality of the image labels, ImageTagger includes a special mode for label verification. The *verification view* allows permitted users to inspect a label and give it a positive or negative verification. As the annotation view, it preloads the images and annotations to reduce the perceived latency. Additionally, it is optimized for mobile usage. A positive verification increases the verification level of a label, while a negative one decreases it. The verification is a binary decision; thus it is much faster than the labeling process itself.

A manually created annotation is automatically positively verified by the user creating it. This results in label data where one positive verification means that at least one human considered the annotation as acceptable. Therefore, a verification count of two or more can be considered as sufficient for most use cases.

### 3.4   Image Management

To keep the high number of images required for most deep learning approaches manageable, images are grouped into *image sets*. Each set has a context, e. g. the same ball and field type, and belongs to a team. The *image set view* consists of an image list like the annotation view, general information, a management section, an export section and links to manage the annotations of the set. Members of the team that owns the image set can update the name, location, and description of the set and upload new images or labels. The *image-lock* option can be selected to disable further image upload to keep sets in a static state, e. g. to provide an immutable benchmarking set.

### 3.5   Collaboration

The labeling process is easy for humans, but it is a tedious and time-consuming task. Thus, collaboration is necessary to reduce the workload on each team. However, different algorithms [4,11,12] usually expect their own specific categories and data representations, leading to a high variance in requirements that the tool has to accommodate. To make labels usable for multiple teams, use cases and processing approaches, ImageTagger allows the creation of custom export formats. For every export format, the creator chooses which label categories to include and whether blurred or concealed labels are included. The user employs placeholders (cf. Table 2) which get replaced with the corresponding values in the export creation. All values representing a measure or coordinate in the image are available in an absolute or relative (to the size of the image) form. Resulting from the variable amount of points in a label, the list of x- and y-values has to be generated following a user-defined pattern. The "concealed" and "blurred" flags can be exported by defining text which is only included in the export of the label when the corresponding flag is (not) set.

**Table 2.** The available placeholders according to their contexts. Each value is provided in an absolute pixel value or as a value relative to the image size. The file name format specifies the format of the name of the export file, which the user can download. The image placeholders are only used when the user selects the option to aggregate the labels by images. The vector placeholders are used to generate the list of x/y values for label types with a variable number of points.

| file name placeholders |
| --- |
| name, team, location and unique id of the image set |

| image set placeholders |
| --- |
| name, team, location, description of the image set |
| the content of the image/label format |

| image placeholders (optional) |
| --- |
| name of the image/image set |
| width/height of the image |
| number of labels for the image |
| the content of the label format |

| label placeholders |
| --- |
| name of the image/image set |
| width/height of the image |
| label category |
| the amount of verifications for the label |
| width/height, center/upper left/lower right point, mean height/diameter of the label |
| representation of the vector |
| alternative text for "not in image" labels |

| vector placeholders (optional) |
| --- |
| the number of the current point |
| x/y-coordinate of the current point |

In addition to a simple list of annotations, the option to concatenate the annotations (cf. Fig. 3) by images is given. Depending on the chosen option, the user has to define an image set format, an image format (only when the label concatenation is used) and a label format. Created export formats can be saved privately or publicly and can be used by other users.

**Fig. 3.** export format composition hierarchy with (**right**) and without (**left**) label aggregation by image

While most of the data management is handled by ImageTagger, some tasks need to be processed locally on a system, e. g. the creation of rosbags or writing the label data into the metadata of the images.

Tools, designed for those tasks can be shared using ImageTagger since some of them can be useful for multiple teams in a shared instance.

A permission management system for users and teams is needed to be able to create and share training data in a controlled way. Read and write permissions of image sets can be set by the owning team.

The variety of collaboration options allows teams to define whether they work together with the whole community in every way, to just share the training data without the possibility to collaborate or to keep the set completely private. The distinction between users and admins in a team helps to coordinate the members. To motivate the users to keep labeling and to detect wrongly labeling users, a scoring system was introduced. The score of a user is the sum of positive minus the sum of the negative verifications that were made on the annotations created by the user. This way good annotations are rewarded and wrong annotations are penalized. In the user explore view and the team view, the users are ranked, based on their score. The team view offers a 30-day user high score to focus on a shorter timespan, to make it possible for new team members to compete with the rest and engage users to keep up their effort over a longer time period.

## 4   Evaluation

We provide a public ImageTagger instance for the RoboCup Soccer environment. The server is open for everyone to log in, to download existing images and annotations, or to upload images, label them and verify the labels. See Table 3 for our current server statistics. At the moment, there are 119 public image sets recorded in the RoboCup environment available for download. They belong to participating teams, most notably Hamburg Bit-Bots, Nao Devils and WF Wolves. Based on these sets, team Bit-Bots recently proposed a ball localization challenge, which gives teams a benchmark to compare their approaches [1]. The training data was used to train neural networks proposed by Daniel Speck [13].

**Table 3.** Current numbers on our instance of the ImageTagger of images and labels (**left**) as well as users and teams (**right**).

| | image sets | images | ball labels | robot labels | goalpost labels | users (50+ labels) | teams | active teams (2+ active users) |
|---|---|---|---|---|---|---|---|---|
| all | 171 | 171,057 | 95,352 | 41,016 | 18,800 | 50 | 61 | 6 |
| public | 119 | 155,602 | 92,588 | 37,981 | 17,004 | | | |

## 5   Conclusion and Further Work

In this paper, we presented a tool which facilitates the production and sharing of labeled image data for supervised learning in object recognition. It is already actively used by multiple teams in the Humanoid and Standard Platform League, and image sets from future RoboCup competitions will be uploaded.

Currently, the tool is only used in the soccer context, but it would be possible to use it for other areas as well, e. g. labeling household objects for the @Home League. The modular design allows the adaption of the labeling interface also for the labeling of RGB-D data while keeping the rest of the framework. In the future, the usability of the tool should be improved for usage on mobile systems to enable precise labeling on tablets and smartphones.

We encourage other RoboCup Soccer teams to use the public ImageTagger instance hosted on our server, to download training sets, and to upload further images and labels: https://imagetagger.bit-bots.de
The project source code is available at:
https://github.com/bit-bots/imagetagger

**Acknowledgments.** Thanks to the RoboCup teams Hamburg Bit-Bots, Nao Devils and WF Wolves for taking part in the development. Thanks to the Server AG. Thanks to the contributors, particularly to Timon Engelke, Rebecca Glaser, Jonas Hagge, Jennifer Meyer, Daniel Speck, and Pascal Wichmann.

This research was partially funded by the German Research Foundation (DFG) and the National Science Foundation of China (NSFC) in project Crossmodal Learning, TRR-169.

# References

1. Bit-bots ball localization challenge. https://robocup.informatik.uni-hamburg.de/en/documents/bit-bots-ball-localization-challenge-2018/. Accessed 31 Mar 2018
2. Labelbox. https://www.labelbox.io/. Accessed 25 May 2018
3. Rhoban tagger. http://rhoban.com/tagger/index.php. Accessed 30 Mar 2018
4. Albani, D., Youssef, A., Suriani, V., Nardi, D., Bloisi, D.D.: A deep learning approach for object recognition with NAO soccer robots. In: Behnke, S., Sheh, R., Sarıel, S., Lee, D.D. (eds.) RoboCup 2016. LNCS (LNAI), vol. 9776, pp. 392–403. Springer, Cham (2017). https://doi.org/10.1007/978-3-319-68792-6_33
5. Budden, D., Fenn, S., Walker, J., Mendes, A.: A novel approach to ball detection for humanoid robot soccer. In: Thielscher, M., Zhang, D. (eds.) AI 2012. LNCS (LNAI), vol. 7691, pp. 827–838. Springer, Heidelberg (2012). https://doi.org/10.1007/978-3-642-35101-3_70
6. Bäuml, M.: Sloth documentation (2014). http://sloth.readthedocs.io/en/latest/
7. Dutta, A., Gupta, A., Zissermann, A.: VGG image annotator (VIA) (2016). http://www.robots.ox.ac.uk/~vgg/software/via/. Accessed 10 Mar 2018
8. Iakovidis, D., Goudas, T., Smailis, C., Maglogiannis, I.: Ratsnake: a versatile image annotation tool with application to computer-aided diagnosis. Sci. World J. (2014). https://doi.org/10.1155/2014/286856
9. Lin, T.: Labelimg. https://github.com/tzutalin/labelImg. Accessed 29 Mar 2018
10. Russell, B.C., Torralba, A., Murphy, K.P., Freeman, W.T.: Labelme: a database and web-based tool for image annotation. Int. J. Comput. Vis. **77**(1–3), 157–173 (2008). https://doi.org/10.1007/s11263-007-0090-8
11. Schnekenburger, F., Scharffenberg, M., Wülker, M., Hochberg, U., Dorer, K.: Detection and localization of features on a soccer field with feedforward fully convolutional neural networks (FCNN) for the adult-size humanoid robot Sweaty. In: Proceedings of the 12th Workshop on Humanoid Soccer Robots, IEEE-RAS International Conference on Humanoid Robots, Birmingham (2017)
12. Speck, D., Barros, P., Weber, C., Wermter, S.: Ball localization for robocup soccer using convolutional neural networks. In: Behnke, S., Sheh, R., Sarıel, S., Lee, D.D. (eds.) RoboCup 2016. LNCS (LNAI), vol. 9776, pp. 19–30. Springer, Cham (2017). https://doi.org/10.1007/978-3-319-68792-6_2
13. Speck, D., Bestmann, M., Barros, P.: Towards real-time ball localization using CNNS. In: Holz, D. et al. (eds.) RoboCup 2018. LNAI, vol. 11374, pp. xx–yy. Springer, Heidelberg (2018)

# Mimicking an Expert Team Through the Learning of Evaluation Functions from Action Sequences

Takuya Fukushima[1(✉)], Tomoharu Nakashima[1], and Hidehisa Akiyama[2]

[1] Osaka Prefecture University, Osaka, Japan
{takuya.fukushima,tomoharu.nakashima}@kis.osakafu-u.ac.jp
[2] Fukuoka University, Fukuoka, Japan
akym@fukuoka-u.ac.jp

**Abstract.** In the RoboCup Soccer Simulation 2D League, the performance of teams highly leans on the evaluation functions used for their decision making process. The aim of this paper is to propose a method that improves the performance of a team by mimicking a stronger one. For this purpose, a neural network is employed to model an expert team's evaluation function. The neural network is trained by using positive and negative episodes of action sequences that are extracted from game logs. In our experiments, we successfully improved the performance (e.g., win rate, scored goal, and so on) of our team by mimicking the winner of RoboCup 2017 soccer simulation 2D league.

**Keywords:** Soccer simulation · Machine learning ·
Supervised learning · Evaluation function · Decision making

## 1   Introduction

In the game of RoboCup soccer simulation 2D league, player agents make a decision at each cycle in real time. A game consists of 6000 cycles (excluding periods of set-play), thus the decision making process of each player is executed about 6000 times. Therefore, the performance of a team highly leans on the decision process of its agents. Akiyama *et al.* [1] implemented a tree search algorithm for the decision making process in the RoboCup soccer simulation. Each node (which corresponds to an action) is assessed by an evaluation function during the tree search. Then, the node with the highest value is selected as the action to take. Evaluation functions are commonly tuned by hand: for example, additional points if the ball is close to the goal, or deducting points if the possibility of an opponent's interception is high. Akiyama and Nakashima [2] also described that using an evaluation function including such rules gives higher team performance than using a simple function with no rules. However, tuning such an evaluation function is laborious and provides sub-optimal results most of the time. In addition, since there is no perfect strategy, it is difficult to win against all teams

© Springer Nature Switzerland AG 2019
D. Holz et al. (Eds.): RoboCup 2018, LNAI 11374, pp. 170–180, 2019.
https://doi.org/10.1007/978-3-030-27544-0_14

with a single game plan. As a result, when implementing a team, it is common to define various strategies. In this case, each strategy might require its own evaluation function. Therefore, it is desirable to have an automatic method to tune them.

In a previous work, we tried to solve this task by using a four-layered neural network [3]. Evaluation functions could be tuned successfully by using supervised learning with a training set that was extracted from an expert team's behavior. However, it did not improve the performance of the team. This was caused by a strong relationship between evaluation functions and action candidates. Action candidates are generated around the kicker or receivers, thus team formations should correspond to the expert players' positioning in order to solve this problem.

The aim of this paper is to solve this problem by proposing a method that makes the team mimic an expert team known to play soccer well. If player agents imitate the experts' behaviors, the team would be able to win against opponents it could not defeat with a simple or hand-coded evaluator. In this work, we model the expert's decision making process by using a neural network. The neural network evaluates the action for the next cycle, and is trained by supervised learning. In the experiments, we evaluate the performance of the team using the modeled decision making process by counting the number of times the ball enters into a target area, scored goals and successful through passes. The proposed method is compared with a team using a simple or hand-coded evaluation function. Moreover, we investigate whether all players should use the same evaluation function or not.

## 2   Related Work

The recent advances in deep learning have allowed the design of successful methods in various control domains by using either supervised learning or reinforcement learning. For example, Warnell et al. [4] proposed a method that uses the representational power of deep neural networks in order to learn complex tasks, such as the Atari game BOWLING, in a short amount of time with a human trainer. Stanescu et al. [5] presented a deep convolutional neural network to evaluate states in real-time strategy games. Silver et al. [6,7] used deep neural networks to evaluate board positions and to select moves in the game of Go. In the case of soccer game, Hong et al. [8] proposed a deep policy inference Q-network that targets multi-agent systems. Their model is evaluated in a simulated soccer game whose field is a grid world. In the RoboCup environment, especially the soccer simulation league, it is difficult to train deep neural networks to evaluate actions because the soccer field is a continuous environment. Therefore, supervised learning and reinforcement learning are applied to simple experimental settings [9,10], such as "one on one" or "keepaway". Deep learning methods are also used for offline game analysis [11]. These researches were applied to improve not team performances but a single player's behavior or decision making. Therefore, it would be difficult to apply these approaches to multi-agent systems.

On the other hand, not an individual policy but team strategies improvement are required to defeat opponents in a soccer game. In soccer simulation 2D league, various strategies are implemented by teams to win the competition, and it becomes difficult to win against all teams with a single strategy. For these reasons, in a previous work, we proposed a model that determines the best player formation for corner-kick situations to switch our strategies [12]. Moreover, we proposed a model that identifies the opponent defensive strategies in an online manner [13].

Floyd *et al.* [14] proposed a case-based reasoning approach to imitate player agents in terms of action selection. Their approach focused on imitating low-level actions (i.e., dash, kick, turn). In this paper, in order to create new strategies, we approximate the evaluation function of an expert team to score high level actions (i.e., pass, dribble, shoot) by using a deep/shallow neural network. Unlike [9] and [10], the neural networks can learn strategies because the training data consist of kick sequences. Moreover, the aim of our method is not improving an individual behavior but mimicking team strategies.

## 3    Action Selection

A cooperative action planning by tree search method [1] is employed to model the players' decision making process. In this model, an action plan is created by generating and exploring a decision tree at the time of kicking the ball. Nodes of the tree correspond to situations of the soccer field, and edges correspond to the actions that players take. An evaluation value is assigned to each node. The action plan is defined as a fixed-length action sequence that the player should perform from the next cycle. In this work, we explore the tree by using a best-first search strategy.

The generation of an action plan is done as follows. First, the current state is stored in the root node of the decision tree. Actions (pass, dribble, shoot, etc.) that can involve other players as well as itself are generated based on the current state and predicted state observed by itself. At this moment, it precisely calculates whether it is an executable action or not. If it is not the case, the action is deleted. Therefore, only possible actions are generated as a candidate. Then, generated actions are evaluated by an evaluation function. The action, the state, and the evaluation value are stored as a child node in the decision tree. Once all nodes have been added, the node with the highest value is selected, and further action candidates are generated from this node with the predicted state. The decision tree is expanded by repeating this procedure, and the action planning is executed. When the depth of the tree reaches a fixed threshold, if an action cannot be generated from the predicted state of the node, or even when an action set in the terminal condition of the action sequence is generated, the child node generation at the leaf node is not performed. Connecting the node strings to the generated decision tree provides action sequences. Once the search process completes, the node with the maximal value in the generated action sequences is taken as the action plan. Thanks to the action planning, players can select higher strategic action by considering the above-mentioned proactive approach.

Figure 1 depicts an example decision tree. For the sake of simplicity, only an evaluation value of each action is indicated in each node and actions are written on the edges. This example shows that actions generated in the soccer field are one dribble and two passes. Then, each action is evaluated by the evaluation function. Since in this example, dribble is the first action that maximizes the evaluation function, executable actions are generated from this action node. In Fig. 1, the resulting action plan would be the sequence of a pass and a shoot.

In this paper, we focus on the efficient development of evaluation functions, which is an important factor of designing decision making. In order to make strong teams, it is necessary for each player to select the best actions. Generally, evaluation functions are almost made by hand. Thus, they are not necessarily optimal. In addition, designing such a function needs a trial-and-error iterative process. Therefore, in this work, we investigate the use of supervised learning to automatically design the optimal function.

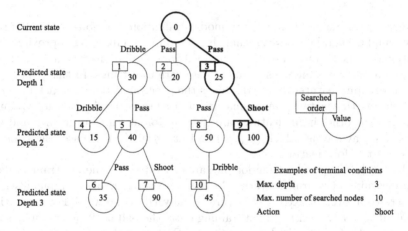

**Fig. 1.** Example of an action plan

## 4    Learning Evaluation Functions by Neural Networks

Positive and negative episodes of kick sequences have to be defined in order to train neural networks by using a supervised learning approach. In this paper, we consider as positive episodes, sequences of kicks that end up into the opponent's penalty area. On the other hand, sequences that end up outside this area, are considered as negative episodes (i.e., opponents' interceptions). The target value for the negative episodes is defined as 0, while that for the positive ones is 1. Figure 2 depicts examples of such episodes, where red lines represent positive episodes and dotted blue lines correspond to negative ones. From Fig. 2, we can see that an episode consists of a series of ball coordinates.

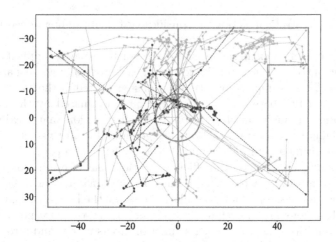

**Fig. 2.** Extracted positive episodes (red lines) and negative episodes (dotted blue lines) (Color figure online)

Neural networks are employed to model evaluation functions. The main reason we employ neural networks is that they are universal function approximators. Additionally, the architecture of a neural network can be easily changed. Therefore, neural networks allow us to investigate various settings. In this paper, two versions of input features are used. One is the position at the next kick $(x_n, y_n)$, which means that a two-dimensional input feature vector is used for training data. And the other input features are the position at the current kick and the ball position at the next kick $((x_c, y_c)$ and $(x_n, y_n))$. In this case, the training data consist of four features.

The extracted episodes from log files are converted to generate training data for the learning of neural networks. As there are two versions of input features as described above, an extracted feature is analyzed in two ways. For generating training data for two-dimensional training data, the ball positions in an episode are separated into individual ball positions. Each of such ball positions is used as a training vector which consists of the ball position $(x_n, y_n)$ as well as a positive/negative target value. This process is shown in the above side of Fig. 3. On the other hand, in the case of four-dimensional training data, a pair of successive two ball positions are used to generate a training vector. The former term of the pair is regarded as the current ball position and the latter is the predicted ball position at the next kick. Each of the two ball positions in the pair is concatenated to generate a four-dimensional input vector $(x_c, y_c, x_n, y_n)$. The target value for the generated vector is determined by the label (i.e., positive or negative) that is associated with the episode that the four-dimensional vector was generated from. The lower part of Fig. 3 shows this process.

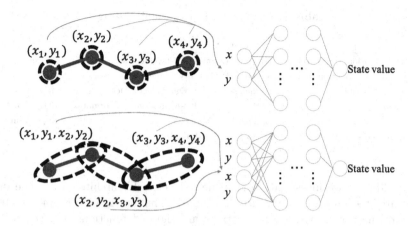

**Fig. 3.** Conversion of an episode into training data

# 5  Experiments

## 5.1  Experimental Settings

We evaluate the performance of evaluation functions modeled by neural networks that are trained with using supervised learning. Performances are evaluated by counting the number of times the ball enters into a target area, scored goals and successful through passes. Training data such as passes and dribbles were extracted from the game logs between an expert and an opponent team. HELIOS2017 [15], which won the RoboCup2017 tournament in soccer simulation 2D league, was employed as the expert. On the other hand, HillStone [16], which won the eighth position was employed as the opponent team. In this experiment, we tried to defeat the target team by making our own team, opuSCOM, mimic the expert team (i.e., HELIOS2017). opuSCOM is developed by Osaka Prefecture University for JapanOpen competitions, which is the Japanese national RoboCup contest. We designated Hillstone as our target team because while it is not a top ranked team, it is much more stronger than our team opuSCOM. On the other hand, we chose HELIOS2017 as the expert team since it is one of the top rank teams for several years. In addition, opuSCOM and HELIOS2017 share the same base code, Agent2D (HELIOS base) [17], which is currently one of the most popular base code for the RoboCup soccer simulation 2D league. Particularly, their formation configuration files are almost the same. Therefore, it should be easy for opuSCOM to copy the HELIOS2017's formation strategies.

In this experiment, we set three types of formation strategies. The first formation consists of four defenders, three midfielders, and three attackers, named as 433-formation that is mainly used by our team. The second is the HELIOS2017's formation, 4231-formation. The last is the 442-formation, that have 2-top attackers. The main reason for employing the last formation is that we want to investigate the effect of using a different number of attackers.

**Table 1.** Summary of experimental settings

|  | Variation | Abbreviation |
|---|---|---|
| Layers (Activation function) | 4-layered (Sigmoid), 7-layered (Leaky-ReLU) | sig, relu |
| Output layer's activation function | Sigmoid (Probability), Linear (Regression) | sig, reg |
| Evaluation function | all kick sequences, One player's kick sequences | all, each |
| Formation | 4231-formation, 433-formation, 442-formation | 4231, 433, 442 |
| Input | $(x_n, y_n)$, $(x_c, y_c, x_n, y_n)$ | 2input, 4input |
| Depth for tree search | Up to 1, 2, 3 and 4 | 1, 2, 3, 4 |

In addition, we investigate several neural network's architectures. The different architectures are summarized in Table 1. The four-layered (2or4-100-100-1) neural networks' activation functions are sigmoid functions. On the other hand, the Leaky-ReLU function [18] is employed as an activation function in the seven-layered (2or4-50-50-50-50-50-1) neural networks to prevent vanishing gradient problems and dead neurons. Moreover, we investigate two types of output layer's activation function. The first one is the sigmoid function, and the second one is a linear activation (i.e., no activation function). The output layer using a sigmoid function outputs values in $[0, 1]$, thus the output can be considered as the probability of entering the opponent's penalty area at the end of the sequence. On the other hand, the output layer with a linear activation outputs an unbounded value. This function is usually employed for regression problem. The learning rate are set as 0.001 for all structures.

In addition, we investigate two types of training procedures. One uses all kick sequences, thus all players have the same evaluation function. The other one uses only the sequences involving the learning player itself. Therefore, players learn their own evaluation functions. While this procedure requires to train several neural networks, the training may be easier.

We assume that players of the expert team consider a team strategy when selecting an action. Therefore, the expert's kick sequences are expected to include the information of the considerations. By modeling each player's action selector to the expert's one, a team behaviors are close to the expert.

Learned evaluation functions are implemented in opuSCOM. We evaluate the performance by making it play against HillStone. Performances are measured over 100 games.

## 5.2 Results

Figure 4 shows the performance of several trained neural networks in comparison with the opuSCOM's default hand-coded evaluation functions. Comparisons are based on three different criteria: the number of scored goals, the number of times the ball entered the opponent's penalty area and the number of successful through passes. Evaluation functions modeled by neural networks outperform those designed by humans regardless the criterion.

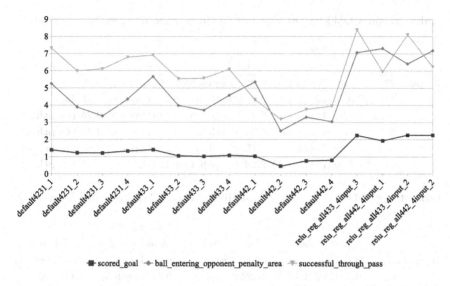

scored_goal    ball_entering_opponent_penalty_area    successful_through_pass

**Fig. 4.** Team performance with various neural network models

Tables 2, 3 and 4 summarize the opuSCOM's win rate against Hillstone for each experimental settings. Automatically designed evaluation functions helped to increase the win rate by a factor greater than or equal to 10%. Neural network evaluators helped to win more than 50% of games, in spite of default evaluators whose win rate is at most 40%. On the other hand, there was also a performance decrease in some experimental settings. This is particularly the case with the sig-sig model when used for formations that involve a few number of top attackers (formation 442).

**Table 2.** opuSCOM's win rate against HillStone when using a hand-coded evaluator

| Formation | Win rate |
|---|---|
| 4231 | 0.27 (Depth 3, 4) |
| 433 | 0.40 (Depth 1) |
| 442 | 0.14 (Depth 3) |

Figures 5, 6, 7 and 8 depict examples of evaluation functions modeled by neural networks trained by supervised learning. Note that the $x - y$ plane represents the soccer field. For example, the area $x > 0$ is the opponent's side while the area is our side when $x < 0$. They represent the functions learned by the models: sig-sig-all-2input, sig-reg-all-2input, relu-sig-all-2input and relu-reg-all-2input according to the abbreviated name in Table 1. In order to draw such visualization, we discretized the soccer field and evaluated every position by using the different trained models. As shown in Figs. 5, 6, 7 and 8, neural

**Table 3.** opuSCOM's win rate against HillStone when using an *"all"* evaluator

| | | 4-layer (sig) | | 7-layer (relu) | |
|---|---|---|---|---|---|
| | | Sigmoid (sig) | Linear (reg) | Sigmoid (sig) | Linear (reg) |
| 2 input | 4231 | **0.39 (Depth 4)** | **0.37 (Depth 3)** | 0.35 (Depth 4) | 0.31 (Depth 4) |
| | 433 | 0.46 (Depth 2) | 0.48 (Depth 4) | 0.41 (Depth 2) | 0.43 (Depth 4) |
| | 442 | 0.01 (Depth 1) | **0.25 (Depth 3)** | 0.22 (Depth 3) | **0.25 (Depth 3)** |
| 4 input | 4231 | 0.16 (Depth 3) | 0.28 (Depth 3) | 0.22 (Depth 4) | **0.40 (Depth 2)** |
| | 433 | 0.30 (Depth 3) | 0.45 (Depth 1) | 0.23 (Depth 2) | **0.53 (Depth 3)** |
| | 442 | 0.00 (Depth 1–4) | **0.24 (Depth 1)** | 0.17 (Depth 3) | **0.30 (Depth 3)** |

**Table 4.** opuSCOM's win rate against HillStone when using an *"each"* evaluator

| | | 4-layer (sig) | | 7-layer (relu) | |
|---|---|---|---|---|---|
| | | Sigmoid (sig) | Linear (reg) | Sigmoid (sig) | Linear (reg) |
| 2 input | 4231 | 0.34 (Depth 3) | 0.31 (Depth 1, 4) | 0.36 (Depth 4) | 0.36 (Depth 2) |
| | 433 | 0.15 (Depth 4) | 0.36 (Depth 3) | 0.43 (Depth 3) | 0.42 (Depth 4) |
| | 442 | 0.02 (Depth 2, 3, 4) | 0.19 (Depth 4) | 0.13 (Depth 4) | 0.11 (Depth 2) |
| 4 input | 4231 | 0.09 (Depth 3) | 0.28 (Depth 4) | 0.33 (Depth 4) | 0.35 (Depth 2) |
| | 433 | 0.07 (Depth 3) | 0.32 (Depth 1) | 0.41 (Depth 3) | 0.48 (Depth 2) |
| | 442 | 0.01 (Depth 3, 4) | 0.13 (Depth 1) | **0.25 (Depth 1)** | 0.18 (Depth 1) |

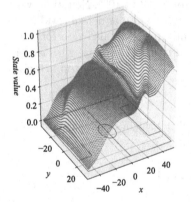

**Fig. 5.** Evaluation function learned by the sig-sig model

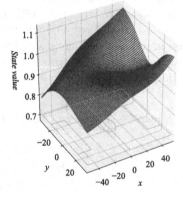

**Fig. 6.** Evaluation function learned by the sig-reg model

networks learned meaningful evaluation functions regardless the experimental settings. Actions that could bring the ball inside the opponent's penalty area have a high evaluation value. On the other hand, actions with a low predicted success probability tend to have a lower evaluation value, even if the ball is close to the goal. The observations suggest the neural networks learn the expert's kick sequences to mimic their action selections. In Fig. 6, the state value produced by the neural network exceeds 1.0 because of an activation function and many

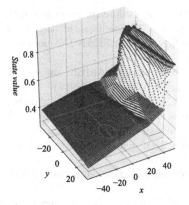
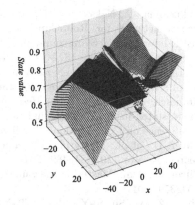

**Fig. 7.** Evaluation function learned by the relu-sig model

**Fig. 8.** Evaluation function learned by the relu-reg model

contradictions in the training data. Some situations (e.g., a corner kick) are labeled differently even though the field information is completely the same.

## 6  Conclusion

In this paper, we proposed a method that improves the performance of a team by making it mimic a stronger one. For this purpose, a neural network is employed to model the team to mimic its evaluation function. The neural network is trained by using positive and negative episodes of action sequences. The proposed method can train the behavior of a given team, and outperform the evaluation function designed by human beings. This method allows to easily and automatically improve the performance of a team. By automatically designing evaluation function, we could focus on the development of efficient strategies. In a future work, we will try to improve our mimic performance by investigating various neural network's structures. In addition, we will consider the use of reinforcement learning in order to outperform the expert team itself.

## References

1. Akiyama, H., Aramaki, S., Nakashima, T.: Online cooperative behavior planning using a tree search method in the RoboCup soccer simulation. In: Proceedings of 4th IEEE International Conference on Intelligent Networking and Collaborative Systems (INCoS), pp. 170–177 (2012)
2. Akiyama, H., Nakashima, T.: HELIOS2012: RoboCup 2012 soccer simulation 2D league champion. In: Chen, X., Stone, P., Sucar, L.E., van der Zant, T. (eds.) RoboCup 2012. LNCS (LNAI), vol. 7500, pp. 13–19. Springer, Heidelberg (2013). https://doi.org/10.1007/978-3-642-39250-4_2

3. Fukushima, T., Nakashima, T., Hidehisa, A.: Learning evaluation functions with neural network for RoboCup soccer situation. In: Proceedings of the First IEEE International Symposium on Artificial Intelligence for ASEAN Development (ASEAN-AI 2018), pp. 18–24, Phuket, Thailand (2018)
4. Warnell, G., Waytowich, N., Lawhern, V., Stone, P.: Deep TAMER: interactive agent shaping in high-dimensional state spaces. arXiv:1709.10163 (2017)
5. Stanescu, M., Barriga, N.A., Hess, A., Buro, M.: Evaluating real-time strategy game states using convolutional neural networks. In: Proceedings of the IEEE Conference on Computational Intelligence and Games (CIG), pp. 1–7 (2016)
6. Silver, D., et al.: Mastering the game of go with deep neural networks and tree search. Nature **529**, 484–489 (2016)
7. Silver, D., et al.: Mastering the game of go without human knowledge. Nature **550**, 354–359 (2017)
8. Hong, Z.-W., Su, S.-Y., Shann, T.-Y., Chang, Y.-H., Lee, C.-Y.: A deep policy inference Q-network for multi-agent systems. arXiv:1712.07893 (2017)
9. Liu, Y., Stone, P.: Value-function-based transfer for reinforcement learning using structure mapping. In: Proceedings of the 21st National Conference on Artificial Intelligence, pp. 415–420 (2006)
10. Hausknecht, M., Stone, P.: Deep reinforcement learning in parameterized action space. arXiv:1511.04143 (2015)
11. Michael, O., Obst, O., Schmidsberger, F., Stolzenburg, F.: Analysing soccer games with clustering and conceptors. In: Akiyama, H., Obst, O., Sammut, C., Tonidandel, F. (eds.) RoboCup 2017. LNCS (LNAI), vol. 11175, pp. 120–131. Springer, Cham (2018). https://doi.org/10.1007/978-3-030-00308-1_10
12. Henrio, J., Henn, T., Nakashima, T., Akiyama, H.: Selecting the best player formation for corner-kick situations based on bayes' estimation. In: Behnke, S., Sheh, R., Sariel, S., Lee, D.D. (eds.) RoboCup 2016. LNCS (LNAI), vol. 9776, pp. 428–439. Springer, Cham (2017). https://doi.org/10.1007/978-3-319-68792-6_36
13. Fukushima, T., Nakashima, T., Akiyama, H.: Online opponent formation identification based on position information. In: Akiyama, H., Obst, O., Sammut, C., Tonidandel, F. (eds.) RoboCup 2017. LNCS (LNAI), vol. 11175, pp. 241–251. Springer, Cham (2018). https://doi.org/10.1007/978-3-030-00308-1_20
14. Floyd, M.W., Esfandiari, B., Lam, K.: A case-based reasoning approach to imitating RoboCup players. In: Proceedings of the 21st International FLAIRS Conference, pp. 251–256 (2008)
15. Akiyama, H., Nakashima, T., Tanaka, S., Fukushima, T.: HELIOS2017: team description paper. In: RoboCup2017 Nagoya, Japan (2017)
16. Kiura, T., Omori, T., Watanabe, N.: Team HillStone2017 in the 2DSimulation league team description paper. In: RoboCup2017 Nagoya, Japan, 6 p. (2017)
17. Akiyama, H., Nakashima, T.: HELIOS base: an open source package for the RoboCup soccer 2D simulation. In: Behnke, S., Veloso, M., Visser, A., Xiong, R. (eds.) RoboCup 2013. LNCS (LNAI), vol. 8371, pp. 528–535. Springer, Heidelberg (2014). https://doi.org/10.1007/978-3-662-44468-9_46
18. Maas, A.L., Hannun, A.Y., Ng, A.Y.: Rectifier nonlinearities improve neural network acoustic models. In: Proceedings of International Conference on Machine Learning (ICML), vol. 30, no. 1 (2013)

# Jetson, Where Is the Ball?
# Using Neural Networks
# for Ball Detection at RoboCup 2017

Alexander Gabel[(✉)], Tanja Heuer, Ina Schiering, and Reinhard Gerndt

WF Wolves, Ostfalia University of Applied Sciences, Wolfenbüttel, Germany
{ale.gabel,ta.heuer,i.schiering,r.gerndt}@ostfalia.de

**Abstract.** The approach of using neural networks in the RoboCup humanoid league for ball detection is investigated in a case study at the RoboCup 2017 competition. A patch-based classification approach is used. Two different ConvNet architectures, the Inception v3 network by Google and AlexNet are evaluated in the context of a ROS-based architecture on a robot with a Jetson GPU board. The aim is to allow for an efficient re-training of neural networks in the context of the competition.

**Keywords:** Ball detection · Neural network · Humanoid league ·
RoboCup

## 1 Introduction

Based on the intention of RoboCup Humanoid league, that in 2050 "a team of autonomous humanoid robots shall play soccer against the human world champion" [5], the complexity of the tasks of RoboCup are increasing. Examples of this increasing complexity are the use of a standard FIFA ball, increasing field sizes and the use of artificial grass. These challenges lead to increasing requirements concerning object detection.

The WF Wolves team previously used the Haar cascade algorithm [21]. This algorithm is integrated in frameworks as OpenCV and allows for a very time-efficient ball recognition when the ball is in medium range. It is not able to cope with far away balls or partial occlusion. In such situations, which will occur more often because of the growing field size and an increasing number of players, the prior approach is unable to reliably detect balls in larger distances (Fig. 1).

A promising approach is the use of neural networks, which were recently investigated in the context of the humanoid league [18]. However, in the past, neural networks, particularly fully-connected ones, were too computationally intensive for usage in image classification. Due to improved architectures (i.e. convolutional neural networks - CNN) and adapted hardware, this has changed in the last decade. However, the usage of deep neural networks for end-to-end learning in the context of the humanoid league was not feasible until the recent introduction of fast embedded GPUs, for (small) mobile robot platforms.

© Springer Nature Switzerland AG 2019
D. Holz et al. (Eds.): RoboCup 2018, LNAI 11374, pp. 181–192, 2019.
https://doi.org/10.1007/978-3-030-27544-0_15

**Fig. 1.** Far balls detected by CNN (pink circles), false positive by Haar Cascade classifier (violet circle). Red line: approximated field outline. Blue squares: patches analysed by CNN. Blue rectangles: goal post hypotheses (Color figure online)

Our approach is based on pre-trained convolutional neural network models, which are fine-tuned[1] to the RoboCup ball classification scenario. Advantages of this approach include vastly reduced training times, higher accuracy and less overfitting, when compared to a model trained from scratch. To localize the ball, not the whole image is classified by the CNN, but the image is divided into patches, which are filtered based on color information.

In this paper the use of neural networks for ball detection, in particular far away balls, is evaluated based on experiences of the RoboCup 2017 competition. The aim of the proposed approach is a CNN based classifier, which is fast-adaptable to on-site conditions. We present the adapted vision pipeline, the machine learning approach and experimental results.

## 2    Related Work

Neural networks are a widespread used technology for object recognition. In the RoboCup soccer league neural network based systems for object recognition have mainly been used in the middle size league. Mayer et al. [12] proposed a neural network for robot detection on the field. Their approach uses the classical feature extraction/classification separation with hand-crafted features designed by humans. Our approach rather uses the more recent, but also more computationally intensive approach of end-to-end learning (deep learning), which also learns the feature extraction from the raw pixels. Furthermore neural networks are sometimes used in combination with other approaches, such as Kalman filters [11,20] to improve performance for objects in motion (i.e. predict their position).

---

[1] https://cs231n.github.io/transfer-learning/.

At present, neural networks become computationally feasible also for the humanoid league and standard platform league for ball and opponent recognition. In the humanoid league the team Hamburg Bit-Bots [18] proposed a CNN approach for ball localization. They used a custom network architecture trained from scratch by using a normal distribution as teaching signal for each coordinate axis. The team AUTMan [6] presented the idea of a CNN model for recognizing opponents. In the Standard Platform League the approach using neural networks was also recently investigated by several teams [1,3,14,15].

CITBrains from Japan are the only team stating the use of CNNs for ball, goal post and opponent recognition for the RoboCup competition in their team description paper for the RoboCup 2017 [16]. Hence until now mainly preliminary lab results about the use of CNNs in the humanoid league are described. Besides the RoboCup, CNNs implemented on a Jetson TX1 board is currently a gladly used approach in a low-power environment [2,13]. The CNN AlexNet is retrained for car plate and person recognition with satisfying results [4,10]. In the following we present our results and experiences from using CNNs during the RoboCup 2017.

## 3 Vision Pipeline

In general, we use a patch-based classification approach, to decide whether a particular region of interest (ROI) in the image contains a (partial) ball or not. To increase computational efficiency, classification is only applied to patches, which potentially contain a ball. Therefore the image is preprocessed and filtered (Fig. 2).

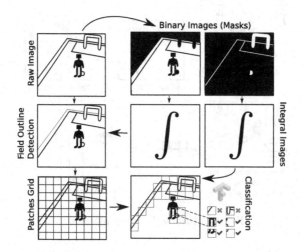

**Fig. 2.** Vision pipeline (Color figure online)

First we generate binary images (masks) by classifying the color of each pixel in the source image. For ball detection the masks for soccer *field green* and for *ball white* are relevant.

To keep rectangular sum calculations in the mask efficient, we transform the masks into integral images. Based on the detection of field outlines, regions outside of the field, without touching it, are not considered as a possible ball region. The image is then divided into a grid of $n \times n$ patches with a default patch size $n$ of 50 pixels (Fig. 5). This hyper-parameter was chosen as a performance/accuracy-trade-off.

For each patch, we determine the number of pixels belonging to the *ball white* color class using the integral image. Patches where this number exceeds a predefined threshold (default: 30), are considered as a *region of interest* (ROI) for classification.

Each of those ROIs is then fed into the classifier, a deep convolutional neural network, which calculates probabilities for the two classes *ball/partialball* and *noball*. The classifier itself is running as a separate ROS[2] node.

## 4   Machine Learning

We evaluated two different ConvNet architectures, the modern Inception v3 network by Google [19] and AlexNet [9], one of the first well-performing deep convolutional neural networks. As we use TensorFlow for our model, all operations in the training refer to the corresponding functions and implementations in TensorFlow (Fig. 3).

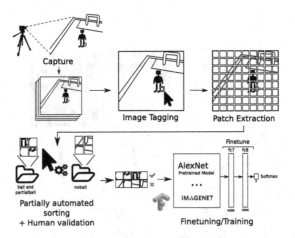

**Fig. 3.** Machine learning pipeline

For both evaluated networks, we did not perform a full training of the network, as the goal during the competition was to be able to relatively fast adjust the network to on-site conditions. Hence we fine-tune models of each network, which were pre-trained for ImageNet. Also these models should be able to generalize better, as they already learned common features for object recognition and overfitting is less likely to occur, as we only retrain the last layer(s). For fine-tuning Inception v3, there is already a script and tutorial provided by TensorFlow[3]. Also for AlexNet there exists a project for fine-tuning[4], where the pretrained model is converted from the Caffe [7] model of BVLC AlexNet[5].

For collecting training images, we use a regular tripod in the height of our robot with the camera of our robot. We capture single images instead of the whole data stream to include common situations, which might also occur during a real game, while avoiding too many pictures of a single perspective, which would introduce an unwanted bias to our dataset, and look for difficult situations like other white objects on/near the field.

After capturing, the images are labeled using the ImageTagger[6] by the Hamburg Bit-Bots team, which allows to build up a shared image database for humanoid soccer competitions. In the tagger application, we annotate balls in the image using bounding boxes.

The images are then divided into small patches (see Fig. 5). To generate training data, no patches are filtered out in this step, as this has proven to result in a better, more flexible model. In an automated labeling patches are labeled as *ball* if the overlap of any ball bounding box with the region is larger than a certain threshold.

As this automated sorting is still error-prone, after this step a human has to validate the resulting patches and potentially to move images to the correct folder. Files where even the human is unsure about classification are removed from the dataset.

In general we do not perform additional preprocessing of the training/validation images (i.e. translation/noise addition/etc.) to reduce the time needed for on-site training. Due to the high amount of patches, we expect to have enough translation variety already present in the dataset.

As the training data is highly unbalanced between the classes, i.e. we have a lot of negative samples, but comparably only a very small percentage of positive (ball) samples, the training process has to be adjusted. Otherwise the classifier might prefer the overrepresented class over the other. This effect is called accuracy paradox.

There are multiple ways of handling imbalanced classes, including oversampling, undersampling, class weights or balanced batches. To cope with the highly imbalanced training data, instead of using *oversampling* on the *ball* class *undersampling* on the *noball* class was investigated. This led to an increased false positive rate due to less negative (*noball*) samples. Using alternatively class weights

---

[3] https://www.tensorflow.org/tutorials/image_retraining.

[4] https://kratzert.github.io/2017/02/24/finetuning-alexnet-with-tensorflow.html.

[5] https://github.com/BVLC/caffe/tree/master/models/bvlc_alexnet.

[6] https://github.com/bit-bots/imagetagger.

led to a more robust model with a reduced false positive rate. Also balanced batches yielded good results for the Inception network.

For fine-tuning AlexNet, we re-train the last two fully-connected layers (fc7 and fc8). Softmax cross entropy is used as loss function. Batches of 128 randomly chosen patches are fed into the network for training. Adam [8] is used as optimization procedure and TensorBoard for monitoring the training and validation accuracy, as well as the cross-entropy loss over time.

## 5    Experimental Results

The presented approach is evaluated in the following based on the experience of the RoboCup 2017. A description of the dataset used for training is provided and the performance of the inference process is investigated based on the built-in Jetson board of the robot.

The proposed CNN-based method (pink circles) is able to detect partially covered balls and far away balls, as shown in Fig. 1, with less false-negatives compared to the Haar cascade approach (violet circles) (Fig. 4).

**Fig. 4.** Close ball detected by Haar Cascade classifier and CNN (Color figure online)

**Fig. 5.** Examples of patches (non-filtered)

### 5.1    Dataset

The images used as the basis for our dataset were recorded at 3 different locations: our lab test field, German Open 2017 and RoboCup 2017 Japan. The original ∼1800 images had a resolution of 640 × 480 respectively 640 × 360 pixels and were all taken with our robot's camera.

The dataset consists of ∼158k patches, where ∼3k were labelled as *ball or partial ball*, and the rest ∼155k patches were labelled as *no ball*. The images contain different kinds of white balls, with difficult situations, such as partial occlusion by robots, sun light from open doors and various shaped and sized objects of white color. We particularly included problematic situations on the RoboCup, where we experienced a lot of false positives.

For evaluation of the different models, we captured an additional dataset consisting of ~1000 images. This dataset, in this paper referenced as 'evaluation dataset', is used for performance testing on whole-frame pictures, as well as for the confusion matrix.

## 5.2  Validation

We evaluated several models varying training epochs/steps[7], validation split and class imbalance handling (Table 1). The true positive rate is defined as the number of correctly detected balls divided by the number of ground truth balls. The false discovery rate is defined as the number of false positive balls divided by the sum of false positive and true positive balls.

**Table 1.** Evaluated models with true positive rate (TPR), false discovery rate (FDR), validation accuracy and training duration (inception has constant bottleneck creation time = only required once for all models). (AlexNet 20 epochs (10% validation data, class weights); Inception v3 500 steps (10% validation data, balanced batches); Inception 4000 steps (10% validation data, balanced batches); Inception 20000 steps (10% validation data, class weights); AlexNet 38 epochs (20% validation data, class weights); AlexNet 64 epochs (10% validation data, undersampling); AlexNet 9 epochs (10% validation data, class weights))

| Model | Haar | AlexNet 20 epochs | Inception 500 steps | Inception 4000 steps | Inception 20000 steps | AlexNet 38 epochs | AlexNet 64 epochs | AlexNet 9 epochs RC2017 |
|---|---|---|---|---|---|---|---|---|
| TPR | 24.135% | 74.382% | 96.34% | 96.736% | 98.811% | 72.908% | 88.131% | 68.546% |
| FDR | 7.925% | 10.9% | 10.724% | 14.06% | 80.697% | 18.568% | 39.346% | 12.278% |
| Val. acc. | - | 99.25% (N = 15776) | 98% (N = 100) | 88% (N = 100) | 93% (N = 100) | 99.48% (N = 15776) | 96.97% (N = 1076) | 99.14% (N = 15776) |
| Train. Dur. | - | ~8, 5 h | 2, 5 h + 1 m | 2, 5 h + 7 m | 2, 5 h + 36 m | ~16 h | ~45 m | ~4 h |

From the Table 1 it can be seen, that the Haar Cascade algorithm has a low TPR, therefore not detecting a large percentage of balls. AlexNet performs better, but with an increased FDR. We suspect that the rather high FDR for AlexNet 64 epochs, is due to less amount of training data caused by undersampling. Inception with 20000 epochs is probably overfitted. We have selected Inception 500 steps and AlexNet 20 epochs, as they have the best trade-off between true positives and false positives[8]. As can be seen in Fig. 6, the Haar cascade algorithm is unable to detect balls at distances larger than 3.50 m, in contrast to both CNN algorithms.

We achieved ~99% validation accuracy during the RoboCup competition (AlexNet 9 epochs). During the RoboCup, the time available for training is very

---

[7] Number of batches (batch size 100) used for training.
[8] Additional results are left out because of page limitations, but can be downloaded from our website (https://www.wf-wolves.de/jetson-rc2017/).

constrained, therefore we only trained for 9 epochs, which already took about 4 h. The TensorFlow *retrain.py* script used for fine-tuning Inception, uses a technique to first generate *bottleneck files,* which are the results of processing each training image through the first layers (which are not changed). This leads to a constant start-up cost, and greatly reduces training time in total. The concept may be applied to AlexNet as well, which might decrease training time by a large portion. However, the false positive rate slightly increases for the CNNs.

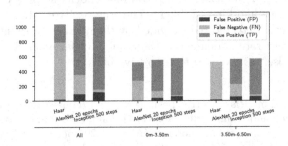

**Fig. 6.** Comparison of three different classifier models: Haar Cascade; AlexNet trained for 20 epochs with class weights; inception v3 trained for 500 steps with class weights

## 5.3   Performance of Inferencing

For the evaluation we investigated Inception v3 and AlexNet as described in Sect. 4. The Inception v3 model might in principle lead to better classification accuracy results, but was too slow for this use case. Figures 7 and 8 show the processing time required for the whole image pipeline (time between publishing of a camera image to the receiving of the debug image).

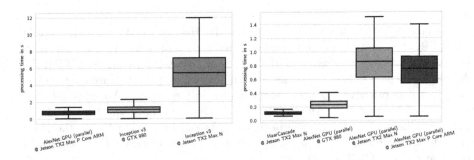

**Fig. 7.** Pipeline performance AlexNet vs Inception v3 (outliers excluded)

**Fig. 8.** Pipeline performance AlexNet vs Haar Cascade (outliers excluded)

Running the Inception network on a CPU, took about 1 s per inference run/patch. Running it on a Desktop GPU, increased the performance to about

0.2 s per patch, which is still slow, when having to handle a large number of patches. Therefore we switched to AlexNet, a more lightweight model, which still promised sufficient classification accuracies, while achieving better real-time performance. With AlexNet, we achieved approximately 0.1 s for the inference time per patch on a CPU. For larger amounts of patches this was still too slow. Using the Jetson TX2 GPU board the duration could be further reduced.

To further optimize the performance, we compared the sequential execution of the network with a parallelized version taking a variable batch of patches as input. The results for this can be seen in Figs. 9 and 10. While the processing time in the sequential version grows linearly, the parallel version has a relatively high amount of outliers. Based on mean execution times, the parallel version offers a huge advantage compared to the sequential method.

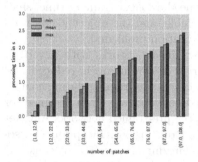 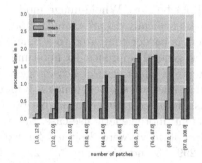

**Fig. 9.** Execution time of sequential AlexNet on the Jetson GPU

**Fig. 10.** Execution time of parallel AlexNet on the Jetson GPU

We used the *Max-P ARM* performance mode of the Jetson TX2, which was the most stable, but at the same time well-performing setting. We also investigated the *Max-N* mode, with which we had stability issues, which may have been caused by current limitations of the power supply. Table 2 gives an overview about the investigated performance modes.

**Table 2.** Tested performance modes of the Jetson TX2

| Mode | ARM | Denver | GPU | Power w/o GPU | Power w/ GPU |
|------|-----|--------|-----|---------------|--------------|
| Max-P | 2.0 GHz | Disabled | 1.12 GHz | 0.6 A | 0.9 A |
| Max-N | 2.0 GHz | 2.0 GHz | 1.30 GHz | 1 A | >2 A |

# 6 Discussion

In general the presented approach was feasible during the competition and the accuracy and model performance is promising. An advantage of the patch-based approach compared to approaches operating on the whole image is, that it is easier to generate an adequate amount of training data, as one image contains already many patches. Also training samples are usually better distributed, as e.g. the ball is not always in the center or often only partly visible. This improves especially the detection of partially covered balls. Still, there may be a bias from other sources, such as illumination and exposure. When choosing a patch size of $50 \times 50$ pixels with a stride-size of 50 pixels, we had an accuracy-performance trade-off in mind. Lowering the stride-size, will lead to more patches, which might simplify the problem for the classifier, but decreases the runtime-performance. Furthermore it might be worth to investigate adaptive patch sizes, for example based on the distances from the robot's view.

A potential disadvantage of the patch based approach are patches containing small parts of a ball without further context in the image, where even humans would not be sure. Whole-image models may need a longer training time, since there are typically no pre-trained models available, and the object localization problem is harder compared to a binary classification problem.

The general approach to fine-tune a pre-trained networks with a verified architecture offers several advantages. The risk of overfitting is reduced and training times are shorter, which is important for on-site training during competitions. However, publicly available pre-trained networks are often designed for a different, more generic use-case. In our case the pre-trained networks AlexNet and Inception v3 were designed for fixed input dimensions. Inception v3 uses $299 \times 299 \times 3$ and AlexNet $227 \times 227 \times 3$ as input dimensions. This is considerably larger than the patch size ($50 \times 50 \times 3$) chosen here. Therefore each patch has to be scaled up to the network's input dimension. This yields to a computational overhead, which would not be necessary in case of a custom designed network. Furthermore the parallelization on the Jetson may suffer from this, as there are more CUDA units necessary to compute the larger network.

To enhance the inference performance, it would be interesting to investigate custom network architectures or available networks with smaller input dimensions, which are pre-trained similarly on a general purpose challenge (e.g. ImageNet Large scale Visual Recognition Challenge) and afterwards fine-tuned to the specific requirements of the RoboCup environment.

Furthermore the performance could possibly be enhanced by adapting models to the specific hardware capabilities. For example TensorRT[9] optimizes trained neural networks for execution on NVIDIA hardware by weight quantization (i.e. quantize floating point weights to 8-bit integers), layer and tensor fusion and other optimizations. However at the time of writing this framework is only available as a release candidate for the Jetson TX2 board currently missing some APIs when compared to the x86 version.

To improve the validation process, the ability to explain the network's decision may be useful. Selvaraju et al. developed Gradient-weighted Class Activation Mapping (Grad-CAM) [17], which highlights regions, that are 'important' for the prediction outcome. Further investigation into explanations of the

---

[9] https://developer.nvidia.com/tensorrt.

network's decision may allow to decide whether a network has actually learned the general concept of a soccer ball, or something else.

## 7 Conclusion

Ball detection by deep neural networks in the RoboCup humanoid league proved promising. The accuracy is adequate for the intended application, leading to less false negatives compared with previous approaches, as the Haar cascade algorithm that was used before. It is possible to adjust the approach to changing on-site conditions during a competition. By including a Jetson board in the robot, the use of CNNs is computationally feasible in a ROS based architecture.

The approach fosters the cooperation between teams by the possibility to build up common training sets and to share ROS nodes with pre-trained classifiers with other teams.

## References

1. Albani, D., Youssef, A., Suriani, V., Nardi, D., Bloisi, D.D.: A deep learning approach for object recognition with NAO soccer robots. In: Behnke, S., Sheh, R., Sariel, S., Lee, D.D. (eds.) RoboCup 2016. LNCS (LNAI), vol. 9776, pp. 392–403. Springer, Cham (2017). https://doi.org/10.1007/978-3-319-68792-6_33
2. Balleda, K., Menon, S.K.: D-face: parallel implementation of CNN based face classifier using drone data on K40 & Jetson TK1 (2015)
3. Cruz, N., Lobos-Tsunekawa, K., Ruiz-del Solar, J.: Using convolutional neural networks in robots with limited computational resources: detecting NAO robots while playing soccer. arXiv preprint arXiv:1706.06702 (2017)
4. Eisenbach, M., Stricker, R., Seichter, D., Vorndran, A., Wengefeld, T., Gross, H.M.: Speeding up deep neural networks on the jetson TX1. In: CAPRI 2017, p. 11 (2017)
5. Gerndt, R., Seifert, D., Baltes, J.H., Sadeghnejad, S., Behnke, S.: Humanoid robots in soccer: robots versus humans in RoboCup 2050. IEEE Robot. Autom. Mag. **22**(3), 147–154 (2015)
6. Javadi, M., Azar, S.M., Azami, S., Ghidary, S.S., Sadeghnejad, S., Baltes, J.: Humanoid robot detection using deep learning: a speed-accuracy tradeoff. In: Akiyama, H., Obst, O., Sammut, C., Tonidandel, F. (eds.) RoboCup 2017. LNCS (LNAI), vol. 11175, pp. 338–349. Springer, Cham (2018). https://doi.org/10.1007/978-3-030-00308-1_28
7. Jia, Y., et al.: Caffe: convolutional architecture for fast feature embedding. arXiv preprint arXiv:1408.5093 (2014)
8. Kingma, D.P., Ba, J.: Adam: a method for stochastic optimization. CoRR abs/1412.6980 (2014). http://arxiv.org/abs/1412.6980
9. Krizhevsky, A., Sutskever, I., Hinton, G.E.: ImageNet classification with deep convolutional neural networks. In: Advances in neural information processing systems, pp. 1097–1105 (2012)
10. Lee, S., Son, K., Kim, H., Park, J.: Car plate recognition based on CNN using embedded system with GPU. In: 2017 10th International Conference on Human System Interactions (HSI), pp. 239–241. IEEE (2017)
11. Li, X., Lu, H., Xiong, D., Zhang, H., Zheng, Z.: A survey on visual perception for robocup msl soccer robots. Int. J. Adv. Rob. Syst. **10**(2), 110 (2013)

12. Mayer, G., Kaufmann, U., Kraetzschmar, G., Palm, G.: Neural robot detection in RoboCup. In: Wermter, S., Palm, G., Elshaw, M. (eds.) Biomimetic Neural Learning for Intelligent Robots. LNCS (LNAI), vol. 3575, pp. 349–361. Springer, Heidelberg (2005). https://doi.org/10.1007/11521082_21

13. Mhalla, A., Gazzah, S., Ben Amara, N.E., et al.: A faster R-CNN multi-object detector on a Nvidia Jetson TX1 embedded system. In: Proceedings of the 10th International Conference on Distributed Smart Camera, pp. 208–209. ACM (2016)

14. Militão, G., Colombini, E., Técnico-IC-PFG, R., de Graduação, P.F.: RoboCup soccer ball depth detection using convolutional neural networks (2017)

15. O'Keeffe, S., Villing, R.: A benchmark data set and evaluation of deep learning architectures for ball detection in the RoboCup SPL. In: Akiyama, H., Obst, O., Sammut, C., Tonidandel, F. (eds.) RoboCup 2017. LNCS (LNAI), vol. 11175, pp. 398–409. Springer, Cham (2018). https://doi.org/10.1007/978-3-030-00308-1_33. Robocup symposium: poster presentation

16. Seki, Y., et al.: CIT Brains (kid size league) - team description paper (2017)

17. Selvaraju, R.R., Das, A., Vedantam, R., Cogswell, M., Parikh, D., Batra, D.: Grad-CAM: why did you say that? arXiv preprint arXiv:1611.07450 (2016). https://arxiv.org/pdf/1611.07450.pdf

18. Speck, D., Barros, P., Weber, C., Wermter, S.: Ball localization for Robocup soccer using convolutional neural networks. In: Behnke, S., Sheh, R., Sarıel, S., Lee, D.D. (eds.) RoboCup 2016. LNCS (LNAI), vol. 9776, pp. 19–30. Springer, Cham (2017). https://doi.org/10.1007/978-3-319-68792-6_2

19. Szegedy, C., Vanhoucke, V., Ioffe, S., Shlens, J., Wojna, Z.: Rethinking the inception architecture for computer vision. arXiv:1512.00567, December 2015

20. Taleghani, S., Aslani, S., Shiry, S.: Robust moving object detection from a moving video camera using neural network and kalman filter. In: Iocchi, L., Matsubara, H., Weitzenfeld, A., Zhou, C. (eds.) RoboCup 2008. LNCS (LNAI), vol. 5399, pp. 638–648. Springer, Heidelberg (2009). https://doi.org/10.1007/978-3-642-02921-9_55

21. Viola, P., Jones, M.: Rapid object detection using a boosted cascade of simple features. In: Proceedings of the 2001 IEEE Computer Society Conference on Computer Vision and Pattern Recognition, CVPR 2001, vol. 1, p. I. IEEE (2001)

# Bridging the Gap - On a Humanoid Robotics Rookie League

Reinhard Gerndt[1]([✉]), Maike Paetzel[2], Jacky Baltes[3], and Olivier Ly[4]

[1] Ostfalia University of Applied Sciences, 38304 Wolfenbüttel, Germany
r.gerndt@ostfalia.de
[2] Uppsala Univeristy, 75105 Uppsala, Sweden
maike.paetzel@it.uu.se
[3] National Taiwan Normal University, Taipei 10610, Taiwan
jacky.baltes@ntnu.edu.tw
[4] University of Bordeaux, 33405 Talence, France
ly@labri.fr
http://www.wfwolves.de, http://bit-bots.de,
http://www.ntnu.edu.tw/ee/erc/, http://rhoban.com

**Abstract.** The 2050 robot-human soccer game is among the most prominent goals of RoboCup. All RoboCup leagues contribute to this goal, for example the Simulation Leagues with research on strategic game play, the Standard Platform League with stable walking and vision algorithms and the Humanoid League with mechatronics of bipedal robots. However, especially in the Humanoid League, the swift improvement in performance of the robots makes it significantly harder for newcomers to enter into this field of research. With robots increasing in size, with new challenges in mechatronics for bipedal robots and software increasing in complexity, the gap for new teams is widening on the course to the 2050 game. There have been many approaches to easy entry, such as the introduction of a two-league system in the Standard Platform (SPL) and Small Size League (SSL) or an 'educational challenge' at regional @home events. While the SPL and SSL approaches require fully developed hard- and software in order to compete, as the @home challenge, we propose an entry-level league with a reduced set of requirements to bridge the gap between the Junior level and advanced Humanoid League. We believe that the Humanoid League can only reach the 2050 goal if new researchers and universities can be attracted on a regular basis. Attracting new researchers requires an easy entry path for new teams, suitable for undergraduate students and universities with a limited budget. The 'Humanoid Rookie (Sub-) League' (HRL) will give new researchers and teams the time to gather experience and funds that are necessary to successfully participate in and contribute to the Humanoid League's development towards the 2050 game. This paper intends to spark discussion about the current state and the roadmap of the Humanoid League within the RoboCup community.

D. Holz et al. (Eds.): RoboCup 2018, LNAI 11374, pp. 193–204, 2019.
https://doi.org/10.1007/978-3-030-27544-0_16

# 1  Introduction

When the RoboCup Humanoid League started in 2002, the competition initially consisted of technical challenges only, exercises that were considered useful elements of a soccer game play [13]. In the following years, the challenges developed into 2 vs. 2 robot soccer games. The games raised considerable attention among researchers and led to the participation of 20 teams in the 2005 RoboCup Humanoid League. At that time, the two robots per team had a size of about 40 cm, the environment was color-coded and the surface was a flat carpet. Moreover, constraints on the robot's body parameters like height of the center of mass and foot size were very favorable for new teams to enter. The current rules allow 4 robots with a height between 40 and 90 cm for the kid size sub-league, 3 robots with a size between 80 and 140 cm in teen size and a single robot of 130 to 180 cm in adult size. However, most successful robots range between 70 and 90 cm. There is no more color-coding, except for the identification of robot teams. The games are now played with white goals on both sides and a regular FIFA-compliant ball. However, there is still a considerable gap between the current requirements in the league and the regular FIFA rule book: The current field size is 9 * 6 m with a playing period of two times 10 min. Aiming for the 2050 game, the field size must increase to about 100 * 60 m within the coming 30 years. Robots will need to reach a height of about 1.80 m or more, and an endurance of 45 min. While the walking speed of the current robots rarely exceeds 1.5 km/h, they must be able to run at a minimum of 15 km/h (sustained) to 36 km/h (burst) as the human competitors in the 2050 game are capable of. In addition, robots must be able to kick the ball at more than 100 km/h and have a vertical leap that is better than 50 cm to be competitive against the best human players. Note that we chose these physical skills since they are easy to measure and we believe that they are necessary, but not sufficient for world class soccer players. Many attributes such as speed with the ball, ability to change direction quickly, and to predict the play are of the utmost importance but too hard to measure experimentally. Table 1 gives an indication of the current value, the 2050 requirements and the required average yearly increase to reach the goal. However, requirements may not increase gradually but rather stepwise. For example the endurance requirement may jump from 10 to 20 min as a next step rather than increasing by 1.2 min every year.

**Table 1.** Necessary robot attributes for the 2050 challenge

| Parameter | 2018 | 2050 | Required average Δ/Year |
|---|---|---|---|
| Height | 40–180 cm | 180–200 cm | ≈1.5 cm |
| Endurance | 10 min | 45 min | ≈1.2 min |
| Running speed | <1.5 km/h | >36 km/h (Burst) | ≈0.9 km/h |
| Kick speed | <2.0 km/h | >100 km/h | ≈3.3 km/h |
| Vertical leap | <1 cm | >50 cm | ≈1.6 cm |

The league already faces stagnation of the number of teams participating. We believe that a main reason is that teams fear both the cost as well as the hardware and software challenges connected to larger robots. New teams enter the Humanoid League almost exclusively through the kid size league and few of them eventually work their way up to teen and adult size, which supports this hypothesis. However, with the increasing level of difficulty in all sub-leagues, it is expected that even this entry-level will become too high for new teams, especially undergraduate student teams, in the very next years. As an evidence, the Humanoid League at RoboCup German Open was cancelled in 2018 after many years of successful competitions due to lack of new teams.

Figure 1 gives an indication of the planed evolution of the robot and the field size in the league as discussed within the league in 2014 [4]. The roadmap is driven by scientific challenges that the Humanoid League TC believes are crucial to accomplish the 2050 goal and that they hope to achieve by controlling the playing field and associated rules of the league. For example, larger playing fields naturally lead to improvements in the running speed of robots and their visual acuity. Furthermore, special scientific challenges are approached via technical challenges (e.g., the 2018 competition includes jumping and kicking a rolling ball challenges as they are crucial scientific goals, but are not currently beneficial in the soccer matches).

However, the increasing number of robots per team will put high demands on each team's logistics and budget. The Technical Committee already addressed this matter by introducing the drop-in games [10], which allows participants to attend the competition with only a single robot. It was inspired by the drop-in challenges introduced by the FIRA United Soccer competition (2011), and the Standard Platform League (where drop-in was introduced in 2013 [2], and later improved [1]). However, rather sooner than later, costs for research, components and equipment even for a single humanoid robot will reach a level that may be too high to be taken in one step. We propose a Humanoid Rookie League, which we will detail in the coming sections, to ease the path for new teams and to guide towards full participation. The HRL will combine elements of robotics and artificial intelligence education and research and shall enable undergraduate teams to develop a robot to participate in the league within the time frame of a year's project. The design follows research on robotics in education, e.g. [14] and [12]. The small rule set [3] will prioritize the principles of robotic entertainment and avoid complex regulations and requirements, such that participation and watching shall be highly attractive.

## 2   Soccer Leagues Development

As the abilities of the robots increase, it is clear that the amount of human interaction with the robots must be reduced for safety reasons alone. New teams must implement a large amount of code to simply fit into the league's infrastructure (e.g., listening and providing status updates to the game controller or automatic referee). Even though established teams publish their code base, this is still a

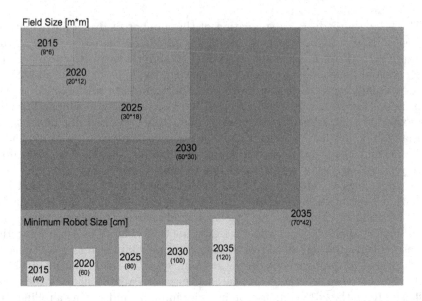

**Fig. 1.** Development of field and robot sizes as stated in the Humanoid League Roadmap from 2014 [4].

non-trivial work that is not at the core of soccer playing robots and thus of little interest to new teams, but still necessary to participate in the advanced leagues during RoboCup.

While league infrastructure is required in all leagues, the Humanoid League is at a great disadvantage when compared to the other RoboCup soccer leagues: Both in 2D and 3D simulation as well as in the Standard Platform League no hardware development is involved, which means that a good solution from a single team can be shared with all other teams and the league can make significant progress in this respect. Most teams in the Humanoid League use their own hardware and software, which makes sharing more difficult. There have been several attempts to use common middle-ware (e.g., ROS) or frameworks (FUmanoids player communication library [6]) to standardize at least some components in the Humanoid League. These attempts have not been very successful. For example, even though a lot of teams are interested in ROS, few teams actually implement it in their robots, first and foremost because updating a whole architecture takes considerable time away from implementing new features to keep up with the rule updates every year. The Technical Committee tried to foster a more collaborative approach within the league in the last years: In 2017, a drop-in challenge was introduced as a mandatory part of the competition for all teams participating in kid and teen size. While team collaboration increased *during* RoboCup, only few adaptations to hardware and software are actually made on-site. By announcing the drop-in teams in advance, the Technical Committee will make another attempt to strengthen the code exchange and development of a common code basis between the teams for 2018.

The increasing level of difficulty in the software development is only one of the development tracks in the Humanoid League. Similar to the Small and Middle Size League, the Humanoid League teams have to develop their own hardware, too. However, in contrast to the other hardware leagues, which

- use wheel-based locomotion,
- allow for non human-like hardware and vision-approaches and
- do rarely include rule changes which forces significant changes in the robot's hardware,

the Humanoid League imposes a very different level of hardware challenges on participating teams.

Even the Standard Platform League with the potential of easily exchangeable code faces a situation with few very advanced teams leaving the majority of other teams behind. The introduction of a Champions Cup creates an option for advanced teams to keep their games challenging, while still enabling new and less successful teams to play balanced games in the classical competitions [8]. A similar approach will be taken by the Small Size League in 2018 for the first time [5]. The idea of introducing a Rookie League, however, proposes a competition scenario at the 'lower' end of the performance range, because the 'higher' end is already defined by the 2050 challenge. A similar approach is followed by the @home Educational Challenge, co-located with the 2018 European RoboCup Junior [9]. Without the HRL, new teams will soon not be able to even meet the requirements for participating before putting in years of development effort and after significant investment. However, we strongly believe that new teams benefit from entering real competitions and networking with other teams during RoboCup events early on. Therefore, we need to provide a possibility for new teams to enter the Humanoid League and play against equally strong opponents while still developing towards the 2050 game for the experienced teams.

## 3   The Humanoid Rookie League

The user story of the Humanoid Rookie League is based on a group of undergraduate or early graduate students, interested in humanoid robotics and robotics soccer. They are assumed to have a yearly budget of a few thousand Dollars and some faculty support and should be able to design, build and program robots to enter the league within a time-frame of one year. With competitions organized at regional, super-regional and international level, the RoboCup Federation already allows for limited traveling budget of new-coming teams. Considering bipedal locomotion the core element of the Humanoid League, bipedal locomotion and kicking or driving a ball should be at the center of the Rookie League. At a lower, yet necessary level we see basic perception, localization with a local map and elementary planing. It is a core idea of the Rookie League that the rules and requirements of the league are simple enough as an entry point while simultaneously clearly guiding the development of a hardware platform and software base which can be used to compete in the regular Humanoid League within two or three years of participating in the Rookie League.

**Fig. 2.** HL Rookie League robot (left) and cardboard goal keeper (right).

### 3.1 Bipedal Locomotion

Constraints on the robots shall be reduced to the minimum. The regular league imposes restrictions on the center of mass (COM), height and foot size, just to mention a few. Except for the requirement of bipedal locomotion and a maximum size and weight, the Rookie League rules may not foresee any further constraints on the robot design. Avoiding or reducing the danger of falling, e.g. by sufficiently large feet, would allow to implement a robot with as few as 4 motors. Avoiding rules requiring to kick the ball, instead of just pushing it, would make robot design and control easier. However, locomotion on the difficult artificial turf used in the Humanoid League is still considered a significant challenge. Figure 2 shows a prototype of a basic 4-DOF bipedal robot for the HRL next to a FIFA size-1 ball. A game shall be played by robot teams of 3–6 robots, with each participant or participating team providing a single robot. Scoring and team building will be done according to the Humanoid League drop-in scheme [7], which awards points for scoring goals and supporting other robots. The range of number of robots per team allows for easy adjustment to the actual number of participants. In this case a competition with multiple games can be held with as little as 6 participating teams (forming 2 teams with 3 robots each). There are 10 different configurations of teams to play against each other with 6 robots, such that multiple games can be played.

### 3.2 Basic Perception

Color coding provides an easy way of identifying objects for a soccer scenario. Color blob detection is among the content of many entry-level computer vision courses. There are even integrated hardware solutions for color blob detection, like CMUCam (PixyCam) smart cameras. As in the earlier Humanoid League times, an orange colored ball, however, now a larger FIFA size-1 ball, shall be used. Coloring the goals is not suitable since this would require additional effort when using the goals of the regular league. Instead, a colored cardboard figure shall be placed in the goal (Fig. 2 right). Goal keepers shall be colored blue and red for the two different teams. This should ease orientation of the robots.

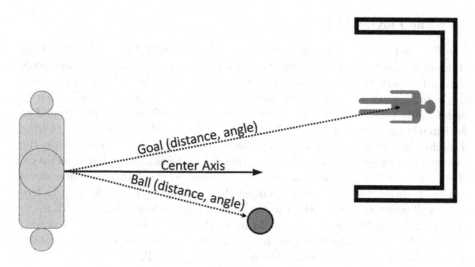

**Fig. 3.** HL Rookie League local map example.

Not having a dedicated goal keeper robot comes with multiple benefits. First, there is no need to implement a dedicated behavior and second, the drop-in scoring scheme becomes much easier and fair, since all robots follow the same behavior. Additional information on the environment can be derived from the fixed size of the objects, such that distances can be estimated with mono vision already.

### 3.3   Localization with Local Maps

Local, ego-centric models may serve as a very basic means of localization. This approach showed to be very easy to acquire for new coming students [11]. Figure 3 gives an example of a robot facing the ball and the opposing goal or more precisely the opposing cardboard goal keeper. From the position and size of the respective color blobs in the image, the position and distance relative to the own position can be estimated. A vector representation lays the base for easy calculations of positions and paths, as well as later decision making and planing.

### 3.4   Elementary Decision Making and Planing

Based on the local map as sketched in the previous subsection, basic decisions can be derived easily by adding and subtracting vectors. For example, in order to identify a suitable position for a goal kick, the robot may calculate the difference between the goal vector and the ball vector and extend it by an offset. After reaching the position the robot has to align to the goal and start driving the ball towards it.

## 3.5    The Playing Field

The Rookie League competitions shall be co-located with the regular RoboCup Humanoid League competitions. Therefore, the same playing field and goals should be used. If needed, the playing field may be reduced in size, e.g. to a single half, playing left to right and moving the goals to the touch lines or maintaining the playing direction with one goal moved to the center line. The field markings may require additional considerations. With a left-right playing direction in one half, temporary field lines may be drawn or taped within the free space between the lines of the current regular field, such that a rectangle of 6 m times 2.7 m without any otherwise misplaced goal box and center circle can be realized. With the main competition moving to larger fields, the free space will increase. Ultimately, the goal box of a full-size FIFA field, with up to approximately 5.5 m times 18 m could be used as afield for the HRL. However, with a strict local model based on the goals and the ball, it is possible for robots to play the game without evaluating field markings at all.

Similar to the field lines, the definition of the goals may impose some challenges. Making use of the same equipment was one of the objectives. However, eventually the main league will arrive at goals with a width of 7.3 m, such that they can not be used for the HRL. Instead we propose to make use of standard soccer goals as used for training purpose.

## 3.6    A Road Towards the Main Competition

While each challenge in itself is kept simplistic on purpose, the setup of the game allows for teams to advance their software and hardware development over time and step by step while still being able to participate in the league. For example, the white goals require more sophisticated vision to differentiate them from the white field lines. The hardware can be extended to using fully developed robots complying with the kid and teen size rules which poses additional challenges in the locomotion. Every year teams participate in the Rookie League they are encouraged to advance in one of the fields, so by the end of the three-year period they are allowed in the Rookie League their robots shall be advanced enough to participate in the regular kid or teen size league. While completely new teams are qualified to participate by default, teams have to demonstrate their advancements in a simplified application process for their second and third year in the Rookie League. This shall ensure that teams actually advance towards being compliant with the main tournament.

# 4    Draft Rookie League Rule Sheet

The guiding principles of the rules are fostering exiting games for participants and visitors and paving new robotics researchers a path to the RoboCup Humanoid League. Aiming for exiting games, robustness of the robots and the robot behavior, as well as minimal human robot handler interaction is crucial.

Attracting many new researchers shall be assured by introducing as few rules as possible to allow for easy implementation of the robot behavior and game play. At the same time they should avoid levering out the competitive advantage of more capable and robust robots. Appendix A shows an initial draft of the rules [3]. In order to guide the participants towards the main Humanoid League, we propose to allow participation to the HRL for a maximum of three years only In order to make robots more easy to handle, rules foresee a limitation to 1 m in size and 10 kg in weight. Robots may be started manually at the touch line, such that human robot handlers do not need to enter the field during start or restart. However, robots listening to the start command of the Humanoid League game controller may be positioned anywhere on the field as an advantage. For start and restart of the game a drop ball is carried out at the center point. The games continue until time is up, a goal is scored or until there is no further progress in the game (stuck game) for whatever reason. Typical scenarios for a stuck games could be robots not being able to find the ball or move it over a longer period of time e.g. because it is too close to a goal post or the goal keeper. Then there is a fresh start. The quality of the overall game play, whilst attempting to make sure that robust robots are not put at a disadvantage by other faster failing robots, is accounted for by restarting, if less than half of the robots of one of the teams are active and on the field. As stable locomotion is of paramount importance and restrictions are few, disallowing to pick up fallen robots, other than during a stoppage of the game, is considered a suitable rule to foster the development of robust robots. If the robot is in danger of damaging itself or others, standing, walking or fallen, it will be removed until next restart. As a default rule, significant authority is given to the referee. It is expected, that during implementation and the first trial run during a competition a few more rules need to be added.

## 5    Conclusions

The Humanoid Rookie League is an attempt to advance the RoboCup Humanoid League towards the 2050 game while still allowing new teams to easily enter with minimal requirements. It bridges the gap between a newcomer's budget of a few thousand Dollars and a 50.000 and more Dollars adult size robot. The HRL competitions provide motivation to new robotics students through manageable challenges and entertaining competitions. The Rookie League is closely linked with the overall league development and sets a clear path towards participation in the main competition after a maximum of three years. In this paper, we laid out the motivation for the Rookie League, presented the guiding principles and discussed a rule draft as a base for a broad discussion within the RoboCup community.

# Appendix A

# Draft of the RoboCup Humanoid Rookie League Rule Sheet

The games in the RC Humanoid Rookie League (HRL) are played as drop-in games for bipedal robots, with a minimal rule set. Every participating individual or group contributes a single robotic player to a robot team. Scoring is according to the HL drop-in rules. Individuals may participate in the Rookie league for a maximum of three years only and must not have participated in the Humanoid league before.

## 1. Field of Play

The HRL league is played on the fields of the RoboCup Humanoid League (currently $9 * 6$ m). Cyan, respectively magenta cardboard figures represent the goal keepers. They are suspended from the respective goals cross bars, reaching the floor. Both figures have the same form. They are positioned by the referee, who may change their position during any stoppage of the game.

## 2. The Ball

The ball is a FIFA size 1 ball with orange colored surface.

## 3. The Number of Players

The teams consist of 3–6 randomly chosen robots and change during the tournament.

## 4. The Players

The robot players are bipedal autonomous robots that walk on two legs and drive a ball by pushing or kicking. The maximum size of the robots is 1 m, the maximum weight is 10 kg. Robots must bring red and blue team markers and must not use blue or red on any part that is not interchangeable. Robots may be started manually at the touch line of their team's own half. Robots that are started by the game controller may be positioned anywhere in their own half After positioning and possibly starting the robots, human team members must not interfere with the game play, except if explicitly called for by the referee. Robots need to be equipped with a handle to be safely picked up by a referee and an emergency switch off that is clearly marked and reachable. Pick-up of robots by robot handler and re-entry only is allowed during stoppage of the game.

## 5. The Referee

Each match is controlled by a team of referees with one head referee, who has full authority to enforce the Laws of the Game.

## 6. The Duration of the Match

A match is played in two half times of 10 min each with a break of 5 min.

## 7. Start and Restart of Play

The play is started and restarted by a drop ball at the kick-off point at the center. The ball is in play for both teams immediately. Goals may be scored immediately. A game is restarted for:

- second half time,
- after a goal was scored,
- after more than half of the robots of a team became inactive or removed after a (re-)start,
- stuck game.

For (re-)start of game robots may be placed and possibly manually started by a robot handler.

## 8. The Ball In and Out of Play

If the ball leaves the field of play, it is returned to field by the referee or an assistant referee, one meter into the field, perpendicular to the point where it crossed the line. There is no stoppage of the game.

## 9. The Method of Scoring

A goal is scored if the ball completely crossed the goal line between the two goal posts.

## 10. Fouls and Misconducts

The following cases are considered as fouls, resulting in a removal penalty until next restart of the game:

- any action posing the potential to significantly damaging a robot, including itself,
- leaving the playing field (field of play and surrounding green surface),
- any other significant offense, e.g. obstructing the game, as considered by the referee.

Robots potentially endangering humans by whatever activity are excluded from the game (red card).

# References

1. Genter, K., Laue, T., Stone, P.: Three years of the RoboCup standard platform league drop-in player competition: creating and maintaining a large scale ad hoc teamwork robotics competition. JAAMAS **31**, 790–820 (2017)
2. MacAlpine, P., Genter, K., Barrett, S., Stone, P.: The RoboCup 2013 drop-in player challenges: experiments in ad hoc teamwork. In: IROS 2014 (2014)
3. N.N. Humanoid League Proposed HRL Rules. http://www.robocuphumanoid.org/wp-content/uploads/HL-rookie-league-2.pdf
4. N.N. Humanoid League Proposed Roadmap. www.robocuphumanoid.org/wp-content/uploads/HumanoidLeagueProposedRoadmap.pdf. Accessed 25 Mar 2018
5. N.N. Laws of the RoboCupSoccer Small Size League 2018 http://wiki.robocup.org/images/4/4f/Small_Size_League_-_Rules_2018_Diff.pdf. Accessed 10 Apr 2018
6. N.N. Mixed Team Communication Protocol. github.com/fumanoids/mitecom. Accessed 10 Apr 2018
7. N.N. RoboCup Humanoid League Rule Book 2018. https://www.robocuphumanoid.org/wp-content/uploads/RCHL-2018-Rules-Proposal_final.pdf
8. N.N. RoboCup Standard Platform League (NAO) Rule Book 2017. http://spl.robocup.org/wp-content/uploads/downloads/Rules2017.pdf. Accessed 10 Apr 2018
9. N.N. RoboCup @home Educational Challenge. www.robocupathomeedu.org/challenges/robocup-home-education-challenge-eurcj-2018. Accessed 22 May 2018
10. Paetzel, M., Baltes, J., Gerndt, R.: Robots as individuals in the Humanoid League. In: RoboCup Symposium (2016)
11. Gerndt, R., Bohnen, M., da Silva Guerra, R., Asada, M.: The RoboCup mixed reality league - a case study. In: Dubois, E., Gray, P., Nigay, L. (eds.) The Engineering of Mixed Reality Systems. HCIS. Springer, London (2010). https://doi.org/10.1007/978-1-84882-733-2_20
12. Gerndt, R., Schiering, I., Luessem, J.: Elements of SCRUM in a students robotics project - a case study. In: Robotics in Education, RiE 2013 (2013)
13. Gerndt, R., Seifert, D., Baltes, J., Sadeghnejad, S., Behnke, S.: Humanoid robots in soccer. IEEE Robot. Autom. Mag. **22**(3), 147–154 (2015)
14. Gerndt, R., Luessem, J.: Designing robotics student projects from concept inventories. In: Robotics in Education, RiE 2017 (2017)

# Context Aware Robot Architecture, Application to the RoboCup@Home Challenge

Fabrice Jumel[1,4], Jacques Saraydaryan[1,4], Raphael Leber[1],
Laetitia Matignon[3,4,5], Eric Lombardi[5], Christian Wolf[2,4,5],
and Olivier Simonin[2,4(✉)]

[1] CPE Lyon, Université de Lyon, Villeurbanne, France
[2] INSA Lyon, Université de Lyon, Villeurbanne, France
olivier.simonin@insa-lyon.fr
[3] UCBL Lyon 1 Univ., Université de Lyon, Villeurbanne, France
[4] CITI Lab., INRIA Chroma, Université de Lyon, Villeurbanne, France
[5] LIRIS Lab., CNRS, Université de Lyon, Villeurbanne, France

**Abstract.** This paper presents an architecture dedicated to the orchestration of high level abilities of a humanoid robot, such as a Pepper, which must perform some tasks as the ones proposed in the RoboCup@Home competition. We present the main abilities that a humanoid service robot should provide. We choose to build them based on recent methodologies linked to social navigation and deep learning. We detail the architecture, on how high level abilities are connected with low level sub-functions. Finally we present first experimental results with a Pepper humanoid.

## 1 Introduction

Most of robotic architectures focus on a specific ability: autonomous navigation, grasping, human-robot interaction, etc. Today, more and more applications and professional or public contexts require a robot to be able to perform several tasks with a high level of abstraction (help a human, execute a human order, serve humans). While AI[1] methods and technologies progress, expectations about service robotics are growing. This is particularly true in complex human-populated environments [1]. In this context we aim to define software architectures that orchestrate and combine different high level abilities and their sub-functions.

Each high-level ability is generally built on sub-functions, that we call also low level tasks or controls. We can mention for instance path-planning computation, SLAM[2] function, object and human detection, or speech output. In this paper we present an architecture which is able to perform high level tasks that require several skills: navigation in dynamic - human-populated - environments, object detection, people detection and recognition, speech recognition, and task

---

[1] Artificial Intelligence.
[2] Simultaneous Localization and Mapping.

© Springer Nature Switzerland AG 2019
D. Holz et al. (Eds.): RoboCup 2018, LNAI 11374, pp. 205–216, 2019.
https://doi.org/10.1007/978-3-030-27544-0_17

planning. Interacting with humans and answering to their orders is a very large and challenging problem. In this paper, as a first step, we limit our study to the high-level tasks proposed in the RoboCup@Home competition, by focusing on social navigation. These tasks are presented in the next section.

Our approach distinguishes two main levels. The first one is the "decision" level which selects the main high level task to do, and potentially in parallel. The second level is defined as a set of general tasks which are required in several high level tasks. We organize this level in a limited set of generic tasks, which are themselves built on sub-functions that can be shared.

The paper is organized as follows. Section 2 presents the context of the RoboCup@Home challenge and its relative tasks. We also discuss existing works on robot software architectures. Then in Sect. 3 we give an overview of the proposed architecture, before to detail in Sect. 4 how the General Behavior Manager orchestrates the execution and selection of tasks. Section 5 details the navigation strategy selection and Sect. 6 gives on overview of methodologies used for human detection and interaction. Section 7 illustrates in details the approach on a complex scenario, then Sect. 8 presents first results in the RoboCup@Home challenge. Finally Sect. 9 concludes the paper.

## 2   Service Robots and Software Architectures

We aim at developing software architectures and AI modules allowing mobile/humanoid robots to navigate in human-populated environments and to carry out high-level tasks. In this context, we focus on tasks proposed in the RoboCup@Home challenge[3], which requires to develop and to connect different modules providing image analysis, decision making and learning, human-robot interaction, and autonomous navigation. These modules must be orchestrated in a whole architecture.

The scenarios driving our research concern mainly tour guide robots [2] and waiter robots [3] which are variants of tasks proposed in the Robucup@Home competition. For example, the cocktail party challenge of the RoboCup@Home [4] consists for a robot to take orders during a private party in a flat. In order to score, the robot has to find the room, ask guests about orders and give them to the bartender located in another room. In order to fulfill this scenario, navigation skill and human-robot interaction skill (principally speech interaction) are required. Other tasks are aimed, that are optional part of the challenge:

- Navigate inside the cocktail party room to find calling guests to take order
- Find a more discreet guest to take order
- Find a missing order (drink) on a table or equivalent (object recognition)
- Find back the guest concerned by the missing order (person recognition)
- Be able to describe the guests to the bartender, so that it can correctly distribute the orders in the cocktail party room (person description).

---

[3] http://www.robocupathome.org/.

A major issue in the design of a robot architecture is to allow the robot to fulfill high level objectives while dealing with a complex and dynamic environment. More precisely, the robot has to simultaneously sense the environment, navigate and detect people to interact, and so on. This requires to define dedicated architectures able to orchestrate several tasks, mostly in parallel. Such an issue requires to build behaviors over a middleware embedded in the robot. In Calisi et al. [5] authors showed that a lot of frameworks have been proposed for robotics software development. More recently, Chitic et al. [6] have underlined that ROS has become a classic middleware to support such a development, with a rich library of functions. Other middlewares, as [7], focus on tasks description language and life cycles. To build a generic architecture, we have chosen ROS as middleware: we inherit the publish-subscribe way of communication, as well as services and actions, and the manager of concurrent processes (or nodes). Our objective is to propose a generic architecture, able to deal with high level tasks, ie. not focusing on a specific task, scenario, or robot. Concerning software architectures dedicated to humanoids, there are, up to now, few generic solutions to manage service tasks. We can mention the work of Natale et al. [8] dedicated to the iCub, where the architecture is turned towards code generation, motor control, and interfaces.

## 3 Overview of the LyonTech Architecture

In this section we present the embedded AI software architecture of LyonTech's team, aiming at managing both high level decisions and low level tasks of Pepper. Figure 1 gives a general view of the proposal. It contains modules which have been developed in different research work of the consortium, completed by off-the-shelf modules which tackle standard tasks, as well as engineering bricks interconnecting these modules.

On top, the **General Behavior Manager** works like an orchestrator and gives orders to other blocks. Their combination allows to achieve high level tasks, as detailed later. The architecture is organized in four principal functionality blocks (cf. Fig. 1), that we detail below.

The **Robot Navigation Manager** is in charge of localizing the robot and allowing dynamic navigation (obstacles avoidance). It uses two sub-functions which are the ROS Navigation layer and the ROS Mapping layer (ie. provided by ROS).

Perception of the environment is performed by the **Object Detection and learning module**, based on deep neural networks [9] and off-the-shelf modules like YOLO-2 [10], which have been retrained and fine-tuned on additional data which we collected specifically for the targeted tasks. Labeled object positions are provided to other blocks. In addition, detailed human information such as human activity, posture, and identity is provided by the complementary People Detection Learning module.

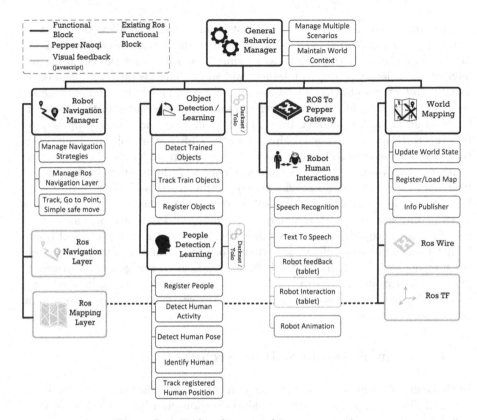

**Fig. 1.** LyonTech software architecture overview

(a)                                                                      (b)

**Fig. 2.** Our recent visual perception work: (a) gesture recognition [11]; (b) activity recognition [12]

All human-robot interactions are managed by the **Robot Human Interaction** block embedded in the robot. The robot also maintains a knowledge database about its environment (humans, objects, and points of interest positions).

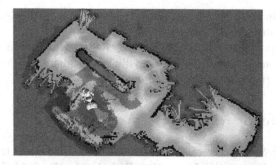

**Fig. 3.** Example of integration scenario including navigation and object recognition.

The last module, called the **World Mapping**, is in charge of mapping the environment, including also semantic information, and relies on the ROS Mapping layer shared with the Robot Navigation Manager.

These modules are built on previous team's work, which can be summarized in four topics:

**Perception:** Our computer vision module brings knowledge in gesture recognition [11] and activity recognition [13], see illustrations in Fig. 2. These methods are capable of running in real time and have been integrated in our platforms of mobile robots. Combined with object detection [10], this allows us to be aware of the objects present in a room, their locations, as well as the ongoing activities in this room (see illustration in Fig. 3).

**Motion planning and Decision making:** This module aims to deal with motion planning in dynamic and uncertain environments, 2D mapping, and 2D localization. We combine our work on autonomous navigation in crowded environments (human-aware navigation) [14] with service delivery strategies [3].

**Human-Robot Interactions:** We have been working for several years on different interactions with robots (from teleoperation to multi-robot orchestration [15,16]). The Naoqi SDK, provided by Softbank Robotics with the Pepper robot, gives a set of API that are mainly used for Robot and Human interactions (speech recognition, text to speech, robot behavior feedbacks). In order to highlight the robot activity, the Pepper tablet gives visual feedbacks (javascript framework). In the context of the RoboCup@Home we use these different functionalities to give a user friendly interaction with robots including Animations, Tablet, and Dialogues.

**Integration:** All components are integrated using the ROS middleware, which is the base system of our architecture. Figure 3 illustrates an integration scenario and its implementation with a Pepper robot.

## 4 General Behavior Manager

The General Behavior Manager acts as an orchestrator of high level tasks. Four main tasks are executed in parallel: Perception Task, Navigation Task, HRI Task, and General Manager Task.

The General Manager task is in charge of loading a scenario description and managing high level call of Perception, Navigation, and HRI tasks. Each task call could interact synchronously or asynchronously with the General Manager Task. This interaction is based on action as defined in ROS Architecture and leads to a task state (pending, success, failure). The scenario description defines the sequence and conditions of task calls including task timeout, multi-conditional success, and target of the task (navigation point, dialogues, object to find, ... ).

With the help of given ontologies, when a task failure occurs, the general manager attempts to change the task target before retrying. As mentioned in [17], ontologies can be used to select objects that share same properties/usages. For example, if the robot was asked to find a coke bottle, and if no one was found, the general manager could provide the alternative target "fizzy drink" (considered as parent class of coke) to the perception task.

## 5 Navigation Strategy Selection

The main objectives of a social aware robot navigation is first to be safe for people around him, to be safe for himself, and then to navigate as quickly as possible while respecting social conventions. The targeted environment can be composed of dynamic obstacles, and of populated or congested areas. To deal with such constraints, we provide our robot with the ability to select a navigation strategy compliant with the current environment. To optimize robot navigation,

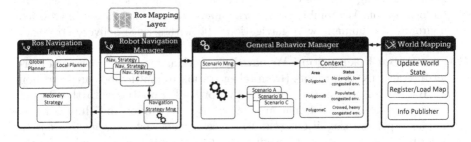

**Fig. 4.** Navigation strategy selection

we propose to maintain a **context of the robot environment**. To do so we distinguish two main dynamic parameters, the human density in the environment and the environment complexity (level of congestion). On one hand, with the help of the built map, we are able to compute the obstacle density of an area. Once the area delimitation is computed, a percentage of obstacle pixel in this area is computed. With the combination of the color distribution entropy [18] we can determine if an area contains a lot of obstacles and how they are distributed in the targeted area (complexity). The higher the obstacle density and dispersion is, the higher the probability to freeze the robot during navigation is. On the other hand, the world mapping function helps to maintain the observed human locations into a map. The area delimitation is then provided by segmentation following the approach of [19].

As shown in Fig. 4, maintaining different contexts into a map allows the general manager to ask the navigation manager to select a navigation strategy according to the goal to achieve and the context of the environment. The Navigation manager holds a set of navigation strategies. Each navigation strategy is focused on different objectives:

- optimize the robot navigation to go as quickly as possible to the objective, while being adapted to the environment.
- ensure a safe navigation including recovery mode in case of freezing (eg. replay last command before robot freeze).
- optimize the robot navigation into populated environment (eg. by following the human flow [14]).

When the General Behavior Manager needs a Navigation Task, a first path is computed from the robot actual position $A$ to the goal $G$. This path, $A \rightarrow G$ is computed by the ROS navigation task service (make_plan service). Once the path is computed, the General Behavior Management gets Context information and the associated areas. Regarding to the path $A \rightarrow G$, crossed areas are considered and become sub navigation goals $S_i$. Then the General Behavior Management asks for a navigation task according to the appropriated navigation strategy $\pi_i$ for each sub goal until the goal is reached: $A \rightarrow S_0, \ldots, S_{i-1} \rightarrow S_i, \ldots, S_{n-1} \rightarrow G$.

# 6 Human Detection and Interaction

The interaction of the robot with close people requires that the robot can collect information about humans. To do so we build interaction abilities from the following functionalities which are finally integrated (see Fig. 5 Human Detection/Learning block):

- Human Detection: with the huge increase of the efficiency of Deep learning based tools, detection of objects and people is quickly carried out using standard RGB camera. For this purpose, we integrate the well known **Yolo-2 model** [10] (in its original C++ *"darknet"* implementation) in order to get estimates of bounding boxes centered on humans in the visual field.

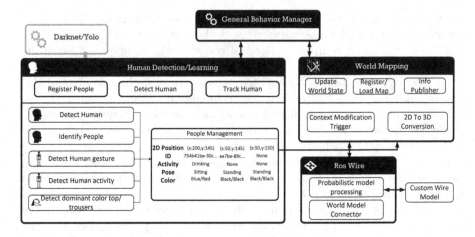

**Fig. 5.** People perception processing organization

- Human Identification (face detection): to allow interaction with human, it is also required to recognize already met people. To tackle this problem, we adapt a module of face recognition to our system. We use the method provided by Adam Geitgey's library[4].
- Human pose: articulated pose provides important information for interaction with humans. The openpose tools[5] are used to extract information about the skeleton of each person, i.e. a set of body key point positions. In addition, we developed a function to determine main people poses like standing, sitting, lying and hand call, by calculating the different key points relative positions. Thanks to camera settings and pose, combined with human 2D normalized data, we can estimate partial 3D pose of people. Therefore, we can improve the posture detection, estimate the depth, and discern the different people groups.
- Human dominant color top/trousers: all different clues are important to discriminate people. Using openpose and a dominant color detection we can detect main colors of specific body position if available (we developed a ROS node including a HSV color transformation and a K-mean color clustering).
- Human activities: we recognize complex human activities with our own method, recently introduced, and getting state of the art performance on standard datasets [13]. This method was specifically designed for robot applications: it is capable of running in near time and requires only standard sensors, i.e. a single RGB camera, while at the same time outperforming other methods, which use multiple modalities.

An additional process is required to track all these data/encountered humans. To do so we customize the world state estimator of detected object *wire*[6]. *Wire*

---

[4] https://github.com/ageitgey/face_recognition.

[5] https://github.com/CMU-Perceptual-Computing-Lab/openpose.

[6] http://wiki.ros.org/wire.

provides a toolset to track various object attributes during the time. Object location, color and label can be tracked through various models including Kalman Filter (e.g for position attribute). All these tools include a model of uncertainty to be robust in real situation. For this purpose, we customize world object model of *wire* to track human position according to a defined Kalman filter and all additional labels (such as id, pose, activity, and dominant color) through uniform distribution models.

With the help of this information, the General Manager updates the context map. The people density of a given area could be computed and the navigation strategies change according this update.

# 7    Step by Step Scenario Execution

In order to illustrate the functioning of our architecture, let's see the execution of an example of a general purpose robot scenario. The following scenario is aimed: after the operator is found by the robot, the operator asks the robot to go to the kitchen, to find Tom, and to say him a joke. First of all, with the existing map, the World Mapping block provides to the General Behavior Manager a Context including different room polygons with associated congestion level and people density (0.5 by default).

The General Behavior Manager starts the 4 main tasks: Perception (using the Object Detection/learning and People Detection/Learning blocks), Navigation, HRI, and **General Manager Task (GMT)**.

The **GMT** loads the targeted scenario, including sequences of executions and task controls. The execution of this scenario is presented in Table 1. In this table, gray rows refer to actions executed by the **GMT** itself and other rows to task calls. Concerning the columns, the id refers to the sequence number of the operation, the operation column to the type of general manager execution, the task type column gives the name of the task called, the mode column can take two values synchronous (Sync.) or asynchronous (ASync.). In the target column, the inputs of the task call is set. Finally, The success conditions are defined by the column of the same name.

After waiting the door is opened (1), the **GMT** computes sub goals and get the associated strategy to go to the living room (2). For each sub goal (3), the Navigation Task is called to go to the current sub-goal $S_i$ applying the associated navigation strategy $\pi_i$. When all Navigation Task succeeded, a Perception Task is called to find a people (4). The **GMT** waits until a people is detected. After that, it is asked to the operator to explain the mission to do (5). When achieved, the **GMT** transforms the given information into a set of actions (6). After recomputing sub goals (7), the robot is asked to detect human around (8) and to go to the kitchen (9). Note that during the robot navigation, human information is collected and transmitted to the World Management Block. When the destination is reached, the **GMT** calls the World Management database to see if there is a human in the kitchen (10). The robot asks to the human confirmation about it's identity (11). However, it is not Tom. The **GMT** tries

**Table 1.** Operation list of the General Manager (gray rows are GMT actions, others are task calls)

| id. | Operation | Task Type | Mode | Target | Success Condition |
|---|---|---|---|---|---|
| 1 | Loop until Success | Perception | Sync. | Opened Door | State=success |
| 2 | Make Path to living Room, Compute sub. goals $S_i$, get navigation strategy $\pi_i$ | | | | |
| 3 | For all $S_i$ | Navigation | Sync. | $S_i, \pi_i$ | State=success |
| 4 | Loop until Success | Perception | Sync. | Human | State=success |
| 5 | Wait Success | HRI | Sync. | Ask for Goal | State=success |
| 6 | Compute task list from results of task.id=5 | | | | |
| 7 | Make Path to Kitchen, Compute sub. goal $S_i$, get Navigation strategy $\pi_i$ | | | | |
| 8 | Loop until Success of task.id=9 | Perception | ASync. | Human | State=success |
| 9 | For all $S_i$ | Navigation | Sync. | $S_i, \pi_i$ | State=success |
| 10 | Call world management and check if human is in the kitchen | | | | |
| 11 | Wait Task End | HRI | Sync. | Ask for Name | Result=Tom |
| 12 | In case of Failure get new HRI Task Target = Human | | | | |
| 13 | Call world management and check if human is in the kitchen | | | | |
| 14 | Wait Task End | HRI | Sync. | Tell a joke | State=Success |

to find a new valid target by changing the level of abstract of Tom resulting into "Human" (12). After checking again if a human is still there (13), the robot tells a joke (14).

## 8   Experimental Evaluation

In order to experiment our architecture with a Pepper humanoid, we prepared Pepper to be controlled by a PC with ROS. The gateway between ROS and the Pepper robot has been customized and allow to gather Pepper sensor information (RGBD data, laser information, odometry,..). The ROS Pepper navigation task has been defined with the ability to map the environment and avoid obstacles. After comparing two object/people detection techniques (tensorflow Single Shot Multibox Detector SSD and MobileNet, Darknet Yolo 2), the Darknet framework with the Yolo 2 model gives currently better results concerning object detection.

Interaction between ROS and Naoqi Dialogue System has been made allowing to test a simple general purpose robot service scenario: detect a people, ask for a task, understand task "Find Maria", navigate to search people, and identify the targeted people.

Preliminary results with these tasks can be shown in the video[7]. In this video, after introducing our research work on perception and navigation, a first

---

[7] https://www.youtube.com/watch?v=TPTh_KjVUJQ.

experimental result with this scenario is shown. On the left side, the Robot navigation is presented including map representation and simple object detection from the robot side view. On the right side, results of object and people detection are shown thanks to the Darknet framework and Yolo 2 model. Finally, in the last part of the video, a simple general purpose robot service is presented.

## 9  Conclusion

In this paper, we offered an overview of the architecture developed by the Lyon-Tech team to target the SSPL RoboCup@Home competition with a Pepper humanoid. After introducing the different AI modules we developed, we presented the architecture which allows to organize them. Then we detailed the navigation strategy selection and the human detection blocks. Finally, we introduced first experimental results in a robot service scenario, including detection of people, navigation and search for a person. The video presented in Sect. 8 illustrates the ability of the Pepper to manage such high level tasks. The last stage of this work has been its evaluation during the Social Standard Platform League (SSPL) competition, in Montreal, June 2018. We achieved fifth place, showing the efficiency of the proposed architecture and its ability to orchestrate several tasks and their sub-functions.

## References

1. Iocchi, L., Lázaro, M.T., Jeanpierre, L., Mouaddib, A.-I., Erdem, E., Sahli, H.: COACHES cooperative autonomous robots in complex and human populated environments. In: Gavanelli, M., Lamma, E., Riguzzi, F. (eds.) AI*IA 2015. LNCS (LNAI), vol. 9336, pp. 465–477. Springer, Cham (2015). https://doi.org/10.1007/978-3-319-24309-2_35

2. Burgard, W., et al.: The interactive museum tour-guide robot. In: Proceedings of the Fifteenth National/Tenth Conference on Artificial Intelligence/Innovative Applications of Artificial Intelligence, AAAI 1998/IAAI 1998, Menlo Park, CA, USA, pp. 11–18. American Association for Artificial Intelligence (1998)

3. Saraydaryan, J., Jumel, F., Simonin, O.: Robots delivering services to moving people: individual vs. group patrolling strategies. In: IEEE ARSO, IEEE International Workshop on Advanced Robotics and its Social Impacts (2015)

4. van Beek, L., Holz, D., Matamoros, M., Rascon, C., Wachsmuth, S.: RoboCup@home 2018: rules and regulations (2018). http://www.robocupathome.org/rules/2018_rulebook.pdf

5. Calisi, D., Censi, A., Iocchi, L., Nardi, D.: Design choices for modular and flexible robotic software development: the OpenRDK viewpoint (2012)

6. Chitic, S.-G., Ponge, J., Simonin, O.: Are middlewares ready for multi-robots systems? In: Brugali, D., Broenink, J.F., Kroeger, T., MacDonald, B.A. (eds.) SIMPAR 2014. LNCS (LNAI), vol. 8810, pp. 279–290. Springer, Cham (2014). https://doi.org/10.1007/978-3-319-11900-7_24

7. Lutkebohle, I., Philippsen, R., Pradeep, V., Marder-Eppstein, E., Wachsmuth, S.: Generic middleware support for coordinating robot software components: the task-state-pattern. J. Softw. Eng. Robot. 1(2), 20–39 (2011)

8. Natale, L., Paikan, A., Randazzo, M., Domenichelli, D.: The iCub software architecture: evolution and lessons learned. Front. Robot. AI **3**, 24 (2016)
9. Moysset, B., Louradour, J., Wolf, C.: Learning to detect and localize many objects from few examples. Pre-print: arXiv:1611.05664 (2016)
10. Redmon, J., Farhadi, A.: Yolo9000: better, faster, stronger. In: IEEE Conference on Computer Vision and Pattern Recognition CVPR (2017)
11. Neverova, N., Wolf, C., Taylor, G.W., Nebout, F.: ModDrop: adaptive multi-modal gesture recognition. IEEE Trans. Pattern Anal. Mach. Intell. (PAMI) **38**(8), 1692–1706 (2016)
12. Baradel, F., Wolf, C., Mille, J.: Pose-conditioned spatio-temporal attention for human action recognition. Pre-print: arXiv:1703.10106 (2017)
13. Baradel, F., Wolf, C., Mille, J., Taylor, G.W.: Glimpse clouds: human activity recognition from unstructured feature points. In: IEEE Conference on Computer Vision and Pattern Recognition CVPR (2018)
14. Jumel, F., Saraydaryan, J., Simonin, O.: Mapping likelihood of encountering humans: application to path planning in crowded environment. In: The European Conference on Mobile Robotics, ECMR 2017, Paris, France (2017)
15. Sevrin, L., Noury, N., Abouchi, N., Jumel, F., Massot, B., Saraydaryan, J.: Preliminary results on algorithms for multi-kinect trajectory fusion in a living lab. IRBM Innov. Res. BioMed. Eng. **36**(6), 361–366 (2015). Special Issue: SI
16. Nauer, E., Cordier, A., Gaillard, E.: Man-machine collaboration to acquire adaptation knowledge for a case-based reasoning system. In: ACM DL (ed.) WWW 2012, 21st International Conference on World Wide Web - SWCS 2012 Workshop, Semantic Web Collaborative Spaces, Lyon, France, pp. 1113–1120. ACM, April 2012
17. Sommaruga, L., Perri, A., Furfari, F.: DomoML-env: an ontology for human home interaction. In: Proceedings SWAP 2005, the 2nd Italian Semantic Web Workshop, Trento, Italy, 14–16 December 2005. CEUR Workshop Proceedings (2005)
18. Sun, J., Zhang, X., Cui, J., Zhou, L.: Image retrieval based on color distribution entropy. Pattern Recogn. Lett. **27**(10), 1122–1126 (2006)
19. Mielle, M., Magnusson, M., Lilienthal, A.J.: A method to segment maps from different modalities using free space layout - MAORIS: map of ripples segmentation. CoRR, abs/1709.09899 (2017)

# From Commands to Goal-Based Dialogs: A Roadmap to Achieve Natural Language Interaction in RoboCup@Home

Mauricio Matamoros$^{(\boxtimes)}$ (iD), Karin Harbusch, and Dietrich Paulus

Active Vision Group (AGAS), University of Koblenz-Landau,
Universitätsstr. 1, 56070 Koblenz, Germany
mmatamorosmc@gmail.com

**Abstract.** On the one hand, speech is a key aspect to people's communication. On the other, it is widely acknowledged that language proficiency is related to intelligence. Therefore, intelligent robots should be able to understand, at least, people's orders within their application domain. These insights are not new in RoboCup@Home, but we lack of a long-term plan to evaluate this approach.

In this paper we conduct a brief review of the achievements on automated speech recognition and natural language understanding in RoboCup@Home. Furthermore, we discuss main challenges to tackle in spoken human-robot interaction within the scope of this competition. Finally, we contribute by presenting a pipelined road map to engender research in the area of natural language understanding applied to domestic service robotics.

**Keywords:** Robotic competitions ·
Natural language understanding · Artificial intelligence and robotics

## 1 Introduction

From its foundation, RoboCup@Home has stressed the importance of natural interaction between humans and robots. With the target perspective that intelligent robots can understand people's orders that fall within their application domain. Thus, Human-Robot Interaction (HRI) has always been pursued in the competition.

However, a detailed evaluation of natural language interactions is not easy. In favor of many other functions in early stages of the robot development, simple straightforward commands often served the purpose of interaction. This, along with (a) the noisy competition environments, (b) the biased, non-native speaker operators; and (c) the use of command generators to instruct robots have impeded the definition of fine-grained evaluation measures RoboCup@Home for natural language understanding in the domain of RoboCup@Home.

In order to achieve this goal, we first analyzed the progression of the league in Automatic Speech Recognition (ASR) and Natural-Language Understanding

© Springer Nature Switzerland AG 2019
D. Holz et al. (Eds.): RoboCup 2018, LNAI 11374, pp. 217–229, 2019.
https://doi.org/10.1007/978-3-030-27544-0_18

(NLU) in the last nine years. Our proposal is based on claims made by the participating teams in their Team Description Papers (TDPs), relevant publications, rulebooks, multimedia material available on-line, and our cumulative experience as participants and referees in RoboCup@Home since 2009.

In this paper we present a road map to pave the way towards a completely natural interaction between humans and robots. This ultimate goal is achieved by defining milestones that promote the use of natural-language interaction. We underpin our strategy by getting the general public involved in the creation of a large annotated dataset of untrained and unbiased operators, inexistent to the extent of our knowledge. Here, the competition plays a fundamental role, since RoboCup@Home sets the perfect scenario to involve the audience in data production for scientific use. We believe this data will foster research in both, Natural-Language Processing (NLP) and HRI.

The paper is organized as follows. In Sect. 2, we briefly introduce the RoboCup@Home league. In turn, we present a summary of the last nine years of the competition, and give an overview of the strategies used by the teams to solve the tests. In Sect. 3 we summarize the main unresolved challenges in human-robot interaction. In Sect. 4 we discuss a roadmap and its milestones to deal with the key problems. Finally, in Sect. 5 we sum up and draw conclusions.

## 2    Speech Recognition and Natural Language Understanding in RoboCup@Home

RoboCup@Home aims at developing service and assistive robot technology by evaluating a robot's performance with a series of **tests** in an unstandardized and realistic scenario. Here, new approaches are tested in a competitive setup where robots have to solve a set of common household **tasks** upon request. Consequently, the competition influences research, even sometimes directing it. Such is the case of ASR and NLU, since they are fundamental to HRI.

In a **test**, a task is divided in a sequential set of subgoals or phases, being necessary to fulfill one goal to advance to the next phase [8]. This approach keeps difficulty reasonably low for newcomers, while still striving for high top level performance [25]. Usually, in the beginning, the **operator** gives a spoken command to the robot. A **command** is typically a short imperative sentence containing all required information to execute a predefined task. Normally, the operator and the **referee** take account of the robot's processing, whereas the scoring is executed by the Technical Committee (TC), which is also in charge of design tests and review rules. Detailed descriptions can be found in [8,27].

In RoboCup@Home, ASR and NLU are closely related. Spoken commands have always been the preferred way to operate a robot and, since robots need to confirm they have understood the command, both abilities are commonly scored together.

The evolution process of Automatic Speech Recognition and Natural-Language Understanding in RoboCup@Home is addressed as follows. In Sect. 2.1, we summarize the last nine years of competition, focusing on the main challenges the teams had to face. In Sect. 2.2, we present an overview on strategies used to solve the tests.

## 2.1 Historical Overview of HRI Testing

Our review starts in 2009. We have chosen this year because the rulebook of 2009 is the oldest available on the RoboCup@Home website[1].

For the competition in **Graz 2009** the guidelines for operating a robot were loose. Most interactions were hardwired, based on each team's preconceptions of what a natural HRI could be. In addition, the use of headsets and wireless microphones was common, and some tests rewarded the use of gestures over speech.

**Istanbul 2010** came with important changes: (a) scoring was made explicit, (b) score sheets were included in the rulebook, and (c) interaction guidelines were included as part of the tasks in each test. For instance, a robot could score for catching the name of a person or room (typically, only the name was given).

But the cornerstone of 2010 was the inclusion of the *General Purpose Service Robot* (GPSR) test. In this test the operator could command the robot to perform any task from any of other test (including those of former years). Moreover, robots had to deal with long sentences and incomplete information for the first time; a big step in NLU and HRI. Notwithstanding, all interactions in GPSR followed the patterns used in the other tests.

For **Singapore 2011** most interaction guidelines had been removed and a **command generator**[2] was developed by the TC for GPSR (teams only had access to a limited version).

No significant changes in NLP or spoken HRI were introduced in the next three years. Nevertheless, the TC noticed a sustained performance decrease in command retrieval.

To help teams, in **João Pessoa 2014** the TC introduced a way to bypass speech recognition in order to solve the task: the *Continue* rule. However, only few teams took advantage of it.

For **Hefei 2015** the use of QR codes to bypass ASR was made compulsory. Moreover, the data recording feature allowed teams to get a scoring bonus and contributing with the league by providing all data acquired by the robot during a test. In addition, a new command generator was open sourced. Notwithstanding, even having access to the verbatim output of the GPSR command generator via the QR Code, many robots remained unresponsive.

In consequence, **Leipzig 2016**, the TC decided to provide open access to the command generator and the generation grammars about one month before the competition. This was a crucial decision due to its direct impact on natural HRI, as explained in Sect. 3. Cloud Computing was another minor but important change. Prior to this year, the availability of an Internet connection through the arena's wireless network wasn't granted. However, in combination with the low

---

[1] http://www.robocupathome.org.

[2] Available on-line: http://komeisugiura.jp/software/2010_GeneralPurposeTest.tgz.

reliability of the network, discouraged teams from exploring solutions based on cloud services.

By **Nagoya 2017**, the previous two years of tests focused on benchmarking had paid off (See Table 2). In addition to an increase in performance in ASR, the relevance of command interpretation and NLU grew with the inclusion of the Standard Platform Leagues (SPL). The out-of-the-box-ready robots allowed teams to focus on high-level problems such as command interpretation, NLU, and task planning and reasoning. This year was the first time in which robots had to answer questions about their environment and previously executed tasks. Moreover, in the Tour-Guide test they also had to attract people outside the competition area, introduce themselves, and answer people's questions without the help of any grammar.

### 2.2   Adopted Strategies and Software Solutions for HRI

Either in face-to-face communication or remotely like by phone, radio, or TV, the hearer decodes the produced sounds of the speaker, trying to match them with the best interpretation given the current context. Similarly, spoken Human-Robot Interaction requires the extraction and analysis of the language elements of the uttered sentence.

**Fig. 1.** One of the most common processing chains for spoken commands

Although possible, dealing with audio signals can be extremely difficult in high levels of abstraction [3,16]. Therefore, the most broadly adopted solution consists in using an Automatic Speech Recognition (ASR) engine to get a text-transcript for further processing as depicted in Fig. 1. Typically, **cardioid microphones** are used as main audio input for the ASR engine to cope with noise. Afterwards, the ASR engine output is preprocessed by some sort of [natural] language processor so the task planner can select the most adequate behavior.

Other than the microphone itself, filters are normally absent and the filtering task is delegated to the ASR engine itself [4]. Although several noise-reduction filters have

**Table 1.** Most used ASR software in 2017

| Usage | ASR engine name |
|---|---|
| 25.81% | CMU [Pocket] Sphinx |
| 16.13% | Google Speech Api |
| 16.13% | Microsoft Speech Api |
| 12.90% | Julius |
| 9.68% | Nuance VoCon/DNS |
| 6.45% | Rospeex |
| 6.45% | Intel RealSense SDK |
| 3.23% | Amazon AWS/Alexa |
| 3.23% | Kaldi |
| 3.23% | iFlyTek |
| 9.68% | Unreported |

been tested in the competitions, we couldn't find any reported successful solution other than **HARK**[3] [2,7,14]. However, HARK is used mostly for sound-source localization and separation.

Continuing with the pipeline of Fig. 1, the most commonly adopted software solutions include Loquendo (now Nuance) ASR [22], and the Microsoft Speech API [17], being most popular **CMU Sphinx** [19,23] as Table 1 shows. However, in 2017, due to the limited computing power of the robots in the SPL, most teams used cloud services (mainly the Google speech API [14,26]) or relied on the built-in ASR system [12,24] which, as the rightmost two columns of Table 2 show, were not as good as other solutions.

**Table 2.** Top-10 scores in ASR-related tests (final rank in parentheses)

| Rank | 2015 | 2016 | 2017 | | |
|---|---|---|---|---|---|
| | | | OPL | DSPL | SSPL |
| 1 | 86.7% (1) | 86.7% (3) | 96.7% (1) | 67.3% (1) | 71.5% (1) |
| 2 | 83.3% (2) | 83.3% (6) | 83.3% (3) | 45.3% (5) | 52.1% (2) |
| 3 | 70.0% (8) | 72.7% (13) | 73.3% (5) | 37.3% (3) | 36.4% (4) |
| 4 | 70.0% (10) | 60.7% (2) | 70.0% (4) | 12.0% (4) | 30.3% (5) |
| 5 | 66.7% (6) | 60.7% (5) | 66.7% (2) | 3.3% (7) | 29.1% (6) |
| Top5 $\bar{x}$ | 75.3% | 72.8% | 78.0% | 33.0% | 43.9% |
| Top5 $\sigma$ | 9.0% | 12.2% | 12.2% | 25.8% | 18.0% |

Despite the remarkable advances achieved in Natural-Language Processing and task planning in recent years, RoboCup@Home has taken little advantage of it. Some reasons include (a) the sequential nature of the tests, (b) the simplicity of the tasks (HRI-wise), (c) the computational power available in the robot, (d) the lack of awareness due to sensors' limitations, and (e) the need of recognizing only a few words. In consequence, most approaches for NLP relied in **keyword spotting** or pattern matching to trigger the execution of a **state machine** [15,20]. At least in the beginning, this strategy seemed to be faster and more robust than its more advanced counterparts, albeit much simpler.

Despite this, robust A.I. solutions have always been in play. As of 2013, it was common to find the task planner and the natural language processor fused in the same module, which doesn't seem to be the case anymore. Common strategies included (a) the use of rules of inference for both, sentence parsing and task planning [11]; (b) probabilistic parsers [5], (c) semantic networks [17], and (d) regular expressions [15] to name some.

Although keyword spotting, **pattern matching**, and state machines are currently used solutions (specially in simple tests), we spotted more powerful and

---

[3] HARK (**H**onda Research Institute Japan **A**udition for **R**obots with **K**yoto University) is an open-source robot audition software that includes modules for ASR and sound-source localization and sound separation. Source: https://www.hark.jp/.

avant-garde approaches. Whilst in 2017 only 39% of the teams didn't mentioned neither NLP nor NLU approaches in their Team Description Paper (TDP), in all other reports the task planner and the NLP are separated. Among the approaches for processing language, we found (a) Probabilistic Semantic Parsers [6]; (b) Multimodal Residual Deep Neural Networks [10], (c) ontology-based parsers over inference engines [18], and (d) probabilistic parsers for syntax-tree extraction along with lambda calculus for semantic parsing [9]. The **Stanford Parser** [21] is the most broadly adopted solution for POS-tagging and syntactic tree extraction, and **LU4R** [1], a Spoken Language Understanding Chain for HRI developed in La Sapienza [13] by participants of RoboCup@Home which is used by several teams.

These newer solutions have increased the robots' performance in the latter versions of GPSR when some ambiguity was added. Nevertheless, the league does not acquire these newer approaches. Most robots are still using grammar-based ASR engines, which limit the input of the NLP unit. Moreover, so far no test requires the resolution of ellipsis or anaphora. Finally, another major inconvenience, is the use of command generators instead of natural interactions. How to develop HRI tests which focus on these problems is discussed in Sect. 3.

## 3   Challenges

As stated in previous sections, several setbacks have been holding back the league's advances in natural language dialogs with the robot. Here we exemplify challenges and come up with guidelines for future research when addressing tougher scenarios.

### 3.1   Noise

One of the most problematic aspects (and to which most attention has been paid) is the noise in the competition environment. Having a separated hall as in 2012 didn't help much. The **ambient noise** produced by over two hundred people greatly exceeds the noise levels of an average apartment.

In the past, several solutions have been proposed to this problem. Having a separate hall, arenas with tall walls, and transform the arena in a sound-proof closed area with glass walls are recurrent examples. However, service robots will also operate in noisy environments such as airports and shopping malls. Thus, we think it is best to deal with this issue in an early stage. For this reason, noise is addressed in the roadmap presented in Sect. 4.

### 3.2   Operators

An aspect that has characterized RoboCup@Home is that the league has always been robot-friendly. People volunteering as operators in RoboCup@Home are often patient and prone to follow the robot's instructions, unconsciously trying to help the robot to succeed (e.g. repeat a given command louder when the robot seems unresponsive). In addition, almost all the operators are specialists, or at least familiar with service robotics. In other words, all testing has been performed by (unconsciously) **biased operators**, making it easier for the robots to accomplish their tasks. However, trying to give a positive impression to the audience, has the disadvantage of voiding the purpose of RoboCup@Home of providing real-case scenarios for testing.

Another important closely related aspect addresses the demographics of the league's participants. An international community will offer **diverse accents** to the robots and styles (which may not be correct). But this diversity comes with a price. With few exceptions, operators having English as second language lack the richness and verbal fluency of a native speaker. Same hold for gender and age.

Therefore bias, variety of speech and diversity of accents, lexicon, and styles, are also addressed in the roadmap of Sect. 4.

### 3.3   Generators

Although the rulebooks never provided interaction templates, suggested guidelines and the sentences produced by the command generators codify biased HRI in a similar way. Besides, officializing the release of the command generator and its **grammars** had the pernicious effect of replacing natural language with a simplistic one, i.e. artificializing interactions. Moreover, the person in charge of the generator (one of the authors of this paper), although proficient, is not a native speaker of the official competition language (US-English). In summary, despite stimulating immediate positive results and supplying the teams with a powerful tool, the careless use of generators might delve into a ballast in the long term. For this reason, the use of command generators is revised in the roadmap of Sect. 4.

In order to overcome the problems discussed in this section, the proposed solution should force robots to deal with a vast diversity of unbiased operators speaking freely and under reasonable conditions of noise, while keeping tests fair and scientifically meaningful. This ultimate goal is analyzed and split into small steps which are presented in Sect. 4.

## 4   Solution Strategy and Roadmap

Ideally, the robots will lead a natural-language dialogue in real-environment conditions. This is the ultimate goal in service robotics regarding NLU. Considering the challenges presented in Sect. 3 we propose a series of specific tests and changes to the existing ones.

In the previous section we identified the biased operators in combination with restricted GPSR as a main obstacle for the stagnation in elaborate HRI. In order to set up a rich corpus of human-robot dialogs, we opt for recruiting untrained English native speakers as **untrained operators**, e.g. selected from the audience. The **unbiased operators** must have little to no previous experience in RoboCup@Home (or preferably in robotics), and be allowed to interact freely with the robot. With these changes, we are solving biasing, variety and diversity of speech, and tackling the artificiality introduced with the command generators.

Needless to say, the proposed changes towards free natural-language dialogs with the robot have to be applied gradually. Therefore, in this section we present a roadmap of three phases that takes as axis the *General Purpose Service Robot* test before changes are propagated and adapted for other tests. Each phase sets a constraint that will rule over the upcoming featured milestones. Milestones present **small increments** in the difficulty of the NLU task, presumably achievable with the data collected in former years. Once solved in GPSR, the constraints of a milestone would become standard practices in other tests. In addition, milestones are planned to respect the two-years-limit established by the founders of the league [8]. Furthermore, the proposed roadmap has the advantage of being adaptable. If sufficient performance hasn't been achieved, the milestones can be shifted forward in time.

In order not to overtax the teams, we propose the following 3-step pipeline to implement the changes by small increments towards free natural-language dialogs with the robots. First, teams test and benchmark with recordings addressing the features of the milestones newly defined; then, those features are tested in GPSR; and finally, propagated to all other pertinent tests.

Hence, the strategy considers also the inclusion of a *Natural-Language Understanding and Action Planning* benchmark in Stage I with a small contribution to the overall score. In this benchmark, a team receives a set of **sound files**, each one containing a task-execution request from an unbiased operator of the same kind that would be given in GPSR. The A.I. of the robot needs to transcribe and analyze these recordings, extracting either a goal, a plan with a set of actions to carry out, or a set of questions or statements to continue the interaction. The score should consider not only the analytical quality of producing transcripts (where applicable penalizing hard-wired constructions in favor of generalized NLP-rules), but also how far the robot went in its planning, and if it was following the right direction. In this way, milestones could be tested one or two years before being implemented in GPSR and propagated to other tests, giving time to teams to prepare. Furthermore, by giving the same recordings to all teams, **fairness** and replicability are addressed, while noise can be tackled by superposing ambient **noise** to the recordings of the operators. It will be up to the TC to decide on the nature and intensity of the noise regarding the league's advances in the subject.

In addition, to support the league and foster research, the proposed strategy exploits the **Data Recording** feature, incorporated in 2015 to the competition. This is deemed as fundamental for the success of our proposal. We think all interactions between the operator and the robot should be recorded and distributed under **Open Access** license as soon as a transcription is available. This includes all benchmarking sets from previous years. In this way, the league supports both, experienced and new competitors. Beyond this obvious assistance the entire scientific community gains relevance. In early stages, teams providing recordings of all speech-based interactions during a test might receive a bonus proportional to the score obtained, as well as an additional bonus or a certificate (as decided by the TC) for annotating the provided data. Later on, such policy should be made compulsory for the roadmap to work with full efficiency, automating the collection process if possible.

Before summing up by means of presenting the roadmap, we have to state some minor clarifications: (1) In all phases, operators with no background in robotics are selected from the audience by the TC. (2) Unless the test specifies otherwise, chosen operators shall be fluent English speakers. (3) Commands, goals, and tasks are generated before the test. A referee must explain all pertinent information to the operators before spoken interactions are recorded and noise overlapped. (4) The TC randomly assigns to each robot a set of generated tasks from the pool. The robot will listen to the recording, but the operator must be present for further (unexpected) interactions.

## Roadmap Phase 1: From Commands to Goal Formulation

The referee gives a specific goal to the operator along with all pertinent information regarding the desired task. For this purpose, a random command generator can be used. When required, the operator can practice with the referee. Referees assist operators in unexpected situations.

The intensity of overlapped noise should increase gradually, starting from relatively quiet environments (country house, city apartment, office, etc.) towards moderately noisy ones (busy office, or a restaurant with background music).

### Yearly Progress

2019 The operator reads the generated command.
**Note:** This vanilla milestone introduces no change to allow the benchmarking of the next milestone in the pipeline.

2020 The operator tries to memorize the command, repeating it to the robot afterwards. Slight variations are expected.

2022 The referee explains the task to the operator, who has to command the robot using their own words (e.g. rephrasing).

2024 The operator requires the robot to accomplish a task, although not necessarily in an imperative way, as if suggesting.

2028 The operator tries to explain the goal to the robot, not specifying what to do, but the expected final result.

While no big changes are expected during the first four years in NLP, we foresee the inclusion of more robust filters and the use of less constrained grammars. However, by the third milestone (2022), operators might unintentionally neglect information, so robots will need to reconcile information as it arrives, making **questions** as needed. Furthermore, people normally make a very efficient use of language, so references are very common. Therefore, we expect the exploration of **reference resolution** such as ellipsis and anaphora by this year. Finally, the latter milestones will keep the pace, slightly moving the focus to task planning while addressing new types of sentences.

## Roadmap Phase 2: Towards Dialog-Based Interaction

The referee gives to the operator a set of examples of what robots can do in a given domain. The operator must propose a similar task for the robot which has to be approved by the referee. The robot may not know how to accomplish the task, in which case the procedure is explained by the operator.

The intensity of overlapped noise ranges from medium to high, with sudden bursts of loud recorded human voices like in shopping malls, grocery stores, and airports are good examples.

### Yearly Progress

2032 After receiving a set of examples, the operator elicits a similar behavior to the robot. The procedure can be explained in detail step by step.

2036 After receiving a topic and a set of examples, the operator requests something of the same difficulty. Sub-goals are detailed to the robot, but not the individual commands. The operator corrects the robot's plan.

In these phases, we continuously add new elements to NLU, integrating it deeper with **planning**, while, at the same time, we are collecting new applications from users (the potential market). Plan-learning using natural language requires the integration of **cardinality**, as well as spatial and temporal relationships (e.g. the operator may request *make me a sandwich*, explaining later on the steps like *grab a slice of bread, spread mayo...*).

In contrast to only presenting an initiated plan to the operator, the tasks stimulate that the operator and the robot have to enter in a **dialog** towards an unconstrained natural interaction.

### Roadmap Goal: Reaching Unconstrained Interaction

In the last phase, the operators only get explained the State-of-the-Art, i.e. the limits of what the robots can achieve. They can request anything crossing their minds within those limits the way they want. The robot may not know how to accomplish the task, in which case the procedure is freely explained by the operator in a dialog.

### Yearly Progress

2040 The operator explains to the robot how to perform an entirely new task and what the results should be.

2044 The operator requires anything from the robot within the state-of-the-art. All planning is left to the robot.

We believe the presented roadmap helps the RoboCup@Home community to push the boundaries of research in HRI.

The first steps will force teams to look for alternatives to grammar-based ASR engines, or at least a less restricted ones. Besides, the continuous analysis of audio signals to separate the operators' voice from noise is also addressed, although dealing with noise can be left as an option for daring teams.

Regarding NLU, the first steps will take current approaches to the limit. Unbiased operators will gradually expose robots to the richness of **free speech**, while the pipeline will grant time to prepare.

Later on, moving from imperative sentences (e.g. *clean the bedroom*) to goal-driven sentences of any kind (e.g. *I need the room clean for tonight, is the breakfast ready?*) will not only have the league working with semantics and pragmatics, but also might foster research in action planning.

Especially, in the second phase, more complex elements of language analysis are incorporated, paving the road towards a dialog-based interaction. On that basis, we stipulate conversational robots in RoboCup@Home. This claim is substantiated in the last phase by widening the domain and removing all constrains from the operators, in order to deal with real-world situations.

Nevertheless the roadmap provides the necessary flexibility for the worst-case scenario where direct instructions can be given to the robots.

## 5 Conclusions

In this paper we provided a historical overview of testing natural-language interactions with robots over the last nine years of RoboCup@Home. We outlined the state-of-the-art Automatic Speech Recognition and Natural-Language Processing. We quantified recent strategies and software solutions adopted by teams to overcome the trials set in the competition.

In these observations we identified a set of challenges that haven't been tackled. Critical components that hamper free dialogs with the robot are posed by the command generator along with the subconscious unintentional bias of the operators. We inspected how individual test features prevent the league from dealing with free natural language. Based on this study, we propose a strategy and a roadmap that formulate key features to implement the in the individual NLP components of the robot (see Fig. 1) to conquer those challenges. Many test details strongly depend on the advancement of ASR engines, neglects non-verbal communication, so there should be an entangled roadmap for these features.

We hope this roadmap will serve as initiative to promote long-term planning in RoboCup@Home. In particular our contribution elaborates on stepstones to elicit thorough NLP to empower robots with strong natural-language skills.

## References

1. Bastianelli, E., Croce, D., Vanzo, A., Basili, R., Nardi, D.: A discriminative approach to grounded spoken language understanding in interactive robotics. In: IJCAI, pp. 2747–2753 (2016)
2. Demura, K., et al.: Happy mini 2017 team description paper. RoboCup@Home 2017 Team Description Papers (2017)
3. Dominey, P.F.: Learning grammatical constructions from narrated video events for human–robot interaction. In: Proceedings IEEE Humanoid Robotics Conference, Karlsruhe, Germany (2003)

4. Doostdar, M., Schiffer, S., Lakemeyer, G.: A robust speech recognition system for service-robotics applications. In: Iocchi, L., Matsubara, H., Weitzenfeld, A., Zhou, C. (eds.) RoboCup 2008. LNCS, vol. 5399, pp. 1–12. Springer, Heidelberg (2009). https://doi.org/10.1007/978-3-642-02921-9_1
5. Gaisser, F., et al.: Delft robotics RoboCup@Home 2013 team description paper. In: Proceedings RoboCup Competition (2013)
6. Hart, J.W., Stone, P., Thomaz, A., Niekum, S.: UT Austin villa RoboCup@Home domestic standard platform league team description paper. RoboCup@Home 2017 Team Description Papers (2017)
7. Hori, S., et al.: Hibikino-Musashi@Home 2017 team description paper. RoboCup@Home 2017 Team Description Papers (2017)
8. Iocchi, L., Holz, D., Ruiz-del Solar, J., Sugiura, K., Van Der Zant, T.: RoboCup@Home: analysis and results of evolving competitions for domestic and service robots. Artif. Intell. **229**, 258–281 (2015)
9. Lee, B.J., et al.: 2017 AuPair team description paper. RoboCup@Home 2017 Team Description Papers (2017)
10. Liu, J., Zhang, Z., Tang, B., Chen, X.: WrightEagle@Home 2017 team description paper. RoboCup@Home 2017 Team Description Papers (2017)
11. Llarena, A., Boldt, J.F., Steinke, N.S., Engelmeyer, H., Rojas, R.: Berlin-United@Home 2013 team description paper. In: Proceedings RoboCup Competition (2013)
12. Martínez, L., et al.: UChile HomeBreakers 2017 team description paper. RoboCup@Home 2017 Team Description Papers (2017)
13. Lázaro, M.T., Iocchi, L., Nardi, D., Hanheide, M., Fentanes, J.P.: SPQReL 2017 team description paper. RoboCup@Home 2017 Team Description Papers (2017)
14. Oishi, S., et al.: AISL-TUT@Home league 2017 team description paper. RoboCup@Home 2017 Team Description Papers (2017)
15. Pineda, L., et al.: The Golem team, RoboCup@Home 2013 (2013)
16. Roy, D.K., Pentland, A.P.: Learning words from sights and sounds: a computational model. Cogn. Sci. **26**(1), 113–146 (2002)
17. Savage, J., et al.: Pumas@Home 2013 team description paper (2013)
18. Savage, J., et al.: Pumas@Home 2017 team description paper. RoboCup@Home 2017 Team Description Papers (2017)
19. Schiffer, S., Niemüller, T., Doostdar, M., Lakemeyer, G.: AllemaniACs@Home 2009 team description. In: Proceedings CD RoboCup (2009)
20. Seib, V., Manthe, S., Memmesheimer, R., Polster, F., Paulus, D.: Team Homer@UniKoblenz—approaches and contributions to the RoboCup@Home competition. In: Almeida, L., Ji, J., Steinbauer, G., Luke, S. (eds.) RoboCup 2015. LNCS, vol. 9513, pp. 83–94. Springer, Cham (2015). https://doi.org/10.1007/978-3-319-29339-4_7
21. Stanford: CoreNLP (2011). http://nlp.stanford.edu:8080/corenlp/
22. Stückler, J., Dröschel, D., Gräve, K., Holz, D., Schreiber, M., Behnke, S.: NimbRo@Home 2010 team description (2010)
23. Wachsmuth, S., Lier, F., Meyer zu Borgsen, S., Kummert, J., Lach, L., Sixt, D.: ToBI - team of Bielefeld a human-robot interaction system for RoboCup@Home 2017. RoboCup@Home 2017 Team Description Papers (2017)
24. Williams, M.A., et al.: UTS unleashed! For RoboCup 2017@home SPL. RoboCup@Home 2017 Team Description Papers (2017)
25. Wisspeintner, T., Van Der Zant, T., Iocchi, L., Schiffer, S.: RoboCup@Home: scientific competition and benchmarking for domestic service robots. Interact. Stud. **10**(3), 392–426 (2009)

26. Yaguchi, H., et al.: JSK@Home: team description paper for RoboCup@Home 2017. RoboCup@Home 2017 Team Description Papers (2017)
27. van der Zant, T., Wisspeintner, T.: RoboCup@Home: creating and benchmarking tomorrows service robot applications. In: Robotic Soccer. InTech (2007)

# RoboCupSimData: Software and Data for Machine Learning from RoboCup Simulation League

Olivia Michael[1] , Oliver Obst[1(✉)] , Falk Schmidsberger[2] , and Frieder Stolzenburg[2]

[1] Centre for Research in Mathematics, Western Sydney University,
Locked Bag 1797, Penrith, NSW 2751, Australia
O.Obst@westernsydney.edu.au

[2] Automation and Computer Sciences Department,
Harz University of Applied Sciences,
Friedrichstr. 57–59, 38855 Wernigerode, Germany

**Abstract.** The main goal of this work is to facilitate machine learning research for multi-robot systems as they occur in RoboCup, an international scientific robot competition. We describe our software (a simulator patch and scripts) and a larger research dataset from games of some of the top teams from 2016 and 2017 in Soccer Simulation League (2D), where teams of 11 agents compete against each other, recorded by this software. We used 10 different teams to play each other, resulting in 45 unique pairings. For each pairing, we ran 25 matches, leading to 1125 matches or more than 180 h of game play. The generated CSV files are 17 GB of data (zipped), or 229 GB (unzipped). The dataset is unique in the sense that it contains local, incomplete and noisy percepts (as sent to each player), in addition to the ground truth logfile that the simulator creates (global, complete, noise-free information of all objects on the field). These data are made available as CSV files, as well as in the original soccer simulator formats.

**Keywords:** Mobile robotics · Multi-robot systems · Simulation · RoboCup · Reinforcement learning · Self-localization

## 1 Introduction

RoboCup is an international scientific robot competition in which teams of multiple robots compete against each other. The RoboCup soccer leagues provide platforms for a number of challenges in artificial intelligence and robotics research, including locomotion, vision, real-time decision making, dealing with partial information, multi-robot coordination and teamwork. In RoboCup, several different leagues exist to emphasize specific research problems by using different kinds of robots and rules.

© Springer Nature Switzerland AG 2019
D. Holz et al. (Eds.): RoboCup 2018, LNAI 11374, pp. 230–237, 2019.
https://doi.org/10.1007/978-3-030-27544-0_19

There are different soccer leagues in the RoboCup with different types and sizes of hardware and software: small size, middle size, standard platform league, humanoid, 2D and 3D simulation [7]. In the 2D soccer simulation league [1], the emphasis is on multi-robot teamwork with partial and noisy information in real-time. Each of the robots is controlled by a separate program that receives sensor information from the simulator as an input and, asynchronously to sensor input, also decides on a next action that is sent back to the simulator, several times a second. This complexity of the environment, with continuous state and action spaces, together with the opportunity to compete against each other, makes RoboCup soccer an interesting testbed for machine learning among many other applications.

To assist automated learning of team behavior, we provide software to generate datasets from existing team binaries, as well as a large dataset generated using 10 of the top participants in RoboCup 2016 or 2017. While it is possible to use the simulator directly for machine learning, it is not easily possible to use the system to learn from existing teams. Our software allows to record data that facilitates this by recording additional data that is not normally available from playing other teams directly. For this, we modified and extended the simulator software to record data from each robots local perspective, i.e., with the restricted views that depend on each robots situation and actions, and also include the sensor noise. In addition, for every step of the game (100 ms), we recorded ground truth information (such as positions and velocities) of all objects on the soccer field, as well as basic actions of each robot. This ground truth information is usually recorded in a binary format logfile, but not available to teams during a match. We also provide scripts to translate these logfiles and the local player information into comma-separated values (CSV) files.

Using this software, we created a dataset from all pairings of the selected teams with 25 repetitions of each game, i.e., 1125 games in total. With 11 robots in each team, a single game dataset consists of 22 local views plus a global (ground-truth) view. These views are made available as CSV files, in addition to the original logfiles, that include additional sensors and actions of each robot recorded as text files.

The provided data are useful for various different tasks including imitation learning (e.g., [3]), learning or testing of self-localization (e.g., [11]), predictive modeling of behavior, transfer learning and reinforcement learning (e.g., [15]), and representation learning for time series data [9]. The next sections describe the environment, robots, and data in more detail.

## 2   Description of the Software Environment

The RoboCup Soccer Simulation Server rcssserver [10] is the software used for the annual RoboCup competitions that have been held since 1997. It is hosted at github.com/rcsoccersim/. We used the rcssserver version 15.3.0 to create our software and the data. The simulator implements the (2D) physics and rules of the game, and also handles the interface to the programs controlling each player.

By default, players use a 90° field of view and receive visual information every 150 ms. Throughout the game, this frequency can actively be changed by each player individually to 75 ms, 150 ms, or 300 ms, by changing the field of view to 45°, 90°, or 180°, respectively. Visual information is transmitted in the form of (Lisp-like) lists of identified objects, with the level of detail of information depending on object distances. Potential objects include all other players on the field, the ball, and landmarks like goal posts, flags, and side lines. Each player also receives additional status information, including energy levels, referee decisions, and the state of the game, every 100 ms. Each robot can issue parameterized actions every 100 ms, to control its locomotion, the direction of its view, and its field of view. A more detailed description of the information transmitted can be found in the simulator manual [6].

## 3    Overview on the Provided Data

In robotics, data collections often comprise lidar data recorded by laser scans. This is very useful in many applications, e.g., field robotics, simultaneous localization and mapping (SLAM) [16], or specific purposes such as agriculture [4]. Other datasets have been collected, e.g., for human robot interaction [2] or human-commentated soccer games [5]. In many contexts, there is not only one but several robots which may be observed. The data from RoboCup that we consider here include information about other robots in the environment and hence about the whole multi-robot system.

Data from multi-agent systems like the RoboCup or the multi-player real-time strategy video game StarCraft [8] provide information on (simulated) environments as in robotics. However, in addition, they contain data on other agents and thus lay the basis for machine learning research to analyze and predict agent behavior and strategies important for multi-robot systems. To provide a diverse dataset, we include several teams from the last two RoboCup competitions, allowing for different behaviors and strategies.

Perception and behavior of each robot during a game depends on the behavior of all other robots on the field. Game logfiles, i.e., files containing ground truth information obtained from recording games, can be produced from the simulator and are recorded in a binary format. Access to individual player percepts, however, is only possible from within the player code. To learn from behavior of other teams, it is useful to use the exact information that individual players receive, rather than the global (and noise-free) information in recorded logfiles. We therefore modified the simulator to additionally also record all local and noisy information as received by the robots on the field in individual files for each player. This information is stored in the same format as it is sent to players. We also provide code to translate these individual logs into CSV files that contain relative positions and velocities (cf. Sect. 6).

We chose ten of the top teams from the RoboCup 2D soccer simulation world championships 2016 in Leipzig, Germany (CSU_Yunlu, Gliders, HELIOS2016, Ri-one) and 2017 in Nagoya, Japan (CYRUS, FRA-UNIted, HELIOS2017,

HfutEngine, MT, Oxsy). Team binaries including further descriptions can be downloaded from archive.robocup.info/Soccer/Simulation/2D.

We played each team against each other team for 25 times, resulting in 1125 games. Generated CSV files from one match vary in size (approx. 200 MB), in total we collected about 229 GB of CSV files (17 GB of data zipped). For each game, we also recorded the original logfiles including message logs. We also generated files with ground truth data as well as local player data in human-readable format. Finally, we made our generating scripts available (cf. Sect. 6), so that they can be used to reproduce our results or to produce additional datasets using other robotic soccer teams. There is also a smaller subset of 10 games where the top-five teams play against each other once (163 MB CSV files plus 217 MB original logfiles). Our software and data is available at

bitbucket.org/oliverobst/robocupsimdata/

with a detailed description of the ground truth and the local player datasets.

# 4  Description of the Ground Truth Data

According to rules of the world soccer association FIFA, a soccer pitch has the size of 105 m × 68 m. This is adopted for the RoboCup soccer simulation league. Nevertheless, the physical boundary of the area that may be sensed by the robots has an overall size of 120 m × 80 m. For the localization of the robot players, the pitch is filled with several landmark objects as depicted in Fig. 1: flags (f), which are punctual objects, lines (l), the goal (g), and the penalty area (p). The origin of the coordinate system is the center point (c). The pitch is divided horizontally ($x$-direction) into a left (l) and right (r) half and vertically ($y$-direction) into a top (t) and a bottom (b) half. Additional numbers (10, 20, 30, 40, or 50) indicate the distance to the origin in meters. Since every soccer game takes place on the same pitch, there is only one file with information about the landmarks for all games that lists all these coordinates, given as a table in CSV format, with name `landmarks.csv`. For example, the row `f r t,52.5,34` says that the right top flag of the pitch has the $(x, y)$-coordinates $(52.5, 34)$.

Further table files provide information about the respective game. The names of all these files – all naming conventions are summarized in Fig. 2 – contain the names of the competing teams, the final scores for each team, possibly extended by the result of a penalty shootout, a time stamp (when the game was recorded), and some further identifier.

The central SoccerServer [6] controls every virtual game with built-in physics rules. When a game starts, the server may be configured by several parameters which are collected in one file with the identifier `parameters`. For example, the row `ball_decay,0.94` denotes that the ball speed decreases by the specified factor (cf. [14]). However, from a robotics point of view, most of the information in this file is not very relevant, like the stamina of the robots, the noise model, or the format of the coach instructions. We therefore skip further details here.

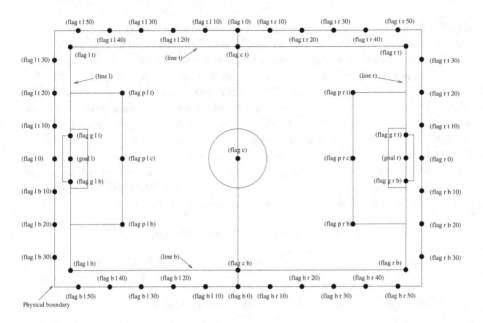

**Fig. 1.** Flags and lines in the robotic soccer simulation (cf. [6]).

1. landmarks: `landmarks` (static information for all games, 1 file)
2. game data: `<time>-<team left>_<score left>-vs-<team right>_<score right>-<id>`
   where `<id>` =
   – `parameters` (server configuration parameters, 1 file)
   – `groundtruth` (logfile information for each game, 1 file)
   – `<team name>_<player number>-<suffix>`
      where `<suffix>` =
      • `landmarks` (relative distances and angles to landmarks, 22 files)
      • `moving` (relative distances and angles to ball and other players, 22 files)

**Fig. 2.** Name conventions for the log and data files.

A soccer simulation game in the RoboCup 2D simulation league lasts 10 mins in total, divided into 6000 cycles where the length of each cycle is 100 ms. Simulations are different from each other even with the same teams, as noise is added to sensor data and player actions, and even attributes of players randomly vary between runs. Games are recorded in logfiles, which comprise information about the game, in particular about the current positions of all players and the ball including their velocity and orientation for each cycle. This information is collected for the whole game in a table with the identifier `groundtruth`. For each time point, the play mode (e.g. `kickoff`), the current ball position coordinates and its velocity is listed. Furthermore, the positions and velocities of each player of the left (L) and the right (R) team including the goalkeeper (G) is stated.

For example, the column with head `LG1 vx` contains the velocity of the left goalkeeper in $x$-direction. Finally, information about the robots body and head orientation and their view angle and quality is included. The absolute direction a player is facing (with respect to the pitch coordinate system) is the sum of the body and head direction of that player.

## 5    Description of Local Player Data

The visual sensor of the players reports the objects currently seen. The information is automatically sent to players every sense step with a frequency depending on the player view width and quality. By default it is set to 150 ms. Thus, in addition to the three files mentioned above, 44 more files are available for each game. For each of the altogether 22 robots (ten field players and one goalkeeper per team), two files with local player data is provided, hosting information about where the respective player sees the landmarks and moving objects, respectively.

The file with final identifier (suffix) `landmarks` provides the distances (in meters) and angles (in degrees) to the respective landmarks relative to the robot head orientation for each step. Analogously, the file with final identifier `moving` provides the actual relative distances and angles to the ball and all other players. Sometimes the player number or even the team name is not visible and hence unknown (u) to the robot. In this case, the respective piece of information is left out. If data is not available at all, then this is marked by `NAN` in the respective table element. The server also provides information about the velocity, stamina, yellow and red cards, and the commands (e.g. dash, turn, or kick) of the robots. In some cases there is also information about the observed state of other robots available, in particular, whether they are kicking (k), tackling (t), or are a goalkeeper (g).

## 6    Code

The soccer simulator communicates with players using text messages in form of lists, via UDP (see also Sect. 2). These individual messages can currently not be recorded, in contrast to the simulator logfiles. One option for developers of teams is to implement recording of messages that their own agents receive. But to collect data from other teams, the simulator software had to be modified instead. Our code contains patches to the simulator that allow recording of visual and body messages in individual files for each player. Messages are stored in their original format to keep the amount of processing during the game minimal. Running a simulation with our additional software will result in a number of recorded files:

-   the visual and body messages (two files for each player). The file names follow the same naming convention as the game data CSV files (cf. Fig. 2) but use the `.rcv` suffix for visual messages and `.rcb` for body messages.

- a recording of the game (the ground truth in a binary format), using the suffix `.rcg`.
- commands from players as received by the simulator (in plain text), using the suffix `.rcl`.

Recording these files for all players on the field into files on a network drive can result in significant traffic, and it may be preferable to record onto a local drive and transfer the data after each match in order to reduce the impact of recording on the simulation.

Three different pieces of code are part of this project:

1. There is the `rcssserver-patch` written in C++ which modifies the RoboCup simulator to also log each player's visual and body sensors.
2. To convert the simulator logfile (ground truth) into a CSV file, we provide `rcg2csv`, a C++ program that is built using the open source `librcsc` library (see osdn.net/projects/rctools/releases/p3777). Logfiles are recorded at regular intervals of 100 ms. Optionally, `rcg2csv` stores all simulation parameters in an additional CSV file.
3. To convert visual messages into CSV files, we provide a Python program `see2csv.py` that translates player visual messages into two files: a CSV file for moving objects (other players and the ball), and a CSV file with perceived landmarks.

## 7  Conclusions

RoboCup provides many sources of robotics data, that can be used for further analysis and application of machine learning. We released software to create research datasets for machine learning from released RoboCup simulation league team binaries, together with a large and unique dataset of 180 h of game play. This package allows a number of problems to be investigated: approaches to learning and test self-localization, predictive world-models, or reinforcement learning. The publicly available research dataset has proven itself instrumental as it has already been used as a testbed for time-series analysis and autoencoding (data compression) by recurrent neural networks [12,13] as well as for the analysis of soccer games with clustering and so-called conceptors [9].

**Funding.** The research reported in this paper has been supported by the German Academic Exchange Service (DAAD) by funds of the German Federal Ministry of Education and Research (BMBF) in the Programme for Project-Related Personal Exchange (PPP) under grant no. 57319564 and Universities Australia (UA) in the Australia-Germany Joint Research Cooperation Scheme within the project *Deep Conceptors for Temporal Data Mining* (Decorating).

# References

1. Akiyama, H., Dorer, K., Lau, N.: On the progress of soccer simulation leagues. In: Bianchi, R.A.C., Akin, H.L., Ramamoorthy, S., Sugiura, K. (eds.) RoboCup 2014. LNCS (LNAI), vol. 8992, pp. 599–610. Springer, Cham (2015). https://doi.org/10. 1007/978-3-319-18615-3_49

2. Bastianelli, E., Castellucci, G., Croce, D., Iocchi, L., Basili, R., Nardi, D.: HuRIC: a human robot interaction corpus. In: Calzolari, N., et al. (eds.) Proceedings of the Ninth International Conference on Language Resources and Evaluation, LREC 2014, pp. 4519–4526 (2014)

3. Ben Amor, H., Vogt, D., Ewerton, M., Berger, E., Jung, B., Peters, J.: Learning responsive robot behavior by imitation. In: International Conference on Intelligent Robots and Systems, IROS-2013, pp. 3257–3264, November 2013

4. Chebrolu, N., Lottes, P., Schaefer, A., Winterhalter, W., Burgard, W., Stachniss, C.: Agricultural robot dataset for plant classification, localization and mapping on sugar beet fields. Int. J. Robot. Res. 36(10), 1045–1052 (2017)

5. Chen, D., Mooney, R.J.: Learning to sportscast: a test of grounded language acquisition. In: Proceedings of the 25th International Conference on Machine Learning (ICML) (2008). http://nn.cs.utexas.edu/?chen:icml08

6. Chen, M., et al.: RoboCup Soccer Server – for Soccer Server Version 7.07 and Later. The RoboCup Federation, February 2003. https://sourceforge.net/projects/ sserver/files/rcssmanual/manual-7.08.1/manual.pdf

7. Kitano, H., Asada, M., Kuniyoshi, Y., Noda, I., Osawa, E., Matsubara, H.: RoboCup: a challenge problem for AI. AI Mag. 18(1), 73–85 (1997)

8. Lin, Z., Gehring, J., Khalidov, V., Synnaeve, G.: STARDATA: a StarCraft AI research dataset. CoRR - Computing Research Repository abs/1708.02139, Cornell University Library (2017). http://arxiv.org/abs/1708.02139

9. Michael, O., Obst, O., Schmidsberger, F., Stolzenburg, F.: Analysing soccer games with clustering and conceptors. In: Akiyama, H., Obst, O., Sammut, C., Tonidandel, F. (eds.) RoboCup 2017. LNCS (LNAI), vol. 11175, pp. 120–131. Springer, Cham (2018). https://doi.org/10.1007/978-3-030-00308-1_10

10. Noda, I., Matsubara, H., Hiraki, K., Frank, I.: Soccer server: a tool for research on multiagent systems. Appl. Artif. Intell. 12(2–3), 233–250 (1998)

11. Olson, C.F.: Probabilistic self-localization for mobile robots. IEEE Trans. Robot. Autom. 16(1), 55–66 (2000)

12. Steckhan, K.: Time-series analysis with recurrent neural networks. Project thesis, Automation and Computer Sciences Department, Harz University of Applied Sciences (2018). (in German)

13. Stolzenburg, F., Michael, O., Obst, O.: Predictive neural networks. CoRR - Computing Research Repository abs/1802.03308, Cornell University Library (2018). http://arxiv.org/abs/1802.03308

14. Stolzenburg, F., Obst, O., Murray, J.: Qualitative velocity and ball interception. In: Jarke, M., Lakemeyer, G., Koehler, J. (eds.) KI 2002. LNCS (LNAI), vol. 2479, pp. 283–298. Springer, Heidelberg (2002). https://doi.org/10.1007/3-540-45751-8_19

15. Taylor, M.E., Stone, P.: Transfer learning for reinforcement learning domains: a survey. J. Mach. Learn. Res. 10, 1633–1685 (2009)

16. Tong, C.H., Gingras, D., Larose, K., Barfoot, T.D., Dupuis, É.: The Canadian planetary emulation terrain 3D mapping dataset. Int. J. Robot. Res. (2013). http:// asrl.utias.utoronto.ca/datasets/3dmap/

# Generation of Laser-Quality 2D Navigation Maps from RGB-D Sensors

Federico Nardi$^{(\boxtimes)}$ (iD), María T. Lázaro (iD), Luca Iocchi (iD), and Giorgio Grisetti (iD)

Department of Computer, Control and Management Engineering,
Sapienza University of Rome, Rome, Italy
{fnardi,mtlazaro,iocchi,grisetti}@diag.uniroma1.it

**Abstract.** The use of RGB-D cameras has become an affordable solution for robot mapping and navigation in contrast to expensive 2D laser range finders. Although these sensors provide richer information about the 3D environment, most successful mapping and navigation techniques for mobile robots have been developed considering a 2D planar environment. In this paper, we present our system for 2D navigation using RGB-D sensors. The key feature of our system is the extraction of 2D laser scans out of the 3D point cloud provided by the camera that can be later used by common mapping or localization approaches. Along with the real experiments we raise the question *"how far can we go with the use of RGB-D sensors for 2D navigation?"* and we analyze performance and limitations of the system compared to accurate, yet expensive, laser-based systems.

**Keywords:** RGB-D sensors · 2D mapping · Educational robots

## 1 Introduction

Robot mapping and navigation in indoor environments are fundamental abilities in many different application scenarios, including home service robots (e.g., cleaning robots) and educational robots. In particular, several competitions in RoboCup require such abilities, especially within the RoboCup@Home and RoboCupIndustrial domains, and other junior competitions would benefit from these functionalities.

Two major components must be developed: a mapping system, able to generate a map of the environment, and a navigation system, able to plan and execute paths in this environment. The quality of these processes depends on the combination of the sensors and the software used. High-quality sensors provide better quality of data that guarantees accuracy and robustness of the mapping and navigation processes. However, high-quality sensors are also expensive, thus increasing the budget to build and maintain robots and the difficulty of teams in participating to robot competitions. Consequently, most applications involving home service robots do not use a proper mapping, localization and navigation system, significantly limiting their functionalities.

© Springer Nature Switzerland AG 2019
D. Holz et al. (Eds.): RoboCup 2018, LNAI 11374, pp. 238–250, 2019.
https://doi.org/10.1007/978-3-030-27544-0_20

Examples of high-quality sensors for robot mapping and navigation are 2D laser-range finders (LRF). Several models exist with different technical specifications (e.g., Hokuyo UTM and URG family, SICK LMS and TIM family). 2D LRFs provide for very precise and accurate measurements and have been extensively used for mapping and navigation in many robotic applications. However, they also have two drawbacks: (1) being planar sensors they are not able to deal with obstacles that are not on the same plane of the laser, (2) they are more expensive than camera-based solutions.

A second type of sensors are RGB-D cameras. Also in this case there is a variety of models with different specifications (e.g., ASUS Xtion PRO LIVE, Microsoft Kinect). RGB-D cameras provide for information about the environment that are not limited to a planar surface and are less expensive than LRFs, but they have the following disadvantages: (1) lower resolution, precision and accuracy of the acquired data, (2) limited field of view and range.

In this paper, we want to fill the gap between LRF and RGB-D technology, by presenting an effective mapping system that is based on RGB-D cameras. The proposed system provides results that are comparable with maps generated by a LRF. With the proposed method, it is thus possible to map and navigate in an environment with performance that is comparable with LRF technology at a reduced cost and with the advantage of using a 3D sensor for obstacle avoidance. This method can be useful on many kinds of robots and in many applications and RoboCup competitions, since it enables the possibility of performing complex tasks with a low-cost robot. For example, RoboCup@Home Education[1] is an initiative aiming at providing support to teams to set-up RoboCup@Home teams with low-cost hardware. In this initiative, robots are equipped only with a single RGB-D sensor. Another example is given by the SoftBank Pepper robot used in RoboCup@Home Social Standard Platform League that is equipped with a laser device providing only a few laser scans and, therefore, navigation tasks highly depend on its RGB-D sensor.

More specifically, the contributions of this paper are: (1) a method to generate 2D laser measurements from the information gathered by an RGB-D sensor based on a projection procedure that allows to extract a scan-line at an arbitrary laser pose (in contrast to ROS[2] tool *depthimage_to_laserscan*[3] which generates the laser measurement from a fixed pose), making it suitable also for tilted or moving cameras, (2) the adoption of a robust SLAM system to deal with lower performance – namely precision and field-of-view – of RGB-D sensors compared to LRFs, and (3) the evaluation of navigation systems of low-cost robots when mapping and navigation are performed with only an RGB-D sensor.

We validate our approach in two sets of experiments. In the first set, we compare the quality of the maps produced with RGB-D sensors with respect to those obtained with an expensive and high accurate LRF sensor, while in the second set we evaluate navigation capabilities of a robot using an RGB-D sensor and a motion model that are different from the ones used for mapping.

---

[1] www.robocupathomeedu.org.

[2] http://www.ros.org/.

[3] wiki.ros.org/depthimage_to_laserscan.

## 2  Related Work

An efficient way to represent an indoor environment for navigation is to use occupancy grids, first introduced in the work of Moravec and Elfes [12]. This technique consists in integrating the range measurements acquired by the robot into a common frame to represent the obstacles in the scene. The use of laser scanners for building such a map allows to obtain high accuracy in the measurements but implies, also, a significant economic expense. Since accurate digital cameras became available at reasonable costs, there have been different contributions in the effort of extracting range measurements from cameras in order to avoid the expense of laser scanners.

Murray and Jennings [13] introduced the first occupancy-grid mapping system that uses a visual sensor to collect dense depth information. They manage to produce depth images with a trinocular camera, which yields accurate results but, of course, requires a specialized rig and a meticulous calibration. Sim and Little [15] use stereo-vision to perform RaoBlackwellised Particle Filter (RBPF) visual SLAM. Although their method can be categorized as feature-based SLAM, the authors describe how to infer the corresponding occupancy grids using a maximum likelihood estimate.

Gastshore et al. [5] were the first to explore the possibility of building occupancy grids with a single camera. In their work, each grid cell represents a vertical line feature and a voting scheme is used to propose the occupancy of each grid cell. The authors, however, don't consider problem of localization with this method. To really obtain range measurements from a monocamera Choi and Oh [3] introduce the visual sonar technique, which consists of projecting in space virtual rays and then detecting where these rays collide with obstacles in 3D space. Asmar and Samir [1] extend the previous approach to deal with variable lighting conditions by using g High Dynamic Range (HDR) images and propose a different segmentation technique to have a better extraction of the ground features.

Since the appearance of the first RGB-D cameras in 2010, robotic researchers have been attracted by the potentialities of this type of sensors for mobile robots navigation. This is because they provide depth information for each image pixel and they are available at a reasonable price. In this context, one of the first works to use this sensor for navigation has been made by Oliver et al. [14], in which they simulate the presence of a laser by extracting a 2D scan from the depth image. Our approach is similar to that of Oliver et al., in addition, we use reliable calibration procedures on our system to obtain precise intrinsic and extrinsic camera parameters. This allows us to obtain accurate maps, which can be used later for navigation as we show in Sect. 4.

## 3  Our Approach

The 2D mapping procedure from RGB-D sensors proposed in this paper can be summarized in the following steps. Firstly, a data acquisition phase is performed while steering the robot in the environment to be mapped, in which the sequence of RGB and Depth images acquired by an RGB-D camera together with the robot odometry are recorded.

Next, each depth image is used to reconstruct the local 3D scene as a point cloud from which a virtual scan is extracted to simulate the presence of a laser device.

The RGB-D scans together with the robot odometry are used as input to our robust laser-based graph SLAM approach to estimate the robot trajectory. The result of this process provides the estimated global robot coordinates from which each depth image (RGB-D scan) was acquired.

Finally, the map of the environment is obtained by fusing the generated scans into an occupancy grid based on the pose-graph computed at the previous step. In the remainder, we describe in detail each component of the system.

## 3.1    Extraction of Scans from Depth Images

The first step of our approach is to generate range measurements for building the 2D map. As mentioned in Sect. 1, ROS provides the package *depthimage_to_laserscan* to perform this operation, which is done by extracting the set of pixels belonging to the middle row of the depth image and back-projecting them in 3D.

It is relevant to notice that this approach is effective only under the assumption of a camera parallel to the ground floor, see Fig. 1. Instead, our approach works by first transforming the depth cloud in the virtual laser frame and consequently extracting scan points. This allows a better flexibility, since the technique can be applied also to a tilted camera, as it is that of the Pepper, and it is possible to extract points whose corresponding pixels fall outside the middle row of the image (see below).

The proposed procedure to generate virtual laser scans is the following. Each pixel $\mathbf{u} = (u_i, u_j) \in \mathbb{R}^2$ with depth value $d_{ij} \in \mathbb{R}$ of the current depth image is back-projected into the corresponding 3D point $\mathbf{p} = (p_x, p_y, p_z) \in \mathbb{R}^3$ using the camera calibration matrix $\mathbf{K}$ [7]:

$$\mathbf{p}^c = \mathbf{K}^{-1} \cdot [u_j d_{ij} \ u_i d_{ij} \ d_{ij}]^T \tag{1}$$

where superscript $\mathbf{p}^c$ denotes the point is represented with respect to the camera frame.

Let $\mathcal{P}^c = \{\mathbf{p}_k^c\}$ be the point cloud containing the collection of $k$ transformed points in the camera frame. Given $\mathbf{T}_c^r$, the pose of the camera with respect to the robot frame and using $\mathbf{T}_v^r$ as the pose of the virtual laser frame from which we want to generate an RGB-D scan, it is possible to obtain the point cloud $\mathcal{P}^v = \{\mathbf{p}_k^v\}$ in the laser frame by applying the following transformation to each point:

$$\mathbf{T}_c^v = (\mathbf{T}_v^r)^{-1} \cdot \mathbf{T}_c^r \tag{2}$$

$$\mathcal{P}^v = \mathbf{T}_c^v \cdot \mathcal{P}^c. \tag{3}$$

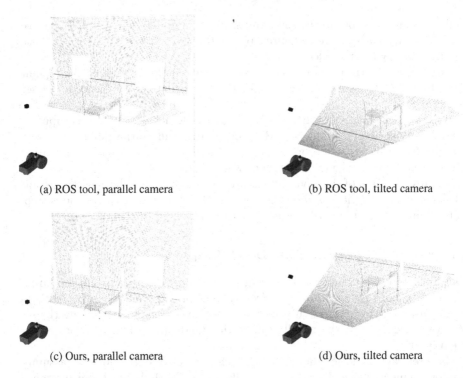

(a) ROS tool, parallel camera

(b) ROS tool, tilted camera

(c) Ours, parallel camera

(d) Ours, tilted camera

**Fig. 1.** Comparison of the extraction procedure with the ROS *depthimage_to_laserscan* tool and our method. The RGB-D camera is represented by the black box on top of the robot, the virtual laser is represented by the 3D model of an Hokuyo sensor.

Finally, we set the 2D scan to lie in the XY plane of the laser reference frame. To this end, we generate the RGB-D scan $s_v$ by considering only the points of $\mathcal{P}^v$ whose height is inside a pre-defined threshold $\varepsilon$:

$$s_v = \{p^v \in \mathcal{P}^v \text{such that } |p_z| \leq \varepsilon\}, \tag{4}$$

where $\varepsilon$ is typically chosen to be close to zero in order to allow for some tolerance.

### 3.2    Estimation of the Robot Trajectory

In order to generate a consistent trajectory of the robot we use our novel graph-based SLAM system [9]. Since describing mathematical details of our SLAM system is out of the scope of this paper, we briefly describe the main pipeline and specific features that make it suitable for mapping 2D environments using scans extracted from RGB-D sensors. The input of the system consists of a stream of laser scans and the robot odometry and the output is the estimation of the trajectory followed by the robot.

In such system, the map of the environment is represented as a graph whose vertices contains robot positions together with a measurement (laser scans in this case) gathered from that position and the edges connecting a pair of vertices represents spatial constraints between them. Then, the goal of the SLAM system is to obtain a global configuration of the vertices that better explains the constraints. This is done by formulating a least-squares minimization problem that can be solved by using optimization methods like Gauss-Newton or Levenberg-Marquardt.

The pipeline of the SLAM system used in this work approaches the following aspects:

**laser tracking.** Is the problem of tracking the position of the laser between consecutive timestamps. This is done by implementing an Iterative Closest Point (ICP) algorithm, which provides the transform that minimizes the reprojection error of the points of the current scan with respect to the previous one.

**local-map generation and management.** Is the problem of generating a consistent local view of the environment out of a small chunk of trajectory. To this end, the scans registered during the laser tracking process are continuously fused into a single 2D point cloud producing a refined representation of the environment. Local map maintenance id done by removing points further than a certain distance from the current tracked pose. When the robot moves for a certain distance, the current local map is stored and associated to a vertex in the graph. The use of local maps in contrast to the use of single laser scans greatly improves the reconstruction of the local surroundings of the robot specially in the case of the use of RGB-D sensors due to their limited field of view.

**relocalization or loop closing.** Is the task of determining if the current local map captures a portion of the environment already seen in the past. To this end our SLAM approach first retrieves which local maps from those already present in the graph are most similar to the current one by selecting the vertices in covariance range with respect to the current one, then it validates the potential matches by performing local map registration. This generates a set of possible *closures* that are finally introduced in the graph as edges connecting non-consecutive vertices after an inlier verification process using a voting scheme described in [11].

**global optimization.** Relocalization events might introduce "jumps" in the estimated trajectory. The global optimization module aims at distributing the estimation error evenly between the vertices. This is done in the SLAM system by solving a pose-graph [6] by means of the **g2o** optimizer [8]. The core idea is to determine the positions of the nodes that better explain the relative transformations arising from laser-tracking and relocalization.

At the end of a run, this mapping process returns an estimate of the robot trajectory $\{\mathbf{x}_{1:t}^r\}$ from which the laser scans were generated. The whole described SLAM process accounts for the transformation $\mathbf{T}_l^r$ to represent the laser scans into the robot reference frame.

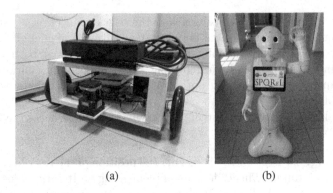

(a)                              (b)

**Fig. 2.** Robots and sensors configuration used for the experiments. (a) MARRtino robot. (b) SoftBank's Robotics Pepper.

### 3.3   Occupancy Grid for Navigation

Once the trajectory is provided by the SLAM system, it is possible to reconstruct the most likely map using the gathered measurements. If we want our robot to navigate safely in the environment, i.e. without hitting obstacles, we have to provide it with the information about free and occupied space. For this purpose, we represent the environment with an *occupancy grid* [12], where each cell contains the probability of being occupied by an obstacle, thus containing values ranging from 0 (free) to 1 (occupied).

This method goes under the name of *occupancy grid mapping* [16], and in the remainder of the paragraph we report a sketch of the procedure. The inputs are the RGB-D scans $\{\mathbf{s}_{v_{1:t}}\}$ and the estimated robot poses $\{\mathbf{x}_{1:t}^T\}$. For each range of the single laser scan, a ray is casted with a straight-line grid traversal algorithm [2] to find the traversed cells. Each cell of the grid stores two values: the number of *hits* and the number of *misses*. If a ray passes through a cell we increment its misses count, while for the end-point of the ray we increment the hits count of the cell where it falls.

Finally, the probability of each cell of being occupied is computed as $\frac{hits}{hits+misses}$. The selection of the appropriate threshold value allows us to discriminate between three types of cells:

- Unexplored: $hits = 0$, $misses = 0$
- Occupied: $\frac{hits}{hits+misses} > threshold$
- Free: $\frac{hits}{hits+misses} \leq threshold$.

which is used to obtain a thresholded grid map compatible with the most commonly used localization and path planning algorithms for navigation purposes.

## 4   Experiments

The main goal of this work is to produce usable 2D navigation maps from RGB-D data. Our key claim is that the proposed mapping system, using data from an

**Table 1.** Comparison of the technical specification of the two sensors.

|  | Hokuyo UTM-30LX | Microsoft Kinect V2 |
|---|---|---|
| Field of view | 270° | 70° |
| Min range | 0.1 m | 0.5 m |
| Max range | 30 m | 4.5 m |
| Frames per second (FPS) | 40 Hz | 30 Hz |
| Power consumption | <8 W | 2.25 W |
| Resolution at 2 m | 1 mm | 5 mm |

affordable RGB-D sensor, can provide comparable quantitative and qualitative results to those that we could obtain with a more accurate and expensive laser range finder. Therefore, in this section, we present real experiments in which our approach is used to create maps of different indoor environments which can later be used to perform common navigation tasks such as localization or path planning, not necessarily with the same robot used to build the map.

The first set of experiments are intended to evaluate the quality of the maps produced by our proposed system. To this end, we used a self-built robot (Fig. 2a) based on the open source and open hardware robotic platform MAR-Rtino Robot[4], and equipped it with a Microsoft Kinect for Windows V2 RGB-D sensor and an Hokuyo UTM-30LX laser range finder. The difference in hardware specifications between both sensors is highlighted in Table 1. We implemented the components of our system in C++ as ROS nodes, publicly available as open source[5,6].

As a prior step before performing the experiments, we calibrated the robot to obtain the extrinsic sensor parameters $\mathbf{T}_c^r$ and $\mathbf{T}_l^r$ using the unsupervised calibration procedure explained in [4].

We tested our approach in two different indoor environments: a domestic environment of $60m^2$ and a corridor of our department at the Sapienza University of Rome, hereinafter denoted as $\mathcal{M}_{home}$ and $\mathcal{M}_{uni}$ respectively. The experimentation and validation is performed in two steps. First, we record a dataset containing the laser scans and the RGB-D data gathered by both on-board sensors together with the odometry provided by the platform while manually driving the robot around the test environments. This dataset is used to produce a map of the environment using our system. Then, once each map is constructed, we record a second dataset where the robot follows a different trajectory than the one used for mapping. We use this second dataset to validate localization with respect to the previously created maps using both sensors.

In order to validate our approach, we compare the map $\mathcal{M}_{our}$, built with virtual scans $\{\mathbf{s}_{v_{1:t}}\}$, with respect to the map $\mathcal{M}_{ref}$, built with the real scans,

---

[4] http://www.dis.uniroma1.it/~spqr/MARRtino/.

[5] https://gitlab.com/srrg-software/srrg_depth2laser_ros.

[6] https://gitlab.com/srrg-software/srrg_mapper2d_ros.

**Table 2.** Translational and rotational localization errors with respect to the robot positions given by a localization system using the Hokuyo data ($\mathbf{s}_{real} + \mathcal{M}_{ref}$)

|                           |        | Home  | University |
|---------------------------|--------|-------|------------|
| Translational error (m)   | Mean   | 0.034 | 0.075      |
|                           | Max    | 0.123 | 0.115      |
|                           | Median | 0.025 | 0.085      |
| Rotational error (rad)    | Mean   | 0.017 | 0.010      |
|                           | Max    | 0.218 | 0.036      |
|                           | Median | 0.013 | 0.009      |

denoted as $\{\mathbf{s}_{r_{1:t}}\}$ and collected from the Hokuyo laser. Results are shown in Fig. 3. We also show that using available ROS tools, i.e. *depthimage_to_laserscan + gmapping*, in these scenarios does not provide a robust solution, since the output maps cannot be used for navigation tasks.

To obtain a quantitative comparison, we compute the percentage difference between the two corresponding images with the following formula:

$$\Delta = 100 \sum_{k=1}^{K} |\frac{u_{our_k} - u_{ref_k}}{K}| \tag{5}$$

where $u_{ref_k}$ and $u_{our_k}$ are the $k^{th}$ pixel values of $\mathcal{M}_{ref}$ and $\mathcal{M}_{our}$ respectively. From the experiments we obtain that the difference of $\mathcal{M}_{ref}$ is 1.86% with $\mathcal{M}_{home}$ and 1.27% with $\mathcal{M}_{uni}$. This shows that if the system is properly calibrated then the RGB-D sensor can return a map that is almost undistinguishable from the one provided by the laser. The main difference between these sensors is in the angular extension of the measurement since the depth camera has a field of view that is less than one third of the laser scanner one. As a direct consequence, the map generated by the laser has some details that could not be detected by the Kinect due to its restricted angle of view, as shown in detail in Fig. 4.

The second set of experiments aim at evaluating the usability of the maps generated from the previous experiments for navigation tasks by robots with different features (Fig. 2). Thus, we choose to test the particle filter based localization system in [10] to estimate the robot motion in different scenarios. To support our claim, we try to localize the MARRtino robot on $\mathcal{M}_{our}$ by using the scans generated from the RGB-D sensor and we compare the resulting trajectories with the ones estimated by the localizer on $\mathcal{M}_{ref}$ using the laser scans, Fig. 5. That is, we measure the translational and rotational error for each robot pose between the reference trajectory and the one obtained with the RGB-D scans. As it is shown in Fig. 6, in some points of the trajectory the localization with the depth camera is less precise than the reference one. To reduce this difference we have accurately calibrated the odometry parameters of the mobile platform, as explained in [4], in order to have a better initial guess of the robot

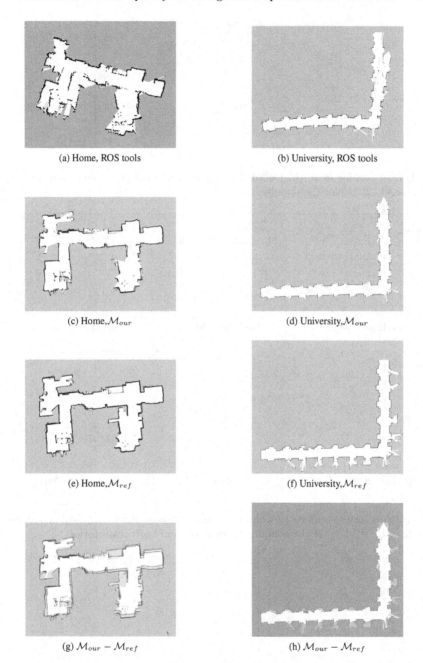

(a) Home, ROS tools

(b) University, ROS tools

(c) Home, $\mathcal{M}_{our}$

(d) University, $\mathcal{M}_{our}$

(e) Home, $\mathcal{M}_{ref}$

(f) University, $\mathcal{M}_{ref}$

(g) $\mathcal{M}_{our} - \mathcal{M}_{ref}$

(h) $\mathcal{M}_{our} - \mathcal{M}_{ref}$

**Fig. 3.** Results of the first set of experiments. First row: maps built using available ROS tools. Second row: maps generated with RGB-D scans. Third row: maps generated with laser scans. Last row: superposition of $\mathcal{M}_{ref}$ on $\mathcal{M}_{our}$, for a qualitative comparison we show in green the reference map on the map generated with our approach. (Color figure online)

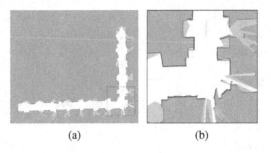

(a)                              (b)

**Fig. 4.** (a) Corridor map. (b) Detail. The figure shows the $\mathcal{M}_{ref}$ (in green) superimposed to $\mathcal{M}_{our}$. (Color figure online)

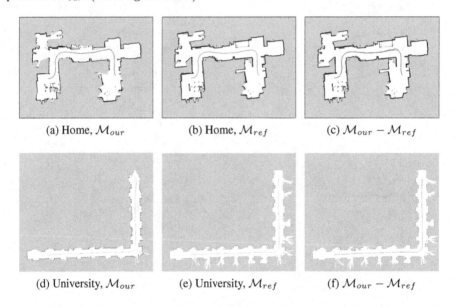

(a) Home, $\mathcal{M}_{our}$          (b) Home, $\mathcal{M}_{ref}$          (c) $\mathcal{M}_{our} - \mathcal{M}_{ref}$

(d) University, $\mathcal{M}_{our}$     (e) University, $\mathcal{M}_{ref}$     (f) $\mathcal{M}_{our} - \mathcal{M}_{ref}$

**Fig. 5.** Trajectories estimated by the localizer. Left column: $\mathbf{s}_{virtual} + \mathcal{M}_{our}$. Center column: $\mathbf{s}_{real} + \mathcal{M}_{ref}$. Right column: superposition of both trajectories.

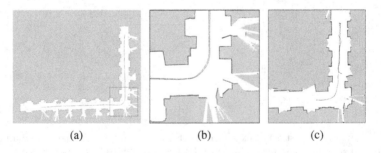

(a)               (b)               (c)

**Fig. 6.** (a - b) Estimated trajectories and zoomed area for the corridor map. (c) Trajectory followed by the Pepper robot during a navigation task at University in map $\mathcal{M}_{our}$.

motion. Results are reported in Table 2, showing overall localization errors of ~5 cm (translational) and ~0.02 rad (rotational).

Furthermore, we test University $\mathcal{M}_{our}$ map during a navigation task with the Pepper robot. Pepper's original laser consists of 45 points with a usable range of ~3 m. As it's shown in Fig. 6c, the trajectory reported by the localization system is comparable with the ones executed by robots with more accurate sensors.

## 5   Conclusions

In this paper, we presented a novel approach to generate accurate 2D maps by using RGB-D cameras. We implemented and evaluated our approach on different datasets acquired in different application scenarios where the use of available packages would not give the same quality of the results. Quantitative experimental results show the effectiveness of the proposed approach, that is able to generate maps whose quality is comparable with the ones generated by laser sensors.

More specifically, we showed that self-localization performance of a robot in different environments are substantially the same when using an RGB-D camera or a laser range-finder. Therefore, this method enables the replacement of laser-based navigation with RGB-D navigation in many applications, yielding a lower cost and improved 3D information for obstacle avoidance.

Despite the results show high effectiveness of the proposed method in the considered situations, we would like to investigate other interesting situations of mapping and navigation for robots equipped with low-cost sensors. Moreover, we want to carry out additional experiments to evaluate in a quantitative way if the performance of depth sensors on typical navigation tasks (e.g., entering a small passages, navigation speed, etc.) are comparable with those of laser-based solutions.

## References

1. Asmar, D., Shaker, S.: 2D occupancy-grid SLAM of structured indoor environments using a single camera. Int. J. Mechatron. Autom. **2**(2), 112–124 (2012)
2. Bresenham, J.E.: Algorithm for computer control of a digital plotter. IBM Syst. J. **4**(1), 25–30 (1965)
3. Choi, Y.H., Oh, S.Y.: Map building through pseudo dense scan matching using visual sonar data. Auton. Robots **23**(4), 293–304 (2007)
4. Cicco, M.D., Corte, B.D., Grisetti, G.: Unsupervised calibration of wheeled mobile platforms. In: Proceedings of the IEEE International Conference on Robotics & Automation (ICRA), pp. 4328–4334, May 2016. https://doi.org/10.1109/ICRA. 2016.7487631, https://gitlab.com/srrg-software/srrg_nw_calibration_ros
5. Gartshore, R., Aguado, A., Galambos, C.: Incremental map building using an occupancy grid for an autonomous monocular robot. In: 7th International Conference on Control, Automation, Robotics and Vision, ICARCV 2002, vol. 2, pp. 613–618. IEEE (2002)

6. Grisetti, G., Kummerle, R., Stachniss, C., Burgard, W.: A tutorial on graph-based SLAM. IEEE Intell. Transp. Syst. Mag. **2**(4), 31–43 (2010). https://doi.org/10.1109/MITS.2010.939925

7. Hartley, R., Zisserman, A.: Multiple View Geometry in Computer Vision. Cambridge University Press, Cambridge (2003)

8. Kummerle, R., Grisetti, G., Strasdat, H., Konolige, K., Burgard, W.: g2o: a general framework for graph optimization. In: Proceedings of the IEEE International Conference on Robotics & Automation (ICRA), pp. 3607–3613, May 2011. https://doi.org/10.1109/ICRA.2011.5979949

9. Lázaro, M.T., Capobianco, R., Grisetti, G.: Efficient long-term mapping in dynamic environments. In: IEEE/RSJ International Conference on Intelligent Robots and Systems, Madrid, Spain, 1–5 October 2018

10. Lázaro, M.T., Grisetti, G., Iocchi, L., Fentanes, J.P., Hanheide, M.: A lightweight navigation system for mobile robots. In: Ollero, A., Sanfeliu, A., Montano, L., Lau, N., Cardeira, C. (eds.) ROBOT 2017. AISC, vol. 694, pp. 295–306. Springer, Cham (2018). https://doi.org/10.1007/978-3-319-70836-2_25

11. Lázaro, M.T., Paz, L.M., Piniés, P., Castellanos, J.A., Grisetti, G.: Multi-robot SLAM using condensed measurements. In: Proceedings of the IEEE/RSJ International Conference on Intelligent Robots and Systems (IROS), Tokyo Big Sight, Japan, 3–8 November 2013. https://doi.org/10.1109/IROS.2013.6696483

12. Moravec, H., Elfes, A.: High resolution maps from wide angle sonar. In: Proceedings of the IEEE International Conference on Robotics & Automation (ICRA), vol. 2, pp. 116–121. IEEE (1985)

13. Murray, D., Jennings, C.: Stereo vision based mapping and navigation for mobile robots. In: Proceedings of the IEEE International Conference on Robotics & Automation (ICRA) (1997)

14. Oliver, A., Kang, S., Wünsche, B.C., MacDonald, B.: Using the Kinect as a navigation sensor for mobile robotics. In: Proceedings of the 27th Conference on Image and Vision Computing New Zealand, IVCNZ 2012, pp. 509–514. ACM, New York (2012)

15. Sim, R., Little, J.J.: Autonomous vision-based exploration and mapping using hybrid maps and Rao-Blackwellised particle filters. In: Proceedings of the IEEE/RSJ International Conference on Intelligent Robots and Systems (IROS), pp. 2082–2089. IEEE (2006)

16. Thrun, S., Burgard, W., Fox, D.: Probabilistic Robotics. MIT Press, Cambridge (2005)

# Towards Long-Term Memory for Social Robots: Proposing a New Challenge for the RoboCup@Home League

Matías Pavez[1(✉)], Javier Ruiz del Solar[1(✉)], Victoria Amo[2], and Felix Meyer zu Driehausen[2]

[1] Advanced Mining Technology Center & Department of E.E.,
Universidad de Chile, Santiago, Chile
{matias.pavez,jruizd}@ing.uchile.cl
[2] Institute of Cognitive Science,
Universität Osnabrück, Osnabrück, Germany
{vamo,fmeyerzudrie}@uos.de

**Abstract.** Long-term memory is essential to feel like a continuous being, and to be able to interact/communicate coherently. Social robots need long-term memories in order to establish long-term relationships with humans and other robots, and do not act just for the moment. In this paper this challenge is highlighted, open questions are identified, the need of addressing this challenge in the RoboCup@Home League with new tests is motivated, and a new test is proposed.

**Keywords:** Long-term-memory · Service robot · Social robot · RoboCup@Home

## 1 Introduction

Long-term memory allows humans to feel continuous and coherent in his/her thoughts, i.e., to be a continuous person with a continuous life. Hence, long-term memory is an essential component of social interaction between people in daily life, it allows remembering names, events, duties, relationships, etc. In fact, when long-term memory does not work properly due to illness (e.g., Alzheimer disease), the ability to interact with other human beings is severely damaged.

Therefore, it seems evident that a key aspect in achieving long-term interaction and social relationship between humans and social robots is the requirement of a long-term memory system for the latter. Memory constitutes an important part of a cognitive system implementation; in fact, it is the link of prior experiences with ongoing and future behavior. As stated by [24], a nontrivial level of social interaction requires that the robot should be able to use both semantic and episodic information. Both, semantic and episodic memories constitute the declarative long-term memory. While semantic memory is a repository for facts, such as knowing that the capital of Chile is Santiago, episodic memory is

© Springer Nature Switzerland AG 2019
D. Holz et al. (Eds.): RoboCup 2018, LNAI 11374, pp. 251–261, 2019.
https://doi.org/10.1007/978-3-030-27544-0_21

the memory of past experiences, i.e., remembering events and their associated context (places, persons, emotions, etc.). Both kinds of memories work together, and both need to be implemented for providing appropriate social skills for social robots. However, in contrast to implementing semantic memories, the implementation of episodic memories for social robots is much less developed, and therefore we focus our work on the latter.

The amount of information to be processed in a lifetime is vast; therefore, efficient methods are required for acquiring, filtering, encoding, storing, deleting and updating a robot's episodic knowledge of its working environment. This information can be encoded in symbolic form and held in a storage module invoking the functionality of an episodic memory system. So far, this challenge has not been addressed appropriately, and the construction of long-term memories for social robots, which include both episodic and semantic components, has not been achieved. In this context, the main goals of this paper are: (i) to highlight the need of building appropriate long-term memory for social robots, (ii) to identify open questions that need to be answered in order to fulfill this first goal, and (iii) to provide basic concepts to address this challenge in the RoboCup@Home League with new tests. We propose the structure of such kind of tests, and give an example of a concrete test. This paper is organized as follows: The basic aspects of human memory are summarized in Sect. 2. Relevant open questions are identified in Sect. 3. The structure of the proposed tests for the RoboCup@Home League is presented in Sect. 4. Finally, some conclusions of this work are outlined in Sect. 5.

## 2   Human Memory

According to [8], memory is "the record of experience presented in the brain". There are multiple memory systems that work in a complementary way. These systems have different functions, and they are characterized by different operating characteristics and brain structures in which they are embodied.

A first categorization is related to the persistency of the stored information. The *Sensory Memory* is able to store information acquired by our sensory systems just for the fraction of a second. This information then enters the so-called *Short-Term Memory*, which support "brief storage and immediate recall of substantial detail" [8]. Part of the stored information is then consolidated into the *Long-Term Memory*. The term *Working Memory* is sometimes used instead of Short-Term Memory, although the working memory concept includes processes and structures used for the temporal storage and manipulation of information [22].

The Long-Term Memory is composed by a *Declarative or Explicit Memory*, which refers to information that is remembered consciously, and a *non-Declarative or Implicit Memory*, which refers to skills, abilities and tasks that can remembered implicitly (e.g., how to ride a bicycle). The Implicit Memory is further divided in *Procedural Memory*, in charge of storing procedures or ways of doing tasks, and *Priming*, which refers to the fact that some experiences are primed or recalled when a given stimuli is received. The Declarative Memory is divided into two complementary memories, the *Episodic Memory* and the *Semantic Memory*. Episodic memory, first defined by Tulving [21], refers to the memory of specific events occurring at a specific place and time and enables human beings to remember past experiences. Semantic memory is basically a repository for facts. Emotional experiences are also stored in the brain and they have influence on how other information is stored. The *memory about emotions* is stored in the declarative memory, while the *emotional memory* belongs to the implicit memory. Detailed explanations about the episodic, semantic and emotional memories can be found in [4,7].

The main functionalities provided by the declarative long-term memory are: (i) the capability of remembering facts, concepts, events, experiences, skills, tasks, emotions, (ii) the ability to feel like a continuous person, (iii) a way of linking prior experiences with ongoing and future behavior, and (iv) the ability to interact with other human beings, i.e. be able to communicate coherently, and to build long-term relationships.

In this article our analysis will focus in the episodic memory, which as already mentioned, is related to the conscious remembrance of context-dependent events that are personally experienced. By context-dependent is it meant the cognitive state—the temporal, spatial and emotional/affective context—, as well as the embodied nature of the experience, i.e. the sensory-perceptual processing of a given experience [1]. For instance, the experience/event of visiting your mother's house for having dinner last night includes a temporal context (last night), a spatial context (your mother's house), an emotional context (spending time nicely with your mother), and sensory-perceptual experiences (how the dinner tasted).

## 3   Open Questions for Implementing Long-Term Memory for Social Robots

During the past decade there have been several approaches that implemented episodic and semantic long-term memory in artificial systems (e.g., [5,6,10,13–16,18,22]). We believe that these works addressed only partially some of the main challenges that poses the implementation of long-term memory for social robots, and that still some of the questions described in the next paragraphs need to be answered.

*How to store events and experiences in the form of episodes in the episodic memory?* It is still not clear how the cognitive state—temporal, spatial and emotional/affective context—associated to events, as well as the embodied nature of them, can be stored by a social robot. Naturally, the temporal context can be easily stored (e.g., using time stamps). The ability to determine and store spatial context has advanced largely in the last few years thanks to the deep learning revolution that allows the recognition of places, objects, and persons more easily. Yet, this has so far not been implemented in social robots that interact continuously with the changing world. Very few works have addressed the task of storing the emotional context and the embodied nature of the experience.

*How to give different levels of relevance to the different episodes in terms of its novelty or the associate emotional state?* As in the case of human beings, the stored episodes have different levels of relevance, which depends in the associate emotional state, among many other factors. Mechanisms for determining autonomously this level of relevance need to be developed.

*How to store emotional states?* In the human brain emotional situations are stored in the explicit and implicit memory systems, and experiences with a strong emotive content produce powerful and vivid memories. Mechanisms for implementing these functionalities need to be developed.

*How to consolidate short-term memory into the long-term memory?* The update of the long-term memory is a complex and time-consuming process that involves the consolidation of short-term memories into long-term ones [2]. In the case of humans this is carried out during the sleep process, and consumes a large amount of brain resources [23]. Therefore, the update of episodic information must be carefully designed and implemented in the robot case. No work has addressed the challenge of long-term memory consolidation for a social robot operating continuously in the real-word.

*Which mechanisms to use for forgetting and repression?* Given that the memory capacity is limited, forgetting mechanisms need to be implemented on basis of the relevance of the stored information. In addition, it must be analyzed if, as in the case of human beings, it is required to implement repression mechanisms that unconsciously block memories in order to protect the self from situations/emotions that she/he cannot cope with [9].

*How to address the ethical issues related to the management of personal information of human beings acquired by social robots?* A social robot with long-term memory will store information related with his/her human mates. It must be analyzed how this personal information will be protected, managed, and eventually, deleted.

## 4    Long-Term Memory in the RoboCup@Home League

In this Section we propose a new test for the RoboCup@Home league. First, we will describe the minimum requirements for an EpLTM (Episodic Long-Term Memory) implementation, how to validate them, and which sources of information are valid when generating memories. Finally, we present a test proposal for the competition, focused on EpLTM, Human-Robot Interaction (HRI) and perception.

### 4.1    Requirements

At present, there is no consensus on the way an EpLTM should be implemented for service robots, but many approaches can be found [9–12,19,20,22]. As the RoboCups goal is to boost research, we propose to evaluate only the core requirements an EpLTM must fulfill, avoiding to force an specific implementation on the teams. The proposed requirements can be separated into 2 categories: I. exclusively episodic, and II. requirements related to historical and emotional relevances.

Category I is build from the 11 design requirements $\{R_1, \ldots, R_{11}\}$ presented by Stachowicz [20]. These were created to match the characteristics every EpLTM system must satisfy and are the minimum points for validation. The requirements (R1, R2, R4) declare that every episode must be recollected and stored by its spatio-temporal context: *what*, *when*, and *where* it happened. Moreover, there are no restrictions on which information the *what* field can contain; For the competition there are useful pieces of data to remember, for example, static information about known people or objects (name, age), and their dynamic state (last location, clothes, emotions). On the other hand, (R3, R6) state how the *what* field can be accessed and modified, while (R5, R7, R8) give some rules about the episode system structure (children episodes, anidation and transposition). In this work, R9 (non intrusiveness), R10 (efficiency), and R11 (scalability) are left out, because they relate to desirable design requirements and are not considered as candidates for validation during a test.

Category II adds the concept of relevance to each episode in memory, which is not covered by category I. Episodic relevance is essential when remembering interesting events, allowing access to episodes by their importance. On the one hand, we propose the historic relevance, which is directly related to the age of an episode; the lower its antiquity is, the higher its importance, which means a high probability to remember recent events. On the other hand, we propose the emotional relevance by assigning an emotion and its related magnitude to each episode; this allows to retrieve older but important events. It is important to stress that knowing *why* the episode is relevant and *how* the emotion relates to the episode is not required, as this depends on the emotion engine implementation.

## 4.2   Required Information for Validation

Next we present a proposal for the minimum data required to be stored for the competition, and the level of detail needed when validating the requirements (categories I and II). The concepts to be delimited are the episode definition, its contents (What, Where, When), and the associated emotions.

Although Stachowicz's requirements do not impose the exact data to be gathered for (What, Where, When) fields, a set of verifiable entities should be defined for the competition. This serves as a way to normalize the validation process, by clarifying which data and format will be required for validation. It is important to highlight that by the following constraints we expect not to impose an implementation to the teams, but just to formalize the minimum required capabilities to any robot in competition.

**Episodes:** In order to provide context to any episodic query or to enable a precise memory description by the robot, we propose at least the following nested episodic levels:

1. *Context:* RoboCup, Stage X, Test Y, Subtest Z. This let us identify generally the spatio-temporal context of an episode. Subtest Z only applies to tests where sub stages are clearly defined, as in: "Stage 1, Test: SPR, Subtest: The Riddle Game".
2. *Tasks:* There must exist an episode related to each task or order executed by the robot. Tasks are defined inside a *Context* or inside other *Task*.
3. *Capabilities:* There must exist an episode related to each high-level robot capability: navigation, manipulation, perception, HRI. *Capabilities* are defined inside a *Task*.

**When:** Just knowing the sequence of episodes is not enough for validation. On the one hand, transposed episodes, i.e. episodes that are simultaneous, cannot be sequenced; on the other hand, the referees need a way to verify that the given episode description relates to the recorded time. Consequently, at least, the temporal information of an episode must consider initial and final timestamps. These can be described in terms of minutes, hours, days, weeks, months or years.

**Where:** Location must be described in a simple way. Using coordinates like (x,y,z) is not allowed. What is allowed:

- The robot can show a map of the arena with drawings marking the interesting locations.
- The robot can describe locations using semantic information, with room names and elements of the arena. Some examples: Inside/Outside the arena, rooms (kitchen, bedroom), furniture (desk, fridge), or by using relative positions (at the left of, over the). For tests which require Simultaneous Localization and Mapping (SLAM) the description can be in terms of known areas, as the "bar" in the Restaurant test.

**What:** As the information to store is not clearly defined, this highly depends on the team implementation. However, at least some entities and fields should be defined by the referees/technical committee, in order to give a normalized base for all queries and validations during a test. Proposed entities to be stored are: people, objects and locations. Fields for each of these can be obtained from capabilities required on previous tests (e.g., age/emotion recognition, last seen location, and face images). Event description can be made verbally or by displaying a graph with the related sub-episodes.

- The verbal description is preferred. This should be related as a story, by saying the associated episode sequence.
- The description should be as specific as possible. E.g.: "I moved" vs. "I moved towards the door".
- Transposed episodes should only be considered if they are in context. These might require more complex verbal explanations to emphasize the concurrence of the actions.

**Emotions:** How emotions are generated for a given robot and how they are associated to any given episode strongly depends on the emotional system used by the team. Therefore, no matter what emotional model is used, we propose to restrict the emotions to just 4 groups: Joy/Trust, Sadness/Fear, Surprise/Anticipation, Anger/Disgust. These are obtained from Plutchik's theory of emotions [17]. This selection is made to have a simple and verifiable set of emotions for the competition. Each episode must be related to at least one emotion and its intensity. Emotion intensity must have at least a resolution of 4 levels: "normal", "a little <happy>", "<happy>", "very <happy>".

**Other Limitations:** There are no proposed rules on how the memories are stored into semantic memory, as it depends on the implementation. There are no rules associated to other concepts.

### 4.3 Episode Generation

There are many sources from where the robot can generate episodes for the EpLTM: preparation for the competition, the travel, setup days, time between tests, non-RoboCup related episodes and the tests in which the robot participated. However, only the last one is a verifiable source of information. Then, we propose to limit the episodes to only the ones related to the tests of the current competition. On the first hand, this lets us simplify the evaluation and veracity of the memories. On the second hand, by only considering these episodes, new participants will compete in the same terms as older teams, this also serves as a regulation between the amount of memories gathered by teams which compete many times in a year.

As the competition lasts only a few days, the number of learning instances to gather episodes is small. In order to increase the amount of episodes, we propose two approaches. First and most important, the EpLTM test must be postponed as much as possible, ideally as the last test of Stage 2. The second proposal is to add a "Memory Setup" stage at the end of the "Setup Days" period, where each robot can generate interesting memories for the queries of the test. E.g.: By maintaining an informal conversation with someone of the committee or by an introduction to the people that it will find through the tests.

Depending on the queries the robot will encounter on the competition, the organizing committee can find new requirements. For instance for queries about people participating in 2 or more tests, the same name should be assigned to them, and they should wear similar but not identical clothes.

Finally, we have proposed to only consider episodes related to the current RoboCup competition, but it is important to mention that adding other events and older RoboCup competitions has some advantages. This directly affects the amount of episodes the robot will recollect. Moreover, this enables us to consider queries based on episodic inference, so the robot can be confronted to tasks requiring extrapolation from similar situations (e.g., Joe usually wants me to clean up the table after a meal). This capability can be added in later competitions, when the EpLTM test is considered solved.

## 4.4   Validation

The introduction of the memory concept is susceptible to cheating, for example, with manually written episodes during the competition or through a random episode generator. To attack this problem, first we consider the Fair Play concept. On the other hand, a strategy to hinder hardcoding is to increase the number of episodes and increase the number of available queries. However, the simple solution is to require evidence of each described episode.

Evidences fulfill two purposes, they hinder the cheating and also simplify the score assignation by the referees. When describing an episode it is desirable that the robot displays related evidence. As an example, the robot can provide a visualization as the one shown on Fig. 1, where location, time, and context are given. Moreover, this can be displayed through the Vizbox [3] application, so that referees and audience can see it.

– Task is validated by displaying the requirement as text.
– Location is validated by displaying a colored map and images.
– Sub-Episodes are validated with images or video.

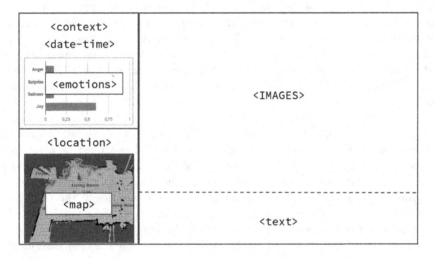

**Fig. 1.** Example of episodic visualization for the competition with fields showing all verifiable information by the referees. In the upper-left panel, the *context* and *date-time* are shown (e.g., "EpLTM Test" - "Wed, July 17, 2019 15:40:15"), followed by a graph with the emotion intensities. In the lower-left panel, location information is displayed using a *map* of the environment and the *location* name (e.g., "kitchen"). In the right panel, the *images* and *text* fields are meant to display images recorded by the robot, interaction subtitles, and other useful information as proof for validation.

## 4.5    Test Proposal: Sick and Elderly Care

Next we present an example of an @Home like test with EpLTM requirements. The test is based on the methodology proposed in this Section. Particularly, it is important to postpone the test as part of Stage 2, so that the robots can collect as much interesting episodes as possible beforehand. We expect that this proposal can be adjusted as needed for the competition.

**Focus:** The robot must help a sick or elderly person with reduced mobility (in bed/wheelchair), by answering questions about the home and recent events at which he cannot attend. The test is focused on EpLTM, perception and HRI.

**Setup:** The test takes place on the @Home arena. The operator is waiting in the bedroom, lying on the bed or sitting on a chair. The arena keeps the same structure and items as in other tests, but with some small changes. Other people are located in the house with which the robot can interact as needed.

**Task:** The robot starts by entering the arena, it moves to the bedroom, approaches the operator and asks if any assistance is needed. The operator explains he is sick/tired and cannot move, so it will make some questions to the robot. After 4 queries, the operator tells the robot to leave the bedroom.

**Considerations:** Queries can be separated into 3 categories, depending on their requirements. The robot should answer at least one question of each category.

- Cat 1: Queries about memories and emotions.
- Cat 2: Queries which require investigating objects in the arena.
- Cat 3: Queries which require interacting with people in the arena.
- We recommend the use of an episodic queries generator, built to match requirements of categories I and II.
- The robot must show evidences when answering, e.g., in a screen or using Vizbox [3], as shown on the official Rulebook.
- Referees must validate the coherence between answers and provided evidence.
- Rooms, people and objects must be set up according to the possible queries.

## 5    Conclusions

The development of EpLTM for social robots is an important challenge for improving human-robot interaction, and @Home has the means to boost the progress. For that reason, we have presented a test proposal focused on EpLTM, its requirements and validation strategies. The proposal is focused on the minimum requirements any social robot implementing EpLTM should fulfill, but trying not to impose an specific implementation to the teams.

# References

1. Allen, P.A., Kaut, K.P., Lord, R.R.: Chapter 1.8 emotion and episodic memory. In: Dere, E., Easton, A., Nadel, L., Huston, J.P. (eds.) Handbook of Episodic Memory, Handbook of Behavioral Neuroscience, vol. 18, pp. 115–132. Elsevier, Amsterdam (2008)
2. Bailey, C.H., Bartsch, D., Kandel, E.R.: Toward a molecular definition of long-term memory storage. Proc. Natl. Acad. Sci. U.S.A. **93**(24), 13445–13452 (1996)
3. van Beek, L., et al.: RoboCup@Home 2017: rules and regulations (2017). http://www.robocupathome.org/rules/2017_rulebook.pdf
4. Dere, E., Easton, A., Nadel, L., Huston, J.P.: Handbook of behavioral neuroscience. In: Handbook of Episodic Memory, Handbook of Behavioral Neuroscience, vol. 18, p. iii. Elsevier (2008)
5. Deutsch, T., Gruber, A., Lang, R., Velik, R.: Episodic memory for autonomous agents. In: 2008 Conference on Human System Interactions, pp. 621–626, May 2008
6. Dodd, W., Gutierrez, R.: The role of episodic memory and emotion in a cognitive robot. In: Proceedings - IEEE International Workshop on Robot and Human Interactive Communication, 2005, pp. 692–697 (2005)
7. Eichenbaum, H.: Learning & Memory. W. W. Norton & Company, New York (2008)
8. Eichenbaum, H.: Memory. Scholarpedia **3**(3), 1747 (2008)
9. Ho, W.C., Dautenhahn, K., Lim, M.Y., Vargas, P.A., Aylett, R., Enz, S.: An initial memory model for virtual and robot companions supporting migration and long-term interaction. In: RO-MAN 2009 - The 18th IEEE International Symposium on Robot and Human Interactive Communication, pp. 277–284, September 2009
10. Jockel, S., Weser, M.: Towards an episodic memory for cognitive robots. In: European Conference on Artificial Intelligence, pp. 68–74 (2008)
11. Kelley, T.D.: Robotic dreams: a computational justification for the post-hoc processing of episodic memories. Int. J. Mach. Conscious. **06**(02), 109–123 (2014)
12. Kim, M.J., Baek, S.H., Cho, S.H., Kim, J.H.: Approach to integrate episodic memory into cogency-based behavior planner for robots. In: 2016 IEEE International Conference on Systems, Man, and Cybernetics (SMC), pp. 4188–4193, October 2016
13. Kuppuswamy, N.S., Cho, S.H., Kim, J.H.: A cognitive control architecture for an artificial creature using episodic memory. In: 2006 SICE-ICASE International Joint Conference, pp. 3104–3110 (2006)
14. Laird, J.E., Newell, A., Rosenbloom, P.S.: SOAR: an architecture for general intelligence. Artif. Intell. **33**(1), 1–64 (1987)
15. Leconte, F., Ferland, F., Michaud, F.: Design and integration of a spatio-temporal memory with emotional influences to categorize and recall the experiences of an autonomous mobile robot. Auton. Robots **40**(5), 831–848 (2016). https://doi.org/10.1007/s10514-015-9496-2
16. Nuxoll, A., Laird, J.E.: A cognitive model of episodic memory integrated with a general cognitive architecture. In: ICCM (2004)
17. Plutchik, R., Kellerman, H.: Emotion: theory, research, and experience. In: Theories of Emotion, p. ii. Academic Press (1980)
18. Ratanaswasd, P., Gordon, S., Dodd, W.: Cognitive control for robot task execution. In: IEEE International Workshop on Robot and Human Interactive Communication ROMAN 2005, pp. 440–445, August 2005

19. Spexard, T.P., Siepmann, F., Sagerer, G.: A Memory-based software integration for development in autonomous robotics. In: International Conference on Intelligent Autonomous Systems, pp. 49–53 (2008)
20. Stachowicz, D., Kruijff, G.J.M.: Episodic-like memory for cognitive robots. IEEE Trans. Auton. Mental Dev. **4**, 1–16 (2012)
21. Tulving, E.: Episodic and semantic memory. In: Tulving, E., Donaldson, W. (eds.) Organization of Memory, pp. 381–403. Academic Press, New York. (1972)
22. Vijayakumar, S.: Long-term memory in cognitive robots. Ph.D. thesis, Universitaet des Saarlandes (2014)
23. Walker, M.P., Stickgold, R.: Sleep-dependent learning and memory consolidation. Neuron **44**(1), 121–133 (2004)
24. Wood, R., Baxter, P., Belpaeme, T.: A review of long-term memory in natural and synthetic systems. Adapt. Behav. **20**(2), 81–103 (2012)

# eEVA as a Real-Time Multimodal Agent Human-Robot Interface

P. Peña[1]([✉]), M. Polceanu[3], C. Lisetti[2], and U. Visser[1]

[1] University of Miami, Coral Gables, FL 33146, USA
pedro@cs.miami.edu
[2] ENIB Brest, UMR 6285, Lab-STICC, 29200 Brest, France
[3] Florida International University, Miami, FL 33199, USA

**Abstract.** We posit that human-robot interfaces that integrate multimodal communication features of a 3-dimensional graphical social virtual agent with a high degree of freedom robot are highly promising. We discuss the modular agent architecture of an interactive system that integrates two frameworks (our in-house virtual social agent and robot agent framework) that enables social multimodal human-robot interaction with the Toyota's Human Support Robot (HSR). We demonstrate HSR greeting gestures using culturally diverse inspired motions, combined with our virtual social agent interface, and we provide the results of a pilot study designed to assess the effects of our multimodal virtual agent/robot system on users' experience. We discuss future directions for social interaction with a virtual agent/robot system.

**Keywords:** Human-robot interaction · Service and social robots · Intelligent virtual agents · Culturally-aware robotics · Culturally-aware virtual agents

## 1 Introduction

Twenty years ago, research has shown that humans respond positively to social cues when provided by computer artefacts [21]. With the emerging introduction of robots in social spaces where humans and robots co-exist, the design of socially competent robots could be pivotal for human acceptance of such robots. Humans are very skilled at innately reading non-verbal cues (*e.g.*, emotional signals) and extrapolating pertinent information from body language of other humans and animals [24]. Although some robots are currently capable to portray a small collection of emotional signals [12], robots social abilities are currently very limited. Recently, the use of virtual interactive social agents as main user interface (UI) has been shown to enhance users' experience during human-computer interactions in contexts involving social interactions (*e.g.*, health assistants, tutors, games) [7,14]. Yet robots intended to engage in social dialogs and physically collaborate with humans do not have virtual social agents as user interface.

© Springer Nature Switzerland AG 2019
D. Holz et al. (Eds.): RoboCup 2018, LNAI 11374, pp. 262–274, 2019.
https://doi.org/10.1007/978-3-030-27544-0_22

We posit that human-robot interfaces that integrate multimodal communication features of a social virtual agent with a high degree of freedom robot might enhance users' experience with, and acceptance of, robots in their personal spaces, are highly promising, and need to be investigated. However, according to Matarić et al. [15], in order to avoid a mismatch between the expectations of the human and the behavior of the robot during human-robot interaction (HRI, henceforth), the natural integration of all the modules of the robot responsible for social, physical, and cognitive abilities is of utmost importance.

We have started to address this social HRI challenge by developing a multimodal human-robot interface for the Toyota's Human Support Robot (HSR, designed to help people in homes or offices) which integrates the RoboCanes agent and the Embodied Empathetic Virtual Agent (eEVA) developed by FIU's VISAGE lab. The RoboCanes agent is responsible for managing and controlling navigation, object manipulation, grasping, among other physical actions, while the VISAGE agent is responsible for recognizing and displaying social cues involving recognizing the user's facial expression and speech, synthesizing speech with lip-synchronization, and portraying appropriate facial expressions and gestures.

We created a greeting context for the pilot study of our first social human-HSR interactions with our RoboCanes-VISAGE interface (described in Sect. 4) by designing a small set of greeting gestures to personalize Toyota HSR with its users greeting preferences (and to establish some initial rapport in future more advanced studies): the Toyota HSR generates greeting gestures from four different cultures such as waving-hand (Western), fist-bump (informal Western), Shaka (Hawaii), and bowing (Japan) greeting gestures (for details see Sect. 4). The HSR's gesture greetings are performed based on the user's spoken selection of one of the four greetings and our pilot questionnaire aims to assess the impact of combining the virtual agent interface on the user's experience (*e.g.*, feelings of enjoyment, boredom, annoyance, user's perception of the robot's friendliness or of competence). Future directions for social interaction with a virtual agent/robot system are discussed in Sect. 5.

## 2   Related Work and Motivation

**Human-Robot Interfaces:** Human-robot interfaces that utilize multimodal features (*e.g.*, nonverbal and verbal channels) to communicate with humans has been a current trend in HRI [1,2,9,22], but has demonstrated to be very challenging due to the high-dimensional space of these channels. Therefore, theories and ideas from plethora of fields (*e.g.*, Neuroscience, psychology, and linguistics) have come together to develop new algorithms to create a more natural interface to communicate with humans. However due to hardware constraints and current A.I. technologies, developing an agent and robot that can communicate with humans at the level of human-human interaction has not been possible. Consequently, human-robot interfaces that are simple yet intuitive have been developed to help with tasks that require assistance for humans. An example of these interfaces is the graphical user interface. Depending on the task, it is easier for the user to interact with a robot using a graphical user interface with 3D graphic rendering of the world to select objects or tasks for the robot to perform [4], than with speech recognition and synthesis as proposed with our approach.

Nagahama et al. [16] developed an interactive graphical interface for users that are not able to grab an object by themselves. The interface allows the user to specify the object the user wants the robot to fetch by clicking on the object on the screen. Hashimoto et al. [8] created a simple interface that has four different modes or windows to give Toyota HSR tasks or monitor the robot.

Nonverbal gestures (e.g., arm gestures) to communicate with the robot and assist with tasks have also been used. Kofman et al. developed a human-robot interface that allows a user to teleoperate a robotic arm with vision [13]. There are also human-robot assistive interfaces developed with haptic and visual feedback [6,23]. Human-robot interfaces that are connected to the human brain have also been developed [20]. Qiu et al. developed a brain-machine interface that is able to control an exoskeleton robot through neural activity. There is also a recent trend of Augmented Reality (AR) human-robot interfaces to help users visualize an environment from another location in their physical environment [25].

Although there has been recurring research in human-robot interfaces, the communication between humans and robots through graphical interfaces is limited because the interaction between the human and the robot is constrained by the screen where the interface resides in, and it does not offer nonverbal and verbal communication as a medium of communication. Augmented and virtual reality is a promising interface but it is also limited by the hardware, equipment, and the lack of physical realism, i.e., virtual characters cannot interact with the physical world. A promising yet an immature technology is the integration of virtual agents which offers the social realism that robots require and integration of robotics which offers the physical realism that virtual agents require.

**Social Virtual Agents with Robots:** Because virtual characters can use their sophisticated multimodal communication abilities (e.g. facial expressions, gaze, gesture) [17], to coach users in interactive stories [10], establish rapport (with back channeling cues such as head nods, smiles, shift of gaze or posture, or mimicry of head gestures) [18], communicate empathically [19], and engage in social talk [11], they have the potential of becoming as engaging as humans [7]. The integration of a virtual agent with social robots has been very limited and only given small attention. On example of a robot with a social virtual agent as a human-robot interface is GRACE (Graduate Robot Attending ConferencE) which was built by Simmons et al. [22] to compete in the AAAI Robot Challenge that required GRACE to socially interact with humans in a conference.

The Thinking Head research [9] was performed in conjunction with artist Stelarc where the facial characteristics of Stelarc were used for the animated head. Cavedon et al. developed an attention model for the Thinking Head that used backchanneling cues and eye gaze [5]. The Thinking Head resides in various robots such as a robot arm's end-effector and in a mobile robot.

Other human-robot interfaces include head-projection systems where a projector projects an animated face onto a mask [1,2]. These systems allow an animated avatar to display complex facial expressions not yet possible with robotic hardware.

However, none of these previous approaches studied robots with manipulative capabilities that are able to produce gestures, appropriately combined with the social verbal and non-verbal cues of a virtual agent. Yet, many of the emerging and future human-robot interactions are or will require socially and culturally appropriate robots. Therefore rather than utilize a robot as a platform for a virtual character to enable movement in the physical world such as the literature discussed in this section, we developed an agent that takes advantage of the social-emotional capabilities of social virtual agents (*e.g.*, anthropomorphic agent, natural language, and nonverbal gestures) with the physical capabilities of the robot (high degree of freedom arm and mobile base of the HSR robot) that can work as a synchronized system which exhibits features from human-human interactions such as simple greetings (*e.g.*, robot greets user saying "hello" and waving arm based on the users' spoken utterance, discussed in Sect. 4) to enhance the social interaction with the user. In the following section, we will explain the architecture of the virtual agent and robot to understand how these two systems interact with each other while it is providing a synchronized interface for the user.

# 3   Modular Architecture for Real-Time Multimodal User-Interface Agents

## 3.1   RoboCanes-VISAGE: Integration of Two Agent-Based Frameworks

The system architecture of the RoboCanes-VISAGE affective robot agent consists of two separate frameworks: one developed by FIU's VISAGE lab (eEVA framework) and the other developed by UM's RoboCanes lab (RoboCanes framework). As described earlier, the RoboCanes agent is responsible for physical actions, such as managing and controlling navigation, object manipulation, grasping. The VISAGE agent is responsible for recognizing and displaying social cues involving recognition of the user's facial expression and speech, speech synthesis with lip-synchrony, and portray of appropriate facial expressions and gestures.

Since our goal is to integrate two existing agent-based systems (namely the eEVA and RoboCanes agents), in order for the integration of eEVA and RoboCanes modules to cooperate seamlessly, a higher-level framework has been designed and implemented to manage both systems accordingly. This was accomplished by integrating the inputs of eEVA and of the RoboCanes agent under one decision making process rather than treating both systems separately. By doing this, eEVA and RoboCanes agent act as one agent and their behavior is synchronized.

More specifically, in order to integrate both systems together, the frameworks communicate through the Standard ROS Javascript Library, roslibjs[1].

---

[1] http://wiki.ros.org/roslibjs.

This library facilitates both frameworks to communicate through web-sockets. Therefore the user input in eEVA is transported from these web-sockets to the RoboCanes framework, and the robot generates motions based on the requests from the user.

### 3.2    eEVA: A Framework for Building Empathic Embodied Virtual Agents

The default HSR user interface (UI) is shown in Fig. 1(a), and it is our aim to use our empathic embodied virtual agent (eEVA) shown in Fig. 1(b) to enhance user experience while interacting with HSR. While eEVA's UI is a 3D animated agent, it is driven by a fully integrated web-based multimodal modal system that perceives the user's facial expressions and verbal utterances in real time which controls the displays of socially appropriate facial expressions on its 3D-graphics characters, along with verbal utterances related to the context of the dialog-based interaction. eEVA's facial expressions are currently generated from the HapFACS[2] open source software developed by the VISAGE lab for the creation of physiologically realistic facial expressions on socially believable speaking virtual agents [3].

(a) HSR default visual screen (with eEVA's added speech recognition and synthesis) as user interface

(b) eEVA visual screen (with eEVA's speech recognition and synthesis) as HSR user interface

**Fig. 1.** Human-robot interfaces

**eEVA Components:** The two basic components of the eEVA architecture consist of modules and resource generic types. The principle of a module is to robustly implement a single concrete functionality of the overall system. A module is defined by the task that it solves, the resources it requires for solving the given task, and the resources it provides (which may be further used for other purposes within the system). In other words, a module receives an input which is the resource it requires and it has an output which is the resource it provides. Modules are further categorized by their resource handling: sensors (*i.e.*, modules which only provide resources), processors (*i.e.*, with both required and provided

---

[2] http://ascl.cis.fiu.edu/hapfacs-open-source-softwareapi-download.html.

**Table 1.** List of eEVA current modules.

| Ref. No. | Type | Short name | Function description |
|---|---|---|---|
| 1 | Sensor | ChromeSpeech | Speech recognition using Google Chrome API |
| 2 | Processor | HapCharacter | Virtual character controller (body and face) |
| 3 | Processor | UserChoice | User interface for interacting with eEVA |
| 4 | Processor | WinSAPISynth | Speech synthesis using Windows SAPI |
| 5 | Effector | WebGLScene | Default 3D scene rendering |
| 6 | Effector | ROSHandler | ROS Communication through roslibjs |

resources), and effectors (*i.e.*, modules which require resources but produce no further data for system use). The list of eEVA modules and third-party libraries is shown in Table 1.

**Sensors:** Sensors are modules that provide an output but do not have a processed input. An example of a sensor in the eEVA framework is the ChromeSpeech module which uses Google Speech API to recognize speech from the user by using the head microphone of HSR as shown in Table 2. The final speech text from the user is processed by this module and provides a UserText and UserCommand resource that can then be required by another module such as an effector or processor. Hence, sensors are modules that receive input from the environment.

**Processors:** Processors are modules that require and provide resources. The modules process inputs from the sensors and then request the effectors to do an action. Hence, these modules extract information and make a decision. Since the interaction in the pilot study is turn-taking, the UserChoice module displays the choices the user can say (*i.e.*, the greetings discussed in Sect. 4). The virtual agent uses Windows SAPI to generate speech. It is important to note that majority of modules fall into the processor category and the collection of these modules define the behavior of the agent.

**Effectors:** The effectors are modules that require resources but do not further process other resources. Effectors are the modules that perform an action on the environment and are responsible for displaying system data such as the 3D virtual scene, the agent's behavior, text, and other information to the user. The effectors are the modules that are visible to the user and affect the perception of the sensors. The communication between eEVA and RoboCanes is done through an effector, ROSHandler. ROSHandler requires UserText resource from a sensor, ChromeSpeech module, and sends this resource through roslibjs (roslibjs deals with wrapping this resource in a format that ROS understands).

## 3.3 RoboCanes Components

On the robotic side, we use Toyota HSR which is an exemplary platform to embody the integration of the University of Miami (UM) RoboCanes agent with the FIU VIrtual Social AGEnt (VISAGE). Our RoboCanes framework is an extension of the ROS[3] architecture that runs on the HSR.

The RoboCanes framework is developed in the ROS environment and it is also modular. In pursuance of gesture synthesis, the RoboCanes framework consists of a motion library node that uses MoveIt![4] and Toyota Motor Corporation (TMC) action servers. The relevant node for this research is the manipulation node.

**Motion Planner:** The motion planner node uses the MoveIt! library and the OMPL[5] library through MoveIt! to generate motions. The motions are requested by the eEVAHandler which handles the communication between both frameworks. The eEVAHandler processes the request from eEVA and decides which gesture to generate based on the input of eEVA. This results in the robot generating motions of the physical robot through ROS. In Fig. 2, eEVA is running on HSR, and Fig. 1(b) shows how eEVA is presented on Toyota HSR. All the relevant HSR components are listed in Table 2. The actuators shown in Table 2 are used in parallel to generate the motions discussed in Sect. 4.

**Fig. 2.** eEVA running on Toyota HSR

**Table 2.** Listing of most significant Toyota HSR hardware components. The highlighted components are used for the pilot study.

| Type | Short name | Function description |
|---|---|---|
| Sensor | Head Microphone | Speech Recognition |
| Sensor | Head 3D sensor | RGBD Camera |
| Sensor | Head Stereo Camera | Perception |
| Sensor | Head Wide Camera | Perception |
| Sensor | Laser Range Sensor | Perception |
| Actuator | Arm | Manipulation (Gesture synthesis) |
| Actuator | Head Display | Displays eEVA |
| Actuator | Head | Tilts and pans (Gesture Synthesis) |
| Actuator | Body | Goes up and down (Gesture synthesis) |
| Actuator | Gripper | Grasping (Gesture synthesis) |
| Actuator | Omni-Directional Base | Motion |
| Actuator | Speakers | eEVA voice |

---

[3] http://www.ros.org/.

[4] http://moveit.ros.org/.

[5] https://ompl.kavrakilab.org/.

# 4  Pilot Study: Culturally-Sensitive Greetings on HSR with RoboCanes-VISAGE

We investigated what the effects of a multimodal virtual agent as a UI are, and whether we can develop a multimodal virtual agent UI that is more enjoyable than a robot without such a UI.

We aimed at testing the following hypotheses:

- **H1:** Users find eEVA's 3D character with speech recognition as the HSR UI more enjoyable and competent over an HSR robot UI with speech recognition without eEVA's 3D character.
- **H2:** eEVA's 3D character as UI with speech recognition does not make the HSR UI with speech recognition more eerie, annoying, or boring compared to the HSR robot default UI with speech recognition.

In our pilot study, the user stood about one meter away from the robot in the lab, and the interaction exhibited turn-taking behavior. Each interaction was initiated by eEVA greeting the user: **"Hi, I am Amy. How is it going? How do you greet?"**. eEVA uses Google Chrome API for speech recognition and Windows SAPI for speech synthesis (see Table 1 and Sect. 3.2). After eEVA received the user's greeting preference, the user greeted the robot from four greetings (see below), and the robot portrayed the corresponding pre-greeting gesture. The interaction is concluded when the robot performs the greeting gesture chosen by the user. When the robot finishes greeting the user, the user is allowed to get greeted by the robot again (study setup is shown in Fig. 3).

We established four short social interactions with the RoboCanes-VISAGE framework. The four greetings identified below represent diverse forms of greeting, which vary to reflect cultural influences via the HSR's robot specific motions, coupled with the eEVA human-robot interface: 1. Japanese greeting (**Bow**) as shown in Fig. 3(a). When the user says, "hello" in Japanese, "Konnichiwa", the robot lifts its torso and bows by tilting its head forward. 2. **Fist bump** as shown in Fig. 3(b). When the user says, "Hey, bro!", the robot lifts its torso and moves its arm forward while closing its fist. The user is able to pound the fist of the robot. (this is the only interaction that involves physical contact with the user). 3. **Shaka**, the Hawaiian greeting as shown in Fig. 3(c). When the user says, "Shaka", the robot performs a Shaka gesture. The Shaka gesture involves the robot lifting its hand and moving it side to side. 4. **Hand Waving** greeting. When the user says, "hello", the robot moves its hand up and down, *i.e.*, simulating a wave arm motion.

## 4.1  Participants

There were a total of 32 participants from the University of Miami Computer Science department that took part in the pilot study (age $M = 41$, $SD = 13$). There was a total of 17 females and 15 males that completed the experiment. Data from one participant was excluded because the participant did not complete the whole questionnaire.

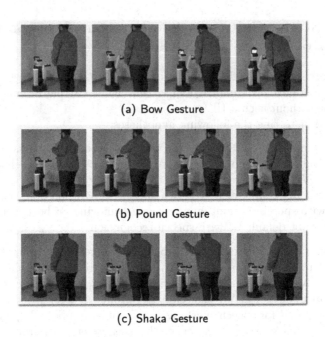

(a) Bow Gesture

(b) Pound Gesture

(c) Shaka Gesture

**Fig. 3.** Gestures used for pilot study

## 4.2 Experiment Design and Procedure

A small number of participants interacted with Toyota HSR with eEVA's voice, and the screen of the robot had the visual default HSR splash screen as shown in Fig. 1(a). We compared their interaction experience with users who interacted with Toyota HSR with eEVA's 3D character as the visual interface element and eEVA's voice as shown in Fig. 2.

We split the participants into two groups: one group of 19 participants (age $M = 40$, $SD = 12$) who interacted with Toyota HSR with eEVA (face and voice Fig. 1(b)) and another group of 13 participants (age $M = 41, SD = 13$) who interacted with Toyota HSR with eEVA's voice and HSR default screen (see Fig. 1(a)). At the end of the interaction, we asked the participants to fill out a questionnaire with 7-point Likert scales about how they felt about the interaction of the robot and their feelings toward the robot itself, and conducted an unstructured interview for qualitative data.

## 4.3 Results

The data was analyzed using the Mann-Whitney test. For this experiment, $n_1 = 19$ and $n_2 = 13$ with a critical $U = 72$. An alpha level of 0.05 was used to analyze the data. There was no significant difference reported for each Likert scale. The competent category was very close to the critical $U$-value but was not significant enough. No significant differences were found between both groups with regards

**Table 3.** Overall impression of eEVA as a human-robot interface

| Category | eEVA | | | eEVA's voice only | | | Mann-Whitney test | |
|---|---|---|---|---|---|---|---|---|
| | Q1 | Median | Q3 | Q1 | Median | Q3 | U ($Critical\ U = 72$) | $p$ |
| Enjoyable | 6 | 6 | 7 | 5 | 7 | 7 | 108.5 | 0.56 |
| Boring | 1 | 2 | 3 | 1 | 1 | 2 | 101 | 0.39 |
| Natural | 2 | 4 | 5 | 2 | 3 | 4 | 108 | 0.55 |
| Friendly | 5.5 | 6 | 7 | 4 | 6 | 6 | 107.5 | 0.54 |
| Competent | 5 | 6 | 7 | 4 | 4 | 6 | 92 | 0.22 |
| Scary | 1 | 1 | 2.5 | 1 | 1 | 1 | 111 | 0.63 |
| Annoying | 1 | 1 | 1 | 1 | 1 | 1 | 105.5 | 0.49 |

*Significant $p < 0.05$ (Likert scales are 7-point scales)

to age ($p = 0.79$) and experience interacting with robots ($p = 0.42$). Details can be seen in Table 3.

## 4.4  Discussion

Although no significant differences were found in all categories, interesting conclusions can be made from this pilot study. First, it is important to note that no significant difference was found in the *scary, annoying,* nor *boring* category. Therefore our second hypothesis **H2**, *eEVA does not make the human-robot interaction more eerie, annoying, or boring* is supported by our results. We concluded that eEVA as an virtual agent human-robot interface might be acceptable to users.

The first hypothesis, **H1**, is not supported by our quantitative results. However the qualitative data we acquired in the study revealed interesting observations that we will investigate in future research. For example, participants in the study requested to interact with HSR for a longer period. One user asked "Will the robot say something else?", and another user asked "Can it do something else?" These observations indicate that a longer interaction might be needed to allow the user to interact with eEVA for a longer period of time to generate an accurate evaluation. This also indicates that users enjoyed the HSR interaction enough to want longer interactions with it, which is a measure of engagement; many users asked, "Can I try all four greetings?" (in fact, 100% of all users used all four greetings). We also noticed that users who interacted with eEVA were trying to get closer to the screen suggesting that the size of HSR's screen might also have an effect on the interaction (*i.e.*, in this case, the HSR screen might be too small to generate an effect in the experience of the interaction).

Another factor in the interaction that might deter our results to be statistically significant is the current hardware of Toyota HSR which evokes aspects of a human face: the two stereo cameras and the wide angle camera on the Toyota HSR resemble two eyes and a nose. During the interaction, users were seen gazing at HSR's stereo cameras rather than the screen. One user mentioned the stereo cameras were distracting when interacting with eEVA.

Henceforth, in future formal studies we plan to investigate the following questions, among others: Does eEVA on different screen sizes on the HSR affect the user's experience such as user's feelings or user's perception of the robot's characteristics? Does HSR's anthropomorphic features (two stereo cameras as eyes and wide angle camera as nose) affect the user's experience such as user's feelings or user's perception of the robot's characteristics? If the answer to the previous question is yes, do users prefer eEVA as a human-robot interface for Toyota HSR without an anthropomorphic face, Toyota HSR with an anthropomorphic face but without eEVA, or both, eEVA and anthropomorphic face?

## 5    Conclusions and Future Work

In this article, we described a system that integrates both frameworks (eEVA and RoboCanes) under one synchronized system that takes human input such as eye gaze and user speech, and outputs a personalized human-robot interface with greeting gestures.

Our pilot study to assess the effects of eEVA as a human-robot interface for Toyota HSR revealed no significant differences in enjoyment, friendliness, competence, uncanniness, and other categories when comparing Toyota HSR with and without eEVA. We concluded that eEVA's character does not make Toyota HSR more uncanny, boring, or annoying.

In our future research, we will make a formal experiment to study further effects of eEVA on Toyota HSR. This will include making the interaction with Toyota HSR for a longer period of time to answer users' wish to interact longer with the robot (with or without eEVA).

**Acknowledgements.** Part of this research was funded by the National Science Foundation grant award No. IIS-1423260 to Florida International University.

## References

1. Abdollahi, H., Mollahosseini, A., Lane, J.T., Mahoor, M.H.: A pilot study on using an intelligent life-like robot as a companion for elderly individuals with dementia and depression. arXiv preprint arXiv:1712.02881 (2017)
2. Al Moubayed, S., Beskow, J., Skantze, G., Granström, B.: Furhat: a back-projected human-like robot head for multiparty human-machine interaction. In: Esposito, A., Esposito, A.M., Vinciarelli, A., Hoffmann, R., Müller, V.C. (eds.) Cognitive Behavioural Systems. LNCS, vol. 7403, pp. 114–130. Springer, Heidelberg (2012). https://doi.org/10.1007/978-3-642-34584-5_9
3. Amini, R., Lisetti, C., Ruiz, G.: HapFACS 3.0: FACS-based facial expression generator for 3D speaking virtual characters. IEEE Trans. Affect. Comput. **6**(4), 348–360 (2015)
4. van der Burgh, M., et al.: Tech united eindhoven@ home 2017 team description paper. University of Technology Eindhoven (2017)
5. Cavedon, L., et al.: "C' Mon dude!": users adapt their behaviour to a robotic agent with an attention model. Int. J. Hum Comput Stud. **80**, 14–23 (2015)

6. Cowan, R.E., Fregly, B.J., Boninger, M.L., Chan, L., Rodgers, M.M., Reinkensmeyer, D.J.: Recent trends in assistive technology for mobility. J. Neuroeng. Rehabil. **9**(1), 20 (2012)

7. Gratch, J., et al.: Can virtual humans be more engaging than real ones? In: Jacko, J.A. (ed.) HCI 2007. LNCS, vol. 4552, pp. 286–297. Springer, Heidelberg (2007). https://doi.org/10.1007/978-3-540-73110-8_30. http://dl.acm.org/citation.cfm?id=1769622

8. Hashimoto, K., Saito, F., Yamamoto, T., Ikeda, K.: A field study of the human support robot in the home environment. In: 2013 IEEE Workshop on Advanced Robotics and its Social Impacts (ARSO), pp. 143–150. IEEE (2013)

9. Herath, D.C., Kroos, C., Stevens, C.J., Cavedon, L., Premaratne, P.: Thinking head: towards human centred robotics. In: 2010 11th International Conference on Control Automation Robotics & Vision (ICARCV), pp. 2042–2047. IEEE (2010)

10. Hill, R.W., Gratch, J., Marsella, S., Rickel, J., Swartout, W., Traum, D.: Virtual humans in the mission rehearsal exercise system. Kunstliche Intelligenz (KI J.) **17**(4), 5–10 (2003). Special issue on Embodied Conversational Agents

11. Klüwer, T.: "I Like Your Shirt" - dialogue acts for enabling social talk in conversational agents. In: Vilhjálmsson, H.H., Kopp, S., Marsella, S., Thórisson, K.R. (eds.) IVA 2011. LNCS (LNAI), vol. 6895, pp. 14–27. Springer, Heidelberg (2011). https://doi.org/10.1007/978-3-642-23974-8_2

12. Knight, H., Simmons, R.: Expressive motion with x, y and theta: Laban effort features for mobile robots. In: 2014 RO-MAN: The 23rd IEEE International Symposium on Robot and Human Interactive Communication, pp. 267–273. IEEE (2014)

13. Kofman, J., Wu, X., Luu, T.J., Verma, S.: Teleoperation of a robot manipulator using a vision-based human-robot interface. IEEE Trans. Industr. Electron. **52**(5), 1206–1219 (2005)

14. Lisetti, C., Amini, R., Yasavur, U.: Now all together: overview of virtual health assistants emulating face-to-face health interview experience. KI - Künstliche Intelligenz **29**(2), 161–172 (2015). https://doi.org/10.1007/s13218-015-0357-0

15. Matarić, M.J.: Socially assistive robotics: Human augmentation versus automation. Sci. Robot. **2**(4) (2017). eaam5410

16. Nagahama, K., Yaguchi, H., Hattori, H., Sogen, K., Yamamoto, T., Inaba, M.: Learning-based object abstraction method from simple instructions for human support robot HSR. In: 2016 IEEE International Conference on Advanced Intelligent Mechatronics (AIM), pp. 468–475. IEEE (2016)

17. Pelachaud, C., Bilvi, M.: Computational model of believable conversational agents. In: Huget, M.-P. (ed.) Communication in Multiagent Systems. LNCS (LNAI), vol. 2650, pp. 300–317. Springer, Heidelberg (2003). https://doi.org/10.1007/978-3-540-44972-0_17

18. Pelachaud, C.: Modelling multimodal expression of emotion in a virtual agent. Philos. Trans. Roy. Soc. London. Ser. B Biol. Sci. **364**(1535), 3539–3548 (2009). http://www.ncbi.nlm.nih.gov/pubmed/19884148

19. Predinger, H., Ishizuka, M.: The empathic companion: a character-based interface that addresses user's affective states. Appl. Artif. Intell. **19**, 267–285 (2005)

20. Qiu, S., Li, Z., He, W., Zhang, L., Yang, C., Su, C.Y.: Brain-machine interface and visual compressive sensing-based teleoperation control of an exoskeleton robot. IEEE Trans. Fuzzy Syst. **25**(1), 58–69 (2017)

21. Reeves, B., Nass, C.I.: The Media Equation: How People Treat Computers, Television, and New Media Like Real People and Places. Cambridge University Press, Cambridge (1996)

22. Simmons, R., et al.: Grace: an autonomous robot for the AAAI robot challenge. Technical report, Carnegie Mellon University (2003)

23. Suero, E.M., et al.: Improving the human-robot interface for telemanipulated robotic long bone fracture reduction: Joystick device vs. haptic manipulator. Int. J. Med. Robot. Comput. Assist. Surg. 14(1) (2018)

24. Wolpert, D.M., Doya, K., Kawato, M.: A unifying computational framework for motor control and social interaction. Philos. Trans. Roy. Soc. B: Biol. Sci. **358**(1431), 593–602 (2003)

25. Yew, A., Ong, S., Nee, A.: Immersive augmented reality environment for the tele-operation of maintenance robots. Procedia CIRP **61**, 305–310 (2017)

# Evaluation of Situations in RoboCup 2D Simulations Using Soccer Field Images

Tanguy Pomas and Tomoharu Nakashima[✉]

Department of Computer Science and Intelligent Systems,
Osaka Prefecture University, Sakai, Japan
mb104079@edu.osakafu-u.ac.jp, tomoharu.nakashima@kis.osakafu-u.ac.jp

**Abstract.** This paper proposes a convolutional neural network (CNN) that assesses the situation at one point of a RoboCup 2D soccer game, predicting which team will score next and when, by only taking soccer field images as input. To train this model, we define a metric, called *SituationScore* that estimates, for a frame, the remaining number of frames before next goal. A dataset containing more than one million RoboCup 2D soccer field images labeled with their SituationScore, from more than 5,000 games has been built to train our CNN. Our CNN-based model manages to predict the *SituationScore* of a frame with an average error lower than the other methods tested in this paper that use raw numerical data from log files.

## 1 Introduction

Since games in RoboCup 2D Soccer Simulation League, or simply RoboCup 2D, are simulated on computer, every piece of information regarding them is stored, and can be easily extracted for analysis purposes. Such logs contain, for example, the coordinates of every player, for every cycle of a game, as well as their velocity and their orientation. Therefore, it is not surprising that log files play an important role when analyzing games and designing strategies.

RoboCup 2D games can be visualized on computers thanks to tools such as soccerwindow2 that displays the position of all players and the ball for every cycle of the game, with one computational cycle corresponding to one frame on it. This tool not only allows audience to visualize games, but also researchers to replay the same game, the same actions, in order to easily analyze them. However, even when working with soccerwindow2, field images are only considered as a representation of numerical data stored in log files, not as data itself.

This paper proposes a model that uses such images as input data in order to assess how good or bad is the situation for both teams playing, without considering numerical data available in log files. A metric, called *SituationScore*, is proposed and used to evaluate the state of the field, estimating the number of remaining frames before the next goal. We decided to build our model by using a Convolutional Neural Network (CNN), given their efficiency for a large range of tasks related to image analysis. To allow comparison with our CNN-based

© Springer Nature Switzerland AG 2019
D. Holz et al. (Eds.): RoboCup 2018, LNAI 11374, pp. 275–286, 2019.
https://doi.org/10.1007/978-3-030-27544-0_23

model, other models using raw numerical data from log files have been built and evaluated, such as fully-connected neural networks and decision trees.

In order to evaluate these models, we built datasets containing more than one million soccer field images and their corresponding raw numerical data from more than 5,000 games. Our CNN leads to slightly better results than the other tested methods. This may indicate that spatial features extracted by our CNN can provide better information than raw numerical data.

The remainder of this paper is organized as follows. Section 2 presents research that shares common points with this paper. In Sect. 3, we detail what is the main objective of our work. Section 4 describes the procedure used to build our datasets and provides the reasons why several datasets are required. In Sect. 5, experiments relying on raw numerical data, as well as our model only training with soccer field images and their respective results are described. Finally, Sect. 6 summarizes our work, its results and limits, and provides an idea to improve it.

## 2 Related Work

CNNs are known to be really efficient for a wide variety of tasks, especially tasks related to computer vision, such as object classification, segmentation, or face recognition. We can mention the work of Krizhevsky et al. [1] who first used CNN in 2012 on the Imagenet dataset [2] and significantly outperformed every other method employed at that time to perform image classification. Their work is particularly appropriate to illustrate the learning power of CNNs, as Imagenet dataset contains millions of images corresponding to 1000 different classes.

More closely related to our work, Stanescu et al. [3] used CNNs to evaluate the state of a Real-Time Strategy (RTS) game, $\mu$RTS. Their CNN has been trained to predict which of the two players is the most likely to win. To do this, it analyzes the state of the game at three different moments. Each of these moments is represented by a $8 \times 8 \times 25$ image stack corresponding to the 25 features that can be found on the $8 \times 8$ map, such as resources, units and buildings of each player. Despite accurately predicting the winner of an RTS game, this prediction only concerns $\mu$RTS, which is a very simple RTS game designed for testing AI techniques.

Other more complex and popular RTS games have also been subjects of research. That is the case of StarCraft on which some researchers applied machine learning methods to estimate the global state of a game. For example, Erickson et al. [4] proposed a logistic regression method to predict which player will win a game by taking the global state of the game into account. To do so, many aspects of the game have been identified and converted into features such as number of units, map coverage and skill of each player. These game states have been taken every 10 s for each of their 400 replays, providing them enough data to evaluate their model on states from particular time intervals. Rivari et al. [5] further improve their results by computing new features and applying gradient boosting regression trees and random forests to estimate the winner of the game.

Another completely different way to predict the winner of a StarCraft game is proposed by Sánchez-Ruiz et al. [6] who use influence maps in order evaluate the state of the game. Influence maps are matrices representing the situation for each player on the StarCraft map. For each unit owned by a player, a numerical influence value is added to its corresponding position on the influence map and its surroundings. In their work, influence maps are then reduced from $128 \times 128$ to $4 \times 4$ matrices. Therefore, the global state of a game is represented by 16 numerical values per player. Several machine learning methods are then used to predict the winner of a game based on these influence maps that are computed every 30 s.

While [4] and [5] extracted numerical values to evaluate the state of a game, other work transform their initial raw numerical data into images. That is the case of Souza et al. [7], who convert time-series into Recurrence Plots (RP), considered as gray images. Several features are then extracted from these images and used as input of a Support Vector Machine (SVM) algorithm that will use this data to classify the time-series. Hatami et al. [8] propose a very similar method that converts time-series into RP images, which are then used as input images of a CNN that will perform a classification of the initial time-series. The main difference between these last two papers is that the latter uses a CNN directly working with RP, without extracting hand-crafted features first.

The work presented in this paper shares a few similarities with some of these researches, as it involves the use of a CNN training on soccer field images that are visual representation of available raw numerical data. However, it is still one of a kind as it aims to evaluate the immediate state of a RoboCup 2D game with only one image.

## 3  Task Definition

In RoboCup 2D soccer games, many different metrics could be defined to tell which of the two playing teams currently has the upper hand, for example considering how many players of each team are on which part of the field, as well as where is and who possesses the ball. However, such analysis, while easily conducted using numerical data from log files, would be much more complicated to conduct working only with field images. Therefore, another metric, independent from players' coordinates, has to be defined to assess the situation of a game.

To this end, we introduce the *SituationScore* of a frame $f$ that is defined by

$$SituationScore(f) = \pm(100 - n), \tag{1}$$

where $n$ is the number of frames between $f$ and the frame corresponding to the next goal. It is assumed in this paper that the considered frames are at most 100 cycles away from the next goal. Therefore, in this formula, $n$ is necessary lower than 100. The *SituationScore*'s sign is determined by the team that will score this goal. We chose to consider a positive score when left team will score next goal and vice versa. An example of a soccer field image and its corresponding score is provided in Fig. 1.

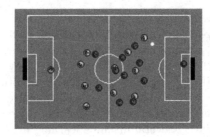

**Fig. 1.** Image taken 35 frames before the left team scores. The corresponding *SituationScore* is +65.

Such definition presents two main assets, the first one being the easiness to assign the correct score to newly produced images, as it does not require any complex computation. The second asset is inherent to our objective to work only with images. This metric does not take into account the state of the field itself at all, only the remaining time, the number of frames, before next goal. Therefore, many situations or formations can automatically be covered by this model.

On the other hand, this score is only defined for the last 100 frames before a goal, meaning that, for most frames of a game, this score is not defined. However, our model estimating such score is built only on valid frames, within 100 frames before a goal. Therefore this problem does not affect the training phase. Then, a solution to bypass this problem is to think of evaluated situations that are more than 100 frames away from a goal as similar to situations with identical scores.

Having defined the *SituationScore*, our goal is to build a model that estimates its value for any given frame. To this end, a dataset containing images associated with their score has first to be created. In this paper, we built a dataset containing more than one million images from more than 5,200 games, as well as other datasets containing their corresponding raw numerical data. Using these datasets, we built several models to estimate the *SituationScore*, in particular a CNN only working on the image dataset.

## 4    Datasets Construction

### 4.1    Procedure

In order for our dataset to cover as many situations and formations as possible, games between several 16 different teams have been simulated.

Dataset creation has been decomposed into several steps:

1. Games between each possible pair of teams are simulated and their log files saved
2. Log files of games where no goal have been scored are deleted
3. For each game, every frame is saved using soccerwindow2
4. A python script is used to analyze their corresponding log files to determine at which cycles goals have been scored

5. Every 100 frames before each of these goals are kept, and their *SituationScores* are computed. These frames are renamed to include their *SituationScore* while the other are deleted.

When using soccerwindow2 in this procedure, some graphic options have been precised, mainly to enhance the frames' quality, removing superfluous information and enlarging the players and the ball. These options include hiding score board, player numbers, view area, stamina and potential yellow card, as well as setting player size to 2, and ball size to 1.3. Size of saved images has also been precised in these options, but minimum size from soccerwindow2 being $280 \times 167$, kept frames have then been cropped to be of size $256 \times 160$. Soccer field images visible in this paper, such as in Fig. 1 offers a good insight of frames contained in our dataset.

A dataset containing about 1.02 million soccer field images taken from 5215 games has been constructed. This dataset has then been split into three parts: a training set containing ∼720,000 images, a validation set containing ∼156,000 images and a test set containing ∼135,000 images. Images from a specific game are all included in only one of these sets. In other words, each of these sets contains images from different games.

## 4.2   Play-On Only Dataset

During a soccer game, there are several phases during which players have some time to replace themselves on the field, while a player is about to make a kick. These phases are typically kick-in, free kicks or corner kicks, and they are implemented in RoboCup 2D Soccer Simulation League. We will refer to them as "Non Play-On" (NPO) phases or events.

These events are quite common and also happen regularly within the last 100 frames before a goal. Therefore, NPO events concern a significant proportion of images of the previously built dataset that systematically gathered the last 100 frames before a goal. However, it is not uncommon that players barely move during these NPO phases, leading to almost identical successive frames, with different *SituationScores*. Figure 2 illustrates this phenomenon, by showing two images that are taken 28 frames apart. Players have barely moved during these 28 frames, thus images are almost identical, but the *SituationScore* is completely different.

Regarding this issue, we decided to build another dataset using the same procedure as for the first one. We decided to call this second dataset "Play-On Only" (POO) dataset, in reference to the play-on phase, which is simply the standard game phase. The only difference with the first dataset that we may refer to as "All Frames" (AF) dataset, is that NPO phases frames, like kick-in and corner kicks frames, are not counted within the last 100 frames before a goal. Basically, this dataset contains the last 100 play-on frames before each goal, which often include frames that are more than 100 frames before a goal.

The POO dataset has been built using the same log files as the all frames dataset, it has also been split in the exact same way into training, validation

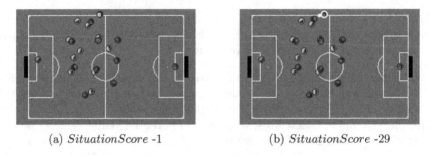

(a) *SituationScore* -1    (b) *SituationScore* -29

**Fig. 2.** Lack of players' movements during a kick-in.

and test sets. Therefore, each of these contains approximately the same number of images as its all frames counterpart.

### 4.3   Raw Numerical Dataset

To allow comparison with our CNN-based model, models using raw numerical data, such as coordinates, also have to evaluated. Consequently, a dataset containing numerical data from the same log files has first to be built.

In order to allow fair comparison with our CNN model, two different numerical datasets have been built. The first one that we will refer to as "coordinates dataset" only contains numerical data that could be retrieved by analyzing just one image. In other words, it contains for one frame, the ball and the players' coordinates along with their body angle, which can be obtained by paying attention to the orientation of their back, the black part of their circle visible on every frame, such as in Fig. 1. The second one that we may call "all numerical dataset" contains the same data as the first one, on top of ball and players' velocities, their absolute neck angle and their view angle range.

The problem of non play-on cycles being exactly the same whether field images or their corresponding coordinates are considered, numerical datasets have also been split into Play-On Only datasets and All Frames datasets. Therefore, four numerical datasets have been built: All Frames Coordinates (AFC), All Frames All Numerical (AFN), POO Coordinates (POOC) and POO All Numerical datasets (POON).

These numerical datasets have been built using the same log files as for the previous images datasets. Splitting into training, validation and test sets has also been done the same way, leading to sets of the same size, corresponding to the same games.

## 5   Experiments and Results

### 5.1   Experiments on Raw Numerical Data

While the main aspect of our work is to use CNN to build a model that accurately estimates the *SituationScore*, most, if not all, work on RoboCup 2D exploits numerical data from log files. Therefore, to allow comparison with our CNN model and to determine if working directly with soccer field images has an interest, models using numerical data have first to be built and evaluated.

Two kinds of experiments using numerical data have been conducted. The first one was experiments using Fully-Connected Neural Networks (FCNN), build with the TensorFlow library. These experiments are similar to our CNN experiments, but with much simpler neural networks, containing only fully-connected layers, up to thirty of them. The only hyper-parameters that were tested during these tests were batch size, learning rate, number of fully-connected layers and number of units within them. These experiments were run on the four numerical datasets presented earlier.

Table 1 includes the best results of these experiments for each numerical dataset, based on the Mean Absolute Error (MAE) between their *SituationScore* predictions and true scores. As expected, using all numerical data available leads to better results than only using data visible on one frame. Moreover, these first results tend to prove the importance of distinguishing NPO phases from standard game phases, as results on POO datasets are significantly better than those on AF datasets.

For the second series of experiments, several models built on these datasets have been tested using various machine learning methods. Experiments were conducted using Scikit-learn Python machine learning library [9]. Tested methods were bagging of decision trees, random forest, extra trees regressor, linear regression, linear SVR and k-Nearest Neighbors. The latter three gave results much worse than the other methods, not being really efficient with huge datasets. In particular, without transformation of the training set, the kNN method need to compute a distance between a situation and every other 720,000 training situations to estimate the score of this situation, making it completely unusable for our task. Random forest, bagging of decision trees and extra trees regressor methods gave similarly good results.

Table 1 presents the best results obtained with all methods implemented and tested with Scikit-learn Python library. The extra trees regressor model gives slightly better results than the other on all datasets, except on the All Frames, all Numerical (AFN) dataset, for which best results are obtained with a Bagging of Decision Trees model. Interestingly enough, this time better results are achieved on AF rather than on POO datasets.

## 5.2  Experiments Using Images as Input Data

Regarding our CNN implementation, we decided to use the TensorFlow library in Python. A CNN architecture similar to the VGG architecture [10], along with appropriate hyper-parameter values leading to satisfactory results have been determined by preliminary experiments. Our architecture is illustrated in Fig. 3. Our CNN was trained with an initial learning rate of 0.0001, decreasing by 5% every 1500 steps, corresponding to batches of size 16. It should also be noted that our CNN takes $160 \times 256$ images as input and contains a 15% dropout term at the end of each convolutional block, as well as after each fully-connected layer.

**Table 1.** Lowest MAE obtained during numerical experiments on every dataset

| Method | AFC | POOC | AFN | POON |
|---|---|---|---|---|
| Fully-connected neural network | 14.91 | 14.39 | 14.07 | 13.79 |
| Linear SVR | 19.89 | 18.79 | 18.52 | 17.59 |
| Linear regression | 20.30 | 19.18 | 18.81 | 17.95 |
| Decision tree bagging | 14.66 | 14.69 | 13.96 | 14.23 |
| Random forest | 14.65 | 14.69 | 13.97 | 14.25 |
| Extra trees regressor | 14.60 | 14.58 | 14.14 | 14.21 |
| k nearest neighbors | 18.56 | - | - | - |

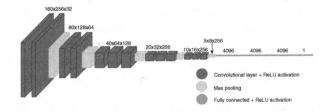

**Fig. 3.** Final architecture of our CNN, composed of the same four convolutional blocks as VGG, but with one more fully-connected layer

From lack of being truly optimal, our final architecture, along with presented hyper-parameter values quickly and consistently leads to a MAE usually between 13.3 and 13.6 that do not rise afterwards.

Table 2 shows the lowest MAE obtained using the presented architecture with its hyper-parameters values along with. Further hyper-parameters adjusting may lead to slightly better results, such as a MAE consistently around 13.3, but systematically getting below this value may be extremely difficult without changing this architecture.

A remark that has to be done regarding these results is that bagging of decision trees, extra trees and random forest can provide lower MAE if trained longer, with more trees. However, their MAE has only decreased by about 0.02 when going from 100 to 200 trees. Therefore an improvement of more than 0.1 is probably not to be expected. Extensive hyper-parameters adjusting, on the other hand, could possibly lead to better results, but that is also the case for FCNN and our CNN-based model.

Besides this issue that may have a slight impact on results, we can also consider the prediction time issue. Indeed, if we want to be able to compute the *SituationScore* in real time, our models have to be fast enough to do it before the next frame is displayed, which is within 100 ms. Even more, if we want the *SituationScore* to be a parameter that a team considers when making choices, prediction time has to be much shorter than 100 ms so that strategic choices can be made in the remaining time. Table 2 includes prediction time of

**Table 2.** Best MAE obtained using our CNN and most efficient methods

| Method | AF | POO | Prediction time |
|---|---|---|---|
| Proposed CNN | 13.31 | 13.27 | ~4.1 ms |
| Fully-connected neural network | 14.07 | 13.79 | ~0.8 ms |
| Bagging of decision trees | 13.93 | 14.23 | ~6.0 ms |
| Random forest | 13.97 | 14.25 | ~5.1 ms |
| Extra trees | 14.14 | 14.21 | ~9.1 ms |

the most efficient methods tested. All of them compute a *SituationScore* in less than 10 ms, which shows that their predictions are fast enough to be used in a team strategy. However, it should be precised that our CNN and FCNN models required a GeForce GTX 1080 GPU to be that fast, while the other methods used a simple Intel(R) Core(TM) i7-7700 CPU @ 3.60 GHz.

### 5.3   Additional Remarks

**AF and POO Datasets.** In some experiments, models built on AF datasets perform better than models built on POO datasets. In particular that is the case in decision tree bagging and random forest experiments. However, the contrary is observed in FCNN experiments. Our CNN-based model, as for itself, gives approximately the same results whether trained on AF or POO dataset. This proves that, contrary to what we could have thought, the POO datasets are not "better" datasets than AF datasets. In fact, it may be possible that ignoring movements of players during NPO phases when some of them move a lot compensates the improvement got by ignoring NPO frames when players barely move.

Indeed, in some NPO phases players barely move leading to many similar frames with different scores. However, in other NPO phases some players move a lot, meaning that ignoring them will bring a discontinuity in the *SituationScore* distribution. There will be frames corresponding to the same goal, with scores different by 1, but some players will seem to jump from one position to a completely another one between those frames, as shown in Fig. 4.

Therefore, both AF and POO datasets have a defect related to these NPO phases. As a consequence, it may be better to only focus on the AF dataset, as it represents everything that happens in the game.

**Distribution of Prediction Error.** Intuitively, the *SituationScore* is more easily estimated on some frames than other. For example, the closer the ball is to the goal, the sooner the goal is likely to be scored and the higher should be the *SituationScore*. Therefore, high *SituationScore* situations, regardless of their sign, are relatively easy to identify. On the other hand, when the ball is far from the goal, position of every player on the field has to be considered to assess the

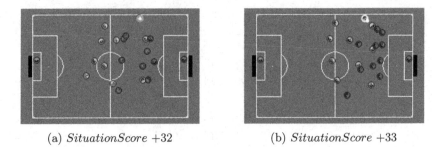

(a) *SituationScore* +32                    (b) *SituationScore* +33

**Fig. 4.** Players' position jumping between two consecutive POO images.

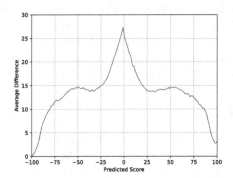

**Fig. 5.** Average error for each computed *SituationScore*.

situation, which makes it considerably more difficult to accurately estimate the *SituationScore*.

By computing the average difference between estimations and true scores for each possible value, this intuition can be confirmed. In fact, when true score is between −10 and +10, average error of our model is above 20 points while it drops below 5 points when true score is either above +90 or below −90, as visible in Fig. 5.

**Situation Score Predictions on Other Frames.** Another problem remains as the *SituationScore* is only defined for the last 100 frames before a goal but games used in our experiments contains more than 3,000 frames for only two goals on average. That means the *SituationScore* is not really defined for more than 90% of frames. This may not be a problem to train our model, as datasets have been built for this purpose, but make our model's predictions harder to interpret for frames that have no true *SituationScore*. A simple solution, when using our CNN on every frame of a game, would be to consider that the situation in the frame is similar to a situation with predicted score, whether or not a goal will be scored soon. However, it is still interesting to have an idea of the probability that a goal will be scored knowing a *SituationScore* estimation.

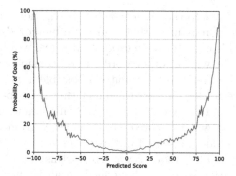

**Fig. 6.** Probability that a goal is scored within next 100 frames for each computed *SituationScore*.

In order to have the beginning of an answer to this question, another dataset, containing all frames from 120 games, totalling 360,612 images where *SituationScore* is not defined and 23,098 images where it is has been built. These first figures confirm that *SituationScore* is properly defined in only about 6% of all frames. After training on the All Frames dataset, our CNN estimated the score of all these frames. Without surprise, the higher the predicted *SituationScore* regardless of its sign, the more likely a goal will be scored soon, and vice-versa. While predicting a score between $-10$ and $+10$ has less than 2% chance to corresponds to an actual frame within 100 frames before a goal, chances that a goal will be scored soon increase with *SituationScore* prediction value. For example, this probability gets higher than 50% if predicted score is below -94 or above 92, as shown in Fig. 6.

Considering a new model, estimating whether or not a goal will be scored in the next $X$ frames could be an interesting extension of this work.

## 6   Conclusion

In this paper, we have introduced the *SituationScore*, a metric that assesses the field situation at one point of a RoboCup 2D game by estimating the remaining number of frames before next goal. Datasets containing frames or numerical data from more than 5,000 games, along with their corresponding *SituationScore* have been built in order to train models estimating this score.

Several models that predict this score have been built. Most of them were trained using raw numerical data and, among them, the decision tree bagging, random forest, extra trees and FCNN performed the best. However, we also focused on the construction of a CNN-based model that outperformed these models by training only on soccer field frames, disregarding numerical data. However, most tested methods could provide slightly better results if trained longer, with extensive hyper-parameter adjusting.

If results using our CNN are satisfactory and able to predict the number of remaining frames before next goal with an average error around 13.5, another problem inherent to the *SituationScore* definition subsists. In fact, the *SituationScore* definition assumes that a goal will be scored within 100 frames. Therefore, our model is not trained to estimate if a goal will be scored soon, but instead assumes that it will. In other words, when considering truly any frame of a RoboCup 2D game, our CNN estimates a possible number of frames before next goal is scored regardless of the probability that it happens.

Thus, this work could be extended by considering a new model that predicts whether or not a goal will be scored in the next $X$ frames. Combining this new model with the model presented in this paper would be a way to complete it, to make it fully usable. Another way to do this would be to update the *SituationScore* definition so that it is defined on all frames of a RoboCup 2D game, for example considering a score of 0 when no goal is scored within the next 100 frames. It would be also useful to investigate the performance of various CNNs that are trained by using games from different years. This would lead some insight into the trend of teams by years. This is also left as a future task.

# References

1. Krizhevsky, A., Sutskever, I., Hinton, G.E.: Imagenet classification with deep convolutional neural networks. In: Advances in Neural Information Processing Systems, vol. 25, pp. 1097–1105 (2012)
2. Russakovsky, O., et al.: Imagenet large scale visual recognition challenge. Int. J. Comput. Vis. **115**(3), 211–252 (2015)
3. Stanescu, M., Barriga, N.A., Hess, A., Buro, M.: Evaluating real-time strategy game states using convolutional neural networks. In: Proceedings of the IEEE Conference on Computational Intelligence and Games, pp. 1–7 (2016)
4. Erickson, G.K.S., Buro, M.: Global state evaluation in StarCraft. In: Proceedings of the Tenth Artificial Intelligence and Interactive Digital Entertainment Conference, pp. 112–118 (2014)
5. Ravari, Y.N., Sander, B., Spronck, P.: StarCraft winner prediction. In: Proceedings of the Twelfth Artificial Intelligence and Interactive Digital Entertainment Conference, pp. 2–8 (2016)
6. Sánchez-Ruiz, A.A., Miranda, M.: A machine learning approach to predict the winner in StarCraft based on influence maps. Entertain. Comput. **19**, 29–41 (2017)
7. Souza, V.M.A., Silva, D.F., Batista, G.E.A.P.A.: Extracting texture features for time series classification. In: Proceedings of the Twenty-Second International Conference on Pattern Recognition, pp. 1425–1430 (2014)
8. Hatami, N., Gavet, Y., Debayle, J.: Classification of time-series images using deep convolutional neural networks. In: Tenth International Conference on Machine Vision (ICMV): Image Analysis and Imaging System, Vienna (2017)
9. Pedregosa, F., Varoquaux, G., Gramfort, A., Michel, V., Thirion, B., Grisel, O., et al.: Scikit-learn: machine learning in python. J. Mach. Learn. Res. **12**(Oct), 2825–2830 (2011)
10. Simonyan, K., Andrew, Z.: Very deep convolutional networks for large-scale image recognition. arXiv preprint arXiv:1409.1556 (2015)

# Near Real-Time Object Recognition for Pepper Based on Deep Neural Networks Running on a Backpack

Esteban Reyes[1]([✉]), Cristopher Gómez[1], Esteban Norambuena[1],
and Javier Ruiz-del-Solar[1,2]

[1] Department of Electrical Engineering, Universidad de Chile, Santiago, Chile
{esteban.reyes,cristopher.gomez,esteban.norambuena}@ug.uchile.cl
[2] Advanced Mining Technology Center, Universidad de Chile, Santiago, Chile
jruizd@ing.uchile.cl

**Abstract.** The main goal of this work is to provide Pepper with a near real-time object recognition system based on deep neural networks. The proposed system is based on YOLO (*You Only Look Once*), a deep neural network that is able to detect and recognize objects robustly and at a high speed. In addition, considering that YOLO cannot be run in the Pepper's internal computer in near real-time, we propose to use a Backpack for Pepper, which holds a Jetson TK1 card and a battery. By using this card, Pepper is able to robustly detect and recognize objects in images of $320 \times 320$ pixels at about 5 frames per second.

**Keywords:** Pepper robot · YOLO · Jetson TK1 · ROS

## 1 Introduction

Environments where service and social robots operate/live are highly dynamic, in part because of the people living in those environments constantly interact with each other and carry out daily life activities. Therefore, service and social robots require perception systems that are highly robust, but at the same time are able to operate in real-time[1]. Object detection and recognition are some of the vision tasks that require at least near real-time operation.

The commercial Pepper robot [1] is a social robot used to research on human-robot interaction in real-world human environments (e.g. it is the official platform of the RoboCup@Home Standard Platform League), but its operation is constrained to the fact that it lacks the computational power necessary to run state-of-the-art vision algorithms.

On the other hand, the uprising of Deep Neural Networks (DNNs) has lead researchers to use them in the development of models that can quickly recognize

---

[1] In the service robot domain, we understand as real-time tasks that have a reaction span that looks natural to people, i.e. ~5 Hz.

© Springer Nature Switzerland AG 2019
D. Holz et al. (Eds.): RoboCup 2018, LNAI 11374, pp. 287–298, 2019.
https://doi.org/10.1007/978-3-030-27544-0_24

objects and persons in a robust manner. However, they are very expensive in terms of computational power, so they cannot be run directly on typical service robots. In particular, most of state-of-the-art DNN models cannot run on Pepper's internal computer, a situation that stands as the problem we address in this paper. Therefore, the main goal of this paper is to propose a solution to this problem that considers two components: First, the selection of YOLO (*You only look Once*) [2], a DNN with real-time detection and recognition of objects and persons, as the most suitable DNN to this task; and second, the development and implementation of an add-on for Pepper, a backpack that permit the attachment of a single board computer onto Pepper, particularly a Nvidia Jetson TK1, which can run YOLO at about 5 FPS when processing images of $320 \times 320$ pixels. The use of an external enhancing device, attached to the robot without modifying its structure, comes as an inspiration from similar projects developed for the NAO robot [3], where a fully replicable backpack was built.

In this work we provide details on how to reproduce the backpack for Pepper, and on how to install and implement YOLO on it, making the backpack CAD model, hardware, software specifications and an installation guide available for replication.

The remainder of this paper is structured as follows. In Sect. 2, we present an overview of the YOLO network. Subsequently, in Sect. 3 we present the process done to adapt and use YOLO on the Pepper's internal computer and in the Jetson TK1 card. Then, in Sect. 4 we address the mechanical design of the Pepper Backpack. Finally, in Sect. 5 we draw some conclusions of this work.

## 2    Robust and Fast Object Recognition Using YOLO

*You Only Look Once* (YOLO) [2], is a computer vision system capable of detecting a wide variety of objects in a single image, with an accuracy similar to RetinaNet [4], but with a superior speed of inference when compared to others state of the art systems such as SSD [5], R-FCN [6] and FPN FRCN [7]. Its speed makes it one of the best-suited systems for real-time object detection needed in systems such as service robots.

One of the main features of YOLO is to treat the detection of objects as a regression problem, where the model is trained to identify bounding boxes (BB), along with probabilities of certainty, in areas that might contain an object. Unlike other systems, where *proposals* or *regions of interest* are generated explicitly as object candidate windows, on which a class inference is executed. This difference gives YOLO advantages in terms of speed, having to process each image only once to perform multiple detections, instead of processing *proposals* individually. Also, the system processes the complete image and not just a region of it, which makes its inferences contemplate the global context of the image, making it less likely to detect background content as an object, which translates into a lower number of false positives in comparison to other systems.

Another distinctive feature of this model is its end-to-end training process, meaning that it has a unique *pipeline* that is trained jointly. Unlike other systems that have different components and need to be trained separately, such as Faster-RCNN [8].

Since the first release of YOLO, there have been 3 major versions of the algorithm, each one aiming to improve accuracy with respect to previous versions. The first version, YOLOv1 [2], achieved 63.4% mean average precision (mAP) over PASCAL VOC 2007 [9], with an inference speed of 45 FPS. Introduction of a fully-convolutional model [5], multi-scale training [10], batch normalization [11], BB dimensions priors [10], among other techniques, raised YOLOv2 [10], which gets an mAP of 48.1% on COCO [12] dataset and 78.6% mAP on PASCAL VOC 2007, while working at 40 FPS. The latest version of YOLO, YOLOv3 [13], includes a larger model with 75 convolutional layers that use residual blocks [14], prediction of BB across 3 different scales by using a procedure similar to feature pyramid networks [7], among other improvements that result in an mAP of 57.9% on COCO, at 20 FPS on the same TitanX GPU that all models where tested. Differences among YOLO versions clearly depicts that performance can be sacrificed to gain processing speed, allowing to choose the best-suited version for a given application. Moreover, there are reduced versions of YOLOv1 and YOLOv2 which are even faster. A review of most versions of YOLO is shown in Table 1.

**Table 1.** Performance of different YOLO versions. Inference speed results (FPS) where obtained when running on a Titan X GPU. Fastest YOLO version is tiny-YOLO v2 at 207 FPS, and most accurate version is YOLOv3 with a 57.9% mAP on COCO dataset.

| Model | Input size | Train set | Test set | mAP | FPS |
|---|---|---|---|---|---|
| YOLOv1 | 448 × 448 | VOC 2007+2012 | VOC 2007 | 63.4% | 45 |
| Fast YOLOv1 | 448 × 448 | VOC 2007+2012 | VOC 2007 | 52.7% | 155 |
| YOLOv2 | 416 × 416 | VOC 2007+2012 | VOC 2007 | 76.8% | 67 |
| tiny-YOLOv2 | 416 × 416 | VOC 2007+2012 | VOC 2007 | 57.1% | **207** |
| YOLOv2 | 608 × 608 | COCO | COCO | 48.1% | 40 |
| YOLOv3 | 608 × 608 | COCO | COCO | **57.9%** | 20 |

# 3   Adapting YOLO to Be Used with Pepper Robots

In spite of YOLO's exceptional performance and speed, it is necessary to take into account that the reported speeds were measured using a platform with a powerful GPU. When running YOLO on a CPU-only system, such as the Pepper's internal computer, the speed of operation decreases considerably. To deal with this situation is that we base our work on the fastest versions of the model (tiny-YOLO), which has only 15 convolutional layers.

### 3.1 YOLO for Pepper

To run YOLO on the Pepper's on-board computer, the Darknet framework [15] must be first installed. Darknet is written in C, a low-level language, so it is easy to port to different platforms. Thus, compilation for Pepper's computer is straightforward.

To easily integrate YOLO with other modules of Pepper, the darknet_ros package from ETH Autonomous System Lab [16] is used. This package operates with an older version of Darknet, however, it is compatible with the most recent versions of Darknet. The YOLO ROS package implements all the tools needed to feed the system with a standard ROS stream of images through a defined topic. Moreover, the information of the detected objects is also published through a ROS topic.

To compile the YOLO ROS package for the Pepper's computer, mild modifications are needed to source and compilation files. A guide to the process can be found in the *Supplementary Material* Section.

### 3.2 YOLO for Jetson TK1

As an alternative strategy to the Pepper's on-board processing of tiny-YOLO, an external processing unit is used, where the only task that directly involves Pepper is to publish on a ROS topic the images from his camera at a rate that depends on the resolution of the images. The maximum resolution that enables a rate of ∼30 Hz is 640 × 480. Jetson TK1 development card is used for the external processing. We select this unit because it has an integrated 2 GB Nvidia GPU, which allows the use of parallel computing platform CUDA [17], accelerating the calculation of certain Darknet operations written exclusively for parallel processing in CUDA.

As a first approach, the original version of Darknet is compiled, it is important to note that its compilation with GPU is immediate, but not the use of the cuDNN library [18] of efficient computing for deep learning. This incompatibility raises because of the CUDA version available for the Jetson TK1 is CUDA 6.5, and the library cuDNN from Darknet uses the CUDA 7.0 version, thus processing speeds will be lower.

Afterwards, YOLO ROS is compiled on the Jetson card, for which ROS Indigo was previously installed by following the ROS Jetson guide [19]. The YOLO ROS compilation without GPU is straightforward, but to enable its use some modifications need to take place. The changes made to YOLO ROS focuses on the file CMakeList.txt, the scripts in C++, the configuration of the CUDA paths and extensions of some ROS Indigo files. Due to the extensive and tedious modifications made to the code, they will be omitted, but these and the entire installation process in the Jetson TK1 are reviewed in detail in the *Supplementary Material* Section.

Finally, a *ROS Network* is configured to connect Pepper to the Jetson through an Ethernet cable. Configuring Pepper as MASTER and Jetson as a HOST. This enables the access of Jetson TK1 card to the topic where images from Pepper's camera are published, then process them with tiny-YOLO to finally publish detection information on another topic that Pepper can subscribe to and use as desired. A diagram that depicts the connections made is shown in Fig. 1.

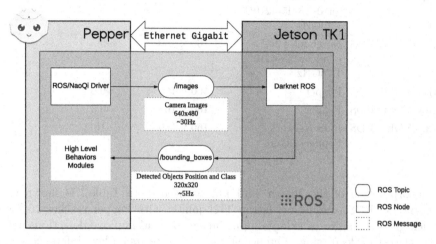

**Fig. 1.** Pepper to Jetson TK1 communication diagram. Through the ROS/NaoQi driver, Pepper publishes images from his camera. The Darknet ROS node runs the YOLO network that feeds from the images. The detected objects and their classes are published in a custom ROS message, which can be easily accessed by software modules running in Pepper's internal computer.

### 3.3   Results

The training process of tiny-YOLO considers input images that vary in resolution. In the process, the images are resized every ten training iterations, to resolutions equal to $320 + 32n$, where $n \in \{0, 1, ..., 9\}$ is chosen randomly. By doing this, images from $320 \times 320$ pixels up to $608 \times 608$ pixels are considered in the training process. This multi-scale property allows to choose the input image resolution at runtime; so the input image size is used as a system parameter to manage the trade-off between inference speed and detection accuracy. The original tiny-YOLO configuration, that considers $416 \times 416$ pixel input images, is first tested on a notebook with a quadcore i5-4210U 1.70GHz CPU, and the inferences speed reached roughly 1 FPS. Then, input images are reduced to $160 \times 160$ pixels, allowing detection of big objects at $\sim$6 FPS, while small ones were not detected. Afterwards, we compared tiny-YOLO and tiny-YOLO ROS in the notebook, Pepper, and Jetson at a fixed input size of $160 \times 160$, these results are summarized in Table 2.

To consider the object detection method as a near real-time system, it must have an inference speed of at least 5 FPS. Table 2 makes clear that the Pepper's on-board computer cannot be used to run the tiny-YOLO ROS system,

**Table 2.** Comparison between different tiny-YOLO systems and platforms. The inference speed and image size are evaluated.

| Model | Computer | Input image size | Inference speed [FPS] |
|---|---|---|---|
| tiny-YOLO | Notebook CPU quadcore i5-4210U 1.70GHz | 160 × 160 | ~6 |
| tiny-YOLO ROS | Notebook CPU quadcore i5-4210U 1.70GHz | 160 × 160 | ~3 |
| tiny-YOLO | Pepper | 160 × 160 | ~0.6 |
| tiny-YOLO ROS | Pepper | 160 × 160 | ~0.3 |
| tiny-YOLO ROS | ROS Network Pepper-Jetson | 160 × 160 | ~16 |

so incorporation of the Jetson TK1 unit is needed. In Table 2 is shown that tiny-YOLO ROS running on Jetson TK1 jointly with Pepper reaches 16 FPS, which gives a margin to enlarge input image size and improve detections accuracy at cost of decreasing inference speed. Experiments on how inference speed decreases when making input image size bigger, are shown in Table 3, where mAP over VOC 2007 test set is calculated to depict that a greater image size means better detection, specifically of small objects. The highest resolution that could be tested was 384 × 384 because a greater one leaves Jetson TK1 without computational resources.

**Table 3.** Speed of tiny-YOLO ROS for Pepper-Jetson TK1 at different input image size. Inference speed decreases as input size increases, but larger images get higher mAP on VOC 2007 test set.

| Input image size | Inference speed [FPS] | mAP |
|---|---|---|
| 160 × 160 | ~15.5 | 24.60% |
| 224 × 224 | ~5.9 | 37.10% |
| 288 × 288 | ~5.8 | 44.72% |
| **320 × 320** | **~4.8** | **47.69%** |
| 352 × 352 | ~4.5 | 50.32% |
| 384 × 384 | ~3.6 | 52.62% |

**Table 4.** Class-wise mean average precision (mAP) on VOC 2007 test set for tiny-YOLO ROS in Pepper-Jetson TK1, with an input image size of 320 × 320.

| aero | bike | bird | boat | bottle |
|---|---|---|---|---|
| 47 | 60.1 | 39.5 | 30.6 | 15.8 |
| bus | car | cat | chair | cow |
| 61.2 | 57.8 | 65.6 | 23.9 | 43.1 |
| table | dog | horse | m bike | person |
| 49 | 59.2 | 66.3 | 63.5 | 52.3 |
| plant | sheep | sofa | train | tv |
| 21.9 | 42.2 | 48.1 | 59.8 | 47.1 |

Table 3 clearly show that tiny-YOLO ROS for Pepper-Jetson TK1 achieves a near real-time inference speed of ~4.8 FPS at an input image size of 320 × 320 while getting 47.69% mAP on VOC 2007 test set. Using this same data, class-wise mAP is calculated on Table 4. This gives a detailed insight on the performance of the system at 320 × 320 resolution, where it is clear that correct detection of small objects like bottles or potted plants is a challenge for the system.

After evaluating the system on classic data sets, we jumped to try it in an indoor environment, a place closer to the reality of what a service robot has to deal with. We analyzed different sizes of the input images, in order to select the one that allows obtaining an acceptable detection rate as well as processing speed. Figure 2a shows how for an image size of 160 × 160, the YOLO based detection system is unable to detect a bottle and it also throws false positives by detecting a non-existing car. On the other hand, when using a resolution of 384 × 384 pixels (Fig. 2b) the YOLO based detection system is able to correctly detect the bottle and also better fits the BB for a person.

(a)                                        (b)

**Fig. 2.** Detection examples of tiny-YOLO ROS for Pepper-Jetson TK1, at different resolution inputs. Color BB with labels shows detected objects. (a) Input image size of 160 × 160 pixels, where the model is unable to detect small objects like the bottle and mistakenly detect a car. (b) Input image size of 384 × 384 accurately detects multiple small to medium size objects. (Color figure online)

When testing the detection system with input image of 320 × 320 pixels, it achieved near real-time inference speed, and it showed robust object detection of people and infrequent false positives. These results are shown in Fig. 3, where multiple sights of the indoor environment where shown to the system. Numerous object detection can be seen in Fig. 3a where 2 people and a chair are correctly detected. On the other hand, false positives that momentarily happen are depicted in Fig. 3b, by detection of a non-existing car. Small object detection difficulties can be seen in Fig. 3c and d, where the bottle is not detected at first, but its recognized after moving it around, straighten it up and putting it closer to the camera of the Pepper robot.

Therefore, we conclude that is very relevant to select an appropriate image size, and that an image size of 320 × 320 pixels allows obtaining a good trade-off between detection accuracy and processing speed.

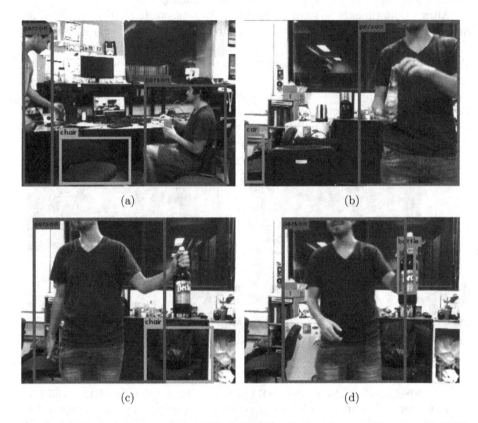

|            |            |
|:----------:|:----------:|
| (a)        | (b)        |
| (c)        | (d)        |

**Fig. 3.** Detection examples of tiny-YOLO ROS for Pepper-Jetson TK1, at ∼4.8 FPS and input image size of 320 × 320. This resolution allows detection of people and medium to large size objects, while struggles with small ones (a) Correct detection of multiple objects. (b) Example of an incorrect car detection, false positives are infrequent. (c) Correct detection of a person and a chair, but the bottle is ignored. (d) Correct detection of a small object when moving bottle from (c) closer to the camera.

## 4   Pepper Backpack

Considering that using an external processing card (Jetson TK1) is the best alternative for implementing a YOLO based object detection system, we decided to design and built a backpack for Pepper, which can hold the card as well as its battery.

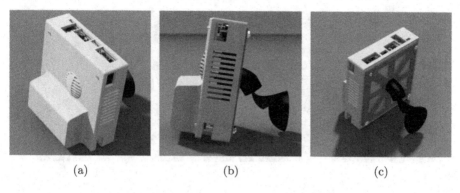

(a) (b) (c)

**Fig. 4.** 3D Renders of the Pepper Backpack. The main enclosure (white) is 3D printed. A commercial suction cup (black) is used to attach the backpack to Pepper. (a) Front view. (b) Lateral View. (c) Back view.

## 4.1 Mechanical Design

The most important restriction to design the Pepper Backpack was to not modify the robot structure. For this reason, the attachment of the backpack to the robot should be non-invasive, therefore, an attachment using a suction cup is proposed.

The main enclosure of the Jetson computer corresponds to one acrylic plate in the base and a 3D printed case with a battery compartment mounted on the front of the board. A custom joint was 3D printed to connect the enclosure of the Jetson and the suction cup structure. Whole backpack renders can be seen in Fig. 4, while perspectives of the backpack attached to Pepper robot through a 5.8 mm of diameter commercial suction cup can be seen in Fig. 5.

The CAD models, list of components and materials required to build the backpack can be found in the Supplementary Material section.

## 4.2 Hardware

**Nvidia Jetson TK1.** The Nvidia Jetson TK1 main processor is a Nvidia Tegra K1 which is a CPU+GPU+ISP single chip. The existence of a GPU in the Jetson allows it to run state-of-the-art Deep Learning algorithms.

The Nvidia Jetson TK1 comes with a power supply that can provide 12 V and 5 A maximum. These requirements are fulfilled by a 3-Cell LiPo battery. The battery is connected to the Jetson through a standard 2.1 × 5.5 mm barrel jack. The typical power-draw of the Jetson does not surpass 10 W [20]. It is important to note that Pepper does not provide a power output, thus using it as a source of power for the Jetson card is not possible without structural modifications of Pepper.

To connect the Jetson computer to Pepper, and enable data stream between platforms, the Ethernet Gigabit port of both is used.

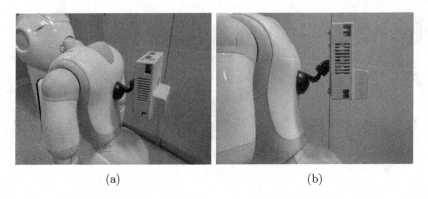

(a)                                          (b)

**Fig. 5.** Pepper robot with the Jetson TK1 backpack attached to its lower back. (a) Perspective view. (b) Lateral close-up tho backpack.

## 5    Conclusions and Future Work

In this work, we studied the use of YOLO on the Pepper's computer, by testing different versions of the model and variation of their parameters. We concluded that it is not possible to surpass the 1 FPS minimum limit in order to achieve near real-time object detection. As an alternative, we introduced external image processing, choosing the Jetson TK1 computer as the device to run tiny-YOLO at an input image resolution of $320 \times 320$, which demonstrated to be the best-suited model to reach high-speed processing of $\sim 4.8$ FPS. By using a smaller input image size we gained speed, at cost of performance, this was reflected on an mAP of 47.69% over VOC 2007 test set, and a low capacity of detection for small objects on real-world indoor environments.

To enable high-speed communication between Pepper and the Jetson TK1 computer we use an Ethernet Gigabit connection. More important is the fact that we directly attached the board onto Pepper through a custom made backpack, which does not affect the movement of the robot.

As a future work task, we propose usage of another external computer besides Jetson TK1, because it may not be the most suitable platform to best exploit inference speed of tiny-YOLO. This statement lies in the fact that the Jetson TK1 is a 32-bit system that supports up to CUDA 6.5 version, which does not allow usage of the deep neural networks dedicated library cuDNN. Platforms such as Jetson TX1 or Jetson TX2 which allow higher versions of CUDA and thus cuDNN usage may outperform results presented in this work.

Finally, all the necessary files to replicate the project will be publicly available.

### Supplementary Material

All the necessary to replicate the project resides in two GitHub repositories. One repository provides the CAD models and list of components to build the Pepper Backpack: https://github.com/uchile-robotics/pepper-backpack. The other repository corresponds to a fork of **darknet_ros** with instructions to run tiny-YOLO ROS on the Pepper-Jetson TK1: https://github.com/uchile-robotics-forks/darknet_ros

**Acknowledgements.** This research was partially funded by FONDECYT Project 1161500.

# References

1. SoftBank Robotics. Pepper. www.ald.softbankrobotics.com/en/robots/pepper. Accessed 20 2017
2. Redmon, J., Divvala, S., Girshick, R., Farhadi, A.: You only look once: unified, real-time object detection. In: Proceedings of the IEEE Conference on Computer Vision and Pattern Recognition, pp. 779–788 (2016)
3. Mattamala, M., Olave, G., González, C., Hasbún, N., Ruiz-del-Solar, J.: The NAO backpack: an open-hardware add-on for fast software development with the NAO robot. arXiv preprint arXiv:1706.06696 (2017)
4. Lin, T.-Y., Goyal, P., Girshick, R., He, K., Dollár, P.: Focal loss for dense object detection. arXiv preprint arXiv:1708.02002 (2017)
5. Liu, W., et al.: SSD: single shot multibox detector. In: Leibe, B., Matas, J., Sebe, N., Welling, M. (eds.) ECCV 2016. LNCS, vol. 9905, pp. 21–37. Springer, Cham (2016). https://doi.org/10.1007/978-3-319-46448-0_2
6. Dai, J., Li, Y., He, K., Sun, J.: R-FCN: object detection via region-based fully convolutional networks. In: Advances in Neural Information Processing Systems, pp. 379–387 (2016)
7. Lin, T.-Y., Dollár, P., Girshick, R., He, K., Hariharan, B., Belongie, S.: Feature pyramid networks for object detection. In: CVPR, vol. 1, p. 4 (2017)
8. Ren, S., He, K., Girshick, R., Sun, J.: Faster R-CNN: towards real-time object detection with region proposal networks. In: Advances in Neural Information Processing Systems, pp. 91–99 (2015)
9. Everingham, M., Van Gool, L., Williams, C.K.I., Winn, J., Zisserman, A.: The PASCAL Visual Object Classes Challenge 2007 (VOC 2007) Results. http://www.pascal-network.org/challenges/VOC/voc2007/workshop/index.html
10. Redmon, J., Farhadi, A.: Yolo9000: better, faster, stronger. arXiv preprint (2017)
11. Ioffe, S., Szegedy, C.: Batch normalization: accelerating deep network training by reducing internal covariate shift. arXiv preprint arXiv:1502.03167 (2015)
12. Lin, T.Y., et al.: Microsoft COCO: common objects in context. In: Fleet, D., Pajdla, T., Schiele, B., Tuytelaars, T. (eds.) ECCV 2014. LNCS, vol. 8693, pp. 740–755. Springer, Cham (2014). https://doi.org/10.1007/978-3-319-10602-1_48
13. Redmon, J., Farhadi, A.: YOLOv3: an incremental improvement. arXiv (2018)
14. He, K., Zhang, X., Ren, S., Sun, J.: Deep residual learning for image recognition. In: Proceedings of the IEEE Conference on Computer Vision and Pattern Recognition, pp. 770–778 (2016)
15. Redmon, J.: Darknet: open source neural networks in C (2013–2016). http://pjreddie.com/darknet
16. ETH Autonomous System Lab. Darknet ROS. https://github.com/leggedrobotics/darknet_ros. Accessed 30 Mar 2018
17. Sanders, J., Kandrot, E.: CUDA by Example: An Introduction to General-Purpose GPU Programming. Addison-Wesley Professional, Boston (2010)

18. Chetlur, S., et al.: cuDNN: efficient primitives for deep learning. arXiv preprint arXiv:1410.0759 (2014)
19. ROS Wiki. Jetson ROS. http://wiki.ros.org/NvidiaJetsonTK1. Accessed 30 Mar 2018
20. eLinux.org. Jetson TK1 powerdraw. https://elinux.org/Jetson/Computer_Vision_Performance#Power_draw_during_computer_vision_tasks. Accessed 30 Mar 2018

# Multimodal Movement Activity Recognition Using a Robot's Proprioceptive Sensors

Robin Schmucker[1]([✉]), Chenghui Zhou[2], and Manuela Veloso[2]

[1] Karlsruhe Institute of Technology, 76131 Karlsruhe, Germany
robin.schmucker@online.de
[2] Carnegie Mellon University, Pittsburgh, PA 15213, USA
{chenghuz,mmv}@cs.cmu.edu

**Abstract.** By recognizing patterns in streams of sensor readings, a robot can gain insight into the activities that are performed by its physical body. Research in Human Activity Recognition (HAR) has been thriving in recent years mainly because of the widespread use of wearable sensors such as smartphones and activity trackers. By introducing HAR approaches to the robotics domain, this work aims at creating agents that are capable of detecting their own body's activities. An activity recognition pipeline is proposed that allows a robot to classify its actions by analyzing heterogeneous, asynchronous data streams provided by its inbuilt sensors. The approach is evaluated in two experiments featuring the service robot Pepper. In the first experiment, a set of base movements is recognized by analyzing data from various proprioceptive sensors. The findings indicate that a multimodal activity recognition approach can achieve more accurate classifications than single-sensor approaches. In the second experiment, a person interferes with the forward movement of the robot by pulling its base backward. This happens in a way that is not detected by Pepper's inbuilt systems. The approach can detect the unexpected behavior and could be used to extend Pepper's inbuilt capabilities. Through its generality, this work can be used to recognize activities of other robots with comparable sensing capabilities.

**Keywords:** Learning from sensory data · Activity recognition · Behavior verification

## 1 Introduction

While the planning layer captures a robot's intended activity execution, it makes no statement about its actual state and activity. Assume a robot wants to move a certain distance forward. During its movement, it might collide with an obstacle and fall over. A robot that recognizes the unexpected behavior can try to recover or call a human operator for help. In another scenario, a robot might be pushed by a human. If the robot recognizes what is happening to its body, it can respond

© Springer Nature Switzerland AG 2019
D. Holz et al. (Eds.): RoboCup 2018, LNAI 11374, pp. 299–310, 2019.
https://doi.org/10.1007/978-3-030-27544-0_25

with a warning when it is being moved in a way that is overly demanding on its mechanics. In case of remote control, the robot might even reject a user command to prevent damage.

Sensor-based Human Activity Recognition (HAR) uses wearable sensors such as accelerometers and gyroscopes to capture human activity and finds application in areas including mobile computing [17], ambient-assisted living [5] and health care [2]. HAR can detect activities of the human activities such as walking, running, riding escalator, eating, opening door, and lifting object [11] by detecting patterns in streams of sensor data. While sensor-based HAR needs to attach and calibrate sensors for each individual user, robots feature a variety of inbuilt sensors that give insight into their physical states.

By combining HAR approaches with a robot's rich sensor data, this work aims at creating an agent that recognizes its own body's activity. A recognition pipeline is proposed that enables the robot to detect its own activities by analyzing asynchronous, heterogeneous streams of sensor data. A Long Short Term Memory (LSTM) [8] based neural network is used for activity recognition. The approach is evaluated in two experiments featuring the service robot Pepper. In the first experiment, a set of 7 movement activities is recognized. Here, the robot detects if it moves forward, backward, left or right, rotates clockwise or counterclockwise or stands still (see Fig. 3). The pipeline combines information from heterogeneous, propriocepetive sensors to achieve accurate classifications. The multimodal sensor data comprises joint states, electrical current, orientation, angular velocity and acceleration data. In the second experiment a human interferes with the forward movement of the robot by pulling its base backward in a way that is not detected by Pepper's inbuilt capabilities. Through its generality, the in this work presented approach can be used to recognize activities of other robots with comparable sensing capabilities.

## 2   Related Work

This work uses a robot's inbuilt sensors to allow it to detect the actions performed by its own body. This is achieved by recognizing activity patterns in streams of sensor data. In robotics, related work can be found in Collision Detection (CD) and Execution Monitoring (EM).

The area of CD uses a robot's sensors to handle intentional or accidental contact of its body with its physical environment [7]. One of the central motivations is to enable robots to share a common work space with humans by preventing injuries caused by forceful impacts as well as preventing damage to the robot's body.

EM (also known as Fault Detection and Diagnosis) observes sensor readings to detect and classify faults and their causes [1,9,15]. Examples are the detection of mechanical jams and the loss of hydraulic fluid. Conventional EM approaches analyze a robot's activities and determine a set of features that indicates correct execution. These features are then monitored to detect anomalies by either comparing them with the expected system behavior or by subjecting them to pattern recognition methods.

While the areas of CD and EM are interested in fault avoidance and fault detection/recovery respectively, this work aims at allowing a robot to recognize the activities executed by its own body. This goal and the used methods in this work are closely related to the field of HAR which uses wearable sensors to gain insight into human activities.

As part of Human Computer Interaction, HAR creates devices that can recognize their user's physical activities. Wearable sensors are used to capture data about a user's body activity which is then subjected to pattern recognition methods. One example is fall detection in ambient-assisted living. Here, a person is equipped with a wearable device that detects falls and calls help if required [19]. Multimodal HAR approaches use data from multiple sensors to capture activities in greater detail. The use of data from a variety of sensors can achieve a higher classification accuracy than unimodal approaches [12–14,16]. Lara [11] and Cornacchia [6] provide comprehensive surveys about HAR with wearable sensors. Conventional sensor-based HAR approaches use sliding window based techniques combined with manual feature engineering. While these approaches achieve satisfying results on simple activities such as lying, standing and walking, it is difficult to recognize more complex activities. This limitation mainly lies in the manually engineered features that are restricted by human domain knowledge [4]. Recent advances in HAR utilize deep learning techniques because of their automatic feature generation and selection. Deep learning approaches such as LSTMs and Convolutional Neural Networks can come up with task specific non-linear features and provide more accurate classification [18].

## 3 Robot Activity Recognition

Inspired by similar approaches in the field of HAR [18], this section formulates the task of activity recognition in the context of robotics. Sensors act as a connection between the physical world and the computer and allow to observe a robot's physical state. During task execution, data streams generated by a robot's sensors can be analyzed to gain insight into the performed activities. Assume a robot is executing a sequence of activities belonging to a predefined set $A$:

$$A = \{a_p\}_{p=1}^n \tag{1}$$

where $n$ marks the number of activity types. The robot's sensor readings are observed over time. The observed sequence $s$ contains $m$ consecutive readings $r_i$, $i \in \{1, \dots, m\}$, that capture the state of the robot during a period of time at equal intervals. The size of $m$ depends on the sampling rate and the observation duration. For example, the recorded sequences used in Sect. 5.2 each capture 10 readings per second over roughly 5 min. The number of readings that are actually used for a prediction at a given time is dependent on the used model and activity types. Each of the $m$ readings features $l$ attributes.

$$s = (r_1, \dots, r_m), \quad r_i \in \mathbb{R}^l \tag{2}$$

The goal is to learn a model $\mathcal{M}$ that generates a sequence of predictions $\hat{A}$ about the performed activity at the time of each given reading $r_i$

$$\mathcal{M}(s) = \hat{A} = (\hat{a}_{r_1}, \ldots, \hat{a}_{r_m}), \quad \hat{a}_{r_i} \in A \tag{3}$$

where the actual performed activity sequence $A^*$ is:

$$A^* = (a^*_{r_1}, \ldots, a^*_{r_m}), \quad a^*_{r_i} \in A \tag{4}$$

A suitable model $\mathcal{M}$ minimizes the discrepancy between predicted sequence $\hat{A}$ and ground truth sequence $A^*$. Here, $A^*$ can, for example, be determined by a human observer or, as in our later experiments, by logging the commands given by the robot's controller. While this formulation assumes that the readings are sampled synchronously at the same rate, a real robot's sensors usually generate readings asynchronously and at different, sometimes even varying, rates. The following section responds to this by introducing a recognition pipeline that can generate a steady data stream by combining and synchronizing readings from multiple, asynchronous sensors.

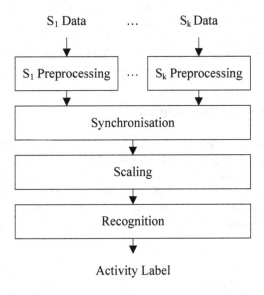

**Fig. 1.** The proposed activity recognition pipeline. It classifies the current activity performed by the robot by analyzing data streams from multiple sensors.

## 4  Activity Recognition Pipeline

A general approach for robot activity recognition is proposed. The architecture features a 4-step pipeline (shown in Fig. 1) that recognizes a robot's activity by analyzing heterogeneous, asynchronous streams of sensor data during runtime. The readings from the individual sensors (Sect. 4.1) are preprocessed separately (Sect. 4.2) and then fused to a combined synchronous data stream (Sect. 4.3). Afterwards, the combined readings are scaled (Sect. 4.4) and subsequently passed to a recognition module (Sect. 4.5) which classifies the activity that is currently performed by the robot. The used scaler and model are intended to be trained offline with data from annotated activity sequences. In the following, the individual pipeline steps are discussed in detail.

## 4.1  Sensor Data

Sensors can capture the state of a robot's body over time. Heterogeneous sensors, such as accelerometers and gyroscopes, provide data streams that can be used to recognize the performed activities. Common variables include acceleration, torque, electrical current, voltage, orientation, joint states and temperature. The individual variables vary in significance based on the class of activity that is to be predicted. For example, acceleration and torque capture information about the forces that act on a robot's body at a given time and are suitable for the detection of motion activity. Meanwhile, temperature can be seen as an indicator for long term engine activity by being dependent on the amount of heat that is generated over time.

The pipeline assumes that a robot features $k$ sensors $S_j$, $j \in \{1, \dots, k\}$. Each sensor $S_j$ samples signal $p_j$ with sampling rate $f_j$ over time. A reading of sensor $S_j$ at given time $t$ provides a $d_j$ dimensional vector:

$$S_j(t) = (v_1, \dots, v_{d_j}) \in \mathbb{R}^{d_j} \tag{5}$$

## 4.2  Preprocessing

The recognition pipeline receives one stream of sensor data from each of the $k$ sensors. It can be favorable to perform sensor specific transformations before learning a model. This can reduce the number of required training samples by adding expert knowledge to the model. Each sensor $S_j$ is associated with a preprocessing function $\Phi_j$ that is implemented in a separate module. Thereby, the sensor readings are transformed to $d'_j$ dimensional feature vectors.

$$\Phi_j(S_j(t)) = (v'_1, \dots, v'_{d'_j}) \in \mathbb{R}^{d'_j} \tag{6}$$

For the evaluation, joint angles and electric current are scaled to unit space based on the respective sensor specifications. A filter is applied to the raw acceleration data generated by the inertial measurement unit (IMU) to separate low frequency gravitational acceleration from high frequency activity acceleration [3].

## 4.3  Synchronization

In the general case, a robot samples its individual sensors at different rates and provides asynchronous data streams. The recognition module assumes all sensors

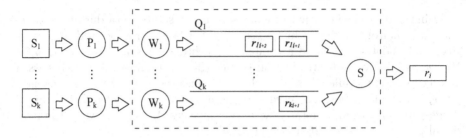

**Fig. 2.** Synchronization module.

to be sampled synchronously at a predefined rate $f$, which makes it necessary to synchronize the individual streams of preprocessed sensor data.

The synchronization module fuses the separate streams to one combined data stream. First, an initial start time $t_0$ is being determined. Subsequently, for each $t_i = t_0 + i*T$ ($T = 1/f$, $i \in \mathbb{N}$), one combined measurement is being interpolated. The module observes all data streams in parallel. For each sensor $S_j$, one reading $r_{j_m}$ (the $m$-th reading of $S_j$) is kept in a buffer together with the timestamp of its creation $t_{j_m}$. When a new reading $r_{j_{m+1}}$ arrives at time $t_{j_{m+1}}$, the condition $t_{j_m} \le t_i < t_{j_{m+1}}$ is checked. If the condition is not met, the synchronization module updates its buffer with $r_{j_{m+1}}$ and continues listening to the stream until another reading matches the condition. If the condition is met, the buffer is updated likewise and a linear interpolation between $r_{j_m}$ and $r_{j_{m+1}}$ is performed to determine

$$r_{j_i} = \frac{r_{j_m} * (t_{j_{m+1}} - t_i) + r_{j_{m+1}} * (t_i - t_{j_m})}{t_{j_{m+1}} - t_{j_m}} \tag{7}$$

where $r_{j_i}$ is the representative feature vector for sensor $S_j$ at time $t_i$ which will be used in the recognition process. Subsequently, the module buffers $r_{j_i}$ in a queue and continues to determine $r_{j_{(i+1)}}$. After one vector $r_{j_i}$ for each Sensor $S_j$ has been determined for time $t_i$, the synchronization module dequeues the vectors, concatenates them and passes the combined reading to the next pipeline step.

A scheme of the synchronization module is shown in Fig. 2. For each sensor $S_j$, $j \in \{1, \ldots, k\}$, a worker process $W_j$ analyzes the stream of data published by preprocessing node $P_j$. For time $t_i$, worker $W_j$ interpolates a representative feature vector as described above and puts it into queue $Q_j$. Subsequently it continues to interpolate an entry for $t_{i+1}$. After one feature vector for each sensor has been determined, synchronizer $S$ dequeues the individual vectors and fuses them to one combined reading $r_i$. This reading is then given to the scaling module for further processing.

### 4.4    Scaling

The scaling module subtracts the mean from the individual features contained in the synchronized readings and scales them to zero mean unit variance. This pipeline step reduces the numerical difficulties in the training process and prevents the features in a greater numerical range to have a negative impact on the model. In the experiments, the StandardScaler implementation of the scikit-learn library was used and trained with data from multiple prerecorded activity sequences.

### 4.5   Recognition

The recognition module receives a stream of synchronized and scaled sensor readings from the previous pipeline step. The stream matches the requirements for the activity recognition formulation described in Sect. 3. Each reading captures the physical state of the robot at a given point in time. Depending on the activities that are intended to be recognized, a suitable model is selected by the programmer. The chosen model analyzes the multimodal sensor data and outputs an activity label that describes the activity the robot is currently performing. The model is trained offline with annotated activity sequences.

In the evaluation, an LSTM based neural network receives a description of the robot's state as an input matrix containing multiple consecutive sensor readings. This matrix is prepared by a small buffer that proceeds the network. The network was trained on 5 readings containing 50 features each. This input goes through two LSTM layers consisting of 32 neurons each. Afterwards, a softmax layer associates each sequence with one of 7 classes (see Sect. 5.2). Each LSTM layer is followed by a batch normalization layer and is regularized by $l_1$ and $l_2$ regularizers each with coefficient 0.05. The categorical cross-entropy function is used to calculate the loss and Adam [10] is the used optimizer. The network is trained over 20 epochs with a batch size of 100.

## 5   Evaluation

An implementation of the activity recognition pipeline is evaluated in two experiments featuring the service robot Pepper. In the first experiment, the pipeline is used to recognize a set of 7 movement activities. The classification accuracy achieved when using single and multimodal sensor data is analyzed. In the second experiment, a human interferes with Pepper's forward movement. It is shown that the pipeline responds to the interference and could be used to verify activity execution.

### 5.1   Pipeline Implementation

The pipeline was realized with the Robotic Operating System (ROS). The modules are implemented as individual ROS nodes which communicate over ROS topics. The ROS community provides a NAOqi/ROS API to communicate with Pepper's NAOqi operating system. The API offers joint state (50 Hz) and IMU (10 Hz) readings via designated topics. An additional wrapper node was implemented which samples electrical current at 10 Hz and publishes the data to a topic. Each reading is associated with the time of its creation.

The recognition module uses an LSTM based neural network (Sect. 4.5). The network is realized with Keras and trained with annotated activity sequence data. TensorFlow serves as Keras backend. During the data collection process, a training script lets Pepper perform an activity sequence and publishes annotation information whenever it sends a command to the robot. The recognition pipeline runs partially up to the synchronization module (Sect. 4.3) and publishes combined readings containing joint state (17 features), electrical current (20 features) and IMU (13 features) data. Two logging nodes store annotation information and synchronized sensor data in a SQLite database. For the training of the model, the readings are annotated corresponding to their timestamps.

## 5.2   Recognizing Movement Activities

The activity recognition approach is evaluated on a set of 7 movement activities executed by the Pepper robot. An activity sequence (shown in Fig. 3) is executed by the robot. Sensor readings are captured, annotated and used to train and evaluate scaling and recognition module. The pipeline uses joint state, electrical current and IMU data for its classifications.

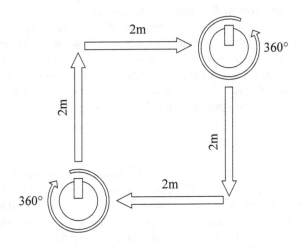

**Fig. 3.** The recorded activity sequence.

**Recorded Data:** A control script lets Pepper perform the movement sequence shown in Fig. 3. The robot performs a full clockwise rotation, moves forward, moves right, performs a full counterclockwise rotation, moves backward and finally moves left to its initial position. Between the individual movements Pepper stands still for 2.5 s. The control allows the robot to perform 5 repetitions of the activity sequence and sends corresponding commands and annotation information. The synchronization module interpolates combined sensor readings at 10 Hz containing joint state, electrical current and IMU data. During the experiments, 10 recordings containing combined sensor readings and annotation information are collected, each capturing little above 5 min of Pepper's movement activity. For evaluation, a 10-fold cross-validation is performed. Each of the 10 folds consists of 2450 annotated samples from one individual recording (350 samples per class picked at random from the respective recording).

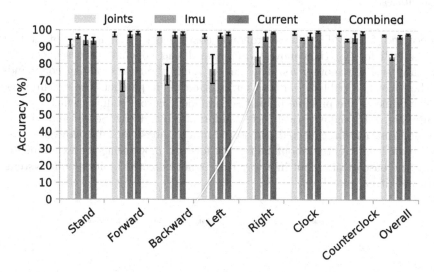

**Fig. 4.** The classification accuracy and standard deviations achieved on Pepper's base movements when using different sensor data for the recognition process.

**Experimental Results:** Multiple neural networks are trained to recognize Pepper's movement activities by analyzing different sensor data. Three single-sensor networks are trained with joint states, IMU and electrical current data respectively. One multimodal model is trained to analyze combined readings. The mean per-class and overall accuracies achieved by the different models and respective standard deviations are visualized in Fig. 4. The combined model achieves an mean overall accuracy of 97.47%, which outperforms the joint states (96.78%), IMU (84.20%) and electrical current (96.05%) model. While the combined model outperforms the others in terms of overall accuracy, there are differences in the individual class accuracies. The IMU model achieves a lower overall accuracy than the other models, but achieves the highest accuracy for the standing activity. Also, the IMU model achieves good results for the rotations while achieving worse results on the directional movements. The joint and current model perform similarly except when recognizing the rotating and right moving robot.

## 5.3 Detecting Human Interference

In this experiment, a human interferes with Pepper's forward movement by pulling its base backward in a way that is not detected by the robot's inbuilt systems. The output of the recognition pipeline is analyzed. It is shown that the approach can detect unexpected behavior that defers from the commands given by the robot's controller and could be used to extend Pepper's inbuilt capabilities.

**Recorded Data:** The Pepper robot is controlled by a simple script. It first stands still for 5 s, then moves 3 m forward and concludes the sequence by standing still for another 5 s. The control sends the corresponding commands to the robot and publishes annotation information in parallel. The synchronization module of the pipeline publishes combined sensor readings which contain joint state, IMU and electrical current information at 10 Hz. Sensor and annotation information are collected and stored in a database for later analysis. After the robot has executed about half of its forward movement, the experimenter grabs the base of the robot in a way that is not detected by its inbuilt systems and pulls it backward.

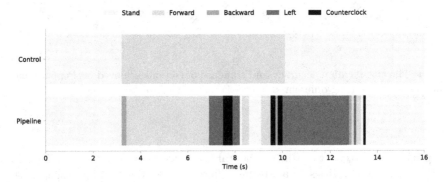

**Fig. 5.** The robot's activity over time as perceived by the robot's controller and recognition pipeline.

**Experimental Results:** For this experiment, pipeline scaler and model are trained with the 10 recordings of the previous experiment (Sect. 5.2). Figure 5 compares the robot activity over time as perceived by control layer and recognition pipeline. The pipeline recognizes the standing activity correctly. At the transition between standing and forward movement, the model makes two wrong predictions (200 ms) before recognizing the forward movement correctly. After about 7 s, the experimenter starts pulling Pepper's base backward. While the control does not respond to the interference, the pipeline recognizes the change in the robot's movement and classifies it first as backward, then left and then backward again. Because the experimenter pulls the robot unevenly, the recognized state then swings for a while between several states which are followed by a long backward movement. After about 10 s, the control sends a standing command and assumes Pepper came to a halt while in reality it is still being pulled by the experimenter. After about 13 s, the interference stops.

To verify correct activity execution, the output of the recognition pipeline can be compared to the robot's commands. If control and pipeline do not agree on the same activity for a certain amount of time (e.g. 0.5 s), an observation system can detect the unexpected behavior of the robot. This can then be used to allow the agent to communicate its problem to a remote supervisor.

# 6   Conclusion

This work introduced a activity recognition pipeline inspired by HAR methods to the robotics domain. The approach analyzes multiple streams of asynchronous sensor data to recognize the type of action a robot is performing and by doing so allows it to detect its own activities in the physical world. The robot could use this capability to verify its own activity execution or to narrate its actions to a remote person.

The recognition pipeline was evaluated in two experiments. In the first experiment, a set of 7 base movements executed by the service robot Pepper was recognized. It was shown how a model can achieve higher classification accuracy by analyzing combined data from heterogeneous sensors. In the second experiment, a person interfered with the forward movement of the robot by pulling its base backward. While the robot's inbuilt capabilities were not able to detect the external interference, the pipeline successfully recognized the unexpected state. This suggests that the approach could be used to extend Pepper's inbuilt capabilities with an additional verification system.

In future work, we want to recognize more complex activities that go beyond simple base movements. In particular, the application of plan detection is of interest to us. Here, we want to analyze how the recognized activities fit into a meaningful context. This work used proprioceptive sensors because they are more homogenous than external sensors and are closely relate to conventional HAR methods. In further research, readings from external sensors such as rgb cameras and depth sensors can be incorporated into the pipeline to enrich the activity information. Another question is if a model that was trained on one robot can provide accurate predictions when deployed on another robot of the same type.

# References

1. Alwi, H., Edwards, C., Tan, C.P.: Fault Detection and Fault-Tolerant Control Using Sliding Modes. Springer, Heidelberg (2011). https://doi.org/10.1007/978-0-85729-650-4

2. Avci, A., Bosch, S., Marin-Perianu, M., Marin-Perianu, R., Havinga, P.: Activity recognition using inertial sensing for healthcare, wellbeing and sports applications: a survey. In: 2010 23rd International Conference on Architecture of Computing Systems (ARCS), pp. 1–10. VDE (2010)

3. Bayat, A., Pomplun, M., Tran, D.A.: A study on human activity recognition using accelerometer data from smartphones. Procedia Comput. Sci. **34**, 450–457 (2014)

4. Bengio, Y.: Deep learning of representations: looking forward. In: Dediu, A.-H., Martín-Vide, C., Mitkov, R., Truthe, B. (eds.) SLSP 2013. LNCS (LNAI), vol. 7978, pp. 1–37. Springer, Heidelberg (2013). https://doi.org/10.1007/978-3-642-39593-2_1

5. Chernbumroong, S., Cang, S., Atkins, A., Yu, H.: Elderly activities recognition and classification for applications in assisted living. Expert Syst. Appl. **40**(5), 1662–1674 (2013)

6. Cornacchia, M., Ozcan, K., Zheng, Y., Velipasalar, S.: A survey on activity detection and classification using wearable sensors. IEEE Sens. J. **17**(2), 386–403 (2017)

7. Haddadin, S., De Luca, A., Albu-Schäffer, A.: Robot collisions: a survey on detection, isolation, and identification. IEEE Trans. Robot. **33**(6), 1292–1312 (2017)

8. Hochreiter, S., Schmidhuber, J.: Long short-term memory. Neural Comput. **9**(8), 1735–1780 (1997)

9. Khalastchi, E., Kalech, M.: On fault detection and diagnosis in robotic systems. ACM Comput. Surv. (CSUR) **51**(1), 9 (2018)

10. Kinga, D., Adam, J.B.: Adam: a method for stochastic optimization. In: International Conference on Learning Representations (ICLR) (2015)

11. Lara, O.D., Labrador, M.A.: A survey on human activity recognition using wearable sensors. IEEE Commun. Surv. Tutor. **15**(3), 1192–1209 (2013)

12. Liu, K., Chen, C., Jafari, R., Kehtarnavaz, N.: Fusion of inertial and depth sensor data for robust hand gesture recognition. IEEE Sens. J. **14**(6), 1898–1903 (2014)

13. Ofli, F., Chaudhry, R., Kurillo, G., Vidal, R., Bajcsy, R.: Berkeley MHAD: a comprehensive multimodal human action database. In: 2013 IEEE Workshop on Applications of Computer Vision (WACV), pp. 53–60. IEEE (2013)

14. Ordóñez, F.J., Roggen, D.: Deep convolutional and LSTM recurrent neural networks for multimodal wearable activity recognition. Sensors **16**(1), 115 (2016)

15. Pettersson, O.: Execution monitoring in robotics: a survey. Robot. Auton. Syst. **53**(2), 73–88 (2005)

16. Radu, V., Lane, N.D., Bhattacharya, S., Mascolo, C., Marina, M.K., Kawsar, F.: Towards multimodal deep learning for activity recognition on mobile devices. In: Proceedings of the 2016 ACM International Joint Conference on Pervasive and Ubiquitous Computing: Adjunct, pp. 185–188. ACM (2016)

17. Shoaib, M., Bosch, S., Incel, O.D., Scholten, H., Havinga, P.J.: A survey of online activity recognition using mobile phones. Sensors **15**(1), 2059–2085 (2015)

18. Wang, J., Chen, Y., Hao, S., Peng, X., Hu, L.: Deep learning for sensor-based activity recognition: a survey. arXiv preprint arXiv:1707.03502 (2017)

19. Zhang, T., Wang, J., Liu, P., Hou, J.: Fall detection by embedding an accelerometer in cellphone and using KFD algorithm. Int. J. Comput. Sci. Netw. Secur. **6**(10), 277–284 (2006)

# Survey of Rescue Competitions and Proposal of New Standard Task from Ordinary Tasks

Masaru Shimizu[1]([⊠]) and Tomoichi Takahashi[2]

[1] Chukyo University, Nagoya, Japan
shimizu@sist.chukyo-u.ac.jp
[2] Meijo University, Nagoya, Japan
ttaka@meijo-u.ac.jp

**Abstract.** This study surveys rescue robot competitions and tracks the changes in the RoboCup Rescue League. The real robot league has been changed because of requests from real disasters; however, the virtual robot league competition basically remains the same as it was in the beginning.

In terms of some elements, the virtual robot league competition has capabilities of reproducing real situations for rescue robot evaluations when compared to the real robot league.

We propose herein a new competition task to mimic actual situations. We used a tank array model as the stage of the competition task after the Fukushima nuclear power plant.

## 1 Introduction

Since the Great East Japan Earthquake of 2011, robots have been used to explore the interior of the Fukushima Daiichi Nuclear Plant (FDNP). The situations encountered at the FDNP in 2011 and after the September 11 attack on the World Trade Center (WTC) proved to be far more challenging than anything anticipated before these disasters. In the tunnel ceiling collapse accident at Sasago tunnel in 2012 in Japan, the disaster area consisted of certain long and curved narrow spaces.

At the FDNP, robots are expected to be used for a variety of tasks for several decades as the nuclear facilities are decommissioned [3]. These tasks include clearing debris, monitoring and mapping the inside and outside of buildings, setting up instruments, shielding and decontaminating, as well as transporting materials, construction pipes, and equipment. The tasks require robot mobility, perception ability, autonomous ability, multi-robot ability, networking ability, maneuvering ability, and safe behavior ability. Therefore, it will be necessary to design new mechanisms and develop sensing algorithms to satisfy the mid- and long-term schedules for decommissioning the FDNP [29].

The use of robots in emergency, ordinary situations and during reconstruction periods not only require mobility of the robot but also other abilities to complete

© Springer Nature Switzerland AG 2019
D. Holz et al. (Eds.): RoboCup 2018, LNAI 11374, pp. 311–323, 2019.
https://doi.org/10.1007/978-3-030-27544-0_26

tasks. For example, these robots could be used to inspect water contaminated with radioactive material, such as those stored in the tanks outside the FDNP [27]. It is necessary to evaluate the abilities of robots to develop better robots. Robot competitions play the role of leaders in developing evaluation methods regarding the abilities of robots.

The RoboCup Rescue Real Robot League (RRRL) and the Rescue Virtual Robot League (RVRL) both possess proper robot evaluation items. S. Carpin et al. discussed the usage of a simulation platform in the urban search and rescue task in 2006 [4, 6, 7]. In the case of the RVRL, using simulation technology, robotic programs, algorithms, and robot behavior can be evaluated before physically constructing the robot. Each league should use its optimum characteristics and fulfill the role expected from disasters that occur.

The robotic tasks at the FDNP include ordinary investigation tasks, such as checking the leak of contaminated water in the tank array area. The task requires rescue robots with three-dimensional mobility, such as a multicopter, an autonomy ability in an unstable Wi-Fi environment, and a multi-robot ability as cooperative by themselves.

We survey the RVRL historical progress, current status, and problems and propose a new competition task based on the scenario of the tank array checking water leaking ordinary investigation task in the FDNP with the tank array, multicopters, ground vehicle robots, and reproduced Wi-Fi behavior. Section 2 describes a survey of the RVRL and rescue competitions and various test methods for evaluating the abilities of response robots. Section 3 describes a proposal for a new competition task based on a realistic ordinary investigation task at the FDNP. Section 4 describes the proposed new competition field. Section 5 discusses the future competition task for the evaluation of robots and a summary of the study.

## 2    Survey of Rescue Tasks

### 2.1    Competitions of Rescue Robots

New robots, devices, programs, and algorithms should be evaluated as soon as possible. After developing a robot, the developers evaluate the ability of the robot in terms of mobility, dexterity, sensing, mapping, and other functions required as a response robot. Already various test methods exist that can be used for evaluating the abilities of each individual robot. The tests comprise the following: mobility tests, wireless communication tests, manipulation tests, human-system interaction tests, and sensing tests. Mobility tests include flat surfaces as well as pitching and rolling ramps, steps, inclines, gaps, stairs, and landings. Sensor tests determine the quality of the video. A previous version of the Quince robot, which participated in the RoboCup Japan Open Rescue Real Robot competition, was actually applied at the FDNP; its use exploring the disaster zone allowed a real-life demonstration of its capabilities [31].

**Table 1.** History of rescue robot competition and test field

| Year | Title of competition | Target Operation | Target Robot Type | Evaluation | Real /Simulation | Background case |
|------|----------------------|------------------|-------------------|------------|------------------|-----------------|
| 1998 | RoboSub | rescue | sea | mobility | real | |
| 2000 | RoboCup (Rescue) | rescue | land/air | mobility /mapping /dexterity | real | Hanshin-Awaji earthquake (1995) |
| 2006 | ELROB | | land/air | mobility | real | |
| 2008 | Rowboat | | sea | mobility | real | |
| 2012 | ICARUS | rescue | land/sea /air | mobility | real | Earthquakes in l'Aquila, Haiti |
| 2013 | DARPA (Robotics Challenge) | rescue | land | mobility /mapping /dexterity | real /simulation | Fukushima nuclear disaster |
| 2013 | euRathlon | rescue | land/sea /air | mobility /mapping | real | Fukushima nuclear disaster |
| 2014 | ARGOS challenge | survey | land | mobility /mapping /dexterity | real | Future plant disaster |
| 2015 | JVRC | survey /rescue | land | mobility /mapping /dexterity | simulation | Sasago falling tunnel ceilings accident |
| 2018 | WRS (Tunnel) | survey /rescue | land/air | mobility /mapping /dexterity | simulation | Sasago falling tunnel ceilings accident |
| 2018 | DARPA (Subterranean Challenge) | survey /rescue | land/air | mobility /mapping /dexterity | simulation | |

Table 1 shows a list of robot competitions [2, 9–15, 17–19, 21–25]. Several competitions were organized after certain large disasters. In these competitions, dedicated competition fields were constructed to evaluate response robots. Thus, each competition field incorporates certain real disaster situations. New competitions have new metrical items owing to new disaster situations.

The investigation tasks consist of routine operations, which are simpler than those undertaken by the Quince robot inside the FDNP in 2011 in a larger area. Several tanks were constructed at the FDNP to store contaminated water for the purpose of cooling nuclear fuel. The tanks were arranged systematically in a 100 m wide area, and each tank measures 10 m in height and 12 m in diameter. The robots designed for these tasks require verification. When developing sensors and robots for search and rescue operations in disaster zones, testing the robots in such environments can aid in determining and improving their performance.

When using tele-operation type response robots, stable Wi-Fi connectivity is essential, in addition to other capabilities such as mobility function. A response robot that moves outside of a Wi-Fi connectable area is uncontrollable, and in the worst case the operator loses it. A response robot with a recovery program, which directs the lost response robot to a Wi-Fi connectable area, requires time for the automatic recovery behavior. The system including the response robots requires a simulator that can estimate the Wi-Fi connectable areas to determine the effective locations of Wi-Fi base stations, which are limited in a disaster area and/or a large destroyed facility such as the FDNP.

Thus, a simulator is an appropriate tool that can be used to observe problems when using a response robot with unstable Wi-Fi connectivity. This approach avoids the difficulties of testing in the real field. The RVRL should use more realistic situations with the Wi-Fi networking.

### 2.2   Standard Test Methods in Robot Competitions

Table 2 shows the relationships between robot competitions and its metrical items:

- Mob. (Mobility): the performance to move on the uneven surface or to climb a ladder.
- Per. (Perception ability): the performance to recognize hazard tags, QR-Codes, and texts in the environment around the robot.
- Aut. (Autonomous ability): the performance to work and produce 3D maps in Wi-Fi blackout areas without human aid.
- Mul. (Multi-robot ability): the performance to work with multiple robots in large size fields and separated fields.
- Net. (Networking ability): the performance to maintain and form the communication link in unstable Wi-Fi areas and Wi-Fi blackout areas.
- Man. (Maneuvering ability): the performance to manipulate, manage, and carry objects.
- Saf. (Safe behavior ability): the performance to move safely and maintain safe behavior with respect to victims and objects in the environment.

Every metrical item is reproduced with a style of robot competitions. For example, National Institute of Standards and Technology (NIST) released Standard Test Methods (STM) for evaluating response robots [1, 16]. STM is used as the

**Table 2.** Competitions and metrical items

| Competitions | Metrical items | | | | | | |
|---|---|---|---|---|---|---|---|
| | Mob. | Per. | Aut. | Mul. | Net. | Man. | Saf. |
| RoboCup (RRRL) | ✓ | ✓ | ✓ | ✓ | ✓ | ✓ | ✓ |
| RoboCup (RVRL) | ✓ | ✓ | ✓ | ✓ | ✓ | | |
| DARPA | ✓ | ✓ | ✓ | | | ✓ | |
| ARGOS challenge | ✓ | ✓ | ✓ | ✓ | ✓ | ✓ | ✓ |
| JVRC | ✓ | ✓ | | | | ✓ | |
| WRS | ✓ | ✓ | ✓ | ✓ | ✓ | ✓ | |
| DARPA (SubT) | ✓ | ✓ | ✓ | ✓ | ✓ | | |

field for evaluation of mobility in the RRRL. A competition that is closed to real situations possesses considerable amount of metric items. Seven metrical items are merged from robot competitions; every robot competition exhibits several abilities such as autonomy ability, perception ability, networking ability, mobility, maneuvering ability, and multi-robot performance. The RRRL and ARGOS challenges contain all metrical items.

## 2.3   Issues of RoboCup Rescue League

Table 3 shows the historical comparisons of the competition content of the RRRL and the RVRL. In the RRRL, the number of metrical items is increasing gradually, and the types of inspection items are also increasing. In the RVRL, the number of metrical items is increasing, and the types of inspection items are not increasing. The RRRL has been evolving at the core of evaluation of rescue robots; the RVRL has been stopping evolution. The RVRL does not contain any critical metrical items that the RRRL already contains. However, the RVRL can prepare some of the metrical elements readily compared with the RRRL.

**Table 3.** Historical comparisons between rescue real robot league and virtual robot league

| Year | Real Robot League | | Virtual Robot League | |
|---|---|---|---|---|
| | Size&Ability | Photos | Size&Ability | Photos |
| 2002 | 10 m x 10 m Mobility Perception Multi-robot Autonomy Safe behavior | | (NOT STARTED) | (NOT STARTED) |
| 2008 | 15 m x 15 m Mobility Perception Multi-robot Autonomy Networking Safe behavior | | 100 m x 100 m Perception Multi-robot Autonomy | |
| 2012 | 30 m x 30 m Mobility Perception Multi-robot Autonomy Networking Maneuvering Safe behavior | | 200 m x 200 m Perception Multi-robot Autonomy Networking | |

The RVRL and the RRRL exhibit the same objective, however, they do not share concepts and schemes with each other. For example, the RVRL should be a tool that the RRRL participating team requires to use for robot development with respect to new autonomous programs, perception algorithms, and mapping systems. The RVRL should use metrical elements that are difficult to prepare at the RRRL and are effective for robot development in the competition. For example, large and realistic situation field models that came from the FDNP and natural Wi-Fi behavior can be realized using already existing simulation items.

In 2009, the wireless communication server (WSS) was introduced to simulate robot behaviors, where the robots receive the Wi-Fi [5]. The WSS was not used at recent competitions in 2016 and 2017.

## 3   New Standard Task from Ordinary Tasks

### 3.1   Use of Wi-Fi in Networking Ability Evaluation

In Fukushima, robots were employed to perform emergency tasks immediately after the 2011 earthquake. At present, robots continue to perform ordinary tasks such as daily investigation jobs. To perform these ordinary tasks, the robots should move freely within a large area. For robot evaluation in the context of these ordinary tasks, the size of the evaluation field should be known, and a controlled unstable Wi-Fi connection status is required.

Quince robots were used to inspect the inside of the FDNP. Because of the Wi-Fi disability in the FDNP facilities, Quince robots were used in tandem [3].

In Table 2, the networking ability was indicated as an item of robot evaluation. Robot behavior stability is evaluated with regard to disconnection of its Wi-Fi connection. In the real response robot working field, the Wi-Fi status has the capability of being unstable in connection [8,25,28]. To reproduce the natural Wi-Fi behavior, the real robot evaluation field should possess a large sized field that has over 100 m in the radius from the Wi-Fi base station to disconnect the Wi-Fi. Therefore, the condition of Wi-Fi disconnection has been managed in an imaginary manner by defining it in the competition rules at a part of the competition area.

The strength of a natural Wi-Fi radio wave exhibits band fluctuation, even when the Wi-Fi base stations and robots do not move. Further, the movement of humans and robots inside a Wi-Fi area increases the band fluctuation of the Wi-Fi radio waves. Fluctuations of the Wi-Fi radio waves within the diffraction area can induce Wi-Fi disconnection in the outer diffraction areas. Thus, to maintain stable Wi-Fi connectivity throughout the Wi-Fi diffraction area, a safety margin is required in the outer diffraction area.

### 3.2   Proposal of New Ordinary Investigation Task

Based on the reported robotic tasks performed at the FDNP, we propose an ordinary investigation task in the large area with high and low places by controlling of the Wi-Fi connection status along with an environmental model that is close to the real scenario at the FDNP, the shape of which can affect the Wi-Fi connection status.

Simulations can be used effectively to evaluate robot performance, as evident from Table 1. In particular, certain real metrical elements that are difficult to prepare and control can be reproduced in a simulation. In addition, a town-size field can be prepared considerably readily in a simulator than in a real-world environment. Controllable environmental phenomena are useful for robot evaluation. Simulations such as that used in the Virtual Robot segment of the RoboCup Rescue competition provides platforms where response robots and algorithms can be tested with respect to the disaster zones where they are intended to operate [20]. Thus, a simulator is a useful tool for identifying problems with response robots under conditions of unstable Wi-Fi connectivity. Therefore, in this study, a new simulated standard task with Wi-Fi behavior similar to the natural case is proposed.

The proposed simulation platform is designed considering multicopters, which exhibit the following characteristics:

- Multicopters can move through a larger area in less time compared with ground vehicles.
- Multicopters can move not only horizontally, but also vertically.
- The Wi-Fi-connectable area is invisible.
- The shape of the Wi-Fi-connectable area or Wi-Fi diablo area is difficult to image.

The real sample situation at the FDNP involves arrays of large tanks storing contaminated water. These tank arrays constitute an unstable Wi-Fi connectivity area. Daily investigative tasks using robots require a stable Wi-Fi connection, and automatization of these daily investigations performed by robots requires a lightweight estimation method to calculate the Wi-Fi connectable areas.

# 4    A New Ordinary Investigation Task Simulation Field

## 4.1    Background of Proposal

At FDNP, robots have been expected to perform ordinary daily investigation tasks. In this proposal, we focus on the multicopter, which is regarded as a standard robot in the RVRL. The multicopter is one of the most suitable robots for ordinary investigation tasks. In an emergency, the multicopter is used as a response robot under restricted conditions of Wi-Fi behavior is not reproduced, these robots can explore the entire model test environment. In contrast, in our proposed simulation platform that reproduces natural Wi-Fi behavior, robots can explore only the Wi-Fi-connectable area.

In the proposed competitive field, a tank array field such as that encountered in the FDNP was used. The following conditions were implemented in the proposed simulation platform:

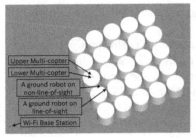

(a) An overview of sample simulation platform.

(b) A real tank array( [30]).

(c) A side close-up view of sample simulation platform.

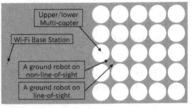

(d) A top overview of sample simulation platform.

**Fig. 1.** An overview of sample simulation platform and original tank array scene

- A 5 × 5 tank array was considered as the test environment.
- Each tank possessed 12 m diameter and 11 m height, similar to those of the real tank array.
- The distance between the tanks was 1 m, as in the real tank array.
- Two multicopters and two ground robots were considered as the test robots.
- Radio wave power attenuated via distance and shadowing via buildings was used to model the Wi-Fi behavior.
- To incorporate the attenuation phenomena of the radio wave power, as affected by distance, the distance was considered as 90 m from the center of the tank array.

Figure 1 presents a sample simulation platform image and an actual tank array image [30]. In detail, Fig. 1(a) shows an overview of the sample simulation platform designed using the above conditions. A Wi-Fi base station is located to the left of the image, two multicopters can be found at the center of the image, and two ground robots are positioned to the right of the multicopters. Figure 1(b) is an image of the actual tank array in the FDNP [30]. This array spans an extremely large area, and an elevated position is required to perform the daily investigation tasks. Thus, a multicopter is an appropriate robot for positioning at the station. Note that the multicopter operator must have access to operate the multicopter properly. Figure 1(c) and (d) show side and top views of the sample simulation platform, respectively.

Figure 2 shows two images of the simulated received signal strengths (RSSs) of the Wi-Fi, as received at the horizontal planes of different heights. In the

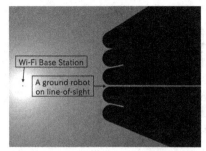
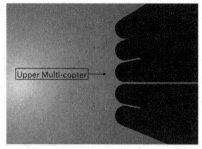

(a) At 0.3-m-high horizontal plane.    (b) At 13-m-high horizontal plane.

**Fig. 2.** Images of simulated received signal strength of Wi-Fi received at different high horizontal planes

simulation of the RSS-treated diffraction and fluctuation phenomenon of radio waves [26], the former WSS did not treat it. The white color in the figure indicates that the RSS value is high, whereas black means the RSS value is less than $-92\,$dB. The robot cannot connect to the Wi-Fi at a location with an RSS value of less than $-92\,$dB. A Wi-Fi base station is located in the center far left of the image. The black areas in the right half of the image corresponding to the Wi-Fi location shadows of the tanks. (a) shows an image of the simulated Wi-Fi RSS at nearly the ground plane. The Wi-Fi base station can be observed on the left of the image (the black dot in the center of the filled white circle), and a ground robot is visible in the line of sight from the Wi-Fi base station. (b) shows an image of the simulated Wi-Fi RSS at a 13 m-high horizontal plane over the tank. Shadows are moving toward the right of the image in (a), and the upper multicopter can be observed in this image.

From (a)–(b), the outline shape of the Wi-Fi shadowed volume is part of a resting cone, which explains why it was exceedingly difficult to tele-operate the multicopters over and between the tanks. Furthermore, this difficulty explains the usefulness and effectiveness of our proposed Wi-Fi simulation platform for evaluating a multicopter system involving a multicopter operator.

## 4.2    Sample Tasks for Networking Ability Evaluation

Figure 3 presents an example of the proposed new standard task incorporating the Wi-Fi behavior. A standard task with a course similar to an ordinary investigation task is illustrated. A multicopter robot should begin at the starting point, from "P1" to "P16" in any order, and return to the destination. A list of sample rules is provided below:

- Obtain a scoring point using the grade of accuracy of the generated 3D map.
- Obtain a scoring point by passing near each checkpoint.
- Obtain a scoring point by reporting changes from "P1" to "P16" for before and after the disaster event.
  Change examples: removal of tank surface paint, broken tank edge

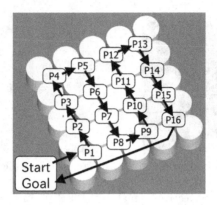

**Fig. 3.** Image of proposed new standard test method

- Obtain a scoring point by returning to the goal in a relatively short time.
- Double the scoring points by developing and using an autonomous software.
- Lose a scoring point by losing the multicopter robot.

The variety and difficulty grades of the field can be established based on the following weather conditions:

- Fine, rain, and snow.
- Day and night.
- Typhoon (strong wind).

The situations, rules, weather conditions, and environmental models for the simulation platform are changeable. Because the proposed platform is implemented on a simulator, it can be used by anyone and modified readily as required.

## 5    Summary and Discussion

Simulations are used to design robots and examine the robot's functions before manufacturing real ones. Rescue robots must be confirmed before being used in disaster situations and reconstruction tasks in FDNP that will continue for decades. This study indicates that the RVRL has been a part of the request of the real world and distinctly mentions the points that should be checked in virtual spaces.

We organized necessary tasks with respect to conducting inspections of FDNP as an example of ordinary tasks and proposed new standard tasks with regard to the RoboCup Rescue League. The tasks would be of interest to the teams of the RRRL and the RVRL with regard to the viewpoint of applying their robots in real fields.

# References

1. Jacoff, A.: Guide for Evaluating, Purchasing, and Training with Response Robots Using DHS-NIST-ASTM International Standard Test Methods (2012). https://www.nist.gov/sites/default/files/documents/el/isd/ks/DHS_NIST_ASTM_Robot_Test_Methods-2.pdf. Accessed 06 Mar 2018
2. ARGOS Challenge (2016). http://www.argos-challenge.com/. Accessed 22 Feb 2016
3. Asama, H.: Robot & remote-controlled machine technology for response against accident of nuclear power and toward their decommision. In: International Conference on Intelligent Robots and Systems (IROS 2012) (2012)
4. Balaguer, B., Balakirsky, S., Carpin, S., Visser, A.: Evaluating maps produced by urban search and rescue robots: lessons learned from RoboCup. Auton. Robot. **27**(4), 449–464 (2009)
5. Balakirsky, S., Carpin, S., Visser, A.: Evaluation of the RoboCup 2009 virtual robot rescue competition. In: Proceedings of the 9th Performance Metrics for Intelligent Systems (PERMIS 2009) Workshop, PerMIS 2009, pp. 109–114. ACM, New York, September 2009
6. Carpin, S., Lewis, M., Wang, J., Balakirsky, S., Scrapper, C.: Bridging the gap between simulation and reality in urban search and rescue. In: Lakemeyer, G., Sklar, E., Sorrenti, D.G., Takahashi, T. (eds.) RoboCup 2006. LNCS (LNAI), vol. 4434, pp. 1–12. Springer, Heidelberg (2007). https://doi.org/10.1007/978-3-540-74024-7_1
7. Carpin, S., Wang, J., Lewis, M., Birk, A., Jacoff, A.: High fidelity tools for rescue robotics: results and perspectives. In: Bredenfeld, A., Jacoff, A., Noda, I., Takahashi, Y. (eds.) RoboCup 2005. LNCS (LNAI), vol. 4020, pp. 301–311. Springer, Heidelberg (2006). https://doi.org/10.1007/11780519_27
8. Carver, L., Turoff, M.: Emergency response information systems: emerging trends and technologies-human-computer interaction: the human and computer as a team in emergency management information systems. Commun. ACM-Assoc. Comput. Mach.-CACM **50**(3), 33–38 (2007)
9. Cubber, G.D., Doroftei, D., Serrano, D., Chintamani, K., Sabino, R., Ourevitch, S.: The EU-ICARUS project: developing assistive robotic tools for search and rescue operations. In: 2013 IEEE International Symposium on Safety, Security, and Rescue Robotics (SSRR), pp. 1–4, October 2013
10. Darpa. Darpa robotics challenge (2012). https://www.darpa.mil/program/darpa-robotics-challenge/. Accessed 31 Oct 2017
11. Defense Advanced Research Projects Agency. DARPA Subterranean Challenge Aims to Revolutionize Underground Capabilities (2017). https://www.darpa.mil/news-events/2017-12-21. Accessed 19 Mar 2018
12. Guizzo, E.: Rescue-robot show-down. IEEE Spectr. **51**(1), 52–55 (2014)
13. International CBRNE Institute (ICI), Fraunhofer Institute for Communication, Information Processing and Ergonomics FKIE. The European Land Robot Trial (2006). http://www.elrob.org/. Accessed 6 Feb 2018
14. Kimura, T., et al.: Competition task development for response robot innovation in world robot summit. In: 2017 IEEE International Symposium on Safety, Security and Rescue Robotics (SSRR), pp. 129–130. IEEE, October 2017
15. Kydd, K., Macrez, S., Pourcel, P.: Autonomous robot for gas and oil sites, September 2015

16. NIST. Robotics Test Facility (2005). https://www.nist.gov/laboratories/tools-instruments/robotics-test-facility. Accessed 6 Feb 2018

17. Okugawa, M., et al.: Proposal of inspection and rescue tasks for tunnel disasters - task development of Japan virtual robotics challenge. In: 2015 IEEE International Symposium on Safety, Security, and Rescue Robotics (SSRR), pp. 1–2, October 2015

18. RoboCup Rescue Robot League. Rescue robot league (2004). http://wiki.robocup.org/wiki/Robot_League. Accessed 13 Feb 2018

19. RoboCup Rescue Simulation Virtual Robot League. Rescue simulation virtual robot competition (2017). http://wiki.robocup.org/Rescue_Simulation_Virtual_Robot_Competition. Accessed 13 Feb 2018

20. RoboCup Virtual Robot League. VR Competitions (2017). http://wiki.robocup.org/Rescue_Simulation_Virtual_Robot_Competition. Accessed 13 Feb 2018

21. Robonation. RoboSub (1998). http://www.robonation.org/competition/robosub. Accessed 6 Feb 2018

22. RoboNation. Roboboat (2008). http://www.auvsifoundation.org/competition/roboboat. Accessed 6 Feb 2018

23. Schneider, F.E., Wildermuth, D., Wolf, H.L.: ELROB and EURATHLON: improving search & rescue robotics through real-world robot competitions. In: 2015 10th International Workshop on Robot Motion and Control (RoMoCo), pp. 118–123, July 2015

24. Serrano, D., Cubber, G.D., Leventakis, G., Chrobocinski, P., Govindaraj, S.: ICARUS and DARIUS approaches towards interoperability two complementary projects that cover the full spectrum of interoperability issues for the integration of unmanned platforms in search and rescue operations (2015)

25. Shimizu, M., et al.: Standard rescue tasks based on the Japan virtual robotics challenge. In: Behnke, S., Sheh, R., Sarıel, S., Lee, D.D. (eds.) RoboCup 2016. LNCS (LNAI), vol. 9776, pp. 440–451. Springer, Cham (2017). https://doi.org/10.1007/978-3-319-68792-6_37

26. Shimizu, M., Takahashi, T.: Databased fluctuating Wi-Fi signal simulation environment for evaluating the control of robots. J. Jpn. Soc. Fuzzy Theory Intell. Inform. $29(2)$, 567–573 (2017)

27. Strickland, E.: Dismantling Fukushima: The world's toughest demolition project. Technical report. IEEE Spectrum (2014). http://spectrum.ieee.org/energy/nuclear/dismantling-fukushima-the-worlds-toughest-demolition-project

28. Takahashi, T., Shimizu, M.: How can the RoboCup rescue simulation contribute to emergency preparedness in real-world disaster situations? In: Bianchi, R.A.C., Akin, H.L., Ramamoorthy, S., Sugiura, K. (eds.) RoboCup 2014. LNCS (LNAI), vol. 8992, pp. 295–305. Springer, Cham (2015). https://doi.org/10.1007/978-3-319-18615-3_24

29. Tokyo Electric Power Company. Mid-and-long-term roadmap towards the decommissioning of Fukushima Daiichi nuclear power units, pp. 1–4 (2011). http://www.tepco.co.jp/en/nu/fukushima-np/roadmap/conference-e.html. Accessed 13 Feb 2018

30. Tokyo Electric Power Company. Water leak at a tank in the H4 area in Fukushima Daiichi nuclear power station (follow-up information) (2013). http://www.tepco.co.jp/en/nu/fukushima-np/handouts/2013/images/handouts_130820_03-e.pdf. Accessed 13 Feb 2018

31. Yoshida, T., Nagatani, K., Tadokoro, S., Nishimura, T., Koyanagi, E.: Improvements to the rescue robot quince toward future indoor surveillance missions in the Fukushima Daiichi nuclear power plant. In: Yoshida, K., Tadokoro, S. (eds.) Field and Service Robotics. STAR, vol. 92, pp. 19–32. Springer, Heidelberg (2014). https://doi.org/10.1007/978-3-642-40686-7_2

# Adjusted Bounded Weighted Policy Learner

David Simões[1,2,3($\boxtimes$)], Nuno Lau[1,3], and Luís Paulo Reis[1,2,4]

[1] IEETA - Institute of Electronics and Informatics Engineering of Aveiro,
University of Aveiro, Aveiro, Portugal
{david.simoes,nunolau}@ua.pt
[2] LIACC - Artificial Intelligence and Computer Science Lab, Porto, Portugal
[3] DETI/UA - Electronics, Telecommunications and Informatics Department,
University of Aveiro, Aveiro, Portugal
[4] DEI/FEUP - Informatics Engineering Department,
Faculty of Engineering of the University of Porto, Porto, Portugal
lpreis@fe.up.pt

**Abstract.** The Weighted Policy Learner (WPL) algorithm has been shown to converge to Nash Equilibria (NE) in several challenging environments with minimum knowledge. However, WPL has trouble converging to deterministic strategies, since the policy update rate approaches zero. We propose a new update rule that bounds this update rate such that, in pure NE games, the algorithm's speed is not slowed down, while its behavior in stochastic NE games remains unchanged. We demonstrate our proposal's behavior in several common game-theoretic environments (with stochastic and deterministic equilibrium policies), in complex maze-related games (where some actions dominate others in most states), against the original WPL as well as other state of the art algorithms. We draw conclusions over the benefits of our solution and its advantages.

**Keywords:** Mixed policy · Multi-agent reinforcement learning ·
Game theory

## 1 Introduction

Reinforcement learning problems can be viewed as decision problems where an agent has to select a particular action at a given state. The agent gets a reward (or a penalty) for executing this action, and that along with the new state observation is the only available information it has from the environment. To learn a policy, the agent samples the underlying reward distribution of each action, and converges to a strategy that maximizes its own pay-off. Traditional reinforcement learning algorithms (such as Q-learning [12]) guarantee convergence to the optimal policy, by assuming that the reward distribution is stationary. However, these theoretical guarantees are lost in multi-agent systems, since the received rewards depend on the remaining agents' actions. Because all agents can change

© Springer Nature Switzerland AG 2019
D. Holz et al. (Eds.): RoboCup 2018, LNAI 11374, pp. 324–336, 2019.
https://doi.org/10.1007/978-3-030-27544-0_27

their policies at any given time, the reward distribution for any given action is not fixed.

In multi-agent systems, the objective is to reach the equilibrium that maximizes each agent's pay-off. However, in non-cooperative environments, a globally optimal equilibrium is not always attainable. A safer and more common alternative is to reach a Nash Equilibrium (NE), where no agent can do better by changing his own strategy, and any static game has at least one Nash Equilibrium [2]. Many multi-agent reinforcement learning (MARL) algorithms have been recently proposed and studied. However, most have unrealistic assumptions, such as knowing the underlying game structure and the game's Nash Equilibrium [4,15], knowing the actions executed and rewards received by other agents [8,10], using hand-tuned heuristics to each problem [5], being unable to achieve mixed strategies [11], or being focused solely on cooperative games [16].

Often, the only information agents have access to is their own actions and rewards, and algorithms that achieve Nash equilibria with only such information have been proposed. State of the art solutions include WoLF-PHC [7], GIGA-WoLF [6], Weighted Policy Learners (WPL) [1], and EMA-QL [3]. WoLF-PHC introduced the *Win or Learn Fast* principle, where different learning rates are used when the agent is winning or losing, a principle also used by GIGA-WoLF and other more recent proposals [14]. However, both algorithms have failed to converge in more complex games, such as the Tricky Game shown in Fig. 3. WPL and EMA-QL have been shown to achieve convergence in such games, but with some setbacks. WPL has no formal analysis and proof of convergence, and EMA-QL features some difficulties learning simpler games with many actions and asymmetric probabilities. These algorithms keep track of action values (as they derive from Q-learning) and of a probability distribution of possible actions. They have distinct update rules and requirements, with WPL being the algorithm that showed best results when adapted to the deep learning paradigm and compared with the remaining algorithms deep learning implementations [13]. However, WPL is biased against pure strategies, and it only converges in the limit, since the policy update rate approaches zero in these cases. We then propose to extend the WPL algorithm with a new update rule that will allow the algorithm to converge to these policies, where some actions are dominated by others, and also to stochastic policies, as before.

The remainder of this paper is structured as follows. Section 2 formally describes the Weighted Policy Learner algorithm and its numerical analysis. Section 3 describes our proposal, implementation, and analysis of two variants for WPL. Section 4 shows the results we obtained, and Sect. 5 draws conclusions and lists future work directions.

## 2    Weighted Policy Learner

The Weighted Policy Learner (WPL) [1] algorithm keeps track of both action Q-values and of an action-probability distribution for each state. This probability may tend to a pure strategy, where the algorithms become the original greedy

Q-learning. WPL has a variable learning rate, and allows the agent to move towards the equilibrium strategy faster than moving away from it. Despite not having a formal proof of convergence due to the non-linear nature of WPL's dynamics, the authors numerically solve WPL's dynamics differential equations and show that it features continuous non-linear dynamics, while experimentally demonstrating it converges in several more complex games.

We denote $Q_t(s, a)$ as the Q-values for action $a$ in state $s$ at time-step $t$, and $\pi_t(s)$ as the policy at time-step $t$ for state $s$, representing a vector of probabilities of picking each action. Each action's probability is represented by $\pi_t(s, a)$. The learning rate and policy learning rate at time-step $t$ are denoted by $\eta_t$ and $\eta_t^\pi$, respectively. A projection function $P(\pi, \epsilon)$ is used to project a policy $\pi$ into the valid probability space, where each probability must have at least a probability of $\epsilon$ over the total amount of actions.

Given a transition at time-step $t$ from state $s$ with action $a$ to state $s'$, which achieved a reward $r$, WPL starts by updating the Q-values using a discount factor $\gamma$ for future expected rewards, with

$$Q_{t+1}(s, a) = (1 - \eta_t)Q_t(s, a) + \eta_t(r + \gamma \max_{a'} Q_t(s', a')). \tag{1}$$

WPL then calculates an increment vector $\Delta(s)$ from the gradients of the value function $V_t(s)$, containing each action's individual increment $\Delta(s, a)$, and uses the vector to compute the new policy $\pi_{t+1}(s)$, with

$$V_t(s) = \sum_{a \in A} \pi_t(s, a)Q_t(s, a), \tag{2}$$

$$\forall a \in A \ \Delta_t(s, a) = \eta_t^\pi \frac{\partial V_t(s)}{\partial \pi_t(s, a)} * \begin{cases} \pi_t(s, a) \text{ if } \frac{\partial V_t(s)}{\partial \pi_t(s,a)} < 0 \\ 1 - \pi_t(s, a) \text{ otherwise} \end{cases}, \tag{3}$$

$$\pi_{t+1}(s) = P\left(\pi_t(s) + \Delta_t(s), \epsilon\right), \tag{4}$$

where $P(\pi, \epsilon)$ is a function that projects a probability $\pi$ into a valid probability space, with a minimum probability value of any action equal to $\epsilon$. The new policy is iteratively computed until convergence has been achieved.

## 2.1   Numerical Analysis

WPL has non-linear dynamics which cannot be solved in closed form. The authors instead perform a numerical analysis to demonstrate the convergence of the algorithm in a set of 2-person 2-action games. The authors solve the general case where Player 2 starts on the equilibrium strategy and, across a time period, the strategy of Player 1 gets closer to his equilibrium strategy while Player 2 ends again on his own equilibrium strategy.

However, the authors are unable to show a solution in closed form. They instead demonstrate an example where Player 1's first action probability equals

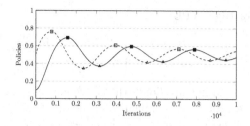

**Fig. 1.** The evolution of the policies of the row player (solid) and the column player (dashed) in a Matching Pennies game (shown in Fig. 3(a)), using the original WPL algorithm. The squared marks represent the maximum probability values, while triangular marks represent the minimum probability values.

0.1, as can be seen in Fig. 1. The plots use the actual algorithm and the marks are predicted by the theoretical model, with an adjusted scale to match the practical values.

## 3    Bounded Weighted Policy Learner

As previously stated, WPL is biased against pure strategies, where the algorithm only converges in the limit. We can easily observe a noticeable delay many trivial learning tasks where some actions are dominated by other actions. This happens since the policy update rate approaches zero in these cases, due to the use of $\pi_t(s, a)$ to adjust the rate.

This has a highly undesirable effect in many scenarios where pure strategies are, in fact, optimal. We propose to modify the update rule, such that the $\pi_t(s, a)$ factor does not approach 0 in such cases, thus removing the asymptotic convergence properties of WPL. We can do so by bounding this factor to an interval different from the original $[0, 1]$, adjusting it while either keeping its mean around 0.5 (changing both the interval's lower and upper bounds) or keeping its upper bound on 1 (and changing only its lower bound). We call these variants, respectively, by *Bounded WPL* and *High WPL*. We adjust the interval in such a way that the original convergence properties of WPL are maintained.

### 3.1    Bounded and High WPL

We can show how the Bounded WPL variant compares against High WPL, by adjusting the $\pi_t(s, a)$ factor to be within example intervals $[0.25, 0.75]$ and $[0.5, 1.0]$, respectively, both of which equal half the original interval's size. From Eq. 3, the new policy update rules for Bounded WPL is

$$\forall a \in A \ \Delta_t(s, a) = \eta_t^\pi \frac{\partial V_t(s)}{\partial \pi_t(s, a)} * \begin{cases} \frac{\pi_t(s,a)}{2} + 0.25 & \text{if } \frac{\partial V_t(s)}{\partial \pi_t(s,a)} < 0 \\ 0.75 - \frac{\pi_t(s,a)}{2} & \text{otherwise} \end{cases}, \quad (5)$$

and, analogously, for High WPL

$$\forall a \in A \ \Delta_t(s,a) = \eta_t^\pi \frac{\partial V_t(s)}{\partial \pi_t(s,a)} * \begin{cases} \frac{\pi_t(s,a)}{2} + 0.5 \text{ if } \frac{\partial V_t(s)}{\partial \pi_t(s,a)} < 0 \\ 1 - \frac{\pi_t(s,a)}{2} \text{ otherwise} \end{cases} . \quad (6)$$

These adjustments do not invalidate the convergence properties of the algorithm, since we have kept the fundamental property of WPL where the probability of choosing an action increases or decreases by a rate that decreases as the probability approaches the boundary of the simplex. In other words, agents move towards their Nash Equilibrium strategy (away from the simplex boundary) faster than they move away from it. We can perform a numerical analysis similar to the one conducted by the authors, by solving these equations for both Bounded and High WPL.

Using the same general example used by the authors, we can see in Fig. 2 the results of the numerical analysis for the above equations, which also demonstrates the convergence properties of our new variants. We can see that Bounded WPL has a slightly slower convergence speed than the original algorithm (which is to be expected, as the convergence speed has now been bounded to a smaller interval), but it maintains a very similar pattern to the original algorithm. However, the High WPL variant overcompensates and thus causes the policies to oscillate a lot more than the original algorithm, since we increased and off-set the average policy update rate. This is a highly undesirable effect, as it may lead to policy divergence in the learning stage, thus requiring adjustments to learning rates, which defeats the purpose of the algorithm.

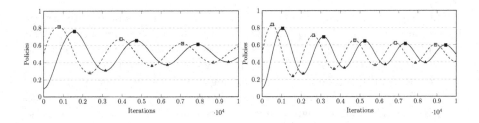

**Fig. 2.** The evolution of the policies of the row player (solid) and the column player (dashed) in a Matching Pennies game (shown in Fig. 3(a)), using the Bounded WPL (left) and High WPL (right) variants. The squared marks represent the maximum probability values, while triangular marks represent the minimum probability values. Simultaneously, solid marks represent the row player and clear marks represent the column player values.

## 3.2   Adjusted Bounded WPL

In order to automatically adjust the interval, such that scenarios with pure equilibria converge faster, and stochastic policy scenarios are not disturbed, we propose an update rule that is based on the Q-values of the actions. Because a pure equilibrium means that one action out-values all others, then Q-values converge such that the dominant action always has a higher Q-value than the remaining actions. In games with mixed policies, the Q-values of actions that belong to the equilibrium oscillate around the same value.

We measure how often those values oscillate, and adjust our policy update based on that. To do so, we average the amount of steps taken for the maximum Q-value's action to change, and start bounding the $\pi_t(s, a)$ factor when an action has remained dominant for more than those steps. The intuition behind this is that the Q-values usually oscillate with a decreasing period $p$ as policies adjust (due to learning rates and action randomicity), and when they are oscillating, the algorithm is converging to a stochastic policy. We do not interfere with the update rule as long as we are within this interval, since we expect the dominant action to change.

If at some point, an action reveals itself as dominant for longer than $p$, the $\pi_t(s, a)$ factor is narrowed until it is a $[0.5 - n, 0.5 + n]$ factor for all actions, where $n$ is an arbitrarily small non-zero positive value. At that point, WPL adjusts probabilities at nearly the same speed for both pure and stochastic policies (which keeps its convergence properties), and no longer asymptotically converges to pure equilibrium solutions. Whenever an action is no longer dominant, the $\pi_t(s, a)$ factor is reset to its original $[0, 1]$, as the solution is once more expected to be a stochastic policy.

Formally, given the dominant action with highest Q-value $a^r_{s,t}$, at time-step $t$, with $t^r$ time-steps elapsed since the last reset (where the dominant action $a^r_{s,t}$ changed), and an expected total $p$ time-steps for the dominant action to be replaced, we can calculate a new bounded $\pi^b_t(s, a)$ factor to be within a $[f_t, 1 - f_t]$ interval by

$$f_t = \begin{cases} f_{t-1} + 0.5/p & \text{if } a^r_{s,t} = a^r_{s,t-1} \text{ and } t^r > p \\ 0 & \text{otherwise} \end{cases}, \qquad (7)$$

$$\pi^b_t(s, a) = \pi_t(s, a) * (1 - 2f_t) + f_t, \qquad (8)$$

where the constraint $f_t = [0, 0.5[$ is enforced outside the equation. We then replace Eq. 3 with

$$\forall a \in A \; \Delta_t(s, a) = \eta^\pi_t \frac{\partial V_t(s)}{\partial \pi_t(s, a)} * \begin{cases} \pi^b_t(s, a) & \text{if } \frac{\partial V_t(s)}{\partial \pi_t(s,a)} < 0 \\ 1 - (\pi^b_t(s, a)) & \text{otherwise} \end{cases}. \qquad (9)$$

To calculate $p$, in order to avoid noise and keep a stable and gradual evolution, we found that a moving average filter with 2 windows and ignoring intervals with $t^Q < \frac{p}{2}$ represented a robust approximation. Noise happens when actions have very similar Q-values, and so oscillate very quickly. This would cause $p$ to decrease to a very small value, when in fact the actions were only oscillating due to randomness in the policies. So, when the time taken for a dominant action to change is too small, in our case, smaller than half of the current $p$, we assume it

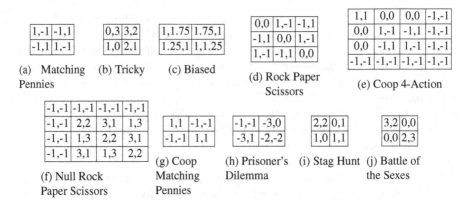

**Fig. 3.** The pay-off matrices of popular Game Theoretic 2-player games. Rows represent the actions of the first player, columns the actions of the second player, and each cell the pay-off $p_0$ of the first player and the pay-off $p_1$ of the second player in the format $p_0, p_1$.

as noise. To make $p$ change gradually, we average the previous and the new value, an approach followed in other algorithms (like CMA-ES [9]) to bind the update step. However, we don't assume this approximation to be the only solution, and many other methods (possibly problem dependent) are expected to work. The algorithm is robust to different initial values for $p$. We used the minimum value 1 in our tests, and larger values simply cause the constraint $f_t$ to change slower, leading to a more conservative initial adjustment of the update rate.

If $f_t = 0$, the algorithm is the original WPL, and this situation occurs when there is no single dominant action. In other words, when the policy should converge to a stochastic policy, WPL's behavior is kept. On the other hand, with a pure Nash equilibrium, the $\pi_t(s, a)$ factor ensures that the policy updates do not decrease as the policy approximates the limit.

Our proposal has increased the state-wise memory consumption of the original algorithm, due to keeping track of several new values per state. However, we believe that the benefits of Adjusted Bounded WPL compensate for its drawbacks, as can be seen in the following section. We published our algorithm's source code at https://github.com/bluemoon93/ABWPL.

## 4    Results

We start by comparing Adjusted Bounded WPL with the original WPL in a set of game-theoretic scenarios, and in a multi-state maze game. Then, we compare our proposal against other mixed-policy algorithms. Unless stated otherwise, plots are shown across epochs of 1000 iterations ($x$-axis), with an exploration rate $\epsilon = 0.05$, a learning rate $\eta = 0.01$, a policy learning rate $\eta^\pi = \eta/100$ and a discount factor $\gamma = 0.9$.

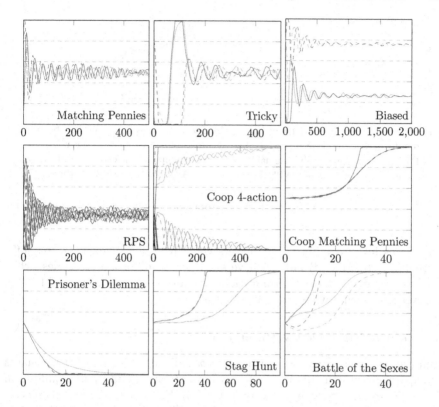

**Fig. 4.** The evolution of the probability of playing the first action ($y$-axis) by 2 players in several 2-player games. For games with more than 2 actions, the probabilities of all actions are shown. The row player (solid) starts with an initial probability $p_0 = 0.1$ or $p_0 = 0.5$, and the column player with an initial probability $q_0 = 0.8$ or $q_0 = 0.5$, depending on the game. The graphs represent the original WPL algorithm (red) and Adjusted Bounded Bounded WPL (blue). (Color figure online)

Figure 3 shows the pay-off matrices of several of these test environments, all of which are known and common benchmarks. They all have unique aspects and represent a well-rounded test suite for any MARL algorithm. Competitive Matching Pennies is a standard 2-action competitive game with balanced strategies (actions should be played with the same probabilities). The Tricky Game has the same NE, but is much harder for algorithms to achieve the it, according to the literature [7]. The Biased Game has unbalanced actions, and Rock Paper Scissors is a balanced 3-action game. The Cooperative 4-action Game is a 4-action game with a dominant action, and Null Rock Paper Scissors is a 4-action game with a dominated action (an action that should never be played, while others should have equal probabilities). Cooperative Matching Pennies is a cooperative game with 2 equilibria where agents have the same expected pay-off, Prisoner's Dilemma has a suboptimal equilibrium (not the Paretto-optimal strategy for players), Stag Hunt has a single optimal equilibrium, and Battle

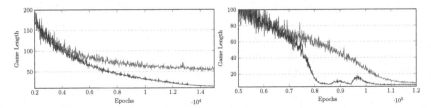

(a) The time-steps (y-axis) taken by two agents to play a complete match of Maz-eRPS. The plots represent the original WPL (red), and Adjusted Bounded WPL (blue).

(b) The time-steps (y-axis) taken by two agents to play a complete a soccer match. The plots represent the original WPL (red), and the Adjusted Bounded WPL (blue).

**Fig. 5.** The MazeRPS and Soccer Kick environments results. (Color figure online)

of the Sexes has 2 equilibria, but players will have different expected pay-offs. Figures 3(a), (b), (c), (d) and (f) have stochastic equilibrium strategies, while the remaining games have deterministic ones. Robust algorithms should be able to converge in such a wide array of scenarios.

## 4.1 Adjusted Bounded WPL and WPL

Given the previous results, we now show how Adjusted Bounded WPL behaves in comparison with the original WPL in both stochastic and pure equilibrium games. We repeat the stochastic games shown in Fig. 4, and also include several widely known environments with pure Nash Equilibria, all of which are described in Fig. 3.

We can see that Adjusted Bounded WPL matches the performance of the original WPL in all stochastic equilibrium games, and outperforms it in all pure equilibrium games. This is the expected behavior of our policy update rule, where we speed up the convergence when an action dominates others, and do

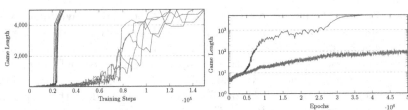

(a) The length in time-steps (y-axis) of a 3v2 Keep-Away match, over training steps (x-axis), for multiple runs. Agents cannot move in this environment, only pass the ball. The plots represent the original WPL (red), and Adjusted Bounded WPL (blue).

(b) The length in time-steps (y-axis, loga-rithmic scale) of a 3v2 Keep-Away match, over training steps (x-axis). The plots rep-resent the original WPL (red), and Adjusted Bounded WPL (blue).

**Fig. 6.** The 3v2 Keep-Away environment results. (Color figure online)

not disrupt the learning process when a stochastic equilibrium causes actions to continuously oscillate.

We now show our proposal compares against WPL in MazeRPS, a repeated game where a complete match consists on two players having to cross a labyrinth, and playing a single round of Null Rock Paper Scissors, shown in Fig. 3(e). Null Rock Paper Scissors has a positive average reward, which makes it a desirable state to reach. We also showcase a 1v1 Soccer Kick environment, where an attacker carries the ball and must feint the defender in order to score. The defender's goal is to reach the attacker and predict the feint. Players lose points as time passes, so they try to reach each other as fast as possible. When they are together, the attacker can hesitate, or shoot straight, left or right. The defender can hesitate or defend straight, left or right. A defense to the side also defends straight shots. If the attacker hesitates and the defender does not, the defender steals the ball and wins the game. As we can see in Fig. 5, Adjusted Bounded WPL outperforms the original WPL algorithm, which prematurely converges and takes much longer to complete its matches. At the end of the game, both algorithms achieve the Nash Equilibrium strategy: avoiding the first action and playing remaining actions with an equal probability for Null Rock Paper Scissors; and feinting/defending to the side, ignoring remaining actions, in the kick environment.

We also show a 3v2 keep-away soccer environment, where 3 defenders with the ball need to cooperate to keep 2 attackers from reaching it. The defenders cannot move outside specific boundaries and lose the game if attackers are close enough to steal the ball. The attackers' strategy is to have one attacker tagging one of the defenders and the other chasing the defender currently with the ball. Defenders are able to move (dribbling the ball with them) or pass the ball. Figure 6 shows the time taken for the attacking team to capture the ball in two scenarios: (a) one where agents cannot move (just pass the ball) and (b) one where movement is allowed. We can once again see how Adjusted Bounded WPL outperforms the original WPL algorithm, achieving the optimal strategy in a fraction of the training steps. The maximum game length was limited to 5000 steps.

## 4.2    Comparing Mixed-Policy Algorithms

Finally, we compare the performance of Adjusted Bounded WPL against WoLF-PHC, EMA-QL, and GIGA-WoLF, other state-of-the-art stochastic search algorithms. Because all algorithms are based in Q-learning and share similar hyper-parameters, we compare all four using the same set of hyper-parameters, where both the original WPL and these algorithms converged to the equilibrium solutions in the games shown in Fig. 7. Since the algorithms keep their own action probabilities, we simply set the minimum probability of each action to be equal to the exploration rate $\epsilon$ divided by the number of available actions. The learning rate $\eta$ affects all algorithms' Q-values in the same way, and the discount factor $\gamma$ represents how important future rewards are. For algorithms that require two policy learning rates (for both winning and losing situations), we set the losing rate $\eta_l^\pi = \eta^\pi$, and the winning rate to $\eta_w^\pi = \eta_l^\pi/2$. In conclusion, the only hyper-parameter that affects the learning process differently for each algorithm is the policy learning rate $\eta^\pi$. Therefore, we evaluate all four algorithms on several magnitudes of the policy learning rate $\eta^\pi$ in Fig. 7. We let policies converge for a number of epochs, and measure the average error of each player's policy in the final quarter of epochs, against their equilibrium policies. We can see that Adjusted Bounded WPL can still match the performance of other state-of-the-art algorithms, for a set of mixed policy games. On all games except Matching Pennies, there is a learning rate for which Adusted Bounded WPL outperforms all other algorithms.

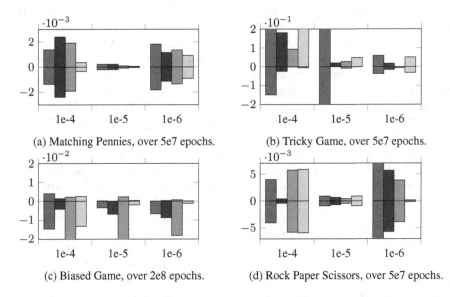

(a) Matching Pennies, over 5e7 epochs.    (b) Tricky Game, over 5e7 epochs.

(c) Biased Game, over 2e8 epochs.    (d) Rock Paper Scissors, over 5e7 epochs.

**Fig. 7.** Average error ($y$-axis) of the average reward of WoLF-PHC (red), AB-WPL (blue), EMA-QL (green), and GIGA-WoLF (yellow) against the expected returns of the Nash Equilibria. The error of player 1 is shown above the 0-line, and of player 2 below, and plots are shown over different policy learning rates ($x$-axis). (Color figure online)

Figure 8 shows the time taken for the same algorithms to converge in pure policy games. Adjusted Bounded WPL is outperformed by WoLF-PHC in most scenarios, but with very small learning rates, WoLF-PHC did not converge to a policy in a Cooperative Matching Pennies game, since it could not decide which equilibrium strategy to converge to. However, our proposal can match the remaining algorithms' performance, and is the only out of all four that converged to a correct strategy in all tested magnitudes of the policy learning rate $\eta^\pi$.

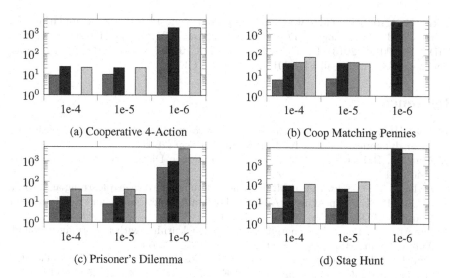

**Fig. 8.** Average time-steps taken ($y$-axis, logarithmic scale) to converge to a pure strategy, for the policies of WoLF-PHC (red), AB-WPL (blue), EMA-QL (green), GIGA-WoLF (yellow), over different policy learning rates ($x$-axis). (Color figure online)

## 5  Conclusion

Reinforcement learning problems are decision problems where agents have to learn to maximize their own pay-off based solely on rewards sampled from the environment. WPL has been shown to achieve convergence in complex 2-player games, in games with up to 100 players, and in deep learning implementations, despite having no formal analysis and proof of convergence. However, it is biased against deterministic strategies, and the policy update rate tends to zero in pure policy games. We extended WPL with a new update rule that allowed the algorithm to converge to both deterministic policies (where some actions dominate others) and stochastic policies, by regulating the policy update rate based on the expected rewards for each action. Despite the increased memory consumption, we show great improvements in the convergence speed of our new variant, and also how it fares against other state of the art algorithms. Adjusted Bounded WPL is robust to hyper-parameter changes, maintains all the convergence properties and speed of WPL in mixed policy games, and is faster in pure policy games.

An interesting work direction for the future is to research how Adjusted Bounded WPL can be extended to the deep learning paradigm, like the original WPL. Examining its behavior in scenarios with more players or other as-of-yet unreported environments may also provide further insights on ways to improve the algorithm's speed even further.

**Acknowledgments.** This work is supported by: Portuguese Foundation for Science and Technology (FCT) under grant PD/BD/113963/2015; IEETA (UID/CEC/00127/2013); LIACC (PEst-UID/CEC/00027/2013); and project EuRoC, reference 608849 from call FP7-2013-NMP-ICT-FOF.

# References

1. Abdallah, S., Lesser, V.: A multiagent reinforcement learning algorithm with non-linear dynamics. J. Artif. Intell. Res. **33**, 521–549 (2008)
2. Aumann, R.J.: Game Theory. The New Palgrave Dictionary of Economics, pp. 1–40 (2017)
3. Awheda, M.D., Schwartz, H.M.: Exponential moving average q-learning algorithm. In: 2013 IEEE Symposium on Adaptive Dynamic Programming and Reinforcement Learning (ADPRL), pp. 31–38, April 2013
4. Banerjee, B., Peng, J.: Generalized multiagent learning with performance bound. Auton. Agent. Multi-Agent Syst. **15**(3), 281–312 (2007)
5. Bianchi, R.A., Martins, M.F., Ribeiro, C.H., Costa, A.H.: Heuristically-accelerated multiagent reinforcement learning. IEEE Trans. Cybern. **44**(2), 252–265 (2014)
6. Bowling, M.: Convergence and no-regret in multiagent learning. In: Proceedings of the 17th International Conference on Neural Information Processing Systems, NIPS 2004, pp. 209–216. MIT Press, Cambridge (2004)
7. Bowling, M., Veloso, M.: Multiagent learning using a variable learning rate. Artif. Intell. **136**(2), 215–250 (2002)
8. Conitzer, V., Sandholm, T.: Awesome: a general multiagent learning algorithm that converges in self-play and learns a best response against stationary opponents. Mach. Learn. **67**(1–2), 23–43 (2007)
9. Hansen, N., Arnold, D.V., Auger, A.: Evolution strategies. In: Kacprzyk, J., Pedrycz, W. (eds.) Springer Handbook of Computational Intelligence, pp. 871–898. Springer, Heidelberg (2015). https://doi.org/10.1007/978-3-662-43505-2_44
10. Hu, J., Wellman, M.P.: Nash q-learning for general-sum stochastic games. J. Mach. Learn. Res. **4**(Nov), 1039–1069 (2003)
11. Kaisers, M., Tuyls, K.: Frequency adjusted multi-agent q-learning. In: Proceedings of the 9th International Conference on Autonomous Agents and Multiagent Systems, vol. 1, pp. 309–316. International Foundation for Autonomous Agents and Multiagent Systems (2010)
12. Russell, S.J., Norvig, P.: Artificial Intelligence: A Modern Approach. Pearson Education Limited, Malaysia (2016)
13. Simões, D., Lau, N., Reis, L.P.: Mixed-policy asynchronous deep q-learning. In: Ollero, A., Sanfeliu, A., Montano, L., Lau, N., Cardeira, C. (eds.) ROBOT 2017. AISC, vol. 694, pp. 129–140. Springer, Cham (2018). https://doi.org/10.1007/978-3-319-70836-2_11
14. Xi, L., Yu, T., Yang, B., Zhang, X.: A novel multi-agent decentralized win or learn fast policy hill-climbing with eligibility trace algorithm for smart generation control of interconnected complex power grids. Energy Convers. Manag. **103**, 82–93 (2015)
15. Zhang, C., Lesser, V.: Multi-agent learning with policy prediction. In: Proceedings of the Twenty-Fourth AAAI Conference on Artificial Intelligence, AAAI 2010, pp. 927–934. AAAI Press (2010)
16. Zhang, Z., Zhao, D., Gao, J., Wang, D., Dai, Y.: FMRQ–a multiagent reinforcement learning algorithm for fully cooperative tasks. IEEE Trans. Cybern. **47**(6), 1367–1379 (2017)

# Towards Real-Time Ball Localization Using CNNs

Daniel Speck[(✉)], Marc Bestmann, and Pablo Barros

Department of Informatics, University of Hamburg, Vogt-Koelln-Strasse 30,
22527 Hamburg, Germany
{2speck,bestmann,barros}@informatik.uni-hamburg.de

**Abstract.** Convolutional Neural Networks (CNNs) have shown promising results for various computer vision tasks. Despite their success, localizing the ball in real-world RoboCup Soccer scenes is still challenging. Especially considering real-time requirements and the limited computing power of humanoid robots. Another important reason is the lack of training and test data as well as baseline models to start with or compare to. In this paper, we propose a state-of-the-art ball detection model and make our training (over 35k images) and test (over 2k images) data sets publicly available.

**Keywords:** RoboCup · Deep learning · Dataset · Ball detection · Ball localization · Fully convolutional neural network · TensorFlow

## 1 Introduction

Ball localization is one of the essential skills in RoboCup Soccer. It has to be precise for close balls to allow the robot to position itself for example to shoot the ball, but it also has to be able to detect balls that are several meters away. The latter will become more difficult in 2020 when the playfield size will be doubled [6]. Additionally, it has to perform on the limited hardware of a humanoid robot in real-time, while still leaving resources for the other tasks of the robot.

Many approaches using neural networks were made since a change in the rules introduced multi-colored balls. Often classifiers are used to detect if a region of interest (ROI) contains a ball [8,10]. To the best of our knowledge, one of the first approaches working on full-scale raw images in RoboCup was proposed by us in RoboCup 2016, Leipzig [13]. It was trained on 1,080 training and 80 test images. The network's output consists of probability distributions that get combined to form a heatmap showing the likelihood of a pixel being part of a ball. While this showed promising results, the runtime performance of the network was too slow to be used on non-GPU ARM hardware robots during a game.

Schnekenburger et al. followed the same approach of taking the full image as input but used an FCCN [12]. This network was only trained on the center points of objects using 2,150 training and 250 test images. It was able to run in

© Springer Nature Switzerland AG 2019
D. Holz et al. (Eds.): RoboCup 2018, LNAI 11374, pp. 337–348, 2019.
https://doi.org/10.1007/978-3-030-27544-0_28

real-time, but the used robot has significantly more computational power. We present a model that is able to run on an NVIDIA Jetson TX2, a hardware that is commonly used in the Humanoid Kid- and Teen-Size League. We train this architecture on 35,327 images and have 2,177 test images for evaluation.

We would like to contribute to the community and support the development of deep learning ball detection architectures. Therefore, we make our training and test datasets publicly available and also share our baseline architectures. This allows benchmarking and comparison of different approaches as well as an easy access to high-quality training data which is especially difficult for new teams.

The remainder of this paper is structured as follows: First, the data sets, as well as the metrics for measuring the detection quality are presented in Sect. 2. Two models for locating balls are then presented in Sect. 3. The results are afterward presented in Sect. 4 and discussed in Sect. 5.

## 2   Hamburg Bit-Bots Ball Dataset 2018

We propose the Hamburg Bit-Bots Ball Dataset 2018. All images and our models have been made public by us to encourage further scientific advances. The data can be accessed via our website[1]. The image sets can also be downloaded separately from our teams profile page on our Imagetagger[2] and the models are accessible at the corresponding GitHub repository[3]. We hope this supports the development and comparability of deep learning based models in RoboCup.

### 2.1   Data

The training dataset consists of 35,327 images (see Fig. 1) and the test dataset of 2,177 images. Moreover, we supply an additional dataset with images only recorded on our robot for testing purposes that consists of another 764 images. We labeled these images with bounding boxes using the Hamburg Bit-Bots Imagetagger[4], an online tool we developed for making image annotation processes easier [3]. The training dataset is split into different so-called *image sets*. Over 14,000 images are from RoboCup 2016, Leipzig, Germany and nearly 8,000 from RoboCup 2017, Nagoya, Japan, over 6,000 images from our new lab, over 5,000 images from Iran Open 2018, and around 1,000 images from our old lab (without artificial turf) in Hamburg. Hence, the training images were recorded at six different locations. To boost the diversity we recorded different types of image sets: two different games from RoboCup 2017, many different sequences (us kicking or rolling the ball), non-moving balls at different angles and positions on the playfield as well as shots taken during preparation phases. Additionally,

---

[1] https://robocup.informatik.uni-hamburg.de/en/documents/bit-bots-ball-dataset-2018/.

[2] https://imagetagger.bit-bots.de/users/team/1/.

[3] https://github.com/Daniel451/Towards-Real-Time-Ball-Localization-using-CNNs.

[4] https://imagetagger.bit-bots.de/.

**Fig. 1.** Images taken from **training dataset** including their bounding boxes (red rectangles). There are 4 different types of balls in total. Most commonly recorded ball type is the Euro 2016 ball, which was the official one in Humanoid Kid-Size League at RoboCup 2017, Nagoya, Japan. (Color figure online)

**Fig. 2.** Images taken from **test dataset**. This dataset mostly covers the Euro 2016 ball and footage recorded from an actual game of the competition in RoboCup Humanoid Kid-Size League at RoboCup 2017, Nagoya, Japan. The whole encounter's footage is just included in the test dataset. The training dataset does not include any of the images of this game. Besides, the test dataset includes another 351 images recorded by the WF Wolves team from a location that is not covered at all in the training dataset.

we have included another 14,886 negative samples, i.e. images covering the playfield, goals, a few robots, ..., but no ball, from RoboCup 2016, Leipzig, Germany, for evaluating models against false positives (Fig. 2).

## 2.2   Metrics

There are several approaches to evaluate object detection frameworks. We supply four different metrics: *Intersection over Union* (IoU; also called *Jaccard index*[5]), *precision*, *recall*, and *radius accuracy*.

---

[5] https://en.wikipedia.org/wiki/Jaccard_index.

For IoU we give the average over the whole test dataset and also the 90th and 99th percentile since the intersection for false positives or false negatives is an empty set, thus heavily affecting the total IoU over the whole dataset. Providing the 90th and 99th percentile is a better measure for the accuracy of pixel-level detection for true positives.

For precision and recall we measure true positives (TP), false positives (FP), and false negatives (FN) with strong restrictions: if the models output contains multiple balls, we only extract the prediction with the highest activation. The center of this predicted ball cluster has to be within the ground truth, i.e. within the original label (ball pixels), to be counted as a TP. Effectively this means that at least 50% of such a predicted ball's pixels have to intersect with the ground truth ball label, otherwise it is counted as FP. If no significant cluster can be found in the model's output, then it is counted as a FN.

The fourth metric we use is radius accuracy. We propose this metric to allow to compare other models to ours that, for example, work on absolute coordinates and cannot produce pixel-level predictions to allow for IoU or other metrics. We hope this allows for comparability with as many models as possible. The radius accuracy is a radial error function. We compute the ball's predicted center and measure whether this point lies within a certain radius $r$ around the ground truth (label). Formally, the accuracy with respect to a certain radius $r$ is the sum (see Eq. 1) over a scoring function $f_r$ (see Eq. 2) that measures if the squared difference between a prediction $p$ and a label (ground truth) $l$ is lower than the square of the radius for every image.

$$accuracy_r = \frac{1}{n} * \sum_{i \in I} f_r \left( (p_i^x - l_i^x)^2 + (p_i^y - l_i^y)^2 \right). \tag{1}$$

$$f_r(x) = \begin{cases} 1 & x < r^2 \\ 0 & x \geq r^2 \end{cases} \tag{2}$$

## 3   Proposed Architecture

Two architectures for neural networks and their implementation in Tensorflow are provided and evaluated against our dataset. Other teams are welcome to use these to compare their own results or improve our proposed architectures.

### 3.1   Model 1 (CNN)

This architecture is an updated version (see Fig. 3) of the ball detection CNN model proposed by us at the 20th RoboCup International Symposium, 2016 in Leipzig [13]. Instead of soft-sign activation, we used leaky ReLU (rectified-linear units) activation, which showed reasonable results for our architecture [9]. The training procedure (teaching signal) stays the same as in the original paper.

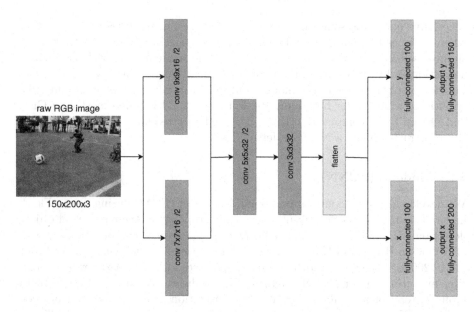

**Fig. 3.** Illustration of our proposed Model 1 (CNN). $7 \times 7$ and $9 \times 9$ convolutions are applied in parallel to the raw RGB input image. The second and third layer use $5 \times 5$ and $3 \times 3$ convolutional kernels respectively, before the information gets flattened and propagated to the fully-connected output channels to build probability distributions for x- and y-dimension. Strides of 2 are applied in the first two layers to reduce dimensionality.

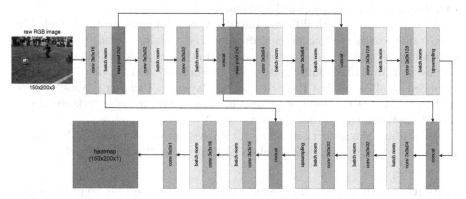

**Fig. 4.** Illustration of our proposed Model 2 (FCNN). Convolutional layers (purple), batch normalization (yellow), concatenation (so-called "skip connections"; blue), 2D upsampling (green), 2D max-pooling (red). (Color figure online)

**Evaluation.** This architecture outputs two different probability distributions that should model a normal distribution where mean $\mu$ is expected to be at the ball's center in x- (first distribution) respectively y-dimension (second distribution). We did not fully utilize the power of the probability distribution (expensive post-processing) in this paper, because this model is already similar when it comes to computational complexity compared to Model 2 (FCNN). We simply used an argmax on the output to find the single neuron with the highest activation and take this as a prediction for the ball's center in x- & y-dimension. Further post-processing of the model's output, i.e. analyzing the probability distributions, would cover better results, but also would be done mostly on CPU and use up more computation time. We tried to streamline the model to also run near real-time on a NVIDIA Jetson TX2.

## 3.2  Model 2 (FCNN)

We developed a fully-convolutional neural network (FCNN) using TensorFlow[6] inspired by the model Schnekenburger et al. proposed in their paper on object detection with the Sweaty robot [12]. Due to the limited computational power of RoboCup Humanoid Kid-Size robots, we propose a model with smaller input ($150 \times 200$ for height and width; original paper uses $512 \times 640$) to allow near real-time execution on our NVIDIA Jetson TX2 hardware. We also feed raw camera input instead of normalized images. An illustration of our model can be seen in Fig. 4. We use 2D max-pooling for dimensionality reduction and 2D bilinear up-sampling in our architecture to get a smoother heatmap as output because strided transposed convolutional layers for up-sampling led to "checkerboard artifacts" in our heatmap for some input images [2]. Xu et al. showed a thorough evaluation of activation functions, which we used as a basis and found Leaky ReLU (rectified linear units) to cover the best results for us [14]. This kind of activation function was proposed by Maas et al. [7].

We experimented with different initialization techniques for the model. The most stable results (test accuracies after finished training varied by only 0.1%) were achieved with Glorot random normal initialization for the convolutional weights and an all-zero initialization for the biases [4]. A dropout rate of 0.5 is applied to all layers but the first and last layer [5]. Padding is always set to "same", i.e. one of the padding options in TensorFlow, in order to keep dimensionality between convolutional layers.

For training the network we compute ellipses out of our bounding box labels in order to get near pixel-precise labels as training feedback for Model 2.

**Evaluation.**  To extract the ball's center we apply several steps onto the heatmap output of Model 2. At first, we apply Otsu's method to binarize and threshold the image [11]. Afterward, OpenCV's contour-finding algorithm is applied to the binary image, which will return clusters for each "hotspot" in the original heatmap. To extrapolate the most significant cluster, i.e. highest activation of the network in the heatmap, we sum up the network's original output over the indices of each cluster. This procedure extracts the "strongest"

---

[6] https://www.tensorflow.org/.

input images

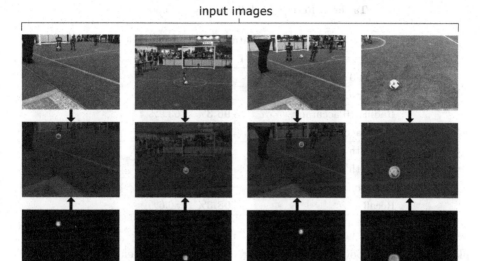

heatmaps (FCNN output)

**Fig. 5. Input images** (test set images; top), **FCNN output** (heatmaps; bottom) and **combined plot** (center) for Model 2. The interval [0.0, 1.0] is the possible range for the network's activation, hence this Figure shows that the network's neurons fire strongly for ball pixels and nearly homogeneously flat out to 0.0 otherwise.

activation in the heatmap, returning the most significant cluster of "ball pixels". Afterward, we extrapolate the center point for a cluster using OpenCV's moments function.

## 4    Experimental Results

### 4.1    Ball Localization

Table 1 shows that the fully-convolutional neural network (Model 2) has a very good ball localization quality throughout the test set, while the older model falls behind. Model 2 also delivers a reasonable performance on the robot test data set, which consists of 764 images recorded only on our robot at IRAN Open 2018. Our robot also walks and moves its camera leading to motion blur in the images.

### 4.2    False Positives

Additionally, we tested our models on a *negative* dataset from Leipzig, i.e. a dataset covering no ball at all. The dataset has 14,886 images covering different

**Table 1.** Results for full training (20 epochs).

| Metric type | Test dataset | | Robot test data |
|---|---|---|---|
| | Model 1 | Model 2 | Model 2 |
| Radius 3 accuracy | 30% | **93.3%** | 39.9% |
| Radius 5 accuracy | 47% | **95.1%** | 46.6% |
| Radius 10 accuracy | 55% | **96.3%** | 63.9% |
| IoU (Jaccard index) | - | **74.3%** | 43.9% |
| IoU 90th percentile | - | **90.6%** | 88.1% |
| IoU 99th percentile | - | **95.7%** | 93.7% |
| Precision | - | **97.9%** | 90.4% |
| Recall | - | **98.3%** | 86.6% |

playfields from RoboCup 2016, Leipzig, recorded at different angles, heights, orientations, and so forth. Considering the size and complexity of the dataset it is a significant challenge to prove a model's robustness against false positives since any detection on this dataset can be considered a false positive. For Model 1 the 99th percentile of output activation showed values of 0.6 with a standard deviation of 0.2, leading to some false positives, even with post-processing applied to the output. Model 2's 99th percentile activation was at 0.003 with a standard deviation of 0.03. Actual balls in an image produce a mean activation of 0.7 (rounded) for Model 2, hence we apply a threshold at 0.5. In our negative dataset, only 1.04% of all images produce an output >0.5. This results in 155 of 14,886 to falsely produce a positive output.

### 4.3 Hardware Benchmarks

The results for inference timings for a CPU and three different GPU types can be seen in Table 2. The NVIDIA Jetson TX2 was chosen since it is used by 7 teams [1] in HL and therefore the most used dedicated GPU. The Intel CPU is comparable to the performance of an Intel NUC which is used by 18 teams in the HL [1]. It shows that CPU inference timings per batch increase somewhat linear with batch size. Additionally, the CPU is considerably slow for many convolutional layers (which is expected, since a CPU has no specific hardware capability of speeding up these computations), rendering Model 2 more computationally expansive than Model 1 without a GPU. The GPU inference timings reveal that for larger GPUs (GTX 1080, Titan X) a mini-batch size of 1, 4 or 8 samples at once is too small to fully utilize the whole GPU. Thus, mean batch time does not increase linearly for these GPU models. Additionally, the Titan X is slightly slower than the GTX 1080 due to the 1080's higher GPU clock speeds. At training time with larger mini-batch sizes the Titan X is of course faster. The Jetson TX2 also performs noticeably well for both models. Model 1 has fewer layers (especially convolutional layers), hence it's computational complexity comes mainly through the fully-connected layers, which can be parallelized

**Table 2.** Inference timings (mean values per batch through 1,000 runs)

| Models | Hardware | GPU | Batch = 1 | Batch = 4 | | Batch = 8 | |
|--------|----------|-----|-----------|-----------|-----------|-----------|-----------|
| | | | Total | Per image | Total | Per image | Total |
| Model 1 | NVIDIA Jetson TX2 | Yes | 0.041 s | 0.014 s | 0.057 s | 0.011 s | 0.089 s |
| Model 2 | NVIDIA Jetson TX2 | Yes | 0.049 s | 0.028 s | 0.112 s | 0.023 s | 0.181 s |
| Model 1 | NVIDIA Titan X | Yes | 0.014 s | 0.004 s | 0.016 s | 0.002 s | 0.016 s |
| Model 2 | NVIDIA Titan X | Yes | 0.015 s | 0.005 s | 0.021 s | 0.004 s | 0.029 s |
| Model 1 | NVIDIA GTX 1080 | Yes | 0.010 s | 0.003 s | 0.011 s | 0.002 s | 0.012 s |
| Model 2 | NVIDIA GTX 1080 | Yes | 0.012 s | 0.005 s | 0.019 s | 0.003 s | 0.026 s |
| Model 1 | Intel Core i5 2500K | No | 0.049 s | 0.025 s | 0.098 s | 0.026 s | 0.204 s |
| Model 2 | Intel Core i5 2500K | No | 0.124 s | 0.130 s | 0.518 s | 0.136 s | 1.085 s |

on the GPU for small batch sizes. This way the mean mini-batch timings for Model 1 do not increase heavily before mini-batch sizes of 8.

## 5   Discussion

Model 1 (CNN) was mainly selected to present a comparison to recent (2016) state-of-the-art models [13] challenged with new, more complex datasets. In comparison to most publications we mainly use footage from actual competitions and not just lab environments and in contrast to Model 1's original test data we now wanted to keep in mind the pending change of the rules that will double playfield sizes. To the best of our knowledge, our training and test dataset is the largest one publicly available for RoboCup. Due to the fact that we did not randomly split train/test data, but hand-picked playfields & games, or even locations in case of German Open footage, the test data is completely novel to the network. This, including our robot test dataset from Iran Open featuring only footage recorded *on* the robot, is more challenging than other test datasets, like the one used in [13]. Hence, it was expected that Model 1 (CNN) shows a considerably lower accuracy. The model performed well on older datasets, but struggles at ball localization on full-size playfields at very high distances with completely new environments, audiences, and so forth. However, despite the increased complexity of test data, this is partly also explainable with us not utilizing the probability distribution output for x- and y-dimension, but just taking the maximum value's index of each distribution respectively. Further post-processing would definitely help to enhance Model 1's accuracy, but also greatly increase runtime performance. On the other hand, Model 1 performs better on CPUs due to its considerably lower amount of convolutional layers, which are only cheap to compute on GPUs. This emphasizes the usage of Model 1 or similar architectures for CPU-based robots, especially since post-processing of mentioned probability distributions is only greatly increasing runtime performance on comparably slow ARM-CPUs like the NVIDIA Jetson TX2. Intel NUC based robots, which are the standard for CPU-based robots, are much faster for the post-processing. Moreover, the lowest detection rates occur for distant balls (more than approx. 5 m). Hence, at least for a goalkeeper (who does not need information about balls on the enemy half of the playfield) Model 1 might be a reasonable choice for fast detection of approaching balls on CPU-based architectures.

Model 2 (FCNN) covers a very high quality in ball localization overall. We wanted to push pixel-level accuracy with this model and supplied reasonable results considering the IoU results presented in Table 1. Model 2 scored 74.3% IoU on the whole test dataset. If we factor out some false positives for which the intersection is zero, hence greatly decreasing the total IoU, we get very high values of 90.6% IoU for the 90th percentile or 95.7% for the 99th percentile. Figure 5 illustrates this pixel-level ball localization. With a precision and recall of 97.9% and 98.3% respectively the results also show that Model 2 has a very low rate of false positives and false negatives. To further present the robustness of Model 2 we additionally benchmarked the model on another 14,886 images from RoboCup 2016, Leipzig, which do not contain any ball, thus any ball detection can be considered a false positive on this dataset. Even on this dataset, the false positive rate is just above 1% in total.

However, one might argue that the test dataset is not complex enough to challenge Model 2 since it does only over three different balls and does not include many very dark images. We included a robot test dataset recorded only on a robot walking over the playfield at Iran Open 2018 (see Table 1). Although the localization quality drops Model 2 delivers a reasonable performance, sufficient for ball localization with a precision of 90.4% and a recall of 86.6%. The drop mainly occurs due to the robot's walking: this introduces motion blur that heavily affects input image quality.

Considering runtime performance on GPUs it is also worth to think about batch processing since it is easier to parallelize batches on a GPU and thus achieve a higher overall utilization of the GPU's computing power. As shown in Table 2 the efficiency per image regarding runtime performance increases with higher batch numbers. Of course, we can not infinitely increase the batch size, because of (1) VRAM limitations, (2) reaching the maximum parallelization performance of the GPU, and (3) latency. On the contrary, it has to be considered that for distant balls at least latencies do not matter, but accuracy does. If the robot always processes batches of 8 images then even if the robot is walking the ball information will be more stable due to the post-processing of the batch. The probability of 8 images being motion-blurred or covering other problems is lower than for single images.

# 6    Conclusion

We proposed a state-of-the-art deep learning architecture to detect & localize balls in complex RoboCup Humanoid Soccer scenes that is able to run in near real-time on NUC- or GPU-based robots, such as the NVIDIA Jetson TX2 based robots we use. We also offer the full training and test dataset, the robot test dataset and the additional negative dataset to test against false positives since we want to emphasize the development and comparison of deep learning architectures in RoboCup. To the best of our knowledge, our datasets are by far the largest and most complex ones publicly available in RoboCup. The results were achieved keeping the limited computational resources of robots of the Humanoid Kid-Size League in mind, thus more complex architectures might very well score even better results. However, we also wanted to push ball detection to a pixel-level localization with Model 2, which comes at the cost of needing a GPU or fast CPU. The models can train 20 full epochs ($20 \times 35{,}327$ images) in less than 4 h on an NVIDIA TITAN X GPU when combined with a parallel data pre-loading algorithm, while also evaluating the test dataset after each epoch. We use a PCI-E SSD card for storing the images to ensure fast loading speeds, but we will also supply HDF5 files that speed up loading from hard disks with the only disadvantage of a larger total file size.

# 7    Future Work

We will release new versions of the dataset each year, to include new environments from each years RoboCup competitions and to increase the difficulty of the test dataset. A large dataset with complex test data eases the transition and prevents a drop of game quality similar to the year when the multi-colored ball was introduced. The datasets also include some, although not many, blurry images. Since a game of RoboCup soccer has to be dynamic recorded images often involve motion blur from the camera itself or simply due to the robot currently walking. Another problem is that different backgrounds, especially light sources, lead to vastly different color spaces. These distortions can heavily affect detection rates of deep learning architectures because the system will focus on learning significant features for ball detection, not de-blurring kernels. We are currently working on neural network based de-noising frameworks to reduce this kind of problems.

For fast moving balls, which will become more common in the future, we will also try to combine neural architectures like the FCNN for detection in combination with fast object tracking architectures. A correlation tracker, for example, is computationally cheap and might produce reasonable results if supplied with accurate regions of interest from an FCNN.

**Acknowledgement.** We would like to thank everyone from our local RoboCup Team, the Hamburg Bit-Bots, who helped with tagging the training data. We are grateful to the NVIDIA corporation for supporting our research[7]. We used the donated NVIDIA

---

[7] https://developer.nvidia.com/academic_gpu_seeding.

Titan X (Pascal) to train our models. This research was funded by the German Research Foundation (DFG) and the National Science Foundation of China (NSFC) in project Crossmodal Learning, TRR-169.

# References

1. Humanoid league team description papers (2018). https://www.robocuphumanoid. org/hl-2018/teams/. Accessed 09 Mar 2018
2. Aitken, A., Ledig, C., Theis, L., Caballero, J., Wang, Z., Shi, W.: Checkerboard artifact free sub-pixel convolution: a note on sub-pixel convolution, resize convolution and convolution resize, July 2017. http://arxiv.org/abs/1707.02937
3. Fiedler, N., Bestmann, M., Hendrich, N.: Imagetagger: an open source online platform for collaborative image labeling. Private Communication (submitted)
4. Glorot, X., Bengio, Y.: Understanding the difficulty of training deep feedforward neural networks. In: AISTATS, vol. 9, pp. 249–256 (2010). 10.1.1.207.2059
5. Hinton, G.: Dropout: a simple way to prevent neural networks from overfitting. J. Mach. Learn. Res. (JMLR) **15**, 1929–1958 (2014)
6. Humanoid Leauge Technical Committe: Humanoid league proposed roadmap (2014). https://www.robocuphumanoid.org/wp-content/uploads/ HumanoidLeagueProposedRoadmap.pdf. Acessed 10 Apr 2018
7. Maas, A., Hannun, A., Ng, A.: Rectifier nonlinearities improve neural network acoustic models. In: ICML 2013. https://pdfs.semanticscholar.org/367f/ 2c63a6f6a10b3b64b8729d601e69337ee3cc.pdf
8. Menashe, J., et al.: Fast and precise black and white ball detection for robocup soccer. In: Akiyama, H., Obst, O., Sammut, C., Tonidandel, F. (eds.) RoboCup 2017. LNCS (LNAI), vol. 11175, pp. 45–58. Springer, Cham (2018). https://doi. org/10.1007/978-3-030-00308-1_4
9. Mishkin, D., Sergievskiy, N., Matas, J.: Systematic evaluation of CNN advances on the ImageNet, June 2016. arXiv:1606.02228
10. O'Keeffe, S., Villing, R.: A benchmark data set and evaluation of deep learning architectures for ball detection in the robocup SPL. In: Akiyama, H., Obst, O., Sammut, C., Tonidandel, F. (eds.) RoboCup 2017. LNCS (LNAI), vol. 11175, pp. 398–409. Springer, Cham (2018). https://doi.org/10.1007/978-3-030-00308-1_33
11. Otsu, N.: A threshold selection method from gray-level histograms. IEEE Trans. Syst. Man Cybern. **9**(1), 62–66 (1979). https://doi.org/10.1109/TSMC.1979. 4310076. http://ieeexplore.ieee.org/document/4310076/
12. Schnekenburger, F., Scharffenberg, M., Wülker, M., Hochberg, U., Dorer, K.: Detection and localization of features on a soccer field with feedforward fully convolutional neural networks (FCNN) for the adult-size humanoid robot sweaty. In: Proceedings of the 12th Workshop on Humanoid Soccer Robots, 17th IEEE-RAS International Conference on Humanoid Robots, pp. 1–6 (2017)
13. Speck, D., Barros, P., Weber, C., Wermter, S.: Ball localization for robocup soccer using convolutional neural networks. In: Behnke, S., Sheh, R., Sarıel, S., Lee, D.D. (eds.) RoboCup 2016. LNCS (LNAI), vol. 9776, pp. 19–30. Springer, Cham (2017). https://doi.org/10.1007/978-3-319-68792-6_2
14. Xu, B., Wang, N., Chen, T., Li, M.: Empirical evaluation of rectified activations in convolutional network, May 2015. arXiv:1505.00853

# Deep Learning for Semantic Segmentation on Minimal Hardware

Sander G. van Dijk$^{(\boxtimes)}$ (iD) and Marcus M. Scheunemann (iD)

University of Hertfordshire, Hertfordshire AL10 9AB, UK
sgvandijk@gmail.com

**Abstract.** Deep learning has revolutionised many fields, but it is still challenging to transfer its success to small mobile robots with minimal hardware. Specifically, some work has been done to this effect in the RoboCup humanoid football domain, but results that are performant and efficient and still generally applicable outside of this domain are lacking. We propose an approach conceptually different from those taken previously. It is based on semantic segmentation and does achieve these desired properties. In detail, it is being able to process full VGA images in real-time on a low-power mobile processor. It can further handle multiple image dimensions without retraining, it does not require specific domain knowledge to achieve a high frame rate and it is applicable on a minimal mobile hardware.

**Keywords:** Deep learning · Semantic segmentation · Mobile robotics · Computer vision · Minimal hardware

## 1 Introduction

Deep learning (DL) has greatly accelerated progress in many areas of artificial intelligence (AI) and machine learning. Several breakthrough ideas and methods, combined with the availability of large amounts of data and computation power, have lifted classical artificial neural networks (ANNs) to new heights in natural language processing, time series modelling and advanced computer vision problems [11]. For computer vision in particular, networks using convolution operations, i.e., *Convolutional Neural Networks* (CNNs), have had great success.

Many of these successful applications of DL rely on cutting edge computation hardware, specifically high-end GPU processors, sometimes in clusters of dozens to hundreds of machines [15]. Low-power robots, such as the robotic footballers participating in RoboCup, are not able to carry such hardware. It is not a surprise that the uptake of DL in the domain of humanoid robotic football has lagged behind. Some demonstrations of its use became available recently [1,5,8,14,16]. However, as we will discuss in the next section, these applications are so far rather limited; either in terms of performance or in terms of their generalisability for areas other than RoboCup.

© Springer Nature Switzerland AG 2019
D. Holz et al. (Eds.): RoboCup 2018, LNAI 11374, pp. 349–361, 2019.
https://doi.org/10.1007/978-3-030-27544-0_29

In this paper, we will address these issues and present a DL framework that achieves high accuracy, is more generally applicable and still runs at a usable frame rate on minimal hardware.

The necessary conceptual switch and main driver behind these results is to apply DL to the direct semantic segmentation of camera images, in contrast to most previous work in the humanoid robotic football domain that has applied it to the final object detection or recognition problem. Semantic segmentation is the task of assigning a class label to each separate pixel in an image, in contrast to predicting a single output for an image as a whole, or some sub-region of interest. There are three primary reasons why this approach is attractive.

Firstly, semantic segmentation networks can be significantly smaller in terms of learnable weights than other network types. The number of weights in a convolution layer is reduced significantly compared to the fully connected layers of classical ANNs, by 'reusing' filter weights as they slide over an image. However, most image classification or object detection networks still need to convert a 2D representation into a single output, for which they do use fully connected layers on top of the efficient convolution layers. The number of weights of fully connected layers is quadratic in their size, which means they can be responsible for a major part of the computational complexity of the network. Semantic segmentation networks on the other hand typically only have convolution layers—they are *Fully Convolutional Networks* (FCNs)—and so do away with fully connected ones, and the number of their weights only grows linearly with the number of layers used.

Secondly, the fully convolutional nature also ensures that the network is independent of image resolution. The input resolution of a network with a fully connected output layer is fixed by the number of weights in that layer. Such a network, trained on data of those dimensions, cannot readily be reused on data of differing sizes; the user will have to crop or rescale the input data, or retrain new fully connected layers of the appropriate size. Convolution operations on the other hand are agnostic of input dimensions, so a fully convolutional network can be used at any input resolution[1]. This provides very useful opportunities. For example, if a known object is tracked, or an object is known to be close to the camera, the algorithm allows for an on-demand up and down scaling of vision effort. Instead of processing a complete camera frame when searching for such an aforementioned object, only an image subset or a downscaled version of a camera frame is processed.

Finally, semantic segmentation fits in directly with many popular vision pipelines used currently in the RoboCup football domain. Historically, the domain consisted of clearly colour coded concepts: green field, orange ball, yellow/blue goalposts. Commonly a lookup-table based approach is used to label each pixel separately, after which fast specialised connected component, scanning, or integral image methods are applied to detect and localise all relevant objects. Over the years the scenario has developed to be more challenging (e.g.,

---

[1] Given that the input dimensions are not so small that any down-sampling operations, e.g. max pooling, would reduce the resolution to nil.

natural light, limited colours) and unstructured, making the lookup-table methods less feasible. Using a semantic segmentation CNN that can learn to use more complex features would allow the simple replacement of these methods and still reuse all highly optimised algorithms of the existing vision pipeline.

## 2  Related Work

The RoboCup domain offers a long history in research on efficient, practical computer vision methods; already the very first RoboCup symposium in 1997 dealt with "Real-Time Vision Processing for a Soccer Playing Mobile Robot" [4], and the 2016 Kid-Size champions still heavily relied on optimisations, e.g., regions of interest and downscaled images, to make vision viable [2]. To ensure keeping track of and participating in a dynamic game of football, the robots ideally should process at least 20 to 30 fps. However, they only have very limited energy resources yielding minimal computational power for achieving that.

Recent developments in low-power, mobile computational platforms, as well as in efficient deep learning, have now made it possible to adopt DL in small mobile robots. One of the first works on DL in the RoboCup domain presented a CNN trained to separately predict the $x$ and $y$ coordinates of a ball in a camera image [16]. Although this network performed relatively well, it could only process a few images per second and operated on heavily downscaled images. At the same time other authors were able to create a CNN-based system that could recognise Nao robots within milliseconds [1]. However, this method relied on a region proposal preprocessing method very specific to RoboCup. This work was later generalised to a different RoboCup league [10], but still relies on the specifically colour-coded nature of the robot football pitch. Instead, the approach taken in this paper is to use CNNs as the very first processing step, and only *after* that step apply domain specific algorithms. This same approach was taken in a recent work very much related to ours [14], but for large humanoid robots with powerful hardware that cannot feasibly be used by smaller size mobile robots, such as Kid-Size humanoids or perhaps drones.

In recent years there has been a growing body of work on creating small, but capable networks, for enabling their use on more restricted hardware. One approach is to try to minimise the complexity of convolutions by first applying a 'bottleneck' $1 \times 1$ convolution layer that reduces the number of features used in the actual $N \times N$ convolution. This idea originated with ResNet [7] to help make training of very deep networks feasible, but at the same time can also reduce run time costs. For networks of the sizes used in this paper however, the computational cost of a bottleneck layer outweighed the benefit of a reduced number of features in the subsequent layer. A different idea is to discretise quantities used in the networks, with the idea that integer operations can be much more efficient in low-end computation devices. The culmination of this idea is in network designs such as XNOR-nets [12] that use very basic and fast bitwise operations during prediction, and DoReFa-nets [17] that further extend this idea to training. We do not study such binary nets here, as at the moment there is

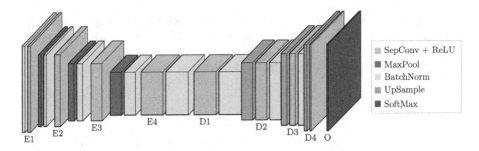

**Fig. 1.** The architecture of the networks used consists of a series of fully convolutonal encoding (E1–E4) and decoding (D1–D4) steps. A pixelwise softmax output layer provides the final classifications. Network variations differ in the actual number of encoding and decoding steps used, filter size and initial depth, filter depth multiplication factor and convolution stride.

no implementation available of the operators required by such networks for the most popular deep learning libraries, and we are interested in systems that can be easily adapted and implemented by the reader using such libraries.

Instead, the optimisations applied to our networks are very much motivated by MobileNets [9]. Most notably, we utilise *depthwise separable convolutions* to significantly reduce the computational complexity of our segmentation networks. Such convolutions split a regular convolution into a filter and a combination step: first a separate 2D filter is applied to each input channel, after which a $1 \times 1$ convolution is applied to combine the results of these features. This can be seen as a factorisation of a full convolution that reduces the computational cost by a factor of $\frac{1}{N} + \frac{1}{K^2}$, where $N$ is the number of output features and $K$ the kernel size. Not all convolutions can be factorised like this, so separable convolutions have less expressive power, but the results of the original MobileNets and those reported here show they can still perform at high accuracy.

## 3   Network Architecture

As mentioned before, our approach is based on fully convolutional semantic segmentation networks. The main structure of our networks is similar to popular encoder-decoder networks, such as U-Net [13] and SegNet [3], mainly following the latter. In such networks, a first series of convolution layers encode the input into successively lower resolution but higher dimensional feature maps, after which a second series of layers decode these maps into a full-resolution pixelwise classification. This architecture is shown in Fig. 1.

SegNet and U-Net both have the property that some information from the encoder layers are fed into the respective decoder layers of the same size, either in terms of maxpooling indices, or full feature maps. This helps overcoming the loss of fine detail caused by the resolution reduction along the way. As good performance is still possible without these connections, we do not use those here. They in fact introduce a significant increase in computation load on our hardware, due to having to combine tensors in possibly significantly different memory locations.

Another modification is to use depthwise separable convolution, as introduced by MobileNets [9], as a much more efficient alternative to full 3D convolution. This is one of the major contributions to efficiency of our networks, without significantly decreasing their performance.

To study the trade-off between network minimalism, efficiency and performance, we create, train and evaluate a number of varieties of the above network, with different combinations of the following parameter values:

1. **Number of Layers (L)**—$L \in \{3, 4\}$, the number of encoding and decoding layers. We always use the same number of encoding and decoding layers.
2. **Number of Filters (F)**—$F \in \{3, 4, 5\}$, the number of filters used in the first encoding layer.
3. **Filter Multiplier (M)**—$M \in \{1.25, 1.5, 2\}$, the factor by which the number of filters increases for each subsequent encoding layer, and decreases for each subsequent decoding layer.
4. **Convolution Stride (S)**—$S \in \{1, 2\}$, the stride used in each convolution layer.

Larger and smaller values for these parameters have been tried out, but we only report those here that resulted in networks that were able to learn the provided task to some degree, but were light enough to be run on the minimal test hardware. Specific instantiations will be denoted with $L_x F_y M_z S_w$ with parameter values filled into the place holders. For instance, $L_3 F_4 M_{1.25} S_2$ is the network with 3 encoding and decoding layers, 4 features in the first feature map, a multiplier of 1.25 (resulting in 4, 5 and 6 features in each subsequent layer) and a stride of 1. Not all combinations are valid: a combination of $L = 4$ and $S = 2$ would result in invalid feature map sizes given our input of $640 \times 480$ images. The total number of network types then is 27. Finally, all convolution layers use $3 \times 3$ filters, padding to have output size the same as input size and no bias.

## 4   Experiments

The networks described in the previous section are trained to segment ball pixels in images taken by a Kid-Size RoboCup robot on a competition pitch. Specifically, the image set `bitbots-set00-04` from the Bit-Bots' Imagetagger[2] was used. It contains 1000 images[3] with 1003 bounding box ball annotations. To derive the target pixel label masks for training the networks, the rectangular annotations are converted to filled ellipsoids. Figure 2 shows an example of the input images and targets.

We use the TensorFlow library to construct, train and run the networks. The networks are trained on an NVIDIA GeForce GTX 1080-ti GPU, with a

---

[2] https://imagetagger.bit-bots.de/images/imageset/12/.
[3] Images taken at the 2016 world championship in Leipzig, Germany.

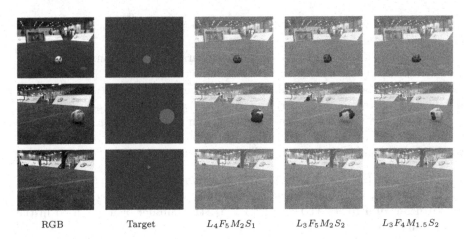

RGB    Target    $L_4 F_5 M_2 S_1$    $L_3 F_5 M_2 S_2$    $L_3 F_4 M_{1.5} S_2$

**Fig. 2.** Examples of input, target and segmentation outputs. The outputs are respectively of the best stride 1 network, the best stride 2 network, and the second best stride 2 network that achieves 20 frames per second on QVGA images.

categorical cross-entropy loss function using stochastic gradient decent with a starting learning rate of 0.1, a decay factor of 0.004 and a momentum of 0.9. The dataset is split in a training set of 750 images, a validation set of 150 and a test set of 100 images. The sets are augmented to double their size by including all horizontally mirrored images. During training, a batch size of 10 images is used. Networks are trained for 25 epochs.

For testing the performance of the networks we map the class probabilities from the softmax output to discrete class labels and use this to calculate the commonly used *Intersection over Union* (IoU) score as $\frac{TP}{TP+FP+FN}$, where $TP$ is the number of true positive ball pixels, $FP$ the number of false positives and $FN$ the number of false negatives. Due to the extreme class imbalance, the networks hardly ever predict the probability of a pixel being part of a ball, $P(B)$, to be above 0.5. This means that if we use the *most probable* class as final output, the IoU score often is 0, even though the networks do learn to assign relatively higher probability at the right pixels. Instead we find the threshold $\theta^*$ for $P(B)$ that results in the best IoU score for each trained network.

Finally, since the original goal is to develop networks that can run on minimal hardware, the networks are run and timed on such hardware, belonging to a Kid-Size humanoid football robot, namely an Odroid-XU4. This device is based on a Samsung Exynos 5422 Cortex-A15 with 2 GHz and a Cortex-A7 Octa core CPU, which is the same as used in some 2015 model flagship smartphones. Before running the networks, they are optimised using TensorFlow's *Graph Transform* tool, which is able to merge several operations, such as batch normalisation, into more efficient ones. The test program and TensorFlow library are compiled with all standard optimisation flags for the ARM Neon platform. We time the networks both on full $640 \times 480$ images and on $320 \times 256$ images.

# 5    Results

We firstly evaluate the performance of semantic segmentation networks trained for the official RoboCup ball. We compare the performance and runtime of the different network instantiations with each other, as well as to a baseline segmentation method. This method is based on a popular fast *lookup table* (LUT) method, where the table directly maps pixel values to object classes. To create the table, we train a *Support Vector Machine* (SVM) on the same set as the CNNs to classify pixels. More complex and performant methods may be chosen, perhaps specifically for the robot football scenario, however we selected this method to reflect the same workflow of training a single model on simple pixel data, without injecting domain specific knowledge. We did improve performance by using input in HSV colour space and applying grid search to optimise its hyper parameters.

Secondly, we extend the binary case and train the networks for balls and goal posts, and compare the network performance with the binary segmentation.

## 5.1    Binary Segmentation

We first analyse the segmentation quality of the set of networks and the influence of their parameters on their performance. The best network is $L_4F_5M_2S_1$ with a best IoU of 0.804. As may be expected, this is the one with the most layers, most filters, highest multiplication factor and densest stride. The least performant network is one of the simplest in terms of layers and features: $L_3F_3M_{1.25}S_1$ with a best IoU of 0.085. Perhaps surprisingly the version of that network with stride 2 manages to perform better, with a score of 0.39. Figure 3 shows the distributions of performance over networks with the same values for each parameter. One can see that overall more complex networks score higher, but that the median network with stride 2 performs better than the median with stride 1.

Figure 4 compares the runtime and IoU scores for all networks. The data points are grouped by stride, resulting in clearly distinct clusters: as expected the networks with stride 2 have a significantly lower runtime requirement. The timings run from 121 to 397 ms per full $640 \times 480$ resolution frame, which is equivalent to approximately 8 and 2.5 frames per second, respectively.

The best performing network in terms of IoU is also the least efficient one, but the second best is a full 74 ms faster with a drop in IoU of only 0.003. The linear fits show that there is indeed a trend within each cluster of better performance given the runtime, but it is clear that this is not generally the case: networks with similar runtimes can vary greatly in achieved performance.

The SVM-based LUT method, though being significantly faster, scores well below most networks, with an IoU of 0.085. This is because such a pixel-by-pixel method does not consider the surrounding area and thus has no way to discern pixels with similar colours, resulting in many false positives for pixels that have colours that are also found in the ball. In contrast, the CNNs can perform much more informed classification by utilising the receptive field around each pixel.

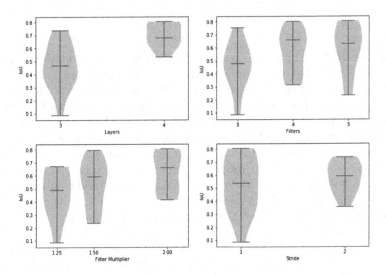

**Fig. 3.** Performance distributions for each network parameter. Horizontal bars show the minimum, median and maximum scores. The lighter area indicates the distribution over the scores through a kernel-density estimation.

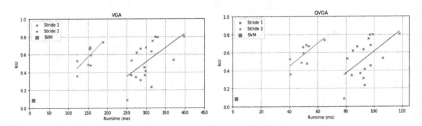

**Fig. 4.** IoU against runtime per image. The mean of the runtime is taken over 100 iterations. Results for networks with stride 1 and stride 2 are split and plotted with blue crosses and orange circles respectively. Additionally, for each group the linear fit to the data is shown. The baseline score of the SVM is marked as a green square. Left: Full VGA ($640 \times 480$), right: QVGA ($320 \times 256$); note the different timescales. (Color figure online)

From this figure we can conclude the same as from Fig. 3, that introducing a stride of 2 does not significantly reduce performance, but with the addition that it does make the network run significantly faster. The best network with stride 2, $L_3F_5M_2S_2$, has an IoU of only 0.066 less than the best network (a drop of just 8%), but runs over twice as fast, at more than 5 frames per second. On the lower resolution of $320 \times 256$ the best stride 2 networks achieve frame rates of 15 to 20 frames per second. Table 1 lists the results for all networks.

**Table 1.** Segmentation scores and runtimes obtained by networks

| Layers | Filters | Mult | Stride | $\theta^*$ | IoU | Time (ms) | |
|---|---|---|---|---|---|---|---|
| | | | | | | 640 × 480 | 320 × 256 |
| 3 | 3 | 1.25 | 1 | 0.07 | 0.086 | 250 | 78 |
| 3 | 3 | 1.25 | 2 | 0.07 | 0.356 | 121 | 40 |
| 3 | 3 | 1.5 | 1 | 0.30 | 0.366 | 261 | 79 |
| 3 | 3 | 1.5 | 2 | 0.25 | 0.529 | 121 | 40 |
| 3 | 3 | 2 | 1 | 0.33 | 0.456 | 295 | 97 |
| 3 | 3 | 2 | 2 | 0.31 | 0.478 | 156 | 52 |
| 3 | 4 | 1.25 | 1 | 0.23 | 0.343 | 273 | 84 |
| 3 | 4 | 1.25 | 2 | 0.31 | 0.487 | 149 | 48 |
| 3 | 4 | 1.5 | 1 | 0.16 | 0.313 | 285 | 92 |
| 3 | 4 | 1.5 | 2 | 0.28 | 0.682 | 155 | 51 |
| 3 | 4 | 2 | 1 | 0.31 | 0.413 | 297 | 93 |
| 3 | 4 | 2 | 2 | 0.26 | 0.660 | 154 | 49 |
| 3 | 5 | 1.25 | 1 | 0.22 | 0.365 | 296 | 90 |
| 3 | 5 | 1.25 | 2 | 0.25 | 0.671 | 155 | 53 |
| 3 | 5 | 1.5 | 1 | 0.49 | 0.233 | 312 | 93 |
| 3 | 5 | 1.5 | 2 | 0.25 | 0.590 | 156 | 49 |
| 3 | 5 | 2 | 1 | 0.42 | 0.538 | 370 | 106 |
| 3 | 5 | 2 | 2 | 0.24 | **0.738** | 188 | 64 |
| 4 | 3 | 1.25 | 1 | 0.43 | 0.531 | 262 | 80 |
| 4 | 3 | 1.5 | 1 | 0.39 | 0.620 | 274 | 84 |
| 4 | 3 | 2 | 1 | 0.49 | 0.754 | 316 | 96 |
| 4 | 4 | 1.25 | 1 | 0.50 | 0.666 | 285 | 87 |
| 4 | 4 | 1.5 | 1 | 0.23 | 0.678 | 299 | 97 |
| 4 | 4 | 2 | 1 | 0.36 | 0.801 | 323 | 98 |
| 4 | 5 | 1.25 | 1 | 0.74 | 0.632 | 313 | 92 |
| 4 | 5 | 1.5 | 1 | 0.41 | 0.794 | 329 | 96 |
| 4 | 5 | 2 | 1 | 0.46 | **0.804** | 397 | 117 |
| SVM | | | | | 0.085 | 10 | 3 |

## 5.2 Multi-class Segmentation

Binary classification is too limited for robotic football, or other real world scenarios. To study the more general usability of our method, we extend the binary-
class segmentation case from Sect. 5.1. The same dataset as before is used, but
with additionally goalposts annotated as a third class. We selected the best
stride 1 and best stride 2 networks to train. These two networks are kept the
same, except for an additional channel added to the last decoding layer and to
the softmax layer.

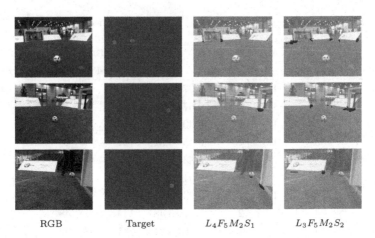

RGB          Target          $L_4F_5M_2S_1$          $L_3F_5M_2S_2$

**Fig. 5.** Examples of input, target and segmentation outputs for goalposts for the two trained networks.

We found it to be difficult for the networks to successfully learn to segment the full goalpost, not being able to discern higher sections above the field edge from parts of the background. Combined with the fact that the robots typically use points on the ground, as they are able to better judge their distance, we select the bottom of the goalposts by labelling a circle with a radius of 20 pixels in the target output where the goalposts touch the field in the images.

Because of the additional difficulty of learning features for an extra class, the IoU score for the ball class dropped slightly for both networks: to 0.754 for $L_4F_5M_2S_1$ and to 0.708 for $L_3F_5M_2S_2$, compared to 0.804 and 0.738 in the binary task. The scores reached for the goalpost class were 0.273 and 0.102 respectively. Although this does not reach the same level as for the ball class, the networks are still able to mark out the bottom of the goal posts in the examples shown in Fig. 5. Because only some additional operations in the last layers, the run times are comparable to the binary equivalents: 414 and 196 ms.

The worse scores on the goalposts are mostly due to false positives, either marking too large an area or mislabelling other objects, especially in the case of the stride 2 network. Several reasons contribute to this. Firstly, the data used is typical for an image sequence of a robot playing a game of football, where it most of the time is focused on the ball. This results in goals being less often visible, and thus in the data being unbalanced: at least one ball is visible in all 1000 images, whereas at least one goal post is visible in only 408 images. Secondly, goal posts are less feature-rich, so more difficult to discern from other objects. Finally, our annotation method does not mark a well-distinguished area, making it harder for the networks to predict its exact shape. Further research is required to alleviate these issues and improve performance, however the results obtained here provide evidence that our approach can handle multi-class segmentation with only little performance reduction.

# 6  Conclusions

We have developed a minimal deep learning semantic segmentation architecture to be run on minimal hardware. We have shown that such a network can achieve good performance in segmenting the ball, and show promising results for additionally detecting goalposts, in a RoboCup environment with a useful frame rate. Table 2 lists the resolutions and frame rates reported by other authors alongside ours. It must be noted that a direct comparison is difficult, because of the different outputs of the used CNNs and the different robot platforms, but our approach is the only one that has all of the following properties:

– Processes full VGA images at 5 fps and QVGA at 15 to 20 fps[4]
– Can handle multiple image dimensions without retraining
– Does not require task specific knowledge to achieve high frame rate
– Achieves all this on minimal mobile hardware

For achieving full object localisation as given by the other solutions, additional steps are still required. However, because the output of the semantic segmentation is in the same form as a lookup table based labelling approach, any already existing methods built on top of such a method can directly be reused. For instance, an efficient—and still task agnostic—connected component based method previously developed by us readily fits onto the architecture outlined here and performs the final object detection step within only 1 to 2 ms.

**Table 2.** Reported resolutions and frame rate of DL application in RoboCup domain

|  | Resolution | FPS | Notes |
|---|---|---|---|
| Speck et al. [16] | 200 × 150 | 3 | Predict separate ball x and y |
| Albani et al. [1] | N/A | 11–22 | Task dependent region proposal |
| Cruz et al. [5] | 24 × 24 | 440 | Task dependent region proposal |
| Javadi et al. [10] | N/A | 240 | No loss: 6 fps; task dependent |
| Da Silva et al. [6] | 110 × 110 | 8 | Predict end-to-end desired action |
| Hess et al. [8] | 32 × 32 | 50 | Focus on generation of training data |
| Schnekenburger et al. [14] | 640 × 512 | 111 | GTX-760 GPU; 19 fps on i7 CPU |
| Ours | 640 × 480 | 5 | $L_3F_5M_2S_2$ |
|  | 320 × 256 | 15 | $L_3F_5M_2S_2$; $L_3F_4M_{1.5}S_2$: 20 fps |

By delaying the use of task dependent methods, one actually has an opportunity to optimise the segmentation output for such methods, by varying the threshold used to determine the final class pixels. For specific use cases it may be desirable to choose a threshold that represents a preference for either high true positive rate (recall), e.g. when a robot's vision system requires complete

---

[4] Actually a resolution slightly larger than QVGA is used, as the stride 2 networks require dimensions that are multiples of 32.

segmentation of the ball and/or it has good false-positive filtering algorithms, or for low false positive rate (fall-out), e.g., when it can work well with only partly segmented balls, but struggles with too many false positives.

# References

1. Albani, D., Youssef, A., Suriani, V., Nardi, D., Bloisi, D.D.: A deep learning approach for object recognition with NAO soccer robots. In: Behnke, S., Sheh, R., Sarıel, S., Lee, D.D. (eds.) RoboCup 2016. LNCS (LNAI), vol. 9776, pp. 392–403. Springer, Cham (2017). https://doi.org/10.1007/978-3-319-68792-6_33
2. Allali, J., et al.: Rhoban football club: RoboCup humanoid kid-size 2016 champion team paper. In: Behnke, S., Sheh, R., Sarıel, S., Lee, D.D. (eds.) RoboCup 2016. LNCS (LNAI), vol. 9776, pp. 491–502. Springer, Cham (2017). https://doi.org/10.1007/978-3-319-68792-6_41
3. Badrinarayanan, V., Kendall, A., Cipolla, R.: SegNet: a deep convolutional encoder-decoder architecture for image segmentation. IEEE Trans. Pattern Anal. Mach. Intell. **39**(12), 2481–2495 (2017)
4. Cheng, G., Zelinsky, A.: Real-time vision processing for a soccer playing mobile robot. In: Kitano, H. (ed.) RoboCup 1997. LNCS, vol. 1395, pp. 144–155. Springer, Heidelberg (1998). https://doi.org/10.1007/3-540-64473-3_56
5. Cruz, N., Lobos-Tsunekawa, K., Ruiz-del-Solar, J.: Using convolutional neural networks in robots with limited computational resources: detecting NAO robots while playing soccer. In: Akiyama, H., Obst, O., Sammut, C., Tonidandel, F. (eds.) RoboCup 2017. LNCS (LNAI), vol. 11175, pp. 19–30. Springer, Cham (2018). https://doi.org/10.1007/978-3-030-00308-1_2
6. Da Silva, I.J., Vilao, C.O., Costa, A.H., Bianchi, R.A.: Towards robotic cognition using deep neural network applied in a goalkeeper robot. In: 2017 Latin American Robotics Symposium (LARS) and 2017 Brazilian Symposium on Robotics (SBR), pp. 1–6. IEEE (2017)
7. He, K., Zhang, X., Ren, S., Sun, J.: Deep residual learning for image recognition. In: Proceedings of the IEEE Conference on Computer Vision and Pattern Recognition, pp. 770–778 (2016)
8. Hess, T., Mundt, M., Weis, T., Ramesh, V.: Large-scale stochastic scene generation and semantic annotation for deep convolutional neural network training in the RoboCup SPL. In: Akiyama, H., Obst, O., Sammut, C., Tonidandel, F. (eds.) RoboCup 2017. LNCS (LNAI), vol. 11175, pp. 33–44. Springer, Cham (2018). https://doi.org/10.1007/978-3-030-00308-1_3
9. Howard, A.G., et al.: MobileNets: efficient convolutional neural networks for mobile vision applications. arXiv preprint arXiv:1704.04861 (2017)
10. Javadi, M., Azar, S.M., Azami, S., Ghidary, S.S., Sadeghnejad, S., Baltes, J.: Humanoid robot detection using deep learning: a speed-accuracy tradeoff. In: Akiyama, H., Obst, O., Sammut, C., Tonidandel, F. (eds.) RoboCup 2017. LNCS (LNAI), vol. 11175, pp. 338–349. Springer, Cham (2018). https://doi.org/10.1007/978-3-030-00308-1_28
11. LeCun, Y., Bengio, Y., Hinton, G.: Deep learning. Nature **521**(7553), 436 (2015)
12. Rastegari, M., Ordonez, V., Redmon, J., Farhadi, A.: XNOR-Net: imagenet classification using binary convolutional neural networks. In: Leibe, B., Matas, J., Sebe, N., Welling, M. (eds.) ECCV 2016. LNCS, vol. 9908, pp. 525–542. Springer, Cham (2016). https://doi.org/10.1007/978-3-319-46493-0_32

13. Ronneberger, O., Fischer, P., Brox, T.: U-Net: convolutional networks for biomedical image segmentation. In: Navab, N., Hornegger, J., Wells, W.M., Frangi, A.F. (eds.) MICCAI 2015. LNCS, vol. 9351, pp. 234–241. Springer, Cham (2015). https://doi.org/10.1007/978-3-319-24574-4_28

14. Schnekenburger, F., Scharffenberg, M., Wülker, M., Hochberg, U., Dorer, K.: Detection and localization of features on a soccer field with feedforward fully convolutional neural networks (FCNN) for the adult-size humanoid robot sweaty. In: Proceedings of the 12th Workshop on Humanoid Soccer Robots, IEEE-RAS International Conference on Humanoid Robots, Birmingham (2017)

15. Silver, D., et al.: Mastering the game of Go with deep neural networks and tree search. Nature **529**(7587), 484–489 (2016)

16. Speck, D., Barros, P., Weber, C., Wermter, S.: Ball localization for robocup soccer using convolutional neural networks. In: Behnke, S., Sheh, R., Sarıel, S., Lee, D.D. (eds.) RoboCup 2016. LNCS (LNAI), vol. 9776, pp. 19–30. Springer, Cham (2017). https://doi.org/10.1007/978-3-319-68792-6_2

17. Zhou, S., Wu, Y., Ni, Z., Zhou, X., Wen, H., Zou, Y.: DoReFa-Net: training low bitwidth convolutional neural networks with low bitwidth gradients. arXiv preprint arXiv:1606.06160 (2016)

# RoboCup Junior in the Hunter Region: Driving the Future of Robotic STEM Education

Aaron S. W. Wong[1,2,3](✉), Ryan Jeffery[2], Peter Turner[1,2,4], Scott Sleap[5], and Stephan K. Chalup[1,2]

[1] Newcastle Robotics Laboratory, The University of Newcastle, Callaghan, Australia
aaron.wong@newcastle.edu.au
[2] Faculty of Engineering and Built Environment, The University of Newcastle, Callaghan, Australia
[3] Faculty of Science, The University of Newcastle, Callaghan, Australia
[4] Tribotix Pty. Ltd., Callaghan, Australia
[5] Regional Development Australia - Hunter, Tighes Hill, Australia

**Abstract.** RoboCup Junior is a project-oriented educational initiative that sponsors regional, national and international robotic events for young students in primary and secondary school. It leads children to the fundamentals of teamwork and complex problem solving through step-by-step logical thinking using computers and robots. The Faculty of Engineering and Built Environment at the University of Newcastle in Australia has hosted and organized the Hunter regional tournament since 2012. This paper presents an analysis of data collected from RoboCup Junior in the Hunter Region, New South Wales, Australia, for a period of six years 2012–2017 inclusive. Our study evaluates the effectiveness of the competition in terms of geographical spread, participation numbers, and gender balance. We also present a case study about current university students who have previously participated in RoboCup Junior.

**Keywords:** STEM education · RoboCup Junior · Engagement · NUbots · Robotics

## 1 Introduction

The National Innovation and Science Agenda [5] is the Australian government's initiative to improve and promote technologically related fields of commercial, industrial, and technical skill development for Australian citizens with a component focusing on the preparation of young school-aged students for studies related to the fields of Science, Technology, Engineering, and Mathematics (STEM). This component has been recognised as the next step in the evolution of the Australian education system. It is understood that the next generation of graduating students will have to be "STEM-ready" to cope with the challenges of a future technologically advanced and internationally competitive workforce.

© Springer Nature Switzerland AG 2019
D. Holz et al. (Eds.): RoboCup 2018, LNAI 11374, pp. 362–373, 2019.
https://doi.org/10.1007/978-3-030-27544-0_30

Educating a STEM-ready workforce is not a trivial task as there are several behavioural factors inherent to modern Australian culture which impede this goal. These include fear of failure [9] (of both students and their teachers), and mathematics anxiety [13]. Students in general should be encouraged at an early stage to take intellectual risk in order to gain life-skills that could be of value for a STEM-related career path [2]. For students, pathways into a STEM related field can be increased by diversifying opportunities and options, so that there is a higher probability of attracting their attention. They could start, for example, with programming websites or building electronic components. In order to help students to access STEM, it is important to explain practical applications and give STEM a purpose. It also should be made clear that mathematics consists of many different disciplines and that they may require very different ways of thinking. There are different options within STEM and similarly within the general area of mathematics, e.g., not everyone who is talented in geometry and visualisations may also be good at memory and number tasks. With these critical thoughts in mind, a STEM-ready workforce has the potential to advance many different aspects of technology.

One aspect of an advanced technology can be found in the field of robotics. Many STEM-related fields and skills are required to develop an autonomous robot. These include sound knowledge of the fundamental concepts of science and mathematics as taught at school. These are also the basis to a successful development of the practical skills required by professional engineers.

Similarly as the Personal Computer (PC) and the Internet had revolutionary impact on our culture, now mobile devices and robots are predicted to be basis of the next technological explosion. Hence, it is important to encourage young students to consider gaining skills in professions related to robotics or to pursue a other career paths that also can lead to a technologically skilled future, i.e., a "STEM-ready" future. For the Hunter region in New South Wales (NSW), Australia, RoboCup Junior [10] is the only annual robotics event that targets young students to actively compete and perform as a team. RoboCup Junior is a project-oriented educational initiative that sponsors regional, state, national and international robotic events for young students, with the goal to encourage the next generation to pursue and take an interest in scientific and technological fields.

In this paper we will investigate the following question: How can the current society be prepared for a sustainable STEM-minded future? How can a community engagement project such as RoboCup Junior Hunter contribute and how can its success be measured?

The subsequent sections show how RoboCup Junior served as a platform for community engagement and for promoting STEM in the Hunter region. By detailing demographic information about the Hunter region it highlights the importance and impact of RoboCup Junior. The results section provides quantitative measures derived from data collected from RoboCup Junior events over the past 6 years. Then a case study of current University of Newcastle students who have previously participated in the competition is presented. The penultimate section discusses the importance and roles of several stakeholders that collaboratively supported RoboCup Junior in the Hunter region and how this led to one of the most successful regional initiatives of its kind in Australia.

## 2    RoboCup Junior in the Hunter Region

RoboCup (est. 1997) is an international competition that fosters research in robotics [8], and the advancement of artificial intelligence within a competitive environment. RoboCup has seen a globally increasing trend in the past decade, see Fig. 1. The goal of RoboCup, in the near future, is to have designed and programmed a team of bipedal humanoid autonomous soccer playing robots, to win against the human world champion soccer team [12]. This goal is yet to mature, and may require some generations of research to achieve, and hence we have RoboCup Junior; the establishment of the next generation of "technologists", with a focus on robotics.

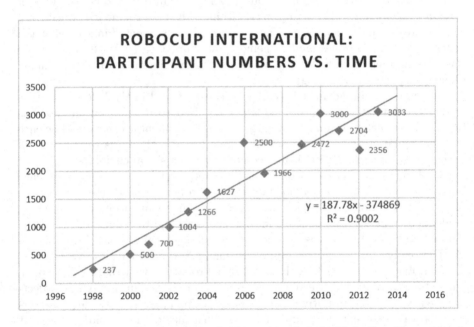

**Fig. 1.** The number of participants who have attended the RoboCup International tournament since its inception [12]: There is a strong linearly increasing trend ($R^2 >$ 0.90) over time with the number of people globally participating in this tournament.

RoboCup Junior is designed to introduce primary and secondary school-aged children to the fundamentals of teamwork and complex problem solving by employing step-by-step logical, rational processes using computers (robots) as a tool to complete a set task. The main objective of RoboCup Junior is to encourage the next generation to pursue and take an interest in scientific and technological fields; to cultivate their interests through a hands-on approach in robot design and creation using platforms including, but not limited to, Lego Mindstorm educational kits. Students are invited to compete in three distinct disciplines; soccer, dance, and rescue.

With the RoboCup Junior initiative, it is possible to create an environment of light-mindedness, experimentation, fun and teamwork that inspires and educates students to expand their horizon through STEM experiences. In this context, there are countless opportunities to establish links to other associated STEM disciplines. It is important that students feel respected as individuals and that they have, at an early stage, access to demonstrations and practical hands-on aspects of STEM careers in a broad manner where they can explore their own career goals. This is one of the key and defining ideals of RoboCup Junior in the Hunter region, NSW.

The Hunter region, NSW, resides approximately two hours north of Sydney and has a substantial rural demography as well as large urban population centres in Newcastle and Lake Macquarie. Although, the Hunter region has been noted to be an innovation hub, e.g. Newcastle as "Smart City" [7], where new smart technologies are being developed as applied solutions to the problems of the world today, the general population includes negatively skewed low social economic status (SES) indicators, when compared to the state's capital, Sydney. For example, Higher School Certificate (HSC) completion rates in the Cessnock Area, within the Hunter region, are with 44% substantially lower than the NSW average of 75% [4]. These low-SES indicators have led the organisers of RoboCup Junior in the Hunter to follow an approach that maintains the core rules of the competition while incorporating additional coaching to promote participation. This allows children to have an attitude of "having-a-go", to have fun, and to enjoy themselves while avoiding anxieties associated with STEM subjects and while subconsciously having a positive experience with STEM and gaining important skills required for a potential career path in STEM.

A career path in STEM does not require direct entry into a university degree, as there are many different pathways into a STEM-related career. However, traditional entry into a university STEM-related degree has generally been perceived to be the fastest arrangement to refine skills, achieve, advance and progress in a competitive STEM workforce. For this reason, the following results section presents information obtained in a case study of currently enrolled students (with their permission) who were past participants of RoboCup Junior, Hunter. This case study together with quantitative results recorded over the past six years corroborates the view that the Hunter RoboCup Junior initiative had substantial positive impact on driving STEM education in the Hunter Region.

## 3   Results

### 3.1   Quantitative Analysis

Over the past six years, 2012 to 2017 (see Fig. 2) there has been a general growth in the number of students, teams, as well as schools, with a total of 1443 student participants in the Hunter Region RoboCup Junior competition. In 2015 the ME program (Sect. 4.2) was not able to support the competition as usual. While in 2017, the date of the competition was significantly earlier then previous years. These factors caused a temporary decline in participation.

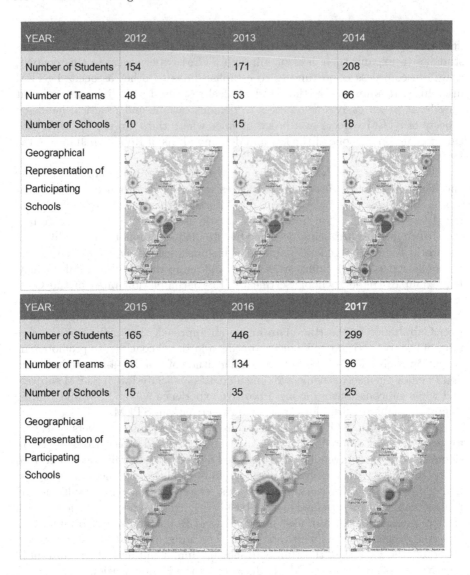

| YEAR: | 2012 | 2013 | 2014 |
|---|---|---|---|
| Number of Students | 154 | 171 | 208 |
| Number of Teams | 48 | 53 | 66 |
| Number of Schools | 10 | 15 | 18 |
| Geographical Representation of Participating Schools | | | |

| YEAR: | 2015 | 2016 | 2017 |
|---|---|---|---|
| Number of Students | 165 | 446 | 299 |
| Number of Teams | 63 | 134 | 96 |
| Number of Schools | 15 | 35 | 25 |
| Geographical Representation of Participating Schools | | | |

**Fig. 2.** Development of RoboCup Junior in the Hunter Region over the past six years (2012–2017 inclusive). There was a general increase in the number of students, teams, and schools. The spatial coverage of the participating schools entering the competition also increased.

Students were as young as 8 years of age in their 3rd school year, and the oldest participating students were up to 18 years of age. The majority of the participating students was aged 14 and 15 (in school years 8 and 9). About 22% of the 1443 participating students were female (2012 = 43, 2013 = 18, 2014 = 46, 2015 = 32, 2016 = 106 and 2017 = 71). For an extra-curricular school activity this fraction can be considered to be relatively high, given that only 13% of all engineers are female [6]. As the geographical representation of participating schools in Fig. 2 shows the geographical distribution of schools participating in the competition increased as the initiative matured over time. Participating schools were from the Central Coast in the South up to Camden Haven in the North. In addition some schools travelled up from the Sydney Region to attend the Hunter tournament in 2014.

With respect to the disciplines offered at RoboCup Junior, the local Hunter region competition comprises all available disciplines that are currently accessible at both state and national tournaments. As a result, the discipline participation distribution follows the identical ranking in proportion with the difficulty of discipline. The ranking from easiest to hardest is as follows; rescue, dance, and soccer. The data from our largest local competition, in 2016, is shown in Fig. 3.

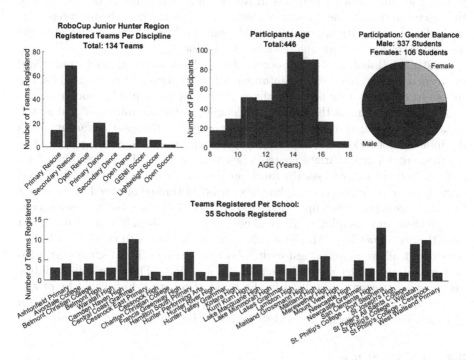

**Fig. 3.** Distributions of registered participants for 2016, RoboCup Junior, Hunter Region: Top Left, a histogram representing the number of teams registered per discipline. Top Middle, a histogram representing the number of participants by age. Top Right, gender distribution for the competition. Bottom, a histogram representing teams registered by school.

RoboCup Junior rescue consists of three sub-disciplines; primary, secondary, and open. Simplest sub-category is primary rescue, predominantly for students who are currently in primary school, while secondary rescue is for participants who are attending high school, or are between 13 and 18 years old. Advanced participants who have participated in at least two tournaments of rescue in previous years compete in open rescue. This hierarchy of sub-categories allows not only for an increase in difficulty, but for different challenges for the different categories of ages. The rescue discipline is very structured, and the task is set by the rules of the competition. This structure was the motivating factor that drove its popularity, with 80 (14 primary, 68 secondary) teams registered to participate in this discipline in 2016.

Like rescue, RoboCup Junior dance also has three sub-categories; primary, secondary and open, with similar age restrictions. This category leaves many open-ended opportunities and flexibility that allow students to explore and experiment with different implementations for their performance. This openness makes it somewhat further challenging when compared to the rescue discipline. Hence, the number of participants in RoboCup Junior dance is smaller than in the rescue category. The number of teams participating in each sub-category is fairly distributed, with approximately 20 teams for primary dance, and 14 teams for secondary dance, with one team for open dance.

Lastly, in RoboCup Junior soccer, the students are required to build and program a small robot team to autonomously play soccer. It is essential for the robots to autonomously adapt to the environment while playing soccer by the rules. This discipline is the utmost challenging of the disciplines offered at the local Hunter regional tournament. However, it is also the most rewarding of all disciplines, as it allows the students to program an autonomous agent, with a requirement for multivariate control algorithm be used. The other disciplines can be, but are not necessarily, much simpler. Due to its perceived difficulty, participation in the soccer discipline has dwindled throughout the history of our local tournament. RoboCup Junior soccer, like RoboCup Junior rescue, consists of three sub-disciplines; GENII, lightweight, and open. The sub-category of GENII only allows Lego Mindstorm NXT or EV3 Robots to compete, whereas lightweight allows modified self-built robots to be used. This includes Arduino based hardware under a certain weight and size limit. The open sub-discipline allows any hardware to be used in the build of robots, which could be of any weight, but within a size limitation. For 2016, we saw the largest cohort, with 18 teams in soccer discipline total (9 GENII, 7 Lightweight, and 2 Open).

## 3.2   A Case Study

A report released in 2015 by the Australian Industry Group, explains a set of key recommendations that can be implemented in order to further encourage school students to study and explore future careers in STEM [2]. A particular key recommendation highlights the need for teachers and schools to be further supported in harnessing students' interest, which is the primary aim of RoboCup Junior and the number of community partnerships involved. Burgher et al. [3] suggest that a hands-on and practical approach to education, results in students becoming more aware of the conceptual theory rather than students being traditionally educated in the format of lectures and traditional classroom exercises.

Exploring this suggestion this study has taken the shape of a questionnaire to current university students (n = 3), who have competed in the tournament in the past. The purpose of investigating this qualitatively was to understand what key factors associated with their participation in RoboCup Junior led the students to develop a deeper appreciation of STEM and finally resulted in their decision to pursue a career in STEM. To begin, all participants had indicated in the questionnaire that they had been encouraged to participate in RoboCup Junior by their schools and teachers. This exemplifies how critical and significant partnerships formed between the organising committee and schools are. Three prevalent themes in the responses consisted of the following areas; Problem solving, Conceptual thinking and Rewarding.

*Problem Solving:* Responses indicated that students had found the nature of the problems presented in RoboCup Junior to be of a "broad nature", which provided further incentive to aid the design of a solution they were presented with during the competition. A critical skill that has been cited is that students had to assess the abstract problem independently which leads into the second theme.

*Conceptual Thinking:* In alignment with Burgher et al. [3] RoboCup Junior being a practical activity, allowed students to gain an additional direct approach to conceptual learning. Results from the questionnaire indicated that the critical skills gained were of a separate nature to a school curriculum. Students also indicated that open-ended problems allowed them to focus on concepts rather than on textbook knowledge. Students also suggested that as a result of it being separate from a school curriculum it allowed focus to bridge gaps between abstract and practical nature.

*Rewards:* Within RoboCup Junior, students are encouraged to use technology to solve a given problem. The nature of responses to the questionnaires indicates that participants find the solutions to be the most rewarding and therefore one of the most encouraging aspects. As STEM is centrally focused around problem solving, students who experienced this during the competition found it further encouraging to seek employment within a career that offers that same sense of reward for solving a broad problem.

## 4    Discussion: Partnerships

The future of STEM in the Hunter region is deemed important by many STEM-related stakeholders of the local region. Several factors that have contributed to the success of the tournament are associated with the partnerships that have been developed with key stakeholders in the period 2012–2017. Some of these key relationships and their impact will be discussed in the following sub-sections.

## 4.1    The University of Newcastle, Faculty of Engineering and Built Environment

The Faculty of Engineering and Built Environment of the University of Newcastle has continuously been the main stakeholder of RoboCup Junior in the Hunter Region since the project's re-inception in 2012. With the university acting as the host, the competition is held on campus at the university's gymnasium, The Forum. The university is also the key supplier of human resources to organise and manage the competition. The faculty has supported the competition with expertise in management, in the form of faculty administrative staff. The faculty manages aspects such as registrations, budget, and covered the majority of costs to run the competition.

Technical aspects of the tournament were administered by members affiliated with the NUbots, the Newcastle University RoboCup team. The NUbots are a senior RoboCup team and comprise several university students and academics [1]. They competed in the Kidsize Humanoid League, and now in 2018, the TeenSize Humanoid League at RoboCup. They are part of the Newcastle Robotics Laboratory, situated in the Faculty of Engineering and Built Environment. The NUbots have participated in RoboCup since 2002. They became world champions in the Standard Platform League using the Aldebaran NAO Robots, in 2008, and were world champions in the 4-Four-Legged League in 2006 using the Sony AIBO robots. This internationally well-recognised team brings over a decade of robotics experience to the local RoboCup Junior Hunter region competition. NUbot members are members of the committee, deliver workshops, and play a crucial role on the Hunter Region competition day in roles such as technical refereeing and judging. Over the past decade, the faculty has had a strong interest in community engagement. With a particular interest in low social-economical-status areas, the faculty has deployed intensive training programs and funding for robotic kits at schools in areas such as, Raymond Terrace in Port Stephens, NSW.

## 4.2    Regional Development Australia (RDA)
##         Hunter – Manufacturing Engineering (ME) Program

RDA – Hunter's ME Program has been a highly successful STEM outreach program that has delivered tangible outcomes in terms of student uptake of STEM-based subjects in upper secondary schools [11]. The ME Program in the Hunter region has supported running of the RoboCup competition whenever possible during 2012–2014 and 2016.

In addition to supporting RoboCup Junior, the ME Program actively supports all aspects of STEM in the Hunter and has produced an innovative school curriculum which integrates the silos of STEM into a Year 9 and 10 elective subject (iSTEM), which was endorsed by BOSTES NSW in 2012. In 2017, there were over 100 schools across NSW teaching iSTEM, which includes robotics programs in a standard curriculum, which also includes RoboCup Junior preparation. As a result of the broader ME Program funding for local schools, it has delivered a substantial quantity of STEM equipment and training (e.g. professional learning for teachers and through the support of Robogals for schools). The hardware provided includes 3D printers, and of course, robotic kits that could be used as part of the RoboCup Junior competition. The 2016 ME Program has included a caveat for any school receiving Lego EV3 robots that they must compete in the RoboCup Junior, Hunter region competition. During 2016, there was a significant increase in the number of schools that received robotic kits as part of the ME program. During 2015–2016, over one hundred EV3 robots were provided to 22 local schools. As a consequence, there was a significant increase in registered participants for the local tournament in 2016.

## 4.3    Robogals Newcastle Initiative

Robogals is an international initiative aimed at promoting gender equality in the fields of STEM through the use of robots and robotic education. Volunteers of the initiative consistently visit different schools and perform their robots at local public events. In addition, they offer free short beginner classes in robotics in using the Lego NXT and EV3 Robots in many school classes. The local chapter of Robogals in the Hunter region is no exception. It consists of many enthusiastic individuals, who are always ready to assist and share when required. The local chapter of Robogals initiative has worked closely with the RoboCup Junior Hunter Region Competition, since the inception of the local chapter in 2013. Robogals have recently signed a Memorandum of Understanding with the ME Program and BAE Systems Williamtown and have been working with ME Program high school and their feeder primary schools. The ME Program also provided 10 EV3 Robots to complement their fleet of NXT units. Volunteers of Robogals have sat on the organising committee for RoboCup Junior, Hunter region, and have also assisted at the events with judging, and holding workshops on the competitions behalf while the competition was running. In addition, training material used to teach classes was shared between RoboCup Junior and Robogals, so that Robogals could concentrate on their goal to achieve gender equality in the fields of STEM. The Robogals initiative in the Hunter region is growing successfully. They have repeatedly reported that there are more schools on their waiting list then they can handle. The result of this partnership, and its growing success, can be seen in the increased female to male ratios (approximately 24% in Fig. 3). It shows the number of females is relatively higher at RoboCup Junior when compared to the number of females enrolled in an engineering course at a later stage, e.g., at university level.

## 4.4    Tribotix

Tribotix is a local robotics company in the Hunter region that sells and builds various robots, mostly for educational purposes. It has a strong interest in the success of RoboCup Junior. The director of Tribotix has personally been involved with the RoboCup Junior since its inception and has also mentored teams in local schools, using a different style of robots than the standard Lego platform.

Tribotix also partners with the national RoboCup Junior Australia committee in the development of state-of-the-art robotic educational kits. This includes, e.g., the DARwIn-MINI, for future use in a possible new Rescue league and a small humanoid league for RoboCup Junior. As more students start earlier with the competition, it would not be too long before these advancing students seek knowledge, information, and new hardware to fulfil their requirements. Tribotix has been a competent partner and helpful supplier throughout all years of the competition.

### 4.5   Community Sponsorship and Membership

Community support was vital for running the event. Support was supplied in terms of funding obtained from community grants, such as Orica (2014), AGL (2015), Newcastle Coal Infrastructure Group (NCIG) (2015), Newcastle City Council (2016), and the Kirby Foundation (2017). Without this funding, the competition itself could not have happened, and therefore no success could have been achieved. Members of the general community represented by teachers and parents of the participants were involved in all aspects of organising the competition. The success of the students comes directly from interacting with their mentors, some of which advise and attend monthly organising meetings which allow us to hear feedback and to incorporate and implement suggestions to make the competition run smoothly. Members of the community are an important part of the Hunter Region RoboCup Junior organising committee and have steered the competition to its current successful state. We acknowledge Mr. Jason Flood, Chair of Local Committee (all years, excluding 2014), for his commitment and extraordinary effort that added to the project's success.

## 5   Conclusion

With decreasing levels of participation in mathematics and science within Australian schools, winning students' interest in the fields of STEM has become an uphill battle. Nonetheless, for the local region of the Hunter, the RoboCup Junior competition gained outstanding success. The partnership of RoboCup Junior Hunter Region with the University of Newcastle, and other key stakeholders such as the RDA Hunter's ME program, stands as a project that will transform the landscape for STEM education in the future. Success of the project to this point is reflected by the increasing number of student participants, a growing geographical distribution, and an improvement of gender balance. In addition, qualitative evidence of the positive influence on students participating in RoboCup Junior explains what impact the competition can play on students' path to a STEM career.

# References

1. Amos, M., et al.: The NuBots team description paper 2018, February 2018. https://www.robocuphumanoid.org/qualification/2018/TeenSize/NUbots/tdp.pdf. Accessed 23 Mar 2018
2. Australian Industry Group: Progressing the skills of stem education (2015). http://cdn.aigroup.com.au/Reports/2015/14571_STEM_Skills_Report_Final_-.pdf. Accessed 23 Mar 2018
3. Burgher, J.K., Finkel, D., Adesope, O., Van Wie, B.: Implementation of a modular hands-on learning pedagogy: student attitudes in a fluid mechanics and heat transfer course. J. STEM Educ.: Innov. Res. 16(4), 44 (2015)
4. Cessnock City Council: Youth unemployment symposium discussion paper. In: The Hunter Valley Youth Unemployment Symposium, pp. 1–16. Cessnock City Council, Kurri Kurri (2015)
5. Commonwealth of Australia: The Agenda: National Innovation and Science Agenda (2016). http://www.innovation.gov.au/page/agenda. Accessed 23 Mar 2018
6. Engineers Australia: UNSW aims to boost female participation in engineering (2018). https://www.engineersaustralia.org.au/portal/news/unsw-aims-boost-female-participation-engineering-0. Accessed 23 Mar 2018
7. Hunter Business Review: Newcastle smart city initiative on track. Newcastle Smart City Initiative on track—Hunter Business Review, May 2016. http://www.hbrmag.com.au/article/read/newcastle-smart-city-initiative-on-track-1974
8. Kitano, H., Asada, M., Kuniyoshi, Y., Noda, I., Osawa, E., Matsubara, H.: RoboCup: a challenge problem for AI. AI Mag. 18(1), 73–85 (1997). https://doi.org/10.1609/aimag.v18i1.1276
9. Michou, A., Vansteenkiste, M., Mouratidis, A., Lens, W.: Enriching the hierarchical model of achievement motivation: autonomous and controlling reasons underlying achievement goals. Br. J. Educ. Psychol. 84(4), 650–666 (2014). https://doi.org/10.1111/bjep.12055
10. RoboCup Junior, Australia: Home: RoboCup Junior Australia (2018). http://www.robocupjunior.org.au/. Accessed 23 Mar 2018
11. Sleap, S.: Advanced manufacturing schools pathways program hunter region new south wales. In: 8th Biennial International Conference on Technology Education Research, vol. 2, Sydney, Australia (2014)
12. Veloso, M., Stone, P.: Video: RoboCup robot soccer history 1997–2011. In: 2012 IEEE/RSJ International Conference on Intelligent Robots and Systems. IEEE, October 2012. https://doi.org/10.1109/iros.2012.6386302
13. Wigfield, A., Meece, J.L.: Math anxiety in elementary and secondary school students. J. Educ. Psychol. 80(2), 210 (1988)

# Distributed Circumnavigation Control with Dynamic Spacing for a Heterogeneous Multi-robot System

Weijia Yao[✉], Sha Luo, Huimin Lu, and Junhao Xiao

Department of Automation, National University of Defense Technology,
Changsha, China
weijia.yao.nudt@gmail.com, lhmnew@nudt.edu.cn

**Abstract.** Circumnavigation control is useful in real-world applications such as entrapping a hostile target. In this paper, we consider a heterogeneous multi-robot system where robots have different physical properties, such as maximum movement speeds. Instead of equal-spacing which is assumed in many existing studies, dynamic spacing according to robots' properties is proposed in this paper. For this purpose, two new concepts - *utility* and *formation guideline* - are presented. Then a distributed circumnavigation control algorithm based on utilities and formation guidelines is designed for any number of mobile robots from random 3D positions to circumnavigate a target. Theoretical analysis and experimental results are provided to prove the stability and effectiveness of the proposed control algorithm.

## 1 Introduction

One of the most prominent research topics on distributed multi-robot system is the formation control problem. Significant efforts have been made on the *circular formation control* and *circumnavigation control* problems. In circular formation control problem, robots remain in their positions after the formation is generated, while in circumnavigation control problem, they still encircle around the target. In this sense, circular formation control could be regarded as a special case of circumnavigation control when the circumnavigation speed equals to zero.

There are already many studies on circumnavigation control (or circular formation control) problems. Most of the existing studies only consider the case where robots are distributed evenly on the formation (i.e., equal spacing), such as [3,7,14]. In addition, the control algorithms proposed in these studies are only applicable on the 2D plane. Nevertheless, [1] proposes algorithms which are still effective in 3D space. The formation spacing, however, is fixed and equal. Although this is effective for a homogeneous multi-robot system, it may not be sufficient for a heterogeneous one where robots have different properties, such as maximum movement speeds. [9] and [10] propose a distributed control law for a multi-robot system to form a circular formation with any desired spacing among robots. However, it assumes that the robots are placed initially on a prescribed

D. Holz et al. (Eds.): RoboCup 2018, LNAI 11374, pp. 374–386, 2019.
https://doi.org/10.1007/978-3-030-27544-0_31

circle and the control algorithm is not applicable in the 3D space. Another major disadvantage is that the desired spacing, which is a global quantity, should be specified for each robot beforehand. If the specified spacing does not sum up to $2\pi$, or if robots are informed of inconsistent specified spacing, they will form an erroneous formation. Moreover, to the best of our knowledge, there are no studies concerning dynamic spacing for a heterogeneous multi-robot system.

In this study, we suppose that mobile robots are heterogeneous in terms of their kinematics abilities, such as maximum locomotion speeds, etc. In a scenario where these mobile robots need to entrap a hostile target, their inter-robot spacing should be different for better performance; those robots with lower mobility are supposed to gather together with smaller spacing than those with higher mobility, so the probability for the target to flee away from the formation is lower. We also consider the deterioration of individual performance due to physical worn-out or damage. Therefore, their spacing should be varied in a dynamic way during the circumnavigation process. Based on this, the goal of this paper is to propose a new distributed circumnavigation control algorithm which is able to control a group of heterogeneous mobile robots from any initial positions to circumnavigate a target with dynamic spacing in the 3D space.

The main contribution of this work is twofold. First, this paper proposes the concept of *utility* and *formation guideline*. Based on these two new concepts, we design a distributed circumnavigation control algorithm which enables robots to adjust their spacing dynamically according to the local variations of their utilities; a pre-specified desired spacing is not necessary (but it is necessary for studies such as [1,9,10]). The control algorithm is distributed and applicable for a heterogeneous multi-robot system of arbitrary size. Second, the distributed control algorithm does not require robots to be placed initially on a prescribed circular trajectory (but it is required in [9,10]). Their initial positions can be arbitrarily chosen in the 3D space rather than being restricted on a 2D plane (which is the case in [9,10]). In addition, the control algorithm can respond effectively to the situation where robots quit or join the circumnavigation process (but it is not studied in much literature such as [3,8–10]).

The remainder of this paper is organized as follows. Section 2 introduces the circumnavigation control problem based on utilities and derives its corresponding mathematical formulation. Section 3 proposes the circumnavigation control algorithm. In Sect. 4, simulation and real-robot experiments are performed and results are analysed. Finally, Sect. 5 concludes the paper and summarizes the future work.

## 2   Problem Formulation

The research question is that a group of $n$ ($n \geq 2$) mobile robots, denoted by $r_i$, $i = 1, \ldots, n$, encircle a target in 3D space with dynamic spacing on a circular formation. Note that $r_i$ is only used to represent the $i$th robot for convenience of narration; it does not correspond to any physical quantities. Suppose each mobile robot is modelled by a 3D kinematic point:

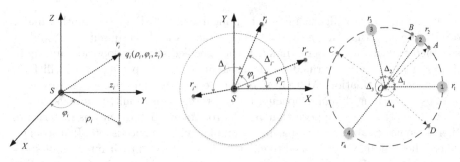

**Fig. 1.** The body reference frame with the target $S$ as the origin.

**Fig. 2.** Robots' projections and the target $S$ on the $XSY$ plane.

**Fig. 3.** The interpretation of the formation guideline.

$$\dot{p}_i(t) = u_i(t), \quad i = 1, \ldots, n, \tag{1}$$

where $u_i(t)$ is the control input to the robot $r_i$ and $p_i(t) \in \mathbb{R}^3$ is its position in the world reference frame $\mathcal{W}$. In this problem, robots are required to maintain on the same plane with the encircled target which is modelled by another kinematic point. Therefore, a (target) body reference frame $\mathcal{B}$ centred at the target $S$ is introduced (see Fig. 1). In addition, the cylindrical coordinate system is preferred to the commonly used Cartesian coordinate system since the former itself embodies three elements of interest: the distance between the projection of the robot on the $XSY$ plane to the target ($\rho$), the height relative to the $XSY$ plane ($z$) and the angle between the $X$-axis and the line joining the projection of the robot on the $XSY$ plane with the target ($\varphi$). The cylindrical coordinates for $r_i$ is denoted by $q_i = (\rho_i, \varphi_i, z_i)^T$ (see Fig. 1). To relate the cylindrical coordinates with the Cartesian coordinates, a vector function is defined as $q(p) = (\rho(p), \varphi(p), z(p))^T$, where $p \in \mathbb{R}^3$ is a generic vector with components $p_x, p_y, p_z$. $\rho(p) = \sqrt{p_x^2 + p_y^2}$, $\varphi(p) = \tan^{-1}(p_y/p_x)$ and $z(p) = p_z$. Note that $\varphi \in [0, 2\pi)$. The Jacobian matrix of the vector function will be used later, which is $J = \frac{\partial q}{\partial p^T} = \begin{bmatrix} \frac{p_x}{\sqrt{p_x^2+p_y^2}} & \frac{p_y}{\sqrt{p_x^2+p_y^2}} & 0 \\ \frac{-p_y}{p_x^2+p_y^2} & \frac{p_x}{p_x^2+p_y^2} & 0 \\ 0 & 0 & 1 \end{bmatrix}$. For better analysis, we label the robots in the counter-clockwise direction according to their initial (angular) positions ($\varphi_i$) in $\mathcal{B}$ as shown in Fig. 2. Note that the subscript $i^-$ and $i^+$ represent the indices of the neighboring robots of $r_i$ in the clockwise and counter-clockwise direction respectively. Especially, if $i = n$, $i^+ = 1$, and if $i = 1$, $i^- = n$. $\Delta_i > 0$ represents the difference between the angular positions of $r_{i+}$ and that of $r_i$. In particular,

$$\Delta_i = \begin{cases} \varphi_{i+} - \varphi_i, & i = 1, \ldots, n-1, \\ \varphi_1 - \varphi_n + 2\pi, & i = n. \end{cases} \tag{2}$$

Also note that $\sum_{i=1}^{n} \Delta_i = 2\pi$,

Before giving the definition of the circumnavigation problem with dynamic spacing, we propose the concept of *utility*.

**Definition 1 (Utility).** *In a heterogeneous multi-robot system, given different kinds of robots, a robot's utility $\mu(t) \geq 0$ is determined by a given criterion (such as its maximum movement speed). The utility reflects the weight of the robot in the circumnavigation process at time $t$.*

For example, suppose a robot's maximum movement speed is the criterion. Let $\mu_i(t) = \frac{v_{mi}(t)}{v_M}, i = 1, \ldots, n$, where $v_{mi}(t)$ is the maximum movement speed of $r_i$ and $v_M$ is the possible greatest movement speed in the heterogeneous multi-robot system. Then $\mu_i(t) \in [0, 1], i = 1, \ldots, n$. When $\mu_i(t) = 0$, the robot $r_i$ cannot continue the circumnavigation process with other robots. In this case, its neighboring robots will neglect its role in the circumnavigation process. $\mu_i(t)$ will increase or decrease due to the enhancement or damage of the robot's locomotion capabilities. To explain directly how utilities are utilized to enable dynamic spacing among robots, we simply regard the utility of a robot to be proportional to its maximum movement speed. For simplicity of writing, the symbol $t$ is neglected from $\mu$ unless it causes confusion. The circumnavigation control problem based on utilities is defined as follows:

**Definition 2 (Circumnavigation Control Problem Based on Utilities).** *In a heterogeneous multi-robot system composed of $n$ ($n \geq 2$) mobile robots, each of the robot's dynamics are modelled by (1). Suppose $f_i : \mathbb{R}^{n+1} \to (0, 2\pi)$, $i = 1, \ldots, n$, is a smooth function of time and the utilities of robots, which maps utilities to the final holistic formation spacing. Assume $\lim\limits_{t \to \infty} f_i(t, \mu_1, \ldots, \mu_n)$ exists, the circumnavigation control problem based on utilities is to seek control laws satisfying the following asymptotic conditions:*

$$\lim_{t \to \infty} \rho_i(t) = \rho^* \tag{3}$$

$$\lim_{t \to \infty} \Delta_i(t) = \lim_{t \to \infty} f_i \tag{4}$$

$$\lim_{t \to \infty} \dot{\varphi}_i(t) = \omega^* \tag{5}$$

$$\lim_{t \to \infty} z_i(t) = z^* \tag{6}$$

*Here, $\mu_i > 0$, $\rho^* > 0$, $\omega^* \in \mathbb{R}$ and $z^* \in \mathbb{R}$. $\rho^*$, $\omega^*$ and $z^*$ denote the circumnavigation radius, the angular speed and the circumnavigation height respectively.*

In this paper, it is required that all robots and the target remain in the same plane in the end. Therefore, the default value of $z^*$ is 0. However, $z^*$ can be different for different robots. Equation (4) manifests that the final formation spacing is not specified manually as proposed in [9] or [13], but instead, it is determined by the $f_i$ function, which will be referred to as $f$ function for simplicity. Note that $f_i$ function depends on the utilities of other robots instead of calculating by each robot alone. The advantage of eliciting the $f$ function is that the spacing among robots can be dynamically adjusted corresponding to the variations of robots' utilities.

The expression of the $f$ function is determined by a *formation guideline*. It is proposed under specific physics background representing the relationship between the utilities of robots and the final formation spacing. In this paper, we suppose that multiple heterogeneous robots circumnavigate a target and try to prevent it from fleeing. In Fig. 3, four robots $r_1, \ldots, r_4$ rotate around a target denoted by $O$. Suppose that the target is intelligent enough to determine the *best fleeing points* denoted by $A$, $B$, $C$ and $D$ in the figure. Obviously, the best fleeing points are related to the utility (i.e., the maximum movement speeds) of robots. The position of $A$, for instance, is calculated by $\angle AOr_2 = \frac{\mu_2}{\mu_1 + \mu_2}$. We also suppose that the probability of capturing the target by a robot is inversely proportional to the time spent on moving from its initial position along the circular trajectory at its maximum speed to the best fleeing point. Therefore, the formation guideline can be defined as

**Formation Guideline 1.** *In the final circumnavigation formation formed by robots, when the target tries to escape via any of the best fleeing point, the two robots adjacent to the best fleeing point have the same probability of capturing the target.*

To understand the above formation guideline, taking Fig. 3 for example, it means the travelling time for $r_1$ and $r_2$ to arrive at the best fleeing point $A$ along the circular trajectory at their maximum speeds (i.e., $\mu_1$ and $\mu_2$ resp.) is the same, or the travelling time for $r_2$ to arrive at $A$ or $B$ along the circular trajectory at its maximum speed (i.e., $\mu_2$) is identical, and hence, the probability of capturing the target is equal. Following this, it can be derived that $\frac{\mu_i}{\mu_i + \mu_{i+}} \Delta_i = \frac{\mu_i}{\mu_i + \mu_{i-}} \Delta_{i-}$. According to this equation, the relationship between the final desired formation spacing and the utilities is $\Delta_1 : \Delta_2 : \cdots : \Delta_n = (\mu_1 + \mu_2) : (\mu_2 + \mu_3) : \cdots : (\mu_n + \mu_1)$. Therefore, given $\mu_1, \ldots, \mu_n$, the formation spacing can be determined, and the $f$ function is expressed as follows:

$$f_i(t, \mu_1, \ldots, \mu_n) = \frac{\mu_i + \mu_{i+}}{\sum_{k=1}^{n} \mu_k} \pi. \tag{7}$$

Other formation guidelines can be similarly defined[1].

*Remark 1.* Note that formation guidelines only reflect the relationship between the utilities of robots and the final formation spacing; it does not determine the utilities of robots.

## 3   Utility-Based Circumnavigation Control Algorithm

First we define a rotational matrix $R_b$, which is the representation of the body reference frame $\mathcal{B}$ with respect to the world reference frame $\mathcal{W}$. Therefore, the

---

[1] Another example of the formation guideline can be found in the full version http://arxiv.org/abs/1805.05395.

following equation calculates the cylindrical coordinates of $r_i$ in the frame $\mathcal{B}$: $q_i = q(R_b^T(p_i - p_b))$, where $p_i$ and $p_b$ are the Cartesian coordinates of $r_i$ and the target in the frame $\mathcal{W}$ respectively. Then the derivative of $q_i$ is the dynamics of robots in the cylindrical coordinates, which is $\dot{q}_i = J_i[\dot{R}_b^T(p_i - p_b) + R_b^T(\dot{p}_i - \dot{p}_b)]$, where $J_i$ is the Jacobian matrix as shown in Sect. 2, i.e., $J_i = \left.\frac{\partial q}{\partial p^T}\right|_{p = R_b^T(p_i - p_b)}$. Note that $\det(J) = \frac{1}{\sqrt{p_x^2 + p_y^2}}$ as long as $p_x^2 + p_y^2 \neq 0$. This means $J_i$ is invertible as long as the distance between $r_i$ and the target is non-zero. This condition can always be guaranteed since the initial positions of the robots and the target do not coincide, and by designing appropriate control algorithms, the distance can be guaranteed to be non-zero all the time. By letting

$$u_i = \dot{p}_i = \dot{p}_b + R_b(J_i^{-1}v_i - \dot{R}_b^T(p_i - p_b)), \tag{8}$$

we can switch our focus to the new control input in the cylindrical coordinates $v_i = \dot{q}_i = (\dot{\rho}_i, \dot{\varphi}_i, \dot{z}_i)^T$ [1]. The advantage of transforming to this control input is that we can control $\rho_i$, $\varphi_i$ and $z_i$ separately, which are the three main variables in the circumnavigation problem.

**Notations.** For positive integers $m$ and $n$, $M_n$ and $M_{m \times n}$ are a set of all $n \times n$ and $m \times n$ real matrices. If all the entries in a matrix is nonnegative, this matrix is called nonnegative. We denote $I_d$ as the $d \times d$ identity matrix. $\mathbf{1}$ and $\mathbf{0}$ are vectors of all 1's or 0's of suitable dimensions respectively. The underlying directed graph (or digraph) of a nonnegative matrix $M \in M_n$, denoted by $\mathcal{G}(M)$, is the directed graph with the vertex set $\{v_i\}, i \in \{1, ..., n\}$, such that there is a directed edge in $\mathcal{G}(M)$ from $v_j$ to $v_i$ if and only if $m_{ij} \neq 0$. A directed graph is called strongly connected if for every pair of vertices, there is a directed path between them [4]. The following is a preliminary result related to any strongly connected digraph.

**Lemma 1 (Theorem 3 of** [6]). *Assume $G$ is a strongly connected digraph with Laplacian $L$ satisfying $Lw_r = \mathbf{0}$, $w_l^T L = \mathbf{0}$ and $w_l^T w_r = 1$. Then $R = \lim_{t \to \infty} \exp(-Lt) = w_r w_l^T \in M_n$.*

**Theorem 1.** *Consider a multi-robot system with robot dynamics described by (1) and (8), by introducing the control input $v_i = \dot{q}_i = (\dot{\rho}_i, \dot{\varphi}_i, \dot{z}_i)^T$ into (8), where*

$$\dot{\rho}_i = k_\rho(\rho^* - \rho_i), \tag{9}$$

$$\dot{z}_i = -k_z z_i, \tag{10}$$

$$\dot{\varphi}_i = \omega^* + k_\varphi(\bar{\varphi}_i - \varphi_i). \tag{11}$$

*Note that $k_\rho$, $k_z$ and $k_\varphi$ are positive gains, and*

$$\bar{\varphi}_i = \begin{cases} \varphi_{i-} + \frac{\mu_{i-} + \mu_i}{\mu_{i+} + 2\mu_i + \mu_{i-}}(\Delta_i + \Delta_{i-}), & i = 2, 3, \ldots, n, \\ \varphi_{i-} + \frac{\mu_{i-} + \mu_i}{\mu_{i+} + 2\mu_i + \mu_{i-}}(\Delta_i + \Delta_{i-}) - 2\pi, & i = 1, \end{cases} \tag{12}$$

*where $\mu_i$ is the utility of the robot $r_i$ and it is piecewise constant. If the $f$ function is shown as (7) (Formation Guideline 1), the circumnavigation control problem based on utilities encoded by (3), (4), (5) and (6) can be solved with exponential convergence speed.*

*Proof.* It is obvious that (9) and (10) do not rely on the states of other robots, and they are basically P control laws with reference input $\rho^*$ and 0 respectively. So according to the classical control theory, $\rho_i$ and $z_i$ will converge exponentially to $\rho^*$ and 0 respectively.

Since $\mu_i$, $i = 1, \ldots, n$, is piecewise constant, it is obvious that $\lim_{t \to \infty} f_i$ exists. We define $\bar{\varphi} = [\bar{\varphi}_1 \ldots \bar{\varphi}_n]^T$ and $\varphi = [\varphi_1 \ldots \varphi_n]^T$, so (11) and (12) can be written into compact forms respectively as follows:

$$\dot{\varphi} = \omega^* \mathbf{1} + k_\varphi (\bar{\varphi} - \varphi), \tag{13}$$

$$\bar{\varphi} = A\varphi + b, \tag{14}$$

$$A = \begin{bmatrix} 0 & \frac{\mu_n + \mu_1}{\mu_2 + 2\mu_1 + \mu_n} & 0 & \ldots 0 & 0 & \frac{\mu_1 + \mu_2}{\mu_2 + 2\mu_1 + \mu_n} \\ \frac{\mu_2 + \mu_3}{\mu_3 + 2\mu_2 + \mu_1} & 0 & \frac{\mu_1 + \mu_2}{\mu_3 + 2\mu_2 + \mu_1} & \ldots 0 & 0 & 0 \\ \vdots & \vdots & \vdots & \vdots : & \vdots & \vdots \\ \frac{\mu_{n-1} + \mu_n}{\mu_1 + 2\mu_n + \mu_{n-1}} & 0 & 0 & \ldots 0 & \frac{\mu_n + \mu_1}{\mu_1 + 2\mu_n + \mu_{n-1}} & 0 \end{bmatrix} \tag{15}$$

where $A \in M_n$ is shown as (15), and $b = 2\pi \begin{bmatrix} \frac{-(\mu_1 + \mu_2)}{\mu_2 + 2\mu_1 + \mu_n} & 0 \ldots 0 & \frac{\mu_{n-1} + \mu_n}{\mu_1 + 2\mu_n + \mu_{n-1}} \end{bmatrix}^T$.

During each time period where $\mu_i$ is constant, $A$ and $b$ are constant matrix and vector respectively. Note that matrix $A$ is a row stochastic matrix and furthermore, it could be considered as the adjacency matrix [4] corresponding to a weighted directed ring denoted by $\mathcal{G}(A)$. It can be readily verified that $\mathcal{G}(A)$ is strongly connected. Next we define the *error signal* as

$$e_\varphi = \bar{\varphi} - \varphi = (A - I_n)\varphi + b = -L_p \varphi + b, \tag{16}$$

where $L_p = I_n - A$, which is the Laplacian matrix of $\mathcal{G}(A)$. Since $L_p$ is constant at each time period, the derivative of $e_\varphi$ is $\dot{e}_\varphi = -L_p \dot{\varphi}$. By substituting (13) and (16) into this equation, we further obtain the *error dynamics* as

$$\dot{e}_\varphi = -\omega^* L_p \mathbf{1} - k_\varphi L_p e_\varphi = -k_\varphi L_p e_\varphi. \tag{17}$$

Note that $\mathbf{1}$ is the right eigenvector associated with the zero eigenvalue of $L_p$, so $-\omega^* L_p \mathbf{1} = 0$. The solution to (17) is $e_\varphi(t) = \exp(-k_\varphi L_p t) e_\varphi(0)$. According to Lemma 1 and also note that $k_\varphi > 0$ only affects the convergence speed but not the convergence value, we have $\lim_{t \to \infty} e_\varphi(t) = w_r w_l^T e_\varphi(0)$, where $L_p w_r = \mathbf{0}$, $w_l^T L_p = \mathbf{0}$ and $w_l^T w_r = 1$. By substituting (16) into this equation, we obtain the following:

$$\lim_{t \to \infty} e_\varphi(t) = w_r(-w_l^T L_p \varphi + w_l^T b) = w_l^T b w_r. \tag{18}$$

Let $w_r = 1$ and $w_l = \frac{w_L}{\sum_{w_L}}$, where the $i^{th}$ entry of $w_L$ is

$$\left[ w_{L_i} = (\mu_{i+} + 2\mu_i + \mu_{i-}) \prod_{j=1, j \neq i, i-}^{n} (\mu_j + \mu_{j+}) \right],$$

and $\sum_{w_L} = \sum_{i=1}^{n} w_{L_i}$. It can be easily verified that $w_l^T$ and $w_r$ are the left and right eigenvector of the Laplacian matrix $L_p$ associated with the zero eigenvalue respectively, and $w_l^T w_r = 1$. Therefore, (18) becomes $\lim_{t \to \infty} e_\varphi(t) = 0$, or $\lim_{t \to \infty} \varphi(t) = \lim_{t \to \infty} \bar{\varphi}(t)$. According to (13), the circumnavigation speed of each robot converges to the desired angular speed $\omega^*$. In addition, under this condition, $\bar{\varphi}_i$ is replaced by $\varphi_i$ in (12) and therefore, for robots with indices $i = 2, ..., n$, the equation $\varphi_i = \varphi_{i-} + \frac{\mu_{i-} + \mu_i}{\mu_{i+} + 2\mu_i + \mu_{i-}} (\Delta_i + \Delta_{i-})$ further becomes $\frac{\Delta_i}{\Delta_{i-}} = \frac{\mu_i + \mu_{i+}}{\mu_i + \mu_{i-}}$. This means a sequence of equations $\frac{\Delta_n}{\Delta_{n-1}} = \frac{\mu_n + \mu_1}{\mu_{n-1} + \mu_n}, ..., \frac{\Delta_2}{\Delta_1} = \frac{\mu_2 + \mu_3}{\mu_1 + \mu_2}$. Assuming $\Delta_1 = k(\mu_1 + \mu_2)$, $k \neq 0$, we have $\Delta_i = k(\mu_i + \mu_{i+}), i = 2, ..., n$. According to $\sum_{i=1}^{n} \Delta_i = 2\pi$, it follows that $2k \sum_{i=1}^{n} \mu_i = 2\pi$, and hence $k = \pi / \sum_{i=1}^{n} \mu_i$. Therefore, $\Delta_i = (\mu_i + \mu_{i+})\pi / \sum_{i=1}^{n} \mu_i = f_i(t, \mu_1, ..., \mu_n)$. So the formation spacing expressed by (4) and (7) can be achieved.

*Remark 2.* Since (9), (10), (11) and (17) typically admit a linear system, the convergence is global and exponential. In fact, for the convergence of $e_\varphi$, a Lyapunov function can be defined as $V(e_\varphi) = e_\varphi^T P e_\varphi$, where $P = \text{diag}\{w_l\}$, so the global and exponential convergence can also be proved using the Lyapunov theorem.

*Remark 3.* In the definition of circumnavigation control problem based on utilities, (4) contains the utilities of all robots. However, it can be seen from (12) that each robot only needs to obtain the utilities of its two neighboring robots. Moreover, it should be noted that robots do not know what the holistic expected formation is; the actual formation (or spacing) among robots adapt dynamically to the variations of the local utilities of neighboring robots. In addition, when a robot joins or leaves the formation, according to (11) and (12), the spacing among robots will adjust dynamically through local update of the utilities of neighboring robots. To sum up, the utility-based circumnavigation control algorithm does not rely on the number of robots, and it is able to dynamically adjust the formation spacing dependent on the change of utilities.

*Remark 4.* When $\mu_\theta = 0$, the robot $r_\theta$ has quitted from the circumnavigation process, and therefore the communication topology has changed. The change of communication topology means the indices of the neighboring robots alter accordingly. When $\mu_2 = 0$, for example, the neighboring robots of $r_3$ change from $r_2$ and $r_4$ to $r_1$ and $r_4$. In this way, the circumnavigation control algorithm based on utilities can well adapt to the cases where there are local variations on utilities or where robots join or quit from the formation. The formation spacing can adjust dynamically based on the selected formation guideline, achieving distributed formation reconfiguration.

Another problem that is worth considering is whether robots preserve their initial orders during the whole circumnavigation process. For the next theorem, the definition of a Metzler matrix [5] is given. For a real matrix $M = [m_{ij}] \in M_n$, if all its off-diagonal elements are non-negative, i.e., $m_{ij} \geq 0, i \neq j$, $M$ is a Metzler matrix.

**Theorem 2.** *During the circumnavigation process, robots always keep their initial orders in the formation. In other words, $\Delta_i(t) > 0, i = 1, \ldots, n$, for $t \geq 0$.*

*Proof.* According to (2), (11) and (12), for $i = 1, \ldots, n$, it follows that

$$
\dot{\Delta}_i = k_\varphi \left[ \frac{\mu_i + \mu_{i+}}{\mu_{i*} + 2\mu_{i+} + \mu_i} \Delta_{i+} - \left( \frac{\mu_{i+} + \mu_{i*}}{\mu_{i*} + 2\mu_{i+} + \mu_i} \right. \right.
$$
$$
\left. \left. + \frac{\mu_{i-} + \mu_i}{\mu_{i+} + 2\mu_i + \mu_{i-}} \right) \Delta_i + \frac{\mu_i + \mu_{i+}}{\mu_{i+} + 2\mu_i + \mu_{i-}} \Delta_{i-} \right],
$$

(19)

where $i^*$ represents $(i^+)^+$, which is the index of the second adjacent robot for the robot $r_i$ in the counter-clockwise direction. Let $\Delta = [\Delta_1 \ldots \Delta_n]^T$, then (19) can be rewritten as $\dot{\Delta} = k_\varphi M_\Delta \Delta$, where $M_\Delta$ is shown in (20).

$$
M_\Delta =
$$

$$
\begin{bmatrix}
\frac{-(\mu_2+\mu_3)}{\mu_3+2\mu_2+\mu_1} + \frac{-(\mu_n+\mu_1)}{\mu_2+2\mu_1+\mu_n} & \frac{\mu_1+\mu_2}{\mu_3+2\mu_2+\mu_1} & \cdots & \frac{\mu_1+\mu_2}{\mu_2+2\mu_1+\mu_n} \\
\frac{\mu_2+\mu_3}{\mu_3+2\mu_2+\mu_1} & \frac{-(\mu_3+\mu_4)}{\mu_4+2\mu_3+\mu_2} + \frac{-(\mu_1+\mu_2)}{\mu_3+2\mu_2+\mu_1} & \cdots & 0 \\
\vdots & \vdots & \vdots & \vdots \\
\frac{\mu_n+\mu_1}{\mu_2+2\mu_1+\mu_n} & 0 & \cdots & \frac{-(\mu_1+\mu_2)}{\mu_2+2\mu_1+\mu_n} + \frac{-(\mu_{n-1}+\mu_n)}{\mu_1+2\mu_n+\mu_{n-1}}
\end{bmatrix}.
$$

(20)

Therefore, the solution of $\Delta(t)$ is $\Delta(t) = \exp(k_\varphi M_\Delta t)\Delta(0)$. Since $M_\Delta$ is a Metlzer matrix, it has been proved that $\exp(k_\varphi M_\Delta t)$ is a non-negative matrix. In addition, due to $\Delta(0) > 0$, it follows that $\Delta(t) > 0$, $t \geq 0$, which means that robots always keep their initial orders in the formation.

*Remark 5.* The significance of this theorem is that it provides a preliminary result for collision avoidance. In other words, if robots are treated as mass points, then collision will not happen since they always keep their initial orders. For real robots with geometric shape, given sufficiently large spacing, the collision will not happen, but this will need further investigation.

## 4    Experimental Results and Analysis

Although it is claimed that formation guidelines correspond to specific physics backgrounds, in the experiment, we do not try to reproduce the specific scenarios. This is because the emphasis here is the stability of the circumnavigation control algorithm based on utilities, and how the global formation spacing reacts dynamically to the variation of the utilities. In the experiments, robots' utilities are supposed to be proportional to its maximum movement speed. However, how the utilities are calculated from the maximum movement speeds is not the interest of the study. Instead, the variation of the utilities are manually specified. Readers can think of an increase in the utilities as an update of robots' locomotion capabilities, while the decrease means the deterioration of performance due to worn-out or damage of robots[2].

## 4.1    Experiment with Soccer Robots

In this experiment, four soccer-playing robots [11,12] are used and Formation Guideline 1 is adopted. Since the soccer-playing robots have omnidirectional movement abilities and they can reach any given velocity instantly, their dynamics can be regarded as the first-integrator model given in (1). In addition, an omnidirectional vision system is equipped on each robot with algorithms for self-localization and the recognition of a yellow football [2]. The position and velocity of the robot itself and the position and velocity of the football are obtained by its own omnidirectional vision system. Moreover, robots are only allowed to receive information from its neighboring robots and the information is transmitted using wireless communication.

|     (a)     |     (b)     |     (c)     |     (d)     |

**Fig. 4.** The real robot experiment. (a)–(d) illustrate the positions of robots at 4 s (Stage 1), 19 s (Stage 2), 39 s (Stage 3) and 61 s (Stage 4) respectively. (Color figure online)

The utilities of robots $r_1$, $r_3$ and $r_4$ remain 20 throughout the whole circumnavigation process, while the utility of the robot $r_2$ varies according to a piecewise constant function. That is, $\mu_2 = 1$, $(0 \leq t < 15)$; $\mu_2 = 20$, $(15 \leq t < 30)$; $\mu_2 = 50$, $(30 \leq t < 45)$; $\mu_2 = 0$, $(t \geq 45)$. For convenience, the four time ranges are denoted by Stage 1, 2, 3 and 4 respectively. Following Formation Guideline 1, it can be calculated the final expected spacing for the four stages is $[62\ 62\ 118\ 118]^T$, $[90\ 90\ 90\ 90]^T$, $[114\ 114\ 66\ 66]^T$ and $[120\ 120\ 120]^T$ (unit: degree) correspondingly. Note that at Stage 4, the robot $r_2$ quits from the circumnavigation process as its utility becomes zero. In this experiment, robots' initial positions are randomly chosen. The experiment parameters are $\rho^* = 2$ m, $w^* = 0.5$ rad/s, $k_\varphi = 2.5$ and $k_\rho = 2$.

The circumnavigation process is shown in Fig. 4. It demonstrates the positions of robots at different stages. The yellow lines connecting each robot's center

---

2 The simulation results are illustrated in the full version http://arxiv.org/abs/1805.05395.

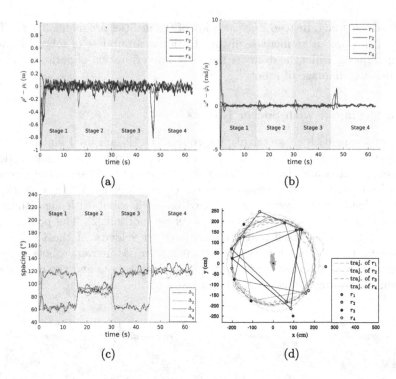

**Fig. 5.** The data plots of the real robot experiment. (Color figure online)

indicate the formation shape. The ball in the middle of the field is the target to be encircled, which is marked by a red circle. The corresponding data plots are shown in Fig. 5. Since robots move on the ground, the error plot of $-z$ is omitted. In Fig. 5d, the red, green, blue and black solid lines connecting the centres of robots represent the formation shapes at Stage 1, 2, 3 and 4 respectively. The dashed lines originated from robots are their trajectories. Note that since $r_2$ quits from the formation at Stage 4 ($\mu_2 = 0$), the data related to $r_2$ is not plotted after 45 s. The circumnavigation radii, angular speeds and formation spacing converge to but fluctuate around the desired values at each stage (see Fig. 5a, b and c respectively). Noticeably, at the last intersection (45 s), the circumnavigation radius and spacing for the robot $r_1$ deviate significantly from the desired values due to the absence of the robot $r_2$ in the formation, but the variations diminish rapidly subsequently (see Fig. 5a and c). The robot $r_4$ is hardly affected as it is not a neighboring robot of $r_2$. In Fig. 5d, the black dot at the center is the real position of the target and the cluster of pink dots are the perceived positions of the target by $r_1$. This manifests that information noise increases the uncertainty of the perceived information. Although there are fluctuations due to the information noise, the real spacing converges to the expected spacing at each stage (see Fig. 5c).

# 5 Concluding Remarks and Future Work

This paper proposes a distributed control law for a multi-robot system to realize circumnavigation process with dynamic spacing based on utilities. Unlike most of the existing study, in this paper, the spacing is not fixed and equal but they are dynamic, which is useful if robots are heterogeneous (e.g. with different kinematics capabilities). The theoretical analysis using graph theory along with the experiments prove the effectiveness of the proposed circumnavigation control algorithm based on utilities.

Although Theorem 2 implies that robots will not collide with each other since their orders are unchanged during the circumnavigation process, this claim is based on the assumption that robots are considered as mass points. The collision avoidance problem taking into account the physical dimensions of robots will be studied in the future.

**Acknowledgements.** Our work is supported by National Science Foundation of China (NO. 61503401 and NO. 61773393), and graduate school of National University of Defense Technology.

# References

1. Franchi, A., Stegagno, P., Oriolo, G.: Decentralized multi-robot encirclement of a 3D target with guaranteed collision avoidance. Auton. Robots **40**(2), 245–265 (2016)
2. Lu, H., Yang, S., Zhang, H., Zheng, Z.: A robust omnidirectional vision sensor for soccer robots. Mechatronics **21**(2), 373–389 (2011)
3. Marshall, B.J.A., Broucke, M.E., Francis, B.A.: Formation of vehicles in cyclic pursuit. IEEE Trans. Autom. Control **49**(11), 1963–1974 (2015)
4. Mesbahi, M., Egerstedt, M.: Graph Theoretic Methods in Multiagent Networks. Princeton University Press, Princeton (2010)
5. Minc, H.: Nonnegative Matrices. Wiley, Hoboken (1988)
6. Olfati-Saber, R., Murray, R.M.: Consensus problems in networks of agents with switching topology and time-delays. IEEE Trans. Autom. Control **49**(9), 1520–1533 (2004)
7. Pavone, M., Frazzoli, E.: Decentralized policies for geometric pattern formation and path coverage. J. Dyn. Syst. Meas. Control **129**(5), 633–643 (2007)
8. Tang, S., Shinzaki, D., Lowe, C.G., Clark, C.M.: Multi-robot control for circumnavigation of particle distributions. In: Ani Hsieh, M., Chirikjian, G. (eds.) Distributed Autonomous Robotic Systems. STAR, vol. 104, pp. 149–162. Springer, Heidelberg (2014). https://doi.org/10.1007/978-3-642-55146-8_11
9. Wang, C., Xie, G., Cao, M.: Forming circle formations of anonymous mobile agents with order preservation. IEEE Trans. Autom. Control **58**(12), 3248–3254 (2013)
10. Wang, C., Xie, G., Cao, M.: Controlling anonymous mobile agents with unidirectional locomotion to form formations on a circle. Automatica **50**(4), 1100–1108 (2014)
11. Xiong, D., et al.: The design of an intelligent soccer-playing robot. Ind. Robot **43**, 91–102 (2016)

12. Yao, W., Dai, W., Xiao, J., Lu, H., Zheng, Z.: A simulation system based on ROS and Gazebo for RoboCup middle size league. In: 2015 IEEE International Conference on Robotics and Biomimetics (ROBIO), pp. 54–59. IEEE (2015)
13. Yao, W., Zeng, Z., Wang, X., Lu, H., Zheng, Z.: Distributed encirclement control with arbitrary spacing for multiple anonymous mobile robots. In: 2017 Chinese Control Conference (CCC), Dalian, China, July 2017
14. Yu, X., Liu, L.: Distributed circular formation control of ring-networked nonholonomic vehicles. Automatica **68**, 92–99 (2016)

# Prediction of a Ball Trajectory for the Humanoid Robots: A Friction-Based Study

Behnam Yazdankhoo[1], Mohammad Navid Shahsavari[1], Soroush Sadeghnejad[1(✉)], and Jacky Baltes[2]

[1] Bio-Inspired System Design Lab, Amirkabir University of Technology (Tehran Polytechnic), No. 424, Hafez Avenue, P.O. Box 15875-4413 Tehran, Iran
s.sadeghnejad@aut.ac.ir
[2] Department of Electrical Engineering, National Taiwan Normal University, 162 Heping E Road Sec. 1, Taipei 10610, Taiwan

**Abstract.** Recent advances in robotics have made it necessary for robots to be able to predict actions like humans. This problem is well presented in international RoboCup competition leagues, especially for humanoid robots in challenges such as Goal-Kick from Moving Ball. In this paper, we proposed double exponential smoothing (DES), autoregressive (AR) and quadratic prediction (QP) as online methods and self-perturbing recursive least squares (SPRLS) as an offline method for prediction of the ball trajectory on ground. These prediction methods are compared in two scenarios by applying LuGre friction model. We simulated our proposed methods by Simmechanics library of MATLAB's Simulink. By comparing results using root-mean-square error and normalized root-mean-square error, we could deduce that methods that were based on predefined models such as QP performed poorly when the friction deviated from the presumed model. Whereas numerical methods such as AR could adapt themselves to variation much better, depending on the friction force variation with time. Also offline methods such as SPRLS are good replacements for online ones when pre-training is possible.

**Keywords:** Humanoid robots · Ball trajectory prediction · LuGre model · Goal-Kick from Moving Ball · Autoregressive · Exponential smoothing

## 1 Introduction

The RoboCup competitions goal for 2050 was started in 1997: a team with fully autonomous humanoid soccer player robots shall win against the winner of the world cup [1]. In order to reach this objective, RoboCup competitions are held every year with incremental steps toward this goal [2,3]. One of the technical challenges in RoboCup competitions is Goal-Kick from Moving Ball. Figure 1

B. Yazdankhoo and M. N. Shahsavari—Contributed equally to this work.

© Springer Nature Switzerland AG 2019
D. Holz et al. (Eds.): RoboCup 2018, LNAI 11374, pp. 387–398, 2019.
https://doi.org/10.1007/978-3-030-27544-0_32

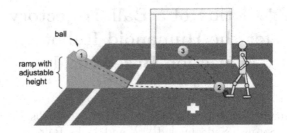

**Fig. 1.** Steps of the RoboCup Goal-Kick from Moving Ball challenge [4].

shows the steps of this challenge; a ball is thrown and the robot should place itself in the appropriate position and kick the ball.

In order to reach this ability, the robot should be able to predict the ball trajectory. Prediction is one of the primary abilities of the human. A psychology study in 1998 showed that a 6-month-old human infant has the ability to predict the trajectory of the objects [5]. This shows the necessity of the prediction in humanoid robots in order to act and think like humans.

A research by Seekircher *et al.* [6] presented an accurate ball tracking using Extended Kalman Filters in order to implement high level behavior in the RoboCup 3D soccer simulation scenario. There is considerable number of works carried out on tracking problem. However, it is different from trajectory prediction. Wang *et al.* proposed an online intention inference algorithm to predict the intention of the human before hitting the ball in a ping-pong match between human and robot [7]. But no algorithm for prediction of ball trajectory is presented in this work. In [8], a method was presented for catching a thrown ball. They focused on the trajectory of the robot to catch the ball by using a least squares method for prediction of the ball trajectory.

Birbach *et al.* [9] presented a method for estimating position and velocity of multiple flying balls for the purpose of robotic ball catching. To this end, a multi-target recursive Bayes filter, the Gaussian Mixture Probability Hypothesis Density filter (GMPHD), fed by a circle detector was used. Finally, they focused on detections that are likely to lead to a catchable trajectory which increases robustness. However, their work was an estimation of the ball position. A predictor based on nearest neighbor regression was presented by Mironov and Pongratz in [10], which does not require an exact physical model of the motion. The challenge of such application consists of a high volume of calculations that are needed to compare the current trajectory with examples from the database.

A research by Baum *et al.* [11] presented a visual tracking and Extended Kalman Filter based prediction method for catching a flying ball with a Hand-Arm-System. In [12], a method was proposed based on probability hypothesis density (PHD) filtering for predicting the ball trajectory.

These studies were estimating the ball position, either predicting the ball trajectory with methods that have a huge amount of calculation or not focusing on rolling ball on ground with variant values of the friction. In this paper, we focused on predicting the soccer ball trajectory rolling on the ground with different values of the friction compared with the constant value of the friction. Also, we presented different possible scenarios for friction force and demonstrate which method is the best solution for each scenario. We will apply all methods to friction scenarios and demonstrate the best method by using root-mean-square error (RMSE) and normalized root-mean-square error (NRMSE) as comparison factors. The main aim of our work is to predict the trajectory of the rolling ball in order to be kicked towards the goal; however, passing the ball to another robot and using it for a goalkeeper can be other possible applications.

The rest of the paper consists of 4 sections: Sect. 2 presents our proposed prediction methods and formulations of them in details. Section 3 contains information about the friction model that is used in our research and formulation of it. Assumptions and parameters of the simulation along with simulation results are presented in Sect. 4. Finally, in Sect. 5, a summary of our work, conclusions and directions for future works are presented.

## 2    Prediction Methods

Ball trajectory prediction could be carried out in two different schemes: online and offline. We use three methods for online scheme and one method for offline scheme, although other methods are also available in the literature, for instance recurrent neural networks [13]. The presented methods are valid while the ball is moving on the ground, in any direction; however, without loss of generality, we denote the position by $x$ assuming the ball is moving in X-direction.

### 2.1    Online Methods

In the online scheme, the trajectory is predicted while the ball is moving, without any a priori knowledge about the environment, i.e. the physical condition of the ground is unknown to the robot.

**Double Exponential Smoothing Method (DES).** In [14], Exponential Smoothing methods are divided into 15 classes based on trend and seasonality. Ball position, in our case, has clearly no seasonality, but it does have an increasing trend. Therefore, we adopt DES as our prediction method here. In this method, we assume that $x$ is the position of the ball at time $t$. The predicted positions based on DES is obtained according to the following relations:

$$S_i = \alpha x_i + (1 - \alpha)(S_{i-1} + b_{i-1}) \tag{1}$$

$$b_i = \gamma(S_i - S_{i-1}) + (1 - \gamma)b_{i-1} \tag{2}$$

where $0 < \alpha, \gamma \leq 1$, and $\hat{x}$ represents predicted position. Also, i = 1, 2, ..., n. $S_i$ and $b_i$ are calculated in n steps and are used to derive predicted position, as follows:

$$\hat{x}_{n+m} = S_n + mb_n \tag{3}$$

Where, m $= 1, 2, \ldots$ is the number of steps ahead. When $0 \leq t < T$, Eqs. (1) and (2) are used and the prediction for future positions is during $t \geq T$ using Eq. (3), where $T$ is determined based on the desired conditions.

There are different ways of calculating the coefficients $\alpha$ and $\gamma$, for instance in [15] an adaptive approach is described. We used constant values for coefficients in this work, because the defined problem is rather simplified and thus constant coefficients suffice. Nevertheless, adaptive prediction which takes prediction updates into account will be one of the important future works we are pursuing.

**Autoregressive Method (AR).** An autoregressive process of order $p$, or AR(p), is one which estimates the future value of a parameter based on a linear combination of $p$ previous values of that parameter. An AR(p) process can be represented according to the following relation,

$$\hat{x}_{i+1} = \phi_1 x_i + \phi_2 x_{i-1} + \ldots + \phi_p x_{i-p+1} \tag{4}$$

where $\phi_j$, j $= 1, 2, \ldots, $p, are the process coefficients and $\hat{x}_{i+1}$ represents the one-step-ahead predicted position.

Some procedures exist in order to determine the appropriate order $p$; however, it has been shown that second derivative of position, i.e. acceleration, can be represented by a first-order AR model [16]. Therefore, in terms of acceleration, we can write:

$$\hat{a}_{i+1} = \psi a_i \tag{5}$$

where $a$ and $\hat{a}$ represent the actual and predicted accelerations, respectively. Also, the relation between $a$ and $x$ in discrete space can be represented as:

$$a_i = \frac{x_i - 2x_{i-1} + x_{i-2}}{(\delta t)^2} \tag{6}$$

where $\delta t$ is the corresponding sample time. Combining (5) and (6), a third-order AR model is obtained for position.

$$\hat{x}_{i+1} = (2 + \psi)x_i + (-1 - 2\psi)x_{i-1} + \psi x_{i-2} \tag{7}$$

Coefficients of an AR(p) model can be obtained through different methods. A well-known and efficient method is the Yule-Walker equations [17]. Considering the notation defined in (4), the Yule-Walker equations can be shown in matrix form as follows ((8b) is the equivalent form of (8a)).

$$\begin{bmatrix} r_1 \\ r_2 \\ \vdots \\ r_p \end{bmatrix} = \begin{bmatrix} r_0 & r_1 & r_2 & \ldots & r_{p-2} & r_{p-1} \\ r_1 & r_0 & r_1 & & r_{p-3} & r_{p-2} \\ & \vdots & & \ddots & \vdots \\ r_{p-1} & r_{p-2} & r_{p-3} & \cdots & r_1 & r_0 \end{bmatrix} \begin{bmatrix} \phi_1 \\ \phi_2 \\ \vdots \\ \phi_p \end{bmatrix} \tag{8a}$$

$$r = R\Phi \tag{8b}$$

In (8a), $r_k$, $k = 0, 1, \ldots, p$, are the autocorrelation functions which are defined according to:

$$r_k := \frac{c_k}{c_0} \tag{9}$$

where $c_k$ are the autocovariance functions which are defined as follows:

$$c_k := E[x_i x_{i-k}] \tag{10}$$

where $E[.]$ denotes mathematical expectation. Theoretically, $E[x_i x_{i-k}]$ should be computed with infinite number of observations. However, since this is not possible during an online prediction, the mathematical expectation could be approximated by proper number of observations (based on the parameter $T$ explained in the previous section). Also note that for autocovariance function, we have $c_{-k} = c_k$.

Using (9) and (10), the corresponding matrices $\mathbf{r}$ and $\mathbf{R}$ in (8a and 8b) can be obtained and, thus, the matrix of coefficients $\phi$ is achieved.

$$\boldsymbol{\Phi} = \boldsymbol{R}^{-1}\boldsymbol{r} \tag{11}$$

For the acceleration model represented by (5), the single coefficient $\psi$ can be obtained by using Eqs. (8a and 8b) to (11). Then, substituting the resulted $\psi$ into (7), the third order model for one-step-ahead position is attained. To predict position $m$ steps ahead, one should repeat the Eq. (7) $m$ times. For instance, for $x_{i+m}$ we can write:

$$\hat{x}_{i+m} = (2 + \psi)\hat{x}_{i+m-1} + (-1 - 2\psi)\hat{x}_{i+m-2} + \psi\hat{x}_{i+m-3} \tag{12}$$

where $\hat{x}_{i+m-1}$ is the predicted position for $m$-1 steps ahead, and $\hat{x}_{i+m-2}$ and $\hat{x}_{i+m-3}$ are also defined in a similar manner.

**Quadratic Prediction Method (QP).** If we consider that the friction is the only force acting on the ball and it follows Coulomb's law, a simplified kinetic model is attained utilizing Newton's second law.

$$a = \frac{\sum F}{m_b} = \frac{-\mu m_b g}{m_b} = -\mu g \tag{13}$$

where $a$ and $m_b$ are the acceleration and mass of the ball, respectively, $\mu$ is the coefficient of kinetic friction, which is considered constant, $\sum F$ represents the sum of the forces acting on the ball, and $g$ is the gravitational acceleration.

The kinematic equation representing this motion is:

$$x = \frac{1}{2}at^2 + v_0 t + x_0 \tag{14}$$

where $v_0$ and $x_0$ denote the initial velocity and position of the ball, respectively, and $t$ represents the time.

According to (13), the acceleration of the ball is constant and, thus, the position of the ball, defined by (14), represents a quadratic model in terms of time. Therefore, we can generally write:

$$x = A_1 t^2 + A_2 t + A_3 \tag{15}$$

where $A_1$, $A_2$ and $A_3$ are constants. If we can record three different positions at three different times at the beginning $T$ seconds of the motion, coefficients $A_1$, $A_2$ and $A_3$ can be readily used in order to form the equation of motion of the ball according to (15). Having the equation of motion, we can predict the position of the ball at each time during the motion for $t \geq T$.

## 2.2   Offline Methods

In offline scheme the ball movement is repeated several times and the robot records the data received from the movements before the desired movement begins and learns how to predict the ball trajectory next time that the ball moves.

**Self-Perturbing Recursive Least Squares (SPRLS).** RLS is a recursive algorithm for determining the parameters of the system. Because of high error of RLS in low variance, we choose SPRLS [18] for predicting the ball position.

$$L_i = \frac{P_{i-1}\Phi_i}{1 + \Phi_i^T P_{i-1}\Phi_i} \tag{16}$$

$$P_i = P_{i-1}(I - L_i\Phi_i^T) + \beta NINT(\lambda e_{i-1}^2)I \tag{17}$$

$$\hat{\theta}_i = \hat{\theta}_{i-1} + L_i(y_i - \Phi_i^T \hat{\theta}_{i-1}) \tag{18}$$

where $e := y - \hat{y}$ is the estimation error with $y := \theta^T \Phi$ and $\hat{y} := \hat{\theta}^T \Phi$ denoting real and estimated outputs, respectively. Also $\Phi$ is vector of input parameters, $\theta$ is vector of estimated parameters, I is identity matrix, $\beta$ is design coefficient, $\lambda$ is sensitivity coefficient, and NINT(.) function is defined as:

$$NINT(x) := \begin{cases} x & x \geq 0.5 \\ 0 & 0 \leq x < 0.5 \end{cases} \tag{19}$$

If we consider that the acceleration is constant, by combination of (13) and (14) we have:

$$x = -\frac{1}{2}\mu g t^2 + v_0 t + x_0 \tag{20}$$

Hence, we can write

$$-2(x - v_0 t - x_0) = \mu g t^2 \tag{21}$$

Comparison between (21) and $y := \theta^T \Phi$ results in:

$$y = -2(x - v_0 t - x_0) \tag{22}$$

$$\theta^T = \mu g \tag{23}$$

$$\phi = t^2 \tag{24}$$

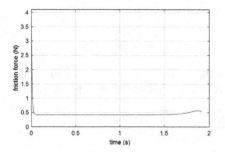

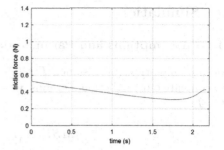

**Fig. 2.** First scenario friction force-time diagram.

**Fig. 3.** Second scenario friction force-time diagram.

## 3   Friction Model

There are several models of friction to use in simulation. Here we have used LuGre model [19] because of simplicity and also good accuracy in many cases. The formulation of this model is:

$$F_f = \sigma_0 z + \sigma_1 \dot{z} + \sigma_2 v$$

$$\dot{z} = v - \frac{\sigma_0 |v|}{s(v)} z \tag{25}$$

$$s(v) = F_c + (F_s - F_c) exp(-(\frac{v}{v_s})^{\delta_{vs}})$$

where $F_f$ is the friction force, $\sigma_1$ and $\sigma_2$ are damping coefficients that are related to the presliding and kinetic friction states, respectively, $v$ is the velocity, the parameter $v_s$ determines how quickly $s(v)$ approaches $F_c$, $F_s = \mu_s m_b g$ and $F_c = \mu_k m_b g$ are static friction force and coulomb friction force, respectively, $\mu_s$ and $\mu_k$ denote friction coefficients and $\delta_{vs}$ is the shape factor of Stribeck curve.

We assumed two scenarios with different friction forces in order to investigate the effect of friction on prediction quality, although many other possible scenarios exist. As shown in Fig. 2, the friction in first scenario is almost constant over time. Whereas Fig. 3 shows that it is variant over time in the second scenario. The common coefficients between two scenarios are (the value for $\delta_{vs}$ is derived from [20], while the others are chosen arbitrarily in order to obtain reasonable friction forces. Also, the mass of the ball is the standard RoboCup ball mass): $m_b = 0.425 \, \text{kg}, v_s = 0.1 \, \frac{\text{m}}{\text{s}}, \delta_{vs} = 1$.

Scenario 1 coefficients are: $\mu_s = 0.25, \mu_k = 0.1, \sigma_0 = 30 \, \frac{\text{N}}{\text{m}}, \sigma_1 = 2 \, \frac{\text{N s}}{\text{m}}, \sigma_2 = 0 \, \frac{\text{N s}}{\text{m}}$ and scenario 2 coefficients are: $\mu_s = 0.15, \mu_k = 0.06, \sigma_0 = 100 \, \frac{\text{N}}{\text{m}}, \sigma_1 = 0.5 \, \frac{\text{N s}}{\text{m}}, \sigma_2 = 0.14 \, \frac{\text{N s}}{\text{m}}$.

# 4   Simulation

## 4.1   Assumptions and Parameters

In our simulation, we assumed $T = 0.5$ s, initial velocity, $v_0 = 2\,\frac{m}{s}$ and in order to compare our prediction methods, we use RMSE and NRMSE which start from $t = T$.

$$RMSE = \sqrt{\frac{1}{M} \sum_{i=1}^{M} (x_i - \hat{x}_i)^2} \tag{26}$$

$$NRMSE = \frac{RMSE}{x_{\max} - x_{\min}} \tag{27}$$

$x$ and $\hat{x}$ are the actual and predicted positions, respectively, and $M$ is the total number of predicted steps. Also $x_{\max} = x(t = t_{end})$ where $t_{end}$ denotes the time at which the ball stops, and $x_{\min} = x(t = 0)$ for offline method and $x_{\min} = x(t = T)$ for online methods.

We assumed DES method parameters as: $\alpha = 0.9, \gamma = 0.5$

For QP method, in order to derive $A_1, A_2, A_3$ we need three equations. After $T$ seconds, using positions at $t_1 = 0$, $t_2 = \frac{T}{2}$ and $t_3 = T$ and (15) we have three equations to derive $A_1, A_2, A_3$ then we have:

$$\begin{aligned}
A_1 &= \frac{(t_3 x_0 - t_3 x_1 - t_2 x_0 + t_2 x_2)}{t_3 t_2 (t_3 - t_2)} \\
A_2 &= \frac{-(t_3^2 x_0 - t_3^2 x_1 - t_2^2 x_0 + t_2^2 x_2)}{t_3 t_2 (t_3 - t_2)} \\
A_3 &= x_0
\end{aligned} \tag{28}$$

In SPRLS method, we assumed $v_0 = 2.5\,\frac{m}{s}$ for training phase and $v_0 = 2\,\frac{m}{s}$ for prediction phase. Also, RMSE and NRMSE are calculated from $t = 0$. Initial values for SPRLS method are: $\hat{\theta}_0 = 1.962, P_0 = 1, e_0 = 1$ and the parameters are: $\lambda = 100, \beta = 30000$.

## 4.2   Simulation Results

We simulated our methods by means of Simmechanics library (second generation) of MATLAB's Simulink. Our vision system frequency is 20 Hz and in order to achieve more real results, we chose this frequency for running the simulation in MATLAB.

As can be seen in Figs. 4 and 5, the QP method has yielded by far the best result for scenario 1, where the friction force is almost constant over time. This fact can be further proved quantitatively by Tables 1 and 2, where the RMSE and NRMSE are obtained to be 0.0036 m and 0.0034, respectively, for this method. This is, however, not surprising since the predefined model in QP method is in great accordance with the friction force which is applied to the ball during the whole motion in this scenario. Apart from this, the offline SPRLS method has resulted in a good prediction with an acceptable NRMSE of 0.1913. The other two online methods, namely AR and DES, showed poorer predictions with NRMSE of 38.68% and 41.52%, respectively.

For scenario 2, Table 2 indicates that online QP and offline SPRLS still lead to more accurate predictions. However, from another perspective, the 4239% rise in the RMSE for QP method from scenario 1 to scenario 2 shows that when the friction force does not comply with the predefined model in QP, the precision of this method decreases drastically. Meanwhile, the 45.6% increase in the RMSE of SPRLS method shows that such a remarkable change has not occurred for this method. The interesting point in scenario 2 is, however, the 30% reduction of the RMSE in AR method in comparison with scenario 1, which demonstrates that this method has adapted itself better to scenario 2. But this is not the case for DES since its performance has deteriorated in scenario 2.

Looking more closely at Figs. 5 and 7, one can obviously observe that both AR and DES methods have predicted a linear trajectory for the ball, which means that the ball will move infinitely and will never stop. The same concept can be interpreted by investigating the relevant mathematical relations presented in Sect. 2.1. This is, however, not compatible with the physical reality of the problem. Therefore, it can be deduced that methods which merely rely on numerical data for prediction often fail to take the physical concepts into account, and are thus suitable for the situations where little data is available about the actual circumstances beforehand. These methods can also be utilized when the prediction is to be carried out not far into the future; linear predictions can be a good approximation of the curved ball position graph (with respect to time) dependent on the applied friction force. Of course, great care should be taken in adopting numerical methods. As discussed in the previous paragraph, AR method yielded a much better result in scenario 2 (the friction force of which was depicted in Fig. 3) than DES method. However, for a different form of friction, the same result is not guaranteed to be attained, which shows the importance of the physical conditions governing the problem.

Ultimately, it can be concluded that when the physical conditions of the ball and ground are known to a good extent beforehand, model-based methods such as online QP are suitable choices for predicting the trajectory of the ball. If, on the other hand, online predicting is not required and the opportunity for pre-training exists, offline SPRLS method provides a good chance to estimate the physical conditions governing the problem and thus to predict the trajectory by an acceptable accuracy. Moreover, online model-free or numerical methods such as AR or DES can also provide us with good predictions, but the precision of the results greatly depend on the variation of the friction force with time (Fig. 6).

**Table 1.** Calculated RMSE for all methods

|       | Scenario1 (m) | Scenario2 (m) |
|-------|---------------|---------------|
| DES   | 0.4405        | 0.5669        |
| AR    | 0.4104        | 0.3154        |
| QP    | 0.0036        | 0.1562        |
| SPRLS | 0.3650        | 0.5316        |

**Table 2.** Calculated NRMSE for all methods

|       | Scenario 1 | Scenario 2 |
|-------|-----------|-----------|
| DES   | 0.4152    | 0.5032    |
| AR    | 0.386     | 0.2800    |
| QP    | 0.0034    | 0.1386    |
| SPRLS | 0.1913    | 0.2688    |

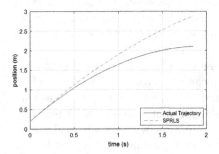

**Fig. 4.** Trajectory predicted using offline method comparing with actual trajectory in first scenario.

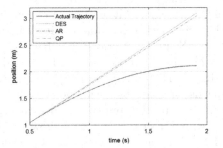

**Fig. 5.** Trajectory predicted using online methods comparing with actual trajectory in first scenario.

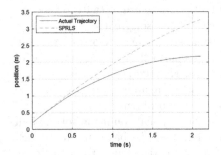

**Fig. 6.** Trajectory predicted using offline method comparing with actual trajectory in second scenario.

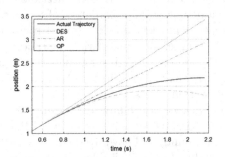

**Fig. 7.** Trajectory predicted using online methods comparing with actual trajectory in second scenario.

## 5   Conclusion and Future Works

In this paper, we aimed at predicting the trajectory of the ball for humanoid robots, which can be used for different goals such as the Goal-Kick from Moving Ball challenge in Robocup. We simulated two different friction forces and compared three online and one offline methods for this aim. The simulated scenarios were presented in one direction; however, the equations are all valid while the motion is completely on the ground.

The results of the simulations indicated that the accuracy of the prediction methods is highly dependent on the frictional condition which governs the motion. However, we concluded that if the physical conditions are known before the start of the motion, online model-based methods such QP are good candidates, while model-free AR and DES methods could be utilized online when either little information about motion is available or the time interval of the prediction is rather small. Offline SPRLS method is also useful when the robot has the opportunity to be pre-trained.

There are many directions regarding future works. First, these methods should be implemented on real humanoid robots to predict the ball trajectory in order to kick, pass or intercept the ball in real-life scenarios, since the explored friction force scenarios in this paper were only two examples of various possible ones. Predicting the three-dimensional trajectory of the ball is also of great interest. As another future direction, more realistic and human-like factors can be taken into account. For instance, the prediction could be updated and improved as the ball moves nearer to the robot by considering proper adaption laws for the presented methods. Also other factors which lead to deviation from ideal circumstances should be considered, such as small obstacles along the path of the ball, lack of perfect roundness of the ball and air drag.

# References

1. Gerndt, R., Seifert, D., Baltes, J.H., Sadeghnejad, S., Behnke, S.: Humanoid robots in soccer: robots versus humans in RoboCup 2050. IEEE Robot. Autom. Mag. **22**, 147–154 (2015). https://doi.org/10.1109/MRA.2015.2448811
2. Baltes, J., Sadeghnejad, S., Seifert, D., Behnke, S.: RoboCup humanoid league rule developments 2002–2014 and future perspectives. In: Bianchi, R.A.C., Akin, H.L., Ramamoorthy, S., Sugiura, K. (eds.) RoboCup 2014. LNCS (LNAI), vol. 8992, pp. 649–660. Springer, Cham (2015). https://doi.org/10.1007/978-3-319-18615-3_53
3. Javadi, M., Azar, S.M., Azami, S., Ghidary, S.S., Sadeghnejad, S., Baltes, J.: Humanoid robot detection using deep learning: a speed-accuracy tradeoff. In: Akiyama, H., Obst, O., Sammut, C., Tonidandel, F. (eds.) RoboCup 2017. LNCS (LNAI), vol. 11175, pp. 338–349. Springer, Cham (2018). https://doi.org/10.1007/978-3-030-00308-1_28
4. RoboCup Soccer Humanoid League Laws of the Game (2017). Robocup Humanoid League. http://www.robocuphumanoid.org/wp-content/uploads/RCHL-2017-final-2.pdf
5. von Hofsten, C., Vishton, P., Spelke, E.S., Feng, Q., Rosander, K.: Predictive action in infancy: tracking and reaching for moving objects. Cognition **67**, 255–285 (1998). https://doi.org/10.1016/S0010-0277(98)00029-8
6. Seekircher, A., Abeyruwan, S., Visser, U.: Accurate ball tracking with extended kalman filters as a prerequisite for a high-level behavior with reinforcement learning. In: The 6th Workshop on Humanoid Soccer Robots at Humanoid Conference, Bled, Slovenia (2011)
7. Wang, Z., et al.: Probabilistic movement modeling for intention inference in human-robot interaction. Int. J. Robot. Res. **32**, 841–858 (2013). https://doi.org/10.1177/0278364913478447

8. Nishiwaki, K., Ionno, A., Nagashima, K., Inaba, M., Inoue, H.: The humanoid Saika that catches a thrown ball. In: 6th IEEE International Workshop on Robot and Human Communication, Sendai, Japan, pp. 94–99. IEEE (1997). https://doi.org/10.1109/ROMAN.1997.646959

9. Birbach, O., Frese, U.: Estimation and prediction of multiple flying balls using probability hypothesis density filtering. In: 2011 IEEE/RSJ International Conference on Intelligent Robots and Systems (IROS), pp. 3426–3433. IEEE (2011). https://doi.org/10.1109/IROS.2011.6094622

10. Mironov, K., Pongratz, M.: Fast kNN-based prediction for the trajectory of a thrown body. In: 24th Mediterranean Conference on Control and Automation (MED), pp. 512–517. IEEE (2016). https://doi.org/10.1109/MED.2016.7536007

11. Bäuml, B., Wimböck, T., Hirzinger, G.: Kinematically optimal catching a flying ball with a hand-arm-system. In: 2010 IEEE/RSJ International Conference on Intelligent Robots and Systems (IROS), Taipei, Taiwan, pp. 2592–2599. IEEE (2010). https://doi.org/10.1109/IROS.2010.5651175

12. Birbach, O.: Tracking and calibration for a ball catching humanoid robot. Doctoral thesis, Universität Bremen (2012)

13. Stolzenburg, F., Michael, O., Obst, O.: Predictive neural networks. arXiv preprint arXiv:180203308 (2018)

14. Gardner Jr., E.S.: Exponential smoothing: the state of the art-part II. Int. J. Forecast. **22**, 637–666 (2006). https://doi.org/10.1016/j.ijforecast.2006.03.005

15. Stakem, F., AlRegib, G.: An adaptive approach to exponential smoothing for CVE state prediction. In: 2nd International Conference on Immersive Telecommunications, Berkley, USA, ICST (Institute for Computer Sciences, Social-Informatics and Telecommunications Engineering), pp. 141–146 (2009). https://doi.org/10.4108/ICST.IMMERSCOM2009.6409

16. Sakr, N., Georganas, N.D., Zhao, J., Shen, X.: Motion and force prediction in haptic media. In: 2007 IEEE International Conference on Multimedia and Expo, Beijing, China, pp. 2242–2245. IEEE (2007). https://doi.org/10.1109/ICME.2007.4285132

17. Cheng, B.: Yule-walker equations. Wiley StatsRef: Statistics Reference Online (2014). https://doi.org/10.1002/9781118445112.stat05549

18. Park, D.-J., Jun, B.-E.: Selfperturbing recursive least squares algorithm with fast tracking capability. Electron. Lett. **28**, 558–559 (1992). https://doi.org/10.1049/el:19920352

19. Piatkowski, T.: Dahl and LuGre dynamic friction models-the analysis of selected properties. Mech. Mach. Theory **73**, 91–100 (2014). https://doi.org/10.1016/j.mechmachtheory.2013.10.009

20. Johanastrom, K., Canudas-De-Wit, C.: Revisiting the LuGre friction model. IEEE Control Syst. **28**, 101–114 (2008). https://doi.org/10.1109/MCS.2008.929425

# Champion Papers

# RoboCup SSL 2018 Champion Team Paper

Zheyuan Huang, Lingyun Chen, Jiacheng Li, Yunkai Wang, Zexi Chen,
Licheng Wen, Jianyang Gu, Peng Hu, and Rong Xiong[✉]

Zhejiang University, Zheda Road No.38,
Hangzhou, Zhejiang Province, People's Republic of China
rxiong@zju.edu.cn
https://zjunlict.cn

**Abstract.** The Small Size League is one of the important events in
RoboCup Soccer. ZJUNlict got the first place in RoboCup 2018. In
this paper, we introduce the new innovations and development we have
made in the past year. These innovations include the mechanical part
which accounted for most of our incredible goals and software part which
enables us to play the game under a terrible vision situation. We also
purpose an interception prediction algorithm to achieve some skills and
improve our ball possession rate.

**Keywords:** RoboCup · Dribbler · Vision prediction ·
Interception prediction

## 1 Introduction

Small Size League (SSL) is an important part of the RoboCup event. It is the
fastest and most intense game in RoboCup's soccer competitions. ZJUNlict from
Zhejiang University has participated in this League for over ten years since 2004.
In RoboCup competition, we have made great progress and won the championship place in 2013 and 2014. After getting third place in the following two
years, we won the championship again in RoboCup 2018 in Montreal. The development of our hardware system during these years is shown in Table 1. The
FPGA handles both motor control and other tasks such as communication and
motion sensor fusion based on embedded Nios II processor. The micro-controller
STM32F407 was added to take over tasks other than motor control since late
2017. Since 2018, a single micro-controller STM32H743 capable of operation frequency up to 400 MHz combined with five BLDC controller Allegro A3930 [4]
was able to handle all the tasks. This paper is organized as follows: First of all,
the major optimization of our mechanical architecture which accounted for most
of our incredible goals are described in Sect. 2. They are "Touching Point Optimization", "Damping System Optimization", and "Dribbler Optimization". Our
detailed improvements in vision module are described in Sect. 3, which enables
us to play the game under a terrible vision situation. The new interception prediction algorithm to achieve some skills is explained in Sect. 4.

© Springer Nature Switzerland AG 2019
D. Holz et al. (Eds.): RoboCup 2018, LNAI 11374, pp. 401–412, 2019.
https://doi.org/10.1007/978-3-030-27544-0_33

402      Z. Huang et al.

**Table 1.** ZJUNlict electrical system configurations

| Configuration | Since 2012 | Since 2017 | Since 2018 |
|---|---|---|---|
| Microcontroller | Cyclone III EP3C25 | Cyclone III EP3C25 | STM32H743 |
| | | STM32F407 | |
| Driving motors | Maxon EC-45 50W | | |
| Dribbling motor | Maxon EC-16 30W | | |
| Encoder | US Digital E4T, 500 CPR | | 1000 CPR |
| BLDC Driver | IR2103S | | Allegro A3930 |
| Motion sensors | Gyroscope | Gyroscope, accelerometer, compass | |
| MOSFETs | IRFR1205 | | IRF8313 |
| Wireless IC | nRF2401A | 2 x nRF24L01+ | |
| Kick Charge IC | UC3843 | | |

## 2  ZJUNlict New Dribbler Design

### 2.1  Typical Dribblers and Existing Problems

The small size league robots do not really have foot like human beings. Instead, they have dribblers. A dribbler is a device that can help dribble and catch the ball. As shown in Fig. 1, a typical dribbler has the following features. A shelf connects 2 side plates and the dribbling motor is fixed on one side plate. Between the 2 side plates is a cylindrical dribbling-bar driven by the dribbling motor. The whole device has only one degree of freedom of rotation and the joints are fixed on the robot flame. Usually there is a unidirectional spring-damping system locates between the shelf and the robot frame to help improve the stability of dribbling as well as absorbing the energy when catching the ball. The dribbling-bar driven by the dribbling motor provides torque to make the ball spin backward when the contact between the ball and dribbling-bar exits so that the ball can be 'locked' by this device in ideal conditions. And the carpet provides supporting force and frictional force and therefore there are 2 touch points on the ball and in this paper we called it a 2-touch-point model (Fig. 2). For the motor control, most teams try to keep the dribbling-bar at a constant rotational speed when dribbling the ball and therefore it is actually an open loop control mode for dribbling. Unfortunately, this 2-touch-point dribbler with unidirectional spring-damping system and passive control mode does not provide ideal dribbling performances. It is quite easy for the ball to bounce back and forth when launching the dribbling motor. The device might also not absorb enough kinetic energy of the moving ball when catching it so it will bounce back and there occurs a catching failure. Actually it is also hard to greatly improve its performance by simply changing the material of dribbling-bar, adjusting the damping and stiffness of the spring-damping system or adjusting the rotational speed of motor. This structure has natural defects with passive control mode.

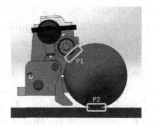

**Fig. 1.** Typical Dribbler (1. Unidirectional damper 2. Dribble motor 3. Connect shelf 4. Dribbling-bar 5. Side plate 6. Rotational joint)

**Fig. 2.** 2-touch-point model

Tigers [4] developed a dribbler with 2 degrees of freedom (Fig. 3). Except for rotational degrees of freedom, the side plates can slide up and down along two damped linear guides with screws covered by thick silicon ring, by doing this, much more kinetic energy will be absorbed by the silicone ring and transferred to the potential energy of the device when catching the ball. It was approved that this device worked quite well with catching and dribbling in static conditions. For example, when the robot stays stilly or just moves back and forth slowly, catching a ball with coming speed up to 5 m/s is quite easy. But considering the real competition environment, the condition will not be that idealistic and more complex movements are needed, indeed. For example, when two robots scramble for a ball, we want our robot able to turn around while dribbling so that it can make space for passing. Also when all shot space is blocked by defenders we want our robot able to do some actions like moving laterally while dribbling to create space to score. In a word, a stronger dribbler is urgently in need.

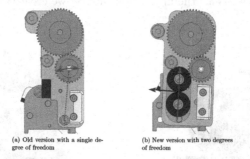

(a) Old version with a single degree of freedom

(b) New version with two degrees of freedom

**Fig. 3.** Energy absorbing by creating a dual freedom [4]

## 2.2   Dribbler Improvements

Considering the purpose above, we devoted ourselves on the dribbler. Firstly, we adjust the geometry parameters of the device so that the ball can touch the chip shovel in steady state, which means both carpet and chip shovel can provide supporting force and frictional force to the ball so we called it a 3-touch-point model (Fig. 4). Normally the dynamic friction coefficient between the ball-carpet surface is greater than that of the ball-chip shove surface. Therefore, when the ball driven by the dribbling-bar moves from the carpet on to the chip shove surface, there will be a sudden drop of frictional force, and the ball will be pushed back on the carpet. And once the ball touches the carpet, there will be a sudden increase of frictional force, the ball will be driven onto the chip shove again. In this kind of state, the amount of spring compression will not change much so that the dribbling system will enter a periodical dynamic steady state. In contrast, with a 2-touch-point system, the friction force will not change much so the ball will enter much more into the dribbler and there will be a bigger compression of the spring-damping system. Therefore the ball will also be pushed back more and totally the bouncing amplitude will be much greater, or even the ball will bounce off the dribbler. In addition, we found that there will be a hard contact between the side plates and the baseplate when the dribbler hits the baseplate. So besides the foam between the shelf and the robot frame, we stick 1.5 mm thick tape between the side plates and baseplate so there will be a soft contact when the dribbler hits the baseplate. Actually this design makes up a bidirectional spring-damping system (Fig. 5) and improves the dynamic behavior of the dribbler. Hopefully it can reduce the bouncing amplitude of the ball when dribbling as well as absorbing more kinetic energy when catching the ball. To improve the dribbling performance when the robot rotates or moves laterally, we also made a dribbling-bar with screw using 3D printing rubber so that it can provide lateral force to the ball when dribbling as shown in Fig. 5. Another key point to make this device better is to change the passive rotational speed control mode to active torque control mode. Instead of keeping the rotational speed with a constant value, we control the motor torque constant according to the current feedback. With the innovations above, we create a quite good active control dribbler.

**Fig. 4.** 3-touch-point model

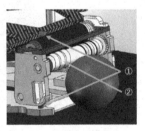

**Fig. 5.** New damper (1. Bidirectional damper 2. Screw dribbling bar)

## 2.3   Tests and Verifications

According to the catching ability tests, the typical 2-touch-point dribbler with unidirectional spring-damping system could catch a ball with coming speed up to 3 m/s and the new 3-touch-point dribbler with bidirectional spring-damping system could catch a ball with coming speed up to 8.5 m/s. The results were quite clear that the new dribbler has better dribbling and catching ability. In addition, we made simple tests to see the effect of screw added on the dribbling bar. The dribbling motor was launched and after the dribbling entering the steady state, we made the robot spin around. The rotational acceleration is 20 deg/s$^2$ and the rotation speed was recorded at the time the ball left the dribbler. This simple test was carried out 10 times for both smooth dribbling-bar and screw dribbling-bar, which were made by some same material. As show in Table 2, the average escape speed of smooth dribbling-bar is 402 deg/s and for the screw dribbling-bar is 622 deg/s. So it was proved that the design of screw could improve the dynamic dribbling performance of dribbler.

**Table 2.** Dynamic dribbling ability comparison between smooth dribbling-bar and screw dribbling-bar

| Dribbling-bar type | 1 | 2 | 3 | 4 | 5 | 6 | 7 | 8 | 9 | 10 | Average |
|---|---|---|---|---|---|---|---|---|---|---|---|
| Smooth dribbling-bar (deg/s) | 400 | 340 | 380 | 360 | 380 | 420 | 400 | 420 | 400 | 520 | 402 |
| Screw dribbling-bar (deg/s) | 600 | 580 | 580 | 580 | 620 | 680 | 620 | 680 | 640 | 640 | 622 |

# 3   SSL Vision Solution

## 3.1   Existing Problems

The existing image recognition system of SSL is shot by cameras (780 × 580 YUV422 60 Hz) which suspended about 4 m above the field. After image acquisition, the vision software provided by SSL official performs color block recognition progress on the ball (orange) and the color code on the top of each robot. The software determines the robot's information (team, id, position and orientation) based on the color code combination at the top of robot, and recognizes the position of the ball based on the orange color patch. Finally the robot and ball information is transmitted to our program for processing in the form of UDP packets.

As the picture (Fig. 6) shows the basic process of the whole SSL vision system. This image system has been used in the SSL competition for around ten years. As the size of the field continues to enlarge, the number of cameras on the field has also increased from 2 to 8 (in this year's competition). Using color block recognition algorithm accordingly will cause the image processed by the graphic processor to survive the following problems:

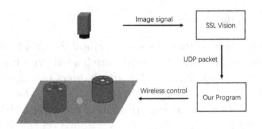

**Fig. 6.** Vision system introduction (Color figure online)

**Noise in the Position Information.** Taking ball as an example, the official vision software recognizes a rectangular orange area as a ball. Therefore, even if the ball itself does not move, the rectangular orange area determined by each frame might still be different, resulting in a small range of jitter in the position of the software recognition. Similarly, there is also jitter in the position of the robot.

Take Fig. 7 as an example. Figure 7.1 is the original image captured by camera. However, as Figs. 7.2 and 7.3 shows, the recognized color block varies from frame to frame.

**Light Interference.** The threshold range of various colors in the vision software needs to manually set, and the difference in light environment will directly affect the performance of different colors recognition. As a result, the official software only works properly in a relatively specific light environment (generally a field lighting with stable brightness). Once the light changes beyond the limit, it needs to manually set the color threshold again.

**Object Missing.** Although the camera is overlooking the scene, there will still be cases where the object is lost in the vision. For example, when the ball is moving at high speed, the color of the ball captured by the camera will become lighter and will form a "fading" phenomenon, which causes the camera fails to recognize the ball. Figure 8 clearly shows the vision output when the ball is moving at a high speed.

In some cases, when the robot takes the ball or while two robots are competing for the ball, the camera will not be able to capture the ball because the robot's body will block the ball, which account for image loss.

**Image Recognition Error.** In some cases within the game, the person's skin color is similar to orange. Therefore the software will recognize a human skin as a ball, thus increasing the wrong information(Fig. 9). When the robot is located at the edge of the camera's coverage, there is a severe image distortion, and the recognition accuracy of the color code is further reduced, and problems such as unrecognizable robot or robot direction recognition errors might occur.

**Tracking from Multiple Overlapping Cameras.** For up to eight cameras, multiple cameras are visible in many areas of the site (maximum of 4). Due to differences in camera parameters and distortion, the position of the same object in different cameras is different.

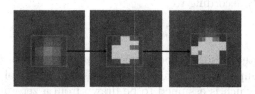

**Fig. 7.** Ball recognition in two different frame

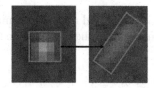

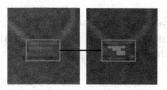

**Fig. 8.** Ball recogintion in high velocity

**Fig. 9.** A non-ball object recognize as a ball

In summary, since the official image recognition software of SSL does not provide us with images of sufficient accuracy we need, we need to process these location information. To this end, we have come up with a complete set of vision solutions.

### 3.2  Solution Introduction

Our image solution provides a code framework that covers the various special cases described above, allowing us to perform algorithmic processing for each situation. After receiving the UDP packet sent by the Graphic Processor, the program will automatically judge the current image quality and suspicious conditions for subsequent algorithm processing.

**Noise Cancellation.** For raw data containing noise, we use a Kalman filter considering noise cancellation.

In order to use the Kalman filter to estimate the internal state of a process given only a sequence of noisy observations, one must model the process in accordance with the framework of the Kalman filter. This means specifying the following matrices:

- $F_k$, the state-transition model;
- and sometimes $B_k$, the control-input model, for each time-step, $k$, as described below.

The Kalman filter model assumes the true state at time $k$ is evolved from the state at $(k-1)$ according to

$$x_k = F_k x_{k-1} + B_k u_k + w_k \tag{1}$$

where $F_k$ is the state transition model which is applied to the previous state $x_{k-1}$; $B_k$ is the control-input model which is applied to the control vector $u_k$; $w_k$ is the process noise which is assumed to be drawn from a zero mean multivariate normal distribution, $\mathcal{N}$, with covariance, $Q_k : \mathbf{w}_k \sim \mathcal{N}(0, Q_k)$

At the same time, because the data noise is effectively eliminated after Kalman filtering, we can also rely on these data for velocity estimation and position prediction.

**Object Confidence.** In order to solve the misjudgment and missed information of the original image itself, we maintained the confidence of the ball and the robot on the field.

$$P_{o,t} = P_{o,t-1} + P(seen, t) - P(lost, t), 0 \leq P_o \leq 1 \tag{2}$$

The above is the mathematical expression of confidence, where:

- $P_{o,t}$ is the confidence of the object o at time t. We set 0 as the initial value of $P_{o,t}$
- $P(seen, t)$ is the probability rise constant of the object o appearing in the image at time t
- $P(lost, t)$ is the probability reduction coefficient of the object disappearing on the image at time t

According to the above formula, we set a confidence threshold of $P_v$, then

$$object = \begin{cases} valid, & P_{o,t} > P_v \\ invalid, & P_{o,t} \leq P_v \end{cases} \tag{3}$$

This solution effectively eliminates the effects of loss of objects due to cameras, light, and the like. At the same time, interference caused by similar objects such as skin is not considered a valid object because its duration is short and its confidence is lower than the confidence threshold.

**Camera Parameter Identification.** Due to the complexity of multiple camera coverage areas on the site, we have adopted an algorithm that automatically identifies camera parameters. While continuously receiving image information, we continuously calculate and update the coverage area, parameters, etc. of the camera.

When an object appears in the field of view of multiple cameras at the same time, we will calculate its actual position by the following formula: $\bar{r}_{real}$

$$\bar{r}_{real} = \frac{\sum_{i=1}^{k} \dfrac{\bar{r}_i - \bar{r}_{cam_i}}{R_{cam_i}} r_i}{\sum_{i=1}^{k} \dfrac{\bar{r}_i - \bar{r}_{cam_i}}{R_{cam_i}}} \tag{4}$$

Among them

- $\bar{r}_{cam_i}$ is the projection coordinate of camera i
- $R_{cam_i}$ is the coverage distance of camera i
- k is the number of cameras that can see the current object

## 3.3   Results

We use the simulation software grSim to test the actual effect of our image module. GrSim can adjust the noise (Gaussian noise) and packet loss rate of the original output image to simulate the effect of real games.

We use the pass success rate to reflect the accuracy of our image module handlers, and we will test the success rate of 100 passes in the current environment.

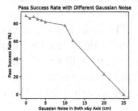

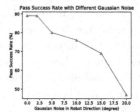

**Fig. 10.** Pass success rate with different Gaussian noise in both X and Y Axis

**Fig. 11.** Pass success rate with different Gaussian noise in robot direction

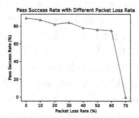

**Fig. 12.** Pass success rate with different packet loss rate

As we can see from the figures above, the pass success rate is above 90% when there's no gaussian noise in x and y axises. When the gaussian noise increases, pass success rate decreases slowly at first. Even when the gaussian noise equals to 10 cm in both axises, which is already a terrible vision input and rarely appears on the RoboCup competition. The pass success rate drops quickly when gaussian noise continues increasing and drops to 0% at about 25 (cm) guassian noise.

When it comes to noise in robot direction, the overall tendency is similar to the former one. However pass success rate drops faster as the noise increases. That's because robot direction determines direction of the passing ball. When there's 15° of gaussian noise in direction, the success rate drops below 70%, which means our program can barely play the game under these situation.

# 4     Interception Prediction Algorithm and Application

## 4.1     Robot Arrival Time Prediction

In our system, we adopted the method used in [5]. First, we carried out RRT global planner, and then the velocity planner based on the path points generated by RRT. For the velocity planner, we use trapezoidal programming. Since it is the omnidirectional wheel that we used, we decompose the translational speed and rotational speed into a 2d planner and a 1d planner. Then, we decompose the translational velocity into two directions with the orientation from the starting location to the target location as the x-axis, which is beneficial for the robot to achieve the maximum velocity in the x-direction, while the velocity in the y-direction decreases to zero as soon as possible. This will reduce the coupling between the two directions. Therefore, we're basically doing three 1d planner, and then combine them together. For each 1d planner, we will use the maximum acceleration and maximum deceleration under ideal conditions to make a trapezoidal program. Therefore, it could reach the target location with the optimal time, which we can accurately predict.

## 4.2     Search-Based Interception Prediction Algorithm

On the basis of realizing the algorithm of accurately predicting the robot's arrival time to a certain destination, we developed a search-based algorithm that predicts the shortest interception time and the best interception point for the robots. In one actual game, according to the movement ability of both sides, we will make an interception prediction for each robot on both sides of the field in each frame. This is very important for the realization of our single robot skills and the realization of multi-robot attack and defense conversion. In order to ensure the feasibility and real-time of this process, we use the search-based strategy to search the time at equal intervals with a fixed minimum interval of $\Delta t$ (such as 1/60 of a second). At a certain moment $t$, we obtain the location and speed of both the robot and the ball, then calculate the location $P_i$ that the ball can reach at any time $t + i\Delta t(i = 0, 1, 2, 3, ...)$ in the future under the action of the frictional force of the field in a straight line motion with uniform deceleration (the acceleration of the ball can be obtained according to the measured friction coefficient of the field). Then, starting from $i = 0$, it traversed the search points to predict the time $T_i$ that would take a robot to reach the point $P_i$. If $T_k \leq t + k\Delta t$ is satisfied after the k-th interval, point $P_k$ is considered to be the best interception point $P_{best}$ of the robot, and $T_k$ is the shortest interception time $T_{best}$ of the robot. Algorithm 1 shows the specific algorithm pseudocode.

There are two extreme cases. One is that the ball has already stopped before the robot intercepts the ball. At this time, the location where the ball stops is the optimal interception location, and the time when the robot reaches the location is the shortest interception time. Another is that the ball has been out of bounds before the robot intercepted it. At this time, in order to ensure that the algorithm can always get a solution, we take the out of bounds location as the best interception location, and the time to the out of bounds location as the shortest interception time. If the prediction of interception time is relatively conservative, such as adding fixed adjustment time $T_m$ to the predicted robot arrival time $T_i$, to ensure a higher success rate of the robot to intercept the ball. It will be found in the actual application that the robot will run more directly to the boundary to intercept the ball.

Figures 13 and 14 shows the interception time of a stationary robot at different positions under two different ball speeds. Darker areas represent shorter interception time, while lighter areas represent longer interception time. In Fig. 13, the initial position of the ball is $(400\,cm, 450\,cm)$, and ball speed is low $(1\,m/s)$, so at a certain time, the closer the robot gets to the ball, the less time it has to intercept the ball. However, when ball speed is high, it has different conclusion. In Fig. 14, the initial position of the ball is $(0\,cm, 450\,cm)$, and ball speed is high $(4\,m/s)$. Robot cannot intercept the ball in most places on the left side, and there is an obvious boundary. If the position of the robot is within the boundary (i.e. the dark area), it can intercept the ball in a short time, but if not, it will cost much, and may never intercept the ball before it out of the field. In the old saying of China, it is called "A little error may lead to a large discrepancy".

---

**Algorithm 1.** Search-Based Interception Prediction

---

**Require:** $\Delta t$, ball initial position $P_0$ and velocity $v_0$, robot initial position $P_r$ and velocity $v_r$

$k \leftarrow 0$

**repeat**

    $P_k \leftarrow predictBallPosition(P_0, v_0, k\Delta t)$

    $T_k \leftarrow predictRobotArrivalTime(P_r, v_r, P_k)$

    $k \leftarrow k + 1$

**until** $T_k \leq k\Delta t$ or $P_k$ out of the field

$P_{best} \leftarrow P_k$

$T_{best} \leftarrow T_k$

---

In [2] we developed a "FSM-based Role Matching" mechanism, using the square of the distance between the current positions of the robots and expected roles' target positions as the cost function. Considering the above situation, it is actually wrong when math robots to intercept the ball if we choose the ball

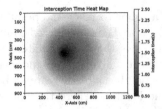
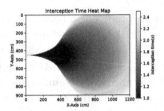

**Fig. 13.** 1 m/s Ball speed interception time heat map

**Fig. 14.** 4 m/s Ball speed interception time heat map

position as the target position. A better way is using the time that robots move from the current positions to the target as a loss function, and if the target is a ball, using Algorithm 1 can match an optimal robot to get the ball, that will improve our ball possession rate.

## 5   Conclusion

In this paper, we have introduced three main optimizations in both hardware section and software section in the competition last year. Our future task is to increase the intelligence and scalability of our system. We are working on changing our microcontroller from FPGA to STM32. And deep reinforcement learning (DRL) will also be used in our algorithm to improve the performance of our robots.

**Acknowledgement.** This work is supported by the Fundamental Research Funds for the Central Universities 2-2050205-19-361, and State Key Laboratory of Industrial Control Technology ITC1904.

## References

1. Li, C., Xiong, R., Ren, Z., Tang, W., Zhao, Y.: ZJUNlict: RoboCup 2014 small size league champion. In: Bianchi, R.A.C., Akin, H.L., Ramamoorthy, S., Sugiura, K. (eds.) RoboCup 2014. LNCS (LNAI), vol. 8992, pp. 47–59. Springer, Cham (2015). https://doi.org/10.1007/978-3-319-18615-3_4
2. Zhao, Y., et al.: ZJUNlict Team Description Paper for RoboCup 2014. RoboCup Wiki as team description of ZJUNlict, João Pessoa, Brazil (2019). Accessed 5 Feb 2014
3. Chen, L., et al.: ZJUNlict extended team description paper for RoboCup 2018. RoboCup Wiki as extended team description of ZJUNlict, Montreal, Canada (2019). Accessed 6 Mar 2018
4. Ryll, A., Geiger, M., Carstensen, C., Ommer, N.: TIGERs mannheim extended team description for RoboCup 2018. RoboCup Wiki as extended team description of TIGERs Mannheim team, Montreal, Canada (2019). Accessed 6 Mar 2018
5. Bruce, J.R.: Real-time motion planning and safe navigation in dynamic multi-robot environments. No. CMU-CS-06-181. Carnegie-Mellon Univ Pittsburgh Pa School of Computer Science (2006)

# Tech United Eindhoven Middle Size League Winner 2018

Yanick Douven, Wouter Houtman, Ferry Schoenmakers, Koen Meessen,
Harrie van de Loo, Dennis Bruijnen, Wouter Aangenent, Jorrit Olthuis,
Cas de Groot, Marzieh Dolatabadi Farahani, Peter van Lith, Pim Scheers,
Ruben Sommer, Bob van Ninhuijs, Patrick van Brakel, Jordy Senden,
Marjon van 't Klooster, Wouter Kuijpers[✉], and René van de Molengraft

Eindhoven University of Technology,
De Rondom 70, P.O. Box 513, 5600 Eindhoven, MB, The Netherlands
{w.j.p.kuijpers,techunited}@tue.nl
https://www.techunited.nl

**Abstract.** The Tech United Eindhoven Middle Size League (MSL) team
achieved a first place at RoboCup 2018. This paper presents a short
evaluation of the tournament and describes the most notable developments made in preparation of the tournament. One development in the
robot's hardware is presented: the realization of our eight-wheeled soccer
player. The following developments in software will be presented: a new
approach to ball state estimation and the human-alike dribble. Additionally, research towards the application of artificial intelligence in opponent
action prediction and opponent recognition will be presented.

**Keywords:** RoboCup soccer · Middle size league · Multi-robot ·
Ball handling

## 1 Introduction

Tech United Eindhoven represents the Eindhoven University of Technology in
the RoboCup competitions. The team started participating in the Middle Size
League in 2006. In 2011 the service robot AMIGO was added to the team to participate in the RoboCup@Home league. In the Middle Size League competitions,
the team has been playing the final for 11 years now, while achieving the first
place four times: 2012, 2014, 2016 and 2018. Before RoboCup 2018, the Middle
Size League team consists of 4 PhD's, 1 PDEng, 8 MSc, 4 BSc, 5 former TU/e
students, 3 TU/e staff members and one member not related to TU/e.

This paper describes the major scientific improvements of our soccer robots
over the past year, and elaborates on some of the main improvements or developments in preparation of the RoboCup 2018 tournament. Additionally, in Sect. 3
some statistics concerning the past tournament will be presented. First in Sect. 2,
an introduction on the hardware and software of our fifth generation soccer robot
is given. The developments in design and control towards our sixth generation

© Springer Nature Switzerland AG 2019
D. Holz et al. (Eds.): RoboCup 2018, LNAI 11374, pp. 413–424, 2019.
https://doi.org/10.1007/978-3-030-27544-0_34

soccer robot, the eight-wheeled robot, are presented in Sect. 4. Improvements to the skills of our robots are presented in Sect. 5. Our progress on including concepts from artificial intelligence into the robot software are presented in Sect. 6. In Sect. 7, we give some insights into one of our main strengths: passing. Section 8 gives concluding remarks and presents our outlook on the coming years.

## 2    Robot Platform

Our robots have been named TURTLEs (acronym for Tech United RoboCup Team: Limited Edition). Currently, we are using our fifth generation TURTLE while we are developing the sixth generation, which is presented in Sect. 4. In this section we will however treat the fifth generation, which makes up the biggest part of our team. Subsect. 2.1 will treat the hardware of this platform, whereas Subsect. 2.2 will treat the software.

### 2.1    Hardware

Development of the TURTLEs started in 2005. Through tournaments and numerous demonstrations, these platforms have evolved into the fifth generation TURTLE, a very robust platform. For an outline of our robot design the reader is referred to the schematic representation published in the second section of our team description paper of 2014 [1]. In 2016, a redesign of the upper body of the robot was made to integrate Kinect V2 cameras and create a more robust frame for the omni-vision unit on top of the robot. This prevents the need for recalibration of mirror parameters when the top of the robot is hit by a ball. A detailed list of hardware specifications, along with CAD files of the base, upper-body, ball handling and shooting mechanism, has been published on a ROP wiki.[1]

### 2.2    Software

The software controlling the robots is divided into three main processes: Vision, Worldmodel and Motion. These processes communicate with each other through a real-time database (RTDB) designed by the CAMBADA team [2]. The vision process is responsible for environment perception using omni-vision images and provides the location of the ball, obstacles and the robot itself. The worldmodel combines the ball, obstacle and robot position information provided by vision with data acquired from other team members to get a unified representation of the world. The motion process is based on a layered software model. The highest level is strategy. Strategy defines actions which are executed by roles deployed on the TURTLEs. These actions consist of a limited set of basic skills such as shooting and dribbling, which require motion control of relevant actuators, the lowest level of the software. More detailed information on the software can be found in [3] or in the flow charts part of the qualification package.

---

[1] http://www.roboticopenplatform.org/wiki/TURTLE.

**Fig. 1.** Fifth generation TURTLE robots, with on the left-handside the goalkeeper robot. (Photo: Bart van Overbeeke)

## 3   RoboCup 2018 Statistics

Five teams participated in the Middle Size League tournament of RoboCup 2018, two teams from China, one team from Portugal and two teams from The Netherlands. A total of 34 matches have been played, of which Tech United played 14 matches. During those 14 matches, Tech United scored 88 goals, an average of over 6 goals per match. The semi-final resulted in a 10-0 score, the final match resulted in a 1-0 score.

By analysing the actions of the TURTLE's, we found 240 attempts for a shot on goal, resulting in a success rate of approximately 37%. During the tournament 15 goals were scored by other teams in our goal. Our goalkeeper, even though always being positioned in the goal, drove 2008 m during all the matches, based on odometry data. The field players on average drove 13 km, with TURTLE 2 driving almost 20 km during the tournament. While driving, the TURTLEs managed to localize in almost 90% of the time, where TURTLE 4 managed to localize 98% of the total time. These numbers are lower than previous tournaments (usually 96%), this is due to the increase in field size. These statistics differ per TURTLE, even though the TURTLEs are similar in hardware and software, this can be due to role, calibration accuracy or total playing time.

## 4   Eight-Wheeled Platform

This section elaborates on the design of the eight-wheeled platform. Subsect. 4.1 will elaborate on some of the design features of the eight-wheeled platform. The challenges faced during the low-level motion control design are presented in Subsect. 4.2.

## 4.1   Design of the Eight-Wheeled Platform

The current platform is equipped with three omni-directional wheels rigidly connected to the base, achieving holonomicity which makes our platform potentially agile. In this configuration, however, not all the torque delivered by the motors is used in the desired movement. Moreover, high forward acceleration causes the front wheels to slip, removing the ability to apply torque from the motors to the field. These drawbacks form the main motivation for the development of the eight-wheeled platform, also presented in [3].

The challenge in designing a platform with four or more wheels is resolving the over-actuated system. The eight-wheeled platform, presented in Figs. 2(a) and (c), has three degrees-of-freedom and is five times over-actuated. To allow five internal movements, each of the wheel combinations is suspended with the rotation point below the ground and the back wheels are suspended over a hinging axle. In this way, the wheels are always in contact with the ground to transfer the torque from the motors to the ground.

## 4.2   Low-Level Control of the Eight-Wheeled Platform

The setup of the platform is graphically represented in Fig. 2(b). In this figure it can be seen that this platform consists of four sets each having two hub-drive wheels. Each pair of wheels can rotate around its suspension by actuating the corresponding wheels in opposite direction. As a result, strictly speaking the platform is non-holonomic, but due to the ability of each pair of wheels to rotate, in a relatively short time-intervals compared to the motion of the platform, a kind of semi-holonomicity is achieved.

In order to manipulate the position $x, y$ and orientation $\phi$ of the center $C$ of the platform, the control strategy of Fig. 3 has been designed. Based on the desired velocity of the platform, $\dot{q}_r = [\dot{x} \ \dot{y} \ \dot{\phi}]^T$, both the reference velocity for each of the eight wheels $v_{w,r} \in \mathbb{R}^{[8 \times 1]}$ and the desired pivot-angle $\delta_r \in \mathbb{R}^{[4 \times 1]}$ can be determined in a feedforward fashion using the inverse kinematics of the platform. As three degrees of freedom are controlled using eight actuators, the system is over-actuated. Therefore, an error in the pivot $\delta$ of each wheelpair leads to undesired internal forces and slip. As a result, if the pivot-error is not within reasonable bounds, the pivot-controller is prioritized over the platform controller, meaning that the wheels are re-oriented before the platform is actuated. In order to correct for this pivot-error, via a feedback controller, a compensation is added to the wheel velocities. The magnitude of this correction term is equal for both wheels in each wheelpair, but they have opposite direction. Finally, by measuring both the wheel velocities $v_w \in \mathbb{R}^{[8 \times 1]}$ and the pivot angle $\delta \in \mathbb{R}^{[4 \times 1]}$, the velocity of the platform can be determined using the forward kinematics of the system.

## 4.3   Results During RoboCup 2018

Unfortunately, we did not manage to employ the eight-wheeled platform during one of the games of RoboCup 2018. The low-level motion control did not meet the

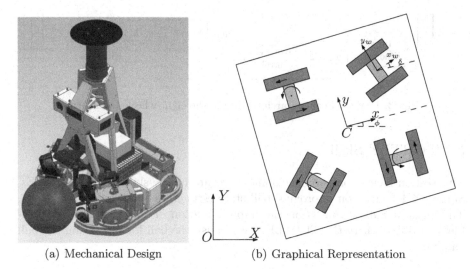

(a) Mechanical Design          (b) Graphical Representation

(c) Realized Prototype

**Fig. 2.** The eight-wheeled platform with four suspended wheel combinations which are able to rotate around its center hinge.

performance requirements for being able to play, resulting in a too low maximum velocity of the platform being. Right after the tournament work reconvened and promising results will ensure playing time for the eight-wheeled platform next year.

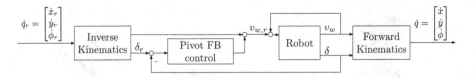

**Fig. 3.** Low-level control architecture of the eight-wheeled platform.

## 5    TURTLE Skills

This section focuses on two developments regarding the skills of the TURTLEs. Subsect. 5.1 focuses on improving ball state estimation (position and velocity). The focus of Subsect. 5.2 is on the implementation of the "human-alike dribble", a dribble where the TURTLEs softly push the ball forward using the ball handling.

### 5.1    Improved Ball State Estimate

A correct ball position and velocity estimate is crucial for the TURTLEs. The performance of the present method is not satisfactory any longer in all situations. The current estimator buffers detections of the ball and fits this with a state trajectory in a least squares sense. In a highly dynamic environment, such as a MSL soccer field, the filter needs to adapt quickly to changing situations. A standard Extended Kalman filter would respond slow on a maneuvering ball depending on the process and measurement noise covariance matrices. To make sure the Kalman filter is able to adapt fast on a changing ball velocity, an Extended Kalman Filter with Inflatable Noise Variance (EKF with InNoVa) [4] is proposed.

Figure 4 presents a comparison between the response of the EKF and the EKF with InNoVa for a disturbance. One can observe from this comparison that the EKF with InNoVa converges to the actual velocity in $x$ direction faster than the EKF. As similar performance is observed in other test cases, the proposed EKF with InNoVa will replace our present algorithm.

### 5.2    Human-Alike Dribble

Within the Middle Size League, robots have a confined dribble space defined as a 3 m radius around the point where the robot intercepted the ball. Currently, the TURTLEs shoot or pass to let go of the ball. However, significant strategical advantages could be gained by softly pushing the ball forward and regaining it again. Previously, our robots had to shoot or give a pass to let go of the ball, therefore a controlled push was implemented.

Before giving a controlled push, the robot has to be aligned and the ball handling levers need to be in a predefined position. In the 70 m/s the wheels have contact with the ball, the wheels ramp up the speed of the ball to about 0.5 m/s

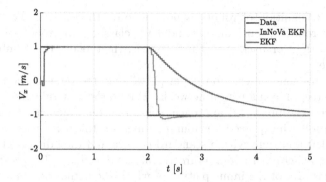

**Fig. 4.** A comparison between the EKF and EKF with InNoVa for a wallbounce, the ball ($V_0 = 1$ m/s) bounces off a wall at $t = 2$ s, the wall is not included in the model.

relative to the robot, to give a controlled push. Slip measurements are performed to determine the maximum acceleration before the ball handling wheels lose grip on the ball. Slip was found not to affect the velocity of the ball below 1.5 m/s which is thus large enough. The proposed control strategy consists of the existing feedback controller combined with a feedforward controller. This control strategy has been found to yield sufficient accuracy for executing the human-dribble.

### 5.3 Results During RoboCup 2018

The human-alike dribble has not been integrated in the software during RoboCup 2018, manpower was distributed to other, higher priority, tasks.

## 6 Artificial Intelligence

We are exploring the possibilities of Artificial Intelligence for this league in two ways. Subsect. 6.1 will elaborate on using Artificial Intelligence (AI) for detailed analysis of the omni-vision images. Another approach, where AI is used to predict the next action of the opponent is presented in Subsect. 6.2.

### 6.1 Detailed Opponent Detection

In last years team description paper we reported on a detection method for opponent label detection using neural networks. Due to the new rule allowing robots to wear shirts, the presented approach was no longer practical. Therefore, we adopted the procedure: first we take pictures of every robot with a normal digital camera, the images are then distorted to resemble the images from the omni-vision system. A normal digital camera will be used to speed up the procedure of taking pictures from opponent robots and prevent us from having to use one of the TURTLEs for this time-consuming task. Every image undergoes additional augmentations in the form of rotations, scaling, color variations and distortions. Recognition of robots is now done on three levels. The first level classifies the robot's team. The second level classifies the robot's orientation in front, left, right or back. The third level is, then again, the number on the number plate.

In last years team description paper [3] we reported on a method for opponent label detection using neural networks. Due to the new rule allowing robots to wear shirts, the presented approach was no longer practical. Therefore, we adopted the following procedure: four pictures are taken for each robot from front, back, left and right with a standard camera and then distorted to resemble the robot images in the omni-directional camera image. This is done using an affine transform of the input picture of which the corner points are mapped onto a corresponding image of the robot in the omni-directional camera. Using rotations, color - and scale variations, the 16 input images per team for each match are augmented to 32.000 28 × 28 color images. These form the input to a three-layer fully convolutional neural network, which is trained to classify single robots to team membership or orientation. The last convolutional layer is fed into a Global Average Pooling Layer, which is used to generate a Class Activation Map. We achieve a 95% accuracy on single robot team classification, against a validation set consisting of single robot images, lifted from omni-directional camera images, shot during test matches. The orientation classification is less reliable since it is depending on the color and shape of the shirts and the protruding ball handling unit, which is not always clearly visible.

This single robot network is then used on the entire omni-directional image by creating a class-activation map in which the highest activation points of each class indicate the position of a robot in the image. We are still working on solving the problem of recognizing our own robots in both classes as a result of the bottom leds.

The entire process of making pictures, augmenting them and training the neural network is completed in 30 min. Using omni-directional images from a robot directly would be better but involves getting both teams on the field, transferring these images, selecting individual robots from them and then train the network. This is not feasible during an actual competition, hence the described approach, which simplifies getting the data in the time available between matches.

To understand the performance of the recognition, a visualization of the feature kernels and activation layers, additionally allowing the fine tuning of the network hyper-parameters. At the moment of writing the first level (team) has a reliability better than 95%, the second level achieves a performance around 80%. Work on the third level did not yield any valuable results yet. Results of the first level have been included here. An omni-vision image as in Fig. 5(a) is input to the neural network, per team(color) a class activated map (CAM) is compiled which shows where certain features are present in the input image, see Figs. 5(b) and (c).

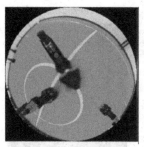
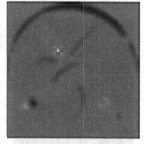
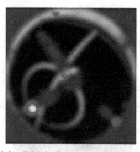
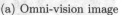

(a) Omni-vision image    (b) CAM features belonging to cyan team    (c) CAM features belonging to orange team

**Fig. 5.** Class activated maps for the detection of robot team, results for the cyan team and orange team are presented. (Color figure online)

## 6.2 Opponent Action Prediction

Being able to predict the opponents action grants a strategical lead with respect to the opponent. To train a network capable of this, the world state information of previous tournaments will be used. The world state information is spatially represented as three 8-bit occupancy grid maps of $28 \times 40$ pixels, the information on opponents, peers and the ball is each stored in a different map. Temporal information is included in the value of the pixel, the longer ago an e.g. opponent arrived at a certain pixel, the lower the value. The three 8-bit occupancy grid maps can be represented as a single RGB image, as in Fig. 6, the ball, opponents and peers are represented by green, red and blue, respectively.

Currently, the achievable performance of an convolutional neural network is determined with an indicative experiment, by recognizing the refbox tasks from this occupancy map. The network was able to classify the correct refbox tasks with an accuracy of 98.5%, a promising result. With this promising result, research will proceed to predicting the opponents action. The neural network operated offline and used data collected during the match as input.

## 6.3 Results During RoboCup 2018

The results presented in this section are proof of concepts, these methods have not been integrated in the software before RoboCup 2018. After the tournament the focus shifted to the actual integration of these algorithms into the current software and into the current processing units.

## 7 Passing

Dynamic teamplay is one of the strengths of Tech United. When in possession of the ball, there are always two robots without the ball (possible pass receivers)

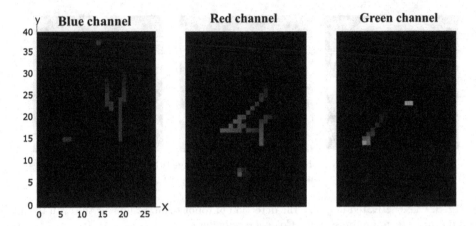

**Fig. 6.** Occupancy grid maps for a specific time instant, from left to right: peer positions, opponent positions and ball position. (Color figure online)

trying to reach a position on the field that is optimal for receiving a pass, continuously trying to avoid opponents blocking any free line between them and the robot with the ball (the pass giver). These passes do not have to be direct, i.e. the ball can be shot into an open area in the field, where the pass receiver will try to dynamically intercept it. This poses additional difficulty for the opponent to block a pass. This section will explain how the robots decide where and who to pass to, and how this pass is handled.

### 7.1  Where and Who to Pass To?

Every robot has a set of cost functions that are evaluated on a grid of positions on the soccer field. For the possible pass receivers, these cost functions combine penalties for being too close to or behind opponents, penalties for being at a position that has a low scoring chance, penalties for being at a position that has no free line for a next pass, penalties for being at a certain illegal position on the field, and a driving cost. These penalties are weighted for two different optimization problems, one for receiving a pass and shooting at goal, and one for receiving a pass and passing to the next robot. E.g. the latter one has zero cost on the penalties for being at a position that has a low scoring chance. The point in the grid with the lowest combined cost, is the position on the field that has the highest probability for receiving a successful pass with corresponding consecutive action (shoot at goal or pass to the next robot). These positions and the corresponding costs are communicated to the pass giver. The pass giver then compares these costs and decides who to pass to. The pass target is the corresponding position. The number of the robot that will receive the pass, and the pass target are then communicated to the rest of the team. The receiving robot will decide for itself what to do next. This way of deciding who and where to pass to is new since RoboCup 2018. Before, the only reason to pass to a robot was that this pass receiving robot had a better chance at scoring. Using this new method, more passes back occur with the intention of passing to the next robot that has a good scoring position. Therefore, in general, more passes occur, letting the ball do the work and making it harder for the opponent to defend.

## 7.2 Pass Handler

When the robots have determined where and who to pass to, the so-called "pass handler" handles the execution of the pass. This is a synchronized state machine between the pass giver and the pass receiver, that has been fully redesigned for RoboCup 2018. The new pass handler has as little states as possible and has a cleaner way to synchronize states, leading to less synchronization issues and more successful passes. The pass giver calculates how long the pass receiver takes to drive ($t_{receiver}$) to the pass target ($x_{pass}$) and adjusts the passing speed ($v_{pass}$) accordingly:

$$v_{pass} = \frac{||x_{pass} - x_0||_2}{t_{receiver} + t_{margin}} \tag{1}$$

Here, $x_0$ is the current position of the pass giver and $t_{margin}$ is some positive time margin to allow for inaccuracies in positioning of the receiver and the actual achieved shooting velocity of the pass giver. To avoid passing too hard and ensure that the ball does not bounce of the ball handling of the pass receiver, the passing speed is limited.

## 7.3 Result During RoboCup 2018

The new pass handler and improved decision making has resulted in dynamic teamplay during RoboCup 2018. Compared to previous years, there were more passes and a higher percentage of successful passes. By having multiple possible pass receivers and giving passes with the intention to directly pass to the next robot, the game became more dynamic and harder to defend for the opponent. This ultimately resulted in the World Title.

# 8   Conclusions

In this paper we have described the major scientific improvements of our soccer robots in preparation of the RoboCup 2018 tournament. Not all of the developments have actively contributed to the result, but the methods developed will be integrated in preparation of future tournaments. The sixth generation TUR-TLE is a robot with 8-wheels, designed for improved agility on the field. The ball state estimation of the TURTLEs has been improved by means of and EKF with InNoVa, achieving better performance for the different dynamic situations. As our current focus is on integrating neural networks into our software, the researches presented towards the application of AI in our software will soon be put to the test. One of our main strengths is passing, which is based on a synchronized state machine between pass giver and receiver. Altogether we hope our progress contributes to an even higher level of dynamic and scientifically challenging robot soccer. The latter, of course, while maintaining the attractiveness of our competition for a general audience. We are determined to create a new generation of TURTLEs with improved agility and ball handling. Meanwhile, our efforts in implementing a configurable strategy framework and applications of artificial intelligence in software will continue. In this way we hope to go with the top in Middle-size league for some more years and contribute to our goal in 2050!

# References

1. Lopez Martinez, C., et al.: Tech United Eindhoven Team Description 2014. Springer, Heidelberg (2014)
2. Almeida, L., Santos, F., Facchinetti, T., Pedreiras, P., Silva, V., Lopes, L.S.: Coordinating distributed autonomous agents with a real-time database: the CAMBADA project. In: Aykanat, C., Dayar, T., Körpeoğlu, İ. (eds.) ISCIS 2004. LNCS, vol. 3280, pp. 876–886. Springer, Heidelberg (2004). https://doi.org/10.1007/978-3-540-30182-0_88
3. Schoenmakers, F., et al.: Tech United Eindhoven Team Description 2017. Springer, Heidelberg (2017)
4. Zhang, J., Welch, G., Bishop, G., Huang, Z.: A two-stage kalman filter approach for robust and real-time power system state estimation. IEEE Transact. Sustain. Energ. 5(2), 629–636 (2014)

# Ichiro Robots Winning RoboCup 2018 Humanoid TeenSize Soccer Competitions

Muhtadin[1]([✉]), Muhammad Reza Arrazi[1], Sulaiman Ali[1],
Tommy Pratama[1], Dhany Satrio Wicaksono[1],
Ahmad Hernando Pradanatta Putra[1], I. Made Pande Ari[1],
Alfi Maulana[1], Oktaviansyah Purwo Bramastyo[1],
Syifaul Qolby Asshakina[1], Muhammad Attamimi[1],
Muhammad Arifin[2], Mauridhi Hery Purnomo[1], and Djoko Purwanto[1]

[1] Institut Teknologi Sepuluh Nopember, Surabaya 60111, Indonesia
muhtadin@ee.its.ac.id, sulaimanali281@gmail.com
[2] Indonesian Institute of Sciences (LIPI), Jakarta, Indonesia

**Abstract.** This paper describes the Ichiro RoboCup Winner TeenSize Humanoid League from the Institut Teknologi Sepuluh Nopember Surabaya, Indonesia. In this paper, the mechatronic design of Ichiro robots, algorithms and robotic behavior will be discussed. At this year, for the first time we took part in a competition on the TeenSize category, our algorithm and robot behavior were simple, but we were able to maximize the algorithm and get the advantages of a fast-computational process and ease of debugging. Therefore, we were able to get four awards: First place Teensize Soccer Competition, Second place TeenSize Technical Challenge, Second place Drop-in Challenge, Third place Best Humanoid Award.

## 1 Introduction

RoboCup Humanoid league has a vision to promote the champion of the league to compete against the winner of FIFA world cup. To facilitate this vision, the rules are getting closer to the rules implemented on FIFA World Cup. These facts motivated many researchers to develop humanoid robots in many aspects, such as mechanical design, robot's perception especially in complex environments, robot's behaviors in soccer game, and so forth. Many challenging fields have attracted the researchers to examine their robots in Humanoid league competitions both on National and International levels.

Team Ichiro specifically develops research in the field of Humanoid Robotics. Members of the team Ichiro were students in undergraduate and diploma programs from the Institut Teknologi Sepuluh Nopember Surabaya, Indonesia. We have participated in various competitions of Humanoid robots at the National level starting in 2013. We began participating in the International level in 2016. That year we received 10 awards with two world records at FIRA RoboWoldCup 2016 in Beijing, China. In 2017, we participated in the RoboCup Humanoid League competition in the KidSize

D. Holz et al. (Eds.): RoboCup 2018, LNAI 11374, pp. 425–435, 2019.
https://doi.org/10.1007/978-3-030-27544-0_35

**Fig. 1.** Left: ichiro robot TeenSize. Right: robot team member at Robocup 2018.

category held in Nagoya Japan. Our participation in the competition opened many insights for us about the development of humanoid robots. In 2018, we had problems with limited funds to finance our team's trip to Canada, therefore, we took part in the RoboCup Humanoid League competition in the TeenSize category (see Fig. 1) which can be done by only two robots with a small number of teams. The amazing results had been achieved from the RoboCup competition in Canada, we won several awards: First place in the TeenSize category, Runner-up at the TeenSize Technical Challenge, Runner-up at the Drop-in Games, finally, we won the third place in Best Humanoid Robot Soccer.

## 2   Mechanical Hardware Overview

Ichiro TeenSize robots was assembled based on a modification from Nimbro-OP [1] (Fig. 2). This robot uses one Logitech camera C922 and two LiPo 4S batteries. There are $20°$ of freedom using Dynamixel Servo. Twelve Dynamixel MX 106 for the robot's legs, six Dynamixel MX 64 for the robot's arms and two Dynamixel MX 28 for the head. Ichiro Teen Size robot has 85 cm of height. This robot is made by cutting and bending with 3 mm thick type 5 Aluminum material.

We made modifications from the Nimbro-OP by reducing its size from 95 cm to 85 cm. With this size, we get many benefits because we can use our robot in many competitions, i.e.: the KidSize category at the national level robot soccer competition (45 cm–90 cm), the AdultSize category at the FIRA International RobotSport robot competition (80 cm–180 cm), as well as the TeenSize category in the Robocup competition (80 cm–140 cm).

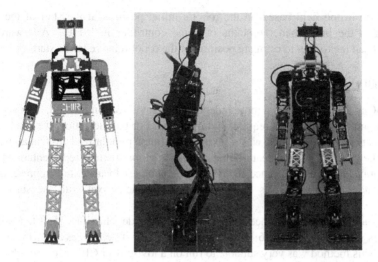

**Fig. 2.** Left: CAD design. Center and right: Ichiro TeenSize.

Ichiro Robot TeenSize uses an Intel NUC mini PC as its main controller. For the visual sensor, we use a standard Logitech C922 camera that plugged on the USB port on Intel NUC.

Since 2017 we have not used a compass because of the regulations that have been applied. For the orientation sensor, we used MPU-6050 where this sensor was quite accurate with a 16-bit analog to digital converse internal hardware facilities for each channel. This sensor combines the 3-axis gyroscope and 3-axis accelerometer on the same chip. To be able to interact with MPU-6050, a microcontroller such as Arduino is needed as an interface for i2c-bus. In our robot, we used Arduino nano to access the orientation sensor.

## 3  Visual Perception

### 3.1  Landmark Detection

For the purposes of localization, we did field extraction for the goalposts and the edge of the field. We got the edge of the field by applying the convex hull to the green area which was the area of artificial grass on the field. The goalposts were detected since the goalposts were at the edge of the field. The goalposts feature was detected by using a Hough line detector in HSV color space. Then we separate the Hough line into the left goalpost and the right goalpost. This method has been discussed in [2] and [3]. Although this method is simple, we get an advantage of fast computing and a good result when the robot is in the middle of the field.

We have difficulties in extracting the line features of the field because the camera on the robot produced only moderate-quality video, video frames were often blurry when the robot moves, so that the lines were often missing and incomplete. Therefore, we did not use lines to estimate the position of robots in the field. The robot estimated its position in the field based on the robot's initial position at the start of the match (looking at the ball when the status of game controller in 'SET'). Afterwards, we employ dead reckoning to estimate position of the robot relative to the starting position.

## 3.2   Ball Detection

In RoboCup 2018, we made a more independent light detection method, high accuracy, low computation and do not require a lot of tuning. For ball detection, we used a Local Binary Pattern (LBP), which was a texture descriptor popularized by Ojala et al. [4]. Unlike the Haralick texture feature that calculates global texture representations based on the gray level co-occurrence matrix, LBP calculates local texture representations. This local representation was built by comparing each pixel with the surrounding pixels.

For the classification process, we use the cascade classifier [5, 6]. Cascading classifiers were trained with $16 \times 16$ pixels of 2832 positive images and 1452 negative images. This method was very suitable to run on a low-power CPU because it has a fast processing speed.

In comparison, as well as backup-plan in detecting the ball, we also use Histogram Oriented Gradient (HOG) features that are popularized by Dalal on [7]. We use the HOG feature extraction as a linear Support Vector Machine (SVM) input to discriminate ball object from non-balls. We prepared these two ball detection methods on our robot, during setup day, we conducted ball detection testing using both methods to choose the most accurate one, then we used it during competition day. Based on our testing at setup day, the accuracy of the LBP feature and HOG feature reaches 94% and 79% respectively. Finally, we used the LBP feature during the competition day.

To reduce noise outside the field, we first segmented the color of the field. From the contour detected, the contour that had the largest area was selected and then Convex Hull was performed. After that, we classify it using the LBP or HOG feature on the object inside convex.

## 3.3   Localization on the Field

There were no more unique features in the field that could be used to discriminate our own area and opponent's area. Magnetometer sensor was also prohibited to be used. This prohibition made it difficult for us to know the orientation of the robot. To overcome this problem, our robots could know their initial position inside the field by estimating their position based on several possible positions that we have defined before.

Figure 3 shows some possible initial position of the robot when entering the field, this method has also been carried out by the Nimbro team [8]. According to the fact that robots always entering their own area when the game starts, our robot will calculate the distance between the robot and the goalposts using the trilateration method as discussed in [3]. Our robot will choose several initial positions that has been defined (Fig. 3) based on the estimated distance of the robot to the goalposts.

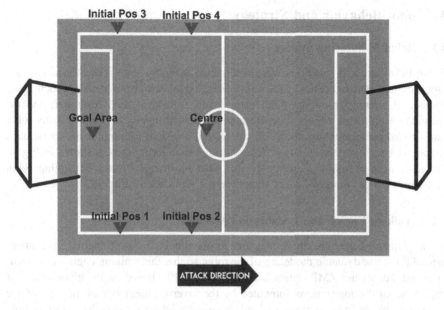

**Fig. 3.** Predefined initial positions of the robot

After the robots know their initial position inside the field, the robot estimates its position based using dead reckoning. The further position was obtained from the estimation of the robot step, the estimation of the robot speed based on anterior step parameters, and the directions of the robot. The method for estimating robot position will be discussed in Sect. 4.2.

Error in estimating robot position often occurs when the robot plays for a long time (about 2 min). However, we can solve this problem by re-estimating the initial position when the game state was "SET", which was usually happen when scoring a goal or a drop ball occurs. Re-estimating the initial position was also done when the robot coming to the field after they had been picked-up or serviced.

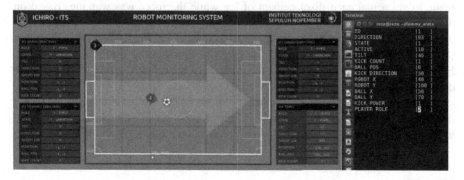

**Fig. 4.** Software for monitoring

# 4 Robot Behavior and Strategy

## 4.1 Robot Monitoring System

Robot behaviors and strategies were determined in many states. The transfer of the robots current state to the next state was determined by various information, such as the number of teammates on the field, game status from the game controller, and the individual teammates robot's state. Because we have difficulty to monitor many robot states based on information received, we created a system to monitor the robot state. Graphical User Interface (GUI) of Ichiro's robot monitoring system shown in Fig. 4. We also make a "dummy" robot to send fake information when debugging robot behavior. GUI of "dummy" robot shown on the right side of Fig. 4.

## 4.2 Walking Engine and Localization Method

We implemented the sinusoidal trajectory to our robot's walking engine. This movement did not use dynamic modeling of the robot so that this walking engine was open-loop and did not use ZMP criterion as described in [9]. Based on the given points of trajectory, all the joints were computed by the inverse kinematics of the legs of the robot. Due to the imperfection of actual dynamics of the robot, we had to tune some parameters in walking engine manually with trial and error. We also implemented the Proportional-Derivative controller (PD) control strategy on both arms and hips of the robot to maintain its pitch at the desired angle to prevent the robot from falling.

We use data from the gyroscope and accelerometer as PD Controller inputs to control the knee, ankle pitch, hip roll, ankle roll on the robot. Validation was done by observing it, then providing a disturbance of stability when the robot was walking. If we felt the robot was less stable, and then we did manual tuning until we got a good stability.

Sensors data and localization module information were needed to design more complex robot behavior. First, we need to use motion capture camera to capture robot's displacement based on given gait command for implementing local localization of the robot. We use Optitrack® Trio[1]. The data was collected by putting the markers on both feet, then we track those markers using the motion capture system. The generated data by motion capture was processed using machine learning with robot's forward kinematic to get actual each displacement of leg while the robot was walking. Based on these motion capture data, we could predict the robot step model based on the gait parameters. This method has been discussed in more detail in [10] and [11]. The robot step model that we have obtained, we tested to estimate the position of the robot. Figure 5 shows the results of testing the position of the robot by using motion capture data as ground truth.

Based on the predictions of the current step model that we have obtained, by fusing this data and orientation data from robot's sensor, robot could estimate a quite accurate location which was used as information of localization module. This method, however,

---

[1] https://optitrack.com/products/v120-trio/.

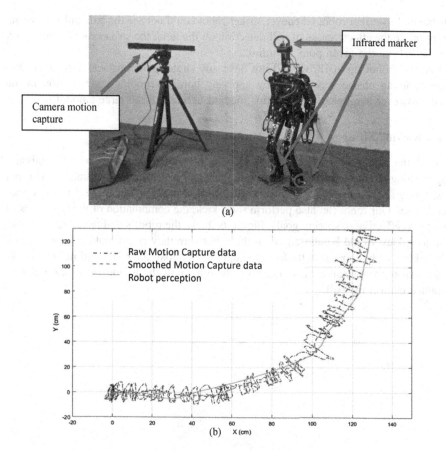

**Fig. 5.** (a) Robot equipped with optical motion capture marker to produce robot's step model data. (b) Comparison of robot position estimation data with motion capture data as ground truth

needs the initial position (discussed in Sect. 3.3) of the robot on the field which was obtained by observing both locations of goal posts at the beginning of the game or whether the robot starts to enter the field.

### 4.3 Teamwork Strategies

The finite state machine was used to design the robot behavior based on current game state, teammates states or location and orientation information from localization module. The communication between the robots was implemented using User Datagram Protocol (UDP) communication which contains information of robot's states. Then in general, the robots were considered as two roles as defender and striker robots. The defender role was chosen by the robot when the striker was active on the field. To reduce power consumption and prevent the absence of players in own field, the defender will stay on his determined position and approaches the ball when the ball was around it. The robot defender was able to give the information of the location of the visible ball to striker robot whenever striker robot could not see the ball and vice versa. To improve the effectiveness of ball detection on the field, the striker robot would look for the ball on the given point coordinates.

At the RoboCup 2018, we did not have any strategy for obstacle avoidance. We tried applying obstacle avoidance by applying non-green color segmentation in the field. However, we failed to apply this method because of the large amount of noise.

### 4.4   Kicking Strategy

One of the weaknesses of our robot was its movement that was slow in walking, approaching the ball, and positioning to the ball. To cover up this weakness, our robot has a long kick (5 m) that can roll the ball from the middle of the field to the opponent's goal. Our robot can also perform short kick, the combination of the two types of kicks was effective in scoring goals. Figure 6 shows the robot's ability to kick the ball. The long kick would be chosen when the robot sure they could make a score from a single kick. If the robot was far from the opponent's goal, the robot will not be able to make a score from a single kick, therefore, the robot will choose the short kick and then regained control the ball.

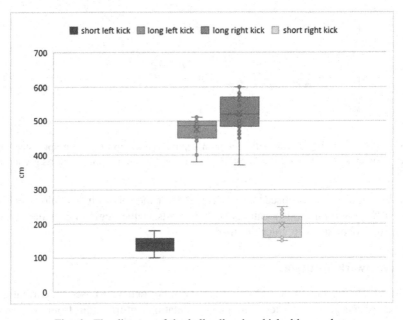

**Fig. 6.** The distance of the ball rolls when kicked by a robot.

When the robot was kicking the ball, the robot will give information about his position, kick direction, and types of the kick to the teammate's robots. Based on that information, the teammates would go to the estimation of the area where the ball will stop.

# 5   Performance in Soccer Tournament

At the RoboCup 2018, there were six teams participated in the TeenSize Humanoid League. In Round Robin, Ichiro had five games against AMN United, NUbots, EDROM, MRL-HSL, and WF Wolves & Hamburg Bit-Bots. On the first day of the set-up day, one of our robots had a problem. The PC was broken due to the short circuit of the power board. Therefore, in round robin we only had one robot. At the first day of round robin, we had three matches against AMN United with a score of 2:0, against NUbots with a score of 3:0, and against WF Wolves & Hamburg Bit-Bots with a score of 1:0 and we won all the match. We used long-kick strategy because we only had one robot. When our robot took control of the ball, our robot would just kick the ball to the opponent's goal according to the robot position. On the second day of the round robin, we won the match against EDROM with a score of 5:0 but we lost a match against MRL-HSL from Iran. They had fast-moving robots; hence we had a difficulty to take control of the ball, and the match ended with score 1:3.

At semi-final round, we successfully repair our second robot and we qualified to the final round after having a good match against WF Wolves & Hamburg Bit-Bots from Germany with a score of 2:0.

At the beginning of the competition, we faced several problems but at the semi-final and final round, our robot could run perfectly. With a good localization, our robot could easily kick the ball to the opponent's goal. At the final round, we had a match against MRL-HSL from Iran for the second time. Finally, we won this match with score 3:0.

## 5.1   Technical Challenges

In Robocup 2018, team Ichiro also participated in the technical challenges. We want to examine the ability of our robot to complete the specific tasks given in the technical challenges. There were four kind of challenges: push recovery, dynamic kick (goal kick from the moving ball), high jump, and high kick. In this year we perform three of the technical challenges.

**Push Recovery:** In this kind of challenge, the objective was to withstand a strong push. An impact was applied to the robot on the level of the Centre of Mass (CoM) by a pendulum. To apply the push, a two kilograms weight of bottle will swing against the robot's body. The pendulum was released from an angle which was the ground projection distance for the pendulum, and the robot must be walking in place during the attempt. The attempt will be a success if the robot returns to a stable standing or walking posture after a push applied. During the attempt, we use the gait as the regular games. Our robot can stand from the push until the distance of 45 cm.

**Dynamic Kick:** The objective of the challenge was to kick a moving ball into the goal. The ball was placed randomly on one of the corners of the field. The pass of the ball was performed by one of our team members to the robot. The robot must kick the ball into the goal before the ball stopped. And here how we faced these challenges:

1. Before the ball passed from the corner, the robot performing pre-kick motion. The robot stands with a single support leg and the other leg folded into the position in order to be ready for kicking the ball.
2. The camera tracking the ball and estimate the time of the ball arrived in the area where the ball can be kicked by the folded leg.
3. Perform the kicking motion when the ball was in the area of the folded leg.

On this challenge, we failed to score. We ran out of time doing a trial on this challenge. When we did a trial, the robot often lost the ball, sometimes the robot could see the ball, but it was late in responding to the ball and too late to kick the ball towards the goal.

**High Kick:** The objective of high kick challenge was to kick the ball into the goal at maximum height. At each attempt, the team must decide how many wooden blocks (related to how tall the obstacle) tries to achieve by the robot. The ball placed on the penalty mark, and the robot placed freely but at least 30 cm away from the ball. Thanks to the ability of our robot to do a powerful kick. At the first attempt, we try 10 cm as the minimum height, and the robot did it very well. At the second attempt, we try 30 cm as the minimum height, the robot also did it well. At the third attempt, we try 45 cm as the minimum height, and the robot successfully finishes the challenge. In this challenge, we reach the highest kick than the other team.

## 6   Conclusions

At Robocup 2018, for the first time Ichiro Robot Team participated in the TeenSize category. Even though we have won first place in the TeenSize category, however, there are many things that we need to improve performance of our robots. We prepare robots in a very short time, so we use several simple algorithms, but we get the advantage of fast computing process and easy debugging. Our mechanical design was also still simple to imitate the design of other robots. As a result, the movement of our robot was slow and less responsive. In the coming year, we will improve the speed of the robot in control and kicking the ball so that our robots have better capabilities. We will change our vision system by using a camera that can produce better images. We will also improve the mechanical system by using stronger parts and more precise metal cutting.

## References

1. Schwarz, M., et al.: Humanoid TeenSize open platform NimbRo-OP. In: Behnke, S., Veloso, M., Visser, A., Xiong, R. (eds.) RoboCup 2013. LNCS (LNAI), vol. 8371, pp. 568–575. Springer, Heidelberg (2014). https://doi.org/10.1007/978-3-662-44468-9_51
2. Muntaha, M.A., Muhtadin, Purnomo, M.H: Self-localization for humanoid soccer robots based on triangulation method. In: Indonesian Symposium on Robot Soccer Competition. Semarang (2013)

3. Zannatha, J.M.I., et al.: Monocular visual self-localization for humanoid soccer robots. In: 21st International Conference on Electronics, Communications and Computers Proceedings of CONIELECOMP 2011. pp. 100–107. Cholula, Puebla, México. (2011)

4. Ojala, T., Pietikainen, M., Maenpaa, T.: Multiresolution gray-scale and rotation invariant texture classification with local binary patterns. IEEE Transact. Pattern Anal. Mach. Intell. **24**(7), 971–987 (2002)

5. Viola, P., Jones, M.J.: Rapid object detection using a boosted cascade of simple features. In: IEEE Computer Vision and Pattern Recognition CVPR (2001)

6. Lienhart, R., Maydt, J.: An extended set of haar-like features for rapid object detection. In: IEEE ICIP 2002, vol. 1, pp. 900–903, September 2002

7. Dalal, N., Triggs, B.: Histograms of oriented gradients for human detection. In: 2005 IEEE Computer Society Conference on Computer Vision and Pattern Recognition, CVPR 2005, San Diego, CA, USA, vol. 1, pp. 886–893 (2005)

8. Ficht, G., et al.: Grown-Up NimbRo robots winning RoboCup 2017 humanoid adultsize soccer competitions. In: Akiyama, H., Obst, O., Sammut, C., Tonidandel, F. (eds.) RoboCup 2017. LNCS (LNAI), vol. 11175, pp. 448–460. Springer, Cham (2018). https://doi.org/10. 1007/978-3-030-00308-1_37

9. Allali, J., et al.: Rhoban football club: RoboCup humanoid kid-size 2016 champion team paper, pp. 491–502 (2017)

10. Behnke, S.: Online trajectory generation for omnidirectional biped walking. In: 2006 IEEE International Conference on Robotics and Automation, ICRA 2006, pp. 1597–1603. IEEE (2006)

11. Schmitz, A., Missura, M., Behnke, S.: Learning footstep prediction from motion capture. In: Ruiz-del-Solar, J., Chown, E., Plöger, Paul G. (eds.) RoboCup 2010. LNCS (LNAI), vol. 6556, pp. 97–108. Springer, Heidelberg (2011). https://doi.org/10.1007/978-3-642-20217-9_ 9

# NimbRo Robots Winning RoboCup 2018 Humanoid AdultSize Soccer Competitions

Hafez Farazi[✉], Grzegorz Ficht, Philipp Allgeuer, Dmytro Pavlichenko, Diego Rodriguez, André Brandenburger, Mojtaba Hosseini, and Sven Behnke

Autonomous Intelligent Systems, Computer Science,
University of Bonn, Bonn, Germany
{farazi,ficht,allgeuer,pavlichenko,rodriguez,behnke}@ais.uni-bonn.de
http://ais.uni-bonn.de

**Abstract.** Over the past few years, the Humanoid League rules have changed towards more realistic and challenging game environments, which encourage teams to advance their robot soccer performances. In this paper, we present the software and hardware designs that led our team NimbRo to win the competitions in the AdultSize league— including the soccer tournament, the drop-in games, and the technical challenges at RoboCup 2018 in Montréal. Altogether, this resulted in NimbRo winning the Best Humanoid Award. In particular, we describe our deep-learning approaches for visual perception and our new fully 3D printed robot NimbRo-OP2X.

## 1 Introduction

The goal of the RoboCup Humanoid League is to develop a team of humanoid robots that can compete against the human World Soccer Champion in 2050. In recent years, there were many rule changes introduced to the league in order to bring the level of complexity closer to human soccer. In the RoboCup 2018

**Fig. 1.** Left: NimbRo AdultSize Robots: Copedo, NimbRo-OP2 and NimbRo-OP2X. Right: The NimbRo team at RoboCup 2018 in Motnréal.

© Springer Nature Switzerland AG 2019
D. Holz et al. (Eds.): RoboCup 2018, LNAI 11374, pp. 436–449, 2019.
https://doi.org/10.1007/978-3-030-27544-0_36

competitions, drop-in games were introduced to the AdultSize class, in which two teams consisting of two robots competed with each other, and several teams performed very well.

For RoboCup 2018, we used two open-source 3D printed robots and an upgraded version of one of our classic robots. Each of our 3D printed robots is equipped with a fast onboard computer and a GPU to perform parallel computations. We extended our open-source software with a deeplearning-based perception system and gait parameter optimization. All of the AdultSize robots are shown in Fig. 1, along with the human members of our team NimbRo.

## 2 Robot Hardware

One of the main contributions to our team's performance at RoboCup 2018 was the hardware capabilities of our design. At the competition in Montréal, we participated with three robots: Copedo, NimbRo-OP2, and NimbRo-OP2X (See Fig. 1). Copedo [1] has a light weight of 10.1 kg, and spring-loaded legs with parallel kinematics make it a dynamically capable robot, which we utilize in, e.g., the jumping technical challenge.

In contrast to the aluminum and carbon-based build of Copedo, the structure of our newest NimbRo-OP2X [2] robot is completely 3D-printed and is a substantial upgrade to the NimbRo-OP2 [3]. The core design principles that made the NimbRo-OP2 a reliable and capable platform remained the same [3]. Both robots share the same kinematic structure, external gearing for increased torque, multiple master-slave actuation pairs and minimal complexity in assembly, diagnostics, and maintenance. Although their appearance may seem similar, the NimbRo-OP2X is a complete redesign that introduces multiple upgrades over the NimbRo-OP2. The main component of the redesign process was the use of a new type of actuator—the Robotis Dynamixel XM-540—which has a heat dissipating metal casing and outputs more torque than the previously used MX-106. This design choice led to the implementation of other features. With a single knee housing eight actuators, a substantial amount of heat is produced during operation. To reduce the possibility of thermal malfunctioning and overheating,

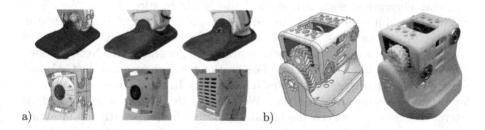

**Fig. 2.** Comparison of various hardware design features. (a) foot and back side of the knee: OP2X(CAD), OP2X, OP2. (b) Finished hip joint along with the CAD model showing the 3D-printed gears on the NimbRo-OP2X.

we have installed cooling fans, which helped to reduce the temperature in the knee by approximately 20 °C. We have also reduced the weight of the 3D-printed parts by making them slightly narrower, rounder and have added dedicated cable pathways, all of which contributed to an increased rigidity. The external gearing necessary to exert enough torque in the ankle and hip roll joints was a bottleneck in the production process of the NimbRo-OP2. We have mitigated this issue by designing low-friction and low-backlash double helical gears, which can be quickly 3D-printed [2]. The SLS (Selective Laser Sintering) printing technology was essential to the robustness of our robots, as no part ever broke, even after several collisions with twice as heavy robots that had a metal exoskeleton with sharp edges. The features mentioned above, along with their comparison between the NimbRo-OP2 and NimbRo-OP2X can be observed in Fig. 2.

## 3   Software Design

Our open-source software based on the ROS middleware [4] has become a well-established framework in the research and RoboCup community since the initial release. Many soccer teams have used our code and ideas in RoboCup [5–7]. We continue to further develop the repository, with the hope that other research groups can benefit from it.

### 3.1   Visual Perception

Each of our robots perceives the environment using a Logitech C905 camera which is equipped with a wide-angle lens. We supersede our previous approach to vision [8] by utilizing a deep convolutional neural network followed by post-processing. The presented perception system can work with different brightnesses, viewing angles, and even lens distortions. Using a recurrent deep neural network, we also are able to track and identify our robots [9].

We developed an encoder-decoder architecture similar to recently proposed pixel-wise segmentation models like SegNet [10], and U-Net [11]. Due to computational limitations, we utilized a shorter decoder than encoder part. Although this design choice minimizes the number of parameters and helps us achieve real-time perception, some fine-grained spatial information is lost. We alleviate this spatial information loss by using a subpixel centroid-finding method in the post-processing steps. To minimize the effort of data annotation, we used transfer-learning in our encoder part, by utilizing a pre-trained ResNet-18 model. Since our task is different from the classification task, we removed the GAP and the fully connected layers in the ResNet-18 model. In the decoder part, we used four transpose-convolutional layers. We followed the U-Net model and added lateral connections between the encoder and decoder parts with the intention to preserve spatial information in the decoder part. The proposed visual perception architecture, which in total has 23 convolutional layers, is illustrated in Fig. 3. The following object classes were detected using the network: goal posts, ball, and robots. For our soccer behavior, we only need to perceive predefined

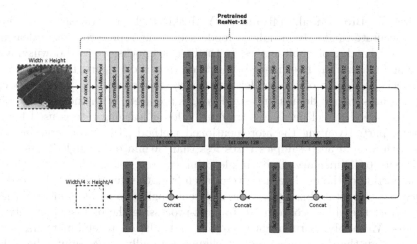

**Fig. 3.** Visual perception architecture. Similar to original ResNet architecture, each convBlock consists of two convolutional layers followed by batch-norm and ReLU activations. Note that for simplicity, residual connections in ResNet are not depicted.

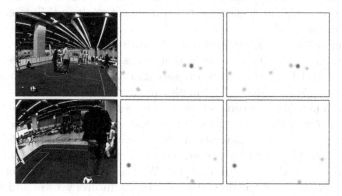

**Fig. 4.** Object detection results. Left column: A captured image from one of our robots. Middle column: The output of the network with balls (cyan), goal posts (magenta), and robots (yellow) annotated. Right column: Ground truth. (Color figure online)

center locations of the interesting objects. Similar to SweatyNet [12], instead of full segmentation loss, we used mean squared error. The desired output consists of Gaussian blobs around the ball center and bottom-middle points of the goal posts and robots.

Although we use Adam optimizer, which has an adaptable per-parameter scale, finding a good learning rate is a challenging prerequisite to training. To find an optimal learning rate, we followed the approach presented by Smith et al. [13].

We used progressive image resizing that uses small images at the start of training, and gradually increase the size as training progresses, a technique inspired by Brock et al. [14] and by Yosinski et al. [15]. In early iterations, the inaccurate randomly initialized model can make rapid progress by learning from large batches of small images. In the first 50 epochs, we used downsampled training images while freezing the weights on the encoder part. During the next 50 epochs, all parts of the models are jointly trained. In the last 50 epochs, to learn fine-grained details, full-sized images are used. With the intuition that the pre-trained model needs less training, a lower learning rate is used for the encoder part. By using the aforementioned methods, the whole training process with around 3000 samples takes less than 40 min on a single Titan Black GPU with 6 GB memory. Two samples from the test set are depicted in Fig. 4. Some portion of the used dataset were taken from the ImageTagger library [16], which have annotated samples from different angles, cameras, and brightness. We extract the object coordinates by post-processing the blob-shaped network outputs. We apply morphological erosion and dilation to eliminate negligible responses on the thresholded output channels. Finally, we compute the object center coordinates. The output of the network is of lower resolution and has less spatial information than the input image. To account for this effect, we calculate sub-pixel level coordinates based on the center of mass of a detected contour. To find the contours, we use connected component analysis [17] on each of the output channels.

We filter detected objects and project each object location into egocentric world coordinates. To minimize projection errors due to the differences between the designed model and real hardware, we calibrate the camera extrinsic parameters, using the Nelder-Mead [18] Simplex method.

In the competition, the robots were able to perceive the AdultSize ball up to a distance of 7 m with an accuracy of 99% and less than 1% of false detection rates. White goal posts are detected up to 8 m with 98% accuracy and with 3% false detections. Opponent robots are detected up to 7 m with a success rate of 90% and a false detection rate of 8%. We are still using non-deep learning approaches for field and line detections [8]. In the future, we will add two more channels to the network output and use a single unified network for all detections. The complete perception pipeline including a forward-pass of the network takes approximately 20 ms on the robot hardware.

**Localization and Breaking the Symmetry:** Our localization method relies on having a source of global yaw rotation of the robot [19]. Instead of a compass, we use integrated gyroscope measurements as the source of yaw orientation. Gyroscope integration is a reliable source of orientation tracking, but it needs a global reference. In order to set the initial heading, we could either use manual initialization or automatic initial orientation estimation. Manual heading initialization can fail during the match since sometimes restarting the operating system of the robot is unavoidable, which will force a reinitialization of the heading. Hence, we reformulated the global heading initialization as a classification task [1]. There are four predefined distinct positions and orientations that the robot can start in or enter the game from. In two of these spots, the robot should start facing the opponent goal, which the location is either near the center circle or the goal area. The other two sets of locations are beside the sideline in the robot's respective half, while facing the field. To choose from these predefined locations and orientations, we employ a multi-hypothesis version of our localization module, which is initialized with four different hypotheses. In the beginning, the robot attempts to discern the most likely hypothesis among all running instances. This process terminates when either the method times out or the robot finds the clearly most probable hypothesis. Ultimately, the vision module keeps the valid instance and rejects the rest. To verify the decision, we double check the result based on the recognized landmarks like the center circle and the goalposts.

## 3.2   Soccer Behaviors

Over the past 2–3 years, we have refined our soccer behaviors to become more robust, flexible, and easier to tune [1,20]. The behaviors are implemented as a highly modularised multi-layer hierarchical state machine and packaged into a ROS module that communicates with other parts of the software, like the vision node and gait motion module, via ROS topics. In this paper, we describe the current state of this architecture which was originally described in [21].

The flow of information and control starts with the ROS topics for which the behavior node is the subscriber, covering predominantly the game state perception, localization and game controller information coming from other nodes. This is captured and read by a ROS interface layer, which abstracts away all ROS-specific knowledge and code. The information is then distilled down into a standardized SensorVars structure, that at the beginning of each cycle is updated and recalculated with the latest direct and derived information about the state of the robot and soccer game. The so-called sensor variables are then used by the upper main layer of the state machine, referred to as the 'Game FSM'. This includes a range of behaviors that determine the soccer gameplay, including ball handling, goalie and positioning skills, which are all required at different times of the game. A standardized set of outputs are provided by the game behaviors that specify parameters like walking targets, ball targets (where to kick or dribble to), whether kicking and/or dribbling should be allowed in the current situation, and so on. These outputs are in turn the inputs to the lower main layer of the state machine, referred to as the 'Behavior FSM'. In this layer, low-level skills are implemented, such as searching for the ball, walking to the ball, kicking and/or dribbling it, and diving for the ball (enabled only for goalkeepers). The Behavior FSM then, in turn, provides a standardized set of outputs that determine where the robot should look, whether the robot should walk or not, and if so, with which velocity in what direction, as well as whether the robot should dive or kick, and if so, which direction of dive or type of kick. This information is then passed back to the ROS interface layer, which ensures that the other nodes are notified of the required actions of the robot.

**Ball Approach:** Walking to the ball, or more specifically, behind the ball while orienting to the correct direction for the ball target, is a Behavior FSM-level skill. It is performed by calculating an orientation-specific halo around the ball and constructing a path plan out of linear and circular arc segments that avoids entering the halo. Further away from the ball, the priority is to turn and walk directly in the direction that the robot needs to go, as forward walking is the fastest and most reliable, but as the robot approaches the ball, it smoothly transitions towards using more omnidirectional walking to approach the desired final position, while also starting to turn to face the direction that the robot wishes to kick or dribble the ball. The ball is aligned with the foot that is closest to the required position for the required action.

**Kicking and Dribbling:** If during the ball approach the ball is detected to be in a suitable region relative to the robot for a suitable amount of time, the kicking and/or dribbling skill behavior is activated. Kicking can only be activated when the robot is standing close to the ball in a suitable position and orientation to kick, but dribbling can sometimes activate up to 2 m away from the ball, so that the robot can follow a dribble approach trajectory and walk right through the ball at speed, leading to smoother, faster and more effective dribbling performance.

**Obstacle Avoidance:** It was a greatly simplifying design choice to implement obstacle avoidance in a completely generic manner, independent of what behavior skill is currently active. The output gait velocity of the Behavior FSM is a combination of a 2D walking vector with a rotational velocity. In the presence of an obstacle within a relevant distance of the robot, the walking vector of the robot is rotated away from the obstacle in a way that limits the maximum radial inwards walking velocity towards the obstacle. Further away from the obstacle (for example 1 m) the limit radial velocity is high, so there is little change to the robot's walking intent, but when very close to the obstacle the limit radial velocity even becomes negative to ensure that the robot will distance itself from the obstacle. A turning component is also proportionally added to the commanded rotational velocity to make the robot turn away from the obstacle, helping it to for example walk past the obstacle if it is blocking the way.

**Obstacle Ball Handling:** The obstacle ball handling was similarly implemented in a completely generic way, but one layer higher in the Game FSM. Given the situation that there is a ball and a ball target, i.e. where the ball should be kicked or dribbled to, then if there is an obstacle that is blocking this possibility, the ball-target is rotated out to avoid the obstacle, more so for closer and more relevant obstacles, and less so for further out obstacles. This enables the robot to identify and kick past a goalkeeper to score a goal. If the obstacle is too close to the robot, or the ball-target has to be rotated more than the amount for example by which a goal can still be safely scored, then kicking is disabled and dribbling is forced to try to take the ball off the opponent, which ideally makes space to then kick the ball towards its intended target.

### 3.3 Bayesian Gait Optimization

The gait is based on an open-loop Central Pattern Generator which calculates a nominal state for the joints using the gait phase angle. The phase angle is proportional to the step frequency [22] and controls the movement of the arms and legs. This approach has been improved by the use of fused angle feedback mechanisms, which introduce corrective actions to counteract disturbances [23, 24]. These fused angle feedback controllers establish new parameters, which need to be tuned. To ensure a high standard of performance, robot-specific parameters have to be tuned for each robot. Moreover, since the robot wears off during extensive use, parameters will become suboptimal, for instance over the course of a RoboCup competition.

As walking is one of the most crucial skills of a humanoid robot, it has to be robust and reliable at all times. To achieve this goal, we optimize the parametrization of the aforementioned fused angle feedback controller autonomously. Using *Bayesian optimization*, we rely not only on real-world experiments but also on simulated experiments to gain useful information, without wearing off the hardware of the robot. This approach has already been successfully applied to the igus® Humanoid Open Platform [25] and the NimbRo-OP2X [2].

Our approach is able to optimize the parameter set in a sample-efficient manner, trading off exploration and exploitation efficiently. This trade-off depends on a *kernel function* $k$ and the parametrization of the underlying *Gaussian Process* (GP). The latter encodes problem-specific values like signal noise and can be measured by a series of initial experiments [25]. The proposed kernel, on the other hand, is composed of two components, where the first term $k_{sim}$ encodes simulation performance and the second term $k_\epsilon$ functions as an error-term resembling the difference between simulation and the real-world performance:

$$k(\mathbf{a_i}, \mathbf{a_j}) = k_{sim}(\mathbf{x_i}, \mathbf{x_j}) + k_\delta(\delta_i, \delta_j)k_\epsilon(\mathbf{x_i}, \mathbf{x_j}), \tag{1}$$

where $\mathbf{a_i} = (\mathbf{x_i}, \delta_i)$ is an augmented parameter vector and $\delta$ is a flag signalizing whether an evaluation has been performed in the simulator or on the real system. If, and only if both experiments have been performed in the real world, $k_\delta$ is defined to be 1, resulting in a high correlation. Due to the error term $k_\epsilon$, it is possible to model complex, non-linear mappings between the simulator and real-world evaluations [26]. For both terms of the composite kernel, we chose the *Rational Quadratic kernel*, since it has been proven to be appropriate in previous work [25]. This composite kernel is then used to perform Gaussian Process regression on the data points.

Since real-world experiments are expensive, we utilize *Entropy* as a measure of information content to sample data points efficiently. In this manner, the next point of evaluation is chosen with respect to the maximal change of entropy, weighted by a factor that trades off the cost of simulated and real-world evaluations [27].

The cost function is a combination of aggregated fused angle feedback, as a stability measure, and a logistic function $\nu$ which penalizes parameters of large magnitude. Furthermore, we consider the sagittal ($\alpha$) and lateral ($\beta$) planes separately to reduce the complexity of the cost function. This results in the final cost functions:

$$J_\alpha(\mathbf{x}) = \int_0^T \|e_{P\alpha}(\mathbf{x})\|_1 dt + \nu(\mathbf{x}), \quad J_\beta(\mathbf{x}) = \int_0^T \|e_{P\beta}(\mathbf{x})\|_1 dt + \nu(\mathbf{x}) \quad (2)$$

which depend on the parameters $\mathbf{x}$ of the fused angle feedback controller. To reduce the impact of simulation noise, we average the cost of $N = 4$ evaluations. Each evaluation is a predefined sequence of movements into forward, sideways and backward directions. In the presented example, we optimize P and D gains of the arm angle corrective actions in the sagittal direction, but the method can be similarly applied on different controllers. We limit the number of real-world evaluations to 15. This limit was reached after evaluating 146 simulations, thus resulting in a total number of 161 iterations. The resulting optimized parameters were validated by comparison with the performance of the old gait parameters over five gait sequence evaluations each. The optimized parameters not only reduce the fused angle feedback deviation by about 18%, but also lead to a qualitatively more convincing gait [2].

The resulting Gaussian Process posterior is depicted in Fig. 5. Note that simulations are important especially in early iterations, even though their impact might not be directly visible in the final posterior [25]. This is proven by the fact that the robot did not fall during optimization, thus confirming that the model is able to utilize information of the simulator effectively.

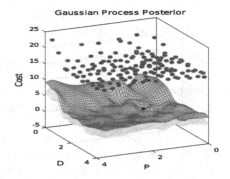

**Fig. 5.** The Gaussian Process posterior of the arm angle optimization. The red dots resemble real-world evaluations, whereas the blue dots indicate the results of simulations. The green mesh shows the predicted cost and the black dot indicates its minimum. The corresponding standard deviation is displayed as the grey mesh. The upper standard deviation has been removed for visibility.

# 4   Performance

In RoboCup 2018, AdultSize robots autonomously competed in one vs. one soccer games, two vs. two drop-in games, and four technical challenges that tested different abilities. The soccer games were performed on a $6 \times 9$ m artificial grass field, which made locomotion challenging. Due to the dynamic lighting conditions, perceiving the environment and localization were also challenging. Our robots performed outstandingly by winning all of the four possible awards, including the Best Humanoid Award. In the main tournament, our robots played a total of six games, including the quarter-finals, semi-finals, and finals. Additional five drop-in games were played, where two vs. two mixed teams were formed and robots collaborated during the game. Our robots officially played 220 min with a total score of 66:5.

## 4.1   Technical Challenges

In the following sections, we discuss four technical challenges at RoboCup 2018: Push Recovery, High Jump, High Kick, and Goal Kick from Moving Ball.

**Push Recovery:** The goal of this challenge is to withstand a strong push which is applied to the robot on the level of the CoM by a pendulum. To define the impulse, a 3 kg weight is retracted by a distance $d$ from the point of contact with the robot. The push is applied both from the front and from the back while the robot is walking on the spot. NimbRo-OP2X was able to successfully withstand a push from the front and the back with $d = 90$ cm.

**High Jump:** The goal of the high jump is to remain airborne as long as possible during an upward jump. In order to successfully complete the challenge, the robot has to reach a stable standing or sitting posture upon landing. The challenge was performed using a predesigned jump motion, which was constructed with our keyframe editor. Copedo has successfully completed the challenge, remaining airborne for 0.147 s.

**High Kick:** This challenge poses the task of scoring a goal over an obstacle positioned on the goal line. The ranking for this challenge is based on the height of the kick. The ball starts at the penalty mark, and multiple kicks are allowed during one trial. We utilized the following strategy: first move the ball closer to the obstacle by a kick of reduced power and then perform a specially designed kick to overcome the obstacle. The kick was manually designed in a way that the foot hits the ball significantly lower on its COM and then moves upwards, which allows to kick the ball into the air instead of rolling it on the ground. We managed to perform a high kick over an obstacle of 21.5 cm. The whole trial took 14.4 s. NimbRo-OP2 performing the challenge is shown in Fig. 6.

**Fig. 6.** High Kick challenge. (a) Initial setup. The ball is positioned on the penalty mark. (b) Ball was kicked to reach the goal area. (c) High kick motion is performed. Note that the foot supports the ball in the air, adding more energy and directing it upwards. (d) Ball passed the obstacle with a large margin. Goal is scored.

**Goal Kick from Moving Ball:** The task of this challenge is to score a goal by kicking a moving ball into the goal. The robot is standing at the penalty mark. At RoboCup 2017 a special ramp was used to direct the ball towards the robot. In contrast, at RoboCup 2018 a human player was giving a pass to the robot from a corner, symbolizing a situation from the real soccer game. Our approach for solving this task was as follows: once positioned at the penalty mark, the robot lifts its foot to be ready for kicking and is standing on the other foot, human player kicks the ball towards the robot; using ball detection and its pose estimation we estimate the velocity of the ball and its approximate time of arrival to the area of a potentially successful kick; given this time, we execute the kicking motion when necessary. Since the robot is initially standing on one foot, with the other lifted upwards, the kick can be performed quickly, which allows for higher speed of the pass and, hence, faster scoring of the goal, which was the primary criterion in team rankings. Standing on one foot, which is also performed by many other teams during this challenge, has two major drawbacks: the robot is not stable in that posture, and it cannot adjust if the pass is not accurate enough. In the future we will work on a more general approach to perform this challenge. NimbRo-OP2X was able to score a goal in 2.78 s after a human player touched the ball (see Fig. 7).

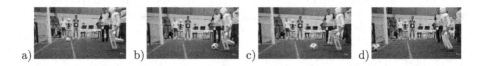

**Fig. 7.** Goal Kick from Moving Ball challenge. (a) Initial setup. The human player passes the ball to the robot. (b) Ball is approaching. Note that the right foot is already moving towards ball's predicted pose in order to kick it. (c) Ball is successfully kicked. (d) Goal is scored, stable posture of the robot is recovered.

The recorded parameters describing our performance at technical challenges are summarized in Table 1.

**Table 1.** Parameters recorded for the technical challenges

| Parameter | Value | Challenge |
|---|---|---|
| Pendulum weight [kg] | 3 | Push Recovery |
| Pendulum swing [cm] | 90 | |
| Obstacle height [cm] | 21.5 | High Kick |
| Time for completion [s] | 14.4 | |
| Time airborne [s] | 0.147 | High Jump |
| Time for completion [s] | 2.78 | Kick from Moving Ball |

# 5   Conclusions

In this paper, we presented hardware and software design that lead us to win all possible competitions in the AdultSize class for the RoboCup 2018 Humanoid League in Montréal: the soccer tournament, the drop-in games, the technical challenges, and the Best Humanoid Award. We presented individual skills regarding the perception, the bipedal gait tuning, and behavior as well as their application in the technical challenges. A video showing the competition highlights is available online[1]. The hardware of the NimbRo-OP2 generation[2] as well as our software[3] were released open-source to GitHub with the hope that other teams and research groups benefit from our work.

**Acknowledgements.** This work was partially funded by grant BE 2556/13 of the German Research Foundation (DFG).

# References

1. Ficht, G., et al.: Grown-up NimbRo robots winning RoboCup 2017 Humanoid AdultSize soccer competitions. In: Akiyama, H., Obst, O., Sammut, C., Tonidandel, F. (eds.) RoboCup 2017. LNCS (LNAI), vol. 11175, pp. 448–460. Springer, Cham (2018). https://doi.org/10.1007/978-3-030-00308-1_37
2. Ficht, G., et al.: NimbRo-OP2X: adult-sized Open-source 3D printed humanoid robot. In: Humanoids (2018)
3. Ficht, G., Allgeuer, P., Farazi, H., Behnke, S.: NimbRo-OP2: grown-up 3D printed open humanoid platform for research. In: Humanoids (2017)
4. Quigley, M., et al.: ROS: an open-source robot operating system. In: ICRA (2009)
5. Razi, M.R.A., et al.: ICHIRO team description paper humanoid teensize league. Technical report, Institut Teknologi Sepuluh Nopember (2018)
6. Dehkordi, M.R.R., Abdollahi, S., Rezayat, M.H., Sajadieh, S.M., Zamani, F.: Unbounded designers teen & kid size team description paper. Technical report, Azad University of Isfahan (2018)

---

[1] RoboCup 2018 NimbRo AdultSize highlights: https://www.youtube.com/watch?v=tPktQyFrMuw.

[2] Hardware: https://github.com/NimbRo/nimbro-op2.

[3] Software: https://github.com/AIS-Bonn/humanoid_op_ros.

7. Chen, X., et al.: RoboCup rescue team description paper NuBot. Technical report, University of Newcastle (2017)

8. Farazi, H., Allgeuer, P., Behnke, S.: A monocular vision system for playing soccer in low color information environments. In: 10th Workshop on Humanoid Soccer Robots (Humanoids) (2015)

9. Farazi, H., Behnke, S.: Online visual robot tracking and identification using deep LSTM networks. In: International Conference on Intelligent Robots and Systems (IROS) (2017)

10. Badrinarayanan, V., Kendall, A., Cipolla, R.: SegNet: a deep convolutional encoder-decoder architecture for image segmentation. arXiv:1511.00561 (2015)

11. Ronneberger, O., Fischer, P., Brox, T.: U-Net: convolutional networks for biomedical image segmentation. In: Navab, N., Hornegger, J., Wells, W.M., Frangi, A.F. (eds.) MICCAI 2015. LNCS, vol. 9351, pp. 234–241. Springer, Cham (2015). https://doi.org/10.1007/978-3-319-24574-4_28

12. Schnekenburger, F., Scharffenberg, M., Wülker, M., Hochberg, U., Dorer, K.: Detection and localization of features on a soccer field with feedforward fully convolutional neural networks (FCNN) for the adult-size humanoid robot sweaty. In: 12th Workshop on Humanoid Soccer Robots (Humanoids) (2017)

13. Smith, L.N.: Cyclical learning rates for training neural networks. In: Applications of Computer Vision (WACV) (2017)

14. Brock, A., Lim, T., Ritchie, J.M., Weston, N.: FreezeOut: accelerate training by progressively freezing layers. arXiv preprint arXiv:1706.04983 (2017)

15. Yosinski, J., Clune, J., Bengio, Y., Lipson, H.: How transferable are features in deep neural networks? In: NIPS (2014)

16. Fiedler, N., Bestmann, M., Hendrich, N.: ImageTagger: an open source online platform for collaborative image labeling. In: Holz, D. et al. (eds.) RoboCup 2018. LNAI, vol. 11374, pp. 162–169. Springer, Cham (2019)

17. Suzuki, S., et al.: Topological structural analysis of digitized binary images by border following. Comput. Vis. Graph. Image Process. 30, 32–46 (1985)

18. Nelder, J.A., Mead, R.: A simplex method for function minimization. Comput. J. 7, 308–313 (1965)

19. Farazi, H., et al.: RoboCup 2016 humanoid teensize winner NimbRo: robust visual perception and soccer behaviors. In: Behnke, S., Sheh, R., Sarıel, S., Lee, D.D. (eds.) RoboCup 2016. LNCS (LNAI), vol. 9776, pp. 478–490. Springer, Cham (2017). https://doi.org/10.1007/978-3-319-68792-6_40

20. Rodriguez, D., et al.: Advanced soccer skills and team play of RoboCup 2017 teensize winner NimbRo. In: Akiyama, H., Obst, O., Sammut, C., Tonidandel, F. (eds.) RoboCup 2017. LNCS (LNAI), vol. 11175, pp. 435–447. Springer, Cham (2018). https://doi.org/10.1007/978-3-030-00308-1_36

21. Allgeuer, P., Behnke, S.: Hierarchical and state-based architectures for robot behavior planning and control. In: 8th Workshop on Humanoid Soccer Robots, International Conference on Humanoid Robots (Humanoids) (2013)

22. Behnke, S.: Online trajectory generation for omnidirectional biped walking. In: ICRA (2006)

23. Allgeuer, P., Behnke, S.: Fused angles: a representation of body orientation for balance. In: IROS (2015)

24. Allgeuer, P., Behnke, S.: Omnidirectional bipedal walking with direct fused angle feedback mechanisms. In: Humanoids (2016)

25. Rodriguez, D., Brandenburger, A., Behnke, S.: Combining simulations and real-robot experiments for Bayesian optimization of bipedal gait stabilization. In: Holz, D. et al. (eds.) RoboCup 2018. LNAI, vol. 11374, pp. 70–82. Springer, Cham (2019)
26. Marco, A., et al.: Virtual vs. real: trading off simulations and physical experiments in reinforcement learning with Bayesian optimization. In: ICRA (2017)
27. Hennig, P., Schuler, C.: Entropy search for information-efficient global optimization. J. Mach. Learn. Res. **13**, 1809–1837 (2012)

# HELIOS2018: RoboCup 2018 Soccer Simulation 2D League Champion

Hidehisa Akiyama[1]([✉]), Tomoharu Nakashima[2], Takuya Fukushima[2],
Jiarun Zhong[2], Yudai Suzuki[2], and An Ohori[2]

[1] Fukuoka University, Fukuoka, Japan
akym@fukuoka-u.ac.jp
[2] Osaka Prefecture University, Osaka, Japan
tomoharu.nakashima@kis.osakafu-u.ac.jp,
takuya.fukushima@edu.osakafu-u.ac.jp

**Abstract.** The RoboCup Soccer Simulation 2D League is the oldest of the RoboCup competitions. The 2D soccer simulator enables to teams of simulated autonomous agents to play a game of soccer with realistic rules and sophisticated game play. This paper introduces the RoboCup 2018 Soccer Simulation 2D League champion team, HELIOS2018, a united team from Fukuoka University and Osaka Prefecture University. The overview of the team's two recent research themes is also described. The first one is the method of online search of cooperative behavior and several approaches to acquire the appropriate evaluation functions. The second one is an opponent analysis in order to adopt the team strategy to the current opponent team online.

## 1  Introduction

This paper introduces the RoboCup 2018 Soccer Simulation 2D League champion team, HELIOS2018, a united team from Fukuoka University and Osaka Prefecture University. The team has been participating in the RoboCup competition since 2000, and won 2010, 2012 [1], 2017 and 2018 competitions. The team released several open source software for developing simulated soccer team using the RoboCup Soccer 2D simulator. A team base code, a visual debugger and a formation editor are available now. The details can be found in [3].

The reminder of this paper is organized as follows. Section 2 introduces the Soccer Simulation 2D League. Section 3 introduces our recent approach of online search of cooperative behavior. Section 4 introduces our approach of opponent analysis. Section 5 concludes.

## 2  Soccer Simulation 2D League

The RoboCup Soccer Simulation 2D League is the oldest of the RoboCup competition [9]. The simulation system[1] enables two teams of 11 autonomous player

---

[1] Available at: https://github.com/rcsoccersim.

© Springer Nature Switzerland AG 2019
D. Holz et al. (Eds.): RoboCup 2018, LNAI 11374, pp. 450–461, 2019.
https://doi.org/10.1007/978-3-030-27544-0_37

agents and an autonomous coach agent to play a game of soccer with realistic rules and game play. Figure 1 shows a screenshot of the 2D soccer simulator. Player agents receive a visual sensor message, an aural sensor message and a body sensor message from the simulation server, and can send few types of abstract action command (kick, dash, turn, turn_neck, and so on). In the game of RoboCup Soccer Simulation 2D League, player agents make a decision at each cycle in real time. A game consists of 6000 cycles, thus the decision making process of each player is executed about 6000 times. The 2D soccer simulator does not model the motion of any particular physical robot, but does capture realistic team level strategic interactions. Therefore, the performance of a team depends on the decision process of its agents. Due to its functions and stability, the 2D soccer simulator is known as a good research and educational tool for multiagent systems and artificial intelligence.

In 2018, up to 16 teams were allowed to pass the qualificaton process. Finally, 13 teams participated in the competition. HELIOS2018 won the championship with 18 wins and 1 loss and 1 draw, scoring 75 goals and conceding 9 goals. CYRUS2018 from Atomic Energy High School won the second place, and MT2018 from Hefei University won the third place.

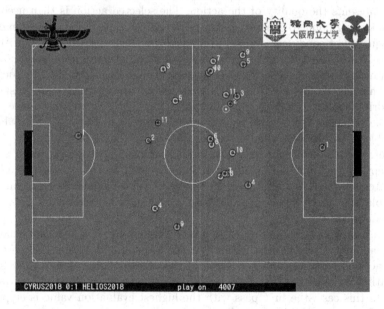

**Fig. 1.** A screenshot of the 2D soccer simulator. This game shows the RoboCup 2018 final between CYRUS2018 (Atomic Energy High School, Iran) and HELIOS2018 (Fukuoka University and Osaka Prefecture University, Japan).

# 3    Online Search of Cooperative Behavior

This section shows an overview of online search of cooperative behavior implemented in our team. First, the model of cooperative behavior and its planning process are described. Then, our recent approaches for acquiring the evaluation function are described.

## 3.1    Action Sequence Planning

In order to model the cooperative behavior among players as action sequence planning, we employed a tree search method for generating and evaluating action sequences performed by multiple players [2]. This method searches for the best sequence of ball kicking actions among several teammate players using a tree-structured candidate action generator and an evaluation function of the candidate actions. A lot of ball kicking action plans are generated during the search process and the best action plan is selected based on the evaluation value. In the current implementation, this planning process is only made by a ball kicker (called a kicker hereafter). First, the candidate actions are generated from the current situation of the soccer field. Each action is assigned an evaluation value that represents the quality of the action. The selected action is then used as a second kicking point to generate further candidate actions. This process expands the sequence of candidate actions in a tree form. Best first search algorithm is used to traverse a tree and to expand nodes. A path from the root node to the branch represents a kick action sequence that defines a certain cooperative behavior. We assume the considered actions are abstracted ones, such as pass, dribble and shoot. Figure 2 shows an example of kick action sequence. The example sequence starts with a pass from Player 10 to Player 7. Then Player 7 dribbles to a position where it passes the ball to Player 9, who finally makes a shoot. Since we consider only ball kicking actions, move actions such as ball interception are omitted in the figure. In our search process, the action plan is generated by the first ball kicker. In Fig. 2, Player 10 generates this plan, and other players cannot know the exact plan or can know it partially by using aural communication.

An example of the planning process is depicted in Fig. 3. The kicker generates three candidates for the first action (i.e., pass, pass, and dribble). Each of the three actions has an evaluation value in the corresponding node. That is, the evaluation value of the first pass is 30, the second pass is 20, and the dribble is 15. In this case, the first pass with the highest evaluation value is employed as the first action. Further candidate actions are generated from the selected pass action. We call the level of the tree as depth of the action sequence. Two actions (pass and dribble) in Depth 2 are added as the candidate action with the corresponding evaluation values. The action sequence is updated as the one with the highest evaluation value among the candidate. In this case, the pass in Depth 2 is selected as it has the highest evaluation of 35. Thus the resultant action sequence is "pass–pass".

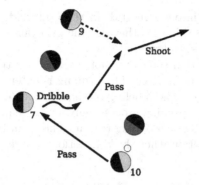

**Fig. 2.** An example of action sequence. This image shows the sequence of four actions: (1) pass from Player 10 to Player 7, (2) dribbling by Player 7, (3) pass from Player 7 to Player 9, and (4) Player 9 shoots to the goal.

The decision of players highly depends on the evaluation function, that computes the evaluation value of each action plan. We have to design an appropriate evaluation function in order to select the action plan corresponding to the team strategy and tactics. However, it is difficult to design an appropriate evaluation function because we have to consider many feature values.

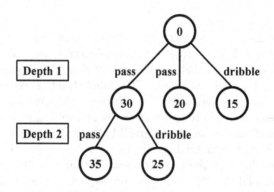

**Fig. 3.** An example search tree of action sequence planning.

## 3.2 Pruning in Action Sequence Planning

We use a pruning approach to restrict actions generated in tree search process. This approach enables to control players' action pattern without adjusting the evaluation function. We propose a pruning method using Support Vector Machine.

In order to clarify position transition of actions, two continuous variables, $x$ and $y$ that represent the coordinate value in the soccer field, are discretized. We divide the soccer field into $n \times m$ grid. In the grid field, if the ball exists in a grid, the grid takes the value 1, otherwise the grid takes the value 0. This grid represents $n \times m$ dimensional vector.

In our approach, action sequences not intended by the team developer are pruned during tree search process. The pruning is determined by a classifier of Support Vector Machine. The labeling method to create a training data set is described in Fig. 4. After pruning process, only action sequences representing the tactics intended by the team developer remain. The input to SVM is a discretized coordinate value of position where kicking action is performed.

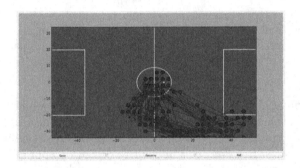

**Fig. 4.** A screenshot of the developed GUI for pruning.

Since SVM is a supervised learning method, we need a training data set to acquire classifier model. We extract action sequences from game log files. Then, the team developers set a label to the extracted action sequences using GUI if that is suitable for their intention. This labeled action sequence is used as a training data. We propose to apply a clustering method in order to classify similar action sequences. This approach reduces the human's action selection procedure. We use Gaussian mixture and EM algorithm with BIC as a clustering method. Figure 4 shows our GUI application. Action sequences organized into one cluster are displayed in the main window. Action sequences intended by the team developer are labeled "1", other action sequences are labeled "−1".

We performed an experiment to evaluate clasification performance of our SVM. Then, in order to evaluate the effectiveness of our pruning approach, we compare the perfomance of two teams, HELIOS2016 with the proposed model and the original HELIOS2016.

In order to evaluate our SVM classifier, we performed simulation games against 8 teams from RoboCup2016. 100 games were performed for each team. Then, extracted action sequences are classified by clustering algorithm. Classified action sequences are labeled by the team developer using our GUI application. Linear kernel and RBF kernel are used as the kernels of SVM. We applied 10-fold cross validation to the obtained training data set. We compared the two types of grid resolutions, $7 \times 7$ and $23 \times 26$. Table 1 shows the result of $7 \times 7$ and Table 2

**Table 1.** Accuracy rate of SVM ($7 \times 7$)

| Kernel | Depth: 1 | Depth: 2 | Depth: 3 | Depth: 4 |
|--------|----------|----------|----------|----------|
| Linear | 80.31    | 81.98    | 83.65    | 84.60    |
| RBF    | 67.93    | 67.93    | 67.93    | 67.93    |

**Table 2.** Accuracy rate of SVM ($23 \times 26$)

| Kernel | Depth: 1 | Depth: 2 | Depth: 3 | Depth: 4 |
|--------|----------|----------|----------|----------|
| Linear | 83.44    | 85.08    | 86.58    | 87.45    |
| RBF    | 67.93    | 67.93    | 67.93    | 67.93    |

shows the result of $23 \times 26$. These results shows Linear kernel is better than RBF kernel and the $23 \times 26$ grids is better than the $7 \times 7$ grids.

In order to evaluate our pruning approach, we performed simulation games against 8 teams. We used the classifier model with Linear kernel and $23 \times 26$ grids field. As a result, we find that HELIOS2016 with the proposed method has a stronger tendency to pass on one side compared with the original team, from the analysis of pass distribution.

### 3.3 Knowledge Sharing in Action Sequence Planning

The problem here is that even though the generated action sequence is good, its execution is not easy. Most of the times, the generated action sequence is intervened during the course of its execution and it is necessary to plan the next action sequence again. One reason for this is that non-ball-kicking players (we call this non-kickers hereafter) do not know the plan of the kicker, which leads the incomplete formation to perfectly execute the plan. In order to tackle this problem, knowledge sharing is employed. Knowledge sharing is to have a common knowledge among different players. In the context of the action sequence planning in this paper, the knowledge sharing means that the action sequence generated by non-kickers are made as close to the one planned by the kicker as possible. To do so, non-kickers focus on obtaining the information around the kicker as much as possible. Then they try to generate the same action sequence as that by the kicker. The non-kicker selects the next action considering the action sequence which will be executed from the current situation.

In order to examine the effectiveness of knowledge sharing, we have done a preliminary experiments using Team opuSCOM, which is based on agent2d. Knowledge sharing is implemented in the opuSCOM players so that all the players are able to expect the action sequence of a kicker when they are non-kickers. In particular, we focus on a situation depicted in Fig. 5. As shown in the figure, action sequences with the depth of less than or equal to two are only considered. Furthermore, it is assumed that all the actions in the plan are passes. This is because it is easier to measure the effectiveness of the knowledge sharing without considering the presence of dribbles, which are difficult to differentiate with self passes.

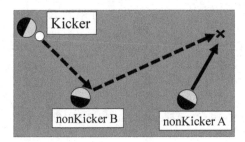

**Fig. 5.** Experimental situation.

Using ten teams that participated in the previous domestic as well as international competitions, the execution rates of the planned action sequences are measured when knowledge sharing is implemented in Team opuSCOM. First, we show the success rates of the knowledge sharing in Table 3. The table shows the average number of planned chain actions as well as successfully shared planned chain actions in 300 games for each opponent team. From this table, we can see that knowledge sharing is achieved with high precision.

**Table 3.** Success rates of the knowledge sharing.

| Opponents | #Planning | Sharing rate (%) |
|---|---|---|
| agent2d | 95 | 89.40 |
| HillStone | 89 | 89.64 |
| Esperanza | 84 | 90.16 |
| Toyosu-Galaxy | 30 | 92.20 |
| WIT | 51 | 89.49 |
| Fifty-Storms | 100 | 90.48 |
| ITAndroids | 84 | 89.81 |
| PersianGulf2017 | 73 | 87.45 |
| Ri-one2017 | 65 | 89.72 |
| opuSCOM (Before) | 114 | 90.29 |

Next, we investigate the execution of the planned action sequences. Table 4 shows the average number of planned action sequences (#Planning), the successful execution rates of the planned action sequences for the depth of one (D1) and two (D2), and the rate of successful execution of the depth-two action sequences over the successful depth-one action sequences (D2 per D1). Table 4 also compares the performance of the two versions of opuSCOM, one without the knowledge sharing (before) and the other with it (after). From this table, we can see that the successful execution increased by the introduction of knowledge sharing with the significance level of 5%.

**Table 4.** Successful execution rates of planned chain actions.

| Opponents | | #Planning | D1 (%) | D2 (%) | D2 per D1 (%) |
|---|---|---|---|---|---|
| agent2d | Before | 101 | 73.37 | 42.12 | 57.40 |
| | After | 95 | 73.39 | 47.15 | 64.25 |
| HillStone | Before | 94 | 71.92 | 39.21 | 54.52 |
| | After | 89 | 70.20 | 45.79 | 65.23 |
| Esperanza | Before | 89 | 72.49 | 43.53 | 60.05 |
| | After | 84 | 73.34 | 48.92 | 66.70 |
| Toyosu-Galaxy | Before | 29 | 74.46 | 30.50 | 40.96 |
| | After | 30 | 75.41 | 37.12 | 49.22 |
| WIT | Before | 51 | 74.06 | 44.36 | 59.90 |
| | After | 51 | 73.57 | 47.56 | 64.65 |
| FiftyStorms | Before | 104 | 67.80 | 37.52 | 55.34 |
| | After | 100 | 68.73 | 43.01 | 62.58 |
| ITAndroids | Before | 91 | 73.63 | 35.61 | 48.36 |
| | After | 84 | 73.95 | 40.65 | 54.97 |
| PersianGulf2017 | Before | 71 | 70.29 | 39.74 | 56.54 |
| | After | 73 | 68.67 | 40.25 | 58.61 |
| Ri-one2017 | Before | 67 | 73.71 | 36.00 | 48.84 |
| | After | 65 | 73.06 | 37.03 | 50.68 |
| opuSCOM (Before) | Before | 120 | 71.13 | 41.04 | 57.70 |
| | After | 114 | 72.43 | 47.14 | 65.10 |

## 3.4  Learning Evaluation Functions by Supervised Learning Method

During the search process, all action sequences are scored by predefined evaluation functions. Usually, human developers manually design the evaluation function for their team. However, manual adjustment does not necessarily produce the optimal function and requires much trial-and error iterative operation. In order to acquire an appropriate evaluation function, we are trying to apply several supervised learning methods.

Learning to Rank algorithm is one of our approaches to acquire the evaluation function that reflects human's tactical intention. Learning to Rank is one of the machine learning techniques which is widely used in information retrieval domain. We applied a linear model of SVMRank [7,8] to acquire the evaluation function for action sequence planning. SVMRank is one of the methods of Learning to Rank, that is classified to the pairwise method. In order to create training data for SVMRank, human trainers are only required to choose preferred action sequences from all generated ones. We developed a viewer application that can visualize generated action sequences and enables us to choose them intuitively. We can observe the list of generated action sequences and their overview on the soccer field (Fig. 6). The details of this approach can be found in [4].

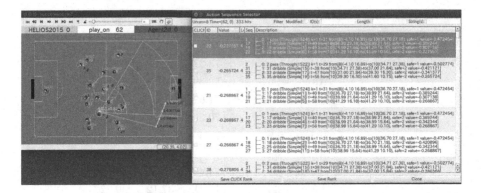

**Fig. 6.** Viewer application to choose preferred action sequences.

In another approach, we employed a neural network to model an expert team's evaluation function [6]. The neural network is trained by using positive and negative episodes of action sequences that are extracted from game logs. We used two versions of input features. One is the position at the next kick $(x_n, y_n)$, which means that a two-dimensional input feature vector is used for training data. And the other input features are the position at the current kick and the ball position at the next kick $((x_c, y_c)$ and $(x_n, y_n))$. These features do not contain player positions.

The extracted episodes from log files are converted to generate training data for the learning of neural networks. For two-dimensional training data, the ball positions in an episode are separated into individual ball positions. Each of such ball positions is used as a training vector which consists of the ball position $(x_n, y_n)$ as well as a positive/negative target value. This process is shown in the above side of Fig. 7. On the other hand, in the case of four-dimensional training data, a pair of successive two ball positions are used as a training vector. The former term of the pair is regarded as the current ball position and the latter is the predicted ball position at the next kick. Each of the two ball positions in the pair is concatenated to generate a four-dimensional input vector $(x_c, y_c, x_n, y_n)$. The target value for the generated vector is determined by the label (i.e., positive or negative) that is associated with the episode that the four-dimensional vector was generated from. The lower part of Fig. 7 shows this process.

This neural network approach tries to mimic other strong team's strategy. However, we often need to modify a part of obtained strategy in order to affect team developer's preference. We are planning to integrate the idea of first approach to the second approach.

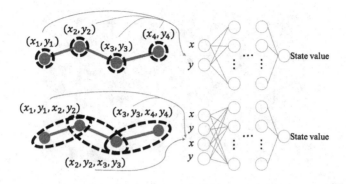

**Fig. 7.** Conversion of an episode into training data

# 4   Opponent Analysis

In this league, one of the essential tasks in the development of a team is to design an effective strategy. The sooner the opponent team's strategy is identified, the sooner the team can adapt its strategy in order to increase its chance to win the game. In this section, we introduce a method for identifying opponent teams' strategies.

We define a team strategy as the player's positioning during a game. To use players'position as the inputs of the learning model requires to consider their uniform numbers. Thus, the order of the players would be a problem in the construction of the model. To cope with this issue, an opponent formation is numerically expressed by discretizing the soccer field by a grid as shown in Fig. 8. Then, the number of players present in each cell is counted. The value of each cell is used as the input of the learning model. The value in each cell shows the number of opponent players at a certain cycle, and the results are integrated. Then, the average value is computed by dividing the integration obtained so far by the number of observed cycles. This set of the average values is used as input data of our identification model. For example, if the field is discretized by a grid of size $6 \times 4$, opponent formation is expressed by a 24-dimensional vector.

The input vectors are used to train a supervised-learning-based classification methods. SVM is employed as our identification model in order to classify the type of opponents teams' formations. The accuracy of the model is high even for short amount of time spent to analyze the opponent formation. The detailed results can be found in [5].

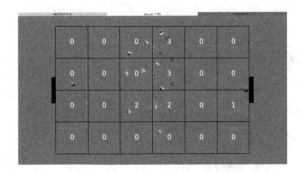

**Fig. 8.** Discretization of the soccer field by a grid of size 6 × 4.

## 5    Conclusion

This paper introduced the champion or RoboCup 2018 Soccer Simulation 2D league. First, the overview of the competition is described. Then, we described our current research topics, online search of cooperative behavior and opponent analysis. The HELIOS team won 3 championships in the past RoboCup competitions. Currently, our released software are widely used in the 2D community not only for the competition but for the research.

## References

1. Akiyama, H., Nakashima, T.: HELIOS2012: RoboCup 2012 soccer simulation 2D league champion. In: Chen, X., Stone, P., Sucar, L.E., van der Zant, T. (eds.) RoboCup 2012. LNCS (LNAI), vol. 7500, pp. 13–19. Springer, Heidelberg (2013). https://doi.org/10.1007/978-3-642-39250-4_2
2. Akiyama, H., Aramaki, S., Nakashima, T.: Online cooperative behavior planning using a tree search method in the RoboCup soccer simulation. In: Proceedings of 4th IEEE International Conference on Intelligent Networking and Collaborative Systems (INCoS), pp. 170–177 (2012)
3. Akiyama, H., Nakashima, T.: HELIOS base: an open source package for the RoboCup soccer 2D simulation. In: Behnke, S., Veloso, M., Visser, A., Xiong, R. (eds.) RoboCup 2013. LNCS (LNAI), vol. 8371, pp. 528–535. Springer, Heidelberg (2014). https://doi.org/10.1007/978-3-662-44468-9_46
4. Akiyama, H., Fukuyado, M., Gochou, T., Aramaki, S.: Learning evaluation function for RoboCup soccer simulation using humans' choice. In: Proceedings of SCIS & ISIS 2018 (2018)
5. Fukushima, T., Nakashima, T., Akiyama, H.: Online opponent formation identification based on position information. In: Akiyama, H., Obst, O., Sammut, C., Tonidandel, F. (eds.) RoboCup 2017. LNCS (LNAI), vol. 11175, pp. 241–251. Springer, Cham (2018). https://doi.org/10.1007/978-3-030-00308-1_20
6. Fukushima, T., Nakashima, T., Akiyama, H.: Mimicking an expert team through the learning of evaluation functions from action sequences. In: Holz, D. et al. (eds.) RoboCup 2018. LNAI, vol. 11374, pp. xx–yy. Springer, Cham (2019)

7. Joachims, T.: Making large-scale support vector machine learning practical. In: Advances in Kernel Methods, pp. 169–184. MIT Press (1999)
8. Joachims, T.: Training linear SVMs in linear time. In: Proceedings of the ACM Conference on Knowledge Discovery and Data Mining (KDD) (2006)
9. Noda, I., Matsubara, H.: Soccer server and researches on multi-agent systems. In: Proceedings of IROS-96 Workshop on RoboCup, pp. 1–7 (1996)

# UT Austin Villa: RoboCup 2018 3D Simulation League Champions

Patrick MacAlpine[1(✉)], Faraz Torabi[2], Brahma Pavse[2], John Sigmon[2],
and Peter Stone[2]

[1] Microsoft Research, Redmond, USA
patmac@microsoft.com
[2] The University of Texas at Austin, Austin, USA
{faraztrb,brahmasp,johnsigmon}@utexas.edu, pstone@cs.utexas.edu

**Abstract.** The UT Austin Villa team, from the University of Texas at Austin, won the 2018 RoboCup 3D Simulation League, winning all 23 games that the team played. During the course of the competition the team scored 143 goals without conceding any. Additionally, the team won the RoboCup 3D Simulation League goalie challenge. This paper describes the changes and improvements made to the team between 2017 and 2018 that allowed it to win both the main competition and goalie challenge.

## 1 Introduction

UT Austin Villa won the 2018 RoboCup 3D Simulation League for the seventh time in the past eight years, having also won the competition in 2011 [1], 2012 [2], 2014 [3], 2015 [4], 2016 [5], and 2017 [6] while finishing second in 2013. During the course of the competition the team scored 143 goals and conceded none along the way to winning all 23 games the team played. Many of the components of the 2018 UT Austin Villa agent were reused from the team's successful previous years' entries in the competition. This paper is not an attempt at a complete description of the 2018 UT Austin Villa agent, the base foundation of which is the team's 2011 championship agent fully described in a team technical report [7], but instead focuses on changes made in 2018 that helped the team repeat as champions.

In addition to winning the main RoboCup 3D Simulation League competition, UT Austin Villa also won the RoboCup 3D Simulation League goalie challenge. This paper also serves to document the goalie challenge and the approach used by UT Austin Villa when competing in the challenge.

The remainder of the paper is organized as follows. In Sect. 2 a description of the 3D simulation domain is given. Section 3 details changes and improvements to the 2018 UT Austin Villa team: variable distance fast walk kicks and

---

P. MacAlpine—The first author did the majority of the work for this publication while a postdoc at the University of Texas at Austin.

© Springer Nature Switzerland AG 2019
D. Holz et al. (Eds.): RoboCup 2018, LNAI 11374, pp. 462–475, 2019.
https://doi.org/10.1007/978-3-030-27544-0_38

a passing strategy incorporating deep learning, while Sect. 4 analyzes the contributions of these changes in addition to the overall performance of the team at the competition. Section 5 describes and analyzes the goalie challenge, while also documenting the overall league technical challenge consisting of both the goalie challenge and a free/scientific challenge, while Sect. 6 concludes.

## 2  Domain Description

The RoboCup 3D simulation environment is based on SimSpark [8], a generic physical multiagent system simulator. SimSpark uses the Open Dynamics Engine (ODE) library for its realistic simulation of rigid body dynamics with collision detection and friction. ODE also provides support for the modeling of advanced motorized hinge joints used in the humanoid agents.

Games consist of 11 versus 11 agents playing two 5 min halves of soccer on a 30 × 20 m field. The robot agents in the simulation are modeled after the Aldebaran Nao robot, which has a height of about 57 cm, and a mass of 4.5 kg. Each robot has 22 degrees of freedom: six in each leg, four in each arm, and two in the neck. In order to monitor and control its hinge joints, an agent is equipped with joint perceptors and effectors. Joint perceptors provide the agent with noise-free angular measurements every simulation cycle (20 ms), while joint effectors allow the agent to specify the speed/direction in which to move a joint.

Visual information about the environment is given to an agent every third simulation cycle (60 ms) through noisy measurements of the distance and angle to objects within a restricted vision cone (120°). Agents are also outfitted with noisy accelerometer and gyroscope perceptors, as well as force resistance perceptors on the sole of each foot. Additionally, agents can communicate with each other every other simulation cycle (40 ms) by sending 20 byte messages.

In addition to the standard Nao robot model, four additional variations of the standard model, known as heterogeneous types, are available for use. These variations from the standard model include changes in leg and arm length, hip width, and also the addition of toes to the robot's foot. Teams must use at least three different robot types, no more than seven agents of any one robot type, and no more than nine agents of any two robot types.

## 3  Changes for 2018

While many components developed prior to 2018 contributed to the success of the UT Austin Villa team including dynamic role assignment [9], marking [10], and an optimization framework used to learn low level behaviors for walking and kicking via an overlapping layered learning approach [11], the following subsections focus only on those that are new for 2018: variable distance fast walk kicks and a passing strategy incorporating deep learning. A performance analysis of these components is provided in Sect. 4.1.

## 3.1   Variable Distance Fast Walk Kicks

This section discusses an improvement to fast walk kicks which were first introduced for the 2017 competition. A fast walk kick is the ability of an agent to approach the ball and kick it without having to first stop and enter a stable standing position. The amount of time it takes for agents to approach and kick the ball is an important consideration as kick attempts that take longer to perform give opponents a better chance to stop them from being executed.

For the 2017 competition the UT Austin Villa team made large improvements by incorporating fast walk kicks and reducing kicking times [6]. In 2017 two different fast walk kick distances were optimized: one for long distance and a shorter distance lower height kick that would not accidentally travel over the goal when taking a shot. New for the 2018 competition, fast walk kicks were optimized for several distances in 1 m increments from 18 m down to 5 m. Kicks were optimized in discrete distances in a similar manner to how the team previously optimized slower variable distance kicks [4] as opposed to learning a kicking skill that adjusts its distance [12]. Having a larger set of distances to kick the ball to provides better passing options for team play.

The UT Austin Villa team specifies kicking motions through a periodic state machine with multiple key frames, where each key frame is a parameterized static pose of fixed joint positions. Figure 1 shows an example series of poses for a kicking motion. The joint angles are optimized using the CMA-ES [13] algorithm and overlapping layered learning [11] methodologies. Kicking motion angle positions were learned for every joint—except for those controlling the position of the robot's head as we wanted to ensure it stayed looking at the ball—over each of 12 contiguous simulation cycles resulting in ≈260 parameters being optimized for each kick distance.

**Fig. 1.** Example of a fixed series of poses that make up a kicking motion.

During learning the robot runs through an optimization task where it performs ten kick attempts beginning from different positions behind the ball, with these kick attempt starting positions being at various offset angle positions one meter from the ball. For each kick attempt the robot walks toward a specific offset position behind the ball from which to execute the kicking motion—the X and Y offset positions behind the ball from which to start the kick are parameters of a kick that are also learned. Once the offset position behind the ball is reached, the robot kicks the ball toward a target position that is the desired kick distance away from the starting position of the ball in the forward direction (toward the opponent's goal) of the field. At the conclusion of a kick attempt a *fitness* value—how good the kick attempt was—is computed, and the overall fitness for a kick is the average fitness of all kick attempts using that kick. The fitness function for a kick attempt at a particular target distance is as follows:

$$\textit{fitness}_{\text{dist}} = \begin{cases} -(\text{targetDistance}^2) & : \text{Penalty} \\ -(\text{kickDistanceFromTarget}^2) & : \text{Otherwise} \end{cases}$$

A penalty condition is one of the following: the agent fell over, the agent ran into or missed the ball, or the kick attempt took too long (over 12 s to make contact with the ball) and timed out. The fitness an agent receives when there is a penalty is the same as if the ball did not move during a kick attempt. A perfect kick's fitness is 0. The relative difference in fitness between kicks does not matter as CMA-ES only uses ordinal ranking of fitness values during learning.

Each variable distance fast walk kick was optimized with CMA-ES by running 300 generations with a population size of 300. The resulting fitness for most of the different distance kicks was greater than $-1$, meaning the average squared error of distance was less than a meter.

Longer distance kicks were learned first using initial parameter seed values from our longest 2017 pre-existing fast walk kick which can travel close to 20 m. Kicks were learned in descending order of distance, and as new shorter distance kicks were learned they were then used as seeds for even shorter kicks.

## 3.2  Deep Learning Passing Strategy

Before the 2018 competition, we used the hand-tuned heuristic scoring function shown in Eq. 1 to decide where to kick the ball for a pass. The equation rewards kicks that move the ball towards the opponent's goal, penalizes kicks that move the ball near opponents, and rewards kicks that move the ball near a teammate. All distances in Eq. 1 are measured in meters. A primary reason for Eq. 1's effectiveness is that it *efficiently* evaluates the value of different kicking locations.

$$\text{score}(\textit{target}) = \begin{matrix} -\|\textit{opponentGoal} - \textit{target}\| \\ \forall \textit{opp} \in \textit{Opponents}, -.5 * \max(64 - \|\textit{opp} - \textit{target}\|^2, 0) \\ -.5 * \max(64 - \|\textit{closestOpponentToTarget} - \textit{target}\|^2, 0) \\ + \max(10 - \|\textit{closestTeammateToTarget} - \textit{target}\|, 0) \end{matrix} \quad (1)$$

While efficient and successful, Eq. 1 is potentially very limited. Firstly, it does not capture the specific positions of players from the kick target. Secondly, the heuristic's restrictive nature forces us to use a different hand-tuned scoring function to handle set plays such as kick-offs. In an effort to tackle these limitations, we used a deep learning based approach for RoboCup 2018.

In our approach, we determine the value of potential passing locations by training a value network. While we evaluate the performance of our network in regular gameplay scenarios, we have trained our network using a supervised learning problem formulation with only indirect kick data against various teams in the league.

Let the total data set $S$ of size $m$ be $\{(x^i, y^i)\}_{i=1}^m$. A single input, $x^i$, to the network is a 49 dimensional feature vector representing the state of the game ie: the play mode, the coordinates of 22 player locations, ball location, and potential pass location. The output, $y^i$, of the network is a single scalar value between $[0, 1]$ that denotes the value of the potential pass location. During our data collection process, we determine a single $y^i$ by repeatedly restoring the state according to $x^i$ ten times. In each of these restorations, the team receives a reward of $+1$ if it scores a goal within 20 s, else it receives a reward of 0. The average reward of these ten runs is $y^i$. Naturally, for each configuration of player and ball locations, there are many valid passing locations; hence, there are many training examples for a single configuration. Here, a valid location is one that is at most 20 m away from the initial ball position and is within the field bounds.

Furthermore, the data was augmented in the following manner:

1. The input into the network is organized in a canonical representation. Specifically, we sort players based on the $x$ coordinates from the left to right of the field.
2. We also pre-process the data to ensure symmetry, which augments our data. Along the $y$ axis, we ensure that inputs into the neural network are such that the $y$ coordinate of the ball is positive by flipping all the $y$ coordinates of the input if the $y$ coordinate of the ball is negative. This allows us to reduce the number of possible data examples by half, which allows us to converge faster.

**Training.** Given that a large network can overfit and be computationally expensive, the best size neural network was based on two factors - its potential to overfit and its compliance with the 20 ms cycle time constraint. Table 1 shows the various fully connected network capacities tested along with their computational cost related metrics.

**Table 1.** The average range of time taken, max time taken, and max packets missed during a *single* forward pass for different networks. Time units are in milliseconds. Bold indicates selected network.

|   | Neurons per layer | Avg. range of time cost | Max time cost | Max missing packets |
|---|---|---|---|---|
| 1 | 128 128 64 32 1 | 0.015–0.04 | 0.095 | 0 |
| 2 | 256 128 64 32 1 | 0.03–0.06 | 0.134 | 0 |
| 3 | **128 128 64 32 16 1** | **0.017–0.05** | **0.102** | **0** |
| 4 | 512 256 128 64 32 1 | ~0.15 | ~0.2 | 5 |

Ultimately, we employed network 3 (in bold) for RoboCup 2018, since its large size would enhance the network's ability to represent complicated functions as well as not cause any agent to miss packets.

Below are the training specifics for network 3:

- Training was offline with the data collected by the method described earlier.
- Data set size: ~4600 states. Nearly ~772000 training examples after augmentation. Network was explicitly trained to handle indirect kicks.
- Training/Test split: 90% and 10%.
- Update Algorithm: Backpropagation.
- Loss Function: Mean Squared Error of the predicted values and true values for a given kick location.
- Optimizer: Adam Optimizer [14].
- Epochs: 10000.
- Architecture: 5 hidden layers with $128, 128, 64, 32, 16, 1$ neurons respectively.
- Activation function: Leaky ReLU.
- Weight initialization: Xavier.
- Learning rate: 0.00001.
- Regularization parameter: 0.00025.
- Mini-batch gradient descent: 64 batch size.
- Deep Learning Framework: Tensorflow.

Once the network is trained, it performs online evaluation of potential passing locations, and an agent kicks to the location with the highest value.

# 4    Main Competition Results and Analysis

In winning the 2018 RoboCup competition UT Austin Villa finished with a perfect record of 23 wins and no losses.[1] During the competition the team scored 143 goals while conceding none. Despite finishing with a perfect record, the relatively few number of games played at the competition, coupled with the complex and stochastic environment of the RoboCup 3D simulator, make it difficult to determine UT Austin Villa being better than other teams by a statistically significant margin. At the end of the competition, however, all teams were required to release their binaries used during the competition. Results of UT Austin Villa playing 1000 games against each of the other six teams' released binaries from the competition are shown in Table 2.

UT Austin Villa finished with at least an average goal difference greater than 2.6 goals against every opponent. UT Austin Villa's strong defense and use of marking [10] limited opponent scoring opportunities, and half the opponents were unable to score any goals against UT Austin Villa. The only team to score more than 100 goals during the 1000 games played against UT Austin Villa was FCPortugal with 499, and of those 452 (over 90%) were scored from a kickoff set

---

[1] Full tournament results can be found at http://www.cs.utexas.edu/~AustinVilla/?p=competitions/RoboCup18#3D.

**Table 2.** UT Austin Villa's released binary's performance when playing 1000 games against the released binaries of all other teams at RoboCup 2018. This includes place (the rank a team achieved at the 2018 competition), average goal difference (values in parentheses are the standard error), win-loss-tie record, and goals for/against.

| Opponent | Place | Avg. Goal Diff. | Record (W-L-T) | Goals (F/A) |
|----------|-------|-----------------|----------------|-------------|
| magmaOffenburg | 2 | 2.648 (0.047) | 939-4-57 | 2708/60 |
| FCPortugal | 3 | 4.572 (0.055) | 997-0-3 | 5071/499 |
| BahiaRT | 4 | 6.734 (0.057) | 1000-0-0 | 6735/1 |
| KgpKubs | 5 | 6.586 (0.052) | 1000-0-0 | 6586/0 |
| Miracle3D | 6 | 5.878 (0.048) | 1000-0-0 | 5878/0 |
| ITAndroids | 7 | 9.104 (0.058) | 1000-0-0 | 9104/0 |

play the FCPortugal team developed that allowed for an almost immediate and unblockable shot on goal. Additionally, UT Austin Villa won all but 60 games that ended in ties, and 4 games that ended in losses, out of the 6000 that were played in Table 2 with a win percentage greater than 93% against all teams. These results show that UT Austin Villa winning the 2018 competition was far from a chance occurrence. The following subsection analyzes the contribution of the new variable distance fast walk kicks and deep learning passing strategy components (described in Sect. 3) to the team's dominant performance.

## 4.1   Analysis of Components

To analyze the contribution of new components for 2018—variable distance fast walk kicks and a deep learning passing strategy (Sect. 3)—to the UT Austin Villa team's performance, we played 1000 games between a version of the 2018 UT Austin Villa team with each of these components turned off—and no other changes—against each of the RoboCup 2018 teams' released binaries. Results comparing the performance of the UT Austin Villa team with and without using these components are shown in Table 3.

Results are mixed in terms of improved performance against the other teams' released binaries when using variable distance walk kicks and our deep learning passing strategy. Both new components help against the top three teams (UTAustinVilla, magmaOffenburg, and FCPortugal), however, which is good as improved performance is more important against better teams. It might be the case that a larger set of passing location options coupled with a better decision on where to pass the ball is beneficial against more skilled teams, while against less skilled teams the best strategy is just to kick the ball as far as possible down the field and then run after it.

**Table 3.** Different versions of the UTAustinVilla team when playing 1000 games against the released binaries of all teams at RoboCup 2018. Values shown are average goal difference with values in parentheses being the difference in performance from the team's released binary.

| Opponent | Released Binary | No Var. Dist. Walk Kicks | No Deep Learn Pass Str. |
|---|---|---|---|
| UTAustinVilla | 0[a] | −0.073 (−0.073) | −0.114 (−0.114) |
| magmaOffenburg | 2.648 | 2.525 (−0.123) | 2.441 (−0.207) |
| FCPortugal | 4.572 | 4.478 (−0.094) | 4.458 (−0.114) |
| Miracle3D | 5.878 | 6.139 (+0.261) | 6.133 (+0.255) |
| KgpKubs | 6.586 | 6.371 (−0.215) | 6.746 (+0.160) |
| BahiaRT | 6.734 | 6.828 (+0.094) | 6.655 (−0.079) |
| ITAndroids | 9.104 | 8.982 (−0.122) | 9.113 (+0.009) |

[a] Games were not played, but assumed to be an average goal difference of 0 in expectation with self play.

## 4.2 Additional Tournament Competition Analysis

To further analyze the tournament competition, Table 4 shows the average goal difference for each team at RoboCup 2018 when playing 1000 games against all other teams at RoboCup 2018.

**Table 4.** Average goal difference for each team at RoboCup 2018 (rows) when playing 1000 games against the released binaries of all other teams at RoboCup 2018 (columns). Teams are ordered from most to least dominant in terms of winning (positive goal difference) and losing (negative goal difference).

| | UTA | mag | FCP | Bah | Kgp | Mir | ITA |
|---|---|---|---|---|---|---|---|
| UTAustinVilla | — | 2.648 | 4.572 | 6.734 | 6.586 | 5.878 | 9.104 |
| magmaOffenburg | −2.648 | — | 0.376 | 2.710 | 2.567 | 4.853 | 4.171 |
| FCPortugal | −4.572 | −0.376 | — | 1.804 | 2.298 | 4.598 | 2.826 |
| BahiaRT | −6.734 | −2.710 | −1.804 | — | 0.581 | 1.761 | 1.266 |
| KgpKubs | −6.586 | −2.576 | −2.298 | −0.581 | — | 0.527 | 0.207 |
| Miracle3D | −5.878 | −4.853 | −4.598 | −1.761 | −0.527 | — | 0.022 |
| ITAndroids | −9.104 | −4.171 | −2.286 | −1.266 | −0.207 | −0.022 | — |

It is interesting to note that the ordering of teams in terms of winning (positive goal difference) and losing (negative goal difference) is strictly dominant—every opponent that a team wins against also loses to every opponent that defeats that same team. Relative goal difference does not have this same property, however, as a team that does better against one opponent relative to another team does not always do better against a second opponent relative to that same team. UT Austin Villa is dominant in terms of relative goal difference, however, as UT Austin Villa has a higher goal difference against each opponent than all other teams against the same opponent.

**Table 5.** Overall ranking and points totals for each team participating in the RoboCup 2018 3D Simulation League technical challenge as well as ranks and points awarded for each of the individual league challenges that make up the technical challenge.

| Team | Overall | | Free | | Goalie | |
|------|---------|--------|------|--------|--------|--------|
| | Rank | Points | Rank | Points | Rank | Points |
| magmaOffenburg | 1 | 42 | 1 | 25 | 3–5 | 17[a] |
| FCPortugal | 2 | 32 | 2 | 15 | 3–5 | 17[a] |
| **UTAustinVilla** | **3** | **30** | **3** | **5** | **1** | **25** |
| KgpKubs | 4 | 21 | — | — | 2 | 21 |
| BahiaRT | 5 | 17 | — | — | 3–5 | 17[a] |
| ITAndroids | 6 | 5 | — | — | 6 | 5 |

[a] Results released from the competition awarded tied teams the points total for the highest rank of the range they finished within. As determining points totals for tied teams was not explicitly specified in the rules, we contend the proper award is instead the average points total across the range of tied for places as is the case for the Standard Platform League technical challenge rules (https://spl.robocup.org/wp-content/uploads/downloads/Challenges2013.pdf) from which the 3D Simulation League scoring system was derived. Teams receive 13 points using the average points total for the range of positions they are tied for, with resulting overall scores being magmaOffenburg 38, FCPortugal 28, and BahiaRT 13.

## 5    Technical Challenges

During the competition there was an overall technical challenge consisting of two different league challenges: free and goalie challenge. For each league challenge a team participated in points were awarded toward the overall technical challenge based on the following equation:

$$\texttt{points}(rank) = 25 - 20 * (rank - 1)/(numberOfParticipants - 1)$$

Table 5 shows the ranking and cumulative team point totals for the technical challenge as well as for each individual league challenge. UT Austin Villa won the goalie challenge and finished third in the free challenge resulting in a third place finish in the overall technical challenge. The following subsections detail UT Austin Villa's participation in each league challenge.

### 5.1    Free Challenge

During the free challenge, teams give a five minute presentation on a research topic related to their team. Each team in the league then ranks the presentations with the best receiving a score of 1 votes, second best a score of 2, etc. Additionally several respected research members of the RoboCup community outside the league rank the presentations, with their scores being counted double. The winner of the free challenge is the team that receives the lowest score. Table 6 shows the results of the free challenge in which UT Austin Villa was awarded third place.

**Table 6.** Results of the free challenge.

| Team | Votes |
|------|-------|
| magmaOffenburg | 14 |
| FCPortugal | 16 |
| **UTAustinVilla** | **18** |

UT Austin Villa's free challenge submission[2] presented the team's use of deep learning to develop a passing strategy discussed in Sect. 3.2. The magmaOffenburg team talked about learning model-free behaviors [15], and the FCPortugal team presented a hybrid ZMP-CPG based walk engine for biped robots [16].

## 5.2  Goalie Challenge

A goalie challenge[3] was held where a goalie faces 12 shots from random starting positions on the field, and then is given a score for the percentage of shots the goalie is able to stop. Starting positions of shots range in one meter increments from 3 to 15 m in the forward direction from the goal, and in one meter increments from 0 to 9 m toward each side of the goal. Target locations for shots are either the center or toward either side of the goal. There are two different shot speeds: slow and fast, and an initial Z velocity as an integer from 0–5 meters per second is added to a shot to determine its height. Given the different shot starting positions, target locations, and velocities, there are a total of 8892 possible shots. Some of the possible shots go over the goal and miss, however, and so for the competition only the shots that will score on an empty goal (8316 possible different shots) are used. At the beginning of the challenge a random seed is selected to determine which 12 shots will be used during the challenge. If after the conclusion of the challenge more than one team has the same score, those teams face a second set of different shots to serve as a tie breaker.

---

[2] Free challenge entry description available at http://www.cs.utexas.edu/~AustinVilla/sim/3dsimulation/AustinVilla3DSimulationFiles/2018/files/UTAustinVillaFreeChallenge2018.pdf.

[3] Framework for running the goalie challenge at https://github.com/magmaOffenburg/magmaChallenge.

The UT Austin Villa team's goalie positions itself to block shots and has three separate goalie diving behaviors for if the ball is kicked straight at, a little to the side, and further to the side of the goalie as described in [7]. Figure 2 shows screenshots of these dives. The diving behaviors consist of a series of fixed poses parameterized by different joint angles. Prior to this year's competition the team's diving behaviors were only hand-designed and hand-tuned. Once on-site at the competition the team decided to optimize these goalie dives for the goalie challenge. Using a training task consisting of a subset of 360 shots chosen to be well distributed across the set of all possible challenge shots, 84 joint angle parameters for the goalie dives were optimized across 200 generations of the CMA-ES [13] algorithm with a population size of 150. After learning, the new goalie dives were able to stop 46.6% of all 8000+ possible shots as compared to being able to stop only 36.4% of shots before learning. These new goalie dives were also added to and used by the goalie during the final rounds of the main RoboCup competition.

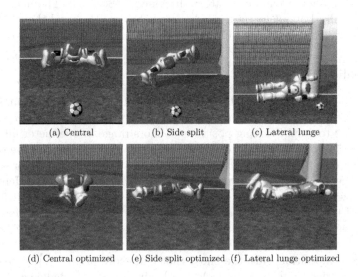

   (a) Central      (b) Side split      (c) Lateral lunge

(d) Central optimized   (e) Side split optimized  (f) Lateral lunge optimized

**Fig. 2.** Screenshots of the original hand-tuned (a–c) and optimized (d–f) goalie diving behaviors.

Results of the goalie challenge are shown in Table 7. UT Austin Villa won the challenge by saving 50% of the shots the goalie faced which is twice as many as any of the other teams competing in the challenge.

**Table 7.** Scores for each of the teams competing in the goalie challenge.

| Team | Score | Score Tie Breaker |
|------|-------|-------------------|
| **UTAustinVilla** | **0.50** | — |
| KgpKubs | 0.25 | 0.08 |
| BahiaRT | 0.25 | 0.00 |
| FCPortugal | 0.25 | 0.00 |
| magmaOffenburg | 0.25 | 0.00 |
| ITAndroids | 0.08 | — |

# 6  Conclusion

UT Austin Villa won the 2018 RoboCup 3D Simulation League main competition as well as the goalie challenge.[4] Data taken using released binaries from the competition show that UT Austin Villa winning the competition was statistically significant. The 2018 UT Austin Villa team also improved from 2017 as it was able to beat the team's 2017 champion binary by an average of 0.171 ($\pm$ 0.042) goals across 1000 games.

In an effort to both make it easier for new teams to join the RoboCup 3D Simulation League, and also provide a resource that can be beneficial to existing teams, the UT Austin Villa team has released their base code [17].[5] This code release provides a fully functioning agent and good starting point for new teams to the RoboCup 3D Simulation League (it was used by two other teams at the 2018 competition: KgpKubs and Miracle3D). Additionally the code release offers a foundational platform for conducting research in multiple areas including robotics, multiagent systems, and machine learning.

**Acknowledgments.** This work has taken place in the Learning Agents Research Group (LARG) at UT Austin. LARG research is supported in part by NSF (IIS-1637736, IIS-1651089, IIS-1724157), ONR (N00014-18-2243), FLI (RFP2-000), DARPA, Intel, Raytheon, and Lockheed Martin. Peter Stone serves on the Board of Directors of Cogitai, Inc. The terms of this arrangement have been reviewed and approved by the University of Texas at Austin in accordance with its policy on objectivity in research.

---

[4] More information about the UT Austin Villa team, as well as video from the competition, can be found at the team's website: http://www.cs.utexas.edu/~AustinVilla/sim/3dsimulation/#2018.

[5] Code release at https://github.com/LARG/utaustinvilla3d.

# References

1. MacAlpine, P., et al.: UT Austin Villa 2011: a champion agent in the RoboCup 3D soccer simulation competition. In: Proceedings of the 11th International Conference on Autonomous Agents and Multiagent Systems (AAMAS 2012) (2012)
2. MacAlpine, P., Collins, N., Lopez-Mobilia, A., Stone, P.: UT Austin Villa: RoboCup 2012 3D simulation league champion. In: Chen, X., Stone, P., Sucar, L.E., van der Zant, T. (eds.) RoboCup 2012. LNCS (LNAI), vol. 7500, pp. 77–88. Springer, Heidelberg (2013). https://doi.org/10.1007/978-3-642-39250-4_8
3. MacAlpine, P., Depinet, M., Liang, J., Stone, P.: UT Austin Villa: RoboCup 2014 3D simulation league competition and technical challenge champions. In: Bianchi, R.A.C., Akin, H.L., Ramamoorthy, S., Sugiura, K. (eds.) RoboCup 2014. LNCS (LNAI), vol. 8992, pp. 33–46. Springer, Cham (2015). https://doi.org/10.1007/978-3-319-18615-3_3
4. MacAlpine, P., Hanna, J., Liang, J., Stone, P.: UT Austin Villa: RoboCup 2015 3D simulation league competition and technical challenges champions. In: Almeida, L., Ji, J., Steinbauer, G., Luke, S. (eds.) RoboCup 2015. LNCS (LNAI), vol. 9513, pp. 118–131. Springer, Cham (2015). https://doi.org/10.1007/978-3-319-29339-4_10
5. MacAlpine, P., Stone, P.: UT Austin Villa: RoboCup 2016 3D simulation league competition and technical challenges champions. In: Behnke, S., Sheh, R., Sariel, S., Lee, D.D. (eds.) RoboCup 2016. LNCS (LNAI), vol. 9776, pp. 515–528. Springer, Cham (2017). https://doi.org/10.1007/978-3-319-68792-6_43
6. MacAlpine, P., Stone, P.: UT Austin Villa: RoboCup 2017 3D simulation league competition and technical challenges champions. In: Akiyama, H., Obst, O., Sammut, C., Tonidandel, F. (eds.) RoboCup 2017. LNCS (LNAI), vol. 11175, pp. 473–485. Springer, Cham (2018). https://doi.org/10.1007/978-3-030-00308-1_39
7. MacAlpine, P., et al.: UT Austin Villa 2011 3D simulation team report. Technical report AI11-10, The University of Texas at Austin, Department of Computer Science, AI Laboratory (2011)
8. Xu, Y., Vatankhah, H.: SimSpark: an open source robot simulator developed by the RoboCup community. In: Behnke, S., Veloso, M., Visser, A., Xiong, R. (eds.) RoboCup 2013. LNCS (LNAI), vol. 8371, pp. 632–639. Springer, Heidelberg (2014). https://doi.org/10.1007/978-3-662-44468-9_59
9. MacAlpine, P., Price, E., Stone, P.: SCRAM: scalable collision-avoiding role assignment with minimal-makespan for formational positioning. In: Proceedings of the Twenty-Ninth AAAI Conference on Artificial Intelligence (AAAI 2015) (2015)
10. MacAlpine, P., Stone, P.: Prioritized role assignment for marking. In: Behnke, S., Sheh, R., Sariel, S., Lee, D.D. (eds.) RoboCup 2016. LNCS (LNAI), vol. 9776, pp. 306–318. Springer, Cham (2017). https://doi.org/10.1007/978-3-319-68792-6_25
11. MacAlpine, P., Stone, P.: Overlapping layered learning. Artif. Intell. **254**, 21–43 (2018)
12. Abdolmaleki, A., Simões, D., Lau, N., Reis, L.P., Neumann, G.: Learning a humanoid kick with controlled distance. In: Behnke, S., Sheh, R., Sariel, S., Lee, D.D. (eds.) RoboCup 2016. LNCS (LNAI), vol. 9776, pp. 45–57. Springer, Cham (2017). https://doi.org/10.1007/978-3-319-68792-6_4
13. Hansen, N.: The CMA evolution strategy: a tutorial (2009). http://www.lri.fr/~hansen/cmatutorial.pdf
14. Kingma, D.P., Ba, J.: Adam: a method for stochastic optimization. CoRR abs/1412.6980 (2014)

15. Baur, M., et al.: The magmaOffenburg 2018 RoboCup 3D simulation team. In: RoboCup 2018 Symposium and Competitions: Team Description Papers (2018)
16. Kasaei, S.M., Simões, D., Lau, N., Pereira, A.: A hybrid ZMP-CPG based walk engine for biped robots. In: Ollero, A., Sanfeliu, A., Montano, L., Lau, N., Cardeira, C. (eds.) ROBOT 2017. AISC, vol. 694, pp. 743–755. Springer, Cham (2018). https://doi.org/10.1007/978-3-319-70836-2_61
17. MacAlpine, P., Stone, P.: UT Austin Villa RoboCup 3D simulation base code release. In: Behnke, S., Sheh, R., Sariel, S., Lee, D.D. (eds.) RoboCup 2016. LNCS (LNAI), vol. 9776, pp. 135–143. Springer, Cham (2017). https://doi.org/10.1007/978-3-319-68792-6_11

# Integrating the Latest Artificial Intelligence Algorithms into the RoboCup Rescue Simulation Framework

Arnoud Visser[1]($\boxtimes$)(iD), Luis G. Nardin[2](iD), and Sebastian Castro[3](iD)

[1] Universiteit van Amsterdam, Amsterdam, The Netherlands
A.Visser@uva.nl
[2] Brandenburg University of Technology, Cottbus, Germany
nardin@b-tu.de
[3] MathWorks, Natick, MA, USA
Sebastian.Castro@mathworks.com

**Abstract.** The challenge of the Rescue Simulation League is for a team of robots or agents to learn an optimal response to mitigate the effects of natural disasters. To operate optimally, several problems have to be jointly solved like task allocation, path planning, and coalition formation. Solve these difficult problems can be quite overwhelming for newcomer teams. We created a tutorial that demonstrates how these problems can be tackled using artificial intelligence and machine learning algorithms available in the MATLAB® and the Statistics and Machine Learning Toolbox™. Here we show (1) how to analyze and model disaster scenario data for developing rescue decision-making algorithms, and (2) how to incorporate state-of-the-art machine learning algorithms into Rescue Agent Simulation competition code using the MATLAB® Engine API for Java.

**Keywords:** Machine learning · MATLAB® · Rescue Agent Simulation

## 1 Introduction

Urban Search and Rescue (USAR) scenarios offer a great potential to inspire and drive research in multi-agent and multi-robot systems. Since the circumstances during real USAR missions are extraordinarily challenging [8], benchmarks based on them, such as the RoboCup Rescue competitions, are ideal for assessing the capabilities of these systems. Thus, one goal of the RoboCup Rescue competitions is to compare the performance of algorithms that coordinate and control teams of either robots or agents performing disaster mitigation tasks.

In particular, the Rescue Agent Simulation competition aims to simulate large scale natural disasters, such as earthquakes, enabling the exploration of new forms of autonomous coordination of heterogeneous rescue teams under adverse conditions. This competition was first demonstrated in the RoboCup

© Springer Nature Switzerland AG 2019
D. Holz et al. (Eds.): RoboCup 2018, LNAI 11374, pp. 476–487, 2019.
https://doi.org/10.1007/978-3-030-27544-0_39

**Fig. 1.** View of disaster scenario in the Kobe map after an earthquake.

2000 [12] and officially launched in the RoboCup 2001. Participating teams have their background mainly from artificial intelligence and robotics.

The competition is based on a simulation platform and a set of complex scenarios representing the conditions of cities after an earthquake (see Fig. 1). In each scenario, fire brigade, police force and ambulance team agents extinguish fires, unblock roads, and rescue civilians trapped inside collapsed buildings, respectively. The final score in the scenario is calculated based on the number of rescued civilians and the number of remaining buildings taking into account the damage caused by the fire. Scenarios typically contain up to 5000 buildings and up to 1000 civilians, as well as agent teams of fire brigades, police forces and ambulance teams composed of up to 50 agents each.

The complexity of these scenarios imposes several challenges to the development of different aspects of multi-agent systems like task allocation with uncertainty, coalition formation, cooperation, distributed control, and communication [1]. Artificial intelligence (AI), in particular machine learning (ML) algorithms are very well suited to cope with some of these challenges. For instance, fire brigades and ambulance teams can optimize their task allocation decisions by estimating, respectively, the danger of fire ignition in different buildings (discrete state—classification) and the chance of rescuing trapped civilians alive (continues state—regression).

The implementation of state-of-the-art AI and ML algorithms, their training, and their integration into the Rescue Agent Simulation competition code can be quite overwhelming for newcomer teams. Hence we propose that competition teams take advantage of existing and well-established AI and ML tools to develop their competition code. Here, we demonstrate[1]

1. how to use MATLAB® and add-on packages, such as the Statistics and Machine Learning Toolbox™, to analyze and model disas-

---

[1] All data as well as Java and MATLAB® code used to generate the results presented in this work are available at https://github.com/IntelligentRoboticsLab/Joint-Rescue-Forces repository.

ter scenario data using both interactive design tools (GUIs) and programming code. The analysis and modeling provide support to the development of more elaborate data-driven rescue decision-making algorithms (see Sect. 2).
2. how state-of-the-art ML algorithms can be directly incorporated into the Agent Development Framework (ADF) [13] using the MATLAB® Engine API for Java (see Sect. 3).

## 2   Interactive Approach

MATLAB® and the Statistics and Machine Learning Toolbox™ can be used in an interactive mode to analyze disaster scenario data and create models that agents can use to base their decisions during the unfolding of these disaster scenarios.

### 2.1   Unsupervised Methods

Unsupervised machine learning methods can be used to analyze and model disaster scenario data. In the Rescue Agent Simulation competition, clustering algorithms are interesting for agents to partition maps into sectors and evenly distribute the search and rescue workload among them [9,10]. MATLAB® implements several clustering algorithms, such as k-means [6], k-medoids [4], hierarchical clustering [5], Gaussian mixture models [7], and hidden Markov models [2].

We can, for instance, use the MATLAB® interactive mode to assess which of these clustering algorithms provides a more evenly distributed number of buildings per sector for a specific city map. This assessment first requires that all $(x, y)$ coordinates of buildings in the city map to be exported into a text file, which can be accomplished including some Java code into precompute phase of the agents code (see `AbstractSimpleAgent.java` lines 79–106). Next, these coordinates are imported into a matrix in MATLAB® using the `textscan` command and subsequently partitioned using one of the clustering algorithms available.

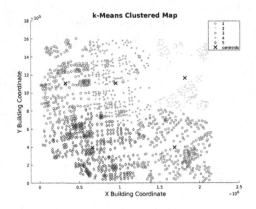

**Fig. 2.** Partitioning of the buildings in the Paris map using MATLAB® k-means clustering algorithm. (Color figure online)

Figure 2 shows the buildings from the Paris map partitioned using the k-means clustering algorithm. The different shapes and colors represent the association of each building to a specific sector. This partitioning were created with the [indices,centroids] = kmeans([x,y], 5) command, and the plot generated with the gscatter(x,y,indices) command (see importBuildingsData.m and building_cluster.m scripts).

## 2.2   Supervised Methods

Supervised machine learning methods can be used to learn associations between variables (part of a causal model of the world). Estimates of variables' value of a world model can be done with discrete states (classification) or continuous states (regression). In the Rescue Agent Simulation, competition teams can use these methods to assess their strategy and the most relevant predictors, for instance, for ambulance teams to estimate the chance that trapped civilians have to survive to a rescue operation by predicting their remaining health points (HP) at the end of a scenario simulation.

To demonstrate the use of MATLAB® to evaluate the strategy of a simple agent team, we collected several metrics from multiple runs in multiple scenarios of this agent team and assessed them using available classification and regression supervised learning algorithms in MATLAB®. The metrics colleted were (see matlab.generator.simple.agent.ambulance.SimpleAmbulanceTeam.java lines 389–420): start and end time of the rescue operation (sTime and eTime), initial and final Euclidean distance to the nearest refuge (sDist and eDist), initial and final HP (sHP and eHP), initial and final damage level (sDamage and eDamage), and initial buriedness (sBuriedness).

In Statistics and Machine Learning Toolbox™, data can be preprocessed with dimensionality reduction methods like principal component analysis and singular value decomposition followed by linear or non-linear regression methods. The results can be visualized with ensembles like random forests, boosted and bagged regression trees. To learn those ensembles several optimization algorithms like AdaBoost and TotalBoost are available. We evaluated the accuracy of different combinations of predictor metrics and concluded that only the metrics with values of the beginning of the rescue operation were relevant to the prediction accuracy (i.e., sTime, sDist, sHP, and sDamage).

To use classification, we discretized the eHP according to the ranges: 0 Dead, 1–3000 Critical, 3001–7000 Injured, and 7001–10000 Stable. Then we trained different classification algorithms in MATLAB® using this data and the most accurate classification was obtained using the Weighted K-nearest neighbors (KNN).

Figure 3 shows the Weighted KNN classification used to predict if a civilian would be dead, in a critical state, injured or in a stable state at the end of a scenario simulation. This classification predicts correctly 78.9% of the civilians' state. Notice, however, that most of the wrong detections (i.e., sum of the numbers in the red cells) are above the diagonal green cells in the right panel of Fig. 3 meaning that this trained classifier predicts a civilian in a less severe state than

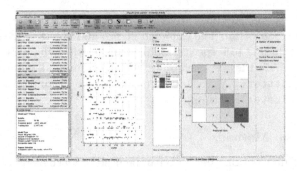

**Fig. 3.** Classification Learner MATLAB® app showing predictions of the injury class of the civilians at the end of the scenario using Weighted K-Nearest Neighbors. **Left panel** shows different assessed classifying algorithms and their respective accuracy. **Middle panel** shows a scatter plot showing the relationship between the initial distance to refuge (sDist) and the time the rescue initiated (sTime) with the model predictions and their correctness. **Right panel** shows the number of predicted versus true (or correct) classification of rescue civilians. The diagonal (green) shows the number of correct classifications, while all other cells represent the number of misclassifications, how they were classified versus the correct classification. (Color figure online)

the civilian really will be. For instance, there are 9 cases in which the civilian will die and the classifier predicted it as injured.

We applied regression methods to the same data without discretazing the eHP and trained different regression algorithms in MATLAB®. Figure 4 shows an ensemble fit into a bagged tree model with the estimate of the remaining health points (HP) at the end of the simulation scenario with a root mean square error (RMSE) between the predicted and true HP values equals 1167.5 (and normalized RMSE equals 0.1228).

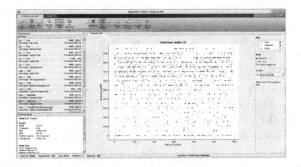

**Fig. 4.** Regression Learner MATLAB® app showing predictions of the chance to survive (remaining HP) of trapped civilians. **Left panel** shows different assessed regression algorithms and their respective root mean square error. **Right panel** shows the prediction versus true HP value of the trapped civilians at the end of a simulation.

## 2.3   Path Planning

If an agent wants to move to a specific location to perform a task, a path plan to that location has to be defined. Two possible approaches to tackle this problem are (1) to use path planning algorithms from the MATLAB® graph and network algorithms[2] or (2) to use graph-routines from Peter Corke's Robotics Toolbox [3].

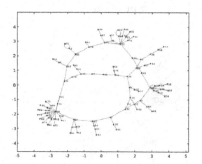 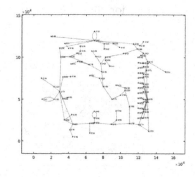

**Fig. 5.** The small Test map of the RoboCup Rescue Agent Simulation competition in MATLAB® as topological (left) and metrical graph (right).

First, however, all the roads of a city map need to be converted to a graph in MATLAB® format. The nodes of the graph are identified by the roads ID and they also store the actual $(x, y)$ location of the road to facilitate the visualization of the results (see Fig. 5). The Java code to generate such a MATLAB® graph is called during the precompute phase of the Rescue Agent Simulation simulation, and its pseudo-code is:

```
For (Entity next: this.worldInfo.getEntities() ) {
    loc = this.worldInfo.getLocation(next.getID());
    matlab.eval("G=addnode(G,table(next.getID(),loc.first(),loc.second());");
}
For (Entity next: this.worldInfo.getEntities() )
    Collection areaNeighbours = next.getNeighbours();

    for(entityID neighbour : areaNeigbours) {
        matlab.eval("G=addedge(G,find(next.getID()),find(neighbour.getID());");
    }
}
matlab.eval("save('graph.mat',G);");
```

Once created, the graph in MATLAB® can be queried, for instance to get the shortest path between two nodes. This can be done by calling a MATLAB® script which contains the function short_path = getPath(from,targets), that loads the graph G, calls the MATLAB® method [TR,D]=shortestpathtree and sorts the resulting paths TR based on the distance D. It is possible to specify in MATLAB® the algorithm to use (Breadth-first or Dijkstra). It is also possible to use A*, which is available in Peter Corke's robotics toolbox [3]. The MATLAB®

---

[2] https://www.mathworks.com/help/matlab/graph-and-network-algorithms.html.

code of this algorithm is open source and well documented making it possible to modify the A* algorithm to Dijkstra's algorithm (by removing the heuristics) or breadth-first (by not sorting the frontier on distance so far). The only thing needed is a script to translate from MATLAB® native **graph**-format to Peter Corke's **Pgraph**-format. For smaller competition maps like Kobe this can be done in 13 s (measurement with a computer with a Intel Core i7-8550U processor), for larger maps like Paris 22 s are needed for this conversion (see Fig. 6). Both are fast enough for the precompute phase of the competition.

**Fig. 6.** Maps of Kobe (left) and Paris (right) in Peter Corke's **Pgraph**-format.

An advantage of this approach compared to the path-planning methods typically applied by the Rescue Agent Simulation competition teams is that each agent can load this *a priori* map and modify the edges based on the blockades observed and/or communicated. This information can even be updated when police force agents clear part of the road.

### 2.4   ROS Interface

A challenge in the Virtual Robot competition is that whenever an agent reaches a building, it has to enter that building [11]. The MATLAB® Robotics System Toolbox allows to directly control robots and realistic simulation via the Robotics Operating System (ROS) interface, as demonstrated in the Future of RoboCup Rescue workshop [14] and the RoboCup@Home Education workshop[3].

Another challenge in this competition is the detection of buried victims from camera images. In the same workshops, victims detection has been demonstrated using the MATLAB® deep learning capabilities, a combination of the Neural Network Toolbox, Parallel Computing Toolbox, GPU Coder, and Computer Vision System Toolbox. Notice that these toolboxes run models deployed to GPU faster than TensorFlow or Caffe, which is a highly desirable for robotic applications[4].

---

[3] http://www.robocupathomeedu.org/learn.

[4] https://blogs.mathworks.com/deep-learning/2017/10/06/deep-learning-with-matlab-r2017b/.

# 3 ADF Integration

In addition to using the MATLAB® models and algorithms in interactive mode, they can also be integrated into the Agent Development Framework (ADF) [13] to run during the simulation execution. ADF is the mandatory agent architecture for all competition teams participating in the Rescue Agent Simulation competition. This agent architecture is composed of several, highly specialized modules responsible for different data processing and decision-making tasks, such as clustering, path planning and task allocation.

The integration of MATLAB® models into the ADF is based on the MATLAB® Engine API for Java®[5], which enables Java programs via `MatlabEngine` class to interact with MATLAB® synchronously (`startMatlab` method) or asynchronously (`startMatlabAsync` method). In addition to start MATLAB®, there is also a possibility to connect synchronously (`connectMatlab` method) or asynchronously (`connectMatlabAsync` method) to an existing shared instance. To share a MATLAB® instance, enter the command `matlab.engine.shareEngine` in the MATLAB® command window. Once connected, it is possible to evaluate a MATLAB® function with arguments (`feval` and `fevalAsync` functions) or evaluate a MATLAB® expression as a string (`eval` and `evalAsync` functions). Additionally, it is possible to interact with the MATLAB® workspace by getting (`getVariable` and `getVariableAsync` functions) or setting (`setVariable` and `setVariableAsync` functions) variables. Once finished the interaction, disconnect from the current session using `disconnect`, `quit`, or `close` functions.

In Sect. 3.1 we show how to integrate the k-means clustering into rescue agents, and in Sect. 3.2 how ambulance team agents can use a trained classifier to decide which trapped civilian has a better chance of surviving a rescue operation.

## 3.1 Clustering Integration

Currently, competition teams need to implement their own version of standard artificial intelligence algorithms from scratch to solve common tasks, such as k-means clustering. However, MATLAB® provides more diverse and robust implementations of these standard algorithms that teams may benefit of to prioritize the development of high-level strategies.

Although diverse and robust, the time constraint imposed on rescue agents demands a more elaborate assessment of the efficiency of the MATLAB® algorithms integrated to the ADF. Here, we have assessed the performance of the k-means clustering algorithm implemented in the Sample ADF using pure Java and in MATLAB® measured in a computer with Intel Core i7 6700HQ 2.6 GHz (8 cores) processor and 16 GB RAM using Arch Linux, Oracle Java JDK 8 and MATLAB® R2017b.

Figure 7 shows the result of this assessment in which the MATLAB® k-means clustering algorithm executes in less time than the Sample ADF Java

---

[5] https://www.mathworks.com/help/matlab/matlab-engine-api-for-java.html.

implementation for all 83 agents. There was significant difference on the execution average time for the MATLAB® (6,095.87 ± 1,178.51 ms) and the Java (8,783.36 ± 1,188.22 ms) implementations; t(164) = 14.63, p < 0.05. Hence, we can conclude that using MATLAB® k-means clustering reduces the effort and maintenance, and increases the performance of the agent teams.

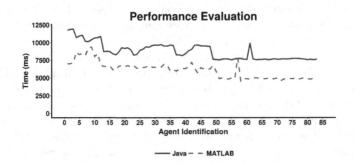

**Fig. 7.** Performance of the k-means implementation in Java and in MATLAB® performed in sequence by 83 agents during the initialization stage of the execution phase of the scenario simulation for the Kobe map.

The k-means clustering can be integrated into the ADF and executed in the precompute phase or execution phase of the scenario simulation. Here, we show how to integrate the k-means clustering algorithm in the agents' initialization stage of the execution phase. The Java code for such integration is

```
// Prepare data for Matlab k−means clustering
double [][] mlInput = new double[this.entities.size()][2];
for ( StandardEntity entity : this.entities ) {
    Pair<Integer, Integer> location = this.worldInfo.getLocation(entity);
    mlInput[i][0] = location.first();
    mlInput[i][1] = location.second();
    i++;
}

// Run k−means clustering
Object[] mlOutput = ml.feval( 2, "kmeans", (Object) mlInput,
                              this.clusterSize,
                              DISTANCE, this.distanceMetric,
                              MAX_ITER, this.maxIter );
double[] mlIndex = (double[]) mlOutput[0];
double[][] mlCenter = (double[][]) mlOutput[1];
```

This code connects the agents to MATLAB® and prepares entities data for clustering (i.e., the x and y entity location). In the initialization, agents are executed in sequence avoiding concurrent MATLAB® connections. Next, the MATLAB® function kmeans is evaluated using the feval method with several parameters: the dimension of the k-means output (set to 2), the number of clusters (set to 10), the distance metric (set to citiyblock), and the maximum number of interaction (set to 100). Once executed, the feval method returns an object array with the indices in the position 0 and the centers in the position 1 that are cast to their respective data types. Finally, the engine is closed, and the indices and the centers can be used to assign agents to specific partitions of the map.

The integration of the clustering algorithm requires only a single call per agent to the MATLAB® engine as its results are stored and used in the remainder of the simulation run. Path planning algorithms, for example, are affected by changes in the environment, and would require reprocessing to account for changes. Because of this characteristic, the MATLAB® path planning algorithm would need to be called every time the agent has to calculate a path in the execution phase of the simulation run, even though the first execution can be performed during the precompute phase. Please see Sect. 2.3 to further details about the path planning.

## 3.2   Classifier Integration

Ambulance teams can also benefit of MATLAB® to optimize their rescue operations by predicting more accurately the chance of trapped civilians to survive a rescue operation. First, however, it is necessary to train a classifier with data collected from earlier runs. This training is performed using the Classification Learner MATLAB® app as described in Sect. 2.2.

We have trained a classifier using the data from rescued civilians collected from several simulation executions of the Paris map using a simple rescue team. The data collected was the time (sTime), the distance to the nearest refuge (sDist), the civilian HP (sHP) and the damage (sDamage) at the start of the rescue operation and the HP of the civilian (eHP) at the end of the rescue operation. We discretized the final HP (eHP) according to the ranges: 0 Dead, 1–3000 Critical, 3001–7000 Injured, and 7001–10000 Stable using the code

```
// TData is the training data
hp_bins = [0 1 3000 7000 10000];
bin_names = {'Dead', 'Critical', 'Injured', 'Stable'};
TData.hp_class = discretize(TData.eHP, hp_bins, 'categorical', bin_names);
```

The trained classifier model (targetSelectorModel) is exported using the Export Model - Export Compact Model feature and validated against a validation dataset with the code

```
// VData is the validation data
predictions = targetSelectorModel.predictFcn(VData);
numCorrect = nnz(predictions == VData.hp_class);
validationAccuracy = numCorrect/size(VData,1);
fprintf('Validation accuracy: %.2f%%\n', validationAccuracy * 100);
```

The training and validation steps comprise an iterative process whose cycle should be repeated until the validation accuracy is satisfactory. Then, the exported model can be saved as a file (targetSelectorModel.mat) and invoked in the function

```
function predictions = selectTargets(time, dist, hp, damage)
  persistent targetSelectorModel
  if isempty(targetSelectorModel)
    load targetSelectorModel targetSelectorModel
  end
```

```
predictors = table(time,dist,hp,damage, ...
        'VariableNames',{'sTime','sDist','sHP','sDamage'});

predictions = int32(targetSelectorModel.predictFcn(predictors));
end
```

The `predictions` function can then be called inside the `calc` method of the `HumanDetector` class for the ambulance team agents in the ADF using the code

```
// rescueTarget is an object containing victim's information
if ( MatlabEngine.findMatlab().length > 0 ) {
  MatlabEngine ml = MatlabEngine.connectMatlab();
  int sTime = rescueTarget.sTime;
  int sDist = rescueTarget.sDist;
  int sHP = rescueTarget.sHP;
  int sDamage = rescueTarget.sDamage;

  int value = ml.feval( "selectTargets", sTime, sDist, sHP, sDamage );

  ml.close();
}
```

This code executes the MATLAB® function `selectTargets` using data about a specific victim and returns a prediction about the state of the victim at the end of the rescue operation coded as 0 **Dead**, 1 **Critical**, 2 **Injured**, and 3 **Stable**. The ambulance team can then combine this prediction with several other information about other victims to determine which victim is worth rescuing first. Possible strategies to use this classification includes (1) classify all known victims, (2) discard the predicted dead, and (3)

a. select one randomly among them
b. select the closest one
c. select the closest one that is predicted **Critical**

Notice that we use `MatlabEngine.findMatlab()` and `connectMatlab()` methods instead of `MatlabEngine.startMatlab()`. This requires that a MATLAB® session is running and shared to the code to work. To share a MATLAB® session, open MATLAB®, enter the command `matlab.engine.shareEngine` in its command window, and leave it open during the execution of the simulation.

## 4   Conclusion

This paper describes the possible uses of existing artificial intelligence (AI) and machine learning (ML) tools to analyze and model disaster scenario data as well as the integration of these tools to the competition code. The examples provided tackle common challenges of the Rescue Agent Simulation competition in which AI and ML tools suit. The approach, however, is extensible to any other algorithm available in MATLAB® or any other tool that provides an interface in Java. For instance, this approach can be extended to integrate deep learning, state machines, and graph node refining algorithms, which may increase the scientific outcomes of the Rescue Simulation League as

(1) teams may focus on high-level strategies to solve rescue challenges and
(2) MATLAB® will provide a performance benchmark against which teams can show their improvements.

# References

1. Akin, H.L., Ito, N., Jacoff, A., Kleiner, A., Pellenz, J., Visser, A.: RoboCup rescue robot and simulation leagues. AI Mag. **34**(1), 78–87 (2013). https://doi.org/10.1609/aimag.v34i1.2458
2. Baum, L.E., Petrie, T.: Statistical inference for probabilistic functions of finite state Markov chains. Ann. Math. Stat. **37**(6), 1554–1563 (1966). https://doi.org/10.1214/aoms/1177699147
3. Corke, P.: Robotics, Vision and Control: Fundamental Algorithms In MATLAB® Second, Completely Revised. Springer Tracts in Advanced Robotics, vol. 118. Springer, Heidelberg (2017). https://doi.org/10.1007/978-3-319-54413-7
4. Kaufman, L., Rousseeuw, P.J.: Clustering by means of medoids. In: Dodge, Y. (ed.) Statistical Data Analysis Based on the $L_1$–Norm and Related Methods, pp. 405–416. North-Holland (1987)
5. Kaufman, L., Rousseeuw, P.J.: Divisive analysis (program DIANA). In: Finding Groups in Data, pp. 253–279. Wiley (2008). https://doi.org/10.1002/9780470316801.ch6
6. Lloyd, S.P.: Least squares quantization in PCM. IEEE Trans. Inf. Theory **28**, 129–137 (1982). https://doi.org/10.1109/TIT.1982.1056489
7. Marin, J.M., Mengersen, K., Robert, C.P.: Bayesian modelling and inference on mixtures of distributions. In: Dey, D., Rao, C. (eds.) Bayesian Thinking Modeling and Computation, Handbook of Statistics, vol. 25, pp. 459–507. Elsevier (2005). https://doi.org/10.1016/S0169-7161(05)25016-2
8. Murphy, R.R., Tadokoro, S., Kleiner, A.: Disaster robotics. In: Siciliano, B., Khatib, O. (eds.) Springer Handbook of Robotics, pp. 1577–1604. Springer, Cham (2016). https://doi.org/10.1007/978-3-319-32552-1_60
9. Parker, J., Nunes, E., Godoy, J., Gini, M.: Exploiting spatial locality and heterogeneity of agents for search and rescue teamwork. J. Field Robot. **33**(7), 877–900 (2016). https://doi.org/10.1002/rob.21601
10. dos Santos, D.S., Bazzan, A.L.: Distributed clustering for group formation and task allocation in multiagent systems: a swarm intelligence approach. Appl. Soft Comput. **12**(8), 2123–2131 (2012). https://doi.org/10.1016/j.asoc.2012.03.016
11. Sheh, R., Schwertfeger, S., Visser, A.: 16 years of robocup rescue. KI - Künstliche Intelligenz **30**(3), 267–277 (2016). https://doi.org/10.1007/s13218-016-0444-x
12. Tadokoro, S., et al.: The RoboCup-rescue project: a robotic approach to the disaster mitigation problem. In: Proceedings of the IEEE International Conference on Robotics and Automation (2000). https://doi.org/10.1109/ROBOT.2000.845369
13. Takami, S., Takayanagi, K., Jaishy, S., Ito, N., Iwata, K.: Design of agent development framework for RoboCupRescue simulation. In: Lee, R. (ed.) CSII 2017. SCI, vol. 726, pp. 185–199. Springer, Cham (2018). https://doi.org/10.1007/978-3-319-63618-4_14
14. Visser, A., Amigoni, F., Shimizu, M.: The future of robot rescue simulation workshop - an initiative to increase the number of participants in the league. University of Amsterdam, Politecnico di Milano & Chukyo University, January 2016

# A Robust and Flexible System Architecture for Facing the RoboCup Logistics League Challenge

Thomas Ulz[1], Jakob Ludwiger[2], and Gerald Steinbauer[3(✉)]

[1] Institute for Technical Informatics,
Graz University of Technology, Graz, Austria
[2] Institute for Control and Automation,
Graz University of Technology, Graz, Austria
[3] Institute for Software Technology,
Graz University of Technology, Graz, Austria
steinbauer@ist.tugraz.at

**Abstract.** In this paper we present the software architecture of the GRIPS team for addressing the challenges of the RoboCup Logistics League. The guiding principles for the development of the architecture origin in the research focus of the involved institutes on dependable intelligent systems. The architecture enables most flexible planning of the tasks as well as a most reliable execution of the generated task list.

## 1 Introduction

Due to increasing demands on flexibility in terms of product configuration as well as delivery time triggered by the trend in e-commerce (e.g. on-line configurators, on-line shopping) production needs to become more flexible as well as more digitized. This trend is well known under terms like *flexible production* or *Industry 4.0*. Usually in order to facilitate reasonable prices for products as well as to guarantee sustainable product quality and fast availability of goods production is heavily automatized. Often, this automation is not very flexible, and thus, in contradiction with the demands on flexibility in configuration (in extreme cases lot size one) and availability. Fortunately, these demands on flexibility and digitization in production require new concepts and open interesting and challenging research questions ranging from Robotics over the Internet of Things (IoT) and multi-agent systems to planning and scheduling. In order to provide an interesting and appealing show case that allows research and teaching in the area of flexible production within the RoboCup initiative [16] a competition called the RoboCup Logistics League (RCLL) was founded. It resembles the setting of a flexible production plant. The RCLL competition posts a number of challenges ranging from Robotics over IoT to Artificial Intelligence and can be used to develop and evaluate new concepts in production.

In this paper we like to introduce the system architecture of the team *Graz Intelligent Robust Production System* (GRIPS) which allowed GRIPS to win

D. Holz et al. (Eds.): RoboCup 2018, LNAI 11374, pp. 488–499, 2019.
https://doi.org/10.1007/978-3-030-27544-0_40

the international RCLL competition in 2018. The team comprises of students and researchers of 3 different institutes of the Graz University of Technology that share a common interest in safe and dependable intelligent systems [2,6,8]. The dynamic setting of the RCLL involving numerous items such as robot and production machines interacting in a real world environment is a perfect testbed for techniques to realize robust complex systems. Thus, in this paper we focus on the aspects of the developed system architecture related to robustness, reactivity, and liveness. We will describe how these properties are achieved on the different system layers ranging from an abstract planning and scheduling module over a robust executive layer to reactive behaviors.

## 2    Logistics League

The RCLL [1,10] is part of the RoboCup initiative and focuses on the stimulation of the development of approaches in Robotics and Artificial Intelligence using robotics competitions. In this league the goal is that a team of autonomous robots in cooperation with a set of production machines produces individualized products on demand. Two teams share a common factory floor of the size of $14\,\mathrm{m} \times 8\,\mathrm{m}$. Each team comprises of up to 3 autonomous robots and owns 7 machines. Machines are represented by Modular Production Systems (MPS) provided by Festo. See Fig. 1 for an example setup.

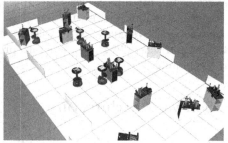

**Fig. 1.** Physical setup of the RoboCup Logistics League.

**Fig. 2.** Simulation setup of the RoboCup Logistics League.

There are different types of machines that resemble different production steps like fetching raw material, assembling parts, or delivering final products. The task of the teams is to develop methods that coordinate the robots (which are mobile) and machines (which are static) that allow producing and delivering requested goods in time. All involved entities are allowed to communicate via WiFi. Robots are cooperative in the sense that they need to interact physically with the machines, e.g. fetching raw material from a dispenser machine or provide an intermediate product to a machine that refines it. Usually teams use some coordination server that collects information from robots, machines, and a central production management system that coordinates the necessary tasks. The products are mimicked by stacks of bases, rings, and caps of different colors. The configuration of the components is flexible and determines the complexity of a product. In general, several refining steps of intermediate products by different machines are required to produce a final product.

This setup for products was selected to have a physical interaction among the robots, the machines, and the products. A central agent named referee box randomly generates product orders with varying configurations and delivery time windows. These orders are communicated to the teams that need to derive a production schedule and distribute the tasks among the robots and machines. Based on the complexity of the product and if the delivery windows was met points are awarded to the teams. For the most complex products usually up to 10 different steps like fetching and delivering material to machines are needed. The actual number depends on the planning representation. Some of them might be parallelized or rescheduled in order to optimize the awarded points. In order to simulate a real world production environment, machines go out of service on a random basis which asks for flexibility in the production planning. The team that collects the most points during 17 min of production time wins the game.

The referee box is able to run games and scoring automatically. Together with a full-fledged simulation [19] (see Fig. 2 for an example setup), it forms an advanced benchmarking system for flexible production approaches [10,11].

The interesting aspect of the RCLL setting is its resemblance to flexible on-demand production sites while abstracting it to not involve any physically changes of the product. Given that, this the RCLL posts challenges in the full range from Robotics (e.g. navigation, precise manipulation) over communication and multi-agent systems (e.g. reliable communication, reliable task execution) to planning and scheduling (e.g. generate production plans, execution monitoring and re-planning).

## 3    Software Architecture

The main aspects for realizing a multi-robot system as required in the RCLL are (1) planning and scheduling, (2) plan refinement and execution, (3) behavior and control, and (4) low-level functionality. In the following sections we are going to present selected topics for all aspects, except low-level functionality such as navigation. A general overview of the software architecture we apply in our system can be seen in Fig. 3. As depicted there, the software architecture spans over multiple physical systems. The planning and scheduling instance is deployed on a so-called *teamserver* which has *global* knowledge of the current game comprising information from the RCLL referee box such as requested orders and from all active robots such as the status of task execution. The teamserver controls all robots and interacts as a gateway between them and the referee box. The modules running on the robots comprises an executive, a behavior and control module, and low-level functionality.

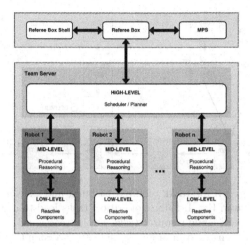

**Fig. 3.** Overview of distributed software architecture in our approach.

## 3.1   Planning and Scheduling

Planning and scheduling in our approach is based on splitting any order that is received from the RCLL referee box into subtasks that cannot be split further. The representation of the task on this level is rather abstract because we like to limit the complexity in planning and there exists a task refinement in the executive layer. This idea is inspired by the concept of hierarchical task network planning [5]. In our system, we distinguish between two subtask categories where we assume that one robot is only able to carry a single item:

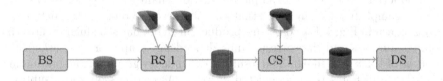

**Fig. 4.** Example production chain for an order of complexity $C1$, adapted from RCLL rulebook [3]. This order requires 2 additional workpieces at the ringstation $RS1$ and a cap loaded at capstation $CS1$.

1. **GET:** A GET task implies that the robot needs to navigate to a given MPS, where a workpiece is fetched by the robot, usually after sending some instruction to the MPS to initiate for instance a material dispense.
2. **DELIVER:** A DELIVER task involves the robot navigating to a given MPS, where the carried workpiece is then deposed. This is usually followed by the robot sending some instruction to the MPS like mounting a ring.

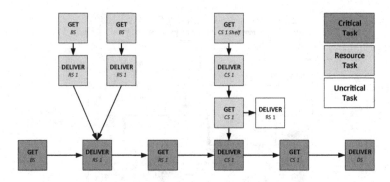

**Fig. 5.** Dependency graph for tasks required to build and deliver a product for the *C1* order that is shown in Fig. 4. Failure of critical tasks lead to complete cancellation of the respective product, while resource tasks can be reassigned. Failure of uncritical tasks have no influence on the overall goal of delivering a complete C1.

Since getting and delivering a workpiece reasonably needs to be done by the same robot, this specific choice of subtask types might seem counterintuitive. However, by separating the pickup and deliver process, MPSs can be freed from a workpiece that would otherwise block the MPS for other robots. The successful execution of these subtasks is then arranged and monitored by the system that will be discussed in Sect. 3.2. For simplicity, we assume here, that this system is capable of providing information of successful or unsuccessful task execution.

**Task Generation.** Any order that is received from the RCLL referee box specifies the color required for each workpiece that is used in the production process. Therefore, any order implicitly defines which MPSs need to be used during the production process. An example production chain for an order of easy-to-medium complexity *C1* (meaning that one ring needs to be mounted before the cap) is shown in Fig. 4. Based on this production chain, our scheduler creates the required subtasks and the corresponding dependency graph for this tasks using the ideas of HTN refinement. The resulting dependency graph for the production chain shown in Fig. 4 is then depicted in Fig. 5. As can be seen there, subtasks belong to one of the following three categories:

1. **Critical Tasks** represent the actual production flow where the requested product is assembled by the MPSs using the workpieces already loaded into the respective MPSs. If such a critical task fails, the product that currently is assembled cannot be reasonably recovered, and thus, production of this product is canceled. Depending on the current game's context, assembly of the same product might be started again.
2. **Resource Tasks** load the MPSs with workpieces that are required for the assembly of products. If resource tasks fail, the actual assembly of the product is not harmed and thus, these tasks can be reassigned until successfully completed. However, assembly of a product might be severely delayed due to resource tasks failing.

3. **Uncritical Tasks** neither influence the successful completion of the currently assembled product, nor do they (directly) influence assembly time of that product. However, if successfully completed, these tasks might have a positive effect by speeding up future assembly processes.

**Task Scheduling.** The assignment of tasks to respective robots in our system is done based on a *request-response* approach. This means, robots that currently do not own tasks request new tasks from the central planning and scheduling instance. For task scheduling, three scenarios might occur that we are going to discuss in the following paragraphs. To do so, we define the following symbols:

- $\tau$: a given task.
- $pred(\tau)$: set of all predecessor tasks of $\tau$ based on the task dependency graph.
- $\tau.type$: the task's type which is one of $\{GET, DELIVER\}$.
- $\tau.state$: the task's state which is one of $\{SUCCESS, FAIL, UNASSIG-NED\}$.
- $\tau.robot$: the robot to which the task $\tau$ was assigned.
- $\tau.machine$: the machine which which the robot interacts in this task. The machine is one of $\{BS, CS1, CS2, RS1, RS2, SS, DS\}$.
- $\xi$: a given product.
- $\xi.\tau$: all tasks that are required to assembly product $\xi$.
- $\xi.machines$: all machines the robots need to interact with during assembly of this product.
- $T$: the set containing all currently active tasks.
- $\rho$: the current robot that is requesting a task.

**1. Task in active assembly.** In the simpler of the two cases, a task in an already active production process for a given product can be found for the robot requesting a new task. That is, the set of tasks $\Phi$ that could be assigned to the robot according to (1) is not empty. In our system, this is the preferred case, and thus, scheduling of tasks is always greedy in a sense that the scheduler aims at finishing products as quickly as possible. Any robot requesting a task is assigned a randomly selected one $\tau \subseteq \Phi$.

$$\Phi = \begin{cases} \Psi, & \text{if } \Psi \neq \emptyset \\ \Theta, & \text{if } \Psi = \emptyset \end{cases} \tag{1}$$

Where $\Psi$ and $\Theta$ are defined as follows.

$$\Psi = \{\tau : \tau.type = DELIVER \\ \wedge \exists\, pred(\tau).robot = \rho \wedge \forall\, pred(\tau).state = SUCCESS\} \tag{2}$$

That is, the set $\Psi$ contains all tasks of type DELIVER for which a successfully finished predecessor task was already assigned to the same robot. In general, the set will only contain one task.

$$\Theta = \{\tau : \forall\, pred(\tau).state = SUCCESS\} \cup \{\tau : pred(\tau) = \emptyset\} \tag{3}$$

That is, the set $\Theta$ contains all tasks for which all predecessor tasks have been finished successfully. Of course, $\Psi \subseteq \Theta$ holds.

**2. Start new assembly.** If no task in the current assembly process needs to be done, the planning and scheduling instance determines whether the assembly of an additional product can be started. To do so, it is determined if a parallel production chain can be found where no machine (besides BS and DS) overlap, such that no deadlock can occur. This mechanism is formalized in (4).

$$\Omega = \{\xi : \xi.machines \cap T.machines = \emptyset\} \tag{4}$$

If the set $\Omega$ contains an additional product for which assembly can be started. Tasks are then selected according to the previous section for the newly to be assembled product. However, considering that any production chain includes mounting a cap to finish the currently assembled product, in our current architecture a maximum of two parallel production chains can be processed. Note that each team has 1 base station, 2 ring stations, 2 cap stations, and 1 delivery station in their MPS set. We did not use the $7^{th}$ machine - the storage station - in this implementation.

**3. "Dummy" task.** If no production relevant task can be found for a robot requesting a new task, that is, if $\Phi = \emptyset \wedge \Omega = \emptyset$, the robot is assigned so-called dummy tasks such that it is not blocking any relevant MPS while having no task. In our system, a dummy task consists of sending the robot to a random zone, such that it is constantly moving while having no production relevant task.

## 3.2   Executive

The bridging between the abstract planning and scheduling and the practical behavior layer is established by an executive layer that runs separately on each robot. The two main functions of the executive are the refinement of the abstract tasks to executable behaviors and the supervision of the entire task execution. The separation of the two functions contributes to the robustness of the overall architecture as the former allows the system to use a flexible abstracted planning approach while the latter allows to reactive to uncertainties and unexpected situations in the interaction between the physical robot and its environment.

We realized the executive layer following the well-known concept of belief-desire-intention (BDI) [4] using the open-source implementation OpenPRS [7]. In order to allow robust and reactive control of robots the approach follows the idea of practical reasoning where the tasks to be fulfilled are represented by goals and goals are pursuit using scripted recipes called procedure. Procedures are represented as directed graph with further sub-goals on the edges. Possible sub-goals are non-primitive goals (further goals), queries (simple queries to a knowledge base), information updates (asserting and retracting facts to the knowledge base), and primitive actions (representing executable behaviors). Goals may also be combined using special modifiers such as maintain where one goal is permanently active until another goal is achieved. The robustness and reactivity of a BDI system results from the execution semantics where the interpreter tries all applicable procedures and valid execution traces within recipes to achieve a given goal and the fact that instead of expensive reasoning (e.g. resolution) a simpler matching process between goals and procedures is used. The response to a posted goal or sub-goal is either success (all sub-goals were achieved) or fail (the interpreter were not able to achieve all sub-goals).

The interaction with the other parts of the architecture works as follows. Any time the robot becomes idle it requests a new task from the planning and scheduling component. The tasks assigned to a robot by this component are mapped to configurable goals. Currently we have corresponding goals for the get, delivery, and dummy task with corresponding hand-crafted procedures. The executable basic behaviors like navigating to a given position, alignment at a machine, or grasping an item are represented by primitive goals that lead directly to a behavior execution. The physical execution is realized using the action-server concept of the Robot Operating System (ROS) [14]. But each primitive goal is wrapped by a safe version of the original goal to achieve dependable execution. These goals comprise additional hand-crafted monitoring and fault-recovery recipes. These safe goals are reused when structuring the recipes for the top-level goals.

The communication between the planning and execution layer is based on abstract positions like C-BS-Input representing the position for the conveyor input of the cyan base station. In order to ground such positions or make conclusions such as that robot is close we use the transformation framework of ROS (there is a proper transformation for each abstract position maintained by the behavior layer) and the concept of evaluable predicates and functions provided by OpenPRS (oracles for the evaluation of predicates and functions are implemented in the behavior layer).

We like to point out the difference in planning and execution to previous attempts reported in [12]. In contrast we use OpenPRS only as an executive to execute tasks while task scheduling is done in the team server. Moreover, in contrast to the Clips-based approach we follow a clear separation of the abstract task scheduling and the task execution rather than performing the overall reasoning in an reactive manner using a rule-based system.

### 3.3   Behavior and Control

Several software components are implemented in the behavior and control layer of the software architecture. These components comprise navigation, alignment to machines, identification and localization of machines, and identifying and manipulation of products. In this paper the control strategy which enables the precise alignment of the robot in front of the machine during production will be explained in detail. This behavior is the base for reliable manipulation of products. In order to grasp or place products during production, the robot needs the ability to align itself at very short distances and with very high precision in front of machines. Achieving these criteria with the usual navigation approaches [9] already implemented in ROS is not possible. However, this is a typical task for classical feedback control. The two parts necessary for feedback control are the error computation and the controller design. These two parts will be described in detail in the following two subsections.

**Error Computation.** To perform closed loop control, the current positioning error has to be computed. The robots are equipped with a laser scanner at the front, which can be used to compute the position of the machine relative to the robot. Given the fact that all machines in the logistics league have the same rectangular base shape and assuming that the robot is roughly facing the machine (this is achieved using the navigation methods mentioned above), the relative position of the machine can be estimated using a very basic clustering algorithm. As the robot faces the machine, the central laser scan measurement is the root of the cluster. Starting from this root, every measurement value with Euclidean distance to the cluster smaller than a predefined threshold is added to the cluster. Applying classical least squares line fitting (see [13]) gives the angular error and using the edge points of the cluster results in the positioning error. Figure 6 shows a typical laser scan reading in gray rays with red tips where the robot faces a machine. The clustered data is depicted in blue and the estimated position of the machine as a green square. Based on the estimate of the machine pose, the three errors for position $e_x$ and $e_y$ as well as the angular error $e_\varphi$ are computed and fed into the controller.

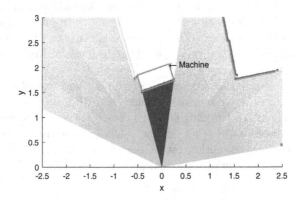

**Fig. 6.** Machine position estimation (Color figure online)

**Control Algorithm.** For each of the three component of the error (position $e_x$, $e_y$ and angular $e_\varphi$) a sliding mode controller is designed (see [18]). Sliding mode control was chosen, because it is a very simple to implement, easy to tune but also represents a robust control strategy. The basic concept of first order sliding mode control will be explained by means of an example. Consider a continuous integrator

$$\frac{dx}{dt} = u + f \tag{5}$$

with state $x \in \mathbb{R}$, input $u \in \mathbb{R}$ and the bounded perturbation $\sup |f| = \bar{f}$. Applying a first order sliding mode control law

$$u = -\rho \operatorname{sign}(x) \tag{6}$$

with parameter $\rho > \bar{f}$ yields the closed loop system

$$\frac{dx}{dt} = -\rho \operatorname{sign}(x) + f. \tag{7}$$

As the parameter $\rho > \bar{f}$, the controller always dominates the perturbation $f$. The reader interested in the theoretical property of sliding mode control exactly compensating perturbations is referred to [15,17,18] and getting familiar with differential inclusions as well as with Filipov's theory. The part $-\rho \operatorname{sign}(x)$ also dominates the perturbation $f$ which results in a movement towards the origin from any initial condition. Typical trajectories for the unperturbed case ($f = 0$) using first order sliding mode control is shown in Fig. 7 for the two initial conditions $x_0^{(1)} = 1.125$ and $x_0^{(2)} = -2.125$. One can see the typical finite time convergence which is also a very good property of sliding mode control. However, the main drawback of this control strategy is also visible in this figure because the state converges to a vicinity around zero and performs a zig-zag motion called chattering. This chattering appears in real world applications due to finite switching frequencies.

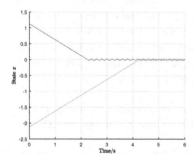
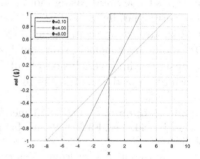

**Fig. 7.** Typical trajectories resulting with first order sliding mode control for two initial conditions and perturbation.

**Fig. 8.** Influence of parameter $\Phi$ on sign function approximation.

In order to reduce this chattering phenomenon, several approximations of the sign function are proposed (see [15]). In the remainder of this paper the $\operatorname{sign}(\cdot)$ function is approximated by the saturation function

$$\operatorname{sat}(\gamma) = \begin{cases} \gamma & -1 \leq \gamma \leq 1 \\ \operatorname{sign}(\gamma) & \text{else} \end{cases} \tag{8}$$

which results in the control law

$$u = -\rho \operatorname{sat}\left(\frac{x}{\Phi}\right) \tag{9}$$

with parameter $\Phi \in \mathbb{R}^+$ specifying the slope of the approximation as depicted in Fig. 8.

*Remark 1.* The parameter $\Phi$ offers a possibility to find a tradeoff between accuracy and chattering alleviation. Please note that $\operatorname{sat}\left(\frac{x}{\Phi}\right) = \operatorname{sign}(x)$ for $\Phi \to 0$.

As the used holonomic robot takes velocity commands, the dynamics of the three errors $e_x$, $e_y$ and $e_\varphi$ can be formulated as integrators (5). In the application the control law (9) is then independently applied to these three systems.

## 4   Conclusions and Future Work

Following the common interest of the institutes involved in the GRIPS RoboCup Logistics League team in a holistic approach to develop methods for dependable intelligent systems we developed a software architecture that allows flexible and robust execution of the demanded production tasks. The basic idea is to separate different concerns such as abstract planning and scheduling, refinement of task execution, and behavioral control and equip each layer with proper motioning and fault-recovery capabilities. The flexible planning and task assignment paired with robust task execution allowed us to realize more complex products reliably and constantly than in the past competitions.

In future work we will aim for an optimization based selection of suitable products to be build (using more context information such as travel time) as well as a better parallelization (using an improved resource management). Moreover, we like to better team up monitoring and recovery between different layers. Often one layer lacks of sufficient knowledge about the actual situation to make a consistent final conclusion about errors and recovery. Sharing and combining information of different layers may help to address this issue.

**Acknowledgement.** The team members in 2018 are Sarah Haas, Vanessa Egger, Stefan Krickl, Leo Fürbaß, Ivan Martin, Thomas Ulz, Jakob Ludwiger, and Gerald Steinbauer.

We gratefully acknowledge the financial support of Graz University of Technology, Knapp AG, IncubedIT GmbH, AccuPower GmbH, and pia automation. In particular, the team is grateful to Knapp AG for the mechanical and electrical design and integration of the GRIPS robot platforms.

## References

1. RoboCup Logistics League. http://www.robocup-logistics.org/
2. Boano, C., Römer, K., Bloem, R., Witrisal, K., Baunach, M., Horn, M.: Dependability for the internet of things - from dependable networking in harsh environments to a holistic view on dependability. e & i Elektrotechnik & Informationstechnik **133**, 304–309 (2016)
3. Coelen, V., Deppe, C., Hoffmann, T., Karras, U., Niemueller, T., Rohr, A.: Rules and Regulations - RoboCup Logistics League. http://www.robocup-logistics.org/rules. Accessed 19 Dec 2018

4. Georgeff, M., Pell, B., Pollack, M., Tambe, M., Wooldridge, M.: The belief-desire-intention model of agency. In: Müller, J.P., Rao, A.S., Singh, M.P. (eds.) ATAL 1998. LNCS, vol. 1555, pp. 1–10. Springer, Heidelberg (1999). https://doi.org/10.1007/3-540-49057-4_1
5. Ghallab, M., Lau, D., Traverso, P.: Automated Planning - Theory and Practice. Morgan Kaufmann (2004)
6. Gspandl, S., Pill, I., Reip, M., Steinbauer, G., Ferrein, A.: Belief management for high-level robot programs. In: Proceedings of the 22nd International Joint Conference on Artificial Intelligence, IJCAI 2011, Barcelona, Spain, pp. 900–905 (2011)
7. Ingrand, F.F., Chatila, R., Alami, R., Robert, F.: PRS: a high level supervision and control language for autonomous mobile robots. In: Proceedings of IEEE International Conference on Robotics and Automation, vol. 1, pp. 43–49 (1996)
8. Ludwiger, J., Steinberger, M., Horn, M., Kubin, G., Ferrara, A.: Discrete time sliding mode control strategies for buffered networked systems. In: 2018 IEEE 57th Annual Conference on Decision and Control (CDC). IEEE (2018)
9. Marder-Eppstein, E., Berger, E., Foote, T., Gerkey, B., Konolige, K.: The office marathon: robust navigation in an indoor office environment. In: International Conference on Robotics and Automation (2010)
10. Niemueller, T., Karpas, E., Vaquero, T., Timmons, E.: Planning competition for logistics robots in simulation. In: WS on Planning and Robotics (PlanRob) at International Conference on Automated Planning and Scheduling (ICAPS), London, UK (2016)
11. Niemueller, T., Zug, S., Schneider, S., Karras, U.: Knowledge-based instrumentation and control for competitive industry-inspired robotic domains. KI - Künstliche Intelligenz 30(3–4), 289–299 (2016)
12. Niemueller, T., et al.: Cyber-physical system intelligence – knowledge-based mobile robot autonomy in an industrial scenario. In: Jeschke, S., Brecher, C., Song, H., Rawat, D.B. (eds.) Industrial Internet of Things: Cybermanufacturing Systems. SSWT, pp. 447–472. Springer, Cham (2017). https://doi.org/10.1007/978-3-319-42559-7_17
13. Penrose, R.: On best approximate solutions of linear matrix equations. Math. Proc. Camb. Philos. Soc. 52(1), 17–19 (1956)
14. Quigley, M., et al.: ROS: an open-source robot operating system. In: ICRA Workshop on Open Source Software (2009)
15. Shtessel, Y., Edwards, C., Fridman, L., Levant, A.: Sliding Mode Control and Observation. Springer, New York (2013). https://doi.org/10.1007/978-0-8176-4893-0
16. Steinbauer, G., Ferrein, A.: 20 years of RoboCup. Künstliche Intelligenz 30(3–4), 221–224 (2016)
17. Utkin, V., Guldner, J., Shi, J.: Sliding Mode Control in Electro-Mechanical Systems. CRC Press, Boca Raton (2009)
18. Utkin, V.I.: Sliding Modes in Control and Optimization. Springer, Heidelberg (1992). https://doi.org/10.1007/978-3-642-84379-2
19. Zwilling, F., Niemueller, T., Lakemeyer, G.: Simulation for the RoboCup logistics league with real-world environment agency and multi-level abstraction. In: Bianchi, R.A.C., Akin, H.L., Ramamoorthy, S., Sugiura, K. (eds.) RoboCup 2014. LNCS (LNAI), vol. 8992, pp. 220–232. Springer, Cham (2015). https://doi.org/10.1007/978-3-319-18615-3_18

# RoboCup@Work 2018 Team AutonOHM

Jon Martin[(✉)], Helmut Engelhardt, Marco Masannek, Tobias Scholz,
Kay Gillmann, and Benjamin Schadde

University of Applied Sciences Nuremberg Georg-Simon-Ohm,
Kesslerplatz 12, 90489 Nuremberg, Germany
{jon.martingarechana,engelhardthe57850,
masannekma61828,scholzto52032}@th-nuernberg.de
http://www.autonohm.de

**Abstract.** This work presents the team AutonOHM which won the
RoboCup@Work competition in Montreal 2018. The tests and main
changes of the 2018 world cup competition are presented and a detailed
description of the team's hardware and software concepts are exposed.
Furthermore, improvements for future participations are discussed.

## 1 Introduction

The RoboCup@Work league, established in 2012, focuses on the use of mobile
manipulators and their integration with automation equipment for performing
industrial-relevant tasks [4]. This work presents our teams major improvements
and changes with regard to last years work [5]. This year, the team has focused
on further increasing the system stability by developing a new gripper, improving
the inventory slots, speeding up task executions and developing a new approach
for the rotating table test.

Section 4 shows the team's hardware concept. In Sect. 5 the main software
modules such as the state machine, localization and perception are presented.
Finally, the conclusion provides a prospect to further work of team AutonOHM
(Sect. 7).

## 2 AutonOHM

The AutonOHM-@Work team at the University of Applied Sciences Nuremberg
Georg-Simon-Ohm was founded in September 2014. In 2018, having most of the
formal members yet taking part on the competition, the main goal was to defend
the German and the World Championship titles. The team is organized so that
each formal member takes care of a specific main task: Team coordination and
state machine, navigation, perception, manipulation and rotating table. Newer
students support the different tasks or develop new packages such as a faster
task planner this year.

In order to retain the titles, the robots hard- and software were improved
based on the knowledge summed during the past tournaments. This includes a

© Springer Nature Switzerland AG 2019
D. Holz et al. (Eds.): RoboCup 2018, LNAI 11374, pp. 500–511, 2019.
https://doi.org/10.1007/978-3-030-27544-0_41

**Fig. 1.** Team AutonOHM at the winners ceremony in Magdeburg

**Fig. 2.** Team AutonOHM with the second (b-it-bots) and third (mrl) placed teams in Montreal

new 3D camera model with a more accurate point cloud. The inventory slots are now more resistant against vibrations. The old gripper mechanism has been replaced by a single motor solution, which enables the robot to grasp heavy objects more reliably. Combined with high precision perception, the team was the only one that never lost the heaviest and most difficult object in the competition. In addition to the hardware improvements, the perception and manipulation for moving objects has been adapted to the new challenges added in the 2018 rulebook.

Even though remarkable changes have been done since the last year, most integration problems and bugs could be solved and the team was able to defend both titles against the strong competitors (Figs. 1 and 2).

## 3  RoboCup@Work

In this section we introduce briefly the tests and most remarkable changes of the 2018 RoboCup@Work world championship. As a common change to uniform the different tasks, the robots must now start in the starting position and end in the finishing position for every run. The 2018 rulebook release [3] contains more detailed information about the changes.

**Arena:** As in previous competitions, the arena has well defined start and finish positions and is entirely shut either by a wall or by yellow-black barrier tape (see Fig. 3). It contains workstations with heights of 0/5/10/15 cm as well as in shelves. The 0 cm areas are marked by the blue-white barrier tape. The Fig. 4 displays the map used by the robot for navigation.

**Basic Navigation Test Removed:** The BNT test had the purpose of demonstrating robots navigation and obstacle avoidance capabilities. However, these abilities can also be proven during any other test and the league has thus decided to remove the BNT test and distribute the points among the following runs. Teams get now 25 points per station reached during the whole competition.

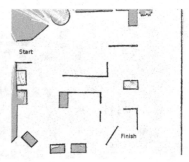

**Fig. 3.** The @Work arena during the RoboCup world cup in Montreal (Color figure online)

**Fig. 4.** Map used for navigation

**Basic Manipulation Test:** The purpose of the Basic Manipulation Test (BMT) is to demonstrate basic manipulation capabilities by the robots. Here, five objects must be grasped and delivered to a nearby workstation.

**Basic Transportation Test:** The purpose of the Basic Transportation Test (BTT) is to assess the ability of the robots for combined navigation and manipulation tasks. The robot receives the start and end positions of the objects to be transported in the arena and autonomously create a plan to perform this grasping and delivery tasks. This test is repeated three times with an increment of the difficulty and penalties during the competition. Here, unknown dynamic obstacles and yellow barrier tapes will limit the mobility of the robot.

**Precision Placement Test:** The purpose of the Precision Placement Test (PPT) is to assess advance perception and manipulation abilities. The robot needs to detect object-specific cavities and introduce the grasped objects into them.

**Rotating Table Test:** The purpose of the Rotating Table Test (RTT) is to assess the robot's ability to detect and grasp moving objects which are placed on a rotating turntable. This year, there are six objects laying on the turntable including three objects to be grasped, such as in previous years, and three extra decoy objects. Moreover, the objects position in the table is now defined by referees. As a result each object has its own circular path, tangential speed and position. The possibility to fix a grasping configuration for the robot in front of the table is eliminated. As in previous years, the direction of rotation of the table is fixed and the speed is set by the referees before just the test starts.

**Final:** The final round is a combination of all the above mentioned tests performed in a single round.

## 4   Hardware Description

Table 1 shows our main hardware specifications. We use the KUKA omni directional mobile platform youBot (Fig. 5), as it provides a hardware setup almost

**Table 1.** Hardware Specifications.

**Fig. 5.** KUKA youBot platform of the team AutonOHM.

| PC 1 | |
|---|---|
| CPU | NUC7i7BNH |
| RAM | 16 GB DDR4 |
| OS | Ubuntu 16.04 |
| *Gripper* | |
| Type | 3D printed, parallel rail |
| Motor | Dynamixel AX-12A |
| *Sensors* | |
| Lidar front | SICK TiM571 |
| Lidar back | SICK TiM571 |
| 3D-cam arm | Intel RealSense D435 |
| 2D-cam gripper | Endoscope Cam |
| 3D-cam back | Intel RealSense D435 |

ready to take part in the competition. Nevertheless, we made some modifications for a better performance.

The platform comes with two PCs with hardware drivers installed, which we replaced by a single Intel NUC i7, because the default processors were outdated and caused performance issues. This main PC is used to control the base and arm of the mobile platform, as well as for image processing and task planning. The KUKA youbot also comes with a Hokuyu 2D-Lidar, which was replaced by two SICK SICK TiM571, one at the front and one at the back of the robot. They are used for mapping, localization, navigation and obstacle avoidance.

The standard endeffector of the Youbot was also replaced by a self developed parallel gripper. The gripper is based on a single Dynamixel servo motor which is attached to a 3D printed rail. Simple mechanics allow an efficient power transmission which enables the motor to grasp with its full torque rather than it being reduced by the lever in the old gripper version. The fin-ray fingers are custom printed out of rubber filament, making them soft and enabling them to close around grasped objects. They are also wider than standard FESTO fin-ray fingers, so they have an enlarged attack surface and therefore have more tolerance for very small and/or moving objects.

Both sides of the gripper mount are also used to mount the cameras used for perception. The main camera is an Intel RealSense D435 which has been chosen due to its ability to provide a 3D point cloud in short distances. The point of view can be changed with different arm positions, enabling different fields of view. The secondary perception camera is an endoscope webcam used to increase the precision while grasping moving objects. Its field of view points directly towards the gripper and therefore enables better timing of gripper controls. For the World Championship, an additional Intel RealSense D435 was mounted at the back of the robot for improving the barrier tape detection.

The robots inventory consists of three identical 3D printed slots mounted on an adaptable rail system. They are equipped with anti-slip pads, which prevent any movement of the objects, even with heavy robot vibrations.

## 5    Software Description

We use different open source software packages to compete in the contests. Image processing is handled with OpenCV library (2D image processing and object recognition) and PCL (3D image processing). For mapping and navigation we use gmapping and navigation-stack ROS-packages[1]. Additionally, robot-pose-ekf package is used for fusing the data from the IMU and the wheel encoders, to provide more accurate data to the navigation and localization system.

The main software packages are based on ROS and explained in the following sections. These include the state machine (Sect. 5.1), global and local localization (Sect. 5.2) and packages for perception (Sect. 5.3) and manipulation (Sect. 5.4). We also improved the rotating table approach (Sect. 5.5). To perform the transportation logistics, a *task_planner* node processes the orders received from the referee box and calculates the best route considering the maximum transport capacity and distances between the workstations. This module finds the optimal solution up to five objects. From six objects on, we need to split the orders in groups of five due to the long computing time of the current solution, resulting on an suboptimal result.

### 5.1    State Machine

The main control of the robot is coordinated over the state machine in Fig. 6. It starts with an initialization state where the robot receives the map and tries to localize itself on it. From there, it moves to the "stateIdle" and waits for new tasks to perform. The Referee Box provides the orders which are processed by the *task_planner* node and sent to the state machine divided into a vector of smaller subtasks. The subtasks *Move, Grasp, Delivery, PreciseDelivery* and *RotatingTable* are now managed in the "stateRunning". Once every subtask is finished it returns to the "stateIdle" to wait again for new tasks to perform.

The first subtask is usually a *Move* action performed over the *navigation* node. Depending on the required accuracy on the localization, the robot may execute a *fine navigation* approach. Both modules are explained in Sect. 5.2. After a specific workstation location is reached, the robot may look for a specific object, container or cavity on the workstation. In case of a *Grasp* subtask, the exact pose of the desired object is identified. For *Delivering* an object, the robot must recognize the exact pose of containers or cavities for *PreciseDelivery*. Once the desired pose is located, the arm manipulation is activated, whether for picking up and storing the object on the robot or for delivering it. The perception and manipulation nodes are explained in Sects. 5.3 and 5.4 respectively. In case

---

[1] http://wiki.ros.org/.

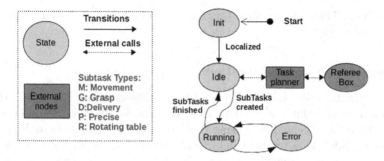

**Fig. 6.** Global overview of the AutonOHM State Machine

of a *RotatingTable* subtask, before grasping an object, a preprocessing step to determine objects velocity and pose in the table is required (Sect. 5.5). Once the manipulation subtask is finished, the robot moves away from the service area and returns to the "stateNextSubtask" to manage the following subtask to do (Fig. 7).

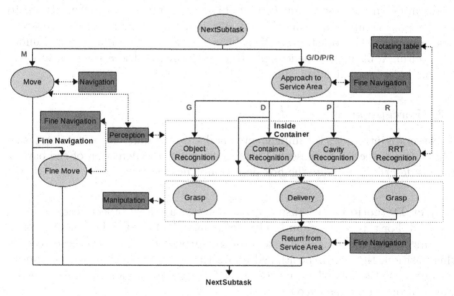

**Fig. 7.** The Running state is divided into substates where the SubTasks are managed

In addition, most of the states have error handling behaviors that manage recovery actions such as in case a navigation goal is not reachable, an object cannot be found or a grasping was unsuccessful. It is important to notice these failures and react to them by repeating the action or triggering planning modifications. The state machine framework can be found on GitHub under our laboratory's repository.[2]

## 5.2   Navigation and Localization

For the navigation, the ROS navigation stack has been used. The localization is based on a particle filter algorithm, close to amcl localization, as described in [1]. The algorithm is capable of using two laser scanners and an omnidirectional movement model. Due to the Monte Carlo filtering approach, our localization is robust and accurate enough to provide useful positioning with an approximate error of about 6 cm, depending on the complexity and speed of the actual movement.

For the fine navigation, such as approximation to service areas and moving left and right to find the objects on them, we use an approach based on the front laser scanner data. Initially, the robot is positioned by means of the particle filter localization and ROS navigation. If the service area is not visible in the laser scan due to its small height, the robot is moved to the destination pose using particle filter localization and two separate controllers for x and y movement. If the service area is high enough, RANSAC algorithm [2] is used to detect the workstation in the laser scan. Out of this, the distance and angle relative to the area are computed. Using this information, the robot moves in a constant distance along the workstation. We achieved a mean positioning error of under 3 cm during a navigation benchmark tests performed in the European Robotics League local tournament in Milan.

## 5.3   Perception

This section introduces the implemented nodes for the different perception tasks. The object detection is presented first. Subsequent the detection of the barrier tape is described. Finally, the box detection is depicted.

**Object Detection:** To grasp objects reliably, a stable object recognition is required. For this purpose, an Intel® RealSense™ D435 RGB-D camera is used.

Firstly, the robot navigates to a pregrasp position. Once the base reaches this position, the arm is positioned above the service area. Due to the limited field of view, the robot base moves first left, then right so all the objects in the workstation can be discovered.

On each position, the plane of the service area is searched in the point cloud using the RANSAC [2] algorithm. Afterwards the detected points are projected to the 2D-RGB image and used as a mask to segment the objects in the 2D-image (Fig. 8a and b).

As all workstations have a white surface, the canny edge detector is used in order to find the concave border of the object in the segmented images for a more

---

[2] https://github.com/autonohm/obviously.

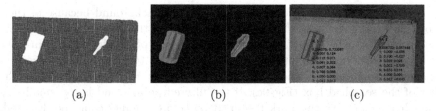

(a)          (b)          (c)

**Fig. 8.** Segmentation mask: The projected point cloud to camera's RGB image (a). Filled border and morphological operations (b). Classified objects (c).

accurate result. To classify an object, the following features are extracted: length, width, area, circle factor, corners count, height and black area. The distance to the workstation surface and the camera calibration matrix is used to calculate distance invariant values. With the help of a kNN classifier and the extracted features, the similarity to each previously trained item is calculated. With this information and the inventory information from the referee box, the best possible fitting combination for the detected object on the workstation is searched. To estimate the location of the object, its mass center is calculated. For the rotation of the object, the main axis of inertia is computed and used. The robot will now move in front of the elected object and activate the object recognition again to obtain a more accurate gripping pose. For the newly introduced challenge of unknown orientation of the objects, the objects are trained from all possible orientations. The corresponding height of the detected object will be passed to the manipulation node for correct grasping. The use of the same features of the corresponding objects is an advantage of this approach. The features of black area and height are not considered, as they are not needed for a successful classification.

**Box Detection:** Some tasks require an object placement into a blue or a red box (see Fig. 9a).

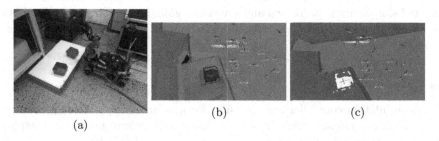

**Fig. 9.** Box Detection: Blue and red box on workstation (a). Point cloud of workstation (b). Red filtered point cloud and mass center (c). (Color figure online)

The boxes are easily distinguishable from the background because of their color. Therefore a different strategy is used instead of the described object detection in Sect. 5.3. The advantage is a faster detection of the drop point. In front of the workstation the robot arm is moved in order to position the camera in a 45° angle to the workstation. Subsequently, the point cloud is filtered by the color of the searched box (Fig. 9c). If the filtered point cloud is too small, the robot drives closer to the workstation. If no colored points could be detected, the robot will move to the left side first, then to the right side, until a significant amount of points is found. After that the mass center of the filtered point cloud is calculated and passed to the manipulation node as the drop point for the object.

**Barrier Tape Detection:** Yellow/black barrier tapes are used to mark restricted areas in the RoboCup@Work competition. If the robot crosses this tape the team is penalized with point deduction (Fig. 10).

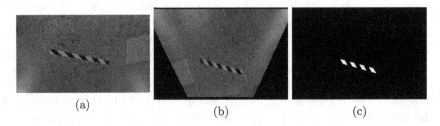

(a)          (b)          (c)

**Fig. 10.** Barrier Tape Detection: Camera image of the barrier tape (a) Birdview (b) Filter for yellow RGB and HSV values and HU-Moments (c) (Color figure online)

In order to detect this barrier tape the camera image is transformed in bird's-eye perspective. Next the image is filtered by RGB and HSV values, which correspond with the yellow part of the barrier tape. For the next step the HU-Moments are calculated and compared to filter out false shapes. Afterwards the detected shapes are transformed and saved in a global map. This gives the robot the ability to avoid the barrier tape even it is not visible in the camera image anymore.

### 5.4   Manipulation

The manipulation controller is responsible for arm and gripper controls, as well as for inventory management. It provides interfaces for arm positions, grasping or placing tasks and for linear arm movements (Figs. 11 and 12).

At the beginning of a grasp or placement process, it receives the target pose from the perception node. A self developed algorithm for the inverse kinematics and interpolation plans a linear and orthogonal trajectory to the workstation, object or container. This prevents the gripper from accidentally touching

**Fig. 11.** Precise placement of objects.

**Fig. 12.** Placing an object below the shelf without causing a collision.

or moving other objects lying on the workstation. Safety behaviors have been implemented during the grasping and placing process to ensure a reliable object handling and inventory management. In specific cases where objects are lost, the affected inventory slot is blocked to further use. The inventory state is broadcasted, so it can be used e.g. by the task planner.

For 2018, the placement process for the shelf workstations was adapted to the changes in the rulebook. Placing an object below the shelf is higher rewarded than placing it on top, because its more likely to cause a collision with parts of the sensor head attached to the gripper. Therefore, a custom placement trajectory has been added to ensure safe operation in the enclosed space below the shelf. Additionally, the grasping process for moved objects was modified to enable more accurate timing and placement of the TCP.

The gripper controller consists of two separated nodes. The driver node runs a microcontroller program which is connected to the Dynamixel servo motors. It initializes and controls the motors position, torque and speed. The microcontroller is connected to the main PC via USB and offers an interface for motor controls and parameter settings. The gripper controller node runs on the main PC and offers dynamic reconfigure options and the grasping services used by the manipulation controller and other nodes. It uses the current torque applied to the motor to determine if an object has been grasped. The torque feedback is also used to prevent the motor from overcurrents by reducing the torque in case of high loads.

### 5.5  Rotating Turntable

As explained in Sect. 3 the rules for this challenge have been significantly changed in 2018. To adapt our system to the changes, the following algorithm considers various parameters such as the rotation speed, rotating direction and the pose of each object on the table.

The robot first navigates to the rotating turntable and extends the manipulator arm to an object detection position. Only performed once, an object recognition preprocessing approach is started to obtain the rotating table speed

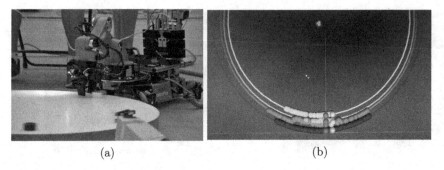

(a)                                          (b)

**Fig. 13.** Rotating Turn Table: Robot in front of the rotating turntable grasping an object (a) All data points, given by the object recognition, and the result of the determined circular paths of all objects on the turntable with different grasp points (red marked) (b). (Color figure online)

and the direction of rotation. First, the 2D position, the time stamp and the type of incoming objects into the camera visual field are recorded over a defined time. Second, the gathered data is used to determine objects circular paths, defining specific grasping position for each circular path. Figure 13b shows a result of this process determining four circular paths with four different grasping positions (red marked).

With the collected data points of each circular path, a RANSAC-based algorithm [2] calculates the rotation speed of the table, its center (blue marked in Fig. 13b) and the radius of each determined path. Having all necessary information and making use of the previously recorded time stamps, it is possible to estimate an approximate moment, when each object passes the object grasping position. To achieve an accurate grasping, an additional stereoscope RGB camera has been attached on top of the manipulator. A background change algorithm is now applied to the image in order to detect the object entrance in the camera view. The previously calculated circular path velocity is used to close the gripper at the right moment.

With the implemented feedback of the gripper the robot recognizes, whether grasping was successful or has failed. In case of success, the object is placed on the robot and the manipulator then moves over the next circular path to grasp the remaining objects. If the grasping fails, the manipulator stays in the position and waits one more time until the same object arrives at the RGB camera. If this retry fails again, the robot tries to grasp the next object on the rotating turntable. The smallest object of the @Work competition, a small nut, was successfully grasped demonstrated a remarkable accuracy.

## 6   Results

Table 2 presents the scorings of the world cup in Montreal 2018.

**Table 2.** Results of the RoboCup@Work world cup competition.

| Place | Team | BMT | BTT1 | BTT2 | PPT | BTT3 | RTT | Final | Total |
|---|---|---|---|---|---|---|---|---|---|
| 1 | AutonOHM | 1043,75 | 900 | 975 | 550 | 1050 | 425 | 1375 | 6318,75 |
| 2 | b-it-bots | 675 | 800 | 900 | 450 | 450 | 225 | 1175 | 4675 |
| 3 | MRL@work | 525 | 550 | 850 | 0 | 875 | 0 | 1050 | 3850 |
| 4 | RobOTTO | 575 | 725 | 1050 | 0 | 0 | 25 | 1075 | 3450 |
| 5 | LUHbots | 675 | 475 | 0 | 37,5 | 1000 | 25 | 650 | 2862,5 |
| 6 | RED | 325 | 75 | 525 | 0 | 0 | 0 | 0 | 925 |
| 7 | RoboErectus | 225 | 0 | 200 | 50 | 350 | 25 | 0 | 850 |

## 7   Conclusion and Future Work

This paper described the participation of team AutonOHM in the RoboCup@
work league. It contains detailed information of the hardware setup and software
packages like navigation, perception and manipulation. We believe that our system stability and repeatability are the key factors to achieve such a regular and
high performance shown in Table 1.

To further increase the system stability and defend the RoboCup@Work
champions title we introduced several improvements in different fields. First, the
new gripper and its feedback function has improved the reliability for correctly
grasping objects, specially during the RTT. Second, the object detection rate
was increased to improve the decoy objects detection during the RTT.

Our main goal for 2019 is to develop a new robot platform to participate
in the German open RoboCup@work, because our Youbot is getting unstable.
Besides, there are several software modules which must be adapted to the new
platform. Additionally, it is planned a software reorganization to make the different modules more modular, independent of each other and reusable.

## References

1. Dellaert, F., Fox, D., Burgard, W., Thrun, S.: Monte Carlo localization for mobile
   robots. In: Proceedings 1999 IEEE International Conference on Robotics and
   Automation (Cat. No. 99CH36288C), vol. 2, pp. 1322–1328, May 1999
2. Fischler, M.A., Bolles, R.C.: Random sample consensus: a paradigm for model fitting
   with applications to image analysis and automated cartography. Commun. ACM
   **24**(6), 381–395 (1981)
3. Hochgeschwender, N., et al.: Work Rulebook (2017)
4. Kraetzschmar, G.K., et al.: RoboCup@Work: competing for the factory of the future.
   In: Bianchi, R.A.C., Akin, H.L., Ramamoorthy, S., Sugiura, K. (eds.) RoboCup
   2014. LNCS (LNAI), vol. 8992, pp. 171–182. Springer, Cham (2015). https://doi.
   org/10.1007/978-3-319-18615-3_14
5. Martin, J., Engelhardt, H., Fink, T., Masannek, M., Scholz, T.: RoboCup@Work
   winners 2017 team AutonOHM. In: Akiyama, H., Obst, O., Sammut, C., Tonidandel,
   F. (eds.) RoboCup 2017. LNCS (LNAI), vol. 11175, pp. 498–508. Springer, Cham
   (2018). https://doi.org/10.1007/978-3-030-00308-1_41

# homer@UniKoblenz: Winning Team of the RoboCup@Home Open Platform League 2018

Raphael Memmesheimer[✉], Ivanna Mykhalchyshyna, Viktor Seib,
Tobias Evers, and Dietrich Paulus

Active Vision Group, Institute for Computational Visualistics,
University of Koblenz-Landau, 56070 Koblenz, Germany
{raphael,ivannamyckhal,vseib,tevers,paulus}@uni-koblenz.de
http://homer.uni-koblenz.de
http://agas.uni-koblenz.de

**Abstract.** We won this year's RoboCup@Home track in the Open Platform League in Montreal (Canada). The approaches as used for the competition are briefly described in this paper. The robotic hardware of our custom built robot Lisa and the PAL Robotics TIAGo, both running the same methods, are presented. New approaches for object recognition, especially the preprocessed segment augmentation, effort based gripping, gesture recognition and approaches for visual imitation learning based on continuous spatial observations between a demonstrator and the interacting objects are presented. Further, we present the current state of research of our Imitation Learning approaches, where we propose a hybrid benchmark and methods for bootstrapping actions. Furthermore, our research on point cloud based object recognition is presented.

**Keywords:** RoboCup@Home · Imitation learning ·
Gesture recognition · Object recognition · Object manipulation ·
RoboCup · Open platform league · Domestic service robotics ·
homer@UniKoblenz

## 1 Introduction

In this year's RoboCup we successfully participated in the RoboCup@Home Open Platform League, where we achieved the first place. After the RoboCup World Cup in Nagoya (Japan (2017)) and Hefei (China (2015)), this is the third time that we won this title. The team consisted of one supervisor and five students. Additionally, two more students were supporting the preparation.

Besides the RoboCup competitions, we also attend the European Robotics League and the World Robot Summit. For this year's participation we focused on imitation learning by observation of humans. We demonstrated this twice. Once at the RoboCup GermanOpen and once in RoboCup@Home Open Platform league. This year we also improved our team's infrastructure by a continuous

© Springer Nature Switzerland AG 2019
D. Holz et al. (Eds.): RoboCup 2018, LNAI 11374, pp. 512–523, 2019.
https://doi.org/10.1007/978-3-030-27544-0_42

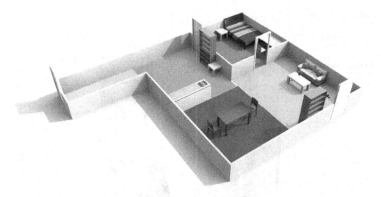

**Fig. 1.** The arena setup from Montreal. Different colors are corresponding to different rooms. Corridor is yellow, kitchen is cyan, dining room is pink, bedroom is red, living room is green (Color figure online)

software integration and built our packages for a variety of processor architectures.

Section 2 gives a short overview of the RoboCup@Home competition. In Sect. 3 we present the robots that we used for this year's participation. A special focus is put on the hardware changes that the robots have undergone. Section 4 describes the architecture and software approaches we are using. An overview of the current research topics is given in Sect. 5. Finally, Sect. 6 summarizes and concludes this paper.

## 2 RoboCup@Home

Domestic tasks are benchmarked in RoboCup@Home. The competition is divided into two stages. An *Open Challenge* and the *Finals* allow to present the current research focus in a practical application scenario. In Stage 1 focuses is on a variety of individual functionalities. The *Speech and Person Recognition* test, benchmarks the speech recognition, sound source localization, person recognition and gender estimation. In *Help Me Carry* robots are supposed to follow a person outside of the apartment to a car. The person hands over a shopping bag in a natural way. On the way back obstacles are put into the path of the robot that should be avoided. In *Storing Groceries* the robot has to pick groceries from a table and sort them into a shelf where items of the same category are already stored. In the *General Purpose* (GPSR) task all possible capabilities are tested. The robot receives a speech command consisting of several sub-commands and has to execute them. Stage 2 consists of the *Dishwasher Test, Restaurant, EE-GPSR* (Extended Endurance General Purpose Service Robot) and the *Open Challenge*. The *Dishwasher Test* focuses on precise manipulation. Robots have to open a dishwasher and store cutlery and plates safely. Further, a dish washing tab should be placed into the dishwasher. The *Restaurant* task takes place outside of the arena in a previously unknown restaurant. The robots are placed

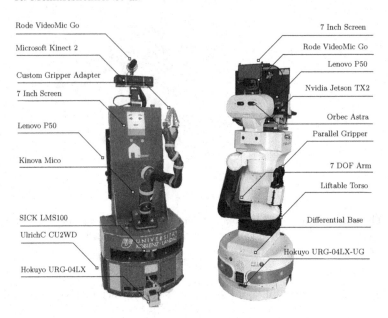

Rode VideoMic Go

Microsoft Kinect 2

Custom Gripper Adapter

7 Inch Screen

Lenovo P50

Kinova Mico

SICK LMS100

UlrichC CU2WD

Hokuyo URG-04LX

7 Inch Screen

Rode VideoMic Go

Lenovo P50

Nvidia Jetson TX2

Orbec Astra

Parallel Gripper

7 DOF Arm

Liftable Torso

Differential Base

Hokuyo URG-04LX-UG

**Fig. 2.** The robots Lisa (left) and Marge (right). Lisa is our main robot inspired by Marge as a successor. Both robots run the same software with minor exceptions like the model descriptions and hardware interfaces.

at an initial location and search for a waving or shouting person. A map in a dynamic environment needs to be created online. The ordering persons should be approached and asked for an order. This is particularly hard as the chosen scenarios are usually quite noisy. The *EE-GPSR* task is an enhanced-endurance version of the GPSR task where multiple robots are operating at the same time. The arena setup from this year's RoboCup in Montreal is shown in Fig. 1.

## 3    Hardware

We use a custom built robot called Lisa and a PAL Robotics TIAGo (Marge). Lisa is built upon a CU-2WD-Center robotics platform. The PAL Robotics TIAGo robot is able to move its torso up and down and has a wider working range. Currently, we are using a workstation notebook equipped with an Intel Core i7-6700HQ CPU @ 2.60 GHz × 8, 16 GB RAM with Ubuntu Linux 16.04 and ROS Kinetic. Each robot is equipped with a laser range finder (LRF) for navigation and mapping. The most important sensors of Lisa are set up on top of a pan-tilt unit. Thus, they can be rotated to search the environment or take a better view of a specific position of interest. Apart from a RGB-D camera (Microsoft Kinect 2) a directional microphone (Rode VideoMic Pro) is mounted on the pan-tilt unit. A 6-DOF robotic arm (Kinova Mico) is used for mobile manipulation. The end effector is a custom setup and consists of 4 Festo Finray-fingers. Finally, an Odroid C2 inside the casing of Lisa handles the robot face

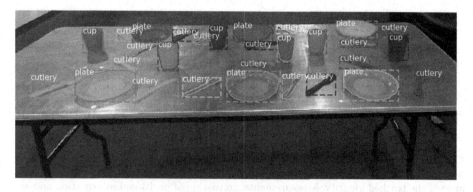

**Fig. 3.** The Mask-RCNN resulting image of cutlery objects as used for the Dishwasher challenge.

and speech synthesis. A Raspberry Pi 3 in combination with a Matrix Creator board was used for the integration of a sound source localization system.

TIAGo has a mobile differential base with a Hokuyo URG-04LX-UG01 laser range finder. We compute the odometry from wheel encoders. In combination with the LRF we can create a map of the environment and localize the robot. The robot has a torso which is lift-able by 40 cm. In case of the toilet cleaning task during the World Robot Summit competition this was a benefit for the use of the sponge-end effector. We could reach the toilet seat with a top-down end-effector pose, but also the ground of the toilet. The 7-DOF arm was used for cleaning the toilet seat, picking up the paper pieces and cleaning the floor of the toilet. The head has a 2-DOF and holds an Orbbec ASTRA RGB-D camera which was used for the segmentation of the toilet seat and the detection of the trash on the floor. Further, we used a Lenovo P50 workstation notebook equipped with Intel i7-6700HQ CPU, 16 GB memory and a 2 GB Quadro M1000 GPU and mounted it on the back of TIAGo. A NVIDIA Jetson TX2 was used to compensate for the low graphical memory available on TIAGO's notebook in order to run multiple models in parallel. The robot setup is depicted in Fig. 2.

## 4    Approaches

This section briefly introduces our approaches. The applied software architecture has been described previously [1–3].

**Object Recognition.** This year we used Mask-RCNN [4] in combination with a custom augmentation approach as a segmentation method for images. The segmented images with the labels are augmented in image space among different backgrounds of the arena. In the background images we ensured that no relevant objects are visible. The use of background images decreases also the false positive detections. This segmentation method is beneficial for more precise manipulation

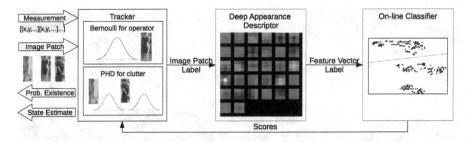

**Fig. 4.** Tracking Overview. We employ a RFS Bernoulli single target tracker in combination with a deep appearance descriptor to re-identify and online classify the appearance of the tracked identity. Measurements, consisting of positional information and an additional image patch serve as input. The Bernoulli tracker estimates the existence probability and the likelihood of the measurement being the operator. Positive against negative appearances are continuously trained. The online classifier returns scores of the patch being the operator.

tasks i.e. for cutlery objects which are not segmentable in the depth images as the height differences are below the separable threshold. As the segmentation method is computationally expensive we calculate the mask proposals on single images only. A faster approach that yields object masks with high frequency is desirable as future work to allow closed loop manipulation. An exemplary segmentation image is shown in Fig. 3. In total 344 images containing containing multiple objects where labeled.

**Speech Recognition.** For speech recognition we use a grammar based solution supported by an academic license for the VoCon speech recognition software by Nuance[1]. We combine continuous listening with begin and end-of-speech with the integrated detection to get good results even for complex commands. Recognition results below a certain threshold are rejected. The grammar generation is supported by the content of a semantic knowledge base that is also used for our general purpose architecture.

**Operator Following.** We developed an integrated system to detect and track a single operator that can switch *off* and *on* when it leaves and (re-)enters the scene [5]. Our method is based on a set-valued Bayes-optimal state estimator that integrates RGB-D detections and image-based classification to improve tracking results in severe clutter and under long-term occlusion. The classifier is trained in two stages. First, we train a deep convolutional neural network to obtain a feature representation for person re-identification. Then, we bootstrap an online classifier that discriminates the operator from remaining people on the output of the state-estimator (Fig. 4). The approach is applicable for following and guiding tasks.

---

[1]    http://www.nuance.com/for-business/speech-recognition-solutions/vocon-hybrid/index.htm.

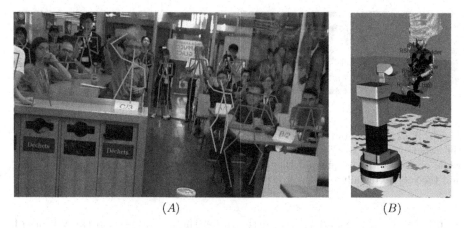

$(A)$ $(B)$

**Fig. 5.** Gesture recognition output: (A) extracted person poses in the *Restaurant* challenge at RoboCup@Home 2018 in Montreal, Canada: detected human poses are marked red, calling persons are highlighted green; (B) projection of the body keypoints into 3D space. (Color figure online)

**Person Detection.** For person detection we integrated multiple approaches for different sensors that can be optionally fused and used to verify measurements of other sensors. A leg detector [6] is applied on the laser data. This yields high frequency, but error prone measurements. For finding persons in point clouds we follow an approach by Munaro et al. [7]. The most reliable detections are by a face detection approach [8], assuming that the persons are facing the camera. For gender estimation we then apply an approach by Levi et al. [9].

**Gesture Recognition.** In this section, we describe the gesture recognition approach as used during RoboCup@Home 2018 in Montreal, Canada. This method differs from our model based approach as presented in [10]. Therefore we give a more detailed description of our approach here. Gesture recognition, and in particular the waving gesture detection, is one of the features that are tested in many RoboCup challenges such as in *Restaurant*, *GPSR* and *EEGPSR*. Human pose features are extracted by Convolutional Pose Machines (CPM) [11] with pre-trained COCO-model from a RGB-image. The extracted features result in the set $F$ with 18 possible body parts represented in the pixel space. We denote the joint keypoint as $\boldsymbol{f}_i \in F$ where:

$$\boldsymbol{f}_i = \begin{bmatrix} x_i \\ y_i \end{bmatrix}, \tag{1}$$

and $i \in \{0, ..., 17\}$. Moreover, we define a vector connecting $i_{th}$ and $j_{th}$ body parts as follow:

$$\boldsymbol{v}_{i,j} = \begin{bmatrix} x_i - y_j \\ y_i - y_j \end{bmatrix}, \tag{2}$$

(A)          (B)          (C)          (E)

**Fig. 6.** Illustration of our effort gripping approach: (A) is the starting position. In (B) the robot prepared to grasp. (C) the arm is moved over the object and downwards while observing the torque and then stopped to grasp. In (D) the arm is lifted again and the success or failure of the grasping is verified.

with $i, j \in \{0, ..., 17\}$ and $j \neq i$. Furthermore, the angle between the vectors of two body parts is calculated exploiting the following formula:

$$a(\boldsymbol{v}_{i,j}, \boldsymbol{v}_{l,j}) = \arccos(\frac{\boldsymbol{v}_{i,j} \bullet \boldsymbol{v}_{l,j}}{||\boldsymbol{v}_{i,j}|| \cdot ||\boldsymbol{v}_{l,j}||}), \tag{3}$$

where $i, j, l \in \{0, ..., 17\}$ and $j \neq i \neq l$. Finally, the given pose is classified as the waving gesture considering angles between particular body parts defined by COCO pose format: *hand-elbow* with connecting vectors $\boldsymbol{v}_{4,3}$ for the right arm and $\boldsymbol{v}_{7,6}$ for the left arm and *elbow-shoulder* with the connecting vector $\boldsymbol{v}_{5,6}$. The angles between *hand-elbow* and *elbow-nose* with connecting vectors $\boldsymbol{v}_{0,3}$ for the right arm and $\boldsymbol{v}_{0,6}$ for the left arm are examined by utilizing Eq. 3 in the following function:

$$call() = \begin{cases} 1, & \text{if } 0 < a(\boldsymbol{v}_{4,3}, \boldsymbol{v}_{0,3}) \leq \theta \wedge 0 < a(\boldsymbol{v}_{4,3}, \boldsymbol{v}_{2,3}) \leq \theta \\ 1, & \text{if } 0 < a(\boldsymbol{v}_{7,6}, \boldsymbol{v}_{0,6}) \leq \theta \wedge 0 < a(\boldsymbol{v}_{7,6}, \boldsymbol{v}_{5,6}) \leq \theta \\ 0, & \text{otherwise.} \end{cases} \tag{4}$$

Based on conducted experiments we found that $\theta = 150$ works well for the *call()* function defined in Eq. 4. The result of the call detection is depicted in Fig. 5(A), where the waving gesture is highlighted in green. To estimate a final position of the gesticulating person we project the average over the body part position into map-coordinates.

The result of the projection is shown in Fig. 5 (B).

A video of this approach during the Restaurant task is available[2]. A model based approach [10] has been proposed later. Currently, we are also working on an extension of the gesture recognition approach to image sequences.

**Effort Gripping.** For gripping tiny objects that are hardly differentiable from the underlying surface in the depth image the estimation of a precise grasp pose is not possible. This is the case for i.e. cutlery or dishwasher tabs. We therefore propose an closed loop effort (in motor-current or force-torque) based

---

[2] Restaurant challenge video: https://www.youtube.com/watch?v=31Tmmhhqo_4.

**1) Observation**

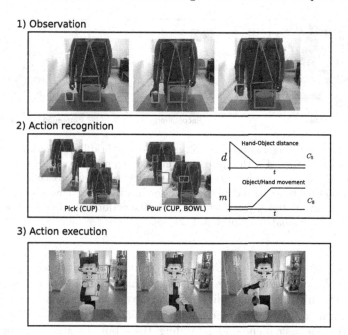

**2) Action recognition**

**3) Action execution**

**Fig. 7.** Approach overview for extracting action informations from 2D image sequences in order to execute them on a mobile robot. Exemplary object detections (yellow, pink) and human pose estimates (green) are observed. Actions are recognized using a set of constraints. For replicating the observed actions we used two mobile robots equipped with an arm. (Color figure online)

grasping approach. An object pose slightly above the object position and the end-effector facing downwards is defined as an initial arm pose. Then the joint efforts are continuously observed while the end-effector is moved downwards approaching the object with Cartesian movements until the joint effort peaks. Freely spoken this approach moves the end-effector downwards to the object until the underlying surface is touched. After the object grasping we observe the joint positions of the gripper in order to verify if the object was grasped successfully. A sequential overview is given in Fig. 6. This approach has proven to be beneficial for small objects multiple times during the challenge and can also be used for safely placing objects on detected surfaces. A video of this approach integrated in the *Dishwasher* scenario is available[3].

**Imitation Learning.** This year in the *Open Challenge* and in the *Finals* we presented a novel approach for imitating human behavior based on visual information of a RGB camera. The human hand and objects are continuously detected. We proposed a visual approach for Imitation Learning [12]. This approach was

---

[3] Effort based gripping approach as used for the Dishwasher challenge: https://www.youtube.com/watch?v=luSMEtMoX7w.

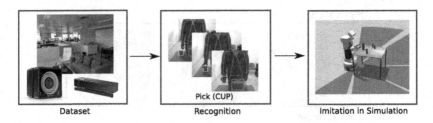

**Fig. 8.** Overview: this figure gives an overview of our hybrid benchmarking model. We provide a dataset recorded with a RGB-D camera and a motion capturing system. The sequences of the dataset are supposed to be interpreted by approaches for imitation learning, which then have to execute the imitation in a simulated environment grounded by the ground truth initial object positions. After the performance in simulation, results are automatically evaluated by provided scripts.

presented during the 2018 RoboCup@Home *Finals* in Montreal. Current robotic systems that lack a certain desired behavior commonly need an expert programmer to add the missing functionality. Contrary, we introduce an approach related to programming robots by visual demonstration that can be applied by common users. Provided a basic scene understanding, the robot observes a person demonstrating a task and is then able to reproduce the observed action sequence using its semantic knowledge base. We presented an approach for markerless action recognition based on Convolutional Pose Machines (CPM) [13], object observations [14] and continuous spatial relations. The actions are executable on a robot that is able to execute a set of common actions. The initial scene analysis allows semantic reasoning in case the required object is not present. Further, this allows executing the same action sequence with different objects which is a major benefit over action sequencing approaches that rely on positional data only. Even though we are demonstrating our approach on 2D observations, the formulations are also adaptable for 3D. Figure 7 gives an overview of our approach. More information is available on our project page[4].

## 5   Current Research

The current focus of research is on Imitation Learning. The previously described visual imitation learning approach is based on spatial relations between the demonstrator and objects and uses a mapping between recognized actions and robot actions. Additionally, we focus on research in benchmarking Imitation Learning and bootstrap actions by observation. Further, we introduce our research activities in point cloud based object recognition methods.

---

[4] Imitation Learning project page: https://userpages.uni-koblenz.de/~raphael/project/imitation_learning/.

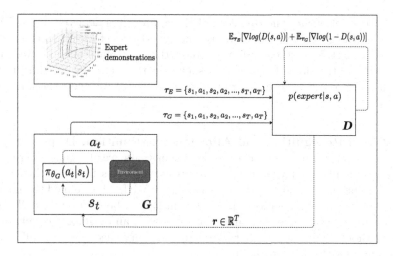

**Fig. 9.** Diagram of the Generative Adversarial Imitation approach for learning robotics tasks from the expert demonstrations. Two neural networks, the Discriminator network $D$ and the Generator network $G$, are trained resulting in an optimal policy $\pi_\theta(a|s)$. $D$ uses the expert trajectories $\tau_E$ for the training to distinguish the expert trajectories from the trajectories $\tau_G$ produced by the policy. $D$ outputs the reward vector $r$ which is used to optimize the policy in the inner loop.

**Imitation Learning Benchmark.** Currently, there is a lack of datasets for Imitation Learning through human observation. We created a benchmark called *Simitate* where we recorded a dataset using a commonly available RGB-D camera calibrated against a motion capturing system. Data was recorded in a domestic real world testbed as used for the European Robotics League. Different people performed daily activities like performing movements with their hand, picking, placing, stacking or moving objects. For the demonstrator's hand and the interacting objects ground truth poses are recorded with the motion capturing system. As ground truth positions of the objects and hand are available we can spawn them into a simulated representation of the environment where simulated robots should imitate the demonstrations. We suggest metrics for effect and trajectory level imitations. The approach is visualized in Fig. 8 and more information can be found on the project page[5].

**General Adversarial Imitation Learning.** Generative Adversarial Imitation Learning (GAIL) was recently proposed by Ho and Ermon [15] as an approach to teach a robot to accomplish the given task using expert demonstrations. In our work we leverage from GAIL and regard the robotic manipulation problem as a sequential decision making task where the robot follows a stochastic parametrized policy $\pi_\theta(a|s)$ that maps observed state $s$ to a distribution over

---

[5] Simitate Imitation Learning project page: https://agas.uni-koblenz.de/data/simitate/.

manipulation actions $a$. The overview of the approach is depicted in the Fig. 9. For training the generative model we use the expert trajectories from the dataset described in Sect. 5. Furthermore, we exploit the Proximal Policy Optimization method [16] in the inner loop as it is shown in the Fig. 9 by utilizing reward vector $r \in R^T$ given by the Discriminator in order to estimate the advantage function.

**Point Cloud Recognition and Affordance Estimation.** Despite the great success of deep learning approaches in the recent years, we also continue research on some classic methods. Classic methods are especially useful if only little training data or computational resources are available. We further refined the nearest-neighbor point cloud recognition presented in [17] to be computationally more efficient and achieve higher classification rates with an optimized codebook filtering method[6]. This approach will be further combined with an affordance estimation algorithm [18] in the future.

## 6   Summary

RoboCup@Home is a robot competition where domestic robots compete in daily tasks. For this year we used two robots, a custom build robot called Lisa and a PAL Robotics TIAGo. We briefly described our approaches and presented our research focus. Novel approaches for gesture recognition, effort based gripping and visual imitation learning where successfully presented in this year's competition. In the finals we further demonstrated that the acquired knowledge by one observing robot is reusable by other robots with a common set of functionalities.

**Acknowledgement.** First we want to thank the participating students Niklas Yann Wettengel, Tobias Evers, Lukas Buchhold, Thies Möhlenhof, Lukas Debald and Anatoli Eckert. A major thanks is given to PAL Robotics SL which supported us with the free loan of a TIAGo robot and further supported us in organizing the shipping to Montreal. Thanks to Nuance Communications Inc. for supporting the team with an academic license for speech recognition. Further, we want to thank NVIDIA for the grant of a graphics card that has been used for training the operator re-identification and the object segmentation.

## References

1. Memmesheimer, R., Seib, V., Paulus, D.: homer@UniKoblenz: winning team of the RoboCup@Home open platform league 2017. In: Akiyama, H., Obst, O., Sammut, C., Tonidandel, F. (eds.) RoboCup 2017. LNCS (LNAI), vol. 11175, pp. 509–520. Springer, Cham (2018). https://doi.org/10.1007/978-3-030-00308-1_42
2. Memmesheimer, R., et al.: Robocup: homer@unikoblenz (germany). Fachbereich Informatik. Technical report 4/2018 (2018)

---

[6] Detailed description and code on https://github.com/vseib/PointCloudDonkey.

3. Seib, V., Memmesheimer, R., Paulus, D.: A ROS-based system for an autonomous service robot. In: Koubaa, A. (ed.) Robot Operating System (ROS). SCI, vol. 625, pp. 215–252. Springer, Cham (2016). https://doi.org/10.1007/978-3-319-26054-9_9

4. He, K., Gkioxari, G., Dollár, P., Girshick, R.: Mask R-CNN. In: 2017 IEEE International Conference on Computer Vision (ICCV), pp. 2980–2988. IEEE (2017)

5. Wojke, N., Memmesheimer, R., Paulus, D.: Joint operator detection and tracking for person following from mobile platforms. In: 2017 20th International Conference on Information Fusion (Fusion), pp. 1–8, July 2017

6. Lu, D.V., Smart, W.D.: Towards more efficient navigation for robots and humans. In: IEEE/RSJ International Conference On Intelligent Robots and Systems (IROS), pp. 1707–1713. IEEE (2013)

7. Munaro, M., Menegatti, E.: Fast RGB-D people tracking for service robots. Auton. Robots **37**(3), 227–242 (2014)

8. Zhang, K., Zhang, Z., Li, Z., Qiao, Y.: Joint face detection and alignment using multitask cascaded convolutional networks. IEEE Signal Process. Lett. **23**(10), 1499–1503 (2016)

9. Levi, G., Hassner, T.: Emotion recognition in the wild via convolutional neural networks and mapped binary patterns. In: Proceedings of the 2015 ACM on International Conference on Multimodal Interaction, pp. 503–510. ACM (2015)

10. Memmesheimer, R., Mykhalchyshyna, I., Paulus, D.: Gesture recognition on human pose features of single images. In: 2018 9th International Conference on Intelligent Systems (IS), pp. 1–7. IEEE (2018)

11. Wei, S.-E., Ramakrishna, V., Kanade, T., Sheikh, Y.: Convolutional pose machines. In: Proceedings of the IEEE Conference on Computer Vision and Pattern Recognition, pp. 4724–4732 (2016)

12. Memmesheimer, R., Mykhalchyshyna, I., Seib, V., Theisen, N., Paulus, D.: Markerless visual robot programming by demonstration. CoRR, vol. abs/1807.11541 (2018). http://arxiv.org/abs/1807.11541

13. Wei, S., Ramakrishna, V., Kanade, T., Sheikh, Y.: Convolutional pose machines. CoRR, vol. abs/1602.00134 (2016). http://arxiv.org/abs/1602.00134

14. Redmon, J., Divvala, S., Girshick, R., Farhadi, A.: You only look once: unified, real-time object detection. In: Proceedings of the IEEE Conference on Computer Vision and Pattern Recognition, pp. 779–788 (2016)

15. Ho, J., Ermon, S.: Generative adversarial imitation learning. In: Advances in Neural Information Processing Systems, pp. 4565–4573 (2016)

16. Schulman, J., Wolski, F., Dhariwal, P., Radford, A., Klimov, O.: Proximal policy optimization algorithms.' arXiv preprint arXiv:1707.06347 (2017)

17. Seib, V., Link, N., Paulus, D.: Pose estimation and shape retrieval with hough voting in a continuous voting space. In: Gall, J., Gehler, P., Leibe, B. (eds.) GCPR 2015. LNCS, vol. 9358, pp. 458–469. Springer, Cham (2015). https://doi.org/10.1007/978-3-319-24947-6_38

18. Seib, V., Knauf, M., Paulus, D.: Affordance origami: unfolding agent models for hierarchical affordance prediction. In: Braz, J., et al. (eds.) VISIGRAPP 2016. CCIS, vol. 693, pp. 555–574. Springer, Cham (2017). https://doi.org/10.1007/978-3-319-64870-5_27

# ToBI - Team of Bielefeld Enhancing the Robot Capabilities of the Social Standard Platform Pepper

Florian Lier, Johannes Kummert, Patrick Renner, and Sven Wachsmuth[✉]

Exzellenzcluster Cognitive Interaction Technology (CITEC),
Bielefeld University, Inspiration 1, 33615 Bielefeld, Germany
swachsmu@techfak.uni-bielefeld.de
http://www.cit-ec.de/de/ToBI

**Abstract.** In this paper, we describe the joint effort of the Team of Bielefeld (ToBI) winning the RoboCup@Home Social Standard Platform League (@Home SSPL) at the world cup in Montreal 2018. The @Home competition consists of benchmarking tests that cover multiple skills required for service robotics and human-robot interaction in domestic environments. The @Home SSPL is one of three different sub leagues – two of those focus on specific standard platforms, the third allows open platforms. In the SSPL the standard platform is the Pepper robot by Softbank. In this contribution, we present our approach and the design decisions for enhancing the standard platform Pepper for the competition. This includes the development and testing environment, the preparation process, the integrated software system as well as the components providing enhanced skills for the robot. We further describe the ideas and techniques used to extend the human-robot interaction by a mixed-reality interface and a first approach to bimanual grasping. Both was presented in the final demonstration of the competition.

## 1 Introduction

The RoboCup@Home competition [1] aims at bringing robotic platforms to use in realistic domestic environments. In contrast to other leagues like soccer, which predefine and standardize the field, robots in the @Home league need to deal with different apartment layouts, changing decorations, unknown sites, unstructured public spaces, as well as cooperating or interfering humans. Human operators are not at all – or only very briefly – instructed how to interact with the robot. Thus, the design and robustness of human-robot interaction is one of the key challenges for the RoboCup@Home competition – and especially for the Social Standard Platform League. In this paper, we treat this issue on different levels. On the level of capabilities, we extend the Pepper platform by using alternative speech recognition, person recognition, and person tracking components to

This work has been supported by the DFG Excellencecluster Cognitive Interaction Technology (EXC277).

D. Holz et al. (Eds.): RoboCup 2018, LNAI 11374, pp. 524–535, 2019.
https://doi.org/10.1007/978-3-030-27544-0_43

improve robustness. On the level of system integration, we use a flexible framework that allows to integrate software components developed in different ecosystems as well as to easily configure and use on-board and off-board computation. On the level of the interaction interface (Open Challenge and Final), we offer an intuitive Augmented Reality device that allows a more transparent inspection of the state of the robot for the user, its integration as an extended sensor device for the robot as well as a human teach-in for the configuration of new scenarios.

The RoboCup@Home competition consists of a set of benchmarking tasks that are adapted or newly defined each year. These typically require multiple capabilities, like navigation and mapping, person recognition and tracking, speech understanding and simple dialogues, object recognition and manipulation. The competition is organized into different stages. Within the first stage, tests focus on a small set of capabilities (e.g. person following and guiding or object recognition and manipulation) scoring the best two tries out of three. The stage is finalized by an integration challenge (GPSR – General Purpose Service Robot) where robots have no predefined task, but need to autonomously sequence a task given by speech. The best 50% of the teams proceed to the second stage. Here, robots are tested in an enhanced and longer version of GPSR (EE-GPSR), in a real restaurant as a waiter, and in an individual open performance (Open Challenge). The final is an extended open challenge that is judged by an internal and external jury. The Team of Bielefeld (ToBI) was founded in 2009 and successfully participated in the RoboCup German Open as well as the RoboCup World Cup from 2009 to 2018 with different robotic platforms. In 2016, the team ended first in the Open Platform League (OPL) [2]. At RoboCup 2017, the team achieved the third place in the OPL competition and the seventh place in the Social Standard Platform League (SSPL). Finally, the team achieved the SSPL world champion award at RoboCup 2018. Thus, our overall approach as been successfully ported to the Pepper platform which has to deal with (i) limited processing capacities on the platform and the low bandwith of the wireless connection to external computing resources, (ii) limited sensor capabilities, e.g., low range and low resolution in space and time of the ultrasonic and laser sensors, (iii) its own ecosystem (NaoQi) which needs to be integrated with other ROS-based components. In the following sections, we will describe our approach to establish an improved development environment for the Pepper robot that allows to support the RoboCup activities as well as the more general research agenda on human-robot interaction.

Bielefeld University is involved in research on human-robot interaction for more than 20 years especially gaining experience in experimental studies with integrated robotic systems [3]. Within this research, strategies are utilized for guiding the focus of attention of human visitors in a museum's context [4]. Further strategies are explored in a project that combines service robots with smart environments [5], e.g. the management of the robot's attention in a multi-user dialogue [6]. A critical property for any human-robot interaction experiment is the reproducibility of the robotic system and its performance evaluation during its incremental development progress. However, this is rarely achieved [7].

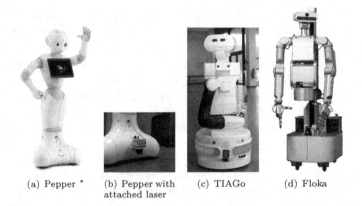

(a) Pepper *       (b) Pepper with       (c) TIAGo       (d) Floka
                   attached laser

**Fig. 1.** Robotic platforms of ToBI. Pepper is 120 cm tall, the overall height of TIAGo is adjustable ≈110 cm–145 cm as well as the Floka platform ≈160 cm–200 cm. (* http://innoventionsblog.blogspot.de/2014/06/meet-pepper-first-personal-robot-who.html)

This applies to experimentation in robotics as well as to RoboCup. A Technical Description Paper (e.g. [8]) – as typically submitted to RoboCup competitions – is by far not sufficient to describe or even reproduce a robotic system with all its artifacts. The introduction of a systematic approach towards reproducible robotic experiments [9] has been turned out as a key factor to maximally stabilize basic capabilities like, e.g., navigation or person following. Together with appropriate simulation engines [10] it paves the way to an automated testing of complete RoboCup@Home tasks.

## 2    Robot Platforms and System Description

During the last years, the RoboCup@Home and related research activities at Bielefeld University utilized different robotic platforms. In 2016, ToBI participated with the two service robots Biron and Floka [2], in 2017 with Biron and Pepper, in 2018 with Pepper. Current research also aims at the TIAGo platform. Figure 1 gives an overview of the three platforms (Pepper, TIAGo, Floka) which are still in the focus of current research activities. Although focusing on the Pepper in this paper, we still aim at the development of platform independent as well as multi-platform robot capabilities. **The Social Standard Platform Pepper** (cf. Fig. 1(a)) has been newly introduced to the RoboCup@Home competition in 2017. It features an omni-directional base, two ultrasonic and six laser sensors. Together with three obstacle detectors in his legs, these provide him with navigation and obstacle avoidance capabilities. Two RGB cameras, one 3D camera, and four directional microphones are placed in his head. It further possesses tactile sensors in his hands for social interaction. A tablet is mounted at the frontal body and allows the user to make choices or to visualize the internal state of the robot. In our setup we use an additional laptop as an external

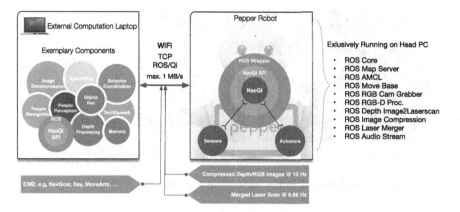

**Fig. 2.** System architecture for the Pepper platform. The software components are partially deployed on an external computing resource. The architecture abstracts from communication protocols and computing ecosystems. Thus, ROS as well as NAOqi processing components can be used on the external computer as well as onboard the robot. Images are streamed in a compressed format in order to meet online processing requirements.

computing resource which is connected to the on-board computer of the Pepper via Wi-Fi. Because the on-board laser is quite short range, we developed a hardware mounting for an external laser sensor (Fig. 1(b)) that can be easily attached or removed. Thereby, the Pepper is enabled to build precise maps of the environment that can be used during competition for navigating with the limited on-board laser sensors. In our research, all three robot platforms are run with the same framework but slightly different robot skill implementations. This allows a transfer of robot behaviors between platforms on an abstract level.

*System Architecture:* Our service robots employ distributed systems with multiple clients sharing information over network. On these clients there are numerous software components written in different programming languages. Such heterogeneous systems require abstraction on several levels. Figure 2 depicts a simplified overview of the system architecture used for the Pepper robot including an external processing resource—a single high performance laptop. In our architecture, the NAOqi framework still encapsulates hardware access to the robot, but we additionally managed to run ROS on the head PC[1] of the Pepper. Our installation includes the entire ROS navigation stack and the depth processing pipeline[2] for instance. This allows a further abstraction across different ecosystems and seamless integration. Software components from both worlds, NAOqi and ROS, can be flexibly deployed onboard or offboard the robot. Skills in the same ecosystem can communicate using ROS or native Qi messages, those in different ecosystems communicate through a ROS wrapper.

---

[1] Intel Atom, 32Bit Gentoo Linux, outdated and streamlined release.
[2] http://wiki.ros.org/depth_image_proc.

(a) MORSE simulation for Pepper          (b) Modeling HRI in MORSE

**Fig. 3.** Simulation of RoboCup@Home tasks for Pepper in MORSE.

The computational resources on the robot's head PC are limited. Thus, only components that are time-critical, e.g. for safe and robust autonomous navigation, are deployed on the head PC, while other skills, like people perception, speech recognition, semantic scene analysis and behavior coordination, are running on the external laptop. In order to meet online processing requirements in certain robot behaviors, e.g. person following, depth and color images are streamed in a compressed format achieving frame rates of approximately 10 Hz.

The robot behavior is coordinated using hierarchical state machines. The hierarchical structure consists of re-usable building blocks that refer to abstract sensors and actors, skills, and complete task behaviors. A typical abstract sensor would be a people detector, while a typical skill would be *person following* that already deals with certain interferences or robot failures like briefly loosing and, then, re-establishing a human operator. As far as possible, we re-use robot skills that already have been used on previous RoboCup@Home or related research systems [2], like Floka or TIAGo. However, this has certain limits if, e.g., a skill *person following* is based on dense, longer-range, high-frequency laser scans. The laser scans of the Pepper platform only achieve a frame rate of 6.66 Hz with a very low resolution and reliable range. Therefore, we already merged the LIDAR with depth information from the camera located in the head of the robot. However, this requires that the robot looks down rather than looking up watching for people. Thus, this conflicts with other robot behaviors introducing new dependencies in the skill and behavior design of the robot. Abstracting skills from task behaviors still leads to a description of task-level state machines that are agnostic with regard to such considerations. The explicit definition of skills further allows to reason about them and track their success during the performance of the robot. Based on this, new elements had been introduced during the last years, like reporting on success and failure of tasks assigned to the robot in GSPR [2].

*Development, Testing, and HRI Simulation:* The continuous as well as incremental software development process is based on the *Cognitive Interaction Toolkit* (CITK) [9]. It provides a framework that allows to describe, deploy, and test systems independent of the underlying ecosystem. Thus, the concepts apply

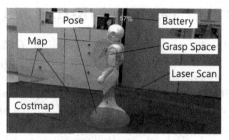

(a) HRI using the HoloLens                     (b) Augmenting the operator's view

**Fig. 4.** Enhanced capabilities of the Pepper system: mixed-reality HRI

for ROS-based components and systems as well as for those defined with, e.g., NAOqi. Combined with an appropriate abstraction architecture, a re-usability of components and behaviors can be achieved across platforms. The CITK framework has already been applied to the Nao platform[3] as well as previous RoboCup systems including the Pepper platform in 2017 and 2018. For the RoboCup@Home SSPL competition we further work on enhancing our simulation approach that allows to easily switch between the real hardware and a simulated environment including virtual sensors and actors. In order to keep our cross-platform approach, we utilized the MORSE Simulation framework [11] that additionally offers extended possibilities for modeling virtual human agents for testing human-robot interaction scenarios [10].

The software dependencies—from operating system dependencies to inter-component relations—are completely modeled in the description of a *system distribution* which consists of a collection of so called *recipes* [9]. In order to foster reproducibility/traceability and potential software (component) re-use of the ToBI system, we provide a full specification of the 2016 system in our online catalog platform[4]. The catalog provides detailed information about the soft- and hardware system including all utilized software components, as well as the facility to execute live system tests and experiments remotely[5]. The MORSE simulation environment [11] allows to conduct human-robot interaction experiments and provides virtual sensors for the cameras and laser-range sensors (see Fig. 3(a)). The virtual image streams and laser scans are published on the equivalent ROS topics which are used by the real sensors. In Lier et al. [10], we show how to utilize this framework for an automated testing of a virtual human agent interfering with the navigation path of a robot (see Fig. 3(b)).

---

[3] https://toolkit.cit-ec.uni-bielefeld.de/systems/versions/nao-minimal-nightly.

[4] https://toolkit.cit-ec.uni-bielefeld.de/systems/versions/robocup-champion-2016-2016-champion.

[5] In order to gain access to our remote experiment execution infrastructure please contact the authors.

## 3    Research on MR-HRI and Bimanual Handovers

*Facilitating HRI by Mixed-Reality Techniques:* Further research is conducted with the Pepper platform in order to explore how human-robot interaction can be facilitated by mixed-reality techniques (Fig. 4) [12,13]. Augmented and Mixed Reality techniques are already applied in various areas of robotics development and debugging [14–17]. Apart from tele-operators and developers, everyday HRI can also be enhanced using AR/MR techniques by displaying virtual avatars on physical robots [18], creating spatial dialogues [19], augmenting a work cell of a industrial robot arm [20] or by communicating intended movements [21]. In our ongoing work, we pick up these ideas but add a novel approach which we suppose to be even more helpful for a human user. Our aim is to not only use a MR headset for visualizing data, but to also integrate its sensor data, giving the user a more direct interface to the robot. This way, on the one hand the user can always be aware of the current robot status and intent. On the other hand, the robot can integrate the human's location in the environment as well as data of the MR headset from, e.g., RGB-D sensors. Moreover, voice instructions can be given remotely, even when the robot is located in another room. For implementing such a scenario, we integrated the Microsoft HoloLens into our robotic framework based on ROS [22]. The Unity3D game engine was used for implementation on the HoloLens. Communication between the MR device and ROS was realized using MQTT. Making use of the room-scale tracking capabilities of the HoloLens, we only initially had to calibrate the coordinate system of the robot and the MR device. This was done by displaying an AR marker on the tablet attached to Pepper. After this marker is detected once, the robot is correctly represented in the coordinate system of the HoloLens and vice versa. Pose updates of the robot are used to also update the representation in the HoloLens. To facilitate interactions with the robot, we use AR in two different ways: like done in previous work, sensor data are visualized to a get a better grasp of the robot's capabilities. Here, we show the map and the robot's localization on it, the costmap and laser scans for giving sensory information. The planned path is shown for making the user aware of the next movements (Fig. 4(b)). Thus, the user is able to understand the reason for e.g. the robot not being able to reach its current navigation goal. This will also help the human to take the correct path, not interfering with the path of the robot. For grasping, the robot can visualize its grasp space when it is not able to reach to an object. This way, the robot can actively ask the user for help, committing information which otherwise would not be obvious. Secondly, since the HoloLens is integrated with the robot's coordinate system, it can be used as an additional sensory and input device. In our example case, by this means the robot gains knowledge about the user's position and orientation in the environment. Wherever the user goes, she can instruct the robot to come and fulfill a task by a voice command interpreted by the AR device. The user's view using the Microsoft HoloLens can be seen in Fig. 4(a). In the RoboCup Open Challenge and Final, we successfully realized a mixed-reality HRI application scenario simulating the business case of a robotic version of Airbnb. In a first run, the owner of an apartment teaches the robot

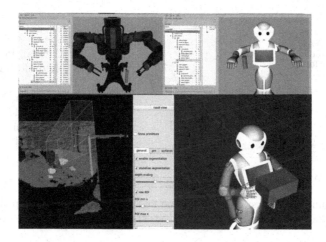

**Fig. 5.** Enhanced capabilties of the Pepper system: bimanual handover

a sequence of behaviors for a procedure for welcoming and introducing a guest. Therefore, she or he uses the HoloLens to teach in places: using the localization of the HoloLens, the owner just walks through the apartment wearing the AR device and remotely instructs the robot what to say at which place in the apartment. After that, when the guest arrives the robot takes the initiative, identifies the guest based on face identification, and proceeds the tour though the apartment in a guiding mode telling the guest the taught-in information about each room. At the kitchen counter the robot is further instructed to check if any drinks are missing. Any feedback information is communicated to the owner's mobile device without the owner being required to be present at the site.

*Bimanual Object Handovers:* Although the Pepper robot is not made for grasping, delivery tasks are a typical use case that is expected from a service robot at home. Regular strategies for grasping do not apply because the Pepper hand is under-actuated offering only a closing or opening, the hand is too small to grasp typical household objects, the large backlash of the arms' gears results in an imprecise control, and finally the depth camera in the head provides no valid 3D data at grasping distance. For the RoboCup@Home competition, we explored two different strategies for compensating the deficiencies of the platform. First, we implemented an interactive strategy for an open loop handover of a customized tray. Here the operator triggers the robot by speech to get into a predefined handover pose. Then the robot takes over and instructs the operator to hang one side of the tray into the right hand and touch the back of the hand. Then, the robot moves the left hand to its final position while the operator hands in the other side of the tray. Finally, the robot closes both hands to hold the tray in front of the robot. This strategy has been successfully used in the restaurant task to carry the drinks and combos from the bar to the guests. In the Final, we further showed an enhanced strategy for an autonomous bimanual

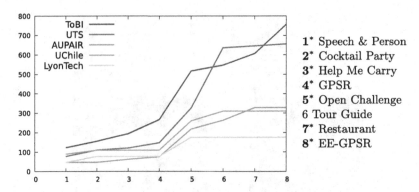

1* Speech & Person
2* Cocktail Party
3* Help Me Carry
4* GPSR
5* Open Challenge
6 Tour Guide
7* Restaurant
8* EE-GPSR

**Fig. 6.** Accumulated scores from the 1st and 2nd stage tests in RoboCup@Home. The numbers on the x-axis refer to tests, the $X^*$-**tests** have been won by the ToBI-Team.

handover strategy. Here, the robot perceives a 3D box presented to the robot, computes appropriate grasping points for both arms, and, plans a synchronized bimanual movement to grasp it. First, the box is segmented using a model-free segmentation algorithm on the depth images [23] combined with a fitting of box- or cylinder-shaped primitives. This step is computed on a larger distance than grasp distance because of the limitations of the depth camera. Figure 5 illustrates the grasping process. As shown in the upper part the manipulation strategy is robot agnostic. It applies the Task Constructor framework of MoveIt! [24]. Here, sub-tasks are defined in *stages* which model atomic movement planning problems. A *generator stage* was used to build a bi-manual grasp generator. The initially generated grasp consists of two poses, one for each end-effector. These are sampled on the object's surface considering that both end-effectors apply enough force on the object between them to hold it. As the Pepper arms only have 5-DoF for computing a 6D-pose, the KDL inverse kinematics solver was patched to deal with low precision requirements in one rotational DoF. The trajectories of each arm where independently generated and then synchronized in a *merging container* combining both into a single trajectory. First successful handovers where shown at the RoboCup 2018 finals.

## 4    Analysis, Lessons Learned and Conclusion

During the RoboCup@Home competition the Pepper robot of our team achieved significant scores in all tests of the competition. In Fig. 6, the results of the 5 best teams of RoboCup@Home SSPL 2018 are shown for the stage-1 and -2 tests. ToBI achieved best performances in the Speech & Person Recognition, Cocktail Party, Help Me Carry, GPSR, Open Challenge, Restaurant, and EE-GPSR tests. For most of the required capabilities, the onboard Pepper components have been exchanged by other available standard libraries that were integrated using the hybrid architecture presented before. The key components (navigation, speech processing, basic person detection) were deployed on the on-board computer so that the team was not severely affected by WLAN dropouts.

The navigation component – we used ROS Gmapping and the standard ROS planning pipeline – robustly worked with the laser and camera depth data which were fused in a preprocessing step. There was only a single dropout in the Tour Guide task, where the robot blocked itself because of a failure in the setup procedure. For speech processing, we used PocketSphinx with context specific grammars that were adapted to each dialogue step. In most conditions this worked quite well. However, in cases where there was too much noise we offered an additional user interface on the Pepper's touchpad where the robot's question and the options for the user's answer were displayed by buttons or menus.

For development and testing, we exploited the dedicated toolchain for reproducible experimentation in robotics described in Sect. 2 [9,25]. In the Cognitive Interaction Toolkit (CITK), there is a versioned description of any – incrementally developed – system distribution including all software and data dependencies which is automatically built on a continuous integration (CI) server. This allowed to track down any system change that might have caused an error or repaired it. Another important aspect is to design robot behaviors for the complete competition and not only for a single test. For example, furniture or persons sometimes blocked navigation goals in the apartment; thus, the robot needed to deal with these situations all the time – not only when mentioned in the rulebook. A general behavior for memorizing and reporting about these events even achieved additional points for the team in the EE-GPSR test. The reasoning about task performances will be a critical capability for future RoboCup@Home developments. The mixed-reality scenario implemented for the Open Challenge and Final has been ranked first by the league internal and external juries. This shows the general interest in possible application scenarios for a standard platform like Pepper.

## 5   Conclusion

We have described the main features of the architecture and technical solution of the ToBI system for the RoboCup@Home Social Platform League (SSPL). There have been several key points that were essential for winning the SSPL competition in Montreal 2018: (i) heterogeneous computing environments: We proposed a general approach – the Cognitive Interaction Toolkit – that allows us to deal with distributed computing and different ecosystems in a unified manner. This allowed us to integrate ROS-based components, on-board NaoQi-skills, and even external sensor devices like HoloLens (with communication based on MQTT) in a systematic, easy to use building process. This is also essential for keeping a vivid exchange to the other sub-leagues, which systems are mainly based on ROS. (ii) Graceful degradation: Even if Wi-Fi breaks down or it is too noisy to recognize speech, the platform must continue to work. This has been realized, e.g., by installing essential components directly on the robot head, or by offering a *continue rule* interface on the robot's touchpad. We further introduced several ways of augmentation of the platform by adding an external laser for mapping, by using a tray for transportation, or by connecting a HoloLens for an extended human-robot interaction. This opens new ways to keep the Pepper platform competitive also to open robot platforms, which is important to develop all sub-leagues towards common goals. (iii) Modular behaviors that are applicable when ever needed, in contrast to programming fixed behavior sequences for pre-defined tasks: An example is the reporting capability of the robot about what went wrong. Such an approach opens up further possibilities to interactively teach a robot appropriate behaviors, which was shown in the Airbnb-scenario in the RoboCup@Home SSPL Final. Overall, the SSPL league has made a larger performance step forward compared to last year, where significantly less scores were achieved. This makes us confident that there is still much potential for further developments, which will significantly profit from an intensified exchange between the RoboCup@Home leagues. We presented several avenues how to technically support this.

# References

1. Wachsmuth, S., Holz, D., Rudinac, M., Ruiz-del Solar, J.: RoboCup@Home - benchmarking domestic service robots. In: Proceedings of the Twenty-Ninth AAAI Conference on Artificial Intelligence, AAAI 2015, pp. 4328–4329. AAAI Press (2015)
2. Meyer zu Borgsen, S., Korthals, T., Lier, F., Wachsmuth, S.: ToBI – team of bielefeld: enhancing robot behaviors and the role of multi-robotics in RoboCup@Home. In: Behnke, S., Sheh, R., Sarıel, S., Lee, D.D. (eds.) RoboCup 2016. LNCS (LNAI), vol. 9776, pp. 577–588. Springer, Cham (2017). https://doi.org/10.1007/978-3-319-68792-6_48
3. Lohse, M., Siepmann, F., Wachsmuth, S.: A modeling framework for user-driven iterative design of autonomous systems. Int. J. Soc. Robot. 6(1), 121–139 (2014)
4. Pitsch, K., Wrede, S.: When a robot orients visitors to an exhibit. Referential practices and interactional dynamics in the real world. In: Ro-Man 2014, pp. 36–42 (2014)
5. Bernotat, J., et al.: Welcome to the future – how naïve users intuitively address an intelligent robotics apartment. In: Agah, A., Cabibihan, J.-J., Howard, A.M., Salichs, M.A., He, H. (eds.) ICSR 2016. LNCS (LNAI), vol. 9979, pp. 982–992. Springer, Cham (2016). https://doi.org/10.1007/978-3-319-47437-3_96
6. Richter, V., et al.: Are you talking to me? Improving the robustness of dialogue systems in a multi party HRI scenario by incorporating gaze direction and lip movement of attendees. In: Proceedings of the Fourth International Conference on Human-agent Interaction, ACM Digital Library (2016)
7. Amigoni, F., Reggiani, M., Schiaffonati, V.: An insightful comparison between experiments in mobile robotics and in science. Auton. Robots 27(4), 313–325 (2009)
8. Meyer zu Borgsen, S., Korthals, T., Wachsmuth, S.: ToBI-team of bielefeld the human-robot interaction system for RoboCup@Home 2016 (2016)
9. Lier, F., et al.: Towards automated system and experiment reproduction in robotics. In: Burgard, W., (ed.) 2016 IEEE/RSJ International Conference on Intelligent Robots and Systems (IROS). IEEE (2016)

10. Lier, F., Lütkebohle, I., Wachsmuth, S.: Towards automated execution and evaluation of simulated prototype HRI Experiments. In: HRI '14 Proceedings of the 2014 ACM/IEEE International Conferenceon Human-Robot Interaction, pp. 230–231. ACM (2014)

11. Lemaignan, S., Echeverria, G., Karg, M., Mainprice, J., Kirsch, A., Alami, R.: Human-robot interaction in the morse simulator. In: Proceedings of the Seventh Annual ACM/IEEE International Conference on Human-Robot Interaction, pp. 181–182. ACM (2012)

12. Renner, P., Lier, F., Friese, F., Pfeiffer, T., Wachsmuth, S.: Facilitating HRI by mixed reality techniques. In: HRI 2018 Companion: 2018 ACM/IEEE International Conference on Human-Robot Interaction Companion. ACM/IEEE (2018)

13. Meyer zu Borgsen, S., Renner, P., Lier, F., Pfeiffer, T., Wachsmuth, S.: Improving human-robot handover research by mixed reality techniques. In: VAM-HRI 2018 The Inaugural International Workshop on Virtual, Augmented and Mixed Reality for Human-Robot Interaction (2018)

14. Collett, H.T.J., Macdonald, B.A.: An augmented reality debugging system for mobile robot software engineers. J. Softw. Eng. Robot. 1(1), 18–32 (2010)

15. Kozlov, A.: Augmented reality technologies for the visualisation of SLAM systems. Ph.D. thesis (2012)

16. Nishiwaki, K., Kobayashi, K., Uchiyama, S., Yamamoto, H., Kagami, S.: Mixed reality environment for autonomous robot development. In: IEEE International Conference on Robotics and Automation, pp. 2211–2212. IEEE (2008)

17. Stilman, M., Michel, P., Chestnutt, J., Nishiwaki, K., Kagami, S., Kuffner, J.: Augmented reality for robot development and experimentation. Technical report, Robotics Institute, Carnegie Mellon University, Pittsburgh, PA (2005)

18. Dragone, M., Holz, T., O'Hare, G.M.: Mixing robotic realities. In: Proceedings of the 11th International Conference on Intelligent User Interfaces (IUI 2006), pp. 261–263. ACM, New York (2006)

19. Green, S.A., Chase, J.G., Chen, X., Billinghurst, M.: Evaluating the augmented reality human-robot collaboration system. Int. J. Intell. Syst. Technol. Appl. 8, 130–143 (2009)

20. Bischoff, R., Kurth, J.: Concepts, tools and devices for facilitating human-robot interaction with industrial robots through augmented reality. In: ISMAR Workshop on Industrial Augmented Reality, vol. 22, October 2006

21. Coovert, M.D., Lee, T., Shindev, I., Sun, Y.: Spatial augmented reality as a method for a mobile robot to communicate intended movement. Comput. Hum. Behav. 34(Supplement C), 241–248 (2014)

22. Quigley, M., et al.: ROS: an open-source robot operating system (2009)

23. Úckermann, A., Haschke, R., Ritter, H.: Realtime 3D segmentation for human-robot interaction. In: IEEE/RSJ International Conference of Intelligent Robots and Systems (2013)

24. Görner, M., Haschke, R., Ritter, H., Zhang, J.: MoveIt! task constructor for task-level motion planning. In: IEEE/RSJ International Conference on Intelligent Robots and Systems (IROS) (2018)

25. Lier, F., Wienke, J., Nordmann, A., Wachsmuth, S., Wrede, S.: The cognitive interaction toolkit – improving reproducibility of robotic systems experiments. In: Brugali, D., Broenink, J.F., Kroeger, T., MacDonald, B.A. (eds.) SIMPAR 2014. LNCS (LNAI), vol. 8810, pp. 400–411. Springer, Cham (2014). https://doi.org/10.1007/978-3-319-11900-7_34

# Author Index

Printed in the United States
By Bookmasters